Quill and Cross in the Borderlands

ANNA M. NOGAR

Quill and Cross in the Borderlands

SOR MARÍA DE ÁGREDA AND THE LADY IN BLUE,

1628 TO THE PRESENT

University of Notre Dame Press
Notre Dame, Indiana

Published in the United States of America

Library of Congress Cataloging-in-Publication Data

Names: Nogar, Anna M., author.
Title: Quill and cross in the borderlands : Sor Maria de Agreda and the Lady in Blue, 1628 to the present / Anna M. Nogar.
Description: Notre Dame, Indiana : University of Notre Dame Press, 2018. | Includes bibliographical references and index. |
Identifiers: LCCN 2018011946 (print) | LCCN 2018013591 (ebook) | ISBN 9780268102159 (pdf) | ISBN 9780268102166 (epub) | ISBN 9780268102135 (hardcover : alk. paper) | ISBN 0268102139 (hardcover : alk. paper)
Subjects: LCSH: Maria de Jesus, de Agreda, sor, 1602-1665. | Nuns—Folklore. | Folklore—New Mexico.
Classification: LCC BX4705.M3255 (ebook) | LCC BX4705.M3255   N64 2018 (print) | DDC 271/.97302—dc23
LC record available at https://lccn.loc.gov/2018011946

For my family.
 AMN

Las virtudes de los Siervos de Dios salen al público medrosas,
hasta que la perezosa volubilidad de los años va limpiando la idea
de ciertas materiales impresiones que le ofuscan el brillante lustre.
 —Francisco Palóu, *La vida de Junípero Serra*

CONTENTS

LIST OF ILLUSTRATIONS

ACKNOWLEDGMENTS

This book has benefited throughout the process from the generosity and support of colleagues, friends, and family; without their help, it would be an infinitely poorer work. I ask pardon in advance for anyone I may inadvertently omit here: there are many to thank.

This book's backbone is built on archival materials from several key repositories, including the Archivo Histórico Provincial de los Franciscanos de Michoacán (AHPFM), Archivo Franciscano Ibero-Oriental (AFIO), Archivo General de Indias (AGI), Biblioteca Nacional de España, Archivo del Ministerio de Asuntos Exteriores (Madrid), Archivo General de la Nación (Mexico), the University of Notre Dame Hesburgh Library Rare Books Collection, the University of Texas at Austin (UT) Nettie Lee Benson Latin American Collection, Fray Angélico Chávez History Library, and the University of New Mexico Center for Southwest Research (CSWR). I am very grateful for the help of the curators and librarians from these collections, whose kind guidance and intervention were most appreciated, in particular Fr. Cayetano Sánchez Fuertes (AFIO), Ana María Ruíz Marín (AHPFM), Christian Kelleher (UT), the late Ann Massman (CSWR), Sam Sisneros (CSWR), and Nancy Brown-Martínez (CSWR). Gracias también a Pilar Ruiz Cacho of the Diputación Provincial de Soria for her generous collaboration from Ágreda. Special thanks to Mariano Chávez, Samia Adelo, Shannon Murray, Martin Varela, and Carol Vogel for their indispensable help regarding the mural at St. Katharine's School in Santa Fe.

Visiting collections, copying materials, transcribing, and organizing texts would not have been possible without financial assistance. Gracias al Research Allocations Committee (University of New Mexico; UNM), the Southwest Hispanic Research Institute (UNM), the Latin American and Iberian Institute (UNM), the College of Arts and Sciences (UNM), the Office of the Vice Provost for Research (UNM), the Northeast Modern Languages Association, the Escuela de Estudios Hispano-Americanos (Seville, Spain), the Hispanic Association of Colleges and Universities, the University of Texas Graduate School and the Center for Mexican American Studies (UT). The National Parks Service Spanish Colonial Research Center at UNM graciously and meticulously transcribed several archival documents; thank you to Joseph Sánchez, Angélica Sánchez-Clark, and their wonderful team for their excellent work.

Finding Sor María in archival hidey-holes was helped along by excellent colleagues who pointed me in the right direction again and again. I am indebted to David Rex Galindo, whose research has informed my own and whose unerring sense for sources has helped me in many ways. Many others signaled important sources: Cory Conover, Tom Chávez, John Morán González, Cristina Cabello de Martínez, Michael Hironymous, John McKiernan González, Jason Scott Smith, Lee Daniels, Jay Harrison, Richard Flores, Dolores García Cárdenas, and David García.

Many, many thanks are due the colleagues and friends who read earlier drafts of this book, and helped me rethink, reshape, and also appreciate this project; special thanks to Cristina Carrasco and Cat Gubernatis-Dannen, who supported me in every way throughout the process. Nicolas Poppe was integral in early drafts of the book, as was Krista Foutz Savoca in organizing primary materials. Without crack editor Sarah McKinney, this project would have remained in its baroque manuscript form; her clarifying eye and excellent humor greatly improved this project.

This book began in 1998 in a class on New Mexico's 400th anniversary that I took with Enrique Lamadrid at UNM. His mentorship and friendship have been at the heart of this project and my time at UNM, and far beyond. The mentorship of my dissertation advisor, José Limón of the Center for Mexican American Studies, professionalized this project (and me), and I am eternally grateful. Under the guidance of dissertation codirector César Salgado, and dissertation committee members Jaime Nicolopulos, Cory Reed, and Domino Perez, this book's first draft was completed. The support of colleagues has been invaluable throughout the entire process. Special thanks go to Celia López Chávez, Diane Rawls, Rosalie Otero, Leslie Donovan, and Gabriel Meléndez, who at different points and for different reasons steered me along this path.

Colleagues and students at UNM have supported my research and teaching in the best ways. Agradezco mucho el apoyo de Mary Quinn, Damián Vergara Wilson, Kathryn McKnight, Anthony Cárdenas, Eliza Ferguson, Len Beké, Andrew Sandoval-Strausz, Cathleen Cahill, and the inimitable Karen Patterson. Colleagues outside of UNM have also been instrumental in the extended process of thinking about and producing this book. I am so very grateful for the support of Ignacio Sánchez-Prado, Nancy LaGreca, Oswaldo Estrada, Ricky Rodriguez, José Ramón Ruisánchez Serra, Irma Cantú, Brian Price, Tamara Williams, Sarah Pollack, Oswaldo Zavala, Matt O'Hara, Steve Hackel, and, especially, Ikue Kina of the University of the Ryukyus, Japan.

I wish to thank my editor at the University of Notre Dame Press, Stephen Little, for his advocacy of this project, and also the late Sabine McCormack for including me in her series at UNDP. I am grateful for the support of the UNDP editorial team, who have been unfailingly kind and patient, and for the careful eye of my copyeditor, Scott Barker.

On a personal level, I am thankful for the friends and family who have made writing this book fun and meaningful, and have gone above and beyond by also scouring the horizon for news of Sor María. To my family, especially my mom, Marcella, thank you for always believing in me and encouraging me. To Joshua and Carmella, thank you for cheering me on, and listening to even the most mundane details of my research with interest. I bet our late father, Nicholas, would have liked this long, weird project. My family, especially my grandparents Mary Ann and Roque, Cathy and Ray, and my wonderful, wonderful aunts, uncles, and cousins: thank you for always being there for me in the best possible sense and for keeping my feet on the ground and eyes on the important things. For the Austin chicas, you know who you are and how much you mean to me. Thanks for the broad perspective from Robert Keller and Brian Dolejsi.

Without the amazing Reyna Evans, I couldn't have finished this or any other project since becoming a mom; thank you from the bottom of my heart.

To Peter, Nico, and Eva, you are the best motivating, cheering crew I could have ever imagined, and I can't believe my good fortune to have you with me. Peter, thank you for lovingly co-captaining this party cruise, and taking it all in stride and good humor . . . and for listening to me talk about the same nun for almost ten years. TQM.

Figure I.1. Creating *The Lady in Blue*, by puppet troupe Puppet's Revenge. Image courtesy Ron Dans.

A Literary Protomissionary in the Borderlands

De mi persona, siempre he tenido grande escrúpulo,
porque yo sé quien soy.

———

I have always been scrupulous regarding my person,
for I know who I am.
— Sor María de Jesús de Ágreda[1]

Colonial-era Spanish accounts tell the story of the Lady in Blue. According to these *historias*, in roughly 1628 a woman dressed in blue or gray religious garb appeared to the Jumano tribe of eastern New Mexico. She instructed the tribe in Catholic beliefs and exhorted them to seek out the Franciscan friars stationed nearby, whom the Jumano had yet to encounter. When the friars and the Jumano did eventually meet, the friars found that the tribe displayed signs of catechesis: its members processed with crosses decorated with flowers, and many made the sign of the cross before the friars had taught them how to do so. The mission's Franciscan administrator in New Mexico, Fray Alonso de Benavides, reported to the Spanish Crown of this "milagrosa conversión de la nación Xumana" (miraculous conversion of the Jumano nation).[2] While attending the court of Felipe IV in Spain in 1630, Fray Benavides heard

1

of a cloistered nun rumored to have traveled spiritually to the Americas. He visited María Fernández Coronel y Arana in her convent in Ágreda, and determined, as others had, that she was the woman who had appeared to the Jumano tribe. Word of this woman, later known as Sor María de Jesús de Ágreda, and the mystical evangelization of the Jumano immediately spread in Spain and its colonies, and persists to the present day.

For many scholars, the account of the "Lady in Blue" is a quaint historical footnote, a throwback to a time when such miracle accounts were commonplace and belief in them motivated any number of behaviors. Historical and literary studies of the American Southwest and Mexico have afforded the Lady in Blue narrative the occasional dismissive chuckle,[3] but the fantastical nature of her story has impeded sustained scholarly cultural and historical inquiry.[4] A different type of analysis, one of a more hagiographic nature, views the narrative as a straightforward historical event but often divorces or abstracts it from its complicated historical context.[5] What has not been recognized in either case—and what this book explicitly articulates—is that the narrative was intimately intertwined with popular readings of Sor María's *writing* in colonial Mexico. From the seventeenth through the nineteenth centuries, the mystical evangelization narrative and Sor María's spiritual writing were understood as two faces of a single coin by Spanish and New Spanish subjects alike.

In this vein, *Quill and Cross in the Borderlands: Sor María de Ágreda and the Lady in Blue, 1628 to the Present* charts the nearly 400-year-long history of the Lady in Blue narrative, examining its trajectory from 1628 to today, and explains how and in what forms it endured and evolved. In these chapters I show that the account of Sor María's apparition to the native tribes of the Southwest was an article of practical belief for Mexican citizens during the seventeenth through nineteenth centuries. Sor María the mystical evangelist functioned as a protomissionary model: her conversions were a touchstone and reference for religious and secular explorers, and the account became a fundamental episode in the history of the region. But the prominence of the Lady in Blue narrative in New Spanish colonization does not fully account for Sor María's ubiquity. In this book, I argue that the survival and propagation of Sor María's mission narrative hinged on the persistent popularity and wide distribution of her writing.

Contrary to how she has been typically understood in the context of colonial Mexico, I posit that Sor María was known in New Spain primarily as an author of spiritual texts. The nun's most famous work, the Marian treatise *La mística ciudad de dios* (*The Mystical City of God*),[6] was vigorously endorsed in Spain by Spanish Franciscans and members of the Spanish monarchy, and this promotion extended to Mexico, where it developed a significant devotional following. Though studies of early modern women writers often consist of close readings of author biographies and writing, I here focus instead on the reading and interpretation of Sor María's writing by others.[7] This analysis is uniquely possible in her case because her oeuvre was extensively printed, circulated, and cited in colonial Mexico for more than a century. Knowledge of Sor María's writing was commonplace: her community of reading was broad, and hers were among the most read texts in New Spain. Despite Sor María's prominence as a writer during the colonial period, she has been largely forgotten as such, with the result that the writerly Sor María has almost vanished from contemporary view.

Past scholarship has tended to frame the Lady in Blue narrative as a regional legend of the U.S.-Mexico borderlands.[8] This characterization is in some ways quite logical, as the events described occurred in New Mexico and Texas, and Lady in Blue lore still exists there, as this book discusses. Preserved and perpetuated primarily among the Indo-Hispano residents of the Southwest, the Lady in Blue legend is in this sense similar to other long-running regional folk narratives, such as those of La Llorona, Juan Soldado, and the appearance of the devil at casinos and *bailes*, and also other accounts that have been passed down over generations.[9]

As legend, the Lady in Blue shares qualities with other miracle narratives retold and preserved in the Southwest. With the Lady in Blue, written and oral histories of the Virgin of Guadalupe, Santiago, and the Santo Niño de Atocha (to name but a few) make up the repertoire of the borderlands miraculous: vernacular religious traditions commingled with secular beliefs and practices.[10] The Lady in Blue is unquestionably a persistent manifestation of miracle discourse born out of the region, written into its historical landscape.

However, when considered solely within the borderlands legend/miracle tale paradigm, the Lady in Blue narrative's true historical scope is constrained. *Quill and Cross in the Borderlands* shows that the narrative traveled far beyond what we now consider the borderlands; it was well known throughout Mexico and other Spanish colonies from the seventeenth through nineteenth centuries. Moreover, reading the Lady in Blue solely as a miracle tale can obscure how it functioned as a model for colonial-era missionaries, conditioning their behaviors and attitudes in the mission field. Furthermore, the narrow view of the narrative as borderlands miracle separates the Lady in Blue from Sor María's writing, when they were in fact closely linked in colonial-era Mexican cultural praxis.

Lastly, when taken as a borderlands miracle story, the narrative's origins are typically attributed to native informants, and the seventeenth-century reports by Fray Benavides are cited as the source for this assertion.[11] Yet postcolonial scholarship informs our understanding of accounts like Fray Benavides's, and advises great care in their reading. These studies make explicit the fact that gradients of power and representation gave voice to colonizing entities, while simultaneously appropriating or silencing those of the native populations who were subjected to extreme violence and displacement.[12] The histories told by those who were conquered seldom emerge explicitly in official historical documents, and they often require deep listening and recuperative efforts to reveal. When divulged, they show that history and narrative do not join so seamlessly.[13]

Keeping all this in mind, *Quill and Cross in the Borderlands* is guided by scholarship on extraordinary narratives in historical sources, cultural practice, and oral tradition, which suggests that such accounts should be read beyond the parameters of the stories themselves to understand their contexts and retellings.[14] Applied in concert with Mexican American cultural studies methodologies, and research into women's writing in colonial Latin America, this book achieves its objective of probing both the narrative and the writing that anchored it in colonial Mexico.[15]

This analysis was initially based on a fundamental juxtaposition: the account of the Lady in Blue features prominently in Sor María's holy biography, or *vita*, a text that prefaced *La mística ciudad de dios*.[16] I show that this had major implications for how and where the narrative was read, for as celebrated seventeenth-century Mexican intellectual Sor Juana Inés de la Cruz observed of Sor María's writing, "corren sus escritos"—her works circulated broadly in New Spain.[17] The robust distribution of *La mística ciudad de dios* throughout Mexico ensured that wherever Sor María's Marian text was found, so was the story of the Lady in Blue. As *Quill and Cross in the Borderlands* proves, this and other written forms of the narrative provided a textual basis for the lore about the Lady in Blue that emerged in the nineteenth and twentieth centuries, contesting the notion that the legend's survival was solely the result of collective remembrance.[18] Yet the singular importance of Sor María's writing in New Spain has not emerged in earlier studies of the Lady in Blue, or of the nun herself. This book seeks to remedy this omission.

We know from scholarship on writing by colonial Latin American women that the elision of Sor María as a writer is far from unusual. As Josefina Muriel commented in 1982, scholarly awareness of women's role in the culture of colonial New Spain has traditionally been one of "[una] ignorancia . . . completa" (a complete . . . ignorance), which she and other scholars have since corrected, revealing "esa parte integrante de la cultura mexicana formada por las mujeres que de manera activa participaron en ella, desde 1521 hasta 1821" (that integral part of Mexican culture formed by women who actively participated in its creation from 1521 to 1821).[19] Debra Castillo quantifies the notable absence of attention to women's writing in traditional literary studies, citing a figure by María Elena and Mario Valdéz that 93.7 percent of the page total of literary histories through 1975 were dedicated to male writers. Invoking Sylvia Molloy's perspective on women writers, Castillo further comments on an "originary instability in describing the woman writer, where the two words put into juxtaposition vibrate on the page as a scandalous oxymoron."[20] Many studies since Muriel's 1946 *Conventos de monjas en la Nueva España* have rediscovered, documented, and problematized the role of women writers in the *colonia*. Asunción Lavrin addresses this in her work by articulating the role of women conventual writers, naming those scholars whose studies have "begun to fill gaps in these women's histories."[21] And historian Lavrin further notes that "the lion's share in the writings on nuns has been done by literary critics,"[22] citing Georgina Sabat de Rivers, Electa Arenal, Stacey Schlau, Kristine Ibsen, Kathleen Myers, Amanda Powell, Elisa Sampson Vera Tudela, Kathleen Ross, Jennifer Eich, and others who have contributed to this body of critical literature on colonial-era writing by women.[23]

Though Sor María was Spanish rather than New Spanish, her shaping of public discourse in colonial Mexico makes her one of its notable literary figures. Sor María participated, as did many like her, in New Spain's cultural milieu: "Women who played an active role in the literary culture of the viceroyalty [of New Spain] were assiduous transmitters of the cultural values that constituted their world, values that were so deeply rooted that they have survived to this day."[24] Sor María's authority seems to have been definitive, for Muriel observes that "the person who wielded the greatest mystical influence [in New Spain], along with St. Teresa, was the venerable María de Jesús de Ágreda . . . her influence on Spanish American Women writers was decisive, even on its greatest figures, such as Sor Juana Inés de la Cruz in Mexico and Sor Francisca del Castillo in Colombia."[25] Muriel saw in Sor María a writer whose impact on New Spanish culture has for too long remained un-examined.

To address these gaps in scholarship on Sor María de Jesús de Ágreda in New Spain, *Quill and Cross in the Borderlands* pursues two complementary lines of inquiry. The first examines the miracle narrative proper over almost four centuries of its existence. In the chapters dedicated to the narrative, I delineate its textual origins, role in colonial Mexico, folkloric manifestations, and contemporary interpretations. Two chapters examine the colonial period, and two focus on relatively recent cultural production, from the nineteenth to the twenty-first century.

The second line of inquiry maps out the promotion, distribution, and reading of Sor María's writing in Spain and Mexico during the colonial period. The two sites are closely linked, as efforts to see the nun canonized extended directly from Spain to Mexico. Using archival materials, I establish that the beatification impetus resulted in a New Spanish distribution network for her texts that, in turn, helped establish a community of readers for her writing in Mexico. The dozens of printings of her writing made in New Spain substantiate my claim that Sor María gained traction as a spiritual author both separate from and in relationship to the Lady in Blue narrative. *Quill and Cross in the Borderlands* uncovers a woman writer of significant authority in New Spain who has all but disappeared from colonial literary history.

In chapter 1, I map the seventeenth-century textual origins of the Lady in Blue narrative through a close reading of several printed and archival sources. The chapter studies who the early authors of the narrative were, what each variation added or omitted, and who the colonial-era audiences for each version were. The analysis of these accounts together illustrates how the narrative developed under Spanish and New Spanish pens. As these early renderings were the sources for seventeenth-, eighteenth-, and nineteenth-century understandings of the narrative in New Spain, they also establish a genealogy for its evolution in text, and respond to questions of the Lady in Blue narrative's provenance.

Chapter 2 explores Sor María's biography, writing, and cultural importance as a religious author in seventeenth- and eighteenth-century Spain, setting the stage for her popularization in New Spain. Spanish Franciscans determinedly advanced her *causa* after her death, taking the remarkable step of establishing a printing press in its name. In this chapter, I create a bibliographic history for the Imprenta de la Causa de la Venerable Madre María de Jesús de Ágreda, which published numerous editions of *La mística ciudad de dios* and Sor María's biography, along with other religious works that earned money towards Sor María's canonization efforts. The chapter shows that the nun's lifelong relationship with Spanish monarch Felipe IV had direct ramifications for the Spanish Crown's advocacy of her case for canonization and endorsement of her writing, energies that extended to New Spanish shores.

Chapter 3 rediscovers Sor María as a spiritual author and religious figure in colonial Mexico. By considering how her diverse community of reading was established and cultivated, I show that the arrival of her writing to Mexico from Spain advanced Sor María's renown as a religious writer in New Spain. This idea gained autochthonous traction through Mexican presses, which published her writing regularly for more than a century, and created accessibility to her ideas for both literate and nonlettered New Spanish citizens. The chapter defines how the texts' circulation resulted in scholarly, religious, and artistic interpretations of their contents, and also fed a devotional community whose investment in Sor María's canonization emerges through religious practices and pious donations.

Chapter 4 returns to the Lady in Blue narrative proper in New Spain, reading it as a historical artifact. I analyze where the narrative was invoked on the northern mission frontier in the seventeenth through nineteenth centuries, and consider who its principal transmitters were. The recovery of Sor María's writing reveals that by the late seventeenth century, the Lady in Blue narrative was cited from both written materials and collective memory. The chapter shows that her writing, found in far-flung religious libraries and personal collections, (fore)shadowed the movement of the narrative through the northern New Spanish borderlands, accompanying the Franciscan mission friars of Propaganda Fide and the Jesuits in Baja California and Sonora. This chapter outlines how the narrative of evangelization and colonization became an essential episode in the exploration and colonization of present-day New Mexico, Texas, Arizona, and the Californias.

History transitions into legend in chapter 5's study of late nineteenth-
and twentieth-century American Southwest lore about the Lady in Blue.
In its "folkloric" manifestation, the bilocation narrative overshadows
Sor María's historical significance as a spiritual writer. I demonstrate
how for many early twentieth-century Mexican Americans—some of
the primary producers of Lady in Blue folklore—the narrative affirmed
group identity and regional primacy in a time of racial oppression. The
chapter illustrates how their accounts, and those by other storytellers
and folklore collectors, are sites where work was done on the narrative,
as the Lady in Blue is ascribed new miraculous abilities and social roles.

The final chapter, chapter 6, delves into the substantial contemporary production that centers on the Lady in Blue. I argue that most
recent renderings are dissociated from Sor María's biography and from
the history of her writing in Mexico; thus detached, the narrative becomes malleable and is readily reinterpreted. The chapter presents a
variety of creative genres—including artwork, children's literature, dance
opera, puppetry (see fig. I.1), public commemoration, and fiction—that
reiterate, reconstruct, or reimagine the Lady in Blue, and I pay particular
attention to the narrative as a memory-artifact in Mexican American cultural production. In consuming these contemporary portrayals, readers
are asked to understand a decontextualized story located within parameters crafted for it by the creators of these works. These conditions sometimes result in challenging renderings of the Lady in Blue and typically
(but not always) erase Sor María as a writer.

Early twentieth-century Texan folklorist J. Frank Dobie considered
the Lady in Blue an example of "sacerdotal humbuggery,"[26] despite the
account's historical background and remarkable longevity. Ethnographer
Enrique Lamadrid more fittingly identifies the Lady in Blue as one of
New Mexico's "foundational milagro narratives,"[27] a legend rooted in
and emerging from the region's early colonial history.[28] The seventeenth-
century mystical narrative linked to Sor María's writing became the story
of record for the nun in New Spain, and in the twentieth and twenty-first
centuries, it has evolved into a site for negotiations of identity, colo-
niality, history, and spirituality. This book documents the material legacy
of a legend that has survived and thrived for hundreds of years, and seeks
to rediscover the writing that was that narrative's herald and counterpart.

CHAPTER ONE

Seventeenth-Century Spiritual Travel to New Mexico

A Miracle Narrative in Text

> Antes de hacerse famosa la monja de Ágreda por sus escritos, por sus cartas, por su correspondencia regia y por la *Mística Ciudad de Dios*, su nombre ya sonaba asociado a las proezas de su misión catequizadora en Nuevo México.

> Before the nun from Ágreda became famous for her writings, for her letters, for her royal correspondence, and for *The Mystical City of God*, her name was already associated with her catechizing mission feats in New Mexico.
>
> —Ricardo Fernández Gracia[1]

The account of the Lady in Blue, in which Sor María de Jesús de Ágreda traveled to the tribes of eastern New Mexico and western Texas and converted them to Catholicism in advance of Franciscan missionaries, continues to be retold even today, but the earliest, colonial-era versions of the narrative provide the basis for understanding it as it was popularized during the colonial period and later. This chapter examines the Lady in Blue narrative through the primary texts that recounted it in the seventeenth century. These texts were chosen because they are foundational sources from which later interpretations of the narrative were drawn. All the works mentioned in this chapter were written by Spanish and New Spanish authors, and several were composed by the same author. These five versions of the Lady in Blue narrative contributed to how Sor María was understood in her time and after, and how she is understood today as a bilocating protomissionary: (1) Benavides's *1630 Memorial*; (2) Zárate Salmerón's *Relaciones*; (3) Sor María's and Benavides's letter to friars in New Mexico; (4) Benavides's *1634 Memorial*; (5) Ximénez Samaniego's *vita* of Sor María.

Franciscan friar Alonso de Benavides's *1630 Memorial* is the first of these texts. Although not the first New Spanish work that treats the Lady in Blue narrative, it is the earliest one that presents the account in detail, and it has therefore been read by many as the primary source for the narrative. The second text, the *Relaciones* by Francisican missionary Fray Gerónimo Zárate Salmerón, predates the *1630 Memorial*, but the work has seldom been read in the context of Sor María's travels to that region. In Zárate Salmerón's text, the brief mention of the Lady in Blue narrative shows awareness within the Church in New Spain of Sor María as a mystical traveler to New Mexico prior to the publication of Benavides's *1630 Memorial*.

By 1631, Benavides had traveled to Spain to present the *1630 Memorial*; there he met Sor María in her convent in Ágreda. With Sor María adhering to her vows of obedience, she and the friar wrote a letter to the friars in New Mexico in which Sor María confirmed her visits to that mission field and asserted the important role of the Franciscan Order there. This letter is the third text. Benavides remained in Europe after meeting Sor María and composed a report for Pope Urban VIII, which derived from his earlier report, but significantly altered the Lady in Blue narrative. This fourth text, therefore, is Benavides's *1634 Memorial*.

The fifth and final version of the narrative examined in this chapter was published around 1670 (after Sor María's death in 1665) as part of her *vita*, or holy biography.[2] Written by Fray Joseph Ximénez Samaniego, who later became the minister general of the Franciscan Order, the *vita* not only explained Sor María's mystical travel in the context of the nun's examination by the Spanish Inquisition, but it also prefaced most editions of her exceedingly popular book, *La mística ciudad de dios*.

Each of the texts discussed here influenced ideas about Sor María as a mystical missionary in the Americas, a concept that continued to evolve from the seventeenth century onward. This book intends to show that the so-called legend of the Lady in Blue was actually an historical artifact whose colonial-era dissemination and long-term survival were related to, if not dependent on, the success of Sor María's writing in co-lonial Mexico. As such, thinking about the audiences for each of these versions of the narrative is important. At the end of this chapter I con-sider who might have read each version, and to what extent they indi-vidually shaped shared ideas of Sor María's travel during the colonial period. We know the written form contributed to the narrative's lon-gevity, internal stability, and consistency across centuries, but which versions were the most influential? The answers to this and like ques-tions, presented in these pages, serve as a foundation for the chapters that follow.

"La mujer que les predicaba" in Fray Alonso de Benavides's *1630 Memorial*

Many scholars cite the detailed rendering of the Lady in Blue narrative in Fray Alonso de Benavides's *1630 Memorial* as the narrative's origi-nary New Spanish source. Published in Madrid in 1631, the *1630 Memo-rial* is a report on the spiritual and material condition of the *custodia* of New Mexico written by its *custos*, or chief religious administrator, Fray Benavides. The document was presented by Benavides at the court of Felipe IV, when the friar had returned to Spain in 1630 to report on behalf of the Franciscan missionaries in New Mexico. The prominently placed section recounting the Lady in Blue narrative is entitled "Con-versión Milagrosa de la Nación Xuamana," and it is one of several miracle accounts woven throughout the *1630 Memorial*.[3] The version of the Lady in Blue in the *1630 Memorial* sets out many of the narrative's basic elements, but it leaves the woman who preached to the Jumanos Indians unnamed. Benavides refers to the female protomissionary as "la santa" (the saint) or "la mujer que les predicaba" (the woman who preached to them). Benavides would modify this and other elements of the narrative in his later writing on the subject.

In his introduction to the *1630 Memorial*, Fray Juan de Santander, then the commissary general of the Indies, states the reader will find within it "descubrimientos de riquezas, así espirituales, como tem-porales" (the discovery of spiritual as well as temporal riches).[4] This intersection of religious and secular issues in New Mexico presented in the *1630 Memorial* no doubt was of interest to its principally European readers.[5] The reports on the arability of the land and the abundant natural resources to be found there, and of the possibility of silver mining (already an important source of income to the Crown in northern Mexico), would have appealed to the Spanish court and to potential investors in New Mexico.[6]

But Benavides had other motives apart from making New Mexico seem like a worthwhile investment. Historical documents contemporaneous to the *1630 Memorial* indicate that one of Benavides's goals was the elevation of the New Mexico *custodia* to a *provincia* (a larger area of religious jurisdiction), and his own appointment as bishop to administer the new *provincia*.[7] To this end, Benavides demonstrates a need for greater administrative autonomy to attend to the numerous new converts in the region.[8] The *1630 Memorial*'s representation of spiritual riches is important: from the successes of the friars among the New Mexican and Texan tribes[9] to the primacy of the Franciscan Order in that mission field,[10] these miraculous incidents serve as further proof of the Franciscans' vital role there and of the need for a province to be established.[11]

Benavides privileges the Lady in Blue narrative amidst these objectives.[12] According to Benavides, what he wrote was based on reports made to him by the mission friars who had contact with the Jumanos. The "Conversión Milagrosa de la Nación Xumana" narrates the incident. Fray Juan de Salas met and was befriended by members of the Jumano tribe during his time stationed in the region.[13] Over the course of six years, the Jumanos repeatedly requested that Salas be sent to them, a petition Benavides granted in 1629.[14] But before Salas and Fray Diego López left to join the Jumanos, the tribe's emissaries were asked why they persisted in requesting friars who would come to the tribe and baptize them. They replied that a woman who resembled a picture of the Spanish nun Madre Luisa de Carrión, which was at the mission, preached to them in their own languages and urged them to seek out the friars.[15] Other tribes that Benavides does not name made similar petitions with similar rationales.

According to Benavides, shortly before the friars and their guides arrived to the Jumano encampment, the devil became upset that he would soon lose the tribe's souls to the friars.[16] He dried up the local water, causing the buffalo they hunted to migrate away, and relayed through the tribe's "hechizeros" (spiritual leaders) that the friars were never going to arrive and the tribe should leave and find another site.[17] As the tribe readied to move, "la Santa," the woman who had visited the Jumanos, told the tribe's captains to remain where they were because the friars would be there soon. Jumano scouts left to search for the friars. When they found them, Salas and López produced a picture of Madre Carrión, and the scouts confirmed that this woman was like the one who visited them, but that the woman they saw was younger and more beautiful.[18]

When the friars arrived to the tribe's encampment, the Jumanos greeted them with a procession led with two large crosses, a gesture Benavides suggests demonstrated that they were "bien industriados del cielo" (well taught in heavenly matters).[19] Salas and López offered their personal crucifixes and a statue of the infant Jesus for veneration by the Jumanos, which the tribal members did "como si fueran Christianos muy antiguos" (as if they had been Christians for a long time).[20] The friars asked for those in the crowd of ten thousand who desired baptism to raise their hands; to the friars' reported surprise, everyone raised their hands, including infants lifted up by their mothers. Over the course of the next several days, other nearby tribes who had also been visited by the protomissionary woman asked that the friars visit them too. Benavides interjects that the Japies and Xabotas had also likely seen her. He notes that the friars reported that the tribes desired to convert and form permanent settlements (the Jumanos were seminomadic), but adds that there were not enough priests to leave the two there, so Salas and López made plans to return to the central missions in New Mexico.[21]

Before leaving, the friars instructed the Jumanos to pray daily before a cross they would leave with the tribe, and to have recourse to it. The tribe's "Capitán mayor" (leader) asked the friars to cure the sick among the tribe, and all through the afternoon, night, and following morning, the two friars healed the ill members of the tribe.[22] With one friar on either side, they made a cross over each individual, recited the *Loquente Jesu*, the *Concede nos*, and the *Deus, qui ecclesiam tuam*.[23] Benavides summarizes the scale of this miraculous event: "fueron tantos los que alli milagrosamente sanaron, que no pudieron reduzirse a numero" (so many were miraculously healed that they were impossible to count).[24] As a result of this, the tribal members' faith in the cross was confirmed to such an extent that they hung crosses in front of their tents. Benavides closes the "Conversión Milagrosa de la Nación Xumana" by expressing jubilant thanks for the miracles the Franciscans witnessed and executed among the Jumanos, and seeing in them the order's particularly blessed role in the mission field: "O bondad infinita! Bendigate los Angeles, que assi quieres honrar a esta sagrada Religion, y a sus hijos, confirmando por su mano, con tantos milagros tu divina palabra. . . . [Bien se infiere] de lo dicho los bienes espirituales tan copiosos, que nuestra seráfica Religión ha descubierto por todo el mundo" (O infinite goodness! May the Angels praise you, that you so wish to honor this holy order [the Franciscans] and its sons, confirming your divine Word through its hand. . . . [One may infer this honor] from what has already been said of the copious spiritual blessings that our Seraphic Order has uncovered throughout the world).[25] Both the Lady in Blue's conversion of the Jumanos, and of other nearby tribes, and the friars' healing of the sick are interpreted by Benavides as evidence of the Franciscan Order's celestial favor in the New Mexico mission.

The version of the Lady in Blue in the *1630 Memorial* is the earliest full version of the narrative and provides many of the details that present-day scholars and cultural producers (such as artists, composers, canonization activists; discussed in chapter 6) draw on. However, Benavides's account was not the first instance when the narrative was invoked in the New Spanish mission context. The mysterious, unnamed "mujer que les predicaba" in his 1630 account appears to have been presaged by a report on New Mexico made a year or two earlier that names Sor María specifically as that mystical evangelizer.

"SANTA MADRE MARÍA DE JESÚS": GERÓNIMO ZÁRATE SALMERÓN'S *RELACIONES*

Fray Géronimo Zárate Salmerón was a Franciscan friar sent with a group of missionaries to New Mexico around 1618 or 1621. A linguist who lived at Jemez Pueblo, he wrote a *Doctrina* in the Jemez language. In 1626 he returned to Mexico City where he wrote *Relaciones de todas las cosas que en el Nuevo-Mexico se han visto y sabido, asi por mar como por tierra, desde el año de 1538 hasta el de 1626* [*An Account of All Seen and Known of New Mexico, By Sea and By Land, From 1538 to 1626*],[26] which was addressed to the commissary general of the Indies, Francisco de Apodaca. The account is dated August 18, 1629; Zárate Salmerón likely wrote it between 1627 and 1629.[27] The *Relaciones* carried the approval of Fray Francisco de Velasco, the provincial of the Province of Santo Evangelio, to which the New Mexico *custodia* pertained.

In the *Relaciones*,[28] Zárate Salmerón summarizes the history of New Mexico "desde el año de 1538 hasta el de 1626"—from 1538 to 1626—recounting early exploration expeditions and documenting the establishment of missions. He begins with Francisco Coronado's expedition, narrates the late sixteenth-century conquest and settlement of New Mexico by Juan de Oñate, and describes the real and fictional regions often then discussed in the context of New Mexico: Florida, the South Sea, and the Strait of Anián.

The Lady in Blue narrative appears in two of the last three paragraphs of the work, under the heading "Relación de la Santa Madre María de Jesús, abadesa del convento de Santa Clara de Ágreda" (Account of the Holy Mother María de Jesús, abbess of the convent of Santa Clara de Ágreda).[29] In contrast to the text that precedes it, which flows easily from one historical episode to another, there is no transition or explanation for why the narrative is included, and the authorial voice is different from that of the earlier text.[30]

The first paragraph briefly describes the region of New Mexico and puts forth the possibility that its inhabitants are in some way instructed in Catholic teachings:

> Es muy probable que en la prosecución del descubrimiento del Nuevo-México, y conversión de aquellas almas, se dará presto en un reino que se llama Tidam . . . que según se entiende está entre el Nuevo-México y la Quivira, y si acaso se errare; la cosmografía ayudará el tomar noticia de otros reinos, llamados el uno de Chillescas, el otro de los Guismanes y el otro de los Aburcos, que confinan con este dicho reino de Tidam . . . se procurará saber si en ellos, particularmente en el Tidam, hay noticia de nuestra santa fe catolica y por qué medio y modos se la ha manifestado nuestro Señor.

———

> It is very probable that in the continued discovery of New Mexico, and conversion of the souls there, one will come upon a kingdom called Tidam . . . which is understood to lie between New Mexico

and Quivira, and if one were to be mistaken, the cosmography will help one find other kingdoms, one called Chillescas, another of the Guismanes and another of the Aburcos, that border on the said kingdom of Tidam . . . one will seek to discover if in them, particularly in Tidam, there is news of our Holy Catholic Faith, and by what means and ways Our Lord has manifested it.[31]

Although this passage does not provide the detailed explanation that the *1630 Memorial* does, or name Sor María, it does implicitly associate the nun with it through the title "Relación de la Santa Madre María de Jesús, abadesa del convento de Santa Clara de Agreda." Zárate Salmerón's version connects specific places (Tidam and Quivira) and specific tribes (Chillescas, Guismanes, and Aburcos) to Sor María and to the project of evangelization. The linkage among Sor María, New Mexico, and conversion in advance of missionaries is quite clear.

An injunction by the archbishop-elect of Mexico, Francisco Manso y Zúñiga, follows. In it, the archbishop orders that the claims of catechesis associated with Sor María be investigated by the friars sent to the New Mexico missions:

Nos, D. Francisco Manso y Zúñiga, electo arzobispo de México . . . encargamos mucho esta enquisición á los reverendos padres, y custodios de la dicha conversion para que la hagan y soliciten, con la puntualidad, fe y devoción que tal caso requiere, y para que de lo que resultare nos hayan dado aviso en manera que haga fe, de que sin duda procederán grandes aumentos espirituales y temporales en honor y gloria de Dios nuestro Señor.

————

We, Don Francisco Manso y Zúñiga, archbishop-elect of Mexico . . . entrust this inquiry to the reverend fathers and custodians of the aforementioned region, that they execute and seek it out with the punctuality, faith, and devotion that it requires, and so that of whatever may result, they will have faithfully advised us, and from which no doubt great spiritual and temporal gains for the honor and glory of the Lord our God will spring forth.[32]

This order is cited in later accounts of the narrative, including others by Benavides. However, its inclusion in Zárate Salmerón's document, produced in the 1620s, seems to acknowledge that in Mexico City in 1628, news of Sor María's travels was already beginning to circulate.[33] It indicates that the possibility of her travel was taken quite seriously within the Church leadership in New Spain as a part of the conversion project in its northern borderlands.

The archbishop-elect's conjecture about what the friars might encounter in New Mexico and the insinuation that their discoveries there would increase faith, and also produce spiritual and material well-being for Spain, are echoed in Zárate Salmerón's conclusion. This final paragraph of the *Relaciones* returns to the friar's voice, closing the work with an exhortation to the king and an appeal to Franciscan leadership, encouraging continued exploration of New Mexico and surrounding areas, for "lo cierto es, que en no acabar de esplorar esta tierra, S.M. pierde una gran mundo" (what remains certain is that, by not completing the exploration of this land, Your Majesty loses a vast world).[34]

The brief account of Sor María by Zárate Salmerón has not received much critical attention, likely because scholarship has tended to focus on the *1630 Memorial*.[35] However, there are several reasons to carefully consider it and its relationship to the Benavides documents. First, by 1628, when Zárate Salmerón was completing the *Relaciones* in Mexico City, Manso y Zúñiga was archbishop-elect of Mexico; inclusion of his order to seek out Sor María of the "Relación de la Santa Madre María de Jesús" fits chronologically. It seems unlikely Zárate Salmerón would have heard of Sor María while in New Mexico, but he might have heard of Salas's story of the Jumanos from the other friars, as Benavides did — though he makes no mention of it. He more likely was informed of her once in Mexico City. Second, the account is bookended in the *Relaciones* by a conclusion written in Zárate Salmerón's voice, which makes it less likely that it was tacked on the end by a later writer or publisher, and no such modifications are noted in its 1856 publication.

News of Sor María's evangelization could have already traveled to Mexico City from Spain. In fact, according to Sor María's biographer[36] and to Benavides,[37] news of her mystical travels circulated within the Franciscan Order in the early 1620s. Sor María's *vita* and her Inquisition records state that she began to experience *exterioridades* (spiritual raptures) involving the conversion of native peoples as early as 1621 and continuing until 1628 or 1630. Sor María had presented these episodes to her confessor, who relayed them to Franciscan superiors in Spain.[38] It seems certain that such information arrived to Mexico by the late 1620s and to the archbishop-elect, suggesting that the Lady in Blue narrative in Zárate Salmerón's *Relaciones* is authentic. This is particularly significant because it predates the *1630 Memorial*.

The chronology of Zárate Salmerón's *Relaciones* raises questions about what Benavides could have known about Sor María's travels when he wrote the *1630 Memorial*. This is difficult to satisfactorily answer, as are many questions about the narrative.[39] It is likely that Benavides was unaware of Archbishop-elect Manso y Zúñiga's letter at the time the events he recounts unfolded: Zárate Salmerón and Manso y Zúñiga were in Mexico City in 1628, while Benavides arrived in New Mexico in 1626 and did not return to Mexico City until 1630,[40] after the events narrated in the "Conversión Milagrosa de la Nación Xumana" took place in New Mexico. Nor is it likely he was informed about Sor María while in New Mexico: the *Relaciones* were not published at that time, and it is improbable that a manuscript copy would have arrived to Benavides while in New Mexico. However, as Benavides completed the *1630 Memorial* while in Mexico City, he may have been informed of Zárate Salmerón's "Relación de la Santa Madre María de Jesús," or of the source material from which it derived.[41] In fact, Benavides would later say that he took a copy of Manso y Zúñiga's letter with him to Spain.

By the time Benavides wrote his *1634 Memorial*, he had modified his version of the Lady in Blue narrative considerably. Among other changes, he includes Zárate Salmerón's exact text of the "Relación de la Santa Madre María de Jesús" (with some stylistic modification) in his newer report on the "Conversión Milagrosa."[42] Benavides states that in 1629, thirty friars sent from Mexico arrived to the mission in New Mexico already informed about Sor María's travel: "les encargo el Arcobispo a los dichos religiosos la inquisicion deste caso dandoles la relacion que dos años antes auia lleuado de españa alas Indias" (the archbishop [of Mexico] entrusted the friars with the investigation of this case, providing them with the account that had arrived to the Indies two years earlier from Spain).[43] Benavides then reproduces the two paragraphs from the "Relación de la Santa Madre María de Jesús," though he attributes them neither to Zárate Salmerón nor to whatever source they might have shared.[44] What exactly Benavides knew before or while writing the *1630 Memorial* is unclear, but by the time he wrote the *1634 Memorial*, Benavides had read Zárate Salmerón's account, or his source material, locating the Lady in Blue narrative in Mexico before 1630.

Reporting under Vows of Obedience in the 1631 Letter

When Benavides traveled to Spain in 1631 to present the *1630 Memorial* at the court of Felipe IV, Benavides tells that Fr. Bernardino Sena, the minister general of the Franciscan Order, had heard of Sor María's miraculous travels when he was the bishop of Burgos, eight years prior. Upon reading Benavides's report on the conversion of the Jumanos, and receiving Manso y Zúñiga's letter, Sena determined that Benavides and Sor María should meet. Sena sent Benavides to Ágreda to speak with the cloistered nun about the conversions in New Mexico, giving Benavides the authority "para obligar a la Bendita madre por obediencia que me manifestase todo Lo que sabia acera del Nuevo Mexico" (to oblige the blessed mother under vows of obedience to declare to me all she knew about New Mexico).[45] The result of this compulsory meeting was a letter written by Sor María and Benavides to the friars in New Mexico in which Sor María's role as the Lady in Blue was confirmed and several specific details of the narrative—which would be reiterated again and again into the nineteenth century—were recorded.[46]

The letter itself is a combination of two documents: a narration by Benavides and a "carta exhortatoria" (exhortative letter) from Sor María to the friars. Benavides's text encircles Sor María's letter and adds many details to the narrative. Sor María's letter repeats some of Benavides's text and encourages the missionaries in the field. Benavides's is the dominant voice, both as it is positioned and insofar as he is the authoritative figure. Sor María's portion, in contrast, begins "Obedesiendo"[47] (obeying) the orders of her male superiors to report to Benavides on her travels to New Mexico.[48] Sor María would twice later be forced by the Spanish Inquisition to explain the information she revealed to Benavides and to justify not only the nature of her travel but also what, if any, material evidence of her voyages remained behind in New Mexico.[49]

The letter opens with Benavides stating that the Franciscan friars in New Mexico are favored by the angels and San Francisco, who intervene "personal, verdadera y realmente" (personally, truthfully, and actually) on the friar's behalf. Then, Benavides names Sor María as the mysterious female visitor to the Jumanos and New Mexico: "Lleban desde la villa de agreda . . . a la bendita y dichosa Madre de la orden de la Concepción franciscana descalza a que nos ayude con su presencia y predicación en todas esas provincia y bárbaras naciones" (They [the angels and St. Francis] bring from the village of Ágreda . . . the holy and blessed Mother from the Franciscan Order of Discalced Conceptionists, so that she might help us with her presence and preaching in all those provinces and barbarous nations).[50] From the beginning of the letter, Sor María is linked to New Mexico and to the conversion of native peoples there. The narrative is positioned as a sign of the divine favor the order and the Crown receive in pursuing conversions there.

Benavides stresses his importance as an emissary from New Mexico, claiming that his *1630 Memorial* was well received at court and alleging that no one previously knew anything of the New Mexico *custodia*: "no agradecia ni sabia lo que vuestras reverencias con apostolico zelo han trabajado en esa viña del Señor" (they neither knew nor gave thanks for all that Your Reverences have accomplished with apostolic zeal in that vineyard of the Lord).[51] Benavides claims that his 1630 text is meant to remedy this ignorance and valorize the missions and friars. He says that four hundred copies of the *1630 Memorial* were distributed in Spain, that a second printing of the text was being considered, and that copies had been sent to Rome.

In the letter, Benavides also describes his visit to Sor María's convent in Ágreda, explaining that before telling the friars more about her visits to New Mexico, he wishes to first explain her family and upbringing, which he views as almost miraculous.[52] He recounts the divine revelation that Sor María's mother, Catalina Coronel, received to convert the family home into a convent, and for all the family members to enter religious life, which she and her husband, Francisco, did: "de su casa ysieron conbento de monjas y ellas [Catalina, Sor María, and her sister Jerónima] quedasen en el. Y ellos [Francisco and Sor María's two brothers] se metiesen frailes" (they made a convent of their home and the women [Catalina, Sor María, and her sister Jerónima] remained in the convent. And the men [Francisco and Sor María's two brothers] became friars).[53] Benavides uses this remarkable family history to frame the discussion of Sor María herself as one that is marvelous. He rapidly transitions into a physical depiction of Sor María—"de hermoso rostro con ser mui blanco, aunque rosado ojos grandes y negros" (a handsome, pale and rosy face with large, black eyes)[54]—that corroborates the rough description of the woman who appeared to the Jumanos: a woman like Madre Luisa de Carrión but "moça y Hermosa" (young and beautiful).[55] He describes her Franciscan habit as "pardo" (gray-brown) with a white overdress, a scapular, and the cord of the Franciscan Order, which is topped by a cape of *sayal* (sackcloth) and black veil and worn with minimal footwear.[56] He states that during her mystical preaching in New Mexico and nearby regions, she would wear the Franciscan habit, though on other occasions she wore "el [hábito] de la Concepción,"[57] a blue habit. He also establishes the timeline for when her travel occurred, beginning in 1620 and continuing through 1631, sometimes occurring several times a day.

Benavides states that Sor María had wished for the conversion of faraway tribes "desde criatura" (since she was very young),[58] and she was brought to them accompanied by St. Michael and St. Francis;[59] once there, "personalmente a predicado por todas las naciones Nuestra Santa Fee católica Particularmente en Nuestro Nuebo Mexico" (she has personally preached our Holy Faith throughout all the [indigenous] nations, particularly in our New Mexico).[60] As if to confirm Sor María's presence among the friars in New Mexico specifically, Benavides recounts anecdotes about the friars in the mission field and the tribes and regions that he maintains Sor María told him about: Benavides baptizing the Piros tribe, Father Quirós appearing, friars Salas and López among the Jumanos, and Fray Ortega's miraculous escape.[61] He adds that Sor María personally told the Jumanos and the Quivira tribe to seek out friars for baptism, echoing his *1630 Memorial* account. Benavides asserts that she describes so many places and climates in New Mexico that "ni aun yo me acordava y ella las truxo a la memoria" (I myself could not recall [them], and she reminded me).[62] Benavides then answers a question that he anticipates the friars would have upon reading the surprisingly intimate information about their fellow New Mexican friars and mission site: Since the native people could see Sor María, why was she invisible to the friars? The answer Sor María provides, according to Benavides, is succinct: the friars did not need to see her to affirm their faith, whereas the tribes did.[63]

Benavides goes on to cite Sor María's recommendations regarding the conversion of tribes to the far west of Quivira, thought to be in the general region of New Mexico-Texas. This section of the letter is one of the most frequently cited sections from the late seventeenth century into the nineteenth century: "en el discurso del camino se convertiran muchas gentes si Los soldados fueren de buen ejemplo y que Nro Padre San

Francisco alcanzó de Nuestro Señor que con solo ver Los Indios a nrs. Frailes se convertirán" (on discussing the road [to the west of Quivira] many nations will be converted if the soldiers are of good comportment; Our Father San Francisco attained a pledge from the Lord that the Indians will convert [to Catholicism] solely upon seeing our friars).[64] This detail is repeated in eighteenth-century Mexican printings of the letter, as I shall discuss in chapter 3, and in chapter 4 I will show how the idea of the need for "soldados de buen ejemplo" in and near the missions was repeated by Franciscan mission friars, as was the notion that indigenous tribes would be converted to Christianity upon laying eyes on Franciscan friars.

Benavides lists the tribes and areas that Sor María visited in New Mexico: "los Rnos. de chillescas, canbujos y jumanos y luego el Reino de Ticlas" (the kingdoms of Chillescas, Canbujos, Jumanos, and then the kingdom of Ticlas), tribes similar (although Benavides does not note it) to those listed in the Zárate Salermón account (Chillescas, Guismanes, Aburcos, and Tidam). Benavides explains this list by acknowledging that these are not the tribes' proper names, but rather ones that sound like them. Recounting what he says was told to him by Sor María, he reports that she left many items behind on her travels, including a monstrance, rosaries, and crosses. This important detail was later cited both by the Inquisition and by missionaries in northern New Spain, as was the curious account Fray Benavides includes concerning two friars who were martyred by a tribe, whose king they had converted and whose (the friars') bones were kept by that king in a silver box.[65] Fray Benavides adds that Sor María was martyred while in the mission field.

Before including the nun's response to his preceding account, Fray Benavides reminds his readers of the vows of obedience she followed in replying:

> después de escritas que me quise despedir de ella se la mostre para que me dixese si en algo me abia equibocado o si era lo mismo que le havia passado entre los dos y para ello le ynterponia la obediencia de Nuestro Reverendisimo que para ello llevava y se la interpuso tan bien el Reverendo Padre Provincial de aquella provincia que alli estaba y su confesor.

―――

After writing down the things she told me, I wished to depart from her company, and I showed her what I wrote so that she might tell me if I might have been mistaken in any point, or if it was written as told during our meeting, and for this purpose I invoked the requirement of obedience imposed by the Reverend Commissary General (which I brought for this reason), as did the Reverend Father Provincial of that province, who was there, and her confessor.[66]

The nun's letter is very different in tone and in apparent aim from the friar's exuberant missive. It is clear hers is the submissive voice, and her message has less to do with New Mexico and native populations specifically and more to do with a desire to participate in the conversions and to encourage the friars in their evangelization. Her tone is self-effacing, as she calls herself "el sujeto mas ynutil e yncapas en su efecto para manifestar la fuersa de su poderosa mano" (the most useless and powerless subject to exercise the force of God's powerful hand). She says that she is obeying the command from her superiors to reveal the contents of her notebooks, in which her travels were recorded. Regarding the conversions in New Mexico, she states, "me mandan diga lo que se contiene en estos cuadernos" (they order that I say what is contained in these notebooks).

Sor María adds little to a narrative ostensibly about her. She comments that she was taken to other places before she appeared in New Mexico, that she first headed east to Quivira and to the Jumanos, and that she was helped in her travels by six angels.[67] She says that some of the indigenous tribes she observed resisted conversion and the Franciscan friars because "el demonio los tiene engañados asiendoles creer que . . . ande estar sujetos y esclabos siendo christianos consistiendo su libertad y felisidad en esta bida" (the devil has them tricked, making them believe . . . that they will become subjects and slaves, though being Christians comprises their liberty and happiness in this life).[68] Sor María repeats the specific recommendation that only soldiers "de buena bida y costumbres y que con apasibilidad sufran las contumelias que se les pueden ofreser" (of good habits and reputable lifestyle, who might patiently suffer the difficulties that may befall them) be allowed into the mission field. She reiterates the dates Benavides set out for her travels, noting that the Quivira and Jumanos were the last nations she visited.

She reminds the Franciscan friars that their mission in New Mexico is particularly blessed, and that they must advance the propagation of the faith: "alégrense Vuestras Paternidades mías, pues el Sr. les a dado la oportunidad, ocasión y suerte de los Apostoles. No la pierdan. Por entender y pensar el trabajo acuerdense lo que le toca obedecer a el altissimo y dilatar y siembre su santa fee" (Rejoice, my dear Fathers, for the Lord has provided you with the opportunity, moment, and fortune of the apostles. Do not lose sight of this. In understanding and thinking about the labor involved, remember what is required to obey the Lord, and spread and sow his Holy Faith).[69]

She assures them that "con sierta siensia y lus que los bien aventurados los ynbidian" (with certain science and light, the faithful departed envy you) for the conversions they accomplish on earth, and that "si pudieran dejar la Gloria que tienen por acompañarles en estas conversiones lo ysieran" (if they could abandon the glory they enjoy to accompany the friars in these conversions, they would), concepts that are later invoked in the mission context in New Spain. Sor María assures them of the value and importance of their work, in which she herself wishes she could participate, and for which she offers "de todo Corazon y alma ayudar con oraciones y ejerisios y los de esta comunidad" (to help with all my heart and soul through prayer and religious devotions, and with those of this religious community).[70] Sor María closes her letter by reiterating that she wrote and gave to Benavides these revelations under a vow of obedience, hoping that her words will stay with the friars in the New Mexico *custodia*, who are particularly blessed.[71]

The letter then returns to Benavides, closing by claiming there is more of Sor María's and his own testimony about her travels, but "son mas para guardarlas en el Corazon" (they are best kept safe in the heart). He brings the discussion back to more mundane issues pertaining to himself and to the New Mexico mission field, referencing the political conflict between religious and secular groups in the region, reminding the friars not to be discouraged by the difficulties they face in the mission field, and mentioning his own desire to return to New Mexico. He assures the friars that he continually works to secure the support of the Crown and the Real Consejo de Indias and that the Franciscan Order considers Sor María's travels a blessing particular to them: "deven tenerse por dichosos de ser patrosinados desta vendita alma Maria de Jesus que alla los a bisto y los encomienda a Dios" (you should consider yourselves fortunate to be championed by that blessed soul, María de Jesús, who has seen you there [in New Mexico] and who entrusts you to the Lord).[72] Benavides reiterates Sor María's and his own wishes for the friars and the tribes,[73] and reminds his readers that the unusual events recounted in the narrative pertain to a very real earthly context, one contested and carefully considered in religious and secular circles.[74] But Benavides still had a few things to say about the Lady in Blue narrative, which he revealed in his *1634 Memorial*.

TWO LADIES IN BLUE: SOR MARÍA DE JESÚS AND LUISA DE CARRIÓN IN BENAVIDES'S *1634 MEMORIAL*

Because the *1634 Memorial* was written with just one audience in mind—Pope Urban VIII—the text's overall emphasis is on spiritual gains rather than material ones.[75] It also focuses particularly on the Franciscan Order's achievements in the New Mexican mission field to establish their primacy there. Other documents written by Benavides, dated 1633 and 1634, indicate that the *1634 Memorial* was one text from a suite of materials regarding the New Mexico *custodia* that promoted its elevation to a province.[76] Pope Urban VIII wielded significant influence over the Spanish Crown and its decisions regarding the allocation of funds and political support of specific religious orders and groups in the Americas. Appealing directly to the pope on behalf of Franciscan missionaries and New Mexican friars was a strategy for gaining support for them from above.

Benavides's 1634 version of the narrative repeats many elements laid out in the *1630 Memorial*: the Jumano procession to greet the friars; the raising of arms to ask for baptism; and the healing of the sick. He specifies by name two neighboring tribes ("naciones comarcanas"[77]) who sought out the Franciscans after they healed the sick—the Xapies and the Quivira—for whom the friars pledged to build a church.[78]

However, the *1634 Memorial* changes the Lady in Blue narrative in two major ways. First, Benavides claims that he had heard the news about Sor María while still in New Mexico in 1629. He states that in 1629, thirty friars arrived from Mexico and brought with them knowledge about Sor María that had been relayed to them by the archbishop of Mexico (Manso y Zúñiga); the archbishop, in turn, had been informed by Spanish sources: "en España corría voz de que una Religiosa llamada María de Jesús . . . era llevada milagrosamente al Nuevo México a predicar nuestra Santa Fe católica a aquellos indios bárbaros" (in Spain, it was rumored that a woman religious named Sor María de Jesús . . . was miraculously taken to New Mexico to preach our Holy Faith to those barbarous Indians).[79] Benavides goes on to reproduce the two paragraphs that appeared in the Zárate Salmerón account nearly verbatim, but without citing any particular source.[80] He adds that Manso y Zúñiga had been informed about Sor María's travels while in Spain by a person of repute ("persona de crédito")[81] and brought news of her when he came to Mexico to occupy the archbishopric in 1629. According to Benavides, when this information arrived in New Mexico, he and the other friars reconsidered "el grande cuidado y solicitud con que los Indios Xumanas nos venían a pedir frailes cada verano para que los fuesen a bautizar era alguna moción del cielo" (the great care and solicitude with which the Jumano Indians would come every summer to ask for friars to baptize them, which we had taken to be a heavenly intervention).[82]

Benavides claims he was convinced the Lady in Blue might be Sor María because of the tribes' shared reaction to the portrait of Luisa de Carrión, whose likeness to Sor María they unequivocally confirmed.[83] Benavides writes that the friars in New Mexico were convinced that "aquella religiosa era la Madre María de Jesús contenida en aquella relación del Arzobispo que merecía ser apóstol de dios milagrosamente" (that woman religious was the Mother María de Jesús contained in the account of the archbishop, who must have been the miraculous apostle of God).[84] In this version of the narrative, Benavides and the friars were convinced that Sor María was the woman who visited New Mexico and converted the Jumano tribe, in conformation with the archbishop's letter, and the friars who arrived to New Mexico in 1630 were aware of this fact and had been charged with investigating it further.

Benavides does not cite Zárate Salmerón as his source for this information and does not mention Zárate Salmerón at all in the *1630 Memorial*, but he does include the friar in the *1634 Memorial*'s chapter on Taos Pueblo, where the friar had worked. This suggests at the very least that Benavides became familiar with Zárate Salmerón at some point, if not that he had read Zárate Salmerón's *Relaciones* and borrowed from it. In claiming that he knew about Sor María while in New Mexico, and then citing the account from Zárate Salmerón's text, Benavides radically changes his presentation of the Lady in Blue narrative in this version; he creates a role for himself in creating institutional knowledge of her in New Mexico.

The second major difference in the *1634 Memorial*'s version of the narrative is unique to this document: Benavides names another female mystical missionary to New Mexico. In the *1630 Memorial*, Benavides reports that a blind child at the Moqui (Hopi) Pueblo had been cured by one of the friars using a cross belonging to the famed Spanish nun Madre Luisa de Carrión.[85] As Benavides explains in the text, the commissary general of the Indies, Juan de Santander, who had given his approval for the *1630 Memorial*'s publication, became convinced that Luisa de Carrión "era la contenida en aquella memoria del Arzobispo de México" (she who was mentioned in the archbishop of Mexico's account).[86] Santander sent Benavides to talk to Madre Carrión's confessor, Fray Domingo de Aspe, while Benavides was in Spain. Aspe showed Benavides a book of revelations[87] that showed that a year and a half before Benavides's arrival in Spain, Madre Carrión "había sido llevada milagrosamente . . . a las conversiones de Nuevo Mexico" (had been miraculously taken . . . to the conversions in New Mexico).[88] Benavides was not permitted to transcribe the contents of the book of revelations, but based on what Aspe shows him, he concludes that Madre Carrión must have shared the ability to mystically evangelize in New Mexico with Sor María.

In response to this new development, Benavides presents the following resolution:

> Infiero por certísimo ser la madre María la que milagrosamente va a predicar a las naciones del Nuevo México que caen al oriente como son los Xumanas, Japies y Quiviras y otros reinos que ella propia me dijo con evidentes señales. Y que la Madre Luisa es asimismo llevada milagrosamente a las conversiones del occidente del Nuevo México como son los Apaches de Navajo . . . y a las provincias de Cuñi y Moqui adonde fue el milagro de la cruz.

———

> I take as absolutely certain that Mother María is she who miraculously travels to preach to the nations of New Mexico that are located to the east, such as the Jumanos, Japies, and Quiviras, and

other kingdoms that she herself told me about with clear indications. And that in the same way, Mother Luisa is miraculously taken to the conversions in the west of New Mexico, such as those of the Apaches de Navajo . . . and to the provinces of Zuñi and Moqui [Hopi] where the miracle of the cross occurred.[89]

According to this version of the narrative, Sor María evangelized in the eastern regions of New Mexico, while Madre Carrión ministered in the west. After this startling revelation and change to the narrative, Benavides offers no further details of their travel or discussion of the matter, adding only that there is more proof which he does not include, as he deems it inappropriate to share while the two women lived.[90]

Madre Luisa de Carrión was a well-known mystic in Spain whose reliquary, including the pictures and crosses Benavides mentions in the *1630 Memorial*, were so prevalent in the Spanish colonies that the Church issued an edict banning their sale and circulation, as Madre Carrión had not been beatified.[91] This may explain her popularity and connection with the idea of the New Mexico mission field. Yet Luisa de Carrión is never again mentioned in a significant manner in later readings of the Lady in Blue narrative.

This may be in part because the *1634 Memorial*'s reading audience was small; the text was meant to be read in Rome by the pope, and there is no evidence it was ever printed. As a result, very few readers then or now are familiar with the extraordinary modifications to the narrative Benavides presented in it. Urban VIII's thoughts on the matter are the subject for another study, but the *1634 Memorial* was Benavides's last major documented work. In spite of his desire to return to New Mexico as its bishop, Benavides left Spain for Goa, India, to assume the position of auxiliary bishop, and is said to have died en route.[92]

Reckoning the Lady in Blue with the Mystical Writer: Joseph Ximénez Samaniego's *Vita* of Sor María

The versions of the Lady in Blue narrative discussed up to this point were all written within a narrow time frame, approximately 1626–34, and from the point of view of early New Mexican missionaries writing with their patrons and superiors in mind. The writers' objectives lay in the development of the missions in and around New Mexico, and the narrative was one part of their complex negotiations, transatlantic and secular/religious. In contrast, the Lady in Blue narrative in Sor María's saint's life, or *vita*, is instead written in relationship to Sor María, the woman who was made answerable for the narrative during her lifetime. Published several decades after the other versions of the Lady in Blue narrative were written, Sor María's *vita* was composed by Franciscan friar Joseph Ximénez Samaniego. Ximénez Samaniego knew Sor María personally during her life and championed her writing and her case for sainthood after her death.[93]

As with any holy biography, the purpose of the *vita* was to show Sor María's spirituality in its best light, and to emphasize those aspects of her life that suggested the type of extraordinary holiness that could lead to her beatification. The Lady in Blue narrative in the *vita* is focused more on the significance of her mystical travel in the context of the nun's life and writing (in particular the difficult questions about the nature of her travel that she was compelled to answer), and less on its impact in relationship to the New Spanish mission field and the Franciscan Order.[94] And, most importantly in terms of the circulation of the Lady in Blue narrative, the *vita* prefaced almost all editions of *La mística ciudad de dios*.

The *vita*'s version of Sor María's travels shares elements in common with the *1630 Memorial* and the 1631 letter, drawing on secondary sources (such as Inquisition documents) that referenced or commented on those texts. The *vita* says little about Benavides, and is silent on Zárate Salmerón; further, Ximénez Samaniego does not appear to have met either friar. Yet Ximénez Samaniego's rise to leadership within the Franciscan Order undoubtedly familiarized him with Sor María's Inquisition process and its documentation. The *vita* he wrote ensured that this remarkable episode from Sor María's youth did not detract from her candidacy for sainthood, or from her authorship of *La mística ciudad de dios*.

The Lady in Blue narrative appears in the twelfth chapter of Sor María's *vita*, contextualized within several chapters dedicated to her early life in the family home/convent and the *exterioridades* she experienced as a young woman. Although its subtitle, "Maravillosa conversión de infieles" (Marvelous Conversion of Infidels), echoes the title Benavides gave to the episode in his two *Memorials*, neither of the friar's texts is cited explicitly. Instead, Sor María's travels are framed as a manifestation of her desire to participate in the work of conversion in far-off places: "se ofrecia a padecer mucho mas y a dar la vida si fuesse necesario para que una sola alma se salvasse" (she offered to suffer much more and even to give her life if it were necessary to save even one soul).[95] Ximénez Samaniego is careful to present Sor María in the least controversial light, and he takes pains to ensure that her spiritual travels are seen as authentic and personal. According to Ximénez Samaniego's version of the narrative, during Sor María's early ecstasies God showed her the entire world, but through neither sight, nor sound, nor physical presence; rather, she observed all through abstract means.[96] Her concern for the souls of the unconverted *infieles* made these experiences "un amargo y cariñoso tormenta" (a bitter and loving torment). During these trips she was shown a group of non-Christians to whom God's mercy was particularly directed: the gentiles of New Mexico and nearby regions.[97] As she visited these places again and again, and achieved a greater understanding of the land and disposition of its people, Sor María prayed strenuously for their conversion. The result of her humble diligence was a miracle of great proportions: "el Señor . . . obró en ella, y por ella una de las mayores maravillas, que han admirado los siglos" (the Lord . . . worked in her and through her one of the greatest miracles seen in centuries). Here, Ximénez Samaniego responds to the skepticism—and shows a bit of the celebrity—with which Sor María's mystical conversions were treated during her lifetime and after.

Circumspect in explaining the nature of Sor María's travels, Ximénez Samaniego recounts how, once while praying, she was suddenly taken to a new place by means unclear to her.[98] It seemed to her she experienced everything in her new environment in a sensory way, seeing "ocularmente, que percibía sensiblemente el temple más calido de la tierra y que experimentaba los demás sentidos aquella diversidad" (visually, that she perceived through her senses the earth's hottest atmosphere and the rest of her senses likewise took in a diversity of impressions). These points of clarification regarding what her travel was like were indirect responses to earlier interrogations by the Spanish Inquisition and superiors in the Franciscan Order regarding the specific means by which she traveled. Sor María channeled her anxiety about this experience into compassion for the people she visited, to whom she preached the Holy Faith.[99] According to Ximénez Samaniego, Sor María thought that she preached to the tribes in Spanish, but they understood her as if she spoke to them in their own language. Before returning to her convent, she was fully occupied in the faraway territories, where "hacía maravillas en confirmación de la Fe que predicaba" (wrought miracles in confirmation of the Faith she preached).

Ximénez Samaniego asserts that the nun made more than five hundred visits to New Mexico.[100] His account reiterates many elements of the Benavides texts, repeating that Sor María converted an indigenous nation and its prince, met the Franciscan friars working in New Mexico, and asked the members of the converted nation to seek out the friars for baptism. Ximénez Samaniego declares that many more remarkable things happened while she was on her travels, but omits them, claiming they were so numerous that it would take too much time to cite them all ("sería muy largo el referir").[101]

As with the preface to *La mística ciudad de dios*, the *vita*'s purpose was to promote Sor María's sanctity, but more specifically to underscore her legitimacy as the author of the book itself (a point that Rome repeatedly questioned after Sor María's death). For this reason, this version of the narrative focused on a specific detail of Sor María's travel that had been of great interest to the nun's critics: the means by which she traveled to and was present in New Mexico. Sor María was examined by the Inquisition twice during her lifetime, and she testified about her travels and her writing. Sometime in the 1650s, she wrote a letter to the vice-commissary general of the Franciscan Order, Pedro Manero, in which she addressed persistent questions about her bilocations.[102] Over time, Sor María's responses to these questions had varied, and reflected not only uncertainty on her part regarding the nature of her travel but, understandably, her caution and reluctance before powerful Inquisition officials. She commented in her letter to Manero that her experiences had been "exaggerated or misunderstood" by Benavides and others who spread the narrative and that "neither then nor now was, or am, I capable of knowing the way [my travels] happened."[103]

In the 1670 *vita*, Ximénez Samaniego cites Sor María's letter to Manero, quoting the nun's own canny reply to questions about whether her travel was corporeal or not: "Si fue ir, o no, real y verdaderamente con el cuerpo, no puedo yo assegurarlo, y no es mucho lo dude, pues San Pablo estaba a mejor luz y confiessa de si fue llevado al tercer Cielo, y que no sabe, si fue en cuerpo o fuera de él" (If the travel were or were not really and truly carried out in my body, I could not myself be sure, and this doubt should not be surprising, for Saint Paul was more enlightened than I, and he did not know whether, if taken to the third Heaven, it was in his body or out of it).[104] Sor María's elegant indirect response underscores the stakes that were riding on the issue of physical spiritual travel, and it highlights her immense knowledge, political awareness, and skill in answering (how could she, a simple woman, know how she traveled if the great St. Paul did not know?). Ximénez Samaniego's citation of Sor María's response shows that his "official" version of the narrative had to take into account how she herself responded to questions regarding her travel, as it calculated how to most favorably present the issue.

Ximénez Samaniego writes that Sor María definitely traveled in some manner, and offers reasons for why she could have traveled in her body, though he avoids making a definitive claim. He reasons that Sor María perceived her surroundings through her senses—she experienced day, night, and weather conditions in various locations, and left rosaries with the people she converted, having them in her possession at the beginning of her raptures and returning without them.[105] The *vita* represents a Sor María who modestly believed that she had voyaged in her spirit, not her body, and later speculated that perhaps she had dreamed the bilocation experiences (though, when asked, she typically confirmed that she had indeed traveled). Sor María's confessor was convinced that she had traveled in her body, and in his account Ximénez Samaniego deduces that her confessor helped circulate this idea throughout Spain, noting that it is difficult to keep secrets of this nature under wraps: "es tan difícil, que secretos de este género, ya conferidos, se guarden" (it is so difficult to keep such secrets, once they are conferred). Given these various complexities and the difficulty of ascertaining the precise nature of her travel—to say nothing of the potential risk for Sor María in laying claim to certain types of travel—Ximénez Samaniego says only that "la verdad cierta" (the honest truth) was that someone, either Sor María or an angel that looked like her, had appeared in New Mexico.[106] Further, this travel was not the work of the devil ("no era cosa del demonio"), for the Lord made very clear to Sor María the integrity of her efforts.[107]

Ximénez Samaniego then recounts parts of the narrative that originated in the *1630 Memorial*. He leaves out Benavides as the author, writing the friar into the background, and adding details. According to the *vita*'s version of the Lady in Blue, the friars in New Mexico were not anticipating the visit from the "infieles," namely, the Jumanos, nor had they heard of Sor María from the archbishop's letter. (These points run counter to what Benavides claims in the *1634 Memorial* but are consistent with what he wrote in the 1631 letter.) The friars then show the tribal members a portrait of Luisa de Carrión, because of her fame in Spain at that time.[108] The friar accompanies the unidentified tribesmen back to their home in the "hasta entonces incógnitas provincias" (until then unknown provinces) after they request baptism from the friars. Sor María's preaching had left the tribes "tan bien catequizados, que sin otra instrucción, pudieron baptizarlos . . . por tener la Sierva de Dios tan bien dispuestos, con tan maravillosa predicación aquellas almas" (so well catechized that without additional instruction, [the friars] could baptize them . . . since the Servant of God had them so well disposed, through her wondrous preaching to those souls). In Ximénez Samaniego's account, Benavides's travel to Spain was motivated by these mysterious conversions, and finding out who had taught them was the primary objective of his visit.[109]

Ximénez Samaniego then makes careful note by name of all the male figures who were involved in the meeting between Sor María and Benavides at her convent, as if to redirect possible critique away from her by reminding readers that she was surrounded by male superiors who elicited and possibly elaborated her testimony. He identifies the Comisario General Fray Bernardino Sena as an "ocular testigo" (visual witness) to Sor María's travels and determines that she was the instrument through which the miracles were accomplished.[110] Ximénez Samaniego lists Benavides; Fray Sebastián Marcilla, the provincial of Burgos and Sor María's former confessor; and Fray Francisco Andrés de la Torre, Sor María's confessor at the time, all who together visited the Ágreda convent and compelled Sor María to cooperate with their questioning: "haciendo sacrificio de su secreto, en obsequio de la obediencia, se confesó con sincera verdad lo que a cerca de la materia le avia sucedido" (sacrificing her secret, in honor of the call to obedience, she confessed with sincere veracity all that had happened to her concerning the event). Out of this meeting, these men composed "una relación de todos estos sucesos y lo que a cerca de ellos la Sierva de Dios avia declarado" (an account of all these events and that which the Servant of God had said about them), and left the account with de la Torre. Ximénez Samaniego does not provide any more information about this report.

Referencing the letter by Benavides and Sor María, Ximénez Samaniego confirms that Sor María helped to compose an exhortative letter to the friars in New Mexico, encouraging them in the constant pursuit of their holy occupation.[111] He attributes the spread of the news about Sor María's voyages to Benavides. The friar, "aunque sabia quan importante era, que tan inauditos secretos no publicassen en España, viviendo la sierva de Dios" (although he knew how important it was not to publicize such secrets in Spain, since the Servant of God was still alive), nevertheless told many people in Spain, and the events were made public ("se hicieron públicos").[112] Although undoubtedly Benavides and others, including Sor María's confessors Fray Marcilla and de la Torre, spread the news of her bilocation in Spain, Ximénez Samaniego's mention of this in the *vita* exonerates Sor María from any suggestion of self-promotion relating to the mystical travels. Ximénez Samaniego reflects—seemingly incorrectly—on Benavides's fate after the visit to Sor María's convent, believing that Benavides returned to New Mexico and personally shared the letter with the friars there.

Ximénez Samaniego adds that Benavides wrote another "relación" (account) regarding these events, which included Sor María's letter in it. Ximénez Samaniego claims that Benavides left a copy of it in the *custodia*'s archive for posterity.[113] Although the title of this later document is not revealed, it would seem he is referring to the 1631 letter from Benavides and Sor María discussed above. The year before Ximénez Samaniego wrote the *vita*, "un tanto" (an excerpt) of that archival letter was sent from the archives by the Comisario General de Nueva España to the *procurador* of the Province of Santo Evangelio, Mateo de Heredia. The document was to be presented at the Real Consejo de Indias as evidence of the Franciscans' work in the region, which was threatened by "cierta emulación, que le pretendía obscurecer esta gloria" (a certain emulation, that sought to obscure this glory).[114] This was perhaps a gibe at the other orders competing for a foothold in the frontier missions. Ximénez Samaniego claims that the letter arrived to him spontaneously, and he clearly incorporated its contents and a discussion about it in the *vita*.[115] In his conclusion, Ximénez Samaniego says of the testimonies concerning Sor María's travels to New Mexico that he has pursued them, thinking this effort worthwhile—"helos proseguido, pareciendome la digression precisa" (I have pursued them, believing the digression necessary)—because such miracles should not be referenced without first looking into them—"prodigios tan singulares no se refieren bien sin su comprobación" (such singular marvels are not well recounted without first being verified). As Ximénez Samaniego frames it, the chapter dedicated to Sor María's spiritual travels of conversion was a digression from the *vita*'s main focus, but was an episode in her life that had to be addressed, both to give it the weight it merited in the context of her biography and to discredit any critique of Sor María on the basis of her travels. In Ximénez Samaniego's version of the Lady in Blue narrative, Sor María's mystical travels were but one part, albeit an important one, of a larger work dedicated to Sor María as a spiritual writer and holy figure.

READING THE LADY IN BLUE IN THE SEVENTEENTH CENTURY: PUBLICATION, CIRCULATION, AND ACCESSIBILITY

Taken together, these early versions of the Lady in Blue comprise the foundation from which the narrative was popularized. But given differences in accessibility to each—and therefore variation in scope of readership—they played different roles in shaping later interpretations of the narrative. Not all versions were equally influential during the colonial period, and some have been attributed more influence than they actually exerted in their time.

As we know, not all of the texts were published: Zárate Salermón's "Relación de la Santa Madre María de Jesús" and Benavides's *1634 Memorial* remained in manuscript form during the colonial period, according to bibliographies and printing records from the epoch. Though recent scholarship draws attention to the manuscript as a prestige literary form during the early colonial period, it does not appear that these two texts circulated to a significant degree in this manner.[116] As a result, these versions were read by the smallest audiences, and they therefore exerted lesser influence on general understanding of the narrative (what was repeated by mission friars, and in later chronicles and histories).[117] We are unlikely to know for certain whether Benavides read Zárate Salmerón's *Relaciones*, or if Zárate Salmerón was his source for information on Sor María, but it is evident that few of his time and later knew about Zárate Salmerón's discussion of the Lady in Blue.[118]

The intended audience of Benavides's *1634 Memorial* was limited to begin with. The fact that virtually no subsequent colonial-era discussion of the Lady in Blue narrative mentions Luisa de Carrión as a mystical missionary contemporary of Sor María's suggests that few outside of Rome read this document. One wonders how Pope Urban VIII and his advisors interpreted the *1634 Memorial*, given Benavides's speedy departure to Goa shortly after submitting the report instead of to the leadership position he sought in New Mexico.[119]

Recent readings of the Lady in Blue narrative argue for the *1630 Memorial*'s popularity during the colonial period. But archival sources do not bear this hypothesis out. In fact, as early twentieth-century historian Henry Raupp Wagner remarked, "very few of the later writers on New Mexico or on María Jesús de Agreda mention [the *1630 Memorial*]."[120] Wagner's assertion bears mentioning to avoid overstating the importance of the *1630 Memorial* in the colonial period, both as a source document and as a means of popularization of the narrative. This misconception may have arisen in Anglophone scholarship due to the repeated publication of the *1630 Memorial* in English translation in the twentieth century, creating the sense that it must have been equally accessible in its day, or simply creating greater accessibility to the document by scholars.[121] This does not appear to have been the case, for although the *1630 Memorial* was printed in four languages in Europe in the early seventeenth century, its circulation outside of Europe appears to have been small.[122] Most significantly, any discussion of Sor María in conjunction with the Lady in Blue would necessarily have been informed by one of the other versions of the narrative, as the *1630 Memorial* does not name Sor María explicitly. Although important in 1630–31 for increasing visibility for the New Mexico missions, the *1630 Memorial*'s Lady in Blue was not as dominant as were later versions of the narrative.

The greatest number of readers of the narrative accessed the 1631 letter to the friars in New Mexico and the *vita* that prefaced *La mística ciudad de dios*. There are many layers of reading for the 1631 letter because it was distributed and read in manuscript and print forms. Archival documents, including some discussed in my later chapters, reference manuscript copies of the letter circulating among Spanish and New Spanish Franciscans in the later seventeenth and early eighteenth centuries. The precise distribution parameters for the manuscript of the letter are difficult to measure, but we get a sense that it arrived to a number of readers within the Church and Franciscan Order. Sor María addressed the claims in a letter to Fray Pedro Manero in the 1650s, suggesting that as a manuscript, it had an influential and significant group of readers in seventeenth-century Spain.

Ximénez Samaniego notes in the *vita* that he received an excerpt of the 1631 letter as he wrote the holy biography. The friar does not specify who sent it to him from the New Spanish archive where the original was located or why it was sent to him, but the fact that he was sent it at all suggests that copying and circulating this text was not uncommon in the later seventeenth century, both in Spain and in Mexico.

The version of the letter Ximénez Samaniego received directly informed the seventeenth- and early eighteenth-century Franciscan missionaries who established missions in the New Spanish borderlands. Ximénez Samaniego was involved in the establishment of the Propaganda Fide colleges in Mexico, where missionaries were trained in the seventeenth and eighteenth centuries. Ximénez Samaniego shared his copy of the 1631 letter with Fray Antonio Llinás, the founding friar of the Propaganda Fide colleges in Mexico. Fray Damián Manzanet, who with Llinás established the Colegio de Santa Cruz de Querétaro, traveled to Texas in 1689 to found missions there. In his a letter to Mexican polymath Carlos Sigüenza y Góngora, Manzanet indicates that he had a copy of the letter given to Llinás before the friars left Spain for Mexico: "Una carta que para en mi poder la qual dieron en Madrid a nuestro Padre Fray Antonio Llinás la cual carta hace mención de lo que la Beata Madre María de Jesús de Agreda comunicó en su Convento al Padre Custodio del Nuevo México Fray Alonso de Benavides y dice la B. Madre como estuvo muchas veces al Nuevo México" (A letter that I have in my possession, which they gave to our Father Antonio Llinás in Madrid, and in which the letter mentions what the Blessed Mother María de Jesús de Ágreda communicated in her convent to the father custodian of New Mexico, Fray Alonso de Benavides, and the Blessed Mother says that she was in New Mexico many times).[123] Manzanet was inspired by the 1631 letter to join in the Mexican mission endeavor: "por estas noticias que yo traía de España y juntamente vine al ministerio de la conversión de los infieles pasé y estuve en las misiones de Coahuila" (on the basis of this news I brought from Spain, and it came to pass that I came to the ministry of the conversion of infidels and I was in the Coahuila missions).[124] Several other seventeenth- and eighteenth-century Propaganda Fide friars also wrote that they had their own copies of the letter, prior to its 1730 publication in Mexico; hence, they must have possessed manuscript copies.

Although Ximénez Samaniego's name is not mentioned directly in Manzanet's letter, he likely sanctioned the 1631 letter's distribution among the mission friars of Propaganda Fide. He certainly appears to have made other efforts to see the 1631 letter associated with the northern New Spanish mission field. A 1776 *Manifiesto* sent from the Propaganda Fide College of San Fernando in Mexico City states that Ximénez Samaniego sent "un tanto" (a selection) of the letter to Fray Mateo Heredia, the procurador of the Province of New Mexico at the Spanish court, so that it could be presented to the Real Consejo de Indias with other documents proving the order's conversion efforts in the New World.[125] In Franciscan and religious circles, and among the Propaganda Fide college friars in Mexico, Ximénez Samaniego's copy of the 1631 letter written by Benavides and Sor María was shared, informing ideas about the northern New Spanish borderlands and its missions. Within this limited but influential group, the manuscript letter's version of the narrative circulated and exercised its effect.

The published version of the letter is a different matter. Published three times in Mexico during the eighteenth century, it reached a much broader audience in New Spain than did the manuscript version of the 1631 letter. Although bibliographer José Toribio Medina documents the publication of the letter in Mexico in 1631, other historians strongly disagree that it was published then, claiming that Medina and other bibliographers cite the same misinterpreted document.[126] Three other documented printings of the letter in Mexico cluster together in the mid-eighteenth century: 1730, 1747, and 1760.[127] The *Tanto que se sacó de una carta* will be examined in greater depth in chapter 3 in the context of works of Sor María's writing published on Mexican presses. In this context, as a document that presented a particular version of the Lady in Blue narrative, it is significant because its publication resulted in greater accessibility to its version of the narrative, and its repeated publication suggests that whoever sponsored its publication pressed for its continued presence in the public sphere. It was clearly very influential in the public perception of Sor María as the protagonist of the Lady in Blue narrative in colonial Mexico.

Sor María's *vita*, part of the preface to *La mística ciudad de dios*, seems to have brought the narrative to the greatest number of general readers. Wagner notes in his discussion of the Lady in Blue, "For the miraculous conversions of which Benavides writes, not his book [the *1630 Memorial*] is quoted, but Ximénez Samaniego's Life of the Nun."[128] Not only was the *vita* published with almost all editions of *La mística ciudad de dios*, it was also printed as a separate document, the *Relación de la vida de la V. Madre Sor María de Jesús*.[129] Many editions of the *Relación de la vida* were published in Spain by the propaganda press dedicated to her case for canonization (discussed in chapter 2), and copies of the *Relación de la vida* were present in the libraries of the College of Santa Cruz de Querétaro, and among the holdings of other colonial-era Mexican collections. Although the *Relación de la vida* did not equal *La mística ciudad de dios* in the extent of its publication, it was nonetheless printed and distributed to an impressive degree, and undoubtedly contributed to the reading of the Lady in Blue narrative by a significant transatlantic audience.

If one were to measure readership of the narrative by considering only the number of copies of the narrative published, then the most robust physical circulation of the Lady in Blue narrative was achieved through *La mística ciudad de dios*. That is, Sor María's *own writing* was the primary vehicle for the popularization of the Lady in Blue narrative. As I will detail in chapter 2, *La mística ciudad de dios*, a Marian treatise written by Sor María that addressed the theological question of the Immaculate Conception of Mary, was repeatedly printed in Spain from the seventeenth through the nineteenth century. Although documented printings of *La mística ciudad de dios* in Mexico are few, the book was sent en masse to Mexico from Spain, as I will show in chapter 3, and its documented presence in libraries, private collections, and other venues suggests a significant community of readers for the text—and its version of the Lady in Blue narrative—in Mexico. New Spanish readers of *La mística ciudad de dios* were familiar with the Lady in Blue narrative through the book's preface, and the two concepts of the nun—mystical missionary and author—complemented each other in New Spanish thought and culture, as chapters 3 and 4 will illustrate.

La mística ciudad de dios was important for reasons other than the circulation of the Lady in Blue narrative. It was frequently published, often read and cited, and rendered into artwork, theater, and even satire. Chapter 2 explores why this was the case and how it came to be in seventeenth- and eighteenth-century Spain.

CHAPTER TWO

Sor María's Rise as Mystical Writer and Protomissionary in Early Modern Spain

No están agotadas, ni con mucho, las pesquisas e investigaciones sobre estos temas. . . . Aunque mucho se conserva en las profusas copias que se hacieron [*sic*] de las obras y cartas de la Venerable Agreda, hay lagunas que revelan la existencia de documentos, cartas, sobre todo, hoy desconocidas, pero quizá no perdidas, sino ocultas o ignoradas.

———

The research and investigation into these topics is by no means exhausted, not by a long shot. . . . Although much has been retained in the profusion of copies of works and letters by the Venerable Ágreda, there are lacunae that reveal the existence of documents and letters as yet undiscovered; perhaps not lost, but rather hidden or ignored.

—Julio Campos[1]

An eighteenth-century painting in Sor María's convent in Ágreda depicts the nun seated at a small table, writing quill in hand. Six angels surround her as she looks slightly upward towards the Virgin Mary, who prompts the nun as she writes. This central image is framed by eighteen smaller vignettes, each of which illustrates an episode of Sor María's life (see fig. 2.1).[2] These vignettes include scenes of Sor María taking the nun's veil, destroying a portrait of herself, and burning her book *La mística ciudad de dios*. Two vignettes at the middle top of the painting depict her travels to the Americas and encounter with native people there. A third shows two friars, perhaps Juan de Salas and Fray Diego López of Fray Benavides's accounts, baptizing the same tribe.[3] This painting has been called a "sermon gráfico" (illustrated sermon), intended to instruct the novices at the convent in Sor María's biography by showing edifying episodes of her life.

The tableau leaves little doubt as to the nun's foremost accomplishment: based on its size and centrality, Sor María's composition of *La mística ciudad de dios* overshadows all else. Although the painting keeps the Lady in Blue narrative in the picture—literally at its front and center—its primary subject is Sor María as the author of this famed and controversial Conceptionist text.

Figure 2.1. Illustrated biography of Sor María de Jesús de Ágreda. Artist unknown. Convento de la Concepción, Ágreda, Soria, Spain. Image courtesy Pilar Ruiz Cacho, Anabel Blanco, and the nuns of the Convento de la Concepción de Ágreda.

Like the painting, I focus here on Sor María as a writer and religious figure, specifically in seventeenth- and eighteenth-century Spain. As the image suggests, her renown in this context is only partially attributable to her famed bilocations to New Mexico. Her writing and its promotion by powerful groups in Spain, and beyond, are the other, perhaps dominant side of the story. These same tendencies carried over to New Spain and to Sor María's popularization as a literary and spiritual figure there.

In this chapter I outline the development of a culture of devotion and reading of Sor María's writing in early modern Spain. A brief discussion of Sor María's biography lays the groundwork for a closer look at her substantial body of writing, including *La mística ciudad de dios*. After her death, the promotion of her case for sainthood led to increased renown for the nun, but it also engendered scrutiny of her writing. Interventions by Spanish Franciscans and the Spanish Crown to see Sor María canonized led to the formal and ongoing posthumous promotion of her writing. These efforts culminated in the establishment of a propaganda press whose profits provided subvention for her *causa*, or case for canonization, in Rome. As a result of this persistent and public advocacy, Sor María emerged as an important figure in early modern Spanish culture. The chapter's conclusion links Sor María's celebrity in Spain with her rise as a writer and religious figure in colonial Mexico.

The Public Life of a Nuanced Nun

María de Jesús Coronel y Arana was born in Ágreda, Soria, Spain, on April 2, 1602, to Francisco Coronel and Catalina Arana (see fig. 2.2, an image from one of the editions of her *vita*). Allegedly of *converso* heritage on her father's side, the family had lived in the city for several generations.[4] María had two older brothers, Francisco and José, and a younger sister, Jerónima. Around 1615, her mother, Catalina, began to contemplate the conversion of the family's estate into a convent, after experiencing visions and under the advisement of a local Augustinian friar, Pedro Otalora. Catalina eventually convinced her fifty-year-old husband of this plan, and the family home formally became a convent in December 1618.[5]

Francisco and his two sons entered a Franciscan monastery in nearby Burgos, while María, her sister, and her mother took simple vows

V.M.SOR MARIA DE IESVS DE AGREDA
murio à.24.de Maio de.1665.de edad de.63.años.
D. Antonius Palomino et Belasco. Pictor. Regis. delineavit.
Greg͞ Fosman et Medina Matritense sculpsit
Matriti anno 1711.

Figure 2.2. Relación de la vida de Sor María (1711). Image by Gregorio Fosman y Medina. Image courtesy of the John Carter Brown Library at Brown University.

and remained in the family's former home, now convent. Soon after, new nun Sor María began to experience intense spiritual raptures, or *exterioridades*, some of which were associated with her mystical travels to New Mexico. News of the *exterioridades* traveled well beyond the walls of the convent, advanced in its spread by Sor María's confessor, Fray Juan de Torrecilla. In a letter to the vicecomissary general of the Franciscan Order, Pedro Manero, Sor María drily describes her confessor as well-intentioned but indiscreet.[6] She goes on to explain that there were significant differences between her raptures as she experienced them and how they were represented by others, suggesting that the expectations of male superiors came to bear on her from a young age.[7]

In 1627, at age twenty-five, Sor María was appointed abbess of her convent, and was subsequently granted a special dispensation to hold that position in 1628 from Urban VIII, required because she was so young.[8] Shortly thereafter, in 1631, Sor María met with Fray Alonso de Benavides at her convent, and together the two wrote the letter to the friars in New Mexico we examined in chapter 1. This moment was pivotal for the Lady in Blue narrative: it was at this point formally associated with Sor María, and the letter circulated within the Franciscan Order and far beyond.

A few years later, in 1635, the Inquisition examined Sor María for the first time. The Inquisition became interested in her primarily because rumors of her travels to New Mexico had spread in Spain: "en los primeros años de la vida religiosa de Sor María—concretamente hacia 1620–1623—las cosas de la monja agredana habían hecho mucho ruido y se habían extendido por toda España" (during the earliest years of Sor María's religious life—around 1620–1623—the Agredan nun's matters had caused a stir and extended throughout Spain).[9] The tribunal seems to have been convened to definitively determine if specific aspects of the nun's mystical travels were true, if Sor María had publicly experienced raptures and had distributed crosses and rosaries with special graces in the Americas, among other activities.[10]

At that time in Spain, accounts of mystical travel were not uncommon; Sor María's case was preceded by that of Franciscan friar Francisco de la Fuente, who also was alleged to have traveled mystically to the Americas.[11] De la Fuente was interrogated in an auto-da-fé in 1632, and the papers from his process were sent to the Inquisition council in Logroño to be examined alongside Sor María's testimony.[12] The two cases were to be compared in order to ensure that Sor María had not been subject to "el mismo engaño y ilusión del Demonio" (the same demonic tricks and delusions) as had de la Fuente.[13]

In comparison to the condemnation of Fray de la Fuente's travel, Sor María's case of bilocation was treated with "prudent benevolence"[14] in Logroño in May 1635, though concern persisted regarding the material evidence of her visits to the Indies—the abovementioned rosaries and crosses. In response to requests from the Supreme Council in Madrid for further information to clarify these points,[15] the Logroño council responded with what appears to have been a manuscript of the letter by Sor María and Fray Benavides: "una relación simple en el que el Padre Custodio, que había venido de las Indias [Benavides], había tratado con Sor María de la prodigiosa evangelización" (a simple account in which the father custodian, who had come from the Indies [Benavides], had dealt with Sor María regarding the prodigious evangelization).[16] The Logroño council also recommended that the padre custodio (Benavides) be contacted so that the documentation might be examined with him present.[17] The Logroño council ultimately was reluctant to press the issue of Sor María' bilocation, and set aside judgment on the matter.

Sor María's response to accusations of false mysticism regarding her travel deepens how we understand her own views on the matter. In her letter to Fray Pedro Manero, which she composed in response to a request for a statement on her experiences in New Mexico, Sor María carefully explains that though the travel legitimately occurred in some spiritual manner, it had happened many years previous, was complicated, and had been misrepresented by many individuals who reported on it.[18] Her reputation as a mystical missionary remained intact throughout her lifetime and beyond, and even influenced real-life Spanish missionaries, such as fellow Ágredan José de Carabantes and Mallorcan Junípero Serra, as we will see in chapter 4.[19]

The renown of Sor María's bilocations eventually reached a royal audience. In 1643, Felipe IV, the king of Spain, stopped at Sor María's convent on returning from Cataluña. There are several possible reasons for this visit, but it seems her fame as a mystical traveler had reached his ears.[20] Felipe IV's interest may also have been piqued by several letters Sor María wrote to him prior to 1643.[21] In any event, this meeting marked the beginning of a twenty-two-year-long written correspondence in which the nun functioned as Felipe IV's spiritual, personal, and at times political advisor, and also as his friend. Felipe IV's will explains his motives for their long relationship:

> Por cuanto yo mantuve una larga correspondencia con la madre Sor María de Agreda, hallando en sus venerables cartas inmensos consuelos, y tal vez conociendo por ellas algunas cosas ajenas de la inteligencia humana, pues como santa profetizaba lo venidero y decía de lo pasado lo que sin ella yo nunca pudiera saber . . . encargo cuanto puedo a mi sucesor ponga todo cuidado en que el dicho libro [de cartas] se conserve y guarde donde se halla, pues está lleno de doctrina sagrada, de amor, de sabiduría, y de avisos y documentos celestiales.

———

> As I maintained a long-term correspondence with mother Sor María de Ágreda, finding in her venerable letters immense consolation, and perhaps discovering through them things foreign to human intelligence, and as a saint who prophesied that which was to come, and told of all that of past that, without her, I would have never known . . . I entrust as much as I might to my successor the protection and conservation of the said book [of bound letters] wherever it may be, for it is full of holy doctrine, of love, of wisdom, of advice, and of celestial documents.[22]

Devoted to Sor María and her counsel, Felipe IV made clear in his will his respect for her writing and mystical knowledge. Although some historians have dismissed Sor María's advisement of Felipe IV as uninformed or exclusively spiritual in nature, historian Luis Villasante finds Sor María's advice generally well defined, prudent, and sensible.[23] Regardless of the content of the letters exchanged between Felipe IV and Sor María, the faithful friendship displayed through them had important ramifications for Sor María's canonization and for the spread of the Lady in Blue narrative for more than a century after their death.

Later correspondence reveals another side to their relationship, one in which Felipe IV functioned as a secure repository for Sor María's writing. By 1637, Sor María had begun writing *La mística ciudad de dios* for the first time. She subsequently burned this text in or around 1646 under the advisement of a confessor, who also ordered the destruction of her other writings.[24] Between 1650 and 1660, Sor María rewrote or recovered the version of *La mística ciudad de dios* that would later be published.[25]

However, letters between Sor María and Felipe IV indicate that she gave an original copy of the text to the king for safekeeping. On this point, their exchange assumed a clandestine tone:

> She would write to the King to tell him that although she had told the tribunal that she had burnt the original copy of her "History of the Virgin Mary," they didn't mention the King's copy, and perhaps they didn't need to know about it: "De la historia de la reina del cielo no han dicho nada; no lo deben saber. Hasta que se aquiete esta tormenta, mejor está oculta" (Regarding the history of the Queen of Heaven, they have not said anything; nor should they know. Until this torment calms, it is better that it remain hidden).[26]

This would not be the last time her writing was protected by the Spanish Crown.[27] It was in fact the starting point for the royal promotion of Sor María's writing in Spain and abroad throughout the seventeenth and eighteenth centuries.

In 1648, the Supreme Council of the Spanish Inquisition began searching for more information about Sor María and contacted the council in Logroño requesting records and judgments from the earlier case. Historians surmise that Sor María's second encounter with the Spanish Inquisition was likely the result of political movements in the Spanish court, as part of a process against the Aragonés pretender to the throne, the Duke of Híjar.[28] At this time, the Supreme Council not only reopened the discussion of Sor María's mystical travel to New Mexico, but it also became interested in the miraculous events attributed to her in Spain and in her writing, specifically *La mística ciudad de dios*.[29]

Sor María's second Inquisition trial formally commenced in 1649, and on January 10, 1650, the Logroño council questioned Sor María regarding "el Memorial de los indios de Méjico" (the account of the Mexican Indians), as the tribunal found the allegations of baptism and conversions of the tribes to be of particular concern from a doctrinal standpoint. When interrogated in her convent by Fray Antonio González de Moral, she responded in the language of visions; she claimed she had

experienced visions of the New World that were "intelectuales, imagi-
narias, y de presencia"[30] (intellectual, imagined, and presential) and that
were absolutely not the work of the devil. Sor María cast the bilocations
as events of her youth, asking pardon for not remembering them in
detail.[31] The Supreme Council interviewed individuals who knew Sor
María personally and who had testified earlier regarding her travels. Her
examiners were ultimately satisfied with Sor María's responses to their
questions and with her demonstrated obedience. In fact, their request
for "cruces y alhajas de recuerdo de Sor María" (crosses and treasures in
memory of Sor María)[32]—souvenirs of their time with her—indicate
their disposition towards her and their ultimate judgment. The *dictamen*
(formal opinion) by the investigators indicated that those who contributed to the letter Sor María wrote with Benavides "añadieron mucho
y supusieron más" (added much and surmised more), effectively shifting
the Inquisition's critical gaze from Sor María to her (male) superiors in
1631. She was found "católica y fiel cristiana, bien fundada en nuestra
santa fe, sin ningún género de ficción ni embeleco del demonio" (a
Catholic and faithful Christian, well founded in our Holy Faith, without
any type of fiction, nor devil's fraud).[33] In her exchange of letters with
Felipe IV after this encounter with the Inquisition, Sor María emphasizes that the events related to her bilocations pertained to her long-past
youth.[34]

By 1655, Sor María had begun the second version of *La mística
ciudad de dios*. With the encouragement of her confessor, Fray Andrés
de Fuenmayor, she completed the text in 1660.[35] The rest of Sor María's
life, with the exception of her interventions for other causes and individuals, was peaceful, and her correspondence with Felipe IV continued
until her death on May 24, 1665. But as her life ended, Sor María's literary legacy began to flourish.

A Mystical Missionary's Prolific Quill

Throughout her lifetime, Sor María wrote prolifically, both personal
texts (letters and documents internal to her convent) and other works.
Although less widely influential because of their smaller reading audiences than Sor María's published texts, her many manuscripts illustrate
the abundance of her wide-ranging spiritual and secular writings. For

example, her *Jardín espiritual y nivel del alma* is in keeping thematically with Sor María's mystical writing,[36] while *Las sabatinas* (a collection of prayers) serves a bibliographic purpose because the text includes an indexing of other works she wrote and destroyed earlier in her life. A manuscript in which Sor María classified the six angels who cared for her illustrates her ongoing interest in the mystical realm.[37] Her *Segundo ejercicio cotidiano* was printed numerous times (including in Mexico), and continued the type of writing presented in her *Ejercicio cotidiano*.[38] Still more spiritual texts, letters, and personal works written by Sor María remain in her convent's archive in Ágreda, and others have more recently emerged in print.[39] Some works were published later than the time period studied in this chapter, among them the *Escala para subir a la perfección* (first published in 1915), *Ejercicio cotidiano* (1879), and *Leyes de Esposa* (1916).

Falling somewhere between manuscript and published work, the *Tratado del grado de la luz y de la redondez de la tierra* is a mystical cosmography in keeping with medieval and Renaissance-era ideas regarding the shape and nature of the heavens and earth.[40] The much recopied *Tratado del grado de la luz* was read by many, yet its date of composition (some suggest as early as 1616,[41] during Sor María's youth) cast doubt as to whether Sor María was indeed its author,[42] as she would have been fourteen when she wrote it.[43] Yet at least one colonial-era Mexican source definitively attributed the *Tratado* to Sor María. Antonio de León Pinelo includes the *Tratado de la redondez de la Tierra, de los Habitantes de ella, i de los quatro elementos* in the *Epítome de la bibliotheca oriental, y occidental, náutica y geográfica, de Don Antonio de León Pinelo*,[44] saying that it was by the "V.M. María de Jesús de Agreda," and claiming it as a primary source for New Mexican history. Citing two colonial Mexican publications (Andrés González de Barcia Carballido y Zúñiga's *Ensayo cronológico para la Historia de la Florida*,[45] and the Agustín de Vetancurt's *Teatro mexicano*),[46] León Pinelo's entry states that the *Tratado* "trata de la America: de que la procedió el deseo de predicar à los Barbaros del Nuevo México, que logró, aunque no pudo discernir, si realmente ò en espíritu" (treats America, which emerged from the desire to preach to the Barbarians of New Mexico, which she accomplished, although she could not determine if it occurred really [in her body] or spiritually).[47] This last point echoes almost directly what Sor María's *vita* (among other sources) states about the nature of Sor María's mystical travel. León Pinelo may have in fact conflated or confused the *Tratado* with an account of the Lady in Blue (from her *vita*, the *Tanto que se sacó de una carta*, or the sources he cites). Yet because Sor María was believed to have traveled to the Americas spiritually, another text describing the geography of the heavens was understood as consistent with her mystical experiences, and a work she could have feasibly penned.

Several of Sor María's texts aside from *La mística ciudad de dios* were reproduced on presses in Spain and abroad. Sor María's *Ejercicios espirituales*, a book of advice on the spiritual life of nuns, was first published in 1676 in Mallorca and was printed eleven subsequent times in Spain in the eighteenth century: a considerable run for a book with a very specific intended audience. Franciscan Antonio Arbiol's citation of the *Ejercicios espirituales* in his book *La religiosa instruida*, a guide for religious women, helped Sor María's message to circulate even more widely.[48] *La religiosa instruida* debuted in 1717, was published once by Sor María's propaganda press in 1753, and was reprinted seven more times in Spain in the eighteenth century. Fray Arbiol enthusiastically cites Sor María's writing, in particular *La mística ciudad de dios*,[49] and presents her devotional practices as an example for younger nuns.[50] Near the conclusion of *La religiosa instruida*, Fray Arbiol juxtaposes Sor María's *Ejercicios espirituales'* devotional practices with those of Santa Teresa de Jesús.[51] Citing the publication of the "highly useful" original in Zaragoza in 1714,[52] Fray Arbiol goes on to quote verbatim the "Propósitos de perfección de la Venerable Madre Maria de Jesús de Agreda, divididas en siete clases" (Resolutions to obtain perfection, by the Venerable Mother María de Jesús de Ágreda, divided into seven types),[53] and follows with a detailed list of devotional practices taken from the *Ejercicios espirituales*. Although the *Ejercicios espirituales* are not often cited as one of Sor María's more influential texts, eighteenth-century reprintings of the *Ejercicios* themselves, and of *La religiosa instruida*, suggest a significant community of reading that extended into New Spain, and included prominent reader Sor Juana Inés de la Cruz.[54]

Without a doubt, however, Sor María's most influential work was *La mística ciudad de dios*, a text of Baroque Marian spirituality. Over its long history, *La mística ciudad de dios* has received significant critical attention from theologians and Church historians; as the *Apuntes para una biblioteca de escritoras espanolas* notes, "pocas obras han dado lugar á tantas polémicas como la *Mística Ciudad de Dios*" (few works have given rise to as many controversies as *La mística ciudad de dios*).[55]

La mística ciudad de dios is concisely described by Franciscan theologian Enrique Llamas as

> una obra hagiográfica—no una teología sistemática—concebida y redactada en la época del barroco; no es una historia propiamente dicha, sino una teología histórica y narrativa, es decir: una descripción del contenido teológico de los misterios de la vida de la Virgen María . . . se trata además de una "mariología mística" o espiritual, fruto de la oración contemplativa.

> ———

> a hagiographic work—not a systematic theology—conceived of and composed during the Baroque epoch; it is not a history, properly speaking, but rather a historical and narrative theology, that is: a description of the theological content of the mysteries of the life of Virgin Mary . . . it furthermore treats a type of "mystical Mariology" or spiritual Mariology, the fruit of contemplative prayer.[56]

But Llamas's reading of the text is not, of course, the only one. Seventeenth-century theologians, in particular Dominicans opposed to the theology of the Immaculate Conception, viewed the work as baseless mysticism and suggested it had been ghostwritten by Sor María's confessors.[57] Contemporary literary critics have read in *La mística ciudad de dios* strategies for the empowerment of women, based on the perspective the work presents of the Virgin Mary as a potential co-redeemer with Christ, while others see an early instance of "fictionalized biography."[58] Ironically, the response by some twentieth-century literary critics—"se ha exagerado mucho al considerarla como un tipo excepcional y la segunda escritora religiosa después de Santa Teresa" (it is an exaggeration to consider Sor María exceptional, or as a women religious writer second only to Santa Teresa)[59]—only confirms the text's consequence.

It was a book that covered many important mystical and theological points, with a particular focus on the Virgin Mary's role in Christ's life and death. A brief summary of *La mística ciudad de dios* from contemporary literary scholar Kate Risse shows that the text as a whole is divided into three parts containing eight books based on the Conception, the Incarnation, the Transfixion and the Coronation. In first person, and with great detail, Sor María tells the story of the Virgin's life, as it was revealed to her, beginning with the Virgin's preordained role as "mystical city of God," and continuing with her birth, youth, marriage to Joseph, role in the early Church, and finally her Coronation as Queen of Heaven.[60]

Even as it elaborated these points, *La mística ciudad de dios* provided new perspectives on a variety of other theological topics of relevance then and now.[61] In the words of Franciscan historian Cyprian Lynch, "*La mística ciudad* purports to give a detailed account of the life of the Virgin Mary—to fill in, as it were, the many gaps in the concise Gospel narrative. The book contains a great quantity of apocrypha interspersed with mystical considerations which are often of a very elevated sort; a disconcerting mixture of fanciful imaginings and what might well be authentic revelations."[62] Sor María's first English-language biographer, T. D. Kendrick, noted of the style and content of the book, "at least nobody could call it dull," and deemed it an "original, lively, and powerful book."[63]

The details of the Immaculate Conception theology are found in the first of its three books, chapters 13 through 19.[64] In the context of St. John the Evangelist's revelations on the Immaculate Conception, Sor María explains why the doctrine had not previously been made known:

Tiempo es ya de que el entendimiento humano se desencoja y alargue en la honra de nuestra gran Reina; y también que el que estuviere opuesto, fundado en otro sentir, se encoja y detenga en despojarla y quitarla el adorno de su inmaculada limpieza en el instante de su divina concepción. Con la fuerza de la verdad y luz en que veo estos inefables misterios, confieso una y muchas veces que todos los privilegios, gracias, prerrogativas, favores y dones de María santísima, entrando en ellos el de ser Madre de Dios, según y como a mí se me dan a entender, todos dependen y se originan de haber sido inmaculada y llena de gracia en su concepción purísima; de manera que sin este beneficio parecieran todos informes y mancos o como un suntuoso edificio sin fundamento sólido y proporcionado. Todos miran con cierto orden y encadenamiento a la limpieza e inocencia de la concepción; y por esto ha sido forzoso tocar tantas veces en este misterio, por el discurso de esta Historia, desde los decretos divinos y formación de María y de su Hijo santísimo en cuanto hombre. Y no me alargo ahora más en esto; pero advierto a todos que la Reina del cielo estimó tanto el adorno y hermosura que la dio su Hijo y Esposo en su purísima concepción, que esta correspondencia será su indignación contra aquellos que con terquedad y porfía pretendieren desnudarla de él y afearla, en tiempo que su Hijo santísimo se ha dignado de manifestarla al mundo tan adornada y hermosa, para gloria suya y esperanza de los mortales.

———

It is now time that human understanding straightens up and stretches in honor of our great Queen; and also that whoever was opposed (based on some other understanding) shrink back and halt in dispossessing and taking away from Her the adornment of Her immaculate conception at the instant of Her divine conception. With the strength of truth and light with which I see these ineffable mysteries, I confess once and many times that all the privileges, graces, prerogatives, favors, and gifts belonging to Holy Mary, coming into them as the Mother of God, according to and as I understand them, all depend on and originate from having been immaculate and full of grace through her immaculate conception; in such a manner that without this benefit all would seem shapeless and faulty, or as a sumptuous building without a proportionate and solid foundation. All regard the purity and innocence of the conception with a certain order and consequence; for this reason, it has been necessary to address this mystery so many times, through the discourse of this history, from the divine decrees and the formation of Mary and her holy Son made into man. And I will not go on about this: but I advise all that the Queen of Heaven so valued the adornment and beauty that her Son and Husband gave to her upon her pure conception, that this correspondence will be her indignation against those who, with obstinacy and stubbornness, intend to strip her of it and disfigure her, at a time when her Holy Son has vouchsafed to show her to the world so bedecked and beautiful, for his glory and the hope of mortals.[65]

Sor María's assurances regarding the validity of the Immaculate Conception found an immediate appreciative audience in the Franciscan Order.[66] When Sor María passed away, her works, including *La mística ciudad de dios*, were left to the Franciscans, who sought to make them accessible to all ("al alcance de las gentes," "within the reach of all people").[67] The ongoing battle over the text's Conceptionist content would shape the destiny of Sor María's book and her case for canonization.

TEXT AND PROCESS ENTANGLED: *LA MÍSTICA CIUDAD DE DIOS* AND THE *CAUSA* DE BEATIFICACIÓN

After Sor María's death, the bishop of Tarazona (Ágreda's diocese) began official proceedings for Sor María's case for sainthood, as her tomb was quickly becoming a pilgrimage site.[68] The initial process ended favorably in 1671 and her case for canonization began to move forward in earnest on June 21, 1672, when it was formally introduced in Rome.[69] Sor María was declared Venerable by Clement X in 1673,[70] but despite repeated attempts by the Spanish Crown from then until the death of Carlos III in 1788 to reconsider her case,[71] it would advance no further, even after the Immaculate Conception theology was declared Catholic dogma by Pius IX in 1854.[72] Indeed, Sor María has the dubious distinction of being the only woman whose cause for canonization was vetoed by two popes: Clement XIV in 1773 and Leo XIII in 1887. Perpetual silence on her *causa* was declared, effectively stopping all further discussion of her anticipated sainthood.[73] At the epicenter of the efforts to see the nun declared a saint, Sor María's writing provided both the force behind this promotion and an obstacle to its success.

By the time the first *procurador*, the official in charge of advancing the *causa*, Franciscan José Sanz de Villaragut, was commissioned by Carlos II in 1681, *La mística ciudad de dios* had already experienced a tumultuous entry into the Spanish reading public, which cast a shadow over the text and its author that affected later promotion efforts.[74] In 1672, coinciding with the introduction of Sor María's case for canonization, the inquisitor general ordered that all extant copies of the book be pulled from circulation to consider the work more carefully before continuing its distribution.[75] This action was taken in part because an early edition of the text was published without the required permissions.[76]

On June 26, 1681, Pope Innocent XI prohibited the book's reading, but this prohibition was short-lived ("[quedó] zanjado"[77]) for several reasons.[78] First, Sor María's biographer, Fray Joseph Ximénez Samaniego, intervened directly to try to revoke the prohibition.[79] Second, Carlos II successfully lobbied to suspend the prohibition in Spain.[80] *La mística ciudad de dios* was removed from the Index of Prohibited Books later that same year,[81] though its inclusion on a version of the Index printed in Venice in 1687 continued to cause confusion about its status until a 1713 decree clarified that it had not been on the Index since 1681.[82]

La mística ciudad de dios came under scrutiny repeatedly, and its publication was once again prohibited a few years later, this time for reasons relating to the book's content and authorship. On December 17, 1685, a meeting of the Supreme Council of the Spanish Inquisition about Sor María's writing issued an *expediente* (official opinion) about *La mística ciudad de dios* and Sor María, asserting that it was worthy of being read and that it in no way intended to deceive its readers: "[la] obra la tienen por digna de que se permita, como las de esta calidad y de otras que tratan de rebelaciones privadas de varones de eximia virtud. Y que a la autora la juzgan incapaz de ilusion actiba ni pasiba, por el crédito de sus grandes virtudes" (the work is understood as worthy of being allowed to be read, as are others of a similar nature and those that treat the private revelations of men of eminent virtue. And they judged the [female] author incapable of active or passive trickery, on the basis of her many virtues).[83] The Supreme Council of the Inquisition classified the impediments against *La mística ciudad de dios* in two categories: *reparos* (questions about the doctrine presented in the work) and *fundamentos* (objections to the idea that it was divinely inspired and/or that it could have been written by a woman).[84] Members of the Dominican Order penned the majority of the fundamentos, including the seventh one, which says *La mística ciudad de dios*'s divine origins are dubious and that the Scotist precepts expressed in it run contrary to Thomistic opinions on such matters.[85] In spite of this opposition, on December 17, 1685, the Inquisition allowed *La mística ciudad de dios* to be printed and read as a work of private revelation.[86]

The decision to reopen printing of *La mística ciudad de dios* was relayed to the Supreme Council of the Inquisition on January 4, 1686. That the book was being printed and read elsewhere during this time did not escape the Inquisition's notice.[87] Inquisitor General Diego Sarmiento de Valladartes published an edict in 1686 declaring that all editions of

La mística ciudad de dios published in other places ("otros Reynos," "other kingdoms"), and Spanish colonies—editions lacking the required permissions—were to be collected and turned in to the Tribunal,[88] because only the 1670 Madrid printing by Bernardo de Villadiego had been authorized.[89] Though these collective initial impediments to reading *La mística ciudad de dios* and to Sor María's beatification deterred neither Spanish readers nor the Spanish Crown nor Spanish Franciscans in their devotion to the nun and her writings, they would continue to ensnare the canonization process for a century.

Discussion of the theological content of *La mística ciudad de dios*, and of its Conceptionist message and other themes, flared again in 1696, when the book was published in France and censured by the Sorbonne's theologians. Among their many criticisms were that

> it gave more weight to the revelations alleged to have been received than to the mystery of the Incarnation; that it adduced new revelations which the Apostles themselves could not have supported; that it applied the term "adoration" to Mary; that it referred all her graces to the Immaculate Conception; that it attributed to her the government of the Church; that it designated her in every respect the Mother of Mercy and the Mediatrix of Grace, and pretended that St. Ann had not contracted sin in her birth, besides a number of other imaginary and scandalous assertions.[90]

Some theological scholars have attributed the Sorbonne's famed censure of the text to a defective translation into French.[91] The critics and supporters involved in the theological discussion and the specific arguments of the debate make up a field of scholarship in and of itself, and indeed many of the defenses and apologia on behalf of *La mística ciudad de dios* were published in the eighteenth century by the propaganda press dedicated to Sor María's canonization.

After the initial burst of interest in Sor María's case for canonization, the process slowed in Spain for several years. This delay in part resulted from *La mística ciudad de dios*'s relationship to the standing of the Immaculate Conception theology and to the Franciscans' involvement with the advancement of both. In 1692, Innocent XII ordered the *procurador* for Sor María's *causa* to respond to the censure emitted by his predecessor, Innocent XI in 1681 (which had led to *La mística ciudad de dios* being included on the Index); however, Franciscans did not submit a response to this request until 1729. It has been suggested that this delay was primarily due to a discussion within the Franciscan Order regarding the terminology to be used in reference to the Immaculate Conception. The wording needed to affirm the theological validity of the Immaculate Conception without challenging Church officials overtly and how the concept was referenced would affect how the response to the censure was framed.[92] Because this issue was so central to *La mística ciudad de dios* and to its defense, the requested response to Innocent XI's censure could not be formulated until a suitable solution had been determined. When in 1729 Benedict XIII convened a commission to consider the long-delayed answer to the censure, a surprise awaited the Franciscans in the commission's response. Instead of deciding in favor of *La mística ciudad de dios* and the canonization of Sor María, as had been anticipated, the commission presented four new critiques of the text in 1734.

With this complicated restart, the canonization process pressed forward, with Spanish Franciscans and the Spanish Crown pushing for the positive resolution of the case, and a wary Vatican cautiously responding.[93] In 1748, Benedict XIV issued a *postulatum* (official recommendation) stating that if Sor María's case for canonization were to be accepted, it had to be proven that Sor María wrote *La mística ciudad de dios* and also that the text did not run counter to the Faith and "buenas costumbres" (good practices).[94] In order to demonstrate the former, all of Sor María's writing, along with *La mística ciudad de dios*, had to be sent to Rome so that the texts could be compared. Neither the Franciscan Order—custodian of her writing—nor the Spanish Crown endorsed this plan, fearing loss or damage to the texts.[95] Though both parties recognized that it was essential in securing acceptance of *La mística ciudad de dios* and Sor María's beatification, they resisted sending her writing, established elaborate security measures for the books once they were in transit and in Rome, and petitioned vigorously for their expedited return to Spain after the analysis was completed in 1755.[96] The response to the analysis of the texts explained in what specific senses Sor María "wrote" *La mística ciudad de dios*. In 1757, Benedict XIV emitted a *tirasonen* (decree) confirming that Sor María had written *La mística ciudad de dios*—that the document was written in her hand. This document was published for the public. In 1771, Clement XIV published a decree stating that Sor María was indeed the author of—the person who composed—*La mística ciudad de dios*.

These moves advanced the work a step closer to legitimacy and Sor María closer to beatification, but by April 1773 her case for canonization was declared perpetually silent by Clement XIV.[97] Near the close of the eighteenth century, correspondence among the Spanish ambassador to Rome, Spanish king Charles III, and the king's confessor debated Clement XIV's right to close the case, and they advocated for Sor María's beatification, attempting every possible means to reopen and advance her *causa*. A final strategy was proposed, separating the canonization case from the issue of her writing, as *La mística ciudad de dios* was still viewed negatively by opponents of the Immaculate Conception theology.[98] But a letter by Spain's ambassador to the Vatican dated May 1, 1778, admitted that Clement XIV's successor, Pius VI, was intractable even on this possibility, seeing the person and her writing inherently intertwined: "hallaba en ella insuperables dificultades . . . diciendo Su Santidad que no entendía cómo se pudiese venir a la separación de dos ramos que siempre han sido indivisibles y deben ser entre sí esencialmente conexos" (He found innumerable difficulties in this possibility . . . His Holiness said that he did not understand how one could arrive at the separation of two branches that have always been indivisible and which in and of themselves should be seen as essentially connected).[99] Given the tenor of past discussions regarding the Immaculate Conception, Pius VI evidently feared the separation of Sor María's writing from her case for canonization could potentially result in a schism within the Church, perhaps because approving of Sor María's beatification would be interpreted as an implicit approval of her writing—and therefore of the principle of the Immaculate Conception.[100] Despite the urgent arguments of the *causa*'s postulador Fray Juan Francisco Aguado regarding the injustice with which the case had always been treated and the misreading of *La mística ciudad de dios* that lay at the root of Benedict XIV's views on it—which was the basis for Pius IV's interpretation—this final effort was ultimately unsuccessful.[101] A final factor also played into the interrogation of Sor María's *causa* and writing: her gender.

A Question of Authorship: Doubting a Woman's Capacity to Write the Immaculate Conception

Although in her outward dealings with Church authorities Sor María behaved in a manner that conformed with the gendered expectations of her time—"[dio] la imagen de su misma que la Iglesia y los hombres [esperaban] que [diera]" ([she presented] an image of herself that the Church and men [anticipated] she [would give])[102]—this did not exempt her from the scrutiny of Church authorities who questioned the authorship of *La mística ciudad de dios* because she was a woman writer. The work's Conceptionist content, in conjunction with doubts about the capacity of a woman to create such an erudite text, fueled its repeated examination. For critics of the work, it was almost inconceivable that Sor María could have been sufficiently educated to formulate the ideas presented in the text. This critique circled back to

> el uso frecuentes de términos escolásticos, el recurso a los autores escolásticos, tantos cómputos cronológicos, tanto hablar de los cielos, Astros, elementos, tantas citas de la Sagrada Escritura, el tratar de cuestiones de teología, citar a los SS padres, todo esto no es propio de una mujer, o de una persona que no haya estudiado.

> ———

> the frequent use of Scholastic terms, the appeal to Scholastic sources, so many chronological computations, so much discussion of the heavens, the stars, the elements; excessive citations from holy scripture, treating theological questions, citing the holy fathers: all of this is not typical for a woman, or for a person who has not studied.[103]

The work's intricacy and studied nature was seen by critics as proof that Sor María could not have been the true author of *La mística ciudad de dios*: her gender was reason enough to question the book's authorship.

The Franciscan Order's avid interest in the Conceptionist ideas presented in *La mística ciudad de dios* made the work doubly suspect. The order's advocacy of an unofficial theology signaled to its detractors that the authorship of *La mística ciudad dios* was vulnerable to the interventions of a much more "capable" author than a convent-bound nun. A more likely scenario, according to Sor María's critics, was that a Franciscan confessor or prelate, knowledgeable in Scotist teachings, had written the work under Sor María's name.[104] This argument observed that a familiarity with Scotist writing informed *La mística ciudad de dios* and that this information could not possibly have been within Sor María's purview. This allegation was declared specious in 1771,[105] after nearly a century of dispute that took Sor María's gender as one of its central arguments.

The Spanish Franciscans did not share this perspective on Sor María's gender, whether as an author or as a mystical protomissionary. For the Franciscans who championed her mystical travels while she was alive, the remarkable fact of Sor María's gender in relationship to her evangelization in New Mexico does not appear to have been emphasized or downplayed, though certainly the uniqueness of her case added particular interest. More generally, mysticism and mystical travel outside convent walls were, if not precisely acceptable modes of religious and social engagement for the early modern woman, at least increasingly common during Sor María's lifetime.[106] Scholars such as Jean Franco and Ellen Gunnarsdøttir have suggested that not only was mystical action within the parameters of "suitable" spirituality for women of the time, but through it a nun could also repurpose her inherent "weaknesses" (a condition of her "naturally" less sophisticated state as compared to men) as the means by which she became closer to God, transcending gender limitations via mystical experience.[107] Under this logic, Sor María's mystical travel experiences absolved her of her feminine frailty and, in a sense, made her more masculine.[108] Indeed in Mexico, the idea of Sor María in the masculine role of missionary was underscored by her iconography in the eighteenth-century printings of the *Tanto que se sacó de una carta*, in which she is posed exactly as her male missionary counterparts (Antonio Margil de Jesús and Junípero Serra) would later be in artwork depicting them as missionaries. For Spanish and Mexican Franciscans, Sor María's mystical evangelization as a woman did not draw untoward attention; in fact, it was quietly celebrated.

Returning to the authorship of *La mística ciudad de dios*, Spanish Franciscans consistently defended Sor María as the author of the work. From their perspective, neither was Sor María a special recipient of the Virgin Mary's autobiography by virtue of her gender nor did her femaleness put her legitimacy as its author in doubt. She was not promoted by the order as a female author per se, but rather as an envoy of the mystical theology represented in the treatise. It seems that for the Spanish Franciscans, Sor María's gender was less significant than what she wrote and how she evangelized in their mission field. Their promotion of her case for sainthood involved unprecedented measures that urged her writing, and with it the legacy of her mystical travel, into the public eye in Spain and its colonies.

Spanish Franciscan Devotion to Sor María: "Los padres franciscanos, que hasta suelen llamar segunda Biblia a su Madre Agreda"[109]

The Franciscan Order in Spain took the *causa* and its advancement as their own: "salió a defenderla desde el primer momento, respondiendo con vehemente impulso a los ataques de los antiagredianos, y dando trabajo a las prensas de toda España" (they sallied forth to defend it from its very first moments, responding with vehemence to anti-Agredist attacks and giving work to all of Spain's presses in their efforts).[110] The order's interest in Sor María's canonization and the spread of her writing was consistent with its historical promotion of the Immaculate Conception, placing the order at the very forefront of efforts on the nun's behalf. In effect, the Franciscan supporters of *La mística ciudad de dios* and of Sor María as a religious figure favored the Immaculate Conception theology (they were "partidarios de la causa inmaculista," "partisans of the Immaculist cause").[111] The ongoing debate between Immaculists/ Conceptionists (supporters of the theology) and Maculists (those who thought it theologically contradictory) roiled in the seventeenth and eighteenth centuries.[112] *La mística ciudad de dios*, with its Conceptionist message, added fat to an already burning flame; it was "uno de los motivos que más exacerbó los ya caldeados ánimos de los teólogos de aquel tiempo" (one of the elements that most exacerbated the roiling tempers of the theologians of the time).[113] The text itself became a lightning rod for rancorous argument over a belief that, though commonly held and commemorated, was not Church dogma. For the Franciscans, Sor María's writing explicitly expressed ideas the order had been advancing for centuries.

Rooted in a long-standing debate between the Dominican and Franciscan orders, the Immaculate Conception theology discussion had early and prominent spokesmen on either side of the debate. The Dominicans advanced the view proposed by Dominican St. Thomas Aquinas (1225–74), and the Franciscans promoted the interpretation of Franciscan John Duns Scotus (1266–1308). At the heart of the Immaculate Conception theology is the belief that, as the mother of God, Mary was born free from sin in order to give birth to Christ. In its simplified form, the Dominican argument claimed that, being human, Mary could not have been conceived free from original sin, though she could have been liberated from sin by divine intervention after her birth. Under this argument, her birth free from original sin would invalidate the need for Christ's redemption of one person, and therefore of all humanity. By contrast, the Scotist perspective argued that Mary could just as well have been born free from sin as been born with original sin, but that the former possibility demonstrated the divine grace with which she was bestowed before she was born in preparation for becoming the mother of God.

From these medieval-era dialogues onwards, the Franciscan Order in Spain endorsed the Immaculate Conception, and also the Scotist school of thought, through formal and informal channels. As early as the late fifteenth century, the prayer office to the Virgin commonly practiced by Spanish Franciscans included a devotion to the Immaculate Conception.[114] The Benedicta prayer, sung on Fridays, also developed Conceptionist characteristics among Spanish Franciscans in the early seventeenth century,[115] while early in the order's history, a special Mass was dedicated to the Immaculate Conception regularly on Saturdays, a rite that became more commonly practiced in the seventeenth century.[116] Unofficially, Franciscan superiors encouraged the establishment of *cofradías* (lay brotherhoods) dedicated to the Immaculate Conception.[117] These brotherhoods promoted the beliefs associated with the theology outside of the formal Church structure, and in conjunction with the Franciscans.

By the seventeenth century, Spanish Franciscan support of the Immaculate Conception had become yet more explicit. The Virgin of the Immaculate Conception was declared the patron of the Franciscan Order on May 26, 1645, codifying the importance of the theology, informed by Scotist thinking, in the order's composition and objectives.[118] On April 5, 1663, Felipe IV directed the *cabildo* of Mallorca to "saludar a la Inmaculada al principio de los sermones" (greet the Immaculate Conception at the beginning of homilies),[119] going against a *parecer* (scholarly opinion) published by the Dominicans of Aragón that was critical of the Immaculate Conception. This move showed overt support of the Spanish Franciscan theological agenda on the part of the Spanish Crown.

For the Franciscans, the theology of the Immaculate Conception was intimately bound to the writings of Duns Scotus, a scholarly attribution that would later be shared with Sor María. From the seventeenth-century publication of *La mística ciudad de dios* onward, Duns Scotus accompanied Sor María in the context of the Immaculate Conception; for the Franciscans, both individuals played prominent roles in divulging the theology. There were, as Patrocinio García Barriuso notes, the two primary figures in the Franciscan Order's vision of the Immaculate Conception: "Juan Duns Escoto y Sor María de Jesús de Agreda son los dos nombres más representativos del empeño de la Orden Franciscana en la defensa del singular privilegio de la pureza original de la Mujer predestinada a ser la Madre del Señor" (John Duns Scotus and Sor María de Jesús de Ágreda are the two names who best represent the Franciscan Order's efforts to defend the singular privilege of the original purity of the woman predestined to be the Mother of God.).[120] Their shared influence is reflected in many pieces of religious artwork created in seventeenth-century Spain and later, which depict Scotus and Sor María as defenders of the theology and related concepts. The Ágreda/Scotus motif would be reproduced in many New Spanish renderings of Sor María. Curiously, Fray Joseph Ximénez Samaniego, the commissary general of the Franciscan Order, was a proponent of Duns Scotus prior to writing Sor María's *vita*. Ximénez Samaniego's biography of Scotus was printed in Spain as early as 1668, before the official publication of Sor María's works; in fact, one of its later reprintings (1741) was made on the Spanish press dedicated to Sor María's beatification process— Imprenta de la Causa de la Venerable Madre María de Jesús de Ágreda, to be discussed shortly.

For seventeenth-century Spanish Franciscans, Sor María's exposition on the theological concept the order had long advocated was the reason its members ardently promoted the nun's beatification and, with it, the publication and circulation of *La mística ciudad de dios*. She became, as Scotus had been, one of the foremost individuals related to that particular devotion, on the basis of her writing. The interest in Sor María's mystical travels as the Lady in Blue (blue being the color of the Conceptionist habit) was another reason that New Spanish Franciscans in particular found her a figure of interest and that the order was at the epicenter of her promotion effort. This was no more clearly the case than in their successful attempts to prompt the Spanish Crown to intervene in beatification efforts.

The Spanish Crown's Intervention in Sor María's *Causa*

Although the Spanish Crown lobbied on behalf of other candidates for sainthood from Spain or its colonies, in Sor María's case, it took extraordinary steps, involving itself domestically, in the Spanish colonies, and in Rome. Because of the Crown's intervention, Sor María's books were printed and circulated in Spain and abroad even while the doctrinality of their contents was still debated in Rome. The Crown's involvement even extended to the exemption of its own taxes on profits garnered for the *causa*, a remarkable decision that I will discuss in chapter 3. The Spanish monarchy was willing to bend its own regulations for Sor María, in order to further the distribution of her writing, advance her popularization throughout the Spanish empire, and respond to antagonism toward her writing. Although Spanish Franciscans would continually press for support for Sor María, appealing to the Crown for centuries, the precedent for the Crown's extended advocacy had personal origins. The decades-long relationship between Felipe IV and Sor María formed the basis for the Spanish Crown's advancement of her *causa*.

Since Felipe IV's death followed Sor María's by just a few months, he did not actively intervene in the advancement of her canonization proceedings. But his family did so, explicitly in the name of his friendship with Sor María. An undated letter by Carlos II, Felipe IV's son, framed his obligation to Sor María's writing and *causa* in terms of his father's relationship with her:

> Siendo tan particular el en que tengo contraído para que se determine favorablemente la causa de los libros que escrivio la Venerable Madre Maria de Jesus de Agreda, por la devoción y afecto que el Rey nuestro Señor y mi padre que ya gloria profesó a esta sierva de Dios, y el que yo la he concedido y tengo como por la aprovación y consuelo con que en estos Reynos han ocurrido sus escritos, os encargo y ruego afectuosamente procureis promover y adelantar por vuestra parte el buen exito de esta materia.

———

> Because the case for favorably resolving the cause of the books that the Venerable Mother María de Jesús de Ágreda wrote is so noteworthy, and on the basis of the devotion and affection that my father, our king, who is now deceased, professed to this servant of God, and the affection that I myself have already conceded, and as I know of the approval her books enjoy and the comfort they have brought to this kingdom, I entrust and affectionately beg you to promote and advance the successful resolution of this matter.[121]

In a March 5, 1679, letter regarding publication permissions for Sor María books, Carlos II summarizes the Spanish Crown's involvement with Sor María's *causa* up to that point, an explanation that prominently featured his father's relationship with her: "por el gran apresio que el Rey mi Señor Padre hizo de esta Prodigiosa Muger en el tiempo que vivió" (on the basis of the esteem in which my father the king held this marvelous woman during his life).[122] He repeatedly echoes that sentiment in later letters to his Roman ambassador and to the pope, underscoring Felipe IV's great devotion to his long-term advisor and to the "ansia fervorosa con que Yo deseo la Beatificación de esta Sierva de Dios" (fervent longing with which I desire the beatification of this servant of God).[123] In a letter pertaining to the Sorbonne's censure of Sor María's writing, Carlos II reiterates that his support of Sor María is based on his father's respect for her: "siendo tan grande el afecto y devozion que el Rey mi señor y mi Padre (que haya gloria) profesó a esta sierva de Dios el qual yo le he continuado . . . he contrayado en defenderlos y procurar su calficazion con la Santa Sede" (because the affection and devotion my father, the king—may he rest in glory—professed for this servant of God was so great, I have continued his efforts . . . I have worked to defend her writing and procure their approval by the Holy See).[124] In a later letter,[125] dated September 22, 1697, pertaining to the same question, Carlos II underscores that his effort was no more than an extension of his father's respect for the nun: "siendo tan de mi empeño . . . y afecto que el Rey mi señor profesó a esta Sierva de Dios y el que io le he continuado" (being so great my efforts . . . and affection that the king my father professed for this servant of God, and which I have continued for him).[126] One step removed from Felipe IV and Sor María themselves, Carlos II took quite seriously the regard his father had for the nun and her writings, assuming personal responsibility for the continuation of the *causa* on the basis of that relationship.

Felipe IV's second wife, Mariana of Austria, shared (or perhaps helped dictate) Carlos II's commitment to Sor María. Mariana of Austria had witnessed her husband's devotion to his cloistered advisor from the beginning of their marriage. As Carlos II was sometimes impeded in executing his royal duties due to a number of physical ailments, Mariana's role in Sor María's *causa* at times overshadowed that of her son. The promotion of *La mística ciudad de dios*, in fact, specifically received her support: "[*La mística ciudad de dios*] tenía la aprobación no sólo de una Orden religiosa en pleno, sino también de innumerables teólogos, y, lo que era de más peso todavía, que gozaba del favor de Da. Mariana de Austria y de su hijo Carlos, por haber sido su autora la gran consejera y confidente del fallecido Felipe IV" ([*La mística ciudad de dios*] enjoyed the approval not only of an entire religious order, but also of innumerable theologians, and, even more importantly, it enjoyed the favor of Doña Mariana of Austria and her son Carlos, as the author had been the great advisor and confidant of the deceased Felipe IV).[127] The support of Felipe IV's wife and son, who were intimately familiar with the king's unique friendship with Sor María and who viewed it as reason enough to support her *causa*, laid the foundation for the Spanish Crown's extended endorsement of the nun and her writing.

In 1735, Franciscan author Fray Pablo de Écija expounded on this royal precedent in his *Sagrado inexpugnable muro de la mística ciudad de dios* (fig 2.3). In the introduction to the *Sagrado inexpugnable muro*, Écija constructs a genealogy of the Spanish Crown's involvement in the *causa* in order to procure the support of Queen Isabel Farnesio, the second wife of Felipe V, the Bourbon king who ended Hapsburg reign in Spain. To this end, Écija invokes the origins of the royal intervention in the *causa* by elaborating the personal relationship between Felipe IV and Sor María and follows with an exposition explaining the support the king's successors had offered for the nun:

Todos los Señores Reyes de esta Catholica Monarquia (de noventa años a esta parte) han tenido grande devoción à esta famosa Abadesa de Agreda, interesándose devotos con la Santa Sede para que se digne de amparar, con sus justisimos Decretos, la causa piadosa de su Beatificación, y de sus Libros. El Señor Don Felipe IV, estimó tanto à la Venerable Madre Maria de Jesus, que movido de la fama universal de sus heroycas virtudes, la visitó tres veces, y la comunicó por cartas, escritas de su real mano, el dilatado tiempo de veinte y cuatro años, siendo este prudente Monarca de la celestial conducta de esta ilustrada Religiosa todos los aciertos de su vasta Monarquia; y aviendo mandado à los primores Maestros de España examinar la Historia Divina, que compuso la Venerable Escritora, leìa frequentemente sus Libros, con notoria utilidad de su alma

————

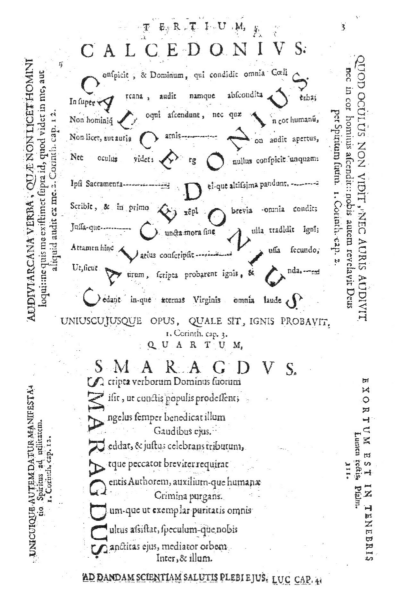

Figure 2.3. Allegorical poem by Ludovic Diez de Lara. In *Sagrado inexpugnable muro* by Fr. Pablo de Écija. Image courtesy of the Biblioteca Nacional de España, Biblioteca Digital Hispánica.

All the Lord Kings of this Catholic monarchy (for the last ninety years) have maintained a great devotion to this famous abbess of Ágreda, devoutly insinuating themselves with the Holy See so that He might shelter, with his ever-just decrees, the pious cause for her beatification, and for her books. King Felipe IV so esteemed the Venerable Madre María de Jesús, that, moved by her heroic virtues, he visited her three times, and communicated with her through letters, penned by his royal hand, for the lengthy period of twenty-four years, this prudent monarch being influenced by the celestial conduct of this enlightened nun regarding all the decisions of his vast monarchy; and having sent the most skilled masters in Spain to examine the divine history [*La mística ciudad de dios*], which the venerable writer authored, and which he frequently read, with well-known benefit to his soul[128]

Écija continues his chronology of Spanish royal involvement in the *causa* with Carlos II, who frequently wrote to popes and cardinals, imposing his royal authority, to examine Sor María's books so that they might be read throughout Christendom: "escrivió muchas veces a los Sumos Pontifices y Eminentisimos Cardenales, empeñando su Regia autoridad en orden a que la Santa Sede los mandasse examinar y los permitesse leer [los libros de *La mística ciudad de dios*] en toda la Christiandad") (he wrote the holy fathers and eminent cardinals many times, imposing his royal authority so that the Holy See would order that [the books of *La mística ciudad de dios*] be examined and read throughout Christendom).[129]

Écija adds that two of the previous queens of Spain—Mariana of Austria and Luisa de Borbón—were involved in spreading the book throughout the Spanish kingdoms, and with their involvement came that of their two august families—the Hapsburgs and Bourbons: "se interessaban en este devoto assumpto las dos más Augustas Casas, que venera, y obedece la mayor parte del Orbe" (The two most august houses, who are venerated and obeyed throughout the majority of the globe, were invested in this devout matter).

Écija's instructive list ends with Felipe V, Isabel Farnesio's husband, the king of Spain, "dueño legitimo de estos Católicos Dominios" (legitimate lord of these Catholic domains).[130] Felipe V followed in established royal footsteps when it came to Sor María, seeking the approbation of

La mística ciudad de dios by the Vatican and the advancement of her case for canonization: "continuó . . . con la misma fervorosa devoción que sus gloriosos Predecessores los Buenos oficios con la Corte Romana, para que finalizada felizmente la causa de estos Libros, se prosiguiesse la de la Beatificacion de esta Venerable Escritora" (he continued with the same fervent devotion as that of his glorious predecessors the efforts at the Roman court, so that once the cause of those books was happily re-solved, the cause for the beatification of this venerable writer could be pursued). After describing the history of royal patronage for Sor María and her writing, Écija delivers a final injunction to Isabel by comparing her with her predecessor. He notes that Felipe V's first wife, Maria Luisa of Savoy, was such a devotee of the nun that she even stopped by the Ágredan cloister, where she remained for a day to view Sor María's in-corrupt body.[131]

Écija's summary of how Spanish royalty had supported Sor María's beatification and her writing for decades had another purpose, namely, he sought a continuation of that support and for this reason his work is dedicated to Isabel Farnesio. Historians not only suggest that she was the power behind the throne as her husband diminished over the course of his reign, but the timing of Écija's entreating work coincides with the Franciscans' renewed involvement with the *causa* in the 1730s. Écija's supplication of the queen was zealous and multifaceted, reflective of efforts the Franciscans exerted on the Crown, and would profoundly affect the path Sor María's beatification took. First, he flatteringly com-pares Isabel to the earlier royal supporters: "no siendo V. Mag. inferior en cosa alguna à las reales Personas que le han procedido (Your Majesty being in no way inferior to the royal personages who have preceded you). He entreats that she too is called to intervene with Pope Clement II on behalf of the books: "favorecer la causa piadosa de los ya referidos Libros, interponiendo su augusto poder con nuestro Santisimo Padre el Señor Clemente II" (favor the holy cause of the abovementioned books, interposing your august power with our Holy Father Clement II). Then, he requests specifically that she intercede to calm the critique of the books within the Vatican and Church circles, in order that Sor María's beatification could proceed unencumbered: "[para que] cessen ya las contradiciones, y se continuen las precisas diligencias en orden a con-seguir la Beatificación de la venerable Madre Maria de Agreda" (so that the contradictions may cease and the necessary tasks required to obtain the beatification of the Venerable Mother María of Ágreda may continue). Next, Écija continues his petition that Isabel protect his own book, the *Sagrado inexpugnable muro*, itself an homage and history of *La mística ciudad de dios*.[132] Finally, Écija ennobles the queen in her projected role as protectress of *La mística ciudad de dios*, comparing her to the "invicta mysteriosa Judith" (the unconquerable, mysterious Judith),[133] the undefeated warrior queen Judith whose defense of Bethulia from the Assyrians is in the Bible. In the same manner, Écija proposes that Isabel would protect Spain's national treasure, *La mística ciudad de dios*, from its detractors. A heroine to her nation and to the Franciscan Order, all Spanish citizens and the Franciscan Order would celebrate her: "podremos todos los Españoles y la religion Seráfica celebrar con Nuevo motivo a V. Mag." (All Spaniards and the Seraphic Religion [the Franciscans] will celebrate Your Majesty with renewed reason); she would be an honor to the Spanish nation and the glorious protectress of the mystical Jerusalem: "Gloria de la Mystica Jersualén . . . y honor excelso de la Nación Española" (Glory of the mystical Jerusalem . . . and sublime honor of the Spanish nation).[134] Écija closes by dedicating the book to the queen and thanking her for her protection of the *causa* and the "heroica benignidad con que ha recibido baxo de su Real proteccion esta piadosa *causa*" (heroic magnanimity with which this holy cause has been received under your royal protection).[135] Écija's invocation is an indirect affirmation of the role the Spanish monarchy played in the *causa* from its inception (even as the royal house changed from Hapsburg to Bourbon rule) and offers a particularly concise view into how Franciscan intervention continually sought the Crown's involvement.[136]

In addition to the early royal support outlined by Écija, the Spanish Crown's advocacy extended to the particulars of her *causa*, to the Immaculate Conception theology, and ultimately to the distribution of her writing in Spanish colonies. One of the ways in which the Crown was involved—and influenced by the Franciscans—was in the appointment of the *causa*'s procurador. A letter dated April 18, 1697, pertaining to Carlos II's request that the Sorbonne's critique of *La mística ciudad de dios* be disregarded, alludes to the role of the procurador in the advancement of the *causa*: "escrivo a Su Santidad la carta inclusa en la forma, que vereis por la Copia, que tambien os remito para que instruido de todo, y de lo que os digere el Procurador que en essa Corte, tiene la Religion para esta causa" (His Majesty wrote the enclosed letter in such a manner, as you will see in the copy of it, that you may all be informed of everything, including the procurador, whom the Franciscans have at this

court, for the advancement of the *causa*).[137] In the correspondence between Carlos II and his ambassador to Rome, Bernardo de Quirós,
dated June 12, 1684, it is clear that Fray Francisco Díaz de San Buenaventura, a Franciscan friar selected by Carlos II, would shortly be sent
to Rome to undertake the "Causa y Justa defensa de los Referidos libros"
(cause for and just defense of the referenced books [*La mística ciudad de
dios*]), for which they expected a happy and quick resolution to a matter
dear to the Virgin Mary and for the benefit of the Spanish nation: "se
deve esperar Feliz y breve expedicion en negocio tan de la gracia de
Maria Santissima y provecho del Pueblo" (one should expect a happy
and brief trip on behalf of a matter so much belonging to Holy Mary's
grace, and for the benefit of the people).[138] However, by 1686, Díaz de
San Buenaventura's efficacy was flagging,[139] and the Crown appointed
his replacement, the Franciscan Benito de Noriega. This appointment is
documented in a letter from Carlos II dated June 26, 1687, in which he
acknowledges the importance of this procurador's mission: "se ha dispuesto que pase luego a esa Corte el Padre Fray Benito de Noriega en
lugar del Padre Fray Francisco Díaz para que asista a todas las diligencias convenientes" (it has been arranged that Father Benito de Noriega
will join this court in place of Father Francisco Díaz so that he may
attend to all advisable steps forward).[140] The Crown, at the encouragement of the Franciscans, would not allow the key function of the
procurador to fall by the wayside.

The earliest correspondence concerning the beatification process reflects the close alignment of the Spanish monarchy with Franciscan interests. One example of this occurs on April 30, 1679, when Carlos II
disregards the placement of *La mística ciudad de dios* on the Vatican's
Index ("Índice"). On writing to a contact in Rome, Cardinal Yúdice, he
orders the cardinal to see the text removed from the Index by whatever
means possible:

> tengo entendido que en agrabio de la autoridad Apostolica los
> émulos de los libros que escrivio esta Sierva de Dios los han puesto
> *como [si] fueran condenados* en el indice de los prohibidos; tambien
> os mando que dispongais . . ., y por los medios que Juzgareis mas
> convenientes se borre la prohibición referida, que yo me dare por
> muy servido de todo lo que executareis a este fin.

———

I understand that, in an affront to Apostolic authority, the rivals of the books that this servant of God wrote have placed them *as if they were condemned* on the Index of Prohibited Books; I also order that you arrange . . . and by the means you deem most advisable, see to it that the aforementioned prohibition is removed. I will be well served by anything you may accomplish to this end.[141]

Later, weighing in on discussion of the contents of the books (their "ciencia infusa," or "infused science," a mystical theological concept) in an undated letter, Carlos II suggests turning the consideration of the books over to the Franciscan Order, to see if the they could settle the matter at hand: "si hallaren alguna dificultad en estos libros, hagan cargo de ella a la Religion Seraphica y que no se pase a dar sentencia, asta ver si la Religion da Satisfaccion" (If any difficulty is found regarding these books, may the Seraphic Religion take care of it, and see that no judgment be passed until the [Franciscans] are satisfied). The Crown's later responses to the Sorbonne's criticism would similarly reflect its tenacious attitude towards such matters and its reliance on the Franciscans to articulate and mount a theological defense.

A letter dated December 1689 from Carlos II to the ambassador, the Marques de Cogollado (the message of which was ultimately intended for the cardinals Aguirre and Salazar), elucidates the Crown's position on the Immaculate Conception and *La mística ciudad de dios*: "en consecuencia de las repetidas ordenes que se os han dado . . . para que su Magestad conceda heco al Misterio de la Concepcion de Nuestra Señora [Octava] y de segunda clase como al de la [Maternidad] para toda la Christiandad . . . he resuelto repetiros [estas orde]nes" (as a result of the repeated orders that have been given you . . . so that his Majesty concede the mystery of the Immaculate Conception of Our Lady [an octave] and a second-class feast day like that of the Divine Maternity of Mary for all of Christendom . . . I have resolved to repeat [these or]ders to you).[142] The endorsement of theology, book, and beatification all fell under the Crown's purview.

The Crown also promoted the circulation of Sor María's writing in its colonies, even as the book underwent formal doctrinal scrutiny in Rome. An undated letter by Carlos II directed at the pope protests the Sorbonne's condemnation of the work for "falsos erróneos y hereticos" (erroneous and heretical falsehoods). At the same time, Carlos II

celebrated that her works were already circulating in his Spanish kingdom: "tengo la aprovacion y consuelo con que en estos Reynos han corrido sus escritos" (I have the approval and comfort of knowing that her
books have spread throughout these kingdoms). Another undated letter
addressed to Ambassador Cogollado alludes to the Crown's commitment to spreading her writing throughout its reign. Though the message
is fragmented because of the physical degradation of the materials, the
message that Sor María's writing had already achieved a wide dispersal
in Spanish reigns, including its colonies, is clear: "y haviendose conse-
guido su [...] y uso en mis Dominios . . . y [haviendo] logrado estos
libros [una] plena [difusión] y aclamacion [Uni . . .] por el [piedo] que se
ha hecho de ellos" (and having achieved their [*illegible*] and use in my
domains and having these books reached a full dissemination and [uni-
versal?] acclamation for the [holiness] that has been derived from them).

   As later examples in this chapter and the next illustrate, the Spanish
Crown engaged in the promotion of Sor María's *causa* until it was closed
in the later eighteenth century, and even beyond.[143] The Crown's early
relationship to these efforts, established through Felipe IV's personal
relationship with Sor María as his advisor and mediated by the Spanish
Franciscans, set the precedent for continued interventions. Manuscripts
from Spain's embassy to the Vatican demonstrate that the Crown continued to appoint and/or accept Franciscan procuradores, lobbied against
sending the original copies of *La mística ciudad de dios* to Rome for examination, petitioned with frequency for their return once they were
sent, continued to ensure that the books circulated to the Americas and
other colonial sites, and commissioned art relating to Sor María and *La
mística ciudad de dios*.

   But if the Crown's efforts were significant, the creation of a press
whose sole purpose was to support Sor María's writing and her case for
canonization was unique and very powerful.

A PROPAGANDA PRESS FOR SOR MARÍA'S BEATIFICATION

In approximately 1720, the Franciscan Order established the Imprenta
de la Causa de la Venerable Madre María de Jesús de Ágreda, a religious
press in Madrid whose purpose was to "[servir] de fondo para costear la
causa": to provide funds to support the advancement of Sor María's
canonization case in Rome.[144] The press's earnings from the sale of its

publications were earmarked to this end, used for expenses relating to the lobby in Rome. The existence of the Imprenta is testament to the efforts leveraged to promote Sor María's case for canonization. No other Spanish candidate for sainthood, male or female, had a press exclusively devoted to his or her canonization at that time, or one that focused so intensely on the publication of works written by that candidate.

The individual to whom the Crown granted permissions to publish through the Imprenta was the procurador for Sor María's *causa*, as is clear in the prefatory materials for the *Manual de confesores ad mentem Scoti* by Fray Juan de Ascagorta, published by the Imprenta in 1758.[145] Royal permission for publication was granted to Fr. Manuel Saenz de Cabezón, the procurador for the *causa* at that time. The same held true in the publication of Fray Juan Blázquez del Barco's *Trompeta evangélica* in 1742.[146] In 1740, procurador Fray Nicolás Ángel published his own work, the *Directorio predicable apostólico*, through the Imprenta. This relationship between the procurador, the Imprenta, and its publications underscores the complex connection between the Franciscans, the Spanish Crown, and the Imprenta in promoting Sor María's beatification.

Information about the Imprenta can be reconstructed from its publications and their paratextual materials, because little has been written on the press itself. The Imprenta was located in Madrid and operated in conjunction with other presses in the capital, including those of Juan Thomas de Jáuregui,[147] Nicolás de Arraztoa,[148] and Joseph de Cueñas.[149] These presses seem to have provided the presses on which the Imprenta produced its publications, and the storefronts that sold the Imprenta's production. The Imprenta's first two publications, both released in 1720, were *La mystica ciudad de dios*[150] and the *Relación de la vida de la V. Madre Sor María de Jesús*.[151] These two works were followed by at least fifty-seven others that were published by the press in the eighteenth century.[152] The Imprenta's last two printings were, again, *La mystica ciudad de dios*[153] and the *Relación de la vida de la V. Madre Sor María de Jesús*,[154] both of which were published in 1765. Over the approximately forty-five years the Imprenta published books, production was fairly steady, at a book or two per year, with a few notable exceptions. After the *Patrimonio seraphico de Tierra Santa* by Francisco Jesús María de San Juan del Puerto in 1724,[155] there was a gap of eight years until the next book was released in 1732, the *Bibliotheca universa franciscana sive alumnorum trium ordinum S.P.N. Francisci* by Juan de Soto and Juan de

San Antonio.[156] In contrast, between 1736 and 1737, seven books were published;[157] 1740 through 1744 saw nine books released;[158] and four books were published in 1747 through 1748.[159] Throughout the eighteenth century, the press continued to produce a number of texts whose sale benefited the *causa*.

One of the Imprenta's explicit goals was to publish Sor María's writing and writing about her in significant numbers in order to cultivate a readership for *La mística ciudad de dios*. The Imprenta was more than successful in this. Twelve of the Imprenta's printings were editions of *La mística ciudad de dios* of various sizes and numbers of volumes. To accompany the 1720, 1721, 1759, and 1765 printings of *La mística ciudad de dios*,[160] the press also released copies of Ximénez Samaniego's *Relación de la vida*,[161] the *vita* that contained the Lady in Blue narrative as part of Sor María's holy biography. Through the press's impressive record of publishing *La mística ciudad de dios* and the biographical texts associated with it, the narrative of Sor María's mystical travel continued to circulate alongside the nun's increasingly published and distributed works. Although other presses in Spain and abroad (including New Spain) would publish Sor María's writing, none did so as consistently in the eighteenth century as did the Imprenta.

The rest of the Imprenta's production covered a range of spiritual matters, but it favored a few select authors and topics. The publication list as a whole unsurprisingly represents Franciscan authors, interests, and theologies, with particular focus on the workings of the Cismontane family.[162] Several works specifically deal with *La mística ciudad de dios* or with the theological discussions concerning it. Among these were *Sagrado inexpugnable muro* (1734) by Fray Pablo de Écija;[163] *Mystica civitas Dei vindicata ab observationibus R. D. Eusebii Amorti* (1747) by Fray Diego González Matheo;[164] *Apodixis agredana pro mystica, civitate Dei technas detegens eusebianas* (1751) also by González Matheo;[165] and *Revelationum agredanarum justa defensio in tres tomos distributa* (1754) by Fray Dalmatius Kick.[166] Some of the other publications, although they do not treat *La mística ciudad de dios* directly, include Sor María's writing in their texts. One such example is Blázquez del Barco's *Trompeta evangélica*, a collection of "sermones de misión, doctrina moral, y mystica," in which citations or readings of her writings are sown throughout, including selections from her "ordinarios ejercicios."[167] Another is *La religiosa instruida* by Fray Antonio Arbiol.[168] Two final examples of texts incorporating Sor María's writing include Nicolás

Ángel's *Directorio predicable apostólico*,[169] and a text by Écija entitled *Novena a la Milagrosa Imagen que con el titulo de Nuestra Señora de los Milagros y misericordias se venera en el coro de el Convento de Religiosas de la Purissima Concepcion de la villa de Agreda* (1745).[170] The latter explicitly supported Sor María's canonization, and was dedicated to the nuns of her convent in Ágreda.

Other topics of interest for the press included the following: (1) Scotist teachings and theology, such as *Vida del venerable padre Juan Dunsio Escoto* by Joseph Ximénez Samaniego;[171] (2) issues relating to Franciscan evangelization in Spain's colonies, such as *El Sol, y año feliz del Perú San Francisco Solano, apostol, y patron universal de dicho reyno* by Pedro Rodríguez Guillen (see fig. 2.4), which celebrated the Franciscan missionary Francisco Solano's work in Peru and Paraguay, and also his canonization;[172] and (3) guides for the administration of sacraments and of religious communities, such as *Manual de confesores ad mentem Scoti* by Juan de Ascagorta,[173] and *La familia regulada con doctrina de la Sagrada Escritura y Santos Padres de la Iglesia Catholica* by Antonio Arbiol.[174] In fact, as the announcement of the publication of Arbiol's *Mystica fundamental de Christo Señor nuestro*[175] on May 26, 1761, indicates, his work was sold with "otras impressiones del mismo autor" (other publications by the same author). The Franciscan friar's works feature prominently among the Imprenta's publications: five works appear under his name, more than any other single author besides Sor María.

In addition to the popularization of Sor María's writing and related theological ideas through the press, the amount of money it generated on behalf of her canonization case was significant. Although a complete summary of the Imprenta's economic contribution to her *causa* is difficult to determine with certainty, the prefatory materials accompanying some of the Imprenta's publications offer an idea of the price of each individual work sold. The *tassas*, or official assessment of a book's market price, was printed as part of a book's frontispiece. These were based on the number of pages each book contained and standardized a book's price. At the time the Imprenta was publishing, each *pliego*, or large sheet of paper, on which a book was printed was valued at six *maravedís* by royal scribes and secretaries; therefore the prices for the books were in denominations of six maravedí. For example, Écija's *Sagrado inexpugnable muro* measured in at forty-two pliegos and was valued at 252 maravedís.[176] Ángel's *Directorio predicable apostolico*, at fifty-seven

Figure 2.4. *El sol y año feliz del Perú: San Francisco Solano* (1735), by Pedro Rodríguez Guillén. Image courtesy of the John Carter Brown Library at Brown University.

pliegos, was assigned the value of 352 maravedís,[177] and the *Manual de confesores ad mentem Scoti* by Juan de Ascagorta, a shorter work, at twenty-eight pliegos, was worth 168 maravedís.[178] The most costly of the texts I examined was Blázquez del Barco's *Trompeta evangélica*, at ninety-four pliegos and 574 maravedís.[179] Though the tassas provide the books' sale prices, without knowing the run of each edition — how many copies of a given book were published — or how many copies of each book were sold, it is difficult to determine with accuracy the Imprenta's total revenue. But what is certain is that these publications were generally lengthy — larger books, rather than pamphlets or prayer devotionals — and that demand was sufficient to justify the press's ongoing activity for almost half a century. Although the maravedí was the smallest unit of Spanish currency during the eighteenth century, valued at 1/34 of a *real*, the income generated by the Imprenta through its numerous publications was significant over the press's existence.

Yet the money earned by the press to advocate for Sor María's *causa* may ultimately have been less important to her legacy in New Spain than was the audience generated by the Imprenta's publication of her writing. Because the Imprenta consistently produced Sor María's most important work, *La mística ciudad de dios*, it became a common text in Spain in the eighteenth century. Further, as chapter 3 will show, the Imprenta's printings of *La mística ciudad de dios* in Spain coincided with monies that were sent back from New Spain and Peru from sales of copies of the books there. This correlation, along with royal orders dictating that *La mística ciudad de dios* circulate in the Americas as freely as it had in Spain, suggests that the Imprenta supplied Sor María's writing to Spanish and American readers alike. It was the nexus not only for fundraising of her *causa* in Spain, and circulation of her writing there, but also for sowing the seeds of her reading in New Spain and beyond.[180]

CIRCULATING NEWS OF SOR MARÍA: THE *GACETA DE MADRID*

The status of Sor María's canonization and her writings were not lost on the early modern Spanish public. Reports on her *causa* appeared periodically in the *Gaceta de Madrid*, the Spanish-government-operated newspaper published in Madrid that began printing in the seventeenth century. Announcements relating to Sor María, her *causa*, the Imprenta, and her writing regularly appeared in the periodical throughout the eighteenth century. The first such news piece was published on April 12, 1729, shortly after the Franciscan Order resumed active promotion activities.[181] The *Gaceta* reported that the pope had sent a decree allowing the *causa* to advance without another examination of *La mística ciudad de dios*. The article further clarifies an ongoing point of confusion, namely, that the book, formerly on the Index, may be freely owned and read in Spain. This last point is especially important because it speaks to the growing readership of Sor María's writing in Spain and New Spain, and to the continued publication of her writing by the Imprenta. The *Gaceta*'s news piece removes any lingering doubts Spanish citizens might have had about *La mística ciudad de dios*'s legitimacy in the eyes of the pope.

The publication of several of the Imprenta's works was heralded in the *Gaceta de Madrid*, alerting readers interested in purchasing the Imprenta's books. These reports noted the titles and press of such works, and frequently mentioned where the books could be bought in Madrid. Among those books announced in the *Gaceta de Madrid* were *Desengaños místicos a las almas detenidas o engañadas en el camino a la perfección* by Fray Antonio Arbiol;[182] the *Manual de confesores ad mentem Scoti* by Fray Juan de Ascagorta;[183] the *Tratado de la vanidad del mundo* by Fray Diego de Estella;[184] and the *Mystica fundamental de Christo Señor nuestro* by Arbiol.[185] The *Gaceta de Madrid*'s mention of these works no doubt stimulated a local Spanish audience to purchase and read these works, and established their significance for the Spanish reading public at large.

On December 2, 1747, the *Gaceta de Madrid* again reported on the progress of the *causa*, noting that a special *Congregación* had been convened specifically to discuss Sor María's beatification.[186] No details are offered regarding the complex processes occurring within the Vatican and between the Spanish embassy and its contacts in Rome, but the brief mention is nonetheless quite important, because news pieces like this one reflected and created general interest in Sor María's beatification and writing in Spain. The *Gaceta de Madrid*'s February 10, 1748, article follows up on the 1747 news piece, noting that the canonization case was ordered to the Congregation of Rites by the pope in order to "tratar de las Virtudes y Milagros de dicha Venerable Madre" (examine the virtues and miracles of the said Venerable Mother),[187] and commenting that a decision regarding the authorship of *La mística ciudad de dios* (that is, whether or not Sor María was its true author) would not be publicized until the pope or one of his successors decided on the findings themselves. The last line of the article states that her books were still circulating in Spain ("los cuales quedan Corrientes," "which are in broad circulation") and reiterates that, until declared otherwise, the books may be freely read, "para que se pueda leer sin reparo alguno" (one might read them without reservation). In reporting this information, the *Gaceta de Madrid* helped to raise and maintain Sor María's profile as a writer for a Spanish reading public.

Later editions of the *Gaceta de Madrid* indicate that interest continued nearly through the official closure of her case in 1777. On April 13, 1762, the *Gaceta de Madrid* printed a status update on the promotion of the case, noting that a decree was emitted declaring that the *causa* might continue to advance ("salió un Decreto . . . declarando que se puede continuar en la Causa," "a Decree came out . . . saying that the *causa* may continue") and offering details about the interpretation of Sor María's *Leyes de esposa*, a compendium of *La mística ciudad de dios*,[188] by the Vatican as part of its examination of all her works. Therefore, that work would be examined because it shared some of the same controversial revelations and doctrines in the source material, *La mística ciudad de dios*: "se haya de sujetar al mismo juicio [de *La mística ciudad de dios*] especialmente sobre las Revelaciones, y otros puntos, que coinciden con las Doctrinas controvertidas de la *Mystica Ciudad de Dios*" (it will be subjected to the same examination [as *La mística ciudad de dios*], in particular regarding the revelations and other points that correspond to the controversial teachings in *La mística ciudad de dios*).[189] As the *Gaceta de Madrid* documents for its reading audience, controversy over the content of Sor María's work was still active as the eighteenth century ended. The *Gaceta de Madrid*'s final report on the standing of the *causa* ran on March 6, 1771, and noted that a special Congregation under the supervision of a Cardinal Cavalchini would be convened on March 9 to "examinar algunos incidentes en la Causa de Beatificacion de la Venerable Sierva de Dios Maria de *Agreda*, Religiosa *Franciscana*, Española" (examine some incidents in the beatification of the Venerable Servant of God María de Ágreda, Franciscan religious, Spanish).[190] Though the process for Sor María's canonization was drawing to a close, interest in it remained keen and public, a fact reflected and encouraged by the *Gaceta de Madrid*.

THE POPULAR SOR MARÍA IN EARLY MODERN SPAIN AND BEYOND

By the end of the eighteenth century, Sor María as a religious figure, her writing, and her case for canonization were squarely situated in Spanish public culture. When Sor María's case for canonization was closing in 1777, her writing was still being read throughout Spain and beyond. An April 7, 1778, letter from a Spanish Court functionary, Manuel de Roda, to the Duque de Grimaldi, Spain's ambassador to Rome, comments on the distribution of copies of *La mística ciudad de dios* in Spain, seemingly critiquing Rome's ongoing misgivings about the work in the reporting:

> Se están repitiendo las impresiones que se extienden por toda España, y si la obra es tan mala como el Papa dice y lo supone la Congregación en el Decreto de 27 de abril de 1773, no es justo que corra y ande en manos de todas clases de gentes.

> ————

> The copies of the book that have already spread throughout Spain are being reprinted, and if the work is as bad as the pope says and as the Congregation of Rites imagines in its decree of April 27, 1773, then it is not fair that it circulate and be in the hands of all types of people.[191]

That numerous reprintings of *La mística ciudad de dios* were already in the hands of "all types of peoples" suggests that reading and knowledge of the text was common in Spain at the time. Regardless of the "official" status of Sor María and her writing within the Church, her persona and her texts exerted pull over Spanish society and cultural production.

This influence should come as no surprise, for the publication of Sor María's writing was not limited to that undertaken by the Imprenta. Other Spanish presses also produced the work in part and in whole, and it was published in other languages and countries. Spanish bibliographer

José Antonio Pérez-Rioja documents twenty-two editions of *La mística ciudad de dios* printed either in its entirety or excerpted in the seventeenth century, seven of which were in Spain. Seventy-two editions were published in the eighteenth century, eighteen of which were in Spain.[192] Among these publications was the 1707 printing in Valladolid of the *Resumen de las más singulares noticias que Christo Nuestro Redentorr y su Santísima Madre escrivió Sor María de Jesús de Agreda*,[193] an excerpted interpretation of *La mística ciudad de dios* notable in part for its place of publication, because the majority of her works published in Spain came out of Madrid rather than out of smaller Spanish cities, such as Valladolid (but interest in Conceptionist topics suggests Valencia as another publication site for Sor María's writing).[194]

Sor María was a popular subject of painting and other artistic works, both religious and secular, in early modern Spain. A complete study of this is well beyond the reach of this book, but art historian Ricardo Fernández Gracia, among others,[195] has documented this artistic legacy, cataloging the many different iconographies into which Sor María was cast, both during her life and much after.[196] The majority of such images depict her in the role of writer and defender of the Immaculate Conception theology, but there are also several that paint her as a missionary in her travels to New Mexico.[197] This artistic production impresses for the sheer number of works featuring the nun, and for the variety of roles Sor María assumes in the paintings. A similar influence emerges in literary works of the period.[198]

Indeed, the *Gaceta de Madrid* documents Sor María's entrance into Spanish popular literary imagination. The January 31, 1736, edition of the paper announced the publication of the first part of *La coronista más grande de la más sagrada historia, Sor María de Jesús de Agreda*, a theatrical version of Sor María's *vita* in verse.[199] The work, a "comedia de santos," or moral play on the life of a saint or holy person, based on Sor María's writing, was intended to be performed.[200] The work was written by Manuel Francisco de Armesto y Castro, secretary of the Inquisition and member of the Spanish court, and the *Gaceta* article further details that it was available in the "Libreria de Joseph de Cueñas,"[201] one of the printers associated with the Imprenta. Ten months later, on October 9, 1736, notice of the second half of the work was published, and both parts were available for purchase on the Plazuela de los Herradores at Cueñas's bookstore.[202] Arnesto's work is an indicator of the degree to which Sor María's writings "corrían" in an exemplary manner in eighteenth-century Spain and influenced theatrical production.

Another example of early creative literary production building upon Sor María's writing is *La caída de Luzbel*, composed by Fray Francisco Muñoz de Villalón and published in 1789. Dedicated to Santa Rosa de Viterbo, the text derives from chapters 7 through 10 of the first part of *La mística ciudad de dios*. In the preface entitled "Advertencia al piadoso lector" (A Warning to the Pious Reader), the author entreats the reader that if the doctrine expressed in the work is unfamiliar, he or she should read *La mística ciudad de dios*:

> Allí verás con verdad
> en los lugares que cito
> que todo ello era escrito
> por mandado de María,
> y que aunque hablo en poesía
> el sentido no la quito.
> No censures la doctrina,
> mira que vino del cielo,
> aquien la lee, da consuelo
> porque de gracias es mina.
>
> ———
>
> There you will see in truth
> in the places I cite
> that all was written
> on the orders of Mary
> and that although I speak in poetry
> the sentiment does not remove the truth.
> Do not disapprove of the doctrine
> see that it came from the Heavens
> it gives comfort to whomever reads it
> because it is a mine of graces.[203]

The reconfiguration of her religious writing into instructive works directed to a reading public speaks to her cultural presence and community of readers in early modern Spain. Works such as *La caída de Luzbel* were important not only because they incorporated Sor María's writing, but also because they demonstrate the creative labor that was applied to them, illustrating that her writing was accessible and inspired creative efforts.

That *La mística ciudad de dios*'s reach extended beyond the borders of Spain is no surprise. Indeed, the influence it had in Mexico is a main premise of this book. However, the scope of its reach was not limited to Spain and its colonies and included other European sites. One note-worthy case of this is Giacomo de Casanova's *Histoire de ma vie*.[204] In his late eighteenth-century biography, the itinerant Italian Casanova, imprisoned in Venice's Piombi prison in 1755 for moral laxity by the Italian Inquisition, is given a copy of *La mística ciudad de dios* by his jailers to improve himself spiritually and morally while jailed.[205] Al-though Casanova had never heard of the book, it interested him a little, and the skeptical lothario began to read, finding "everything that the ex-travagance of the heated imagination of an extremely devout Spanish virgin, given to melancholy, shut up in a convent, and guided by igno-rant and flattering confessors, could bring forth."[206]

Casanova remarks that if the book was supposed to turn his heart towards religious matters, it was not quite successful. He has no truck with the book's author, because "everything is told in perfect good faith" and "they are the visions of a sublimated cerebellum which, without a trace of pride, drunk with God, believes that it reveals nothing but that the Holy Spirit dictates to it."[207] Casanova found the book and its author sufficiently intriguing that he himself traveled to Ágreda in 1767 after escaping from the prison. Yet, in spite of his interest in the text, it did not quite accomplish the ends of moral betterment the Italian Inquisition had intended: "Far from increasing or exciting in my mind a fervor or a zeal for religion, the work tempted me to regard as fabulous all that we have in the way of mysticism and of dogma as well."[208] Casanova's dis-missal of the text and its author are framed by his distaste for the Vene-tian Inquisition and for the conditions under which he was impelled to read the book: "The Spanish woman's book is just what is needed to drive a man mad; but for the poison to take its effect, he must be con-fined under the Leads alone, and deprived of any other occupation."[209] For the purposes of my treatment here, however, the ironic fact that Casanova is compelled to read the nun's mystical treatise of the Virgin Mary's life is suggestive of the work's broader European audience in the eighteenth century.

Casanova's case reveals Sor María's standing as a writer outside of Spain and offers a view into the widespread culture of reading of her works beyond Spain. As I will show in chapter 3, the reach of the Sor María's writing created a type of cultural momentum that drew the Lady in Blue narrative with it into New Spain. I will examine the historical mechanisms that laid the groundwork for her culture of devotion in New Spain, consider how it took shape, and question how the Lady in Blue narrative began to assume particular importance in the context of her community of readers in New Spain.

CHAPTER THREE

"Como si fuera natural de México"

Publication, Reading, and Interpretation of Sor María's
Writing in Colonial Mexico

Y en las Indias, a donde esta testigo vivió ocho años poco más o
menos, en la ciudad de México, eran tan públicas e individuales las
noticias de las excelentes virtudes y prodigiosa vida de la dicha
Sierva de Dios y se hablaba con tanta publicidad y veneración de
ella, como si fuera natural de México, y como la nombraban ordi-
nariamente era la santa monja de Ágreda y por este nombre era conocida de todos generalmente.

———

And in the Indies, where this witness lived for eight years, more or
less, in the City of Mexico, news of the excellent virtues and prodigious life of the Servant of God María de Ágreda was so public and
specific, and she was spoken of publicly with such veneration, it was
as if she were a native of Mexico, and they ordinarily called her the
holy nun of Ágreda, and everyone generally knew her by this name.
—Francisca Ruiz de Valdivieso[1]

As the chapter epigraph attests, in seventeenth-century New Spain
public knowledge of Sor María de Jesús de Ágreda was such that she was
regarded as if she were a New Spanish citizen. Francisca Ruiz de Valdivieso, a courtier of the Duke and Duchess of Alburquerque who traveled with them to Mexico when they assumed the viceroyalty of New

Spain, found that there "se hablaba con tanta publicidad y veneración de ella, *como si fuera natural de México*" (she was spoken of publicly with such veneration, *it was as if she were a native of Mexico*). But in what sense was this the case and how did it come to be? This chapter treats how Sor María's influence spread beyond Europe to New Spain, and addresses how the nun was known as a writer and religious figure in colonial Mexico.

To a significant extent, this was the result of a growing community of reading for her writing and devotional interest in her as a religious figure. We know from historian Josefina Muriel's studies of female conventual life in colonial Mexico that Sor María's *La mística ciudad de dios* could reliably be found at most institutions for religious women there: "fue tan divulgada que no hubo convento, colegio, beaterio o recogimiento en el que no existieran varios ejemplares de ella" (it was so widely disseminated that there was no convent, college, religious community, or sanctorum in which numerous copies of the book could not be found).[2] For almost two centuries, Sor María's writing pervaded colonial Mexican letters, gaining her a prominence afforded few other spiritual writers in the Spanish Americas. But why were Sor María's texts so prevalent in New Spain? And how did they affect not only New Spanish women religious but also colonial Mexican culture generally?

When Sor María's writing emerged in New Spain in the second half of the seventeenth century, both as an import from Spain and as a product of Mexican presses, it did so within the broader context of the extant Lady in Blue narrative. By the late 1600s, the Lady in Blue was already part of the history of the northern borderlands of New Spain, as news of it had been reported and re-reported since 1631. Yet the advent of the nun's writing later augmented her profile there; it inspired works and practices based on her thinking, and lent further stability to the narrative itself.

In this chapter, I examine the cultural phenomenon of Sor María as a writer and spiritual figure in New Spain. First, I explain how Sor María's writing traveled from Spain to Mexico under the sponsorship of the Spanish Franciscans and Spanish Crown. The influx of her texts into New Spain was accompanied by the large-scale publication of her works on Mexican presses, and this chapter studies the reproduction of her writing in colonial Mexico, which continued for well over a century. The influx and growth of Sor María's writing in Mexico gave rise to a vigorous community of reading for her texts, and that engagement was manifested in written works and in New Spanish art. The chapter closes with an exploration of how the prevalence of Sor María's writing in religious communities for women influenced nuns, *beatas*, and other women religious, including Mexico's famed *décima musa*, Sor Juana Inés de la Cruz.

Sowing the Seeds of Devotion in the Americas: Transatlantic Trade on Behalf of Sor María's *Causa*

In chapter 2, I discussed how efforts on behalf of Sor María's canonization cultivated an audience for her writing and placed her squarely in the Spanish public eye throughout the seventeenth and eighteenth centuries. This advocacy was not limited to Spain, however. Spanish Franciscans were instrumental in the circumoceanic circulation of Sor María's writing and in the collection of pious donations on behalf of her *causa*. The Spanish Crown also advanced these ends by exempting donations remitted back to Spain from royal import taxes. This exchange began in the late seventeenth century, not long after Sor María's case for canonization was opened and *La mística ciudad de dios* was removed from the Vatican's Index of Prohibited Books. The direct result of these actions was the growth of Sor María's writing in New Spain, as archival documents reveal.

In 1707, Fray Alonso Garcés, then the procurador for Sor María's *causa*, requested a continuation of royal permission to "pedir limosna" (collect pious donations) in New Spain and Peru. These funds were earmarked to pay expenses incurred in Rome as part of Sor María's beatification process. Fray Garcés's 1707 petition was based on precedent; he included in his letter a copy of the first *real cédula* (royal proclamation) allowing this practice, dated 1683. Authored by then-procurador Fray Antonio de Jesús, the cédula announced consent to collect *limosna* for Sor María's case for canonization in New Spain and Peru.[3] The cédula states that Carlos II originally authorized this practice for a period of six years, starting in 1683: "Rey Don Carlos segundo que esta en Gloria por despacho de 7 de Noviembre de 1692 (cuyo traslado presenta) se sirvió conceder licencia para que por tiempo de seis años se pudiese pedir limosna en las Provinzias del Perú y Nueva España para los gastos de la

Beatificación de la dicha Venerable Madre" (King Carlos II, who now resides in the glory of God, wrote in a letter on November 7, 1692 (a transcription of which is here presented) granting permission that for a period of six years pious donations might be collected in the provinces of Peru and New Spain for expenses relating to the beatification of the said Venerable Mother).[4] This original cédula authorized Franciscan friars Francisco Saez and Juan Ruiz to solicit such donations in New Spain and Peru at the end of the seventeenth century.[5]

Luis Manuel de Quiñones, the royal scribe, clarifies where in the Spanish colonies the pious donations were permitted to be collected:

> [Antonio de Jesús] ha representado que se hallan con falta de medios para los muchos, y precisos gastos de su Beatificación, suplicándome [al Rey Carlos II] fuesse servido de concederle licencia para que en las Provincias del Perú y Nueva España se pueda pedir limosna para este efecto. Y haviéndolo visto por los del Consejo de Indias, he tenido por bien concederle . . . por tiempo de los seis años referidos se pueda pedir, y pida limosna en todas, y qualsquier partes de las Indias Occidentales, Islas y Tierra firme del Mar Oceano, Y mando à los Virreyes, Presidentes, y Oidores de mis Audiencias Reales, Governadores, Corregidores, Alcaldes mayores, y ordinarios, y otros qualesquier Juezes y Justicias: Y ruego, y encargo a los Arçobispos, y Obispos, y sus Vicarios, y Provisores, y demás Juezes Eclesiasticos de todas, y qualesquier partes de las dichas Indias, à cada uno de ellos en sus distrito, y jurisdicción, que durante los dichos seis años dexen pedir limosna à las personas que tuvieren poder del dicho Fray Antonio de Jesus.

> [Antonio de Jesús] has reported that they find themselves without the funds to support the many and demanding expenses relating to her beatification, asking me [Carlos II] if I would concede permission so that in the provinces of Perú and New Spain pious donations might be collected for this effort. And having consulted with the Consejo de Indias on the matter, I have decided to grant it . . . for the aforementioned period of six years, pious donations may and must be solicited, in all and whichever parts of the Western Indies, Islands, and Tierra Firme of the Ocean Sea. And I order that the

viceroys, presidents, and judges of my royal audiences, governors, mayors, magistrates, and all others judges and justices: and I beg and entrust the archbishops and bishops, and their vicars and proxies, and the rest of the ecclesiastical judges, and all other parts of the Indies, each in his district and jurisdiction, that for the said six years, they permit the collection of this pious donation by those endowed with such power by the aforementioned Father Antonio de Jesús.[6]

In effect, all Spanish colonies were included as legitimate sites where the donations could be sought. Furthermore, both Church and secular officials were ordered to facilitate collection of the limosna. Under royal orders, the reach of Sor María's devotional community suddenly extended from Spain to the Americas.

Farther along, the cédula includes specific instructions for how donations were to be collected from these sites and remitted back to Spain:

Para que se consiga mejor, nombren otra de confiança, que también la pida todos los días señalados, con orden de que metan la cantidad que juntaren en una caxa de tres llaves, que la una tenga la Justicia de tal Lugar, otra el Cura, y la tercera el Escrivano del Cabildo, ù otro del Numero, ù Publico, y que en cada Parroquia se ponga caxa con las mismas tres llaves, donde se eche la limosna, encomendándola los Curas en los ofertorios de la Missa, de modo, que con lo que quede esta limosna procediere aya buena cuenta, y razón, teniendo cuidado que cada año se saque lo que huviere en la caxa, dando fee de ello el Escrivano, y con testimonio del se embie à estos Reynos por cuenta à parte en cabeça del dicho Fray Antonio de Jesus, dirigido al Presidente, y Juezes Oficiales de la Casa de la Contratacion de la Ciudad de Sevilla, para que de allí se le acuda, ù à quien su poder tuviere, entregándole la limosna que allí se hallare, y juntare cada año, que en ello seré servido. Fecha en Madrid à siete de Noviembre de mil seis cientos y ochenta y dos años. YO EL REY.

——————

So that the pious donations might best be collected, name another trustworthy individual, who also requests pious donations on the indicated days, with the order that they place the amount gathered in a box with three keys, one key belonging to the judge of that

place, another to the secular priest, and the third to the notary of the
city council, or another officer, or public servant, and that in each
parish, the same sort of box be placed, with the same three keys,
where the donations will be deposited, with the priests commending
this donation at the offertory during Mass, such that, with what is
gradually collected, there will be a goodly amount, and, of course,
taking care that each year the amount collected is removed from the
box, with the notary ensuring its safe transfer, and with documentation, it be sent to this kingdom with a tally, in the name of the
aforementioned Fray Antonio de Jesús, and directed to the president and officials of the Casa de Contratación in the city of Seville,
so that from there it might be referred to Fray de Jesús, or to whoever occupies his position, and the funds that are found and collected each year be conveyed to him. In this, I will be well served.
Dated Madrid, November 7, 1682. I THE KING.[7]

Through the cédula, Fray Antonio de Jesús's authority was effectively
transferred to the Franciscan commissaries and provincials of the many
colonial sites where limosna collection was authorized: Perú, Nueva
España, Santo Evangelio, San Joseph de Yucatán, Tucumán, Chile,
Quito, and Lima.[8] The detailed rules for handling the limosna lay out an
involved process, probably so designed to encourage as many donations
as possible be collected, and to ensure that the monies donated in the
Americas would arrive back to Spain. Accordingly, the *sindicos*, or agents
charged with collecting the pious funds, were vital in securing a legitimate process; they may have also played a role in increasing Sor María's
profile in each of the sites specified in the cédula, perhaps as informal
fundraisers. Through this document, the mechanism for a large-scale donation system in Spain's colonies was set in place; yet for such collection
to be profitable, Sor María as a writer and religious figure would have to
be promoted. The 1683 cédula also addresses this issue, stating that four
hundred copies of the royal permission were to be printed, "para re-
mitirlos à los dichos Reynos de Indias, interponiendo para ello vuestra
magestad su autoridad" (to send them to the aforesaid kingdoms of the
Indies, imposing His Majesty's authority through them).[9] Fray de Jesús
specifies that the order was given in Madrid on December 22, 1682, and
that the copies of the cédula were to be placed in public spaces, where
they would draw attention in New Spain and other Spanish colonies.

Since the original period began in 1683 and lasted for six years, by 1698, the permission had lapsed. Although the Archivo General de Indias, the source for these documents, does not house papers requesting to extend the cédula between 1689 and Fray Garcés's 1707 petition, it is possible either that the permission had already been renewed in the intervening period or that donations were collected without formal authorization. Neither option would have been unusual at the time.

Fray Garcés was successful in his 1707 request to renew: a note on the petition manuscript remarks "por otros seis años se le concede,"[10] extending the permission to collect limosna in New Spain and Peru for another six years, until 1713. In Mexico, the manuscript collection at the Biblioteca Nacional de México confirms this through a *patente*, or official confirmation, sent from Fray Lucas Alvarez de Toledo, the comisario general de Indias in Madrid. Directed to the comisario general de Nueva España and dated February 20, 1708, it confirms that Fray Garcés's efforts to rekindle limosna collection in New Spain were successful. On December 14, 1707, it was extended another six years.[11]

The 1683 cédula is the earliest case of direct, institutional advocacy of Sor María's *causa* in the Americas. However, renewing the permissions for New Spanish collection of limosna was an ongoing effort; the Franciscans in Spain took it up at least two more times, in 1711 and 1724. On December 22, 1711, the comisario general de Indias, Fray José Sanz, issued a patente confirming an October 18, 1711, cédula granting ten more years to amass donations in New Spain.[12] Thirteen years later, in 1724, another patente was sent from Fray Juan de Soto, then the comisario general de Indias, and directed to the comisario general of New Spain. The patente requested collection of limosna for Sor María's canonization beyond the ten years that had already been granted in 1711.[13] Although the collection of pious donations was in place in early eighteenth-century Mexico, it was the advent of Sor María's writing that changed her from the subject of religious veneration into a central figure in New Spanish belief and thought.

In fact, the exportation of Sor María's writing from Spain was specially protected by the Spanish Crown, in defiance of strict restrictions governing the importation of books into New Spain.[14] An illustrative case in point concerns a letter sent in 1724 to Joseph Patiño, the port master of the Spanish port of Cádiz, by Fray Alonso Garcés, the procurador for Sor María's *causa*, and their subsequent exchange. Fray Garcés's letter is an appeal to load sixteen crates containing copies of *La mística ciudad de dios* onto two ships destined for New Spain and Tierra Firme (modern-day Panamá, Costa Rica, and Nicaragua). The friar's request was unusual; he wished to load the books onto *naves de aviso*, or warships, which at the time were forbidden by the Crown from transporting commercial goods. The ensuing conversation among Fray Garcés, Joseph Patiño, and Port Consulate Antonio Sopena brings to the fore the crux of the issue: the procurador's wish that the books arrive to New Spain as soon as possible, on the warships; the port master's reluctance to use the warships for that purpose, enforcing that order ("la Prohibición de que semejantes Navios lleven Mercaderias ni frutos algunos," "the prohibition forbidding ships of this type from transporting merchandise or any type of sellable goods");[15] and the ultimate intervention of the Spanish Crown, which disregarded its own exportation policy when it came to Sor María's writing.

Fray Garcés's letter to the port master sought a significant exception from the policies applied to all other cargo destined for Spanish colonies. Yet, when he writes to the Spanish king in order to contest Patiño's and Sopena's protests, Fray Garcés seems unfazed. His letter to King Luis I confidently references the Crown's historical stance on Sor María as the basis for his appeal. Here, he invokes the royal house's past promotion of her writing in the Americas:

> los gloriosos progenitors de Vuestra Magestad, que Dios guarde, han solicitado los adelantamientos de dicha Causa; y singularmente la leyenda de sus libros, y difusión por todo el Orbe, como expresan repetidas Cartas de sus Magestades a los Sumos Pontifices, y Cardenales, especialmente escritas desde el año de 1690 hasta el de 1705. Dize: que conforme al voluntad eficaz de sus Magestades para que dichos libros se difundan en los Reynos de Nueva España, y Perú, donde mas se necesitan, tiene prevenidos en Cádiz diez y seis cajones de â tercio; y no los han embarcado en los Galeones por faltar la voluntad expresa de Vuestra Magestad.

> ———

> Your Majesty's glorious progenitors, may God keep them, have sought the advancement of the said *causa*; and especially the reading of her books and their diffusion throughout the globe, as repeated

letters from Their Majesties to the supreme pontiffs and cardinals, especially those written from 1690 to 1705, express. Therefore: that in conformation with desired will of Their Majesties that the said books be distributed in the kingdoms of New Spain and Peru, where they are most needed, there are sixteen third-size crates waiting in Cádiz; they have not yet been loaded onto the galleons for lack of Your Majesty's express order.[16]

Fray Garcés clearly enumerates the Spanish Crown's far-reaching advocacy for Sor María's writing, emphasizing that Luis I's predecessors urgently ordered *La mística ciudad de dios* to the American colonies, specifically to New Spain and Peru, "donde más se necesitan" (where they are the most needed).[17] Given this pattern of advocacy, Fray Garcés implies, the reigning king would simply be following precedent by ordering the port master to load the sixteen crates of *La mística ciudad de dios*, waiting patiently on Cadiz docks, onto the navíos de aviso. Patiño, resolutely enforcing royal orders forbidding precisely that, would not budge unless the king himself intervened: "no los [cajones] ha embarcado en los Galeones, por faltar la Voluntad expresa de Vuestra Magestad" (I have not loaded the boxes onto the galleons for lack of Your Majesty's express will).[18]

Fray Garcés's petition closes with the proviso that, if the books were not to be embarked on the naves de aviso, then they must nonetheless make their way to New Spain and Peru as soon as possible on any other ships heading to those lands ("otros qualesquier navios que vayan â aquellos Reynos," "whatever other ships may be going to those kingdoms").[19] One way or another, *La mística ciudad de dios* would arrive to New Spain and Peru, sites where, Fray Garcés affirms again, Sor María's writing was critically lacking.[20]

The conclusion to this case was a happy one for Fray Garcés and for Sor María's *causa*. The books were eventually loaded onto the warships despite the standing prohibition, because the motives for their shipment—the advancement of Sor María's beatification, and the dissemination of her writing—were virtuous, according to the king: "por ser una causa tan piadosa" (as it is such a pious cause).[21] The official order to Port Consulate Sopena and to Port Master Patiño makes clear whose orders they were to follow, and how they were to proceed: "Viene el Rey en dar su permiso para que sin embargo de esta Prohibision se embarquen en estos dos avisos esos 16 cajones de libros y que se den las ordenes a Patiño y prevenga al consulado que por ser una causa tan piadosa, que no puedo ni debo hacer ejemplar, lo ha Resuelto Su Magestad así" (The king gives his permission that, prohibition notwithstanding, those sixteen boxes of books be loaded onto these two warships; because the motives are pious, an example should not be made of this case. His Majesty has thus resolved it).[22]

Two weeks later, Sopena received confirmation that the crates had shipped. The terse note sums up the exceptionality of what transpired: the books had been loaded onto the ships "en la parte que alcanza nuestra rendida y ziega obediencia a . . . esta horden, como a todos las que son de el mayor agrado de Su Majestad" (in a show of our unconditional and blind obedience . . . to this order, as to all orders that please Your Majesty).[23] The deliberate movement of *La mística ciudad de dios* from Spain to New Spain and Tierra Firme, in violation of the Crown's own edicts on shipping, illustrates one way Sor María's writing received special protection from the Spanish Crown.

Fray Garcés's letters concerning this shipment include details about the dimensions and contents of the cargo that provide an idea of the relative number of copies of *La mística ciudad de dios* that were exported to New Spain in the 1724 shipment. The crates carrying *La mística ciudad de dios* were "a tercio," or one-third the normal size, which was typical for heavy cargo such as books. The copies of *La mística ciudad de dios* were of "diferentes juegos,"[24] that is, sets of varying numbers of books. Sor María's Imprenta had produced an eight-volume edition of *La mística ciudad de dios* in 1723 and a five-volume one in 1721, and it is possible that both these editions (and perhaps others) were part of this literary shipment.[25] The three-volume editions, larger in size and heavier, were typically intended for institutional use, whereas smaller, multivolume versions appeared in personal libraries and private collections in New Spain.

In 1597, Mexican Franciscans received *thirteen* crates of an assortment of book titles that were intended to satisfy the needs of the entire order stationed in New Spain.[26] By comparison, the 1724 shipment provided a windfall of Sor María's works for New Spanish and Peruvian readers. The sixteen crates containing solely *La mística ciudad de dios* are representative of how demand for that text and other pieces of her writing was fed and/or generated in New Spain through early Spanish efforts. There are no other records at the Archivo General de Indias that so explicitly document the movement of Sor María's books from Spain to the Americas, based on the prevalence of *La mística ciudad de dios* in New Spain, but more volumes undoubtedly made the transatlantic trip (the text in its entirety was published only once in Mexico in the eighteenth century, so extant copies there likely arrived from Spain).

This incident is the tip of the iceberg in a vigorous transatlantic exchange that centered on the sale of Sor María's books and collection of limosna on her behalf in the Americas, and the transfer of money collected through these efforts back to Spain. This trade is extraordinary on its own, showing a brisk interest in Sor María in the Americas during the eighteenth century. But what distinguishes Sor María's case from that of other Spanish writers read in colonial Mexico is that the funds remitted to Spain were typically exempted from royal taxation. Frequent petitions to the Spanish Crown requested taxation immunity for money collected in the colonies on behalf of Sor María's canonization and from the sale of her books. When granted, this pardon allowed the petitioner to retain the amount owed to royal taxes owed to the Crown on colonial trade. Many such appeals were made between 1760 and 1778. Their regularity suggests that the Spanish Crown readily approved these requests for taxation remission, and the archive confirms that this was the case.

Records of the trade in Sor María's books and limosna originated in the Casa de Contratación, and several are archived at the Archivo General de Indias. Many are dated, yet several undated records in that collection preliminarily define the contours of Sor María's devotional community in New Spain. In one instance, the cargo aboard the *navío de guerra* (warship) *La Assia* included 507 pesos, and 3 pesos "de plata doble,"[27] all earmarked for Sor María's *causa* in Rome. These monies originated from the sale of *La mística ciudad de dios* in Puebla de los Ángeles, Mexico.[28] Although the individual charged with managing the funds, Francisco Joseph Lanasquito, is not explicitly named as the *síndico* for the *causa* in Puebla, it appears Lanasquito functioned as such.[29] According to the request for taxation remission, copies of *La mística ciudad de dios* were sent to Puebla from Spain so that profits from their sale would be returned to Spain. Lanasquito signed off on the collected funds in an official capacity, suggesting that the formal system of donation and collection was in place in Puebla. The proportionately large quantity of money originating from the small city points to a localized mid-eighteenth-century readership for Sor María's writing there. This was in fact the case, as will be borne out later in this chapter: *poblano* presses published many works and devotionals deriving from Sor María's work throughout the eighteenth century, and Puebla's citizens individually made charitable donations directly to Sor María's convent in Ágreda.

In October 1760, the merchant ship *El Tridente*, sailing from New Spain, and the *Príncipe San Lorenzo*, arriving from Lima, anchored in Cádiz. Two requests submitted by procurador Fray Manuel Saenz de Cabezón requested taxation emancipation for the part of the two ships' cargo that contributed to Sor María's *causa*: 2,000 pesos on the *Tridente* and 400 pesos on the *Príncipe San Lorenzo*. These monies were amassed from the sale of *La mística ciudad de dios* in Mexico and Peru, respectively (the books having been sent from Spain), and from the collection of beatification limosna there.[30] On this point, Fray Saenz de Cabezón was crystal clear, specifying that the funds aboard the ships were the "producto de varios libros de la Mistica Ciudad de dios, que se han enviado de Yndias para subvenir a los crecidos gastos que en Roma se originan, para lograr la canonización de la Venerable Madre" (the product of the various books of the *La mística ciudad de dios*, [the funds] have been sent from the Indies to provide subvention for the growing costs originating on Rome, to see the Venerable Mother canonized).[31]

Fray Saenz de Cabezón's request has a tone of urgency, cautioning that the monies should not be taxed because the *causa* found itself in dire financial need, which would be alleviated by New Spanish donations: "hallándose la referida Causa necesitada de medios para su prosecución por los excesivos gastos que se han ocasionado estos años . . . y en consideración a que por falta de medios no se suspenda el curso de causa tan gloriosa" (the aforementioned *causa* finding itself in need of means in order to continue, the result of the excessive expenses that have accumulated these recent years . . . and in consideration that the course of this glorious cause not be suspended for lack of means).[32] Saenz de Cabezón sought to ensure that the full amount collected in New Spain and Peru would arrive to the advocates for Sor María's *causa* in Spain and Rome. This request highlights the direct relationship between funds collected in the two Spanish viceroyalties and the political activities under way in the later eighteenth century in Rome, and also the Crown's apparent willingness to refrain from benefiting from the transaction.

An undated petition for taxation remission confirms that the limosna collected on behalf of the *causa* in New Spain was a significant source of money by itself, suggesting the growing strength of her devotional communities there.[33] Procurador Fray Pedro García's request concerned 4,000 pesos imported aboard the ships *La Capitana* and *Alma Santa*, and details that the funds were assembled not only through book sales at various colonial sites but also through what New Spanish citizens donated on behalf of Sor María: "lo que a dispensado, y dispensa la piedad" (what charity dispenses, and what is dispensed by charity).[34]

The shipment of 700 *pesos de oro* that arrived from Lima to Cádiz on August 18, 1767, offers a glimpse into the identities of some of the individuals involved in the funds' handling on both sides of the Atlantic. The money was embarked on the *navío de registro* (trade ship) *La Ventura* by Don Domingo de Zaldívar, the sindico in Lima. The pesos de oro were then claimed in Cádiz by the port's sindico, Nicolás de Moya, who would continue to receive such shipments from American devotional sites for many more years. In this case, the petition for tax relief emphasized that Sor María's canonization was of particular interest in, as Zaldívar calls them, all of "estos reinos de España" (these kingdoms of Spain).[35] Fray Tadeo de Lievenna, the future procurador for the *causa*, formally presented his request to the royal treasurer, Julian de Arraiga:

> que dicha limosna es para Causa tan piadosa, que se considera muy del agrado de Dios de su Santíssima Madre, y de especial honor para estos Reynos de España Suplica a Vuestra Magestad rendidamente se te digne liberarlos de los derechos que corresponden a Vuestra Magestad, mandando se le entreguen a dicho sindico Don Nicolás de Moya.

> ⎯⎯⎯⎯

> Since said pious donation is for such a holy cause, that is considered very pleasing to God by his Holy Mother, and a special honor for these kingdoms of Spain, we humbly beg His Majesty if he would deign to free them from the obligations owed to His Majesty, and once so ordered, send them to the aforementioned agent Don Nicolás de Moya.[36]

On August 25, the request was granted: "ha resuelto el Rey que se entreguen libres de derechos los setecientos pesos en oro que para dicha

Causa dice embarcó en Lima en el Registro La Ventura" (the king has resolved that the 700 pesos de oro destined for the said *causa* that were embarked in Lima on the ship *La Ventura* be given over free from royal taxes).[37] Through this transatlantic network of agents and promoters, the *causa* retained all 700 American gold pieces collected on behalf of Sor María.

When in August 1768 the navío de guerra *La Castilla* arrived in Cádiz, it brought with it 4,000 pesos dedicated to Sor María's case for canonization.[38] *La Castilla* had set out from the Mexican port of Veracruz, and the funds were there loaded by the Mexican sindico, Andrés García de Allende. The money was collected through the sale of copies of *La mística ciudad de dios* in "aquel reino" (that kingdom, i.e., Mexico),[39] indicating that Spanish presses continued to supply New Spanish readers with copies of *La mística ciudad de dios* well into the late eighteenth century. In this particular exchange, the archive articulates the petition's outcome; Sor María's canonization case, again "de especial honor de estos Reynos" (a special honor for these kingdoms)[40] entitled the 4,000 pesos freedom from import taxation.

The ship *El Hercules* brought with it two *tejos* (ingots) of gold from Lima on December 4, 1770. As the value of any given tejo varied and was determined by its weight, the request for taxation remission specifies that they weighed in at "309 Castellanos y 3 tomínes," or an estimated 31 pounds of gold.[41] The two tejos were sent by the Limeñan sindico, Manuel de Zaldivar, to Nicolás Moya in Cádiz.[42] In spite of assurances made by procurador Fray Pedro García in his petition that this major contribution was indeed to be exempted from all royal taxes—as previous contributions had been—an anonymous commentator was piqued by Fray García's request. The commentator remarks in the margins of the petition that he does not believe the entire fortune merited reprieve from taxation: "Vease la orden por que me parece no de el todo del valor de los dos tejos vale ese regalo" (Look at the order, because it does not seem to me that the exemption covers the entire value of the two tejos).[43] No reasons are stated for the commentator's intervention, but the two tejos de oro might have been seen as too excellent a treasure to freely turn over to the *causa*.

Although most New Spanish donations were collected from geographical jurisdictions (such as those outlined in the 1683 cédula), assembled, and sent to Spain through established official channels, financial donations were also made by individuals, with no surviving documentation of their passage through the Casa de Contratación. In 1773, the mayor of Oaxaca, Luis Veremundo Soriano, sent 3,000 reales on behalf of a local Mexican priest "con la condición de que sean para el retablo de nuestra Santa Madre [Sor María] cuando Dios sea servido se canonice" (under the condition that they are for a retablo of our Holy Mother [Sor María] when, God willing, she is canonized).[44] This contribution anticipating Sor María's canonization suggests support for her *causa* in Oaxaca along with the means and incentive to send such a donation outside of the typical New Spanish system of collection.

On August 27, 1775, the cargos of two ships captained by Don Adrian Cuadrón Cantín, the *Astuto* and the *San Miguel*, passed through the Puerto Rican port of San Ildefonso. On arriving in Cádiz, relief from royal taxes on the 2,000 *pesos reales* they brought from unspecified locales on behalf of Sor María was requested. Records do not explain which ship carried the funds for Sor María's canonization case, and the *Astuto*'s provenance is not mentioned. Yet, we do know that the *San Miguel* belonged to the Compañía Guipuzcoana de Caracas, a trading company headquartered in the Basque country, and that it passed through the Venezuelan port of La Guayra, which was controlled by that company, on its return trip to Spain. It is possible that monies for the *causa* were collected in Venezuela, or from other sites that traded through La Guayra, suggesting interest in Sor María south of New Spain.

Finally, in September 1778, *El Aquilés* returned to the port of Cádiz with 2,000 *pesos fuertes* that were to be conveyed to Fausto Gutierrez Gayón, by then the sindico for the *causa* in Cádiz. According to the request exemption, these funds arrived from Lima and were sent by its sindico, Manuel Zaldivar.[45] They had been collected through the sale of copies of *La mística ciudad de dios* that had been sent there in 1775 by Fray Tadeo de Lievenna.[46] Fray Lievenna's petition for remission emphasized the regularity both of the arrival of such American funds and of their pardoning from royal taxes. Fray Lievenna asks that the 2,000 pesos be turned over to Gutierrez Gayón "libres de derechos . . . como lo ha hecho en otras ocasiones" (free from taxes . . . as they have been on other occasions).[47] Fray Lievenna's perfunctory tone implies that the outcome for such petitions was typically in favor of the *causa*; a letter dated October 2 of the same year, sent to the former *visitador* to New Spain, and member of the General Council on Commerce, Joseph de Gálvez, confirms that the funds were indeed pardoned from royal taxes.[48]

This last exchange confirms that Sor María's Spanish advocates were still sending copies of *La mística ciudad de dios* to the Americas as late as 1775, when promotion of the *causa* in Rome was being met with resistance and failure was imminent. The above cases furthermore confirm that the Spanish Crown continued to advocate for the *causa* in the form of taxation remission on funds originating in New Spain and Peru at least through 1778. Indeed, the formal mechanisms for collection and remittance of funds remained in place through that date, as the sindicos continued to gather the products of late eighteenth-century New Spanish devotion to Sor María.

Out of this precedent, Sor María's communities of reading and devotion in colonial Mexico developed quickly and gained deep roots.[49] The unfolding of Sor María's literary and spiritual presence in New Spain is the focus of the rest of this chapter.

"Corren sus escritos": Mexican Presses and Sor María's Writing in New Spain

Although Spanish presses were the first to provide Sor María's writing in significant volumes for New Spanish audiences, the long-running publication of her writing on Mexican presses provided the foundation for her community of reading in colonial Mexico. Sor María's works are woven throughout Mexican literary records—bibliographies, library catalogs, private collections—from the late seventeenth century to the early nineteenth century. Indeed, famed New Spanish writer and nun Sor Juana Inés de la Cruz remarked of the popularity and accessibility of Sor María's writings in seventeenth-century Mexico that "corren sus escritos" (her writing is everywhere).[50] New Spanish patrons of Sor María's writing and *causa* ensured the reproduction of her texts on their presses, resulting in the creation of many editions of her writing that were read and interpreted well into the nineteenth century.

There are several important considerations regarding the breadth of Sor María's community of reading in colonial Mexico. First, among the literate, the sheer quantity of Sor María's texts, both those shipped from Spain and those printed in Mexico, made them more likely to have been read than less common texts. Because her writing was readily at hand, the incidence of its reading was more likely.

Second, the Mexican publication of Sor María's writing consisted primarily of excerpts of *La mística ciudad de dios*, with her spiritual exercises a distant second. In these publications, selections of Sor María's texts were accompanied by prayers; together, they were used as guides for spiritual regimens, Stations of the Cross, or devotional prayers (novenas, triduos, septenarios, etc.). Given the oral and collective nature of many of these prayer practices, nonreading New Spanish citizens were exposed to Sor María and her theological and mystical concepts through the ritual of communal prayer. In a similar vein, Mass attendees who heard readings of her writing—the Franciscan friars from Propaganda Fide colleges, among others, wrote and presented such sermons—were also passively instructed in ideas and tropes originating in Sor María's writing.

Third, many New Spanish artists reproduced concepts unique to Sor María's writing in their paintings, either because they read it directly or because they were exposed to interpretations of her texts. These art pieces made the contents of her writing accessible to a nonreading public. Thus, the "community of reading" for Sor María's writing in colonial Mexico was not limited to the literate. Keeping this in mind, the impetus for the popularization of Sor María as a writer and spiritual figure in colonial Mexico can still be traced back to her writing, namely, the Ágredan texts published on New Spanish presses.

The rough bibliography of her writing that follows draws on a variety of sources that cite Sor María as an author of a published work. When possible, physical copies of indexed works have provided additional information about the texts' contents and their patrons. It is very likely that many other published works (and even more manuscript ones) borrowed from Sor María's writing either do not credit her or cite her only within the text, but not as an author. The potential for future scholarship in this area is considerable.[51] This literary mapping begins with the only complete edition of *La mística ciudad de dios* made on a New Spanish press, and then documents other New Spanish publications of her writing in chronological order.[52]

Published in 1731 by Joseph Bernardo de Hogal's Mexico City press, the *Escuela mystica de María en la mystica ciudad de dios*[53] is notable because it is the only documented Mexican edition of *La mística ciudad de dios*. Spanish American literary historian Hortensia Calvo notes the Spanish Crown tightly regulated local publishing in its colonies, with

La V. Madre Sor María de Iesus de Agreda

Soto Mayor. esc,

Figure 3.1. Escuela Mystica de María en la Mystica Ciudad de Dios (1731). Image by Francisco Sylverio de Sotomayor. Image courtesy of the John Carter Brown Library at Brown University.

the end of preserving profits and control over ideologies: "The Crown's control of local publishing kept colonial scholars heavily dependent on European presses for publication of original works."[54] In the context of remittance of devotional funds back to the devotional site, the lack of other Mexican editions of *La mística ciudad de dios* would also be logical; it might also explain why other Spanish colonial sites apparently did not publish the complete text.

The publication of the *Escuela mystica* may have resulted from personal devotion to Sor María by an influential figure in the Mexican Church. According to its preface, the book was commissioned by Bishop Juan Ignacio Castoreña y Ursúa, then head prelate of the Yucatán province, who harbored a well-documented interest in the nun.[55] Castoreña y Ursúa's will requested that upon his death, his tongue, heart, and brains be placed in a lead box, then inside a wooden box, which were to be sent to the convent in Ágreda, and interred next to Sor María's body.[56] The December 1729 edition of the *Gaceta de México* reported that Bishop Castoreña y Ursúa celebrated a Mass of thanksgiving in the Convento Grande de San Francisco in Mexico City to commemorate the granting of permission to read Sor María's writing freely in New Spain and elsewhere.[57]

The image accompanying the *Escuela mystica* illustrates the content of the text and reiterates Sor María's role as its author. The engraving, by New Spanish artist Francisco Sylverio de Sotomayor, depicts Sor María in the foreground, seated, smiling, and writing (see fig 3.1). The Virgin of the Immaculate Conception is above and behind her, alluding to the *Escuela mystica*'s Conceptionist message and Sor María's role in transmitting it. In comparison to the many Spanish editions of *La mística ciudad de dios* that we discussed in chapter 2, the sole New Spanish printing could seem paltry in comparison, yet it placed Sor María's famous and controversial work within easy reach of New Spanish readers, and Joseph Bernardo de Hogal's press published a great deal more of Sor María's writing after 1731.

In fact, the publication of excerpts of *La mística ciudad de dios* was common in New Spain, from as early as the late seventeenth century—coinciding with the first permission to collect American limosna for Sor María's *causa*—and continuing well into the nineteenth century. The *Compendio de la sagrada pasión y muerte de N. Señor Jesu-Christo, sacado de la mystica ciudad de dios y historia divina de N. Señora* is the earliest instance of this type of publication. It was first printed in 1693,[58] and was republished in 1717.[59] The *Compendio* is a meditation on Christ's passion, deriving from the sections of *La mística ciudad de dios* that narrate that event; the full title clarifies which parts: "de la segunda parte, libro quatro, desde el Capítulo nono, hasta el vigésimo quarto de dicha historia" (from the second part, book four, from the ninth chapter to the twenty-fourth of that book).[60] Meditations and prayers accompany the selections taken from *La mística ciudad de dios*. The *Compendio* was compiled by Fray Joseph de San Antonio y Flores, a Franciscan from the province of Santo Evangelio, the site of the Lady in Blue's alleged travel and evangelization.

Francisco de Aguiar y Seijas y Ulloa, the archbishop of Mexico in 1693, officially acknowledged the text in its front matter. Readers were given forty days of indulgence for praying the *Compendio*, which effectively incentivized reading Sor María's writing.[61] The indulgences are significant for another reason; they suggest that *La mística ciudad de dios* was more than just a favorite of the Franciscans and that it enjoyed the support of the secular clergy in New Spain. Through these indulgences, the institution advocated for Sor María's writing, in spite of the theological debate over *La mística ciudad de dios* under way in Europe at that time. The 1717 edition does not specify if indulgences were still issued for reading the text, but by then Sor María was already a popular devotional figure in Mexico.

In 1696, prolific New Spanish *cronista* and Franciscan friar Agustín de Vetancurt produced an annotated, abridged edition of *La mística ciudad de dios*—*Chronografía sagrada de la vida de Cristo Nuestro Redemptor*, published by Doña María de Benavides, Viuda de Juan de Ribera, in Mexico City.[62] The *Chronografía sagrada* reproduces key episodes from *La mística ciudad de dios*, narrating the marriage of St. Anne and St. Joachim; Christ's death and resurrection; the beginning of the apostles' evangelization; the composition of the Gospels; and Mary's death and burial.[63] The *Chronografía sagrada* is framed by a Concepcionist orientation: it is dedicated to St. Joachim and St. Anne, "los primogenitores de una Aurora, que tuvo el parto del mejor Sol . . . De los que son mina de cristal de que se formó el espejo sin mancha . . . Padres de la mejor Madre, y Abuelos de el [*sic*] Nieto más precioso" (the primogenitors of a Dawn, who gave birth to the brightest Son . . . they who were a mine of crystal from which a stainless mirror was formed . . . parents of the best mother, and grandparents of the most precious grandson).[64] In keeping with this theme, Vetancurt cites Sor María in discussing Mary's physical conception by St. Anne, the formation of Mary's body, and the creation of her sinless soul: "el sábado siguiente, ocho de Diciembre, se hizo la segunda concepción puríssima, creado el Altissimo la alma de su Madre, infundiendola en su cuerpo, con que se entró en el mundo la más pura criatura" (the following Saturday, the eighth of December, the second pure conception occurred, the Almighty creating the soul of his Mother, filling her body with it, so that she entered into this world the most pure child).[65] Vetancurt's abridgement of *La mística ciudad de dios* made some of the most memorable and iconoclastic portions of Sor María's original text available to New Spanish readers.

As intriguing as the selections Vetancurt presents from *La mística ciudad de dios* are, the reconfiguration of dates (cronografía) he presents is fascinating. The *Chronografía sagrada* provides revised dates for a number of apocryphal, liturgical, and historical events. Fray Vetancurt clarifies he is not the primary architect of this modified calendar ("nada será mío," "nothing is of my own making"),[66] stating that it is based primarily on dates proposed in *La mística ciudad de dios* and complemented by other chronologies, including those of Calixto Placentino and Jesuit scholar Juan Bautista Riciolio.[67] Vetancurt's chronological recalculations (which, as we recall from chapter 2, was one of the critiques levied against Sor María and *La mística ciudad de dios*) may have been a model for later New Spanish writing of this nature. Mexican prelate Cayetano Verdiguer's *Matemática demostración de las letras dominicales y exactas desde el principio del mundo hasta el año 1760 y siguientes* (1760)—examined later in this chapter—likewise drew on Sor María's sense of chronology to reassign dates for world and religious events.[68]

Finally, in Vetancurt and his Mexican publications, we see a concrete correlation between Sor María's writing and the idea of the Lady in Blue, a confirmation that the author and mystical missionary were understood as one and the same. Vetancurt published the *Chronografía sagrada* around the same time as his histories of the Franciscan Order in early New Spanish missions, the *Teatro mexicano* and *Menologio franciscano* (1697–98).[69] In the *Teatro mexicano*, Vetancurt describes Sor María's mystical travels to New Mexico in the context of Franciscan mission work there, and details the meeting between Sor María and Fray Benavides in Spain.[70] Although Fray Vetancurt cites the *1630 Memorial* as his source, he includes other details of her mystical travels from her *vita*, suggesting that he read that version of the Lady in Blue narrative, either as part of the *La mística ciudad de dios* or as a separate publication. Between the *Chronografía sagrada* and the *Teatro mexicano*, Fray Vetancurt presented both Sor María the writer and her complement, the Lady in Blue, to a late seventeenth-century Mexican reading public.

By the early eighteenth century, several works of devotional literature drawing on Sor María's writing had been published. In 1711, Francisco de Rivera Calderón's press published the *Ave María novena divina de la Sacratissima Virgen María*, a forty-six-page guide for a nine-day prayer practice.[71] Attributed to Miguel Yañez Remusco, the novena is a meditation on and elaboration of the incarnation of Christ as explained in *La mística ciudad de dios*.

Nine years later, the *Ocupación angélica dolorosa de los mil angeles . . . según la V.M. de Agreda* debuted,[72] its publication announced in the *Gaceta de México* in 1722.[73] The text was credited to the same Juan Ignacio Castoreña y Ursúa that commissioned the 1731 printing of *La mística ciudad de dios*, but who in 1720 was cathedrático de prima de la Sagrada Escritura. The Jesuit College of San Ildefonso in Mexico City republished the *Ocupación angélica dolorosa* in 1763 under the slightly altered title *Novena angélica dolorosa*.

The year 1726 saw the first printing of the *Septenario al Gloriosissimo Patriarca Sr. S Joseph de los siete privilegios de su Patrocinio, que refiere la V.M. Maria de Jesús de Agreda en su Mistica Ciudad de Dios*.[74] The *Septenario* was one of the most frequently published works of Sor María's writing in Mexico in the eighteenth century. Subsequent editions were published in Mexico City in 1768, 1774, 1785, and 1808.[75] In 1771, the Real Seminario Palafoxiano published its own edition in Puebla.[76] The *Septenario al Gloriosissimo Patriarca Sr. S Joseph* is a compilation of writing by Santa Teresa and Sor María, "dos plumas de dos Escritoras discretisimas de los dos siglos antecedentes" (the two pens of two sober women authors from the two previous centuries),[77] who through their writing "afianzan el Patrocinio de este gran Santo [San José] y remiten a la experiencia el desempeño de su protección" (perfect the patronage of this great saint [St. Joseph] and vouchsafe the prayer for his protection).[78] The preface to the *Septenario al Gloriosissimo Patriarca Sr. S Joseph* lauds the two mystics' spiritual writing on St. Joseph, including his celestial transit as described in the fifth book of *La mística ciudad de dios*.[79]

A 1785 printing of the *Septenario al Gloriosissimo Patriarca Sr. S Joseph* was commissioned by "un Eclesiastico de la Venerable Congregación de Nro. P.S. Felipe Neri de esta Ciudad de Mexico" (a clergyman from the Venerable Congregation of our Holy Father San Felipe de Neri of this City of Mexico), a member of the Congregation of Oratorians of San Felipe de Neri. Part of the congregation's mission was to preach in public, often in the streets of Mexico City in *oratorios*, or public spaces of worship. In this sense, the congregants of San Felipe propagated religious concepts and practices through the spoken word. Since the *Septenario al Gloriosissimo Patriarca Sr. S Joseph* was commissioned by an Oratorian, it was likely read and prayed in public, led by a congregant of San Felipe. Shared with both (Spanish) reading and non-reading inhabitants of Mexico City, the community of people exposed to Sor María's writing extended well beyond the lettered classes. The text's long life in print, from 1726 to 1808, indicates that New Spanish citizens were hearing, reciting, and/or reading Sor María's devotional to St. Joseph for almost a century.

In 1727, Francisco de Rivera Calderón's press published the *Exercicio devotissimo de la muerte, que la Venerable Maria de Jesús de Agreda hacía todos los días*.[80] The small book, also known as the "Disposición de buen morir," or "Guide for a Happy Death," derived not from *La mística ciudad de dios*, but rather from Sor María's own daily devotional exercises. Although a second edition was published in 1765 in Puebla, perhaps its most significant legacy was among the founders of the Propaganda Fide colleges of Santa Cruz de Querétaro and Zacatecas.[81] As I shall discuss in chapter 4, the founder of several Propaganda Fide colleges in Mexico, Fray Antonio Margil de Jesús, was a devotee of Sor María and her writing, and prayed this devotional on a regular basis, both alone and in the company of other friars. Margil de Jesús also incorporated the practice into his spiritual advisement of nuns in Querétaro, among them Francisca de los Ángeles, whose claims to bilocation to Texas will also be examined in chapter 4.

Two announcements in the *Gaceta de México*, in November 1729 and December 1729, publicized the approval of Sor María's beatification by the Congregation of Rites and announced official permission to read *La mística ciudad de dios* to New Spanish audiences.[82] Through the *Gaceta de México*, New Spanish readers were reintroduced to a Sor María who could "legitimately" be read, at the same time that Spanish Franciscans renewed their public involvement with Sor María's *causa*.

Mexican presses responded to the new freedom to publish, producing four works in rapid succession that together represented the many facets of Sor María.

Miracles associated with *La mística ciudad de dios* are the subject of the first of these publications, *Traducción verídica, y auténtica de tres sucesos prodigiosos . . . en que la bondad divina se ha dignado de acreditar los libros de la Mystica ciudad de Dios*.[83] Translated from Latin to Spanish in Mexico by an anonymous "Sacerdote de la Metropolitana de Mexico" (secular priest from the City of Mexico),[84] it is the account of three *prodigios* (miracles) associated with *La mística ciudad de dios*. It is possible that these prodigios had already been presented in Rome as part of her canonization cause and were being made accessible to the general public through this text. Published by Joseph Bernardo de Hogal in 1729, it was announced in the *Gaceta de México* in March 1729.[85]

The *Traducción verídica* promoted *La mística ciudad de dios* as a work of spiritual writing that produced miracles, a framing that reflected favorably on Sor María and supported her case for sainthood. The introduction to the *Traducción verídica* makes clear this intent by locating Sor María among a list of canonized female religious writers, elevating her writing, and the nun herself, through the comparison: "Que las mugeres de eximia virtud han sido Prophetizas y han escrito con eminencia, como Santa Matilde, Santa Brígida, Santa Cathalina de Sena, Santa Theresa, Santa Magdalena de Pazzi, con otras muchas insignes en virtud y letras, como la Venerable Madre María de Jesús" (Women of exemplary virtue have been prophetesses and have written with eminence, such as Saint Matilda, Saint Brigid, Saint Catherine of Sienna, Saint Therese, Saint Magdalena of Pazzi, with many other notables in virtue and in letters, such as the Venerable Mother María de Jesús).[86] After establishing Sor María as an equal of these female saint-writers, the text presents three miracles associated with *La mística ciudad de dios*.

The first occurred in 1719 in Castelnovo, Italy, to two priests who regularly read *La mística ciudad de dios*. Fray Felipe Blassi borrowed a copy of the book from Abbot Buenaventura Masei and, accidentally spilling lamp oil on it, prayed to the Virgin to help him. Fray Blassi recognized any miracle as a sign that the book contained the Virgin's true revelations. Sometime later, when the abbot returned to reclaim his book, it was miraculously free of oil and once again legible, a clear sign for Friar Blassi that *La mística ciudad de dios* was authentic.

The second prodigio involved the minister general of Mallorca, Fray Martín Frontín, who was advised by an older priest to take the third volume of *La mística ciudad de dios* with him on his travels. If under attack by Moorish ships, Fray Frontín was to protect himself and the boat by following specific instructions: "abralo al instante en el Capítulo, en que refiere la navegación de la Bienaventurada Virgen María que hizo a Efeso, y formando la señal de la Cruz, muéstrelo a los Moros" (open the book that very instant to the chapter that discusses the voyage that the Blessed Virgin Mary made to Ephesus, and making the sign of the cross, show it to the Moors).[87] When Fray Frontín's ship was threatened by three Moorish vessels, he did as instructed, opening *La mística ciudad de dios* to the page in which the Virgin Mary's passage to Ephesus is described. Amazingly, the attackers were kept at bay with the help of the wind. Once safely returned to Mallorca, the crew of the Spanish ship named Sor María the boat's patroness. After that, *La mística ciudad de dios* protected them from danger: "llevaba a su Patrona [Sor María] en todas sus Navegaciones, y en ellas le sacó de muchos peligros" (they brought with them their patroness [Sor María] on all their travels, and she saved them from many dangers in their course).[88]

The final prodigio describes a French nun, Margarita de San Salvador, who without knowing any Spanish translated *La mística ciudad de dios* into French with the help of the Virgin Mary and angels. When translating the chapter of *La mística ciudad de dios* that describes the Immaculate Conception, Margarita suffered a pain so severe in her right arm that she stopped work for three days. Upon praying for relief so that she might continue, her arm's abilities were returned to her and she began to write again, "speedily" (velozmente).[89] This miracle ends with a note certifying that the nun's French translation was sent to the procurador of Sor María's *causa* in Spain.[90]

In addition to the miracles ascribed to *La mística ciudad de dios* and the contextualization of Sor María among sainted women writers, the *Traducción verídica* is unique because it connects promotion efforts in Spain with those under way in New Spain. Fray Pablo de Écija's *Sagrado inexpugnable muro*, published by the Imprenta de la Causa de la Venerable Madre Sor María de Jesús de Ágreda in Madrid in 1729, narrates these same miracles at greater length;[91] the *Traducción verídica* and *Sagrado inexpugnable muro* probably share the same source. Both authenticated and publicized miracles that gave weight to the claims of Sor María's sanctity vis-à-vis her writing, and shared that information across the Atlantic Ocean.

Figure 3.2. Verdadero retrato de nuestra Señora de Tepepan. Artist unknown.
From the *Aurora alegre del dichoso día de la gracia María Santísima* (1730), by
Antonio de Vereo. Image courtesy of the John Carter Brown Library at Brown
University.

In 1730, the *Aurora alegre del dichoso dia de la gracia Maria Santísima, Digna Madre de Dios . . . Epítome de los Libros Mystica Ciudad de Dios y Vida de la Virgen Madre de Dios* was published by Joseph Bernardo de Hogal's press.[92] Attributed to Franciscan Fray Antonio de Vereo of the Province of Santo Evangelio, the text opens with a summary of a 1729 *tirasonen* (declaration) by the Vatican announcing that Sor María's cause would continue to advance in the Congregation of Rites "without a new examination of *La mística ciudad de dios*" (sin nuevo examen de los Libros de la Mystica Ciudad de Dios). The *tirasonen* also specified "que los mismos Libros se pueden tener y leer" (those same books may be owned and read).[93] The rationale for the *Aurora alegre* is developed in the "Razón de la obra," a short political history of *La mística ciudad de dios* through 1730. The "Razón" informed Mexican readers of the Franciscan Order's central role in promoting Sor María's case for sainthood,[94] and of the critiques and prohibitions against *La mística ciudad de dios* that had emerged in Europe, to which the *tirasonen* responded.[95]

The main text of the *Aurora alegre* is an *epitome*, or concise annotated summary, of *La mística ciudad de dios*. Its stated purpose was to place the most valuable parts of Sor María's writing in the hands of as many New Spanish readers as possible to make up for the early prohibition against its reading: "para que pues no todos pueden adquirir los dilatados tomos, no se priven de el fructo de este arbol de la vida" (so that although not all may acquire the late-arriving books, no one will lack the fruit given by this tree of life).[96] The *Aurora alegre* is divided month by month, with each section consisting of a reading from *La mística ciudad de dios* and accompanying prayers. It concludes with a guide for "ejercicios para algunos días festivos" (observances associated with particular liturgical feast days).[97]

The *Aurora alegre* also stands out for how it intersected with local Mexican religious devotion, specifically to the Virgin of Tepepan. This Virgin was the patroness of a small town in Xochimilco, and the text was dedicated to her. She adorns the frontispiece (see fig. 3.2) of the *Aurora alegre*, and part of the image's miraculous history is narrated in the *Dedicatoria*:

> Como es tradición de los antiguos, aviendo los hijos naturales del País traido furtive de la puerta de Xochimilco la dicha Imagen; aun

llevada por dos vezes a Mexico, y encerrada por el mismo Provincial, milagrosamente se bolvió, y halló la Santa Imagen sobre el monte, y se levantó en título del milagro con el nombre Nuestra Señora de Tepepam [*sic*].

––––––

As the elders say, the native sons of this country furtively took this image from the gates of Xochimilco; and, taken to Mexico City twice, and locked up by the same provincial, it miraculously returned and the holy image was found upon the mountain, and in name of that miracle, the image was called Our Lady of Tepepan.[98]

Drawing from the Virgen de los Remedios, the earliest major Marian devotion in Mexico, and commissioned by Franciscan friar Pedro de Gante, the Tepepán Virgin holds a scepter in one hand and the child Jesus in her other arm.[99] St. Francis holds them above his head, a cloud encircling his shoulders.

The connection between Sor María's writing and the Virgin of Tepepan in the *Aurora alegre* resides in the association of the Xochimilco Virgin with the Immaculate Conception theology and the Franciscan Order. The description of the Virgin explains this correlation in great detail:

Para que se vea, que si Jacob levantó la piedra en el monte de Bethel, en este monte de Tepepan se vennera en ombros del Serafico Jacob Francisco la piedra levantada en vuestra milagrosa imagen. Alli en título, y memoria de un beneficio, aqui para recuerdo de tantos; alli por mano de Jacob levantada la misma piedra, en que avia puesto la cabeza; aqui la que como piedra limpia en su Concepcion tuvo siempre en su cabeza, como tal concebida, y en plumas de su Religion toda defendida el Jacob llagado.

––––––

So that it may be understood well, if Jacob lifted up the rock at the mountain of Bethel, in this mountain of Tepepan, in the arms of the Seraphic Jacob Francisco, the rock in the miraculous image is venerated. There, in the name and memory of a beneficiary; here, for the memory of the many. There, by the hand of Jacob, who raised the stone on which he had laid his head; here, a rock that, pure as

Her conception, always adorned her head, conceived as such, and by the pens [of the Franciscans], defended by the wounded Jacob.[100]

The description of the Virgen de Tepepan goes on to explain the relationship between the precious stone and the Immaculate Conception:

> Y si esta piedra levantada sobre sus ombros, esta el monte sobre el monte: porque está el preparado monte para Casa de Dios, Maria sobre los montes de Santidad en ombros de un S. Francisco; esta el Jacob de la gracia, o por escabel de la Escala (Imagen de Maria) o con lo grave de la limpidisima, y primaria piedra (symbolo de la pureza) predicandola a lo rethórico, como defensor de la gracia de Maria.

_____

> And if this stone is lifted atop his shoulders, the mountain lays atop the mountain; because the mountain is prepared as a home for God, Mary upon the mount of Holiness in the arms of a Saint Francis; there is Jacob, full of grace, or as a footstep of the ladder (image of Mary), or with the solemnity of the purist one, and the first stone (a symbol of purity), preaching through rhetoric, as a defender of Mary's grace.

Antonio de Vereo continues, invoking the indigenous word for "gem" in his explanation of the image and its implicit connection to the Immaculate Conception:

> Asi lo confessamos agradecidos, Dulcisima Madre: y que con vuestra Sagrada Imagen vino tambien a este lugar el Cordero, que de la piedra del desierto pedia Isais: pues traxo la Imagen al Hijo en los brazos de la misma material, y piedra _Chalchihuitl_, que si en mexicano es lo mismo que en latin _Gemma_, claro está, que como hijo de la Madre a lo natural, y humano se avia de vestir el Hijo de la misma material de la Madre; que por esso para venir el Cordero al desierto humanado: de la material de la Madre: preparó a la Madre de ante mano, la adornó, y enriqueció de la mas preciosa piedra de la gracia en su Concepción.

_____

We thus gratefully confess, Sweet Mother; that with your Holy Image the Lamb also came to this place, as Isaiah asked for the stone of the desert; thus the image brought to the Son in the arms of the same material and rock, *Chalchihuitl*, which in the Mexican language is the same as the Latin *Gemma*, it is clear that as the natural Son of the Mother, and as he was made of the same human material as his mother; and for this reason, the Lamb became human and came to the desert: made of the Mother's material; the Mother prepared the image beforehand, she adorned it, and enriched it with the most precious rock of grace in her conception.

Interestingly, similar gemological cross-referencing to Mary is found in Écija's *Sagrado inexpugnable muro*, published in Spain in 1735.

In 1730, the first edition of the *Tanto que se sacó de una carta* was published in Mexico, and through it Sor María was presented to New Spanish readers as a protomissionary.[101] The text is an adaptation of the 1631 letter by Sor María and Fray Benavides for the New Mexican friars that told of her travels to New Mexico and conversion of the tribes there. The *Tanto que se sacó de una carta* cleaves close to (but is not the same as) the original, which also reported on and substantiated Sor María's mystical evangelization in New Mexico.

The image on the text's cover informed readers that Sor María was to be understood as a missionary to northern New Spain (see fig. 3.3).[102] The picture of Sor María prefigured iconography of New Spanish Franciscan missionaries to those regions, such as Fray Antonio Margil de Jesús and Fray Junípero Serra. Their *vitae* (published in 1737 and 1787, respectively) included representations of them as American missionaries, posed similarly to Sor María in the *Tanto que se sacó de una carta*.[103] In the printing, Sor María is positioned superior to tribal members who look up to her as she gazes slightly downward at a crucifix she holds in her hand. In a caricature of indigenous peoples of Mexico, the native observers in the image wear feathered headdresses, their mouths agape, apparently in awe of Sor María. One of the women pictured carries a child in her arms, perhaps alluding to the moment in Benavides's narration of the Lady in Blue when the Jumano mothers offered their children up for baptism by raising their arms.

The title beneath the image references Sor María "predicando a los Chichimecas del Nuebo Mexico" (preaching to the Chichimecos of New

Figure 3.3. *La Venerable Madre Sor María de Jesús de Ágreda, Predicando a los Chichimecos del Nuevo-Mexico* by Antonio de Castro. Frontispiece of the *Tanto que se sacó de una carta* (1730). Image courtesy of the John Carter Brown Library at Brown University.

Mexico).[104] The historical Chichimecos were an indigenous, semino-madic tribe or tribes in north-central Mexico who successfully resisted Spanish conquest for decades. The Chichimecos are not mentioned in the *Tanto que se sacó de una carta*, which specifies that Sor María visited the Jumanos and other tribes in New Mexico, or in the other primary accounts of Sor María's travels. The use of the tribe's name in the *Tanto que se sacó de una carta* may reflect a tendency to use the expression "Chichimeco" as a generic term for nomadic and seminomadic indige-nous groups opposing Spanish incursion.[105]

The *Tanto que se sacó de una carta* was published twice more, in 1747 and 1760. The 1760 edition bears a slightly different image than the 1730 printing, though the content and format of the pictures are similar.[106] The three printings of the *Tanto que se sacó* are unique among Sor María's publications in Mexico because they describe *only* Sor María's mystical travel to New Mexico. There is no mention of *La mística ciudad de dios*, Sor María's other writing, or her case for canonization. The text disar-ticulates Sor María completely from that most important facet of her identity—her writing—by framing her exclusively as a protomissionary. At the same time, these printings made the Lady in Blue narrative emi-nently accessible and easily decipherable (given its imagery) for New Spanish readers. The details within the letter regarding Sor María's travels to New Mexico, which we explored in chapter 1, and the urgent and sacred nature of the Franciscan friars' mission labors there, were made accessible to a new community of readers through the letter's pub-lication. If prior to 1730 the letter had only circulated in manuscript form, primarily within the Franciscan Order, its entrance onto a much larger stage via the printing press meant that many more Mexican readers became aware of it. The letter's publication helped impress the Lady in Blue narrative onto the imagination and history of colonial Mexico.

The last of this cluster of Mexican publications relating to Sor María is the *Escuela mystica de María en la mystica ciudad de dios*, the New Spanish edition of *La mística ciudad de dios* discussed above.[107] Taken together, these four documents painted a complete picture for Mexican readers of who Sor María was and what she wrote. These publications resulted in increased engagement with her writing and beatification pro-cess by cultivating a community of readers for her. An update on the status of Sor María's *causa* in the May 1731 *Gaceta de México* only em-phasized her growing profile among New Spanish citizens: "y con esta

tan plausible, y desseada noticia se ha ya juntado mas numero de cuatro-
cientas cartas conducentes á el efecto que (especialmente España) aspira"
(and with this praiseworthy and much-desired announcement, more
than four hundred letters to that effect—to which Spain and others
aspire [her beatification]—have already been collected).[108] Through the
production of New Spanish presses, Mexicans became increasingly invested in Sor María's writing, her mystical travels, and her beatification
process.

Throughout the rest of the eighteenth century and early nineteenth
century, Sor María's texts continued to inform New Spanish readers.
The publications produced on Mexican presses shaped devotional practices and encouraged adherence to specific ideas and theological concepts posed in *La mística ciudad de dios*. One example of this is the
*Novena en honor de los mil angeles de guarda de la Santissima Virgen
Maria*,[109] a nine-day prayer pertaining to the Virgin Mary's guardian
angels, printed in Puebla in 1747.[110] The names, natures, and occupations
of angels was a concept Sor María elaborated at length in her other
works of writing,[111] and in *La mística ciudad de dios*, namely "part. 1 lib.
1 cap. 14 desde num. 201 hasta el num. 207" (part 1, book 1, chapter 14,
from number 201 to 207). The angels are a topic in their own right, and
they directed readers' attention back to the Immaculate Conception,
as the portion describing them immediately precedes the chapter describing Mary's conception: "Como el Altissimo manifestó a los Santos
Angeles el tiempo determinado y oportuno de la Concepción de María
Santissima, y los que le señaló para su guarda" (How the Almighty
manifested to the Holy Angels the determined and opportune time for
the Conception of Holy Mary, and those who He indicated for her protection).[112] The angel motif as explained in *La mística ciudad de dios*
would be reiterated in later publications deriving from her writing, and
interpreted through New Spanish art.

The *Peregrinación christiana por el camino real de la celeste Jerusalén*, attributed to Fray Joachín de Osuna, a discalced Franciscan from
the Province of San Diego de México, is an example of devotional prayer
incorporating Sor María's writing. The Biblioteca Mexicana published
the text in 1756 and again in 1760.[113] In the latter printing, Sor María is
featured on the text's cover accompanied by Fray Osuna, in an engraving
by José Benito Ortuño (see fig. 3.4). The two kneel at the foot of a
cross, with a thin sword running its length and three arrow tips at the

bottom of the cross and one on each end of the horizontal piece. The cross is labeled "INRI," and the text below the two figures suggests the *Peregrinación* is a guide to the Via Crucis, or Stations of the Cross. This would not be the last guide to the Stations of the Cross rooted in *La mística ciudad de dios* published in Mexico.

In 1758, the Bibliotheca Mexicana in Mexico City published two devotional texts reinforcing the Immaculate Conception theology; both derived from *La mística ciudad de dios*. The *Novena sagrada, que a la Inmaculada Concepción de la serenissima reyna de los angeles Maria Santissima Nuestra Señora, que consagró la afectuosa devoción de los Religiosos Descalzos de N.S.P.S. Francisco*[114] was excerpted by "un Esclavo de la Reyna de los Angeles" (a slave of the Queen of Angels), possibly Fray Augustín Bernal, at whose behest the novena, printed in small book format, was published.[115] Praying the novena entitled the suppliant to indulgences, presumably for the prayer's advocation of the Immaculate Conception theology, as the cover of the book included a woodprint of the Virgin of the Immaculate Conception.

Fray Joachín de Osuna is the author of the second Conceptionist devotional, *Perla de la gracia y concha del cielo*.[116] A meditation and prayer guide, with instructions to be recited on the eighth and twenty-fifth of each month, it included a septenario, or seven-day prayer, dedicated to the Immaculate Conception, followed by a novena relating to the incarnation of Jesus. The source material for the meditations and prayers was "sacado todo de las Obras de la V.M. Agreda" (taken from all the Works of the Venerable Mother Ágreda). Osuna dedicated *Perla de la gracia* to the "doce Angeles de los mil Custodios de la Emperatriz Celestial" (twelve Angels of the thousand Guards of the Celestial Empress),[117] perhaps an allusion to the twelve doors in the Celestial Jerusalem referenced in the book of Revelation according to St. John, and another linkage to the ideas about angels explored in Sor María's texts.[118] In the book's dedication, Osuna cites part 1, book 1, chapter 23 of *La mística ciudad de dios* at length in a metaphorical discussion of the purity of the Virgin Mary. A Mercedarian friar, Fr. Manuel de Alcaraz, the prelate who authorized the publication of *Perla de la gracia*, affirmed that one of the purposes of the text was to advance devotion to the Immaculate Conception and the incarnation of Christ: "adelantar los cultos a la Soberana Señora en el primer Mysterio [la Inmaculada Concepción] y promerlos [*sic*] en el Segundo [la Incarnación de Cristo]" (to advance

Figure 3.4. *Peregrinación christiana por el camino real de la celeste Jerusalén.*
Image by José Benito Ortuño. Frontispiece of *Peregrinación cristiana* (1760), by
Joachín Osuna. Image courtesy of the John Carter Brown Library at Brown
University.

the devotional cults to the Sovereign Queen in the first mystery [the Immaculate Conception] and promote them in the second [the incarnation of Christ]).[119] Through these two examples, and many subsequent publications, Sor María's writing became a primary vehicle for the popularization of the Immaculate Conception theology in eighteenth-century Mexico.

This is not necessarily surprising. By the time the *Novena sagrada* and *Perla de la gracia* were published, the Virgin of the Immaculate Conception had already been declared patroness of the Americas in 1761.[120] The popular promotion of the theological principle, which had not yet been declared Church dogma, may have driven the surge in later eighteenth-century publications deriving from Sor María's Conceptionist writing. The *Triduo mariano mensual en honor, y reverencia del Felicissimo Transito, entierro y assumpcion de la Reyna del Cielo y tierra María Nuestra Señora, para alcanzar mediante su Protección una dichosa muerte*[121] is one example of this fervent interest in *La mística ciudad de dios* as a Marian work. Composed by Br. D. Francisco Marín, a "clérigo domicilario" (diocesan cleric) from Puebla, the *Triduo mariano* was to be prayed the thirteenth, fourteenth, and fifteenth of every month, "para alcanzar mediante su protección, una dichosa muerte" (to achieve, through [the Virgin Mary's] protection, a happy death). The three days of prayer are meditations on the Virgin Mary's death, burial, and assumption, derived from *La mística ciudad de dios*'s treatment of those topics.

The eight editions of the *Triduo mariano* made it one of the most frequently published of Sor María's texts in colonial Mexico. It was issued for the first time in Puebla in 1761 on the press of Cristobal Ortega,[122] and was reprinted four more times in that city: in 1790, 1796, and 1817,[123] by Pedro de la Rosa's press, and once by the Herederos de la Viuda de Miguel Ortega in 1774.[124] In Mexico City, the *Triduo mariano* was published three times—in 1783, 1790, and 1817.[125] The first two Mexico City editions were by Joseph de Jáuregui, and Alejandro Valdés published the last. Notably, the 1790 Jáuregui edition carried with it the privilege of eighty days of indulgences for each of the three days of prayer, issued by the archbishop of Puebla, Sr. Domingo Pantaleón Álvarez de Abréu. This official approbation for Sor María's writing indicates that it remained at the heart of colonial Mexican devotional practices, even into the close of the eighteenth century.

But the most frequently published text deriving from Sor María's writing was the *Modo de andar la via sacra*.[126] It was first issued in 1763 by the Biblioteca Mexicana, with at least *fourteen* subsequent editions (and likely more) published in the late eighteenth and early nineteenth centuries: 1773, 1774, 1777, 1779, 1789, 1793, 1806, 1808, 1809, 1815, 1817, 1819, 1821, and 1826.[127] Most editions were published in Mexico City by Joseph de Jáuregui's family presses, with the exception of the 1817 printing, made in Guadalajara. The subtitle specifies which part of *La mística ciudad de dios* provided source material ("part. 2. lib. 6. cap. 12," "part 2, book 6, chapter 12"). As this remarkable bibliographical record indicates, *La mística ciudad de dios* influenced the devotional practice of the Stations of the Cross in Mexico for more than six decades.

The subtitle of the *Modo de andar la via sacra* provides a sense for who composed the guide: "uno de los fundadores del Colegio de la Sta. Cruz de Querétaro" (one of the founders of the College of Santa Cruz de Querétaro). The devotion of the founders of the Propaganda Fide colleges to Sor María, which will be a topic central to chapter 4's discussion of Mexican Franciscan promotion of her and her writing, connects their work at mission sites to the production of the Mexico City press. The 1789 edition offers further insight into the colleges' involvement in the frequent republication of the *Modo de andar la via sacra*, stating that it was republished "a devoción de los Misioneros del Colegio Apostólico de S. Fernando de esta ciudad de México" (owing to the devotion of the Missionaries of the Apostolic College of San Fernando, of this City of Mexico). The San Fernando College, like its sister Propaganda Fide colleges in Querétaro and Zacatecas, implemented Sor María's writing in its curriculum and taught its missionaries about her mission work on the northern New Spanish frontier.

Four more publications demonstrate the consistency with which Sor María's writing was published up to the close of the colonial period in Mexico, engaging her Mexican community of reading well into the nineteenth century through texts on Marian ideas derived from *La mística ciudad de dios*. *Ofrecimiento de la corona en honra de la Purísima Concepción* (1777)[128] derived from the first part of *La mística ciudad de dios* and continued the promotion of devotional practices associated with the Immaculate Conception theology. The *Elogios a la reyna del Cielo María Santísima, sacados Del Libro intitulado Exercicios Espirituales de Retiro* (1784)[129] derived from another of Sor María's texts, the *Ejercicios espirituales*, which had already been popularized in Querétaro convents and also among key elite readers (including Sor Juana Inés de la Cruz) in Mexico. The *Oraciones a María Santísima, y Señor Joseph, para saludarlos y alabarlos, y para alentar nuestras confianzas* (1785)[130] were "deducidas de varias partes de la Venerable Madre Sor Maria de Jesús de Agreda" (taken from various parts of the work of the Venerable Mother Sor María de Jesús de Ágreda)—that is, from *La mística ciudad de dios*—and are an example of popular Josephine devotional practice derived from Sor María's writing.[131] Released in 1816, the *Viernes de Maria en obsequio de su glorioso Tránsito, provechosa devoción para conseguir una buena muerte*[132] was taken from book 8, chapter 18, number 745 of *La mística ciudad de dios*, and is a meditation guide intended to lead readers to a happy death. The attribution for the work— "por un vecino de Celaya" (by a neighbor of Celaya)—indicates that it was likely produced in conjunction with the neighboring Propaganda Fide College of Santa Cruz de Querétaro.

One exceptional nineteenth-century work of Agredana merits special attention not for what is relates but for who commissioned its publication and to whom profits from its sale were directed. Fray Diego Bringas y Encinas, a Franciscan and member of the College of Santa Cruz de Querétaro, is attributed with the 1815 edition of the *Modo de andar la via sacra*. A Spanish loyalist, he also published *Sermón político moral* (1813), a text that gained fame and notoriety by arguing against Mexican independence from Spain.[133] Apart from revealing Bringas y Encinas's conservative political views, the *Sermón político moral* reveals the close connection that still existed between the friars of Propaganda Fide and Sor María well into the nineteenth century. The sermon's subtitle dedicates the work to "la admirable y heróica virgen Sor María de Jesús de Ágreda" (the admirable and heroic virgin Sor María de Jesús de Ágreda) and indicates that any profits made from the sermon's publication were earmarked for the benefit of her convent: "al socorro de las actuales urgencias del religiosísimo convento de monjas de la Purísima Concepción de la Villa de Ágreda" (to relieve the pressing present needs of the strict religious convent of the nuns of the Immaculate Conception in the village of Ágreda).[134]

Bringas y Encinas's personal devotion to Sor María, likely nurtured through his tenure at the college, was manifested in other works he published, namely, the *Índice apologético de las razones que recomiendan la obra intitulada Mística Ciudad de Dios* (1834).[135] Published in Valencia, Spain, the *Índice apologético* is a summary spanning many years of the theological and political debates concerning *La mística ciudad de dios*, and is also a defense of the work ("índice *apologético*," "apologetic catalog") that responded to many of the work's early critiques. In the second part of the book, Bringas y Encinas presents a synopsis of Sor María's *vita*. He builds on the Lady in Blue narrative included in the *vita*, and includes a version of the *Tanto que se sacó de una carta*, apparently taken from Écija's *Sagrado inexpugnable muro*. He carefully adds to that version of the narrative the specification that although Fray Benavides claimed Sor María traveled in her body to evangelize in New Mexico, "la Ven. Madre creía ser solo en espíritu" (the Venerable Mother believed that she traveled only in spirit),[136] an important detail from a dogmatic perspective that Bringas y Encinas is careful to underscore.

The continued devotion to Sor María as an author of Marian spirituality in the nineteenth century is evidenced by the last documented Mexican publication of her writing I found—*Compendio histórico, y novena de Maria santisima nuestra Señora que con la advocacion de la cueva santa se venera en el Seminario de la Santa Cruz de la ciudad de Querétaro* (1834), published in Puebla by the Hospital de San Pedro.[137] Another work originating with the College of Santa Cruz de Querétaro, the novena is dedicated to the veneration of the image of "nuestra Señora de la Cueva Santa" (Our Lady of the Holy Cave). The section "Ejercicios que prescribe la concordia espiritual de la buena murete, erigida bajo la protección de nuestra Señora de la Cueva Santa" (Exercises prescribed for spiritual well-being leading to a good death, chosen under the protection of Our Lady of the Holy Cave) offers Sor María's writings as the source for practices associated with private preparation for death, and in association with the veneration of the Virgin of the Holy Cave:

> Estos obsequios, y el fin á que se dirije esta importante concordia son muy del agrado de la soberana Madre de Dios, como se puede ver en los libros de la Mística Ciudad de Dios "Hija mia (dice la soberana Reina á la venerable Sor María de Jesus de Agreda), sobre lo que as escrito declararte otro privilegio que me concedió mi Hijo santísimo en aquella hora" (9 parte n., 741.745).

─────

These spiritual gifts, and the end to which this important harmony is directed, are very pleasing to the sovereign Mother of God, as one can see in the books of *La mística ciudad de dios*, "My daughter (the sovereign Queen says to the Venerable Sor María de Jesús de Ágreda), beyond that which you have already written, declare another privilege that my Son conceded to me at that hour" (9th part, numbers 741–745).[138]

The work is laced with allusions to Sor María's writing, and to her inspiration by the Virgin Mary.

The depth and persistence of Sor María's Mexican community of reading is evidenced even after Mexican independence. In 1844, several publications and public discourses associated with them coincided with the publication of the first complete edition of *La mística ciudad de dios* in Mexico[139] since 1731. Perhaps in response to the book's reemergence, the Mexican newspaper *El Constitucional* published a famous seventeenth-century critique *of La mística ciudad de dios* by French bishop and anti-Agredist Jacques Bénigne Bossuet in 1844. Sor María's supporters strenuously opposed the reopening of that commentary. Jesuit Basilio Arrillaga published his *Defensa de La mística ciudad de dios*[140] the same year in response, countering Bousset's negative appraisal of Sor María's writing by providing a summary of the text and its historical course, and chastising the paper for hauling the criticism back into the spotlight. It is important to note that although we have seen some indication of Jesuit support of Sor María's writing and *causa* through the Mexican publication record, in chapter 4 I will show how the order's engagement with the Immaculate Conception theology led to the popularization of *La mística ciudad de dios* among its friars, including those located at New Spanish missions.

Moving west across the Pacific from Mexico, and returning briefly to the colonial period, one finds an echo of the Mexican printing bonanza of Sor María's writing in the Philippines. Because the activities of Franciscans in the Philippines were dictated in significant part by Franciscans in Mexico during the colonial epoch, the expansion of Sor María's devotional community in the Philippines is closely related to New Spanish publications, beliefs, and practices.[141] The trade route along the Nao de China passed through Mexico's port of Veracruz, and several artifacts point to a community of reading for Sor María's writing in the Philippines that may have resulted from Mexican influence. One example of this is a printing of Sor María's family tree, designed and produced in Manila in 1759 (see fig. 3.5).

The image's creator, Laurencio Atlas, was a prominent printmaker in Manila at the time, and was commissioned by the Franciscan friars of the Province of Saint Gregory the Great to produce the image. The "árbol genealógico" (family tree) features Sor María's three siblings, her parents, and the nun herself, who is pictured holding the three volumes of *La mística ciudad de dios*. The family members are arranged around an actual tree, with her parents, Francisco and Catalina, at the tree's roots, and the family home resting on the crux of its trunk. The Virgin of the Immaculate Conception is positioned at the top of the image. As the text below the image explains, praying one Hail Mary to Sor María's family tree entitled the supplicant to forty days of indulgence, which were granted by the archbishop of Manila, Manuel Antonio Roxo-Del Río y Vieyra. As in Mexico, the Philippine Church's involvement in issuing indulgences demonstrated a degree of institutional acceptance for Sor María's writing.[142] The family tree motif is well known within the corpus of Sor María's iconography, and its very existence opens the possibility that other artwork featuring more universal Agredan themes was also produced in the Philippines and, with it, perhaps Sor María's writing.[143]

The New Spanish publications discussed above are essential to understanding Sor María as a public figure in colonial Mexican culture. Through them, she became a source of theological and spiritual ideas that permeated Mexican spiritual thought and a model for evangelization on New Spain's northern borders. Taken together, these texts illustrate that Sor María's community of reading had much material penned by the nun at the ready, prepared by Mexican presses, and the concepts in her writing infused colonial Mexican art, thought, belief, and religious practice.

Reading about and Writing through Sor María in Colonial Mexico

Owing to the prevalence of her writing and to her increasing public profile, the fortunes of Sor María's *causa* and the status of her writing remained fixed in the New Spain imagination, as Antonio de Robles's *Diario de sucesos notables (1665–1703)* reveals.[144] In the *Diario*, canon

Figure 3.5. Árbol genealógico de la familia Coronel y Arana (1759), by Laurencio Atlas. Image courtesy of the Archivo Franciscano Ibero-Oriental, Madrid, Spain.

lawyer Robles documented the most recent and relevant news of the day, which in June 1682 happened to be the banning of *La mística ciudad de dios* by the Vatican and the order to collect her books in Mexico: "se han mandado recoger los libros de la monja de Agreda" (it has been ordered that the books by the nun of Ágreda be collected).[145] Robles's journal likewise records the beginnings of devotion to Ágredan objects in New Spain in the late seventeenth century, commenting in September 1690 that Church authorities had recently prohibited popular devotional objects attributed to Sor María. Robles wrote of three edicts issued barring the circulation of scapulars, prayer books, books, and crosses attributed to Sor María, an announcement read publicly by the royal scribe in front of the cathedral in Mexico City: "Se leyeron tres edictos de la Inquisicion prohibiendo los escapularios, oratorios y libros de la monja Agreda y cruces" (Three Inquisitorial edicts were read prohibiting scapulars, oratories, and books by the nun from Ágreda, and crosses).[146] Robles's account also demonstrates that interest in Sor María in New Spain had already taken hold by the late seventeenth century, coinciding with the publication of texts such as Vetancurt's *Chronología sagrada*.

Sor María's ascendancy as a public figure continued in the eighteenth century, and updates relating to her case for beatification and the status of *La mística ciudad de dios* were newsworthy information in colonial Mexico. In May 1757, a proclamation reporting Vatican officials' confirmation of Sor María's authorship of *La mística ciudad de dios* and the return of the original manuscripts to Spain was made public and commemorated in Mexico. The *Crónica de la provincia de n.s.p.s. Francisco de Zacatecas*,[147] authored by Franciscan friars José de Arlegui and Antonio Gálvez, revealed that the recently elected Franciscan provincial of Zacatecas, José Manuel de Estrada, followed orders from the father general of the Franciscan Order, which mandated celebrating this event in Franciscan communities:

> y el reverendísimo padre general atendiendo al honor que de esta resolución tan respetable resultaba á la venerable de Agreda, y á todo el Orden, mandó (y el reverendo Estrada publicó su órden) que se cantase una misa solemne, y un Te Deum en accion de gracias, y que en habiendo oportunidad se colectasen limosnas para continuar la causa de la beatificación de la venerable madre.

―――――

And the very reverend Father General, responding to the honor that this very respectable resolution meant for the venerable Ágreda, and for the whole order, ordered (and the Reverend Estrada published his order) that a solemn Mass be recited, and a Te Deum be prayed in thanksgiving, and whenever the opportunity presented itself, that pious donations be collected to continue the cause for beatification of the venerable mother.[148]

As per the father general's order, Franciscan sites (including those in Zacatecas and other parts of Mexico) were to celebrate a solemn Mass and pray the Te Deum to celebrate an important step in the forward movement of Sor María's *causa* in Rome. In addition, no time was to be lost in funding the process; it was advised to make the most of the moment to solicit pious donations for the *causa* from parishioners also.

Yet Sor María's pervasive cultural presence in colonial Mexico was more than a news item, or cause for masses and the collection of limosna. Literate members of her New Spanish community of reading reinterpreted her writing, as had happened in Spain. A 1760 Mexican manuscript by Verdiguer, *Matemática demostración*, shows how Sor María's writing was internalized and transformed by New Spanish readers (see fig 3.6). In this case, Cayetano Verdiguer, a "nacional de México" (Mexican citizen) associated with the Jesuits,[149] followed in the footsteps of Fray Agustín de Vetancurt's 1696 *Chronografía sagrada*, which used information provided in *La mística ciudad de dios* and other texts to present alternative dates for religious and world events. *Matemática demostración* follows this mold, using other texts in complement to *La mística ciudad de dios* to determine when certain biblical and historical moments occurred, and illustrating these using tables and calendars.

The objective of the work is made clear in the dedication of the text to the Virgin of the Immaculate Conception: "A La Siempre Virgen Maria, Madre de Dios, Concebida Sin Mancha de Pecado Original" (To the Always-Virgin Mary, Mother of God, Conceived without the Stain of Original Sin).[150] Verdiguer's prologue acknowledges the 1757 Vatican declaration that Sor María was the author of *La mística ciudad de dios* (the same declaration the Franciscans celebrated) to demonstrate the legitimacy of Sor María as the primary source for the *Matemática demostración*.

Figure 3.6. Matemática demostración de las letras dominicales y exactas desde el principio del mundo hasta el año 1760, y siguientes (1760), by Cayetano Verdiguer. Image courtesy of the Biblioteca Nacional de España.

The majority of the text consists of modification of religious and world calendars, adjusted to conform to dates for particular events given in *La mística ciudad de dios*. Verdiguer appears to have prepared the document for presentation at the Spanish court: in his prologue, he addresses the "muchos doctos Mathematicos de esta corte" (many educated scholars of this court), and implies that the *Matemática demostración* is destined for a circumscribed, attentive readership: "Conosco la corta esfera de mi trabajo y la mucha observacion que le espera" (I recognize the limits of my work and the many observations that await it).[151]

In Verdiguer's chronography, Sor María's calculations are supplemented not only by studies made by European scholars and clerics, but also by native Mexican knowledge.[152] Verdiguer names some of the other sources for his computation, including Mexican polymath Carlos Sigüenza y Góngora and the Italian scholar of pre-Columbian Mexico Lorenzo Boturini Bernaducci (of the Codex Boturini), to whom Verdiguer attributes "la averiguacion de antiguos indios calculos" (the verification of ancient Indian calculations):

La computacion de los setenta sagrados interpretes esta aprobada por el Senor Sixto Quinto; la sigue la Iglesia en el Martyrologio Romano al dia veinte y cinco diciembre; apoyala el chronicon Emilianense; acomodanse a ella el Cavallero Boturini en la averiguacion de antiguos indios calculos; el insigne mexicano Siguenza; el Dr. Don Diego de Torrres en sus reportorios; y muchos doctos Mathematicos de esta corte. No confunde ni se opone su quenta, a la acertada y util correccion Gregoriana, que hoy guardamaos, y debemos venerar; antes registrada con curiosa reflexa la tabla de las Epactatas, se halla la verisimilitud mas propia de la conjunciones de sol y luna hasta estos tiempos, y en el mismo orden proviene los venideros que Dios quiera. Conosco la corta esfera de mi trabajo y la mucha observacion que le espera; serame mucha gloria el que mis yerros motiven en otros, los mas plausibles aciertos.

––––––

The computation of the seventy holy apostles has been approved by Pope Sixtus V; it is followed by the Church in the Roman Martyrology on the twenty-fifth of December; it is supported in the Códice Emilanense; the gentleman [Lorenzo] Boturini takes it into account in his interpretation of ancient Indian calculations; the distinguished [Carlos] Sigüenza [y Góngora]; Dr. Diego de Torres in his indices; and many studied men of this court. The fitting and useful Gregorian correction, which we use today, neither confuses nor opposes its count, and we should respect it; previously regarded with curiosity, the tables of epacts [days added to the lunar calendar to calculate the solar year], one now notes the important similarities in the conjunctions of the sun and moon up through the present day, and in the same way, others that, God willing, will come. I recognize the limitations of my work, and the critique that awaits it; I would be gratified if my mistakes were to motivate others through its most plausible assertions.[153]

Later, Verdiguer includes the founding of Mexico among the select world events he puts forth in his tables: "Este mismo año [1187] los indios chichimecas, se internaron en las tierras que los tultecas [toltecas] havian dexado. Fue principio de la fundacion de Mexico" (This very year [1187] the Chichimec Indians moved inland to the lands that the

Toltecs had abandoned. This was the beginning of Mexico's founding).[154] He incorporates several other moments in indigenous Mexican history throughout the chronology, suggesting the applicability of Sor María's writing to a specific Mexican context, at least in Verdiguer's view.

Verdiguer's reconciliation of Sor María's dates with those of many other calendars is nuanced:

> Sea escopo, y fundamento de estas tablas las palabras aqui puestas, y citadas â los margenes, para advertir los respectivos principios que son el del Año natural distinto del Civil; el de el Dia como lo comenzaban los Hebreos, diferente de el principio que le dieron en la ordinacion Juliana, restableciendo el usso antiguo de Romanos, y Egipcios: Consideremos el año natural al punto que el Sol toca el primero de Aries, y en circulando hasta otro tal, será esse mismo punto fin de un año, y principio de otro. El civil comienza al dividirse la noche que antecede al primero dia del mes Enero, y fenece del mismo modo. El Dia natural lo comenzaron los Astronomos desde el medio dia de sus meridianos, àcaso porque Juzgaron haver sido creado el Sol sobre el territorio que despues se llamò Campo Damasceno (donde fuè formado el primer hombre) en cuyo Zenith comenzò su giro. Este principio, y fin del dia natural sirve aqui mucho, para la tabla de las Epactas.

———

> May the words placed here, and cited in the margins, serve as the chisel and foundation of the tables, to signal the respective starts of the natural year as distinct from the civil year; the beginning as the Hebrews determined it, which is different from the beginning dictated by the Julian calendar, which reestablished the ancient Roman and Egyptian practices; let us consider the natural year the point when the sun touches the first of Aries, and the end of the year its circling back to that same point, and the beginning of another year. The civil year begins by dividing the night that precedes the first day of the month of January, and comes to an end in the same way. Astronomers started the natural day from the middle of its meridians, perhaps because they believed the sun to have been created in the area that was later called the Damascene Field (where the first man was formed) and at whose zenith the sun began its rotation. This

principle, and the end of the natural day, are important here, for the table of epacts.[155]

However, the principal role Sor María's writing played in the document's formulation is unmistakable. Its opening pages cite sections from *La mística ciudad de dios* that Verdiguer used as the foundation for the *Matemática demostración*'s calcuations. He references the date of the creation of mankind per Sor María in *La mística ciudad de dios*, part 2, book 3, chapter 11, number 138: "Sucedió esto Viernes à veinte y cinco de Marzo al romper el Alva . . . à la misma hora que fue formado nuestro primero padre Adan" (This happened on Friday, the twenty-fifth of March, at daybreak . . . at the same hour that our first father, Adam, was formed).[156] Another citation, this time from part 2, book 6, chapter 21, number 1359, establishes the date the world began: "Conforme à este computo, la creación del Mundo fue en Marzo, y del dia en que fue criado Adan hasta la Encarnacion del Verbo, passaron cinco-mil ciento noventa y nueve años; y añadiendo los nueve meses, que estuvo en el vientre virginal de su Madre Santísima." (According to this computation, the creation of the world was in March, and five thousand and ninety-nine years passed from the day Adam was created to the incarnation of the Word; and adding the nine months that [Christ] remained in the virginal womb of his Holy Mother).[157]

From his firm footing in *La mística ciudad de dios*, Verdiguer continues with a series of tables (*tablas*) that compare various chronologies—the "Cuenta de los Romanos," and the "Cuenta natural," for example. The last chart, "Años de la Encarnación," is fashioned from dates provided in *La mística ciudad de dios*. This table is followed by a century-by-century listing of religious and world events assigned new dates based on Verdiguer's reconciliation of these calendars, among them the creation of the world and the great flood, and also the date when Sor María wrote *La mística ciudad de dios*[158] (see fig. 3.7). The events Verdiguer chooses to rechronologize, from episodes in Jesus's and Mary's lives, to the births and deaths of various popes and saints, merits its own study, in particular his attention to important moments in the histories of Mexican indigenous peoples. Yet Verdiguer's careful treatment of Sor María's writing, and his integration of it into the unfolding of world, biblical, and Mexican history, speaks volumes regarding Sor María's intellectual influence in colonial Mexico. This same cultural impact is observed in New Spanish arts.

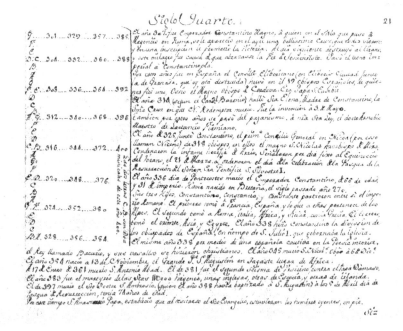

Figure 3.7. Table of dates of world events recalculated using information derived from *La mística ciudad de dios* in the *Matemática demostración* by Cayetano Verdiguer. Image courtesy of the Biblioteca Nacional de España.

Portraying Sor María: Author and Missionary in Colonial Mexican Art

Spanish art historian Ricardo Fernández Gracia has noted of paintings of Sor María in colonial Mexico that "la proyección del *opus magnum* de sor María [*La mística ciudad de dios*] llegó a los pinceles y los buriles de artistas figurativos" (the reach of Sor María's opus magnum [*La mística ciudad de dios*] reached the paintbrushes and chisels of artists),[159] but that the full extent of her influence over New Spanish art remains to be systematically examined: "está aún por valorar [en] su auténtica dimensión" (its true breadth is yet to be appreciated).[160] The few works of art depicting Sor María examined here hint at a much greater body yet to be examined, both pieces that depict her and others works that portray ideas and themes originating in her writing. Here, I examine pieces of Mexican art that reproduce the aesthetics described in *La mística ciudad de dios*, depict episodes from the lives of Jesus and Mary specific to *La mística ciudad de dios*, represent Sor María accompanied by symbols or images relating to the Immaculate Conception, and present the nun alone as a writer, spiritual figure, and/or protomissionary.

Mexican art historian Antonio Rubial García notes that Sor María's writing left a lasting impression on colonial Mexican art, "[dejó] una fuerte huella en [la] iconografía [de ella]" (it left a strong footprint in the artwork depicting her), specifically for how ideas from her writing were translated into aesthetic effects throughout New Spanish artwork.[161] The graphic descriptions of Christ's flagellation and crucifixion in *La mística ciudad de dios*, for example, were manifested in the depiction of suffering Christ figures in several New Spanish works.[162] Mexican art historian Francisco de la Maza observes this influence in an image of Christ, the *Señor del Aposentillo* in Acolman, in which the Christ figure is rendered hanging from his arms ("colgado de los hombros por unas cuerdas," "hung from the arms by some rope").[163] This image, de la Maza asserts, was inspired directly from Sor María's writing: "fue inspirado en los escritos de Sor María de Jesús (Capítulo XVII del libro citado) la cual resulta ser una fuente principalísima de inspiración para los temas pasionarios del Barroco" (the work was inspired by the writing of Sor María de Jesús—chapter 17 of the cited book [*La mística ciudad de dios*]; she was a principal source of inspiration for Baroque passion themes).[164] Reflecting on the repeated publication of the *Modo de andar la via sacra*, which was based on her writing, this hypothesis makes sense. De la Maza also cites part 2, book 6, chapter 20 of *La mística ciudad de dios* as a general source for the images of a bloodied, beaten Christ prevalent in colonial Mexican art.[165]

De la Maza goes on to explain the origin of some particularly unique elements of New Spanish images of the Virgin Mary and St. Joseph that derived from *La mística ciudad de dios*: "[Sor María] fue, quien inventó que, para la concepción del Niño, ante el anuncio del arcángel, tres gotas de sangre corrieron del corazón de la doncella escogida a su matriz y de ellas se formó el cuerpo del Verbo [y] que San José traía pendiente del cuello, en un relicario de oro, el prepucio del Niño cortado en la circuncisión" (Sor María was she who invented the idea that, for the conception of Christ, before the archangel's annunciation, three drops of blood ran from the chosen young woman's heart to her womb, and out of them were formed the body of the Word [and] that Saint Joseph wore around his neck, in a reliquary of gold, the foreskin of the Child Jesus that was removed during the circumcision).[166]

New Spanish artist Juan Correa's (1646–1716) paintings depict angels whose vestiture may have derived from explanations of angels' appearance explained in *La mística ciudad de dios*. Art historian Elisa Vargas Lugo suggests that Correa painted his angels' clothing drawing on Sor María's descriptions of them, and other sources, with the result that "influyeron definitivamente en la manera de vestir a los ángeles dentro del arte barroco español" (they definitively influenced how angels were dressed in Baroque Spanish art).[167] Although angels in Italian Renaissance painting were often nude, angels in colonial Mexican art were frequently completely dressed in elaborate garments, echoing the Spanish tendency to depict them as covered and richly adorned: "púdica[s] en las formas corpóreas y ostentosa[s] en las vestiduras" (modest in their corporal forms and ostentatiously dressed).[168] Several art historians posit that Correa's tendency to dress his angels richly and show their bodies with modesty may have derived from Sor María descriptions of angels' garments.[169] De la Maza cites Sor María's explanation of the angel Gabriel's clothing as an example of the aesthetic reproduced by Correa and others: "el vestido era rozagante, y como si fuera todo resplandor, semejante a un lucidísimo y brillante oro esmaltado o entrepuesto con matices de finísimos colores con que hacían una admirable y hermosísima variedad para la vista" (the dress was radiant, as if it were all alight, similar to a splendid and brilliant gold, enameled or interposed with contrasting color, with which he created an admirable and handsome variety for the eye).[170]

Yet if Sor María's writing influenced New Spanish painters' aesthetic sensibilities in their representation of Christ and angels, other works of colonial Mexican art manifest specific episodes and ideas unique to *La mística ciudad de dios*. These were worked into images destined for broad audiences, exposing nonreaders to some of the key ideas of *La mística ciudad de dios*. Many of these paintings treat events in the life of the Virgin Mary, but others focus on elements of Christ's life or on theological concepts as narrated by Sor María in *La mística ciudad de dios*.[171]

Correa's *La comunión de María*, an image the artist would paint several times, illustrates the emergence of Sor María's Mariology in New

Spanish art.[172] One version of this painting, currently at a diocesan sanctuary in Zacatecas, is considered one of Correa's best pieces, "una de las más sugestivas creaciones de Correa, en la que logró un tono de irrealidad" (one of Correa's most masterful works, in which he achieves a tone of irreality).[173] Against the dark background of the Last Supper, the Virgin Mary receives a host from the angel Gabriel, wings outspread, and the somber contrast between the light illuminating the Virgin and the darkness behind establishes the atmosphere for the piece. Vargas Lugo recounts Sor María's description of this event: "María adoró la Eucaristía en cuanto ésta fue instituida por Cristo y que una vez que tuvo lugar la Comunión entre los apóstoles, Jesús partió otro pedazo de pan consagrado y lo dio a san Gabriel, para que comulgase María que se encontraba en un aposento contiguo" (Mary adored the Eucharist as it was instituted by Christ, and once Communion had taken place among the apostles, Jesus broke another piece of the blessed bread, and gave it to Saint Gabriel, so that María could take communion in a nearby room).[174] The Virgin Mary's reception of Holy Communion during the Last Supper by the angel Gabriel was not a theme widely reproduced in colonial Mexican artwork, in part because the idea was not a dogmatic one.[175] However, Correa adheres closely to Sor María's description of it on canvass.

Correa likewise painted *San Pedro administrando la communion a Elías y Enoc*, an episode from *La mística ciudad de dios* in which the Old Testament figures receive the Eucharist. (In *La mística ciudad de dios*, this scene immediately follows the Virgin Mary's reception of Holy Communion.)[176] Correa's paintings of the *Tránsito de la Virgen*, in which Mary is depicted as she dies, looking at Christ, are other examples of detailed interpretation by him of scenes described in *La mística ciudad de dios*.[177]

Cristóbal de Villalpando (1649–1714), Correa's contemporary, reproduced Sor María's narration of a major event in the Virgin Mary's life in his 1706 painting *La anunciación*.[178] The painting depicts the encounter between Mary and the angel Gabriel as Sor María explains it in *La mística ciudad de dios*. In that description, Gabriel is accompanied in his visit by "millares de ángeles hermosísimos que le seguían en forma visible" (thousands of handsome angels who followed him [the angel Gabriel] in visible form).[179] In Villalpando's *La anunciación*, row after row of angels circle above Gabriel and Mary, echoing the sense of an angelic host expressed in Sor María's work, and lending what de la Maza called "una atmósfera celestial" (a celestial atmosphere) to the piece.[180] Villalpando's work is a departure from other New Spanish renderings of the Annunciation in which the Virgin Mary and Gabriel are depicted alone or accompanied by the Holy Spirit.

In a similar vein, José Rodríguez Carnero's (1649–1725) painting of *La adoración de los pastores* (1725) drew from Sor María's narration of the arrival of shepherds to view the infant Jesus and Mary, and to announce his birth.[181] In *La mística ciudad de dios*, angels, including the archangels Gabriel and Michael, inform several individuals of Christ's arrival: Mary's parents, St. Anne and St. Joachim; Mary's cousin Elizabeth and her husband, Zacharias; Jesus's cousin John the Evangelist; and Anna the prophet, among others. In the same chapter in *La mística ciudad de dios*, Gabriel greets shepherds near where Christ was born, and a host of angels gathers to witness the infant and his parents.[182] In the foreground of the Carnero painting, two angels share in the adoration of the Christ child. Against a dark background, elements of Sor María's description are presented. The archangel Michael visits saints Anna and Joachim, and an angel announces Christ's birth to resting shepherds. Elizabeth and Zacharias also figure into the composition, completing Carnero's interpretation of Sor María's rendition of the event.[183] Renowned Sor Juana portraitist Miguel de Cabrera (1695–1768) also painted an *Adoración de los pastores* that shares several Ágredan compositional elements with Carnero's work.[184]

Famed eighteenth-century Poblano *casta* painter José Joaquín Magón painted a significant episode from Mary's life as explained in *La mística ciudad de dios*: the baptism of Mary by Christ. Magón's *Bautismo de la virgen* depicts Mary's baptism, which God the Father and the Holy Spirit witness, as described in two complementary episodes in *La mística ciudad de dios*.[185] The initial description of the Virgin's baptism is brief: "Y como adelante diré también bautizó el Señor a su madre María Santíssima antes de esta promulgación en que declaró la forma del bautismo que había ordenado" (And as I will soon explain, the Lord baptized his Holy Mother before this promulgation in which he declared the type of baptism that had been ordered). Sor María explains Mary's baptism in detail, and her account includes the intervention of the three members of the Holy Trinity: "Pidióle también la Beatísima Señora a su Hijo que le diese el sacramento del bautismo . . . el mismo

Cristo bautizó a su Purísima Madre por la divina disposición y orde-
nación . . . Luego se oyó una voz del Eterno Padre . . . Otra voz del Espíritu Santo dijo: 'Esta es mi esposa, escogida entre millares'" (The Most
Holy Mother also asked her Son to give her the sacrament of baptism . . .
and the same Christ baptized his Most Pure Mother through divine disposition and ordination . . . later the voice of the Eternal Father was
heard . . . another voice, of the Holy Spirit, said: "This is my wife, chosen
from among thousands").[186] All three figures and the Virgin, who receives baptismal waters at her son's hand, are clearly visible in the image,
as are the "multitud de los coros angélicos en forma visible" (multitude
of angelic choruses in visible form) that aided Christ in blessing his
mother, according to Sor María's account.

The Virgin's baptism is part of a triptych of baptisms narrated in *La
mística ciudad de dios* that Magón painted. In addition to the Virgin's
baptism, Magón also portrayed Christ's baptism by St. John the Baptist
(a favorite and oft-painted episode in Renaissance art), and the far more
rare scene of Christ baptizing St. John in return. The baptism of St. John
by Christ is specific to Sor María's writing, and immediately precedes
the Virgin Mary's baptism in *La mística ciudad de dios*: "Cristo nuestro
Señor, después de haber sido bautizado, dio a su Precursor [San Juan
Bautista] el bautismo que le pidió" (Christ our Lord, after having been
baptized, gave to his precursor [St. John the Baptist] the baptism he
asked him for).[187] In Magón's painting, Christ is shown pouring baptismal water on his cousin's head, in the presence of God the Father and
the Holy Spirit, and of several angels and humans. Magón's paintings of
the baptism of the Virgin and Christ's baptism of St. John are both located in Tecamachalco, Puebla.[188]

Unique events from Christ's life, and ideas relating to the Holy
Trinity originating in *La mística ciudad de dios*, also emerged at the
hands of New Spanish painters. The source for Juan Patricio Morlete's
(1713–72) graphic rendering of a scourged Christ, found at the Pinaco-
teca Virreinal de San Diego de México, is derived from *La mística ciudad
de dios*'s detailed description of that moment of Christ's passion.[189] In
the painting as in the text, a brutally flayed Christ is aided by angels who
both support him and collect fragments of his flesh and blood from the
floor. A similar example is found in a series of paintings of Christ's passion that surrounded a fountain in the Bethelmite Convent in Mexico
City. The paintings were described in the *Gaceta de México* in December

1732 as "corpulentos lienzos" (large canvasses), painted by the "Célebre Ybarra" (probably José de Ibarra, 1685–1756). The brief description mentions the source material for the paintings: "historiada [la Pasión] según la V. Agreda" (as depicted [in the Passion] by the Venerable Ágreda).[190]

An eighteenth-century painting of the Last Supper, attributed to artist Luis Berreuco, depicts an Agredan idea of the Trinity in relationship to Christ's final meal with the apostles.[191] In Berreuco's piece, God the Father and the Holy Spirit are present, superior to Christ, who is situated in a Last Supper tableau. In seeking out the inspiration for this unusual scene (the other two persons of the Trinity are not typically included in representations of the Last Supper), art historian María del Consuelo Maquívar found a likely source in Sor María's description of the event in *La mística ciudad de dios*: "Estando juntos todos los que he dicho, esperando con admiración lo que hacía el Autor de la Vida, apareció en el Cenáculo la persona del eterno Padre y la del Espíritu Santo, como en el Jordán y el Tabor" (As all those I have mentioned were together, awaiting with admiration what the Author of Life was doing, the persons of the Eternal Father and of the Holy Spirit appeared in the cenacle, as at the Jordan and [Mount] Tabor).[192] Though these are but a few examples, other paintings commissioned by or intended for Sor María's New Spanish community of reading likewise drew on distinctive apocryphal episodes of Christ's life described in *La mística ciudad de dios*.

The artwork that accompanied *La mística ciudad de dios* also influenced New Spanish paintings of the Immaculate Conception. Though the images accompanying the volume varied from edition to edition, a Conceptionist theme is relatively consistent across the board. The image accompanying the 1696 Antwerp printing of *La mística ciudad de dios* is representative (see fig. 3.8). In it, the Virgin of the Immaculate Conception is in the upper left corner; Sor María is prominently featured, accompanied by St. John the Evangelist (and his symbol, the eagle), and Duns Scotus. Sor María holds a quill in one hand and a book in the other, indicating her role as an author of the Immaculate Conception theology alongside others associated with it: Duns Scotus, for his thirteenth-century advocacy of the theology, and St. John, whose book of Revelation provided the foundation for Conceptionist imagery. The walled city framing the Virgin is an allusion both to St. John's New Jerusalem and to Sor María's Mystical City of God, or it can be read as a conflation of the two ideas. It is likely that the Antwerp image and similar variations are based on the frontispiece to the 1670 Madrid edition of *La mística ciudad de dios*.[193] As chapter 4 will show, this motif was reproduced in architecture and in art, in the churches and missions of the Franciscan friars of Propaganda Fide. Through New Spanish artist Cristóbal de Villalpando, however, the image achieved its aesthetic apogee.

Villalpando's *La mística Jerusalén* (1706), created for the Propaganda Fide College of Guadalupe de Zacatecas, develops this theme in rich color and detail (see fig. 3.9).[194] In the painting, St. John's and Sor María's roles as authors of the Mystical City of God and the Immaculate Conception take center stage. St. John sits to the left and Sor María to the right, each with a quill in one hand and holding a book in the other. Behind them sits the New Jerusalem, and Mary of the Immaculate Conception is above all, with the moon and sun behind her. The Virgin is surrounded by the three persons of the Holy Trinity, an idea reflected in *La mística ciudad de dios*'s assertion that the Trinity was present at the moment of Mary's sinless conception to honor her.[195] The angels Gabriel and Michael round out the scene. In terms of its thematic composition, the stunning painting draws directly from Sor María's writing ("en plena sintonía con los escritos de sor María," "in full symphony with Sor María's writing"),[196] reproducing not only the imagery of the typical cover art for *La mística ciudad de dios* but also specific details of Sor María's text. Villalpando represents St. John and Sor María with parity: they are mirror images of one another in the painting, contributing equal visual weight and accorded equal importance in the image.[197]

Another unique representation of Sor María in relationship to the Immaculate Conception borrows several elements from the cover of *La mística ciudad de dios*—the Virgin, Duns Scotus, and Sor María—but adds the figure of St. Francis as the Atlas Seraphicus (see fig. 3.10). A frieze located above the entrance to the old cloister of a former Franciscan convent in Ozumba, Mexico, features these figures as it places the role of the Franciscan Order in defending the Immaculate Conception theology into high relief. St. Francis holds three blue spheres above his head, likely representing three branches of the Franciscan Order (Franciscan friars, Poor Clares, and tertiaries) and their support of the theology. The Virgin of the Immaculate Conception is located just above the topmost sphere.[198] Duns Scotus and Sor María flank St. Francis,

Figure 3.8. Cover of 1696 Antwerp printing of *La mística ciudad de dios*. Image courtesy Artstor. Physical repository: Rijksmuseum, Amsterdam.

Figure 3.9. La mística Jerusalén (1706), by Cristóbal de Villalpando.
Image courtesy Cristina Cruz González.

each with a book and quill in hand. Duns Scotus's text reads, "Potuit Decuit Voluit ergo (Fecit)," a reference to his view that the Immaculate Conception was possible and fitting, and that therefore that it was accomplished.[199] Sor María's book states, "Tota Pulcra [*sic*] est Maria," reiterating her claim of the Virgin Mary's purity from the moment of her conception.[200] A painting sharing this theme is located at the Propaganda Fide College of San Fernando in Mexico City, as we shall discuss in chapter 4.

The idea of Sor María as author and defender of the Immaculate Conception theology was developed in other works of New Spanish art, including the *Carro triunfal de la Inmaculada*, a 1777 painting by Poblano artist Juan Manuel Yáñez (Illanes).[201] The painting features Sor María helping to pull an ornate cart occupied by the Virgin of the Immaculate Conception. Sor María is dressed in Conceptionist blue, and is tucked in alongside St. Clare, the founder of the order of Poor Clares. Several other Franciscan promoters of the Immaculate Conception theology, including St. Francis, follow the nuns. Franciscan figures St. Bonaventure and Duns Scotus feature in the collective. The painting, located at the former Franciscan convent of San Martín de Texmelucan (Puebla), was likely commissioned to commemorate Clement XIII's appointment of the Virgin of the Immaculate Conception as Spain's patroness. The 1760

Figure 3.10. Duns Scotus, Saint Francis, and Sor María (*left to right*). Artist unknown. Ex-Convento Franciscano de la Inmaculada Concepción, Ozumba, Mexico. Image courtesy Cristina Cruz González.

papal declaration was made at the request of Carlos III, who leads the procession in the painting with Clement XIII.[202]

If Yáñez's *Carro triunfal de la Inmaculada* contextualized Sor María among the Franciscan Order's major defenders of the Immaculate Conception, this role is reprised in an undated Franciscan family tree located in Puebla.[203] The Virgin of the Immaculate Conception, with the Holy Trinity positioned above her, lies in the middle of a rough genealogy of the Franciscan Order and its devotees. Rows upon rows of Franciscan religious (priests, nuns, brothers, bishops) and faithful involved with the order surround the central image. Sor María is included among a cluster of Poor Clares located in the lower left portion of the painting.[204]

Other works of New Spanish art focused on Sor María alone, frequently representing her as a writer. An anonymous, undated portrait of Sor María located at the Museo Nacional del Virreinato in Tepozotlán shows her in her posture as the author of *La mística ciudad de dios* (see fig. 3.11).[205] Perhaps the most intriguing aspect of this simple portrait is the biography below it. Details of Sor María's life are selectively included in the brief text: her birth, the establishment of her convent, and her authorship of *La mística ciudad de dios*. The brief *vita* goes on to cite Sor María's authorship of "otros cuadernos místicos para utilidad común de las Religiosas y personas espirituales" (other mystical tomes of common use for religious sisters and spiritual individuals), suggesting that the painting may have originally been intended for or hung in a religious community of women.[206] The text concludes with an acknowledgment of the status of her ongoing case for canonization: "se entiende en la Causa de Beatificación" (she is understood to be in the beatification process),[207] ensuring that viewers of the painting would read it in the context of the nun's canonization process in Rome.

A similar image located in Saltillo, Coahuila, also depicts a figure that appears to be Sor María as a Conceptionist author.[208] The likeness is a portion of what was a larger painting, made by an anonymous artist in the second half of the eighteenth century. In it, a seated woman dressed in a blue habit writes and looks upward into the distance. Art critic Rogelio Ruíz Gomar concludes from this that Sor María is the probable subject of the painting fragment.[209] Perhaps, as in similar art that depicts Sor María writing *La mística ciudad de dios*, the nun in the Saltillo painting originally looked to the Virgin of the Immaculate Conception, and that more popular image was cut away.

Figure 3.11. Sor María de Jesús de Ágreda, author of *La mística ciudad de Dios*. Artist unknown. Museo del Virreinato, Tepozotlán. Image courtesy Cristina Cruz González.

Mexico City artist José de Páez (1727–90) depicted Sor María as an evangelizing protomissionary in *El don de la ubicuidad de la Venerable Sor María de Jesús de Ágreda* (ca.1770) (see fig. 3.12). The painting shows the nun in a blue habit, her veil and cape trailing backwards behind her as if pushed back by her sudden movement toward a group of unidentified native people. In contrast to the frontispieces to the *Tanto que se sacó de una carta*, which the painting echoes thematically, Sor María is positioned less superior to her indigenous audience. The brightness with which the tribal members are rendered in the painting (particularly a young woman with a small child, evoking the *Tanto que se sacó de una carta* image; see fig. 3.3) lends them visual weight. One of the nun's hands brandishes a cross towards the neophytes, and the other points in the direction of the cross and the tribal members, leaving no doubt as to the Lady in Blue's purpose. Páez's painting captures the side of Sor María that would become her lasting legacy in the northern New Spanish borderlands and elsewhere.

Our last instance of Sor María in New Spanish artwork concisely illustrates the ideational intersection of protomissionary and writer that existed in colonial Mexico. An anonymous, undated portrait of Sor María, located at the Museo Nacional del Virreinato in Tepozotlán, depicts her simply as an author, standing to the side of a high table, or *bufete*, covered in red velvet (see fig. 3.13).[210] She wears a blue Conceptionist cape and holds a quill in her hand, positioned to write in the book before her. Her face—youthful, serene, and poised—is directed towards the viewer. The representation is clearly one of her authorship of *La mística ciudad de dios* and is characteristic of that iconography, yet the inscription above her head reveals another identity to Mexican audiences.

The text reads: "La V.M. María de Jesus, De Edad 20 Años Y De Esta Predico A Los Yndios De El Nuevo Mexico" (The Venerable Mother María de Jesús, at Twenty Years of Age and Who Preached to the Indians of New Mexico). This brief summary explains that, although the author of *La mística ciudad de dios* portrayed in the painting is not surrounded by "Chichimecos," it is in fact she who traveled to and

Figure 3.12. El don de la ubicuidad de la Venerable Sor María de Jesús de Ágreda (ca. 1770), by José de Páez. Image courtesy of the Museo Soumaya.

Figure 3.13. Sor María depicted as writer and missionary. Artist unknown. Museo del Virreinato, Tepozotlán. Image courtesy Cristina Cruz González.

converted the tribes of New Mexico. The viewer understands that writer and missionary are one and the same. Although the work may have been destined for a limited viewership (at least one art historian concludes that the painting was originally intended for one of the Franciscan Propaganda Fide colleges),[211] the portrait's multiple meanings would not have been lost on other New Spanish audiences. As we shall see in chapter 4, Propaganda Fide friars shared the idea posed in this painting with the communities near their colleges, and carried it into the northern New Spanish mission field.

Private Piety, Public Bequests: New Spanish *Donativos* for Sor María's *Causa*

As the works of art examined above attest, New Spanish interest in Sor María was manifested in a variety of ways that reflected the breadth of her community of reading. Mexican devotion to the nun was also revealed through private donations, including works of art and other valuables, that were contributed by New Spanish citizens to her *causa* and her convent in Ágreda. In contrast to the funds generated and processed through official channels that we examined earlier in this chapter, these contributions came from individuals or families and were often sent directly to Sor María's religious community. Through these pious gifts, devotion to Sor María in New Spain assumed a more personal form.

One significant source of such donations consisted of money willed to the *causa* through New Spanish estates. Mexican citizens with the means or need to commission a last will and testament specified the payment of *mandas forzosas* (compulsory donations). The *mandas* were essential to New Spanish estate allocation, referred to in most wills as the "mandas forzosas y acostumbradas" (compulsory and customary donations). The funds generated from the mandas directed small contributions from estates to religious (and later, civic) causes. The mandas' beneficiaries were generally determined by local custom, and could be influenced by the intervention of nearby religious orders or organizations. In some urban centers in colonial Mexico, the diocese where one lived or registered one's will determined the mandas, and the disbursement of the donation from the estate was managed by religious officials. As is evident in three wills drawn up in Mexico City, Sor María's case for canonization was often included along with more typical mandas speci-fied by local dictates.

The earliest will, dated October 13, 1722, is that of the painter Juan Correa. It includes the directive that two silver *tomínes* were to be given toward each *manda*, which are left unspecified, but would presumably have been familiar to the executor. It goes on to order that an additional tomín be donated on behalf of Sor María's *causa*, and that similar small donations be disbursed to other *causas* for New Spanish candidates to sainthood.[212] The will of Mexico City painter Antonio de Torres like-wise dedicated two tomínes apiece for each of the mandas, and allocated another two for the canonization of the "venerable madre María de Jesús de Ágreda."[213] The October 1740 will of Mexico City architect José Miguel Rivera Saravia bequests a peso to each manda and earmarks an additional gold peso on behalf of Sor María's canonization.[214] Although by no means an exhaustive list of all wills that specified donations to Sor María's case for canonization, these three point to an intriguing trend in early eighteenth-century New Spanish devotional practice that merits closer inspection.

In each case, the donations to Sor María are juxtaposed with be-quests to Mexican religious figures, including Felipe de Jesús (sixteenth-century Mexican martyr in Japan), Gregorio López (sixteenth-century New Spanish hermit), sixteenth-century Mexican Franciscan lay brother Sebastián de Aparicio, and seventeenth-century bishop of Puebla, Juan de Palafox y Mendoza. Sor María's inclusion among these exclusively Mexican candidates suggests a conceptual linkage between Sor María (the protomissionary to New Spain's northern frontiers) and the exem-plary Mexicans whose cases for canonization were being presented in Rome at the same time as Sor María's. Though this linkage may simply have been Franciscan interest in these figures, it may also be that she was indeed perceived "como si fuera natural de México" (as if she were from Mexico).

Individual New Spanish citizens also contributed nonfinancial do-nations on behalf of Sor María.[215] Many of these bequests—such as a box made of *caray* (tortise shell) and silver designed to store copies of *La mística ciudad de dios*,[216] and a painting of the Virgin of Guadalupe by Mexican painter José de Juarez[217]—consisted of precious goods rather than money, yet all exemplify the devotional posture towards Sor María prevalent in colonial Mexico.[218] Among the most prominent early patrons of Sor María's convent were the Dukes of Alburquerque, who reigned as viceroys of New Spain from 1653 to 1660. Their generosity to Sor María's convent intensified through their tenure in Mexico and was encouraged by a member of their entourage, Francisca Ruiz de Valdivieso, a native of Ágreda who became a nun in Sor María's convent after returning to Spain.[219] Over the course of many years, the Dukes of Alburquerque contributed money, gilded church objects, and elaborate pieces of religious artwork to the convent in Ágreda.[220]

Puebla de los Ángeles, where many imprints of Sor María's writing were published, was an important site of pious interest in Sor María. Lorenzo de Ávila, a son of Spanish immigrants to Puebla, and his family donated art and money to the convent in Ágreda, some of these intended to support Sor María's beatification and others for the benefit of the religious community.[221] De Ávila, administrator of the Franciscan tertiaries in Puebla and an avid reader of *La mística ciudad de dios*,[222] personally contributed a great deal to the convent, including 50 doblones (in 1694), 200 dobloncillos de a cuarto (in 1702), an elaborate silver altar hanging and six candlesticks (also in 1702), and 500 pesos, sent posthumously in 1709 on behalf of the "obra pía" (pious work) he founded.[223] His nephew Pedro de Echeverría y Orcolaga, executor of his will, corresponded with the nuns in Ágreda after de Ávila's death, principally about the advancement of Sor María's *causa*.[224] The remaining de Ávila family living in Puebla continued to send money and precious goods to her convent through 1753.[225]

Many New Spanish private donations were intended either for the convent itself or for the veneration of an important icon located there, *La Virgen del Coro*.[226] An eighteenth-century bishop of Yucatán, Ignacio de Castoreña y Ursúa, a Zacatecas native, made regular financial contributions to the convent over two decades, including 100 pesos intended for chocolate for the nuns.[227] He also sent a portrait of the Virgin of Guadalupe, one of several the convent received from what were presumably New Spanish donors. His unusual posthumous arrangements for his body, published in the *Gaceta de México* in August 1733 and discussed earlier in this chapter, likewise exemplified his pious interest in Sor María and her convent.[228] Poblano Juan Miguel de Arnaz conveyed artwork and money to the convent between 1765 and 1774 on behalf of *La Virgen del Coro*.[229] An anonymous "sacerdote de Indias" (priest of the Indies) dispatched 3,000 reales between 1771 and 1773 for a painting of Sor María to be made there on the occasion of her future canonization: "cuando Dios sea servido que se canonice" (whenever God may be served by her canonization).[230] These monies and precious objects reflect the Mexican devotional culture that developed out of Sor María's writing in the seventeenth through nineteenth centuries.

Women Reading a Woman Writing a Woman: Sor María and New Spanish Women Religious

For her women readers in New Spain, Sor María's writing assumed a unique significance, one that sets that group apart from her broader communities of reading and devotion in Mexico.[231] *La mística ciudad de dios* was a core text in many New Spanish religious communities for women, promoted by confessors, spiritual directors, and religious authorities.[232] In addition to the influence *La mística ciudad de dios* exerted within that context, Sor María's rules and guidelines for convent life, drawn from her own experience as abbess in Ágreda, were implemented in whole and in part in many New Spanish religious communities.

The nuns, beatas, tertiaries, and others who read or were taught Sor María's writing understood her as a model nun, Conceptionist author, and protomissionary. Some, like Sor Juana Inés de la Cruz, gravitated to the bold elements of Sor María's writing, namely, its focus on the Virgin Mary as a protagonist in Christ's life and in the cultural history of the Catholic Church. Many comprehended the legitimacy *La mística ciudad de dios* had achieved within New Spanish religious and secular circles, and leveraged it to their advantage when confronted with scrutiny by authorities. And two women religious identified closely enough with the Lady in Blue narrative to place themselves in Sor Maria's figurative mystical missionary habit.

Sor María's ascendancy among these women readers was in part due to the ubiquity of her writing in their communities, but it may also be attributed to the application of her guidelines for convent governance within their walls. Many institutions implemented the suggestions in *La religiosa instruída*, a guide for conventual administration and the spiritual direction of nuns by Fray Antonio Arbiol. Published by Sor María's Imprenta in 1753, *La religiosa instruída* included several of Sor María's rules dictating prayer and religious life, and it presented Sor María as a model nun and abbess. The work was commonly found in convents in Spain and was almost certainly (given the prevalence of both Sor María's and Arbiol's writing in New Spain) applied in New Spanish female enclosures.

Entitled "Propósitos de perfección de la Venerable Madre María de Jesús de Agreda, divididos en siete clases" (Aims to Perfection by the Venerable Mother María de Jesús de Ágreda, divided into seven types), book 3, chapter 21 of *La religiosa instruída* derives in its entirety from Sor María's devotional practices. Fray Arbiol notes that the practices described in the chapter were those used in the convent in Ágreda: "con estas siete clases de santos propósitos, hacían entretenimiento virtuoso, y juego espiritual en el felicisimo Convento de nuestra Venerable Madre María de Jesús de Agreda . . . puede ser ejemplo utilísimo para otras comunidades" (With these seven types of holy intentions, the nuns entertained themselves in virtue and spiritual play in the happy convent of our Venerable Mother María de Jesús de Ágreda . . . it may be a useful example for other communities).[233] Chapter 22 consists of thirty-three *avisos* (one for each year of Christ's life) for the betterment of the nuns' individual spiritual states. All the avisos were to be read daily, and their advice ranged from spiritual injunctions—"3. Ponderar lo mucho que me importa el ser buena, y el dar gusto á Dios, y lo que merece su Divina Magestad" (3. Ponder how important it is to me to be good, and give pleasure to God and what his Divine Majesty deserves)[234]—to more unusual directives—"No mirar al rostro á ninguna criatura, sino al pecho, que es adonde habita el Señor" (Do not look at the face of any living creature, but rather at the chest, which is where the Lord resides).[235] Chapter 23 communicates Sor María's recommendations for living a holy life ("sentencias . . . para governar perfecta y prudentemente las acciones de la vida," "maxims . . . to perfectly and prudently govern daily life"),[236] included among them the pious observation that "el buen ánimo es reverenciador de Dios; y el dilatado Corazon emprende grandes cosas" (the good soul is reverential toward God; and the vast heart undertakes great things);[237] and more earthy observations: "Peores son las enemistades encubiertas, que las manifiestas, y menos daño al enemigo hablador, que el callado" (Hidden enmity is worse than overt, and less harm a chatty enemy than a quiet one), and "Nunca te entristezcas por el bien ageno: porque no te conviene sacar mal del bien" (Never become sad because of happiness that is not yours; because it does not behoove you to derive bad from good).[238] These chapters are followed by two on St. Teresa's spiritual insights and advice for conventual life, once again juxtaposing Sor María favorably with the great sixteenth-century mystic.

Invocations of Sor María's personal piety are woven throughout *La religiosa instruída*. Her pious practices are presented as ideal examples for other nuns to emulate, as in the description of how she carried out her penance after confession, kneeling on bare knees on the ground while saying specific penitential prayers: "La Insigne, y V.M. María de Jesús de Agreda siempre cumplía la penitencia con las rodillas desnudas sobre la tierra, y decía, que aquellas son oraciones distintas de todas las demás" (The Distinguished and Venerable Madre María de Jesús de Ágreda always completed her penance with her bare knees on the ground, and would say that these prayers are different from all others).[239] In other instances, the details of her actions as an abbess are recounted.[240] Among the numerous allusions to Sor María's spiritual principles and behaviors, Fray Arbiol regularly weaves in references to *La mística ciudad de dios*, primarily when describing rituals that Sor María attributed to the Virgin Mary.[241]

The conventual administration described in *La religiosa instruida* was emulated by certain New Spanish abbesses. In 1790, Pobalana María Josefa Pantaleón requested a copy of the Constitutions of the Order for Sor María's convent in Ágreda, which Sor María had composed, so that Pantaleón could establish a similar religious community in Puebla.[242]

Although *La religiosa instruída* exerted some influence among women religious, *La mística ciudad de dios* was far more influential, especially among women scholars and writers, such as Sor Juana Inés de la Cruz. In Sor Juana's celebrated letter defending women's right to intellectual engagement, the *Carta de respuesta a Sor Filotea de la Cruz* (1691), the learned nun depicts Sor María as a fellow female scholar and writer. In the letter, a response to the bishop of Puebla, Manuel Fernández de Santa Cruz (Sor Filotea de la Cruz), Sor Juana invokes a number of female intellectuals, "[citing] an extensive list of illustrious women of the past in order to justify [her] own literary activity," according to literary critic Nina Scott.[243] Sor Juana selected women writers and scholars from the classical era to the seventeenth century in order to create a learned genealogy, "a sisterhood among women across the centuries."[244] Sor Juana positions "la monja de Ágreda"[245] amid the female religious writers—including St. Gertrude the Great, St. Teresa de Jesús, and St. Brigid of Sweden—who were examples for educated women who followed them, including Sor Juana herself.

Sor Juana takes the legitimization of Sor María as a woman intellectual a step further. Sor Juana observes that, from her perspective as a New Spanish reader, Sor María's writing and that of María de la Antigua were permitted by the Church, though neither woman was canonized: "ahora vemos que la Iglesia permite escribir a las mujeres santas y a las no santas, pues la [monja] de Ágreda y María de la Antigua no están canonizadas y corren sus escritos" (now we see that the Church allows women who are saints and also those who are not saints to write, for the [nun] from Ágreda and María de la Antigua are not canonized, and yet their writing is everywhere).[246] Sor Juana continues: "ni cuando Santa Teresa y las demás escribieron, lo estaban [canonizadas]" (neither Santa Teresa nor the others were canonized when they wrote), suggesting that women's writing was valuable even before they were formally acknowledged by the Church as holy individuals.[247] Sor Juana's aside further implies that St. Teresa was declared a saint in part *because* of her writing; prohibiting or discouraging writing by noncanonized women therefore made little sense.[248]

Sor Juana's inclusion of Sor María in the *Carta de respuesta a Sor Filotea* is important for several reasons. First, Sor María's works benefit from the contextualization among these women, in particularly St. Teresa's canonical works; Sor María's writing is framed as of comparable merit from Sor Juana's perspective. Second, in Sor Juana's offhanded assertion that Sor María's writing commonly circulated in Mexico ("corren sus escritos") twenty-six years after Sor María's death, there is casual confirmation that *La mística ciudad de dios* and perhaps others of Sor María's works were common in colonial Mexico. Yet for Sor Juana, Sor María was more than one of several predecessors to her own scholarly career. Sor Juana read Sor María's works and incorporated some of the ideas in them into her own theological works, including the *Ejercicios devotos*.[249]

Scott notes that Sor Juana alluded to *La mística ciudad de dios* in "some devotional exercises she composed in honor of the Virgin,"[250] and it seems that Sor María's influence over Sor Juana was significant in this sense. Sor Juana's *Ejercicios devotos* promotes the Immaculate Conception theology, sharing with *La mística ciudad de dios* that central idea, and Sor Juana's text explores the relationship of that idea to the incarnation of Christ.[251] It shares with Sor María's text a valorization of the Virgin Mary's wisdom, and centers on the idea of an *imitatio Mariae* (instead of the more typical *imitatio Christi*), a prayerful emulation of the Virgin Mary's faith and behaviors.[252] Sor Juana cites *La mística ciudad de dios* in the "Introducción al intento" to the *Ejercicios devotos*, emphasizing Sor María's important role in recording the many favors given to the Virgin Mary by her Son: "la Venerable Madre María de Jesús cuenta los inefables favores que Su Majestad Divina hizo a su escogida y carísima madre" (the Venerable Mother María de Jesús tells of the ineffable favors that His Divine Majesty granted his chosen and dear mother).[253] Literary critic Grady Wray asserts that "the *Mystical* informs the *Exercises*" and that Sor Juana was "intimately versed in her Spanish foremother's work."[254] He argues that Sor Juana delves into and reworks themes Sor María presents in *La mística ciudad de dios*: "Sor Juana deliberately reframes Ágreda's topics to fulfill her own agenda, namely the proclamation of Mary's wisdom,"[255] emphasizing the emulation of Mary's humility before Christ as a means of achieving the wisdom embodied by Mary herself.[256]

In the *Ejercicios devotos*, Sor Juana builds on theological and practical elements that derive from Sor María's work. In *La mística ciudad de dios*, the Virgin Mary asks that Sor María follow the example of Mary's and Christ's humility, sorrow, and wisdom, even as the Virgin imparts her wisdom to Sor María directly. In Wray's reading of the *Ejercicios devotos*, Sor Juana takes this concept a step further, proposing that seeking knowledge and wisdom is a means of imitating the virtue of Mary: "The pursuit of wisdom, one of Mary's most outstanding attributes, as well as her humility, becomes a legitimate goal for imitation by Sor Juana and her exercitants."[257] Focusing on uniquely feminine spiritual agency was in keeping with Sor Juana's other writing, including the *Carta de respuesta a Sor Filotea*, and with Sor María's representation of the Virgin Mary. Yet the extrapolation from Sor María's writing is a fascinating insight into how Sor Juana—and her conventual contemporaries in Mexico—might have interpreted and expanded on the groundbreaking representation of the Virgin Mary in *La mística ciudad de dios*.[258]

If Sor María's conventual rule and spiritual practices conditioned New Spanish women religious institutionally, Sor Juana's example indicates that religious women also read and understood *La mística ciudad de dios.* They demonstrated their familiarity with it in their writing and by referencing Sor María as a well-known authority. During the height of the New Spanish campaign for Sor María's canonization in the first half of the eighteenth century, Dominican nun Sor María Anna Águeda de San Ignacio (1695–1756) showed that appreciation for Sor María's writing flourished even within a religious order opposed at the time to the Immaculate Conception theology. A native of Puebla, Sor María Anna was a prolific writer, and several of her works were printed and circulated during her lifetime.[259] Her writing shared with Sor María's a focus on the Virgin Mary, as "she [Sor María Anna] presents the Blessed Virgin Mary as the central figure of mediation through whom salvation is achieved."[260] Sor María Anna drew on Sor María and St. Ignatius of Loyola for the structure of some of her works,[261] and she created a sense of legitimacy for herself as a female spiritual author by alluding to Sor María as a literary predecessor, just as Sor Juana did.[262] Given Sor María Anna's writing on Marian topics, including her *Devoción en honra de la Purissima Leche con que fue alimentado el Niño Jesús*,[263] and Mary's centrality to her theological discussions, Sor María Anna may have drawn from Sor María's ideas in other ways.[264] Indeed, in Sor María Anna's *vita*, her biographer Fr. Joseph Bellido favorably compares Sor María Anna with Sor María.[265]

Other Mexican religious women did not so much borrow from Sor María's spiritual writing for its ideas as they did capitalize on the legitimacy it had achieved in colonial Mexico. In so doing, they implicitly confirmed their own familiarity with it and its recognition by the individuals they appealed to. As evidenced through Inquisition records, Mexican beatas (unprofessed religious women) Josefa Palacios and María Rita Vargas demonstrated both their knowledge of *La mística ciudad de dios* and their awareness of the credence Church officials gave to it.[266] Josefa Palacios was a beata from Pachuca who was accused of being an *ilusa*, or "false mystic," by the Inquisition in 1788. Not only was Palacios familiar with Sor María's *doctrina* ("religious practices and writing"), so was her confessor Fray Eusebio Villarejo, and both used this knowledge in her defense.[267]

During the course of Josefa Palacios's trial, Fray Villarejo, a missionary from the Propaganda Fide college in Pachuca, was accused of being unduly influenced by Palacios's visions. Although she had discussed the topic of demons at length with her confessor, Fray Villarejo had concluded that she was not possessed: "no estaba energumena" (she is not possessed by the devil).[268] In the Inquisitorial testimony, Fray Villarejo accepted the beata's claims that demons entered churches in the form of men and women by ascribing this idea to Sor María's writing on such matters: "del todo no dudaba [Fray Villarejo], porque teniendo presente por doctrina la Venerable Madre Agreda, segun le parece que los demonios entran en el Templo, por lo que padecen atentar a las almas con permiso del Señor, fundando en esto, y en otros casos, algo se inclinó a creerlo" ([Fray Villarejo] did not doubt all of it, for he knew from the Venerable Mother Ágreda's doctrine that it seemed that demons could enter the Temple with the permission of the Lord in order for a soul to attempt to suffer, and, based on this and on other cases, he was inclined to believe it).[269] Fray Villarejo's knowledge of Sor María's *doctrina* predisposed him to take his confessant's claims seriously and defend her before Inquisitorial authorities on that basis.[270]

During Josefa Palacios's trial, another witness, Fray Antonio de Torrijos, recalled an occasion when Palacios's identification with Sor María was revealed and was interpreted as a sign of her demonic possession. On questioning Palacios about a particular devotional practice that he had understood she learned from a younger "sister," Fray Torrijos asked her about it.[271] Palacios responded: "dixo al Padre mire vuestra merced lo que este demonio me dice, que essa hermanita es Sor María de Jesús de Agreda, . . . y como de ella la [devoción] aprendió, y fue de su orden, por eso la trataba como hermana, y decía que ella le enseño aquella devoción" (she said to the priest, look Your Honor, what this demon tells me, that this little sister is Sor María de Jesús de Ágreda, . . . and how from her [Sor María], she learned [the devotion], and she was from her order, so for this reason she treated her as a sister, and she said that she taught her that devotion).[272] The testimony continued, stating that this conclusion was drawn based on her familiarity with Sor María's writing, which she had read: "lo que le hizo insistir en su idea, como que intelectualmente determinó aquella especie a la venerable Madre Agreda, en cuyas obras havia leído la Doctrina de que se trataba hablando de aquella devoción" (what made her insist on this idea was that she had intellectually determined that the visitor was the Venerable Mother Ágreda, in whose doctrine she had read about that devotional practice).[273] From Palacios's affirmation that she learned the devotional practice from a younger sister, who may have been Sor María, Fray Torrijos concluded that she was, in fact, possessed: "[mantuvo] el firme concepto de ser verdadera Energumena su confesada la Palacios" (he was firm in his conviction that his confessee Palacios was in fact possessed by the devil).[274]

In spite of her testimony citing Sor María's writing as an explanation for her beliefs and behaviors (and similar assertions by Fray Villarejo), Josefa Palacios was eventually found guilty of false mysticism and sentenced to ten years of exile[275] for her ecstasies and claims of mystical encounter.[276] There were numerous ways the Inquisition and Church authorities induced women to reframe their agency in terms of mystical practices and writing, while at the same time excluding them from any possibility of claiming power or voice, and Josefa Palacios's case is an example of this. Yet between the lines of her Inquisition testimony, one finds that in the late eighteenth century, Pachuca was still a site of reading of Sor María's work, and that women religious who read her understood the sway her writing could exert over male superiors.

Beata María Lucía Celis, brought before the Inquisition in 1802 for charges of false mysticism, used Sor María's writing in a similar manner in her testimony. Celis defended herself by claiming that the works that informed her visions were doctrinal: she was reading Church-sanctioned materials, including Sor María's writing, and these formed the basis for the mystical experiences she related to her confessor, Padre Antonio Rodríguez Colodrero. Celis describes some of the unusual visions she would relate to him, "estas representaciones del esposo en figura de niño, de acostarse con él, darle de mamar y las demás cosas" (these representations of the [divine] husband in the shape of a child, of lying down with him, and nursing him, and other things).[277] Yet in the course of explaining her visions' origins, Celis is careful to cite a known source for the ideas that influenced her: "y como ella no tenía otras ideas que las que leía, que eran la venerable madre Agreda, las materializaba y lo mismo le contaba [al Padre Colodrero]" (since she had no ideas other than those in what she read, which was the Venerable Mother Ágreda, she produced them and told them [to Father Colodrero]).[278] Under the extreme pressure of Inquisitorial examination, Celis was encouraged to reconsider what she saw and eventually declared the unsuitability of her visions: "Pero ahora mejor instruida por el señor inquisidor conoce y confiesa que los malos efectos que sentía en su naturaleza con estas representaciones (But now, better instructed by the lord Inquisitor, she realizes and confesses the ill effects that she felt in her being with these representations).[279] It is telling, however, that for nineteenth-century beata María Lucía Celis, citing Sor María's writing was a means of explanation during the course of her difficult trial.

Another beata, María Rita Vargas, shared Colodrero as a confessor at the convent of San Lorenzo in Mexico. A local nun brought Colodrero and his two confessants before the Inquisition on the basis of accusations made against Colodrero. Colodrero shaped the religious formation of both beatas, and Vargas's diary reflects this, and historian Eldemira Ramírez notes that their relationship can be read as forced, based on their dependency on their confessor priest: "un acto forzado . . . La Vargas y la Celis no escriben para reflexionar o conocerse a sí mismas . . . Lo hacían para mantener una relación de dependencia espiritual y material con su confesor [Padre Colodrero]" (a forced act . . . Vargas and Celis do not write to reflect or to get to know themselves. . . . They did it to maintain a relationship of spiritual and material dependency with their confessor [Father Colodrero]."[280] His influence over what the two women read is revealed in Vargas's diary, which shows that they were encouraged by the priest to read Sor María's writing: "Vio [Vargas] una niña hermosísima que ponía el pie en la principal cabeza de las siete que tenía aquella horrible serpiente, y que ésta se sepultó por una boca que se abrió en la tierra; y que dijo la serpiente con voz muy espantosa, ya nos viene a echar de aquí esta niña. Que le llevó el padre las obras de la venerable Agreda" ([Vargas] saw a beautiful girl who put her foot on the first of seven heads of that horrible snake, and then it was swallowed by an opening in the earth; and then the snake said in a frightening voice that this girl has come to throw us out of here. That the priest brought her the works of the Venerable Ágreda).[281] According to Vargas's diary, a male superior intentionally introduced her to Sor María's writing—Celis, Vargas, and Colodrero were all well aware of what Sor María wrote. For these two late eighteenth-century beatas, familiarity with Sor María's writing was encouraged by their male superior and was seen as a legitimate source of religious visions by Inquisitorial authorities.

For two New Spanish religious women, Sor María's allure as a writer was enmeshed with her appeal as a female missionary to native tribes. Both Querétaran mystic Francisca de los Ángeles (1674–1744) and the indigenous abbess of the Convent of Corpus Christi in Mexico City, Sor Felipa de Jesús, framed themselves in the mold of Sor María's missionary actions as the Lady in Blue. Francisca's experiences were by far the more involved of the two. She claimed to have spiritually traveled to Texas on many occasions to complete the conversion work that Sor María had begun there. Under the spiritual direction of Fray Antonio Margil de Jesús, a founder of the College Santa Cruz de Querétaro, Sor Francisca's fascinating case is closely linked to the Franciscan Propaganda Fide colleges, missions, and staff, and therefore we will examine them in chapter 4.

The second case is that of Sor María Felipa de Jesús, an early eighteenth-century indigenous Mexican nun who headed a religious community in Mexico City. Her convent was founded exclusively for indigenous aristocracy (*cacicas*) in order to provide them a spiritual space with minimal Spanish and criollo involvement. The invocation in Sor María Felipa's *vita* of Sor María undoubtedly reflects the reading of Sor María's writing among colonial women religious, but it also calls upon the Lady in Blue narrative, and in such a way that reveals the colonizing effects it exerted as a concept in New Spain, including among women religious.

The lives of several of the nuns at the Convent of Corpus Christi are recorded in a manuscript published in 1963 by Josefina Muriel, *Las indias caciques de Corpus Christi*, and Mónica Díaz's more recent (2010) study offers a contextualized historical analysis of the convent and its writing.[282] The Corpus Christi convent was continually subjected to scrutiny and regulation by Church authorities, a rigorous critique predicated on the nuns' indigenous identity. *Las indias caciques* offers proof of the community's conformity to Catholic doctrine and ability to self-govern, a tacit argument for the retention of their community. Recounting the lives of eight of the convent's nuns, including Sor María Felipa, served a tactical end: it was "a means of defending the noble indigenous women as capable not only of living in the community but also leading an exemplary and, in some cases, even saintly life."[283]

Among the *vitae* in *Las indias caciques*, Sor María Felipa's stands out, "so formally presented that it gives the impression of having been prepared for publication, perhaps even as a work separate from the others."[284] Sor María Felipa's *vita* presented the prominent abbess as the consummate example of the indigenous nun-convert. It illustrated the rigor and constancy of her Catholic faith, carefully distinguishing between pre-Columbian principles and unconverted indigenous peoples and the nun's own beliefs and practices. Her biographer takes care to elaborate the "happiness that had come to her [Sor María Felipa] as a result of the [Catholic] conquest of those lands [Mexico]."[285] This message of absolute adherence to Catholic conversion transmitted through Sor María Felipa's *vita* is also articulated through the incorporation of the Lady in Blue narrative.

In a section entitled "De su grande amor al próximo y cello de la salvación de las almas" (Regarding her great love for neighbor and zeal for the salvation of souls),[286] Sor María Felipa is depicted praying for the conversion of Mexican gentiles and heretics:

> Entre éstos tenían muy especial lugar los mecos [Chichimecos], ya porque decía que la conversión de éstos era más fácil considerándolos como los [consideraba], con menos impedimentos para recibir la luz de la fe y de aquí venía aquel regocijo de que se llenaba, tanto que salía a lo exterior, cuando oía hablar con esperanzas de que se propagase entre ellos el cristianismo. Desde que leyó en las cartas de la madre Agreda a los pueblos de Indios mecos que están por el Nuevo México y que no se han descubierto, se le excitó en su corazón un vivísimo deseo, de que se internaran los operarios evangélicos en aquellas partes, para que aquellos miserables recibiesen la luz del evangelio, y como en las mismas cartas expresa la misma venerable madre las buenas disposiciones que tienen aquellos infelices para ser reducidos, fue su deseo acompañado de una congojosa y santa impaciencia que le afligía mucho y la misma que la espoleaba poderosamente a pedir a Dios, con instante oración, para que su misericordia no tardase más en enviarles el remedio.

––––––

> Among these, the mecos [Chichimecos] held a special place, for it was said that their conversion was the easiest, considering them, as they were thought of, with fewer impediments to receiving the light of faith. And from here emerged the joy that filled her, so much so that it emerged exteriorly, whenever she heard hopeful talk about the propagation of Christianity among them. Ever since she had read in the letters from Mother Ágreda about the meco Indian pueblos that are in New Mexico and which have not yet been discovered, a lively hope awoke in her heart, that evangelical laborers

would be committed to those parts, so that those miserable souls would receive the light of the gospel, and as how in those same letters the same venerable mother expresses the good disposition those unhappy souls to be converted, it was her desire, accompanied by a painful and holy impatience that greatly afflicted her, which powerfully spurred her to ask God, with insistent prayer, that His mercy not tarry in sending them the remedy.[287]

Because it refers to an indigenous group called "mecos," Sor María Felipa's biographer (and/or the nun herself) almost certainly had read or seen the *Tanto que se sacó de una carta*, in which the tribes in New Mexico are described as such. According to Sor María Felipa's *vita*, the indigenous nun sees Sor María as a model evangelizer of native peoples. The Sor María Felipa of the *vita* accepted what Sor María was alleged to have said about the ability and disposition of the "mecos" to convert, and she urgently prayed that the tribe receive Christian instruction, which she frames as a cure to their spiritual ills. Her biographer uses Sor María's conversion of the "mecos" to depict the indigenous reader Sor María Felipa projecting the colonizing message of the Lady in Blue narrative onto other native groups.

It is as important to read Sor María Felipa's *vita* with an understanding of the purpose for which it was written—to illustrate the earnestness of her Catholic convictions for critics who doubted it based on her indigenous origins—as it is to recall that as the leader of her religious community, the qualities she embodied reflected back onto the convent's members and their perception by others. Sor María Felipa's desire for the conversion of the "mecos" as presented in the *vita* must be read as entangled with the convent's project of self-preservation and self-determination, and with the question of who the *vita*'s author was. In this context, the invocation of Sor María as the model for actions of conversion illustrates how the narrative was put into practice conceptually.

As this chapter has shown, the impact of Sor María as a spiritual writer in colonial Mexico was significant and has not been comprehensively addressed in previous scholarship. The next three chapters speak to how the Lady in Blue narrative first complemented and then later supplanted the well-established idea of Sor María as a spiritual writer. As we shall see in chapter 4, the two sides of Sor María—writer and protomissionary—were simultaneously present for colonial-era explorers and missionaries on the northern New Spanish frontier, even as the proto-missionary figure became part of the colonial-era history of northern New Spain. Chapters 5 and 6 will show how the Lady in Blue narrative later eclipsed Sor María's writing in folklore and in contemporary cultural production throughout Mexico, Greater Mexico, and beyond.

CHAPTER FOUR

"Aquella voz de las conversiones"

Writer and Missionary on the New Spanish Frontier

Daré primero un sucinto diseño del principio de su admirable vida con el cual se les dé así el ascenso debido como que sirva de estímulo, celo y fervor a los operarios evangélicos y entran a sacrificar sus vidas en la conversión de tantas y tan innumerables gentilidades.

———

I will first give a succinct summary of the beginning of her admirable life, from which one may derive the proper inspiration, that it might serve as stimulus, zeal, and fervor for evangelical workers, that they might join in the sacrifice of their lives in the conversion of so many innumerable gentiles.

—Juan Mateo Manje, *Luz de tierra incógnita*[1]

As we saw in chapter 3, Sor María's writing—especially *La mística ciudad de dios*—was read across a broad spectrum of colonial Mexican society for well over a century. In addition to her identity as an author of an important spiritual text, Sor María was also understood as a mystical missionary. This view of her was especially prevalent on New Spain's northern frontier, in what would become New Mexico, Texas, Arizona, California, and Mexico's northern states, where Sor María's conversion of indigenous tribes in the region was as significant as her writing. The Lady in Blue narrative was already widespread by the late seventeenth century, and it carried special meaning among missionaries and explorers to northern New Spanish provinces, who viewed Sor María as an essential figure in the history of the region's missions.

Historical documents show the Lady in Blue narrative at the forefront of mission thought and behavior, but not far removed from Sor María's writing. Most seventeenth- and eighteenth-century missionaries and explorers who discussed the Lady in Blue narrative were also conversant in what she authored. This chapter therefore opens by mapping colonial-era libraries and collections in northern Mexico that had copies of *La mística ciudad de dios* and related works, and I discuss the evidence of their reading at those sites.

Many Franciscan friars in New Mexico and Texas were trained at the Propaganda Fide College of Santa Cruz de Querétaro, where they engaged with Sor María as both writer and missionary. The college's involvement with Sor María produced a ripple effect in the neighboring community of Querétaro: local *beata* Francisca de los Ángeles followed explicitly in Sor María's mystical missionary steps. But Santa Cruz was not the only Propaganda Fide institution that dedicated special attention to Sor María and her writing: the colleges of Guadalupe de Zacatecas and San Fernando de México showed similar tendencies. In fact, famed *fernandino* Fray Junípero Serra's devotion to Sor María followed him from the Sierra Gorda to Alta California. A consideration of the Propaganda Fide colleges' involvement with Sor María follows.

Yet the Franciscans were not the only mission order in the region that looked to Sor María as a protomissionary. Jesuits in Baja California and Sonora openly discussed the Lady in Blue, and Sor María's writing emerges in eighteenth-century Jesuit mission libraries there. Expeditions involving Jesuits friars (including Fray Eusebio Kino) reported on Sor María's evangelization in Arizona and Sonora. This chapter closes with readings of colonial-era secular and religious histories on northern New Spain that indelibly inscribed Sor María into official historical narrative as the Lady in Blue.

"Corren sus escritos," Part 2: *La mística ciudad de dios* in the Colonial Mexican North

The circulation of Sor María's texts was by no means limited to the urban centers in Mexico where they were printed. In New Spain's northern territories, even small and remote collections boasted copies of *La mística ciudad de dios* and works relating to Sor María's writing. The private library of Diego de Vargas, New Mexico's late seventeenth-century governor, is one such example. De Vargas, a native of Madrid, was sent to New Mexico in 1689 to resettle the territory after its abandonment by Spanish colonists following the 1680 Pueblo Revolt. By 1692, under de Vargas's leadership, the communities surrounding the presidio of Santa Fe were again occupied by Spanish settlers. After an exile imposed by his successor, Pedro Rodríguez de Cubero, de Vargas resumed the governorship in 1703. His library was inventoried upon his death in 1704 as part of his last will and testament.

Although de Vargas's small library consisted of only thirty-three texts, including Spanish American histories and political tracts, it included the "tres tomos de la Madre María de Jesús de agreda" (three volumes of the Mother María de Jesús de Ágreda)[2] that made up *La mística ciudad de dios*. Based on the inventory's date, de Vargas's edition must have been printed in Spain, which suggests either that he brought it with him when he traveled to Mexico or that he acquired it in New Spain once he arrived, perhaps one of the editions shipped to Mexico from Spain by the promoters of her *causa*. Regardless of how he came to possess it, Sor María's writing was essential reading to have been among the precious few books de Vargas brought to New Mexico.

Evidence of the presence of Sor María's writing was manifested in New Mexican artwork. Eighteenth-century paintings made on animal hide suggest the influence of an early Dutch edition of *La mística ciudad de dios* in the territory. The work of an anonymous New Mexican artist, whom art historian Kelly Donahue-Wallace calls the "Wavy Hem Painter,"[3] was inspired by images printed in the 1736 Antwerp edition of *La mística ciudad de dios*.[4] Donahue-Wallace traces the thematic origin of the Wavy Hem Painter's *Christ Washing the Feet of the Disciples* to an image by the Flemish engravers Jan and Hieronymous Wiericx that appeared in the 1736 edition published by the Viuda de Verdussen.[5] The Wiericx brothers had originally designed that image and others for a sixteenth-century illustrated version of the Bible by the Spanish Jesuit Jerónimo Nadal entitled *Adnotationes et meditationes in Evangelia quae in sacrosanto missae sacrificio toto anno leguntur*.[6] More than sixty images from the Nadal Bible were reprinted in the 1736 Verdussen edition of *La mística ciudad de dios*.[7] Donahue-Wallace correlates the distinctive composition of the three scenes depicted in *Christ Washing the*

Feet of the Disciples—Christ removing his outer robe, Christ kneeling and washing the feet of Peter, and the Last Supper—with illustrations of the same in the 1736 Verdussen printing. She concludes that "the *Mystica ciudad de Dios* becomes the most likely source for the print of Christ and the disciples seen by the hide painter."[8]

In 1776, Fray Atanasio Domínguez, a prelate sent from the Franciscan provincial office in Mexico City, conducted an inventory of the mission libraries in New Mexico as part of his report on the Custodia of San Pedro y San Pablo (New Mexico).[9] Fray Domínguez documented the books at each mission site; the smaller missions, he noted, possessed the bare minimum necessary for offering Mass and administering the sacraments.[10] However, in the custodia's primary library, located at Santo Domingo Pueblo (between Albuquerque and Santa Fe), Fray Domínguez found 256 works, many of which were still present when the library was reinventoried in 1788,[11] but by then the number of books had increased to 384.[12] Although no copies of *La mística ciudad de dios* are explicitly documented in the 1776 inventory, several texts about Sor María's writing are. Two texts dealt directly with the debate over *La mística ciudad de dios* and defended Sor María's book. The first of these Fray Domínguez cataloged as *Certámen mariano de Arbiol*, an argument in favor of *La mística ciudad de dios* in response to the Sorbonne's critique of the text.[13] Penned by Fray José Antonio Arbiol, it was published in Spain in 1698.[14] The 1788 inventory indicated that the mission library also had a copy of *Fr. José Nicolás Cavero Anti-Agredistae Parisiense Expugnati*, another response to the Sorbonne's critique. It was authored by Franciscan José Nicolás Cavero, and was also published in Spain in 1698.[15] Because the apologia of her writing numbered among the holdings of the region's primary religious library, it is fair to conclude that, at least as an idea, *La mística ciudad de dios* was present in eighteenth-century New Mexico.[16]

La mística ciudad de dios reached as far as California, shadowing the progress of famed Franciscan missionary Fray Junípero Serra along the west coast. In Serra's February 5, 1775, report to the Mexican viceroy Antonio María de Bucareli y Ursúa, he states that, among the improvements made to the new five California missions, Mission San Luis de Obispo had recently acquired "los tres tomos de la Mística Ciudad de Dios, para la librería" (the three volumes of *La mística ciudad de dios*, for the library).[17] Fray Serra's twentieth-century biographer Maynard

Geiger confirms that copies of the book were seeded throughout the California missions in the eighteenth century: "There was a set [of *La mística ciudad de dios*] at Mission San Diego in 1777 and another at Mission Santa Barbara in 1834. In 1777, Mission San Diego also had a life of the Venerable María de Agreda."[18] The Online Archive of California lists a 1744 edition with the inscription "Fr. Thomas de la Pena Saravia. Del Colegio de San Fernando"[19] among the holdings of the collection at Mission Santa Clara, which was founded in 1777. The finding aid confirms that the text was in the possession of the library in 1851, when the collection was inventoried.

As in Alta California, eighteenth-century Baja California missions did not lack for *La mística ciudad de dios*. However, there was a significant difference in the missions' administration: the southern missions were under Jesuit control from the late seventeenth century until the suppression of the order and its 1767 expulsion from the Spanish colonies. At that time, the Baja California missions were handed over to the Franciscan Order. When the Dominicans took possession of the missions in 1773, their libraries were inventoried, revealing that Sor María figured significantly in their collections. At the library at the Jesuits' primary site, Misión Nuestra Señora de Loreto, there was a seven-volume edition of *La mística ciudad de dios* and a copy of Sor María's *vita*.[20] Misión San Francisco Xavier Vigé-Biaundó and Misión San José de Comandú each had a three-volume edition of *La mística ciudad de dios* among their very limited holdings.[21] Misión Santa Rosalía de Mulegé had the *Obras de la Venerable Madre María*, which one can assume consisted of or included *La mística ciudad de dios*, while Misión Santa María de los Ángeles contained a nine-volume edition of the text.[22] Misión Nuestra Señora de Guadalupe de Huasinapí had both *La mística ciudad de dios* and another text identified as the *Hystoria de la Virgen*, which may have been another edition of Sor María's work.[23] All in all, of the thirteen mission libraries originally pertaining to the Jesuits, six had books by or about Sor María.

The library inventories were taken after the Franciscans had been at those missions for more than a decade, so it is possible that the Franciscans could have brought *La mística ciudad de dios* with them to the Baja California mission libraries. However, as chapter 3 showed, the Jesuit Order often supported the Immaculate Conception theology before it became dogma in the eighteenth century, and many Jesuits in Mexico were familiar with *La mística ciudad de dios*. It is plausible that the Jesuits themselves brought the text with them to the missions. Regardless of which order brought *La mística ciudad de dios* and other Ágredan texts to Baja California, the effect was considerable: it made Sor María's writing available to missionaries, settlers, explorers, and neophytes on the far northern New Spanish frontier.

The Missionaries' Missionary: The Exemplary Sor María, Evangelist, in Colonial New Mexico and Texas

As Sor María's writing (and its readers) were dispersed throughout New Spain's northern frontier, so were reports of the Lady in Blue in the region. In Texas, Franciscan friars from the colleges of Propaganda Fide in Mexico brought with them their vision of Sor María both as an author and as a model for their evangelization. While in the mission field, friars in Texas marked out the mission space, its inhabitants, and the objectives of colonization within Sor María's purview. Although most Franciscan friars in New Mexico were not trained in the same way as those in Texas, many nonetheless understood Sor María as an integral part of the history of the region, and they invoked her in their historical reports and accounts.

In 1686, several years after the 1680 departure of Spanish settlers from New Mexico, the *custos* of the region, Fray Nicolás López, was charged with a difficult task. In his report on New Mexico for Felipe V, the Franciscan friar needed to justify the continued presence and growth of New Mexico's mission sites in spite of the recent indigenous revolt, headed by Taos tribal leader Popé. To explain why New Mexico still merited investment by the Spanish Crown, Fray López composed his *Memorial . . . acerca de la repoblación de Nuevo Méjico y ventajas que ofrece el reino de Quivira*,[24] in which he described conditions in New Mexico and extolled the virtues of Quivira, the rich, semi-mythological neighboring "kingdom." The Quivira in Fray López's letter was an enticement to explore and expand settlement, the counterargument to the obstacles to colonization and trade that the 1680 Pueblo Revolt manifested. But before explaining Quivira, the friar first apologizes for his "inutilidad" (uselessness) in preventing the many "daños, pérdidas y menoscabos que se han seguido después de dicha pérdida del Nuevo

México" (damages, losses, and discredit that followed the aforementioned loss of New Mexico),[25] transitioning from the failures of the past to the possibilities of the future in New Mexico. Fray López enters into a discussion of the missions in New Mexico, his work there, and the material and spiritual opportunities that would abound in Quivira.

In explaining the latter, he references a royal cédula dated 1678,[26] which cites Fray Benavides's *1630 Memorial* as an authoritative source regarding the region, and alludes to the fourteen-year custodianship of Fray Alonso de Posada, whose own report on the New Mexico territory also quotes the *1630 Memorial*.[27] In his *Informe á S. M. sobre las tierras de Nuevo Méjico, Quivira y Teguayo* (1686), Fray López explains how friars were sent to seek out the Jumanos in 1632 because they seemed to be "amigables [y] mostraban inclinación á ser cristianos" (friendly and inclined to become Christians).[28]

Fray López offers information on the Jumanos through a paraphrasing of the *1630 Memorial*'s account of the "Milagrosa conversión de los jumanos": "en la sazón hallé treinta y tres capitanes infieles de la nación Jumanas y otros que venían á pedir el baptismo, que esta nación, Señor, fué la que en tiempo de Fr. Alonso de Benavides, acompañada de otras, vino á pedirlo mesmo, enviando dicho Padre religiosos á estas conversiones" (to this effect, I found thirty-three unbelieving captains of the Jumano nation and others who came to request baptism; for this nation, Sir, was that which in the times of Fray Alonso de Benavides, accompanied by others, came to ask of them the same, and the same father sent friars out for those people's conversion).[29] Fray López concludes that the conversions among the Jumanos were not successful during Fray Benavides's tenure as *custos* in the late 1620s because "no debía de haber llegado la hora"[30] (it must not have been the appointed time) for their conversion; this explained why the Jumanos were still seeking baptism from Fray López and his friars decades later.

Jumping ahead to his own mission work in and around New Mexico, Fray López explains how, in 1683, he established a mission at La Junta de los Ríos (present-day southwestern Texas)[31] to address the demands for conversion made by many tribes in that area: "muchas naciones pedían el agua del Bautismo" (many nations were requesting the waters of baptism).[32] Among the seventy-six nations requesting baptism from the friars at La Junta, Fray López notes that the Tejas tribe sent representatives on its behalf. (The "Tejas" were one or several Hasinai tribes living in eastern Texas who were often conflated with the Jumanos in colonial-era accounts because the two tribes traded in overlapping areas.) Fray López's description of the Tejas reveals his familiarity with the Lady in Blue and with Sor María's writing.

Fray López writes about the Tejas by contextualizing them within the narrative of the Lady in Blue's evangelization:

> Y fuera de estas naciones tuvimos embajadores de los Texas, reino poderoso adonde catequizó la Madre María de Agreda muchos indios, que se refiere en sus escritos. Y por su intercesión fueron en años pasados á dar dos religiosos de mi orden á aquel reino, que baptizaron muchos indios, siendo su mesmo príncipe el primero que recibió el baptismo.

> And aside from these nations, we received ambassadors from the Tejas, a powerful kingdom where Mother María de Ágreda catechized many Indians, as is discussed in her writings. And through her intercession in years past, two friars from my order were sent to that kingdom, where they baptized many Indians, their very prince being the first who was baptized.[33]

Fray López attributes the Tejas' motives for baptism to their previous catechesis by Sor María, corroborating Sor María's earlier evangelization. In fact, as he describes it, Fray López simply builds on the groundwork previously laid by the Lady in Blue. The friar's understanding of nearby tribes and their apparent desire for baptism, and also his role as the region's *custos*, were informed at their very core by the Lady in Blue narrative.

Fray López cites Sor María's writing as his source for this information. Whether Fray López had read *La mística ciudad de dios* or the 1631 letter that circulated informally within the Franciscan Order, the friar was informed of the Lady in Blue narrative via Sor María's texts. Stationed in the New Mexico-Texas mission field well before the arrival of Propaganda Fide friars, Franciscan Fray López was aware of Sor María as an author, and his own reading of her indicates the wide distribution her works had already achieved in Mexico. Sor María's texts, and the perception of her as an essential element of the New Mexico mission en-

deavor, were already well established on the northern New Spanish frontier in the late seventeenth century.

This characterization of Sor María as a protomissionary carried over
into neighboring provinces. Several decades after Fray López, Franciscan
friar Benito Fernández wrote from the San Antonio de Béxar mission in
Texas about her in the same manner. A letter Fray Fernández wrote in
1741 protested the behavior of newly arrived Canary Island settlers who
were conscripting native inhabitants to work their lands.[34] This worked
against the friars' objectives of conversion, which was based on "zeal
for the holy faith,"[35] which Fernández contrasts with the colonists' more
material objectives. Fray Fernández explains that the San Antonio friars'
approach to evangelization was modeled on that used by friars in New
Mexico, who in turn implemented methods based on Sor María's actions in the mission field: "The old Fathers of the Province of the Holy
Gospel [New Mexico] in planting the faith among the savages and the
many nations of New Mexico decided on this method in the enlightened
and exalted spirit of Venerable María de Jesús de Ágreda."[36] He cites the
1730 printing of the *Tanto que se sacó de una carta* as his source for information on how to carry out mission conversions in an "enlightened"
and "exalted" way: "This can be seen in a copy of a letter which Father
Alonso de Benavides, custodian of New Mexico, sent to the Religious
of the Holy Custody of the Mission of San Pablo of the Kingdom, from
Madrid in 1631. It was printed in Mexico by Joseph Bernard de Hogal
in 1730."[37] The emulation of behaviors based on Sor María's actions as
a protomissionary illustrates how Fray Fernández and perhaps other
missionaries in the region perceived her. Sor María was seen as a true
authority on conversion practices in the colonial Mexican north.

In the late eighteenth century, a report by Franciscan friar Silvestre
Vélez de Escalante revealed Sor María's centrality to colonial-era discourse regarding the New Mexico territory. Fray Vélez de Escalante was
stationed in New Mexico, and reported on conditions there in an April 2,
1778, letter and memorial directed to Reverend Lector Juan Agustín
Morfi.[38] Fray Vélez de Escalante's history of New Mexico draws on
previous historical texts and reports on the region. In describing conditions in New Mexico in 1707, Fray Vélez de Escalante recounts growing
hostilities between the Spanish and the Hopi and Navajo nations. The
New Mexican governor, Juan Ignacio Flores, had heard that "en algunos
pueblos habían los indios reedificado sus estufas" (in some pueblos, the

Indians have reconstructed their kivas [underground places of wor-
ship])[39] after the spaces had been destroyed by missionaries and Spanish
soldiers. In response, Flores ordered the structures destroyed and
weapons collected from all but a few Christianized tribal members. Fray
Vélez de Escalante reported that Flores then convened secular and religious leaders to consider whether they should prohibit the same "indios
reducidos" (converted tribal members) from painting their bodies and
from using "monterrillas de piel" (large pieces of leather that covered
packs carried on the back). In the governor's view, the pack covers provided the opportunity to steal from the Spanish and otherwise subvert
Spanish authority. Fray Vélez de Escalante interjects at this point, dismissing the governor's allegation as utterly lacking in substance, "sin el
más débil fundamento" (without the slightest support).[40] The soldiers
sided with the governor, while the majority of the Franciscan friars were
opposed to the measures, requesting that the viceroy be consulted lest
this act of little faith cause "a grave and general uneasiness" (una grave y
general inquietud)[41] among the tribes.

Fray Vélez de Escalante then quotes one of the mission friars, Fray
Antonio Miranda, "un religioso de una vida muy ejemplar, de experiencia y activísimo celo" (a friar with an exemplary life, with experience
and very active zeal),[42] who offered his recommendation to the governor.
Fray Miranda, a missionary at Acoma pueblo, counseled that depriving
the tribe of its centuries-old traditions was neither savvy nor compassionate. Rather, he advised that the tribes should be treated "con la pa-
ciencia con que un hortelano cultiva una huerta recién planteada" (with
patience with which a gardener cultivates a recently planted field),[43] invoking the metaphor of the neophyte as a new garden to be carefully
tended. Fray Miranda continued in this vein, and ultimately deferred
authority on the matter of conversion to Sor María: "Muy repetidas
vienen las consultas contra este nuevo-verjel, de los naturales del Nuevo-
Mexico, huerto á que Dios se inclina como lo dice la madre Ágreda.
Y pues Dios se inclina a estos naturales, alguna cosa buena mueve la
voluntad" (The accusations against this flowering garden of the native
sons of New Mexico are frequent, a garden towards which God is inclined, as Mother Ágreda says. And so as God is well disposed towards
these natives, something good moves their will).[44] According to Fray
Miranda, since Sor María testified that the tribes of New Mexico were
favored for and inclined towards conversion, they should be treated

gently, like a recently planted garden. The Hopi and Navajo, therefore, should be allowed to retain their practices. As argued by Fray Miranda and reported on decades later by Fray Vélez de Escalante, Sor María's authority regarding moderate approaches to conversion rebuffed the New Mexico governor's "muy repetidas consultas" and his calling for the tribes' punishment.

Although these examples are illustrative of the general perception of Sor María as a mission authority, her colonial-era fame as a protomissionary and writer expanded exponentially through the involvement of friars trained at the Propaganda Fide colleges in Mexico. The friars from these colleges established and operated missions from Texas to California. Sor María was central to their conversion enterprise and to their theological training. The Propaganda Fide friars' familiarity with Sor María was rooted in their education, which trained them in her writing and informed them about her travels.

The College of Santa Cruz de Querétaro and Sor María in the Texas Mission Field

The Mexican Colleges for the Propagation of the Faith came into being in the late seventeenth century as a result of efforts by Fray Antonio Llinás, a native Mallorcan who for fifteen years had been a lector in Michoacán, Mexico. As a result of his experiences, Fray Llinás saw an acute need to establish schools in New Spain where missionaries would be trained for the field.[45] In 1681, Fray Llinás presented his proposal to the minister general of the Franciscan Order, Fray Joseph Ximénez Samaniego, Sor María's biographer and the promoter of her writing. Fray Llinás asked that twelve missionaries, he included, be sent to the northern frontier of New Spain. Ximénez Samaniego considered the request and ordered the founding of a college or training institute relatively close to the proposed mission field to ensure the longevity and success of the mission endeavor by training its friars.[46]

Another Santa Cruz founder, Fray Isidro Félix de Espinosa, commented in his *Crónica de los Colegios de Propaganda Fide de la Nueva España*[47] that Fray Ximénez Samaniego was central to the colleges' establishment: "jugó papel principalísimo en la institución de los Colegios apostólicos de misiones" (he played a principal role in the establishment of the apostolic mission colleges).[48] Fray Espinosa makes clear in the *Crónica* the relationship between Fray Ximénez Samaniego and Sor María, in particular in regard to his authorship of her *vita*, which included the Lady in Blue narrative: "la edición [de *La mística ciudad de dios*] fue encargada al P. Samaniego en 1668 y salió a la luz en 1670, procedida del citado prólogo galeato [donde se encuentra su vita], que se ha incluido después en todas las ediciones posteriores" (the edition [of *La mística ciudad de dios*] was entrusted to Father Samaniego in 1668 and came to light in 1670, preceded by the cited *Prólogo galeato* [where her *vita* is found], which has been included in all later editions [of *La mística ciudad de dios*]).[49] Fray Espinosa praises Fray Ximénez Samaniego for his discernment in mystical matters, specifically those related to Sor María: "[su] circunspección en materias místicas es notoria, y con luces meridianas lo da a conocer el Prólogo Galeato prefijo en las Obras de la V. M. María de Jesús de Agreda" (his circumspection in mystical matters is well known, and he makes that known with crystal-clear light in the *Prólogo galeato* that forwards the *Obras de la Venerable Madre María de Jesús de Ágreda*).[50] To Fray Espinosa, the connection between the founding of the Santa Cruz de Querétaro college, Fray Ximénez Samaniego, and Sor María (as both writer and mystical missionary) is intimate and clear.

Fray Ximénez Samaniego's involvement in the establishment of the college is important for several reasons, not the least of which is that he or someone near him provided a copy of Sor María's 1631 letter to Fray Llinás prior to the friar's departure from Spain. Certainly, Ximénez Samaniego had shared the letter in other circles influential in the New Spanish missions. A 1776 *Manifiesto* sent from the Propaganda Fide College of San Fernando states that in the late seventeenth century, Fray Ximénez Samaniego sent "un tanto" (selection) of the letter to Fray Mateo Heredia, who was the procurador of the provinces of New Mexico at the Spanish court. Sor María's evangelization was proof of the Franciscans' mission success in the New World. Fray Ximénez Samaniego or someone near him ensured that the New Spanish missionaries under Fray Llinás were well informed of the Lady in Blue narrative in preparation for their encounter with the tribes she had previously instructed.

In 1685, a French expedition into Texas headed by René Robert Cavelier, Sieur de La Salle, landed near Bahía de Espíritu Santo. News of the suspicious French party arrived quickly to Querétaro, and Captain Alonso de León was dispatched to take stock of the region. Fray Damián Manzanet, along with other friars from the College of Santa Cruz, accompanied de León.

In his 1689 letter to Mexican polymath Carlos Sigüenza y Góngora, Fray Manzanet explains that he was stationed at the Caldera mission in Coahuila prior to the expedition, where he awaited information about "tierra adentro" from de León's two previous, unsuccessful attempts to arrive at the Bahía de Espíritu Santo. Fray Manzanet's prior knowledge of "tierra adentro" was based on information given to Fray Antonio Llinás in Spain; this derived directly from Sor María's 1631 letter: "noticias que tenía de una carta que para en mi poder la qual dieron en Madrid a nuestro Padre Fray Antonio Llinás la cual carta hace mención de lo que la Beata Madre María de Jesús de agreda comunicó en su Convento al Padre Custodio del Nuevo México Fray Alonso de Benavides y dice la B. Madre como estuvo muchas veces al Nuevo México" (news regarding a letter that I have in my possession that was given to Father Antonio Llinás in Madrid. The said letter makes mention of what the Blessed Mother María de Jesús de Ágreda communicated in her convent to the father custodian of New Mexico Fray Alonso de Benavides, and the Blessed Mother says how she visited New Mexico many times).[51] Fray Manzanet's letter describes the tribes he anticipated the expedition would encounter in tierra adentro, reiterating ideas from Sor María's descriptions of the tribes. Fray Manzanet's expectations of the Texas mission field (and those of his fellow Santa Cruz friars) were informed by the Lady in Blue narrative prior to his arrival in New Spain.

Fray Manzanet closes his letter to Sigüenza y Góngora by recounting an unusual episode that merited special attention; it was for him "lo más particular [de la misión]" (the most exceptional thing [about the mission]).[52] It concerned an exchange between Fray Manzanet and a Tejas tribal leader about burial wrappings. The Tejas man asked Fray Manzanet for a special piece of fabric to wrap his mother in when she died: "un pedaço de vayetta açul para [a]mortaja[r] y enterrar a Su Madre, cuando muriese" (a piece of blue vachette in which to wrap and bury his mother, when she died). When offered a piece of "paño" (plain cloth) instead, he insisted on blue fabric for her future burial. Fray Manzanet reports that he asked the man why the color of the fabric was so important ("que misterio tenía el color açul," "why the color blue in particular"); the man replied that his tribe loved the color blue. According to Fray Manzanet, they preferred to bury their dead in blue because a woman dressed in blue used to visit them, and they wished to be like her: "en otro tiempo los yba ha uer una Mujer mui hermosa la Qual bajaua De lo alto Y dicha Mujer Yba bestida de açul y que ellos querían ser como dicha mujer" (in the past, a beautiful women used to come down from the heavens to see them, and that woman was dressed in blue, and they wanted to be like that woman).[53] When Fray Manzanet asked how long ago the woman had visited the tribe, the Tejas man replied that it had not been during his lifetime, but in the previous generation: "su Madre que era bieja la hauia bisto y los demas viejos" (his mother, who was old, had seen her, as had the other older people).[54] Fray Manzanet fills in the blanks regarding the dates of the mysterious visitations of the Lady in Blue: "las últimas veces que estuvo [la mujer] fue el año de 1631 como consta de su misma declaración que hizo a dicho Padre [Fray Benavides]" (the last time [this woman] was here was in 1631, as we know from the declaration she made to the said father [Fray Benavides]).

For Fray Manzanet, the identity of the visitor dressed in blue is obvious: it must have been Sor María, for "se ve claramente fue la Madre María de Jesús de agreda la cual estuvo en aquellas tierras; muchisimas veces como ella misma confesó al Padre Custodio de Nuevo México" (one clearly sees that it was the Mother María de Jesús de Ágreda who was in those lands; she confessed as much many times to the father custodian of New Mexico). For Fray Manzanet, and for the Propaganda Fide friars who would later follow him to Texas, Sor María's evangelization of the region's tribes was a reality of mission life and of the historical landscape. However, the Santa Cruz friars were not the only ones who framed the region and its tribes in light of Sor María; so did the secular authorities that gave permission for the de León expedition.

The governor of Florida, Juan Marquez de Cabrera, issued a cédula in 1685 permitting de León to preliminarily explore the region. Marquez de Cabrera refers to Sor María implicitly when he describes the limits of de León's purview: "Refiero que habiendo enviado a la Predicación y Conversión de la Nación Jumana y de los Japies que dice están ciento y doce leguas al oriente de la Villa de Santa Fe centro del Nuevo México y en trienta y siete grados de altura al norte llegó también aquella Voz de las Conversiones al Reyno de Quivira y al de los Ayjaos que estaban allí" (I refer to the fact that, having sent out friars for the preaching and conversion of the Jumano nation and the Japies, who are, they say, one hundred and twelve leagues east of the village of Santa Fe, in the center of New Mexico, and at thirty-seven degrees north, the voice of the conversions also arrived to the kingdom of Quivira and to that of the Aixaos who were there).[55] Although Marquez de Cabrera does not name Sor María directly, in the *1630 Memorial*, the "Conversión milagrosa de la nacion Jumana," the episode in which the Lady in Blue's conversion of the Jumanos is described, immediately preceded the chapters on Quivira and Aixaos. "Aquella voz de las conversiones"—Sor María as the Lady in Blue—is used in the cédula to frame the geographical space that de Léon could explore, from the Bahía del Espíritu Santo to the rich kingdom of Quivira.

Although de León himself does not mention Sor María in his reports on the 1689 expedition, the reception of his testimony was couched in terms of the Lady in Blue.[56] A 1689 letter from the Mexican viceroy Gaspar Melchor Baltasar de la Cerda Silva Sandoval y Mendoza to his brother Gregorio de Silva Mendoza IX informed the latter of the discovery of an abandoned French colony in the Bahía de Espíritu Santo. In the same letter, the viceroy also comments on the alleged desire of the nearby Tejas tribes to receive Franciscan missionaries because they had already received some catechesis: "según la tradición, antes habían sido evangelizados por la venerable María Jesús de Ágreda" (according to tradition, they had been evangelized by the Venerable María Jesús de Ágreda).[57] This statement is included to help explain why missionaries should continue to be sent to the area. Here, Sor María plays a small, but undeniably important role in how the region and its native inhabitants were understood by Spanish officials in charge of allocating resources and allowing exploration.

Several years after Fray Manzanet's experience, a group of friars originally from the Santa Cruz college[58] were sent to east Texas to reestablish a chain of missions there: San Francisco de los Tejas, Nuestra Señora de Guadalupe de los Nacogdoches, Nuestra Señora de los Dolores de los Ais, San Miguel de los Adaes, and Nuestra Señora de los Dolores de los Texas. In 1716, Fray Isidro Félix Espinosa, Fray Antonio Margil de Jesús, and Fray Francisco Hidalgo, among others, made their way to the Misión Nuestra Señora de la Puríssima Concepción, the Santa Cruz friars' Texas mission headquarters.[59] Two years later, in response to a perceived French threat to the Texas settlements, the Spanish Crown sent an expedition led by Martín de Alarcón to resupply the missions and settlers, and provide military support. Fray Francisco Céliz, a friar from Coahuila who served as the party's chaplain, kept a diary of the journey, which lasted from 1718 to 1719.[60] Throughout his diary, Fray Céliz refers to the village and mission at "La [Misión] Concepción de Agreda."[61]

The Santa Cruz friars' choice of name for Misión Concepción de Ágreda is in keeping with their awareness of Sor María as a Conceptionist writer and as a mystical protomissionary. In a 1719 letter penned by Fray Margil de Jesús and Fray Espinosa, and addressed to the viceroy of New Spain, Baltasar de Zúñiga Guzmán Sotomayor y Mendoza, the Ágreda mission name is again invoked.[62] The letter explains the importance of the Texas missions as sites of religious instruction and also as defensive outposts to prevent French incursion. They explain that they wished to remain at the Texas missions because they had high hopes of successful conversion of the tribes there ("teníamos buena esperanza concebida," "we had very positive expectations"),[63] a view undoubtedly influenced by Sor María's assurances that the tribes would be convinced upon seeing the Franciscan friars. They sign off the letter from the "Misión de la Purísima Concepción de Ágreda Presia de las Nuevas Filipinas y de los Tejas."[64]

Several years after the Alarcón expedition, on August 18, 1721, in a letter thanking the viceroy for supplies and support sent to the Texas missions, Fray Espinosa again calls the mission site "Misión Concepción de Ágreda."[65] Eventually, the mission was referred to as "Misión Concepción de Acuña,"[66] and from approximately 1724 on, it was simply called "Misión Concepción" in official reports and documents. But, for the friars from the College of Santa Cruz de Querétaro, the idea of Sor María was early inscribed into the Texas mission field.

For one of the founding Santa Cruz friars who participated in the Alarcón expedition, the location and nature of the kingdom of Quivira was irrefutably informed by Agredan authority. Fray Francisco Hidalgo wrote several *relaciones* ("accounts") while stationed at the San Francisco de los Texas mission, including a letter to the New Spanish viceroy, and an accompanying report on Quivira. Both documents illustrate the friar's earnest understanding of Sor María's explanation of Quivira, and his view of her knowledge of the geography and native inhabitants of Texas and New Mexico.

In his letter, Fray Hidalgo attempts to dissuade the viceroy from cutting off support of the friars in Texas, suggesting that the friars' spiritual work would produce an economic yield: "el negocio según la carne, no según Dios, que tiene en su Evangelio prometido el ciento por uno, no solo en lo eterno y espiritual, sino en lo temporal" (the business according to the flesh, not according to God, who has promised in his gospel one hundred for one, not only in the eternal and spiritual sense but also in the temporal one).[67] To explain how this would be the case, Fray Hidalgo unfolds the spiritual and material possibilities of Quivira, including those implied by "la Venerable Madre María de Jesús en la Carta que escribió a los Religiosos del Nuevo México" (the Venerable Mother María de Jesús in the letter that she wrote to the religious in New Mexico).[68] Fray Hidalgo notes that he has his own copy of the 1631 letter with him at the mission ("tengo copia de su carta," "I have a copy of her letter"), reinforcing the idea that the Santa Cruz friars were provided with Sor María's letter before entering the mission field.

Fray Hidalgo clarifies that the area he describes is "Quivira, no Gran Quivira" (Quivira, not Gran Quivira). To accurately distinguish between the two, he refers to the respected informant on the subject, Sor María: "dice así en substancia, a los últimos Reinos que fue llevada fue al Reinos de Quiviras y Jumanas: no dice Gran Quivira, si por decir la Venerable Madre reino, queremos entender grande" (in its substance, it says that the last kingdoms to which she was taken were the kingdoms of the Quiviras and Jumanos: she does not say "Gran Quivira," as if by the Venerable Mother saying "kingdom" we were to understand "Great"). After a brief discussion of whether "Gran Quivira" was so named for its geographical size, for the riches hidden there, or for the number of souls to be converted, Fray Hidalgo returns his attention to the question at hand: Where was Quivira located, and who lived there? To clarify the description, he names actual tribes and locates them in the region, incorporating other more fanciful notions of indigenous kingdoms and their inhabitants, such as the Tártaros, and animals that look like unicorns for the horns on their heads (perhaps buffalo). Given the possibility for speculation about where or if Quivira could be found, Fray Hidalgo reassures the viceroy of certain unequivocal truths about its location: "lo cierto es que según la Venerable Madre citada hay Quivira a dónde está según su novissima relación, hago juicio que estará de esta provincia doscientas leguas" (what is certain is that, according to the cited Venerable Mother, Quiriva lies where it is according to her recent account; I would guess that it is about two hundred leagues from this province).

In Hidalgo's letter, the nun's testimony on Quivira is understood in a serious and authoritative light; it establishes her as one of the primary sources on Quivira that Fray Hidalgo invokes in his accompanying account about the kingdom, the *Relación del Padre Hidalgo de la Quivira, hecha al señor Virrey, pretendiendo su descubrimiento*.

Fray Hidalgo's report on Quivira is elaborate; he cites a number of published texts on the topic, including Fray Agustín de Vetancurt's *Crónica de la Provincia del Santo Evangelio de México* (1697), Fray Juan de Torquemada's *Monarquía Indiana*, along with personal letters and anecdotal descriptions from other informants.[69] The 1631 letter and Fray Benavides's *1630 Memorial* are both referenced, though Fray Hidalgo significantly privileges Sor María's account in several ways: by its placement in the document (her letter is the first work quoted in the text, and her travel is cited at its close), and by citing her in the margins of the text, using her words to counter sources that reported on Quivira.

Fray Hidalgo begins by describing the second *entrada* of Governor Diego Terán de los Ríos (ca. 1691–92) to the region alleged to be Quivira. Terán de los Ríos was accompanied by the mission friars of Santa Cruz de Querétaro, including Fray Manzanet, who were in turn informed about the area by the "Indio Juan Tajano," telling them about the riches of "tierra adentro" (the inland region).[70] In the margin of the text, Fray Hidalgo qualifies this information, perhaps substantiating Juan Tajano's testimony, by citing Sor María: "Relación, le dio dicha Madre relación de la Gran Quivira, de la Gran Tollan de doce naciones muy populosas que están por descubrir con grandes riquezas" (The account, that the said Mother gave about Gran Quivira, about the Gran Tollan of twelve populous nations of great riches, which had yet to be discovered). Fray Hidalgo goes on to explain that another expert on Quivira cited Sor María's description of the region: "Cita esta relación del Padre Fray Agustín Betancurt [*sic*] así como he dicho" (Here is cited the account of Father Agustín Betancurt, as I have said).

In discussing certain old maps of the Bahía del Espíritu Santo and the Mississippi River, Fray Hidalgo attempts to provide a precise geographical location for Quivira.[71] He then transitions into a brief history of how the *1630 Memorial* came to be, and how Fray Benavides met Sor María and heard of her travels. As he recounts it, "el año de 30 del siglo pasado el Padre Custodio de la Nueva Mexico; reconociendo las maravillas que Dios nuestro Señor obraba por un Alma en diversas provincias y Reynos confinantes al Nuevo México pasó con este designio a España a ver si Dios le deparaba esta Alma consulto con el General de la orden quien le dio noticia de ella pasó con despachos del General de la orden a Agreda" (in the year 30 of the previous century the father custodian of New Mexico, recognizing the miracles that God our Father had wrought for a soul in the faraway provinces and kingdoms coterminous with New Mexico, traveled with this design to Spain to see if God had brought this soul, and consulted with the father general of the order, who told him of her [Sor María] and relayed a dispatch from father general of the order to Ágreda). In returning to the geography of Quivira, Fray Hidalgo again has recourse to Sor María's authority.

Fray Hidalgo determines the location of Quivira using a calibration derived from the nun's account: "se la contó [el lugar] a un Republicano de Querétaro, quien me la contó a mí con muchas circunstancias que aquí no pongo está de pobladores que cita por la Venerable Madre Maria de Jesús: habremos de entender la distancia de doce grados que es la que le puede corresponder a seiscientas leguas" (the location was told to a citizen of Querétaro, who told me about it with many conditions that I will not include here; it is a place with inhabitants who are cited by the Venerable Mother María de Jesús: we must understand that the distance of twelve degrees is that which corresponds to six hundred leagues). In continuing the discourse on the space in and near Quivira, Fray Hidalgo includes an anecdote about an anonymous past Franciscan commissary general (possibly Bernardino Sena) who also placed much store by Sor María's account of Quivira:

> Dio razón antiguamente en el siglo pasado el Reverendisimo Comisario General a un [*sic*] su amigo que traía en su compañía de nación gallego: diciendo que había leído en los manuscritos de la Madre María de Jesus, que en este siglo en que estamos se había de descubrir la gran Quivira, que está a los cuarenta grados.

> ——

> A century ago, the Reverend Commissary General attended to a friend from Galicia whom he had in his company: saying that he had read in the manuscripts of Mother María de Jesús that in this current century we were to discover Gran Quivira, which lies at forty degrees.

Fray Hidalgo goes on to square Sor María's explanation of Quivira's location with that presented in other accounts, always giving her version greater weight: "En diferentes tiempos, tengo oído que la Gran Quivira está avecindada a la Mar; las revelaciones hechas a la Venerable Madre no nos dizen si dicha Ciudad está vecina a la Mar" (At other times, I have heard that Gran Quivira lies next to the sea; the revelations made to the Venerable Mother do not tell us if the said city neighbors the sea).

Near the report's close, Fray Hidalgo again references Sor María in clarifying the location of Quivira in relationship to a kingdom of what he concludes are wealthy *tártaros*. Fray Hidalgo seeks to explain Quivira's whereabouts relative to the "Panni" and "Arricara" tribes. He explains,

> Siguiendo el rumbo [fuera de las tribus] al oriente según la carta de la Venerable Madre María de Jesús desde los Pani pasados unas naciones belicosas que están en el camino . . . haciendo mensura de los dos rumbos y sus intermediarios: bien se pueden contar las seiscientas leguas y se hace el rumbo del diario para el poniente de buscar aquella gran ciudad de los 40 grados muy cumplidamente.

> ———

> Continuing in the same direction [away from those tribes] to the east, according to the letter of the Venerable Mother María de Jesús, from the Pani, passing several bellicose nations that lie along the way . . . taking measure of the two courses and their intermediaries: one may well count six hundred leagues, and head out from the usual one to the west to seek out that great city at 40 degrees quite readily.

After definitively triangulating the city of Quivira according to Sor María's descriptions, Fray Hidalgo continues with a differentiation between the "Quivira pobre" of Francisco Coronado's expedition and Torquemada's history, and "la Gran Quivira rica de grandes edificios y de mucho oro y plata: que hace Relación la Venerable Madre María de Jesús de Ágreda y apunta el Padre Fray Agustín Vetancurt Cronista de la Santa Provincia llamada Santo Evangelio" (the Gran Quivira full of large buildings and of much gold and silver; the Venerable Mother María de Jesús de Ágreda makes account of this, as does Father Agustín Vetancurt, the historian of the holy province called Santo Evangelio).

Fray Hidalgo's *relación* closes by invoking Sor María's letter, this time as an exhortative tool, reminding the viceroy of the potential threat posed to Quivira by other countries, which signified financial loss for the Spanish Crown. He comments:

> Si cuanto antes su Majestad Católica no envía gente a atajarlo por dicho Rio de San Andrés, como en la carta adjunta digo a Vuestra Señoría no menos la pérdida de todo el Norte y occidente, Parral, Nuevo México, Rio del Missuri, Quivira, y las grandes poblaciones que refiere la Venerable Madre María de Jesús de Ágreda que se miran al oriente de la Quivira todo se pierde y ya España podrá cesar de sus conquistas superiores.

> If his Catholic Majesty does not send people to take the shortcut to Quivira via the aforementioned Rio de San Andrés as soon as possible, as I say to His Honor in the attached letter, no less than all of the north and west, Parral, New Mexico, the Rio Missouri, Quivira, and the great populations that lie to the east of Quivira that the Venerable Mother María de Jesús de Ágreda refers to will all be lost, and Spain will conclude its mighty conquest.

Fray Hidalgo specifies that a few competing European countries also had their eyes on Quivira's riches: "cerca de este estrecho [Anián] ay un castillo de dinamarqueses que vido el clérigo aragonés [un testigo citado anteriormente en la relación], de donde inferí en la carta adjuntada ser la ciudad de dinamarqueses" (close to this strait [the Strait of Anián] there is a Danish castle that the aragonese cleric [a witness cited previously in the relación] saw; I inferred in the attached letter that the Danish city lies there). He also suggests that the Crown should take advantage of the fact that many other countries are not yet aware of the places, peoples, and potential riches outlined by Sor María: "Deja blanco esta relación para descubrir las naciones de la Venerable Madre, que los franceses hasta ahora se ignoran de ellos, y del Reino de Anián y Reino de la Quivira" (I leave this account open to discover the nations named by the Venerable Mother, as the French at this time ignore them, and the kingdom of Anián and the kingdom of Quivira).[72] For Fray Hidalgo, Sor María's descriptions of the Texas mission field were proof of places and people meriting exploration and colonization by the Spanish Crown, her credibility the result of her mystical travels there.

For friars Manzanet, Espinosa, Margil de Jesús, and Hidalgo, Sor María was an authoritative presence in the field—a missionary's missionary. This view of her on the northern New Spanish frontier and within the colleges of Propaganda Fide would continue to spread for another hundred years, as subsequent generations of Franciscan missionaries brought with them Sor María's writing and the idea of her as a protomissionary. The longevity and continuity of these beliefs and practices related back to the education the friars received at the Mexican colleges of Propaganda Fide.

The Propaganda Fide College of Santa Cruz de Querétaro

With typical "humor servandino" (servandine humor),[73] late eighteenth-century Dominican friar Servando Teresa de Mier describes in his *Memorias* the esteem in which the Mexican Franciscans held Sor María and her writing.[74] He notes of their commitment to her as a spiritual writer such that "los Padres franciscanos la citan [a Sor María] hasta en los púlpitos como Santo Padre" (the Franciscan friars cite her [Sor María] even in the pulpits as if she were a Holy Father).[75] Fray Servando himself was familiar not only with the contents of *La mística ciudad de dios* but also with the theological debate over it,[76] and he gleefully cites all the ways in which the text was considered lacking in past centuries, including the "cuarenta y ocho proposiciones que le censuró la Sorbona, y nada menos la llama sino errónea" (forty-eight points on which the Sorbonne censured the work, and called it nothing less than erroneous).[77] He rattles off the contradictions between Sor María's vision of the Immaculate Conception and those of the mystics St. Catherine and St. Brigid.[78] Fray Servando's satirical commentary on Agredan devotion among Mexican Franciscans culminates in a telling pronouncement on the friars' beliefs and practices: "los padres franciscanos, que hasta suelen llamar segunda Biblia a su Madre Agreda, son dueños de creer lo que se les antoje" (the Franciscan fathers, who go so far as to call their Mother Ágreda the second Bible, are perfectly capable of believing whatever appeals to them).[79] In Fray Servando's estimation, the admiration for and emulation of Sor María by Mexican Franciscans knew no limits.[80]

Fray Servando's characterization should draw our attention, both for the tone with which he writes and for what he says. The Franciscan

friars of the colleges of Propaganda Fide in Mexico were primary prac-
titioners of the Agredan devotion Fray Servando describes. This was
clearly the case at the Colegio de Santa Cruz de Querétaro. There, Sor
María's writing was a staple of the friars' theological preparation, even
as the Lady in Blue was presented as a protomissionary model. Sor
María's writing made up the very fabric of the institution itself. For
more than sixty years, instruction in Sor María's *doctrina* (writing and
spiritual practices) was central to the curriculum for mission friars. In
this way, the College of Santa Cruz de Querétaro cultivated a focused
community of reading for Sor María.

The college's institutional records show how Sor María's writing
was prioritized in college instruction. The *Libro bezerro de provincia*,[81]
located at the college's archives, recorded the personnel involved in the
administration of the provincia de San Pablo y San Pedro de Michoacán
as reported during the *capítulos provinciales*, or biennial meetings of the
province. The *Bezerro* therefore provides a wealth of institutional information about the college's structure, staffing, and instructional objectives. At the October 23, 1729, provincial meeting, the *Bezerro* records
a new faculty post at the College of Santa Cruz,[82] the "Elucidator Mysticae Civitatis Dei, scriptae a Venerabili Matre Maria a Jesu de Agreda"
(Elucidator of the *Mystical City of God*, written by the Venerable
Mother María de Jesús de Ágreda). The Elucidator position was a *cátedra* (professorship) dedicated to teaching *La mística ciudad de dios* at
the Colegio de Santa Cruz de Querétaro. The December 1729 *Gaceta de
México* reported the creation of the position,[83] which was intended for
the teaching of Sor María and Duns Scotus, by a retired lecturer: "los
Venerables Agreda y subtil Escoto, de cuya doctrina también se hace ex-
planación, por un Lector Jubilado" (the Venerable Ágreda and Subtilis
Scotus, whose doctrine will be taught by a retired lector).[84] The *Gaceta*
elaborated the utility of the courses taken by students at the college: they
qualified towards students' graduation with a degree from the University of Mexico.[85]

The creation of the *cátedra* at Santa Cruz de Querétaro doesn't
mean that Sor María's writing—*La mística ciudad de dios* in particular—
had not already been taught at the school; in fact, the accounts described
earlier in this chapter suggest the opposite. But by 1729, teaching Sor
María's doctrine merited the creation of a permanent position, revealing
that her writing was highly valued among the teaching friars at the

college. The *Libro Bezerro de Provincia* shows no other spiritual writer (much less a woman) that merited a *cátedra* dedicated to instruction on their works alone. The prioritization of this position likewise demonstrates that the Franciscan leadership within the Propaganda Fide college desired its graduates to be well versed in Agredana before entering the mission field.

The Elucidator professorship existed at the College of Santa Cruz de Querétaro from 1729 to at least October 1793, or sixty-four years. By May 1795, the position was no longer listed among the faculty positions in the *Bezerro*. Its disappearance is attributable to an overall contraction of the college's faculty. The last *padre lector* to hold the position, R. P. Fray Joseph Plancarte, became the *regens omnium studiorum* (dean of students) in 1795.[86]

Though the overall number of faculty teaching at the Colegio de Santa Cruz varied from year to year (from capítulo to capítulo, as documented in the *Bezerro*), the April 1733 *Gaceta de México* provides a useful snapshot of the overall composition of the faculty. It lists a total of thirty *cátedras*, including twenty in areas such as philosophy, grammar, and indigenous languages. The article then lists a separate ten positions for specific types of instruction: "Diez Cathedras de Theologia, y de ellas dos Canónicos, y una de la Doctrina de la V.M. María de Jesús de Agreda" (Ten theology professorships, and of them two canonical and one for the doctrine of the Venerable Mother María de Jesús de Ágreda).[87] In January 1735, the number of faculty was slightly reduced to twenty-eight,[88] and the Elucidator position was described in the *Gaceta* as "una de la Mystica de la Venerable Agreda" (one for teaching *La mística* [*ciudad de dios*] by the Venerable Ágreda).[89] Within this limited number of faculty, instruction in Sor María's writing was prioritized to the extent that it continued to demand a *cátedra* addressing it.

Most of the friars who taught the *La mística ciudad de dios* and Sor María's *doctrina* had held the title of lector of theology when appointed Elucidator *Mysticae Civitatis Dei*. Though several friars held the position for extended terms, in its early years (1729–40), the Elucidator position rotated through a cadre of experienced *lectores*. Almost without exception, the position was filled in its early years by a senior, well-placed friar who, prior to, during, or following his tenure teaching Sor María's works, became rector of Santa Cruz. Whether the Elucidator

Mysticae Civitatis Dei position itself conferred prestige or whether it was simply a good appointment for qualified instructors, it is clear that the post and the material taught through it were respected within the college.

The prominence of the individuals who occupied the Elucidator *Mysticae Civitatis Dei* post signals the weight accorded to the faculty position. Elucidators uniformly occupied highly placed posts within the college concurrent with, before, or after their tenure as *cátedra* of Sor María's texts. The first individual to hold the post was R. P. Fr. Ignatius de Frías, a retired professor (*lector jubilado*) whose previous position in the college was the *Summa Theologica* master. Many subsequent Elucidators filled the roles of the padre guardián and/or vice-rector of the college previous to or following their instructional terms. Several, including Fr. Christopher de Urrutia (Elucidator from 1736 to 1738), Fr. Andreas Picazo (1765–68), and Fr. Joachim Delgado (1738–40), held the positions of padre guardián and vice-rector of the college simultaneous to their faculty appointment. A long-term instructor of Agredan doctrine, Joseph del Valle (1745–52 and 1754–62), was simultaneously the master of students for many of his terms, while others, like Fr. Joseph Plancarte (1774–78 and 1787–93), had previously been *cátedra* of sacred theology, a position requiring extensive theological preparation.

The long existence of the Elucidator position within a small number of faculty and narrow range of teaching specializations at the Colegio de Santa Cruz de Querétaro indicate a true institutional valorization of Sor María's writing. This same appreciation for and active implementation of Sor María's writing is likewise evinced by the contents of the college's libraries, inventoried in 1766 and 1803.[90]

The libraries' catalogs show that Sor María's works, and texts about her or her writing, are represented to an extent conferred to few other writers in the Santa Cruz libraries. The 1766 inventory of the college's Biblioteca Común reveals that its modest holdings included numerous copies of *La mística ciudad de dios*, including six copies of the three-volume edition,[91] several loose volumes from those printings,[92] one copy of a six-volume edition,[93] four copies of an eight-volume edition,[94] and two copies of the *Escuela Mística de María Santíssima* (the Mexican printing of *La mística ciudad de dios*).[95] These were listed mostly under "Historia eccelsiástica y profana," not, it should be noted, under "Mysticos," a different category.[96] The Biblioteca Común also held two copies of the *Aurora alegre* by Fray Francisco Antonio de Vereo, the abridged monthly reading of *La mística ciudad de dios* that included accompanying prayer practices published in Mexico.[97] The library also boasted four copies of Fray Joseph Ximénez Samaniego's *Vida de la Venerable Madre Sor María de Jesús de Ágreda*.[98]

In addition to these core Agredan texts, the Biblioteca Común held an impressive array of commentaries and apologia for *La mística ciudad de dios* and other texts that feature Sor María prominently. Such texts include Fray Diego González Matheo texts *Apodixis Agrediana pro Mystica Civitatis Dei* (1751), *Mystica Civitatis Dei Vindicata* (1736), and *Responsio ad censuram Super libros Mystice Civitatis Dei* (1747);[99] Fray Dalmatius Kick's *Deffensio Revelationum Agredanarum* (1750–54);[100] and Fray Juan Riquelme's *Deffensorio de la primera parte de la Mystica Ciudad de Dios* (1697).[101]

Two Spanish Franciscans who had published their works with the Imprenta de la Causa de la Venerable Madre María de Jesús de Ágreda in Madrid also emerged in the Santa Cruz Biblioteca Común's collection. Fray Écija's *Verdadera compendiosa relación de la portentosa sagrada imagen de Nuestra Señora de los Milagros* (published by the Imprenta in 1743) was dedicated to the nuns at Sor María's convent, and it makes extensive reference to Sor María throughout the text. Fray Arbiol's works figure significantly into the Biblioteca Común, from his defense of *La mística ciudad de dios* in the *Certamen Marianum Pareisiense* (1698)[102] to other works that incorporate or discuss Sor María's writing, such as *La religiosa instruída*.[103] The library also includes multiple copies of Fray Arbiol's works on mysticism and the mystic tradition in which Sor María is referenced as an ideal mystic model: *Desengaños místicos* (1706, 1761)[104] and *Mystica fundamental de Christo Señor nuestro, explicada por el Gloriosos, y Beato Pdre S. Juan de la Cruz* (1761),[105] both published by the Imprenta.[106]

A 1803 inventory of Santa Cruz's Biblioteca Chiquita shows that the smaller library followed the precedent of collecting Agredan writing. Under the "Libros de historia y vidas de los santos" (History books and lives of the saints), the library's catalog lists nine complete copies of *La mística ciudad de dios* and two copies of Sor María's *vita*.[107]

With these two libraries, the College of Santa Cruz was well equipped to support a curriculum that taught Sor María's writing as a special subject. In 2009, a fire destroyed most of the college's collection. Within the surviving library, I found three-volume editions of *La mística ciudad de dios*, whose large dimensions were meant for public reading, and many copies of the five- and seven-volume editions of *libros del bosillo*. The remaining library contents still reflect the college's original vigor in acquiring Sor María's writing and associated texts. In addition to populating the college's libraries, the physically smaller editions (printed on 8° and 16° sheets of paper) are likely to have followed the friars out of the college; these books they may have been able to afford for themselves, and therefore could take *La mística ciudad de dios* with them into the mission field as part of their personal possessions. Certainly, we know that California missionaries Fray Junípero Serra and Father Thomas de la Peña Seravia—graduates of the College of San Fernando—took their copies with them to California.

Sor María's authority as a spiritual writer and intellectual at the College of Santa Cruz manifested in other ways. The sermons and writing assignments the friars composed there consistently refer to the Agredan works in the college libraries. In the margins of the friars' writing, their notes and comments show that they considered Sor María an irrefutable source for many of their theological arguments, in particular those relating to the Immaculate Conception and other Marian themes. The serious study of Sor María's writing infused the friars' scholarly work with her sensibilities; it led them to cite the nun with equal confidence and authority as they did doctors of the Church, theologians, mystical writers, and the Bible. An exhaustive survey is beyond the scope of this book, but a few examples provide a useful sense of this.

Fray Antonio de Losilla's "Sermón de las excelencias y glorias de Maria Santíssima, especialmente su Asumpción Gloriosa" (Sermon on the excellencies and glories of Holy Mary, especially her glorious assumption)[108] quotes at length and line by line from *La mística ciudad de dios* in discussing the relationship between the Virgin Mary's body and soul. Fray Losilla meticulously documents throughout his text exactly which part, book, section, and line of *La mística ciudad de dios* he draws on to support his theological argument. He quotes Sor María at key points, showing that his thesis turned on certain vital arguments that originated in her writing and for which no other authority superseded Sor María. The precision and consistency with which he refers to Sor

María's writings demonstrates a deep comprehension and masterful application of *La mística ciudad de dios* as an authoritative spiritual text.

Similarly, the margins of a notebook of talks and sermons belonging to Fray Juan José Sáenz de Gumiel,[109] a friar who left Ágreda, Spain, and entered into Santa Cruz in 1749, are filled with references to Sor María and *La mística ciudad de dios*. The same rigorous referencing occurs in the *Amenissimus Sacrae Theologiae Tractatus Dei param Virginem Mariam D.N. alucidans ad mentem S.N. Marianique Doctoris elaboratus dictatusque hoc in Celayensi Liceo a RP Fr. Ferdinando Rivera*,[110] a series of *tratados* (scholarly treatises) written in 1775 by Fray Juan Murga for Fray Fernando Rivera. The text argues for certain subtleties of Marian theology, drawing on *La mística ciudad de dios* (and other Marian texts) extensively. The *tratados*, *sermones*, and letters of friars Losilla, Gumiel, and Murga and their fellow seminarians illustrate the incredibly strong sway Sor María's writing held over the scholarly imagination of the friars at the College of Santa Cruz de Querétaro.

Beyond the intellectual study of Sor María's writing at the college, the spiritual practices of several of its founding friars show how the nun's principles contributed to the community's self-perception and foundational rhythms. Fray Isidro Félix Espinosa's *Crónica de los Colegios de Propaganda Fide de la Nueva España* provides brief *vitae* for some of the college friars. In these biographies, ideas associated with Sor María frequently emerge and her recommended spiritual devotions are often implemented. In documenting the life of Fray Melchior López, Fray Espinosa describes the friar's personality and sensibility as "una cruz bien formada a manos de su penitencia y mortificación" (a well-formed cross made at the hands of his penitence and mortification).[111] Fray Espinosa conjures up the image of Fray López with a *báculo* (crosier) in his right hand and a small stick in his left, "como llevaban los Apóstoles en sus caminos, según refiere la V.M. María de Jesús de Agreda" (as the apostles carried in their travels, as the Venerable Mother María de Jesús de Ágreda says).[112] The missionary Fray López is cast in a mold that Fray Espinosa draws from Sor María's writing.

Other friars' devotional practices relating to Sor María's writing provide further evidence of her influence over those living and studying at the College of Santa Cruz. In documenting the death of "protomártir" Fray Casañas de Jesús María, Fray Espinosa notes that Fray Casañas de Jesús engaged in Sor María's prescribed "ejercicios de la muerte" prior to his death:

Tenía tiempos algunos días que dedicaba a hacer ejercicios semejantes a los de la V.M. María de Jesús de Agreda, especialmente el de la muerte, en cuya profunda meditación se consideraba como la cerca de los últimos lances de la vida, y se disponía como si acabado aquel ejercicio hubiesse de partir su alma a la eternidad.

———

He had time some days that he dedicated to completing exercises similar to those of the Venerable Mother María de Jesús de Ágreda, especially those in preparation for death, the deep meditation over which he considered the last of his final efforts at life, and he was disposed that his soul depart to eternity upon completing them.[113]

Founding friar Fray Francisco Frutos's personal devotion to Sor María's mystical writing is also evident: "En la lección de libros sagrados se ocupaba todos los ratos que podía cercenar de las obligaciones de su ministerio, y éstos eran los de la *Mística Ciudad de Dios*, las obras de la Mística Doctora Santa Teresa de Jesús, el libro de oro de San Juan de la Cruz" (He would spend all the time he could set aside from his ministerial obligations in the reading of sacred books, and these books were *La mística ciudad de dios*, the works of the mystical doctor Santa Teresa de Jesús, and the book of gold by San Juan de la Cruz).[114] Fray Frutos was Fray Espinosa's teacher and mentor, and as Fray Frutos was dying, he asked a special favor of his student:

> me mandaba que en un librito escrito de mano, donde tenía trasladadas las doctrinas que dio María Santísima a su sierva la Venerable María de Jesús de Agreda, le leyesse una, puesto de rodillas; y luego que la acababa, me mandaba lo dejasse solo y no dejasse entrar persona alguna a la celda hasta que él me llamasse. Quedábase en este tiempo en oración, rumiando lo que había oído en la doctrina.

———

> he told me of a little handwritten book, where he had written down the doctrines that Holy Mary gave to her servant the Venerable María de Jesús de Ágreda, and asked me to read him one, kneeling; and as soon as it was over, he ordered me to leave him alone and not let anyone else enter his cell until he called me. He remained praying at that time, ruminating over what he had heard in the doctrine.[115]

For the next fifteen days prior to his death, Fray Frutos repeated this practice again and again, meditating on Marian revelations penned by Sor María.[116]

Like many of his fellow early friars of Santa Cruz, Fray Antonio de los Ángeles was also a devotee of Sor María's teachings.[117] In Fray Juan Domingo Arricivita's *Crónica apostólica y seráfica del colegio de Propaganda Fide de la Santa Cruz de Querétaro* (1792), Fray de los Ángeles's devotional practices are described as such: "He respected the Divine Lady [Mary] as a teacher, and every day he read with profound meditation some one of the teachings that she gave the Venerable Mother Ágreda."[118] A Santander native, de los Ángeles professed at the college in 1690[119] and shared nightly prayers with Fray Antonio Margil de Jesús for the four years Margil de Jesús was prelate of the college. During this practice, "At eleven in the evening he [Fray Margil] would call me. We read the doctrine of Mother Ágreda. He would sit as if my teacher, and I would confess my sins."[120]

The preparations he made for his death showed the rigor of Fray de los Ángeles's devotion to Sor María's writing. As his health failed, Fray de los Ángeles, like Fray Frutos, contemplated Sor María's reflections on death: "[He] reflected on its [death's] agony and prepared himself with particular care of it, using the same exercises that the Venerable Mother Ágreda had practiced."[121] To further explain Fray Antonio de los Ángeles's pious practices, Fray Arricivita provided more explanation: "This earnest devotion induced him [Fray de los Ángeles] to ask for permission to go into retirement for ten days in order . . . to reawaken his spirit in the exercises arranged by the Venerable Mother Ágreda. In these, he centered his attention in learning how to die well."[122] Fray Antonio's spiritual life as a whole is couched within the context of *La mística ciudad de dios* in the Arricivita chronicle: "This was what illuminated his soul . . . for he follows the footsteps of the Almighty and His Most Holy Mother through the history of the Venerable Mother Ágreda."[123]

Of the Quereteran Sor María devotees, few possessed a passion for Sor María equal to that of Fray Antonio Margil de Jesús. His own devotion to Sor María's writing and to her mystical conversions emerged in his personal spiritual practices, in his advisement of other religious men and women, and in his view of the mission field, both within and outside of the College of Santa Cruz. In addition to the Agredan prayer regime he shared with Fray Antonio de los Ángeles, Fray Margil de Jesús cultivated and shared his devotion to Sor María with the other Propaganda Fide colleges, where he was sent as an administrator.

Once chosen as padre guardián of the College of Guadalupe de Zacatecas in 1706, Fray Margil de Jesús personally continued to practice the precepts set forth in Sor María's writing and encouraged others to follow him: "To imitate Mary, as he did Jesus, he took special care in observing the doctrines, which in the *Mística Ciudad de Dios* unravel the excellence of their virtues, with which he also aroused souls to emulate them."[124] Indeed, Fray Margil took this emulation a step further at the Colegio de Zacatecas: the Virgin of Guadalupe was elected as the college's principal prelate, which meant that her authority surpassed that of Fray Margil de Jesús. This decision on behalf of the community, led in the process by Fray Margil de Jesús, imitated Sor María's renunciation of the election to abbess of her convent in favor of appointing the Virgin of the Immaculate Conception as leader over all. Fray Margil de Jesús's actions at the College of Guadalupe de Zacatecas were thus "in conformance with the most pious circumstances that are read in the Venerable Mother María de Jesús."[125] Under his tutelage, the other friars at the community began to observe Sor María's prescribed practices, "whose imitations they all embraced happily."[126] The Zacatecas college's relationship to Sor María's writing will be further explored later in this chapter, but Fray Margil de Jesús's important role in its foundation was determinative in its leanings towards Sor María.

Fray Margil de Jesús likewise brought his Agredan devotion with him when he established the Propaganda Fide college in Guatemala in 1692. In a letter of spiritual consolation sent from Fray Margil de Jesús to an unnamed recipient at the college, the friar quotes extensively from *La mística ciudad de dios*, adding in the margin of the letter "Ojo aquí" before a section citing Sor María at length.[127]

Fray Margil de Jesús continued to promote devotion to Sor María's writings and to the idea of her as missionary even outside of the Propaganda Fide colleges where he lived. His influence as a spiritual advisor in the community of Querétaro meant that Sor María exerted sway well beyond the walls of the Santa Cruz college, in particular in the life and writing of his advisee Francisca de los Ángeles.

A Bilocating Mexican Beata: Francisca de los Ángeles and the Friars of Santa Cruz de Querétaro

Francisca de los Ángeles was a charismatic spiritual figure well known in the Querétaro region for her mystical experiences. Among the many remarkable elements of Francisca's life, her bilocations to the missions of Texas and New Mexico are perhaps the most unusual, drawing the attention of the Mexican Inquisition. There, explicitly following in Sor María's footsteps, she advanced and completed the work of the Propaganda Fide missionaries.

Francisca maintained close relationships with the Franciscan friars of the nearby Propaganda Fide college, especially Fray Francisco Frutos and Fray Antonio Margil de Jesús, who were her confessors and spiritual advisors. Her spiritual guides were well versed in Sor María's writings, and in the nun's protomissionary evangelization, and imparted this knowledge to Francisca: "The community's great role model, Madre María de Jesús de Ágreda, the famed Spanish nun, had experienced . . . bilocations to New Mexico between 1620 and 1631. With the help of angels she had been taken to several faraway kingdoms located beyond hostile lands."[128] Counseled by the college's missionaries and leaders, the idea of Sor María as a mystical missionary intrigued Francisca. When in the 1690s she claimed that she physically traveled on regular Thursdays to the Tejas tribes, Francisca was celebrated in Querétaro for her raptures, very similar to those of Sor María.[129] In describing her travels, Francisca was convinced of the nature of her travels, "more confident than her distinguished Spanish model, who claimed to be unsure as to whether she had traveled in body or not."[130] Francisca explained why it seemed to her fellow beatas that she remained in Querétaro when she was actually carrying out baptisms on the northern frontier: Santa Rosa de Viterbo occupied her place in her religious community while she traveled to Texas.[131]

Letters from Francisca to her confessors reveal in more extensive detail the nature of her travel and its relationship to Sor María's example. A letter she wrote to Fray Margil de Jesús around 1700 parallels her travels explicitly to those of Sor María, showing that she was aware of the connection between her and the Spanish nun, and expected the confessor to likewise recognize the similarities.[132] However, Francisca's experience was more involved, and more specific than Sor María's: Francisca claimed to have baptized the tribes she encountered, and to have administered other sacraments to them. Francisca preached Christian doctrine and met with older people in New Mexico who, according to Francisca, had already been baptized by Sor María during her travels nearly seventy years earlier.[133]

Francisca maintained that she continued to travel to Texas in the 1690s, after the return of Franciscan missionaries to Querétaro in 1693 in the wake of an unsuccessful attempt to establish missions in Texas. Her detailed descriptions of her travels discuss the nature of the people she encountered, the construction of a church modeled after Santa Cruz de Querétaro,[134] and her preaching and administration of the sacraments. In another account, Francisca told of a tribesman who tried to remove Francisca's rosary from her habit. He was unable to do so, but Francisca promised new rosaries on her return; this episode echoed the tradition relating to Sor María that she left behind *cuentas* on her voyages to the Jumano tribe.[135]

At the time, it was accepted in Querétaro that Francisca had traveled to New Mexico and Texas; she was alleged to have advised Fray Damián Manzanet's two expeditions into Texas, drawing upon her familiarity with the people there.[136] However, in 1694 Francisca was accused of *alumbradismo* (false visions). One of the charges against her was based on rumors of rosaries from the Santa Cruz college that were said to have had indulgences associated with them because Francisca had personally given the rosaries to Christ, and He had blessed them. In the course of Inquisition testimony about the rosaries, Francisca cited the indulgences associated with Sor María's reliquary as precedent for her rosaries: "esto es sin toto lo demas que consedio su magestad en dichas cuentas que es el que sean cuentas como las de la madre Agreda originales que se pueden tocar" (this is without all the rest that his majesty conceded in the aforementioned rosaries, which is that they be rosaries like the Madre Ágreda's original ones that can be touched).[137] Clearly, the narrative of the Lady in Blue, and the idea of Sor María as a proto-missionary model were not limited to the Colegio de Santa Cruz de Querétaro. For Francisca, her Propaganda Fide advisors influenced how she conceived of herself as a missionary and how the surrounding community of Querétaro understood her.

Agredan Avocation and Its Mission Manifestations for Other Mexican Propaganda Fide Colleges

Sor María's influence within the colleges of Propaganda Fide in Mexico was not limited to the Colegio de Santa Cruz de Querétaro. Sor María emerged in the colleges of Guatemala, Guadalupe de Zacatecas, and San Fernando de México as both writer and agent of conversion.

At the Colegio de Guatemala, Sor María's expertise in mission administration was invoked in a discourse concerning sites managed by the college's friars. As recorded in Fray Espinosa's *Crónica*, Fray Francisco de San Joseph and Fray Pablo Rebullida wrote to the padre guardián of the Guatemala college expressing their frustration with the presence of soldiers and settlers at the mission site. The letter states that although great numbers of soldiers might lend the appearance of supporting the mission endeavor, Sor María's advice concerning missions and settlements recommended a different approach. They explained: "Es consejo de la V.M. María de Jesús de Agreda que los soldados para las conversiones sean pocos y de buen ejemplo" (It is the recommendation of the Venerable Mother María de Jesús de Ágreda that soldiers sent to missions be few and of good character).[138] The friars add that only a few soldiers are necessary for Franciscan mission sites because, per Sor María's assurances, the Franciscan Order was divinely ordained for success in the mission field: "tiene concedido privilegio a N.P. San Francisco para que todas las naciones se conviertan con sólo ver su hábito" (Our Father San Francisco was granted the privilege that in order for all the nations to be converted, they need only to see his habit [the Franciscan habit]).[139] In their letter, friars Rebullida and San Joseph make clear that they defer to Sor María on matters of secular and religious interactions in recommending that the governor refrain from sending soldiers to their mission.

At the College of Guadalupe de Zacatecas, devotion to Sor María is manifested in the institution's walls.[140] The entrance to the college, which was dedicated in 1721,[141] features a carved bas-relief of the Virgin of Guadalupe, centered over the doorway (see figs. 4.1 and 4.2). St. Francis holds her aloft on his shoulders.[142] The Virgin is flanked by four figures, two on each side, all of which were associated with Marian writing or theology.[143] To the Virgin's right are St. John the Evangelist and St. Luke.

Figure 4.1. Entrance to the College of Guadalupe de Zacatecas. Image courtesy Flikr user Catedrales e Iglesias.

(We discussed St. John's relationship to the Virgin of the Apocalypse/ Immaculate Conception (and therefore Guadalupe) in chapter 3.) St. Luke may be associated with this image because, according to pious tradition, he carved the Virgin of Guadalupe of Extremadura, Spain. To the Virgin of Guadalupe's left are Duns Scotus and Sor María, paired together as in the cover art for *La mística ciudad de dios.*

Figure 4.2. Detail of the entrance to the College of Guadalupe de Zacatecas. Image courtesy Cristina Cruz González.

In the cases of the colleges of Guatemala and Guadalupe de Zacatecas, the incidence of these Agredan gestures allude to the devotion that underpinned those institutions, a ready area of future research. Indeed, other Propaganda Fide colleges that are not discussed in this book (Pachuca, Zapopan, and Cholula) might well be other sites of Agredan development, though their later founding dates (some were established after Sor María's case for canonization case was closed) might have mitigated against this.

The College of San Fernando de México was originally a hospital for Franciscan friars. Located in Mexico City, it became an official college under the leadership of Fray Espinosa in 1733. In the latter half of the eighteenth century, San Fernando college friars were sent to mission regions previously inhabited by Jesuits: the Californias, Arizona, Sonora, and the Sierra Gorda. A painting of Sor María, still located at the college, offers insight into the nature of institutional devotion to her there (see fig. 4.3).[144]

Figure 4.3. Sor María with Virgin of the Immaculate Conception and St. Francis as Atlas Seraphicus. Artist unknown. College of San Fernando, Mexico City. Image courtesy Flikr user Jicito.

The late eighteenth-century painting centers on the Virgin of the Immaculate Conception, who is supported from beneath by St. Francis, again in the posture of "Atlas Seraphicus." He holds aloft three blue spheres representing the three branches of the Franciscan Order. The Virgin rests just above the three spheres, a position alluding to the order's long-standing support of the Immaculate Conception theology. To the left of the Virgin, Sor María sits at a *bufete*, wearing a blue veil, and holding a pen that she uses to write in the open book before her: *La mística ciudad de dios*. Duns Scotus is similarly positioned to the Virgin's right. As depicted for the San Fernando friars, Sor María was central to the Immaculate Conception theology and to Franciscan zeal for it.

Missionaries from the College of San Fernando, including Fray Junípero Serra, would take their passion for Sor María with them into the mission field.[145] One of the earliest manifestations of Sor María's ideological presence at San Fernando is located on the façade of the Santa María de la Purísima Concepción del Agua Mission in Landa in the Sierra Gorda. This mission church, completed in 1768, was one of five constructed in the region under the supervision of the College of San Fernando. The college constructed missions at Jalpan, Tilaco, Concá, Tancoyol, and Landa in the mid- to late eighteenth century. Although it is unclear who designed and supervised the construction of the Landa church (both Fray Junípero Serra and mission superior Fray Miguel de la Campa influenced its development), its stone façade prominently displayed the college's devotion to Sor María for neophytes and friars alike.[146]

A large, recessed octagonal window above the church's entry doors immediately draws the eye (see figs. 4.4 and 4.5). The Virgin of the Immaculate Conception sits between the window and the door, and angels pull away a curtain to expose her to the viewer. The two Franciscan Conceptionist defenders, Sor María and Duns Scotus, sit just above and flanking her.[147] As in the painting at the College of San Fernando, each is seated at a *bufete* with an open book on the table before them. Their hands are poised with quills to write, presumably about the Immaculate Conception, the image maintaining the connection between Sor María, Scotus, and the Immaculate Conception. In this bas-relief, Sor María is incorporated into the very structure of the Landa church as an essential signifier in the mission field.[148]

In addition to Sor María's representation at the Landa church, themes specific to Sor María's writing were inscribed onto other Sierra Gorda churches. On the façade of the Jalpan mission church, both La Virgen del Pilar (patroness of Spain) and the Virgin of Guadalupe (patroness of Mexico) appear. Art historian Monique Gustin suggests that the atypical appearance of the Virgen del Pilar in novohispanic architectural design may be in reference to an episode appearing in *La mística ciudad de dios*. Sor María dedicates particular attention to the narration of the Virgen del Pilar's bilocation to Spain to help Santiago (St. James) in converting the native Iberians to Christianity. The narrative is one of Spain's foundational accounts, but Sor María attends to it in detail in *La mística ciudad de dios*.[149] This allusion to Sor María is less overt than the Landa façade, but it nonetheless implies Sor María's powerful mission presence for the Franciscan friars of the College of San Fernando. In fact, her influence as a writer and a protomissionary achieved perhaps its greatest circulation and visibility in northern New Spain through the college's famous student, Fray Junípero Serra. For Fray Serra, Sor María was a true mission muse who guided his steps in the mission field.

Figure 4.4. Façade of Santa María de la Purísima Concepción del Agua Mission, Landa, Mexico. Image courtesy Wiki Commons, author GAED.

Figure 4.5. Detail of Landa façade. Image source Flikr user Teenek.Ecoadventures.

FRAY JUNÍPERO SERRA, THE COLLEGE OF SAN FERNANDO, AND THE ALTA CALIFORNIA MISSIONS

Fray Serra's devotion to Sor María as a writer and protomissionary was profound, rooted not only in the instruction he received at the College of San Fernando, where he was educated as a missionary, but also in his previous knowledge of the nun. In the *Relación histórica . . . del Venerable Padre Fray Junípero Serra*,[150] Serra's biography by his longtime companion Fray Francisco Palóu, the friar's life as a missionary is bookended by Sor María's writing. Here, and in Fray Serra's letters and diary, the nun's presence is palpable, as are her interventions in the friar's actions and attitudes.

In the second chapter of Fray Palóu's *Relación histórica*, the friar details Fray Serra's call to mission work in the Americas, explaining how Fray Serra determined the genuineness of his vocation: "si era de Dios dicha vocación, tocase el corazón á alguno que lo acompañase en la empresa de tan dilatado viage" (if this calling were from God, that He touch the heart of another [Palóu] who would accompany him in this far-flung

voyage).[151] Fray Palóu, of course, heard the call and accompanied Fray
Serra, but they both were inspired to become missionaries to Mexico in
part because of Sor María's assurances. As both friars knew, Sor María
informed New Mexican friars in her 1631 letter that mission work on the
northern Mexican frontier was the desire of the faithful departed: "[una]
felicidad tan grande que en sentir de la Venerable Madre es envidiable
de los Bienaventurados" (a joy so great that, in the opinion of the Venerable Mother [Sor María], it is the envy of the faithful departed).[152] Fray
Palóu cites the letter for this idea directly: "como lo escribió dicha Sierva
de Dios a los misioneros de Nuestra Seráfica Religión empleados en la
conversión de los Gentiles de la Custodia del Nuevo México" (as the
said Servant of God wrote to the missionaries of our Seraphic Order
[the Franciscans] employed in the conversion of the gentiles in the
custodia of New Mexico).[153] Fray Palóu goes on to say that he will include the letter in its entirety in the *vita*, "á lo último si tengo lugar" (at
the end, if I have space).[154] He notes of this powerful document that it is
particularly valuable as a recruitment tool for new missionaries: "es bas-
tantemente eficaz para animar á todos á que vengan al trabajo de la Viña
del Señor" (it is sufficiently effective to motivate all those who would
come work in the Lord's vineyard).[155] For Fray Palóu and Fray Serra,
Sor María affirmed the work already under way at Franciscan mission
sites—"confirma y aprueba el régimen que acostumbramos en estas
Misiones" (confirms and approves of the regimen to which we are accus-
tomed in theses missions)[156]—reassuring current and future missionaries
of the spiritual value of their work there.

Towards the end of the *Relación histórica*, Fray Palóu includes the
entire *Tanto que se sacó de una carta*. In spite of his concern that the
Relación histórica as a whole might not have encompassed all of Fray
Serra's many virtues, Fray Palóu presses the text to accommodate
the famous and much-cited Agredan document. Fray Palóu reveals in
the process that he was granted permission from his superiors to publish
Sor María's text, because they too believed it would stimulate interest in
the California mission work Fray Serra began: "movería á muchos á
alistarse para Operaciones de la Viña que plantó este exemplar Misio-
nero" (to ready themselves to work in the vineyard planted by that extraordinary missionary [Serra]).[157] But Fray Serra's own reading of Sor
María extended beyond the view of her as a missionary; he regularly put
her recommendations for spiritual practices into action.

Fray Palóu tells us that his companion religiously followed specific practices outlined by Sor María in *La mística ciudad de dios* while in the Sierra Gorda missions. For example, when in Mexico City at the College of San Fernando, Fray Serra wore sandals or shoes; however, in the Sierra Gorda missions, he used *alpargatas* (hemp shoes), in imitation of Christ in his evangelization, as described by Sor María: "[empezó] su oficio de la predicación á imitación de Jesu Christo de las sandalias, como nos lo dice la V. Madre Maria de Jesús de Agreda en su Mística Ciudad (part. 2, lib. 4, cap. 28, num. 685)" ([Serra commenced] the office of preaching in imitation of Jesus Christ and [Christ's] hemp sandals, as we are told by the Venerable Madre María de Jesús de Ágreda in her *Mystical City*, part 2, bk. 4, chap. 28, num. 685).[158] This anecdote is couched in a longer episode explaining Fray Serra's humility, a quality that Fray Palóu also links to Sor María's writing. He says of Fray Serra's implementation of her practices that "esta divina doctrina [la de Sor María] de tal manera se imprimió en su corazón . . . que desde luego propuso en su corazón imitarlo, siguiendo su doctrina en quanto le fuera posible, poniéndola en práctica" (This divine doctrine [by Sor María] in this manner imprinted itself upon Serra's heart . . . such that from that moment on, he set forth in his heart to imitate it, following the doctrine to the extent he could, putting it into practice).[159] Fray Palóu confirms that Fray Serra took copies of *La mística ciudad de dios* with him to the Sierra Gorda, where, as we have already seen, Sor María's writing inspired the design of mission structures.[160]

At the time Fray Serra was sent to the Sierra Gorda, the College of San Fernando had several editions of *La mística ciudad de dios* in its library collection.[161] Not only did Fray Serra and Fray Palóu each have their own set of *La mística ciudad de dios* with them in the Sierra Gorda, but additional copies were also sent to them at the Jalpan mission from the college.[162]

While in the Sierra Gorda and Alta California, Fray Serra continued to conceive of his work as a missionary in light of Sor María's writing on conversions and the mission experience. In 1769, as Fray Serra traveled from Loreto, Baja California, to what would be San Diego, he discussed Sor María in his personal diary, and in a letter to the padre guardián of the San Fernando college, Fray Juan Andrés. On May 18 of that year, Fray Serra recounted in his diary that after baptizing a tribal leader and forty-three of his followers, the leader was renamed "Francisco" in

honor of St. Francis. This was done in recognition of the saint's intervention in the Franciscan Order's conversions, about which Sor María
had provided much information: "de cuya intercesión [la de St. Francis]
píamente creí provenir aquella feliz novedad como cumplimiento de la
palabra que le tiene dada Dios Nuestro Señor en estos últimos siglos
(según afirma la Venerable Madre María de Jesús de Agreda) de que los
gentiles con sólo la vista de sus hijos se han de convertir a nuestra santa
fe católica" (through whose intercession [that of St. Francis] I piously
believed to have resulted that happy circumstance, in fulfillment of the
word attributed to God the Father in these last centuries—as the Venerable Mother María de Jesús affirms—that the gentiles, upon looking at
the sons of St. Francis, would convert to our Holy Faith).[163] Fray Serra
understood the willingness he perceives among the tribes to convert to
Christianity as evidence of Sor María's assurances regarding the friars'
mission labors.

In his letter to Fray Juan Andrés, dated July 3, 1769, Fray Serra says
as much, but he assumes that the recipient will understand what he refers
to when he describes the Franciscans' impact on the tribes. Fray Serra
says of the conversions at the new San Diego mission: "y con la gracia
de Dios me parece que se hará cuanto se quisiere, y que le cumplirá
Dios Nuestro Señor la palabra dada a nuestro Seráfico Padre San Francisco de que con sola la vista de sus hijos se conviertan en estos últimos
siglos los gentiles" (with God's grace, it seems to me that one may convert as many as one wishes, and that God the Father will make good
on his promise given to our Seraphic Father St. Francis in these last
centuries that solely upon seeing his holy sons, the gentiles will be converted).[164] For a confrere, additional explanation of the origins of this
belief was unnecessary; Fray Juan Andrés would have been as aware of
the origins of this belief as were Serra and Palóu.

In 1770, Fray Serra wrote to future minister of the Indies Joseph
Gálvez from Monterrey during the celebration of Corpus Christi. His
letter reveals a truly startling insight into the friar's deep identification
with Agredan mission perspectives. Finding that he lacked the candles
needed to light the Mass, Fray Serra remembered that there was one
lantern in the ship's cabin and he set about searching for it. Fortunately,
and to everyone's great surprise, the searching crew opened a box they
thought contained medical supplies, and instead found several lamps: "se
halló ser de faroles de vidrio sin esttrenar, de que nadie tenía noticia"

(they found glass lamps that had never been used, about which nobody was aware).[165] Finding lamps when least expected would seem simple enough, but Fray Serra's response reveals his deep internalization of Sor María's mission narrative. He says of these lamps that "si no lo[s] trageron los Angeles al menos a nosottros se nos hizo como llovido" (if angels had not brought them, at least to us it seemed as though they had been rained down from heaven).[166] The friar's gentle allusion to angels bringing lamps to the missionaries is based on an anecdote associated with Sor María, which Fray Serra refers to at the outset of the episode, "teniendo pressente el caso que se refiere de los dos religiosos nuesttros llevados al remoto reyno de Titlas" (keeping in mind the well-known case of the two Franciscan friars who were taken to the remote reign of Titlás).[167]

In his preface, Fray Serra reminds Gálvez that the two friars in Texas had found a *custodia* (monstrance) that had arrived there under unusual circumstances: "les fue llevada desde España por manos de Angeles y de la Venerable Madre de Agreda" (that was brought to them from Spain by the hands of angels and by the Venerable Madre Ágreda).[168] In comparing lamps in Monterrey with a monstrance in Texas, Fray Serra does not anachronistically suggest that Sor María brought the lamps to the Monterey mission; rather, he posits that their appearance was as miraculous as her delivery of the monstrance. The parallel Fray Serra draws between the two demonstrates how he conceived of himself and his labor as a continuation of Sor María's protomissionary tradition. Further, the phrasing of the letter assumes that Gálvez—charged with the administration of large portions of northern New Spain where the narrative of Sor Maria's evangelizing travel had long formed part of the historical landscape—would understand Fray Serra's references to the Agredan anecdote and also see the unmistakable similarities between the two incidents.

A 1772 letter from Fray Serra to Fray Palóu, written while the former was at the Monterrey mission, discusses the progress of the project there. In the text, Fray Serra continues to liken his experience and the success of the friars in converting native tribes to Christianity. For him, the manifestation of Sor María's assurances is real and palpable: "Y sobre todo, la promesa hecha por Dios en estos últimos siglos á N.P.S. Francisco (como dice la Seráfica M. María de Jesús) de que los Gentiles con solo ver á sus hijos se han de convertir á nuestra Santa Fé

Católica, ya me parece que la veo y palpo" (And above all, as regards
the promise made by God in these last centuries to our Holy Father
Francis—as the Seraphic Mother María de Jesús says—that the gentiles,
only upon looking at his sons, will convert to our Holy Catholic Faith,
it already seems to me that I see it and touch it).[169] Sor María's assertion
that the Franciscan Order would be effective in the mission field because
it was divinely mandated was being realized under Fray Serra's leadership in California—and Fray Serra himself was carrying out the nun's
charge.

In this same vein, a later letter discussing efforts to move the San
Carlos de Monterrey mission from its previous location to the Carmel
River addresses Fray Serra's responsibilities as an Agredan missionary.
In the letter, Fray Palóu comments that Fray Serra did not foist the
heavy responsibility for this work onto other friars, but rather he himself engaged in the labor. According to Fray Palóu, Fray Serra did so in
part because Sor María declared that such actions were particularly
worthy: "se dirigen á tan noble fin, y son muy del agrado de Dios (como
dice en su citada Carta la V.M. María de de [sic] Jesús)" (it is directed
to such noble ends and [is] pleasing to God—as the Venerable Mother
María de Jesús says in her cited letter).[170] For Fray Serra and Fray Palóu,
the Monterrey conversions and the later relocation of the mission are
conceived of in terms of Sor María's authority on such matters.

The 1771 founding of the Mission San Antonio de Padua is a final
poignant moment when Fray Serra earnestly models his behaviors on
Sor María's protomissionary work. Upon selecting the mission site,
Fray Serra had the church bells immediately unloaded, hung from a
tree, and then he vigorously rang them. When a fellow missionary, Fray
Miguel Pieras, chided Fray Serra for his jubilant turn, Serra replied that
he was simply doing as his mission muse would have in his situation:
"Déxeme, Padre, explayar el corazon, que quisiera que esta campana se
oyese por todo el Mundo, como deseaba la V. Madre Sor María de Jesús
de Agreda," (Allow me, Father, to express my heart's will, which is that
this bell be heard throughout the whole world, as the Venerable Mother
Sor María de Jesús de Ágreda herself desired).[171] This ringing incident
shows that Fray Serra truly viewed his world as a missionary through
lenses colored by Sor María, and behaved in ways he believed to be consistent with her conversion mandates. For Fray Serra, the Sor María who
converted the Jumanos was an authority on his own missions, and her
writing remained with him throughout his life, and his progress along

the California coast can be mapped by where copies of *La mística ciudad de dios* were left at its missions.

"Que descuido . . . decir como quien no quiere la cosa que la relación de la Vuestra Madre Agreda es fabulosa": The College of San Fernando and Sor María in Late Eighteenth-Century Alta California

Fray Serra's and Fray Palóu's devotion to Sor María in the California missions is well documented, but they were by no means the only members of the College of San Fernando who held the nun's writing and the legacy of the Lady in Blue in high esteem. Other San Fernando mission friars later reported an addendum to Serra's Agredan experiences in California. The episode took place at the Mission San Antonio and was likely recounted to Fray Palóu by friars who were stationed there, including Pieras and Verger.[172] The friars reported that a very old woman around one hundred years old, named "Agueda," arrived to the San Antonio mission to be baptized by the friars there.[173] She claimed that a long time ago, a man dressed like the friars, but who had the ability to fly, visited her tribe and instructed them in the doctrine the missionaries were teaching. According to the friars at the mission, other members of her tribe confirmed this account. Fray Palóu concludes in his explanation of the encounter that the individual who visited this tribe must have been one of the two Franciscan friars who traveled to "Titlás," as reported in a 1631 letter from Sor María and Alonso de Benavides to the friars in New Mexico.[174] A 1776 letter sent from the College of San Fernando to Carlos III reiterated this same idea:

> La de dos religiosos que dice la misma sierva de Dios que por su intercesión llevó Nuestro Santo Padre San Francisco al reino de Titlás el que según la misma Venerable Madre deberá estar al oriente de la gran Quivira y tal vez puede ser que alguno de estos padres sea el que vieron aquellos gentiles en el paraje en que hoy día está la misión de San Antonio de Padua, pues sucedió según parece en aquel mismo tiempo como consta de la Relación de la misma Venerable Madre impresa en esta capital el año de 1730.

———

The account of the two friars that the same servant of God says were taken to Titlás by Our Hold Father Saint Francis through her intercession, [Titlás being a place that] according to the same Venerable Mother should lie to the east of Gran Quivira, and it may be that one of these friars could have been he whom the gentiles from the place which is now Mission San Antonio de Padua saw, as it seems to have taken place at that same time, as we know for a fact from the *Relación* by the same Venerable Mother printed in this capital [Mexico City] in 1730.[175]

Other Californian friars from the later seventeenth and early eighteenth centuries continued to reference Sor María, and many cited tribal histories that recalled a Catholic evangelization predating Fray Serra and Fray Palóu, including the well-known account of "the padre of the *mamas*" (the priest with breasts).[176]

The 1776 *Manifiesto* demonstrated the College of San Fernando's continued dedication to Sor María as a writer and authority on the college's Alta California mission purview in other ways.[177] It was written by several San Fernando friars, many of whom participated in the California mission project and reported on exploration and discoveries in Alta California.[178] As a point of reference for new information about Quivira and the Strait of Anián, Sor María's authoritative expertise on Quivira is invoked throughout the *Manifiesto*, and the San Fernando friars ardently defend her knowledge of the mission field.

In fact, the *Manifiesto* deploys Sor María's history, writing, and authority on the region as a framing device. At the beginning of the document, the friars reference Sor María's 1643 petition to Felipe IV requesting that the Virgin Mary be named patroness of the Spanish Crown.[179] The *Manifiesto* notes that although Sor María was unsuccessful in this attempt, many years later the Virgin of the Immaculate Conception was declared patroness of Spain and its colonies.[180] The friars' linking of a prescient Sor María and the later establishment of the Immaculate Conception as patroness shows how well versed the San Fernando graduates were in Sor María's biography and relationship to the Immaculate Conception theology.

Farther along, the *Manifiesto* discusses the Strait of Anián (northern passage to the east),[181] which was thought to be close to Alta California. It compares several different reports on it, including the *Historia de la*

California (1757), written by Jesuit Miguel Venegas. Fray Venegas's account discounted other reports on the strait, namely, *Monarquía Indiana* by Fray Juan de Torquemada, and Sor María's description in the 1631 letter. The critique of Sor María piqued the ire of the *Manifiesto*'s authors, who found Fray Venegas's assessment of her utterly unacceptable: "y lo que más sentimos atropellando lo que de su firma dejó escrito la Vuestra Madre Sor María de Jesús de Agreda" (that which most offends us [in Venegas's text] is [the critique of] what the Mother Sor María de Jesús de Ágreda left written and signed by her own hand).[182] To Fray Venegas's accusations that those reports on Anián were "de puras conjecturas" (of pure conjecture),[183] the San Fernando friars indignantly responded: "¡Quién ha de creer que procedio por puras conjecturas escribiendo ciudades fabulosas! Nosotros no lo pensamos así" (Who could believe that this was pure conjecture, coming up with fantastical cities [such as Quivira]! We do not see it this way).[184] Further along in the *Manifiesto*, the friars continue to energetically reject Fray Venegas's assessment of Sor María:

> La censura [de Fray Venegas] si carece de apoyo, y piedad: de apoyo por que no se funda en razón, ni autoridad; y de piedad por que por su antojo dice ser fabuloso lo que la Vuestra Madre Sor María de Jesús de Agreda afirma haber visto. Esta Sierva de Dios desde el año de 1620 hasta el de 1631 innumerable veces fue llevada por ministerio de Angeles a predicar el Santo Evangelio a los indios de Nuevo México y otros de este Reino como se ve en su vida escrita por el Ilustrissimo Samaneigo paragrafo 12 y en una relación que cita el padre custodio fray Alonso de Benavides impresa después en esta ciudad de México año 1730 cuyo original para en el archivo de la custodia del Nuevo México.

———

> The censure [of Fray Venegas] is baseless and lacking in piety; baseless because it is not founded in reason, nor in authority; and lacking in piety because it capriciously says that what Our Mother Sor María de Jesús de Ágreda confirms having seen is confabulation. This Servant of God was, from the year 1620 to 1631, taken innumerable times by the ministry of angels to preach the Holy Gospel to the Indians of New Mexico and to others of this kingdom as one

sees in her *vita*, written by the Illustrious Samaniego, paragraph 12, and in another *Relación* [*Tanto que se sacó de una carta*], that cites the Father Custodian Fray Alonso de Benavides, printed later in this City of Mexico in 1730, the original of which is located in the archive of the custodia of New Mexico.[185]

The emphatic defense of Sor María as a reliable source on Quivira continues. The San Fernando friars considered petty those who, like Fray Venegas, would discredit Sor María's account. Ultimately, they declare baseless his critiques of the nun's expertise and double down on her importance as an historical actor in Spain's (and all of Christianity's) history:

> Que descuido tambien premeditado, y que sagacidad la de este autor para decir como quien no quiere la cosa que la relación de la Vuestra Madre Agreda es fabulosa, y consiguientemente lo es tambien la gloria, y honor que de ella resulta no solamente a la religión seráfica como mas interesada sino a toda la nación Española, y aun al cristianismo entero.

> ———

> What premeditated carelessness, and what craftiness of this author to say, as one who does not love the thing, that the account of Our Mother Ágreda is confabulation, and that, consequentially, so are the glory and the honor that through her is reflected not only onto the Seraphic Religion, as a most interested party, but also on the entire Spanish nation, and even onto all of Christendom.[186]

Then, in a revealing twist that shows their allegiance to Sor María as a writer, the San Fernando friars bring the proven legitimacy of *La mística ciudad de dios* to bear on her authority regarding Quivira.

The *Manifiesto* enumerates the numerous examinations of *La mística ciudad de dios* by Church officials, noting that Sor María's critics were convinced of the book's legitimacy: "El crédito mayor de estos libros son ellos mismos: más no es pequeña confirmación el haber sido tan examinado, y aprobado el espíritu de la Venerable Madre Sor María de Jesús que los escribió" (The greatest quality of these books is the books themselves: it is no small thing to have been so closely examined and to have the spirit of the Venerable Mother Sor María who wrote the books proven).[187] Turning the tables on Jesuit Venegas, the San Fernando friars invoke Fray Andrés Mendo, a Jesuit examiner of *La mística ciudad de dios* and influential proponent of Sor María's writing, using a member of Fray Venegas's own order to discredit his views on Sor María.

The *Manifiesto* continued to develop the case for Sor María's authority on Quivira by pointing to other examples of her influence, including her lifelong correspondence with Felipe IV: "Grande apoyo es también de la seguridad del espíritu, y de los escritos de esta Sierva de Dios el haber tenido con ella por muy largo tiempo (veinte, y dos años) frecuente comunicación por cartas el Señor Felipe IV" (Another show of her wholeness of spirit and for the writing of this Servant of God is having shared for a very long time—twenty-two years—frequent communication through letters with King Felipe IV).[188] The San Fernando friars bring Sor María's biography as a writer and royal confidant to bear directly on the question of her knowledge of the mission field, erasing any doubt as to whether she should be considered a credible source.

For further evidence of Sor María's unimpeachable character, the San Fernando friars argued, one need look no further than her obedient response to Fray Benavides when questioned about her travels to New Mexico:

> Preguntada confesó que a el mismo con los otros religiosos habia visto en ellas [las regiones de Nuevo México] señalando el día, hora y lugar en que le habia cisto [*sic*] la gente que llevaba en su compañía, y las señas individuales de cada una como lo dice el citado Samaniego con otras circunstancias que nos hacern [*sic*] creer ser verdadera la dicha relación, y consiguiente la existencia de la Quivira.

> ———

> When asked, she confessed that she had seen him [Benavides] with the other friars in those [regions of New Mexico] explaining the day, hour, and place in which she had seen the people he had in his company, and the individual characteristics of each, as the cited Samaniego says, which, along with other circumstances, make us believe the said account is true, and by extension, so is the existence of Quivira.[189]

Citing these virtues of obedience to superiors, and the honesty and completeness in recounting her travels to New Mexico, the *Manifiesto* presented an irreproachable Sor María whose descriptions of Quivira were beyond censure. The San Fernando friars conclude their argument by associating Sor María's geographical expertise with her renown as the author of *La mística ciudad de dios*: "En atención a lo dicho no dudamos sino que piadosamente creemos con toda aquella firmeza que nos es permitida que la consavida Venerable Madre Sor María de Jesús habrá presentado en el cielo los obsequios de Vuestra real Majestad para la Inmaculada Virgen" (Regarding what has already been said, we do not doubt—in fact we faithfully believe with all the conviction we can muster—that the well-known Venerable Mother Sor María de Jesús will have presented gifts from Your Royal Majesty to the Immaculate Virgin in heaven).[190] In resting their case for Sor María's vision of Quivira, the San Fernando friars show their manifest devotion to the nun as spiritual author, a woman whose influence was felt in the mission field and beyond.

Throughout the late seventeenth and eighteenth centuries, the Propaganda Fide colleges of Santa Cruz de Querétaro, Guadalupe de Zacatecas, and San Fernando sent Franciscan friars to New Spain's northern frontier, who brought with them a muse, mission exemplar, and spiritual writer in Sor María de Jesús de Ágreda. Yet the Franciscans were not the only order stationed in the area that understood Sor María as an author, and also knew of the parallel "tradición" of her mystical travels there. In the writings of Jesuit friars and their military escorts in Arizona, Baja California, and Pimería Alta, Sor María emerged in mission discourse.

"Ay tradisión de que vino desde España milagrosamente":[191] The Lady in Blue in Northern New Spanish Jesuit Missions

Although Franciscan enthusiasm for Sor María was far greater than that of other orders in New Spain, the Jesuits were also familiar with *La mística ciudad de dios* and the narratives associated with Sor María. Mexican Jesuits' awareness of the book was in part due to its prevalence in New Spain and also resulted from the order's advocacy of Immaculate Conception theology; the nineteenth-century transformation of the doctrine into dogma depended on several key arguments by Jesuit theologians. In chapter 3 we showed that Jesuit Basilio Arrillaga's 1844 *Defensa de La mística ciudad de Dios* responded to a negative critique of the text published in the Mexican newspaper *El Constitucional*.[192] For some Jesuits in northern New Spain, Sor María was a historical proto-missionary understood in relationship to the Jesuits' mission environment and objectives of conversion.

Shortly after Damián Manzanet's and Alonso de León's late seventeenth-century Texas expeditions, Jesuit missionary Fray Eusebio Kino traveled to "Pimería Alta," present-day Arizona and Sonora. Fray Kino was accompanied by Lt. Juan Mateo Manje, Jesuit friar Luis Velarde, and other Jesuit missionaries, and his brief account of the Lady in Blue in Pimería Alta has been frequently cited. In book 6, chapter 6 (February 7, 1699), Kino explains his party's exploration to the Río Azul and Hopi territory, and mentions Sor María.[193] Kino refers to the "tradición" of Sor María in the context of that region and of the Franciscan Order:

Grasias a infinita bondad del Señor, tan patentemente logramos el deseado desengaño de si los naturales del Rio Grande o del Rio de los Apóstoles y sus contornos tatemavan y comian gente, que el Señor Theniente Juan Mateo Manje, en su curiosa y aseada relacion que escrivió de esta entrada, por aver tanta afabilidad, amor y cariño destas nuevas gentes, dize era de parezer que años antes la Venerable Madre de Jesús de Agreda les avia venido a domesticar e instruir, como ay tradision de que vino desde España milagrosamente a instruir algunas otras Naciones del Nuevo México. Que los Rev. Padres de San Francisco las allavan ya algo catequizadas.

——————

Thanks to the infinite goodness of the Lord, we discovered the wished-for disillusion regarding whether the natives of the Río Grande or of the Río de los Apóstoles [Gila River] and their periphery roasted and ate people; Lieutenant Juan Mateo Manje, in the inquisitive and orderly account he wrote of this exploration, and out of the geniality, love, and affection among these new peoples, says that it seems that years before, the Venerable Mother María de Jesús de Ágreda had come to them to domesticate and instruct them, as there is a tradition that she came from Spain miraculously to instruct other nations of New Mexico. That the Reverend Fathers of Saint Francis found them already somewhat catechized.[194]

Immediately after this explanation, Fray Kino offers another explanation for the tribes' "afabilidad, amor y cariño" (geniality, love, and affection) toward the Jesuit friars. According to Kino, the tribes' willingness to convert could have been the fruit of concrete Jesuit mission efforts: "otros an sido de parecer que la venturossa sangre del V.P. Francisco Xavier Saeta, fertilisa y zazona todas estas tan dilatadas mieses" (others are of the impression that the fortunate blood of the Venerable Father Francisco Xavier Saeta fertilizes and ripens these vast fields).[195] Kino draws from his biography of Francisco Javier Saeta, who was killed at the Caborca mission four years before, and suggests his brother Jesuit's influence may also have produced the much-desired conversions. Fray Kino nonetheless shows that he was aware of the relevance of the "tradición" of Sor María to the region.

In contrast with Kino's tentative and brief discussion of Sor María, his military escort Juan Mateo Manje's description is as extensive as any Franciscan mission friar's. In Manje's report on the expedition, the *Luz de tierra incógnita en la América septentrional y diario de las exploraciones en Sonora*, Manje discusses Sor María both as a missionary and in relationship to her writing.

In the text's second volume, Manje explains why he believes Sor María must have visited the Pima Indians prior to the arrival of his expedition. When questioning the Pimas as to whether they had encountered Spanish explorers in the area before Fray Kino's group, Manje anticipated that the Pimas would have some memory of Juan de Oñate's expeditionary parties, which had been in the near vicinity of Pimería Alta in the early seventeenth century. Manje reports that the Pima offered a different account instead:

Añadieron (sin ofrecernos preguntar la tal cosa) que siendo ellos muchachos, vino a sus tierras una mujer blanca y hermosa vestida de blanco, pardo y azul, hasta los pies y un paño o velo con que cubría la cabeza, la cual les hablaba y gritaba, y reñía, con una cruz, en lengua que no entendían y que las naciones del río Colorado la flecharon y dejaron por muerta dos veces y que resucitada se iba por el aire sin saber donde era su casa y vivienda, y a pocos días volvía muchas veces a reñirlos; lo mismo nos habían dicho días antes en la ranchería de San Marcelo a que no dábamos ascenso, pero confirmando éstos lo mismo y en lugares tan apartados, discurrimos si acaso la venerable María de Jesús de Agreda, por decir en la Relación de su vida que por los años de 1,630 predicó a los indios gentiles de esta Septentrional América y contornos del Nuevo México, y habiendo pasado 68 años hasta el corriente en que nos dan esta noticia los viejos que parecen según el aspecto de 80 años pueden acordarse.

————

They added (without us asking anything about it) that when they were young boys, a beautiful white woman dressed in white, gray-brown, and blue down to her feet, and with a cloth or veil covering her head, came to their lands, and she spoke to them and shouted at them, and scolded them, with a cross, in a language they did not understand; and that nations from the Río Colorado shot her with arrows and left her for dead twice, and once she had resuscitated she would head off in the air without knowing where her home and dwelling place were; and a few days later she would come back several times to scold them. We had been told the same thing five days previous at the San Marceló settlement, but did not put much store in it, but the confirmation of it by these people, who were so far from the first group, led us to ponder if by chance the venerable María de Jesús de Ágreda, as it says in the *Account* of her life, that around the year 1630 she preached to the Indian gentiles of this Northern America and outskirts of New Mexico, and since 68 years had passed between that year and the present in which we were informed of this account, the older folks who seemed to be about 80 years old can recall.[196]

Manje asserts that the Pima offered this anecdote without prompting, and he corroborates their story with a similar one he had heard five days earlier from tribes living near the San Marceló settlement. According to Manje, both versions recalled a beautiful veiled woman dressed in white, gray-brown, and blue who visited carrying a cross, and would scold ("reñía") the tribes in an unknown language. The tribes shot her with arrows twice, and both times she rose up into the air and returned to rebuke them. Manje corroborates this account with the dates when Sor

María had traveled to New Mexico, calculating how far back his informants' memory might have extended, and estimating whether they could have witnessed the events themselves.

Manje continues to develop the idea of Sor María's presence in Pimería Alta, referencing the *vita*'s version of the Lady in Blue narrative. He finds a small inconsistency between the two, which he strives to resolve. In the Pima account, the mysterious woman harangued the tribe in a language they did not understand; in contrast, Sor María's *vita* assured that, although she was unsure how she communicated with the tribes, they definitely comprehended what she was telling them. Manje suggests that the difference in the Pima narrative did not describe a lack of comprehension on the tribe's part. Rather, he suggests various reasons why it might have seemed to the Pima they didn't understand or they expressed the idea that they did not understand, when in fact the tribe had fully grasped Sor María's message:

> Solo reparamos el añadir no la entendían por que Dios obrando el mayor milagro de ser conducida a estas regiones desde España, no hace las cosas imperfectas y le había de dar el don de lenguas para ser entendida, así, pues, a lo principal sigue lo accesorio de ser ella, pero como ha pasado tanto tiempo y ser entonces muchachos harían poco concepto en lo que les enseñaba o el Demonio, caos de confusión, los confundió después borrándoles la memoria, o será los que notamos en estas naciones, en que hablándoles en distinta lengua a la suya, aunque la entiendan usan de la frase de no la entienden, para explicar que no es su lengua. Apunto sólo esto, por si en algún tiempo se hicieran más individuales pesquisas con las naciones del Norte.

––––––

We must hasten to add that they did not understand her because the Lord, working the greater miracle of bringing her to these regions from Spain, does nothing imperfectly, and must have given her the gift of languages to make herself known; thus, therefore, the foremost aspect is followed by the more incidental fact of being her, but as so much time has passed, and since they were children then, that would have had little idea of what she taught them, or the devil—chaos of confusion—confused them later on, erasing their memories, or perhaps it is a case of what we observe among these nations, that when speaking to them in a language different from their own, although they understand, they use the expression that they do not understand, to show that it was not their language. I note this only in case at some point additional inquiries are made into the nations of the north.[197]

For Manje, the passing of years and the possible intervention of the devil, and the tribes' means of explaining the differences among languages, were all explanations for why their account of the Lady in Blue did not square with Sor María's *vita*.

In other parts of *Luz de tierra incógnita*, Manje proves to be a devotee of Sor María's writing. Little is known about Manje's life aside from what he himself says; thus it is difficult to ascertain where he acquired his knowledge of Sor María.[198] Manje may also have been influenced by Franciscan friars in Mexico, and he cites the 1631 letter from Sor María to the New Mexican missionaries that would be published in 1730 as the *Tanto que se sacó de una carta*. At the time Manje composed *Luz de tierra incógnita*, between 1694 and 1701, the letter had not been published yet in Mexico; it was, however, distributed as a manuscript in Franciscan circles. Manje knew the letter well, and sees in its message concerning evangelization in the borderlands an affirmation of the Jesuit friars' work in Pimería Alta: "dice el Señor por la Venerable María de Ag(r)eda, que el servicio más grato a su Divina Majestad y a quien da más grados de gloria, es a las almas que se emplean en convertir a otras y las obras que recibe con más agrado y complacencia que dirá su carta" (the Lord says through the Venerable María de Ágreda that the most pleasing service one can offer his Divine Majesty, and to whom he gives the greater degree of glory, are the souls employed in the conversion of others, and these are the works He receives with the greatest pleasure and satisfaction, as her letter says).[199]

Manje details the narrative of La Virgen del Pilar, a theme that Sor María develops in *La mística ciudad de dios*, in explaining the conversions the Jesuits' experience. Manje develops a parallel between the conversion of the Apache nation by Jesuit friars and the conversion of the "cesaragustanos,"[200] or Zaragozans, of Spain by St. James the Greater (Santiago). Santiago, discouraged at the Zaragossans' unwillingness to convert, is revived by the appearance of La Virgen del Pilar, who travels from Jerusalem to Zaragoza. Manje surmises that such miracles occur "por que entendamos que [los] mandatos [de Dios] embeben diferentes sentidos que nuestra limitada comprensión alcanza" (because we understand that [God's] commands draw in different senses, other than those our limited understanding can grasp).[201] Bringing the account to bear on the Jesuits and Apaches, Manje concludes that the nations that are the most difficult to convert are also those whose conversions are the longest-lasting, a double metaphor for the Apaches yet to be converted and the Spanish that Santiago evangelized.

Manje's "Protesta del autor" (author's protest) exhibits the lieutenant's nuanced understanding of Sor María's provisional status within the Catholic Church. Sor María's case for sainthood was well under way when Manje wrote in the late seventeenth century, but the status of both the *causa* and *La mística ciudad de dios* were uncertain. Recognizing this and perhaps anticipating criticism for his discussion of Sor María, Manje cites a prohibition warning against "dar culto de santidad o de mártires o varones que de esta vida pasaron sin estar declarado por tales en el oráculo del Espíritu Santo" (giving rise to a devotional cult of sanctity or martyrdom or [saintly men] who passed through this life without being declared as such in the oracle of the Holy Spirit).[202] In reference to the bull, Manje declares that, although he calls individuals in his text by the titles "Santo," "Beato," and "Venerable" (as in the case of Sor María), "no es [mi] intención (ni que lo entiendan otros) caigan tales elogios sobre las personas" (it is not [my] intention—nor should others understand it to be—that unearned praise fall upon these persons).[203] He reaffirms that the titles he employs are not intended to suggest sanctity, as the right to determine that quality "está reservado, toca y pertenece a la infalible decisión de la Santa Sede Católica" (is reserved, belongs to, and pertains to the infallible decision of the Holy See).[204] Though he refers to Sor María almost exclusively as the "Venerable Madre" and esteems her, Manje ensures such references are not misread as official endorsements of her.

The majority of *Luz de tierra incógnita*'s first book summarizes other histories of discovery and exploration in the Americas prior to Manje's expedition, discussing variously the end of the Spanish Reconquista,[205] and the Spanish presence in Peru and Chile,[206] the Philippines,[207] and New Mexico.[208] Manje describes the geography and flora and fauna of the Americas,[209] the nature of the religious hierarchy there,[210] and various specific cases of indigenous conversion to Christianity.[211]

His fascinating narration about the creation of the magnetic compass needle in his chapter 4 (which he claims was used for the conversion American populations) provides Manje the opportunity to cite *La mística ciudad de dios*. Echoing chronographies by Fray Agustín de Vetancurt and Cayetano Verdiguer that were based on Sor María's writing, Manje draws on *La mística ciudad de dios* to support the claim that 5,200 years had elapsed between the creation of the universe and the birth of Jesus. For the next twenty-three chapters, Manje recounts the history of exploration and conversion on the northern frontiers of Spain's empire—the Californias, Florida, and New Mexico. He reserves the last two chapters of this first book, chapters 26 and 27, for Sor María, her life, and her travels to New Mexico.

These chapters on Sor María were meant to "coronar esta obra" (crown this work).[212] Manje includes ideas about New Mexico attributed to Sor María because, according to him, they provide vital information on "las gentilidades de esta América Septentrional" (the peoples of this North America).[213] In chapter 26, Manje presents a biography of Sor María, seemingly derived from her *vita* and the 1631 letter to New Mexican friars. Manje details her birth, family history, and the founding of the religious community in her family's home. He cites texts other than *La mística ciudad de dios* that Sor María wrote, including "el tratado que por obediencia escribió que llamó escala" (the treatise she wrote out of obedience, entitled *Escala*), probably a reference to the *Escala para subir a la perfección*.[214] The chapter recounts the physical trials that Sor María experienced as a young woman, detailing how her increasingly intense spiritual *exterioridades* culminated in ecstatic experiences during which the tribes of New Mexico were revealed to her. Manje continues in this vein, commenting extensively on Sor María's mystical experiences: her conversions in New Mexico,[215] her blue robes,[216] the debate regarding whether her travels were corporeal or spiritual,[217] and her eventual meeting with Fray Alonso de Benavides at her convent in Ágreda.[218]

In chapter 27, Manje cites two paragraphs relating to Sor María that originated in Fray Gerónimo Zárate Salmerón's 1628 *Relaciónes*.[219] These were attributed to Mexican archbishop Manso y Zúñiga and addressed the possibility of mystical evangelization in New Mexico by Sor María. Manje provides context for these two paragraphs, explaining that many native people continued to ask about the woman missionary after 1628: "Lo que yo sé acerca de esto, no por revelación que soy muy malo . . . digo que no llegó indio alguno de la tierra adentro del Nuevo México que no le preguntase los secretos de ella" (what I know of this is not from revelations, for I am very bad [poor in spirit] . . . I say that there was no Indian who came to us from the inland area of New Mexico who did not ask about her secrets).[220] Manje interjects an intriguing commentary on the loss of a collection of documents pertaining to New Mexico's history during the 1680 Pueblo Revolt. He claims that a copy of the 1631 letter and a "cuadro" (painting) disappeared,[221] suggesting that additional records of Sor María's travels to New Mexico at one pointed existed. Manje also includes an excerpt of "la carta exhortatoria de la Venerable Madre,"[222] the 1631 letter to the New Mexican friars, and selectively cites specific portions: Sor María's obedience to her male superiors, the kingdoms she visited and converted, the divine importance of the friars' work for conversion, and her recommendations regarding mission settlement. He specifies that Sor María admonished "que los gobernadores pudieran ordenar, los acompañen [a los frailes] algunos soldados de buena vida y costumbres" (that governors may order that the friars are accompanied by a few soldiers of good character and habits)[223]—perhaps also reflecting on himself as Kino's military escort, and referring to the 1631 letter. As Manje's many references to a variety of sources that discussed Sor María show, the lieutenant was well-read in the Lady in Blue narrative and Sor María's writing.

The chapter transitions into a lamentation of the absence of missionary zeal and rigor, which, according to Manje, Sor María had exhorted the New Mexican friars to preserve. Manje's writing here arrives at its apogee, pulling from the momentum of Sor María's text to confirm the importance of the missionaries in the mission field. Manje concludes by echoing Sor María's assertion that the work of conversion in the northern New Spanish frontier was the envy of the faithful departed, and in such mission labor one can see reflected the "Gloria de los evangélicos ministros que se emplean en la conversión de las almas gentílicas" (Glory of the evangelical ministers who are employed in the conversion of gentiles),[224] an extension of Sor María's idea on the matter.

The first book of *Luz de tierra incógnita* makes evident that Juan Mateo Manje not only viewed Sor María as a major historical figure in the region, on par with explorers such as Juan de Oñate and Francisco Coronado, but also that he had a working knowledge of her writing and viewed her as an exemplary missionary figure.

There are similarities between Manje's report and that of Fray Luis Velarde, a Jesuit friar who accompanied Manje and Kino. Fray Velarde's text on Pimería Alta, completed May 30, 1716, (after Kino's death)[225] is very similar to Manje's in terms of how it discusses the Lady in Blue, but it includes some additional details:[226]

Lograráse averiguar que misterio tendrá lo que dicen los Pimas del Norte, de una mujer española que en años pasados salía a temporadas de una casa de la otra banda del Colorado a predicar lo que predican los padres y a enseñar a aquellos naturales gentiles el camino del Cielo, lo cual conviene con lo que se lee en la vida de la Venerable Madre María de Jesús, conocida por el nombre de la Venerable Agreda, y mucho más por sus celestiales escritos que muchas veces fue vista en las partes del Nuevo México y adyacentes, predicándole quizás y repartir rosarios y otros donecillos a los indios, lo cual se averiguó en la manera que se escribe en su vida a que me remito y de aquí puede ser se origine la divisa de los crucíferos.

———

Seek to understand what is meant by what the Northern Pimas say, regarding a Spanish woman who years ago would go out periodically from a house belonging to the other community of the Colorado [River] to preach what the friars preached, and to teach to those natural gentiles the path to heaven, all of which agrees with what one reads in the life of the Venerable Mother María de Jesús, known as the Venerable Ágreda, and even more so for her heavenly writings, who was seen many times in parts of New Mexico and nearby areas, preaching perhaps and distributing rosaries and other gifts to the Indians, all of which may be seen in how it is written in her *vita*, which I return to myself, and it may be that this is the source of the cross motif.[227]

In discussing the possibility that Sor María converted the tribes of Pimería Alta before the Jesuits' arrival, Fray Velarde specifies that they might have also received some of the rosaries she was rumored to have distributed when she traveled to New Mexico. He offers the tentative hypothesis that her travels might have also influenced the cross-like motif ("la divisa de los crucíferos," "the cross emblem") he observed among the Pima.

Fray Velarde's version of these events differs from both Kino's and Manje's accounts. He is more sanguine than Kino, affirming that "muchas veces fue vista en las partes de Nuevo Mexico y adyacentes" (she was seen many times in parts of New Mexico and nearby) and suggesting that she traveled in her body. However, he is less assertive that Manje, saying that the Pimas' report happens to coincide with the Lady in Blue narrative: "conviene con lo que se lee en la vida de la Venerable Agreda" (it agrees with what we read in the *vita* of the Venerable Ágreda). Interestingly, Fray Velarde notes that the nun's fame and the rumor of her sanctity were primarily the result of the popularity of her writing; she was "conocida por el nombre de la Venerable Agreda, y mucho más por sus celestiales escritos" (known by the name of the Venerable Ágreda, and much more for her celestial writing). Fray Velarde's comments imply that he had read Sor María's writing himself, or he was at the very least aware of it.

The Kino/Manje expedition was not the only Jesuit report on the northern New Spanish frontier to mention the Lady in Blue narrative and Sor María's writing. Jesuit missionary José Augustín de Campos's account draws on prior reports of Sor María in the region. In a 1723 proposal by Fray Campos pertaining to the settlement of Pimería Alta—directed to the New Spanish viceroy, the Marquis of Casafuerte—he includes the Lady in Blue in a discussion about the region of "Florida."[228] Fray Campos had already been a missionary for thirty years when he composed the account, having accompanied Fray Kino in his 1693 expedition. In 1695, Fray Campos accompanied Domingo Jironza to assess the damage at the Misión Nuestra Señora de la Concepción del Caborca, after Jesuit Fray Francisco Javier Saeta's death there in April of that year.[229] Fray Campos himself narrowly avoided Fray Saeta's fate at Mission Dolores shortly thereafter. He had been stationed in the region, rebuilding and administering missions, and he was later sent to Mexico City in 1722.[230]

Clearly no stranger to the Pimería Alta missions, Fray Campos's account is "un plan para colonizar el noreste de la Pimería, con la fundación de una villa en el remate donde el río Terrenate entra en el Gila" (a plan to colonize the north of Pimería, with the foundation of a town at the point where the Terrenate River meets with the Gila River) and a proposal for the "reducción" (establishment of permanent mission settlements) of the Moqui (Hopi) nation of east-central Arizona.[231] In the midst of a description of the indigenous nations living near the Río Colorado, Fray Campos includes the following anecdote:

Decía el mismo Padre haberle contado los indios esta rareza: haber una casa o salón, donde vive una mujer sola, que ya no habla con nadie. Venla salirse como a pasear, y se vuelve. Dan a entender suele estar escribiendo en su casa; que antiguamente les hablaba y enseñaba varias cosas, y solía repartirles algunos donecillos. Discurría el padre si sería la venerable madre María de Jesús de Agreda. Fundábase en lo que en su vida, por el padre Samaniego, se refiere de su transmigración, por virtud divina, a las regiones del Nuevo México, y el caso de los rosarios. Cotejado el convenir indios ignorantísimos de historias distantes tantas mil leguas de España, con la relación de su vida, parece impele a una probable verdad. Esta, Dios la sabe y sus fines.

———

The same priest said that the Indians told him this oddity: there was a house or room, where a woman lived alone, who no longer spoke with anyone. They would see her go out as if to walk, and she would return. She was understood to be writing in her house; in the past she spoke with them and taught them many things, and would distribute some small gifts among them. The priest reflected whether it could be the Venerable Mother María de Jesús de Ágreda. He based this on what was said in her *vita*, by Father Samaniego, where her transmigration by divine means to the regions of New Mexico is discussed, as is the case of the rosaries. Comparing the Indians, who are ignorant of distant histories so many thousands of leagues from Spain, with the account of her life, it would seem to impel a probable truth. This, God knows and its ends.[232]

Although Fray Campos gives credit to another friar for the account he heard, what he shares adds much to previous Jesuits' reports on Sor María in Pimería Alta. Notably, Fray Campos's story involves an individual who was still alive at the time he wrote. This mysterious woman lived and wrote, but no longer spoke with or taught the people as she did in the past, nor did she share small gifts with them. In spite of the fact that Sor María had died more than fifty years previous, Fray Campos surmises that perhaps the solitary individual is Sor María, who had remained there after the "transmigración" described in her *vita*, which he is knowledgeable enough about to reference. Most remarkably, he finds this correlation between Sor María and the woman described in the account he hears "una probable verdad." This bold assertion is even more surprising when taken in the context of his assurances elsewhere in the document that he scrupulously distinguishes between fact and fiction in the text: his petition presents "lo cierto como cierto, lo dudoso como dudoso" (the certain as certain, and the doubtful as doubtful).[233] For Jesuit Campos and his facts-only text, a complete report on the area near the Gila River demanded mention of Sor María and of her continued presence there.

The Jesuits' vision of Sor María in their mission field extended beyond the order itself, circulating back to neighboring Franciscans. Two decades after Fray Campos wrote, Fray Carlos Delgado, a Franciscan stationed at the San Felipe Presidio in New Mexico, cited reports from Jesuit missionaries who had occupied areas neighboring the Hopi tribe. Writing in 1746, Fray Delgado recounts what he had heard from the Jesuits nearby:

> Los honorables Padres Jesuitas me dijeron . . . cómo nuestra Madre María de Agreda se halla todavía en las vertientes de Moqui en vía corpórea, cuia noticia tienen de los Indios gentiles q' por allá transitan . . . noticia que puede alegrar a Vuestra Ilustrísima para q' vea cómo nuestra apreciada misionera nos está ayudando a cultivar la Viña del Señor.

> ———

> The honorable Jesuit priests told me . . . about how our Mother María de Ágreda is still found in the outer slopes of Moqui in corporal form, which they have heard about from the gentile Indians who pass through that area . . . news that may cheer Your Grace so as to see how our esteemed missionary is helping us cultivate the Lord's vineyard.[234]

The Franciscans' "apreciada misionera" was reported by the Jesuits to still be physically present at or near Hopi mission sites in the mid-eighteenth century, perhaps an ongoing recollection of what Campos reported. Fray Delgado sees in the Jesuits' account a positive reflection on the Franciscan Order and its missionaries—*especially* "nuestra apreciada misionera" (our esteemed missionary [Mother María de Jesús de Ágreda]).

"La Madre Mariana de Jesús, de Ágreda, Predicadora de la Nueva México": Sor María the Protomissionary Inscribed into New Spanish History

As this chapter has illustrated, for the Franciscans and many Jesuits in the northern New Spanish mission field, Sor María the protomissionary was a reality in their world, emerging with regularity in mission discourse from Texas to California. Many religious informants were familiar with Sor María's writing in addition to the Lady in Blue narrative, and they regularly referenced both. Starting in the late seventeenth century and continuing throughout the eighteenth century, Spanish and Mexican historians would further legitimate and propagate the Lady in Blue narrative in secular and religious histories about New Spain.

Yet unlike the reports from the missions, many of these historiographical texts separate the Lady in Blue narrative from Sor María's writing. Although the persistence of the narrative into the present day is indebted to these historical texts, the works' focus on the conversion narrative by itself heralds the eventual erasure of the nun's writing in folklore and contemporary production treating the Lady in Blue.

The Lady in Blue appears in two early Franciscan histories: *Teatro mexicano: Crónica de la Provincia del Santo Evangelio de México* (1697) and *Menologio franciscano* (1697), both by Franciscan Fray Agustín de Vetancurt.[235] Vetancurt was well read in Sor María's writing, particularly in *La mística ciudad de dios*, as his *Chronografía sagrada* (1696) amply demonstrates.[236] In spite of this, however, Vetancurt documents Sor María only as a mystical missionary, and not as a writer, in his two Mexican histories.

In the fourth part of the *Teatro mexicano*, in a section describing the various custodiae of the province (which included the custodia of New Mexico), Fray Vetancurt summarizes *1630 Memorial*'s account of the conversion of the Jumano tribe. He cites a 1630 Mexican printing of the *1630 Memorial* as his source material,[237] adding to that text the important detail that it was Sor María de Jesús de Ágreda who appeared to the tribe. Since the *1630 Memorial* did not name Sor María as the mysterious female evangelist, Fray Vetancurt must have drawn on other sources besides the *1630 Memorial*—perhaps her *vita* or the 1631 letter.[238] Fray Vetancurt's *Teatro mexicano* provides another detail that is not explicitly mentioned in the *1630 Memorial*. He states that the Jumano tribe arrived to the Isleta mission specifically on the 22nd of June, 1629. Though this point would later emerge in folklore and legend, Fray Benavides did not state it this way in the *1630 Memorial*.

Although Fray Vetancurt takes pains to ensure that Sor María is included in his religious history of Mexico, Fray Benavides's role as the *custos* of the New Mexico custodia is emphasized over Sor María's actions as a protomissionary. In fact, in the *Menologio Franciscano*, the "abadesa del convento de Ágreda" (abbess from the convent of Ágreda)[239] is mentioned only as a part of the encyclopedic entry on Fray Benavides; she did receive her own entry among the great Franciscan figures of early Mexico. Nonetheless, Fray Vetancurt's inclusion of the Lady in Blue narrative in his chronicles of Franciscan missions in New Spain brought the narrative into the order's formal history.

The Lady in Blue narrative also emerged in secular histories about New Mexico and neighboring regions. A 1698 history by Juan de Villagutierre Soto-Mayor, the Relator del Real Consejo de las Indias (royal historian of the Spanish colonies)[240] wrote Sor María the protomissionary into his *Historia de la conquista, pérdida y restauración del reino de la Nueva México en la América Septentrional*. His history recounts the conquest and settlement of New Mexico through 1698 and includes the events of the 1680 Pueblo Revolt and the resettlement of New Mexico in 1692. Like many historians of the Indies, Villagutierre Soto-Mayor never traveled to the Americas.[241] He relied instead on available sources to compose his *Historia* from Madrid, drawing on Gaspar Pérez de Villagrá's epic poem *Historia de la Nueva México* (1610), Sor María's *vita*, and many other documents. The Lady in Blue's presence in Villagutierre Soto-Mayor's royal history suggests that the narrative was sanctioned by Spanish government officials. Through the *Historia*, Sor María as the Lady in Blue becomes an integral part of his secular history of New Spain.

Although Villagutierre Soto-Mayor's accounting of the Lady in Blue derives primarily from Sor María's *vita*, the royal historian says almost nothing about her writing, not even of *La mística ciudad de dios*. As in Fray Vetancurt's histories, the *Historia* disarticulates the literary Sor María from her New Spanish history. In spite of this major omission, the history elevates the Lady in Blue to a role that nearly equals that of the male explorers who preceded her.

The *Historia*'s third book seamlessly transitions from a description of the late sixteenth-century *entrada* (settlement expedition) of Juan de Oñate into New Mexico, to the Franciscan friars and their missions in the region, and then to Sor María's evangelization there. The *Historia* quotes as its source for the material on Sor María "Samaniego, en la 'Vida de la Madre María'" (Samaniego, in the "Life of Mother María"), which makes the omission of her literary legacy even more glaring.[242] The *Historia* summarizes the *vita*'s version of Sor María's conversions in New Mexico, linking her actions to the *Historia*'s mission narrative. In Villagutierre Soto-Mayor's account, Sor María's evangelization was so effective that friars stationed in the custodia had little to do other than administer baptism to the expectant tribes: "por tener ya la sierva de Dios tan bien dispuestas aquellas almas con su maravillosa predicación, habiendo dejado tan poco que trabajar con ellas fueron innumerables las que en cortísimo tiempo bautizaron los religiosos" (for the Servant of God already had those souls so well disposed with her marvelous preaching, having left so little work that the priests were able to baptize innumerable souls in a very short time).[243] This opinion echoed the message repeatedly invoked by Franciscan missionaries, attributed to Sor María, that "con solo ver á sus hijos [de San Francisco] se han de convertir á nuestra Santa Fé Católica" (merely upon seeing the sons [of Saint Francis], they will convert to our Holy Catholic Faith). Villagutierre Soto-Mayor even enters into the controversial question of how Sor María traveled to New Mexico—whether in body or spirit—a point Fray Ximénez Samaniego discussed at length in the *vita*. The royal historian proposes that "tenía muchos fundamentos"[244] (there were many reasons) to believe she physically traveled in her body to New Mexico, in spite of Sor María's expressed doubts regarding the nature of her travel.

Near the end of the *Historia*, Sor María's role as a missionary is again invoked, as Villagutierre Soto-Mayor discusses the "secession" of some Tejas tribes from the Spanish Crown. In recounting this incident, the *Historia* casts Sor María's actions in the language of the mission: she was there to convert the tribes in preparation for Franciscan friars. Some of the Tejas who were no longer Christian had been converted by Sor María herself[245]—he refers to them as "los indios que la misma Madre María había reducido" (the Indians that the very same Mother María had converted)[246]—but they nonetheless rebelled against the Franciscan friars. Here and elsewhere in the *Historia*, Villagutierre Soto-Mayor leaves no doubt as to the nun's singular role in the context of New Mexico's early history. He states that those in New Mexico call her "La Madre Mariana de Jesús, de Ágreda, *Predicadora* de la Nueva México" (the Mother Mariana de Jesús de Ágreda, Preacher of New Mexico),[247] a female preacher in the male mission field.

Villagutierre Soto-Mayor's secular history of early New Mexico places Sor María on equal ground with other, male explorers and missionaries, drawing no essential distinction between the sixteenth-century *entrada* of Juan de Oñate and the Lady in Blue's conversions. Although Villagutierre Soto-Mayor comments of the singularity of Sor María's mystical conversions that "en ninguna otra parte de los dilatadísimos imperios de la América, no se habrá oído que haya sido practicado" (in no other part of the far-flung empires of America has such a thing been done),[248] he nonetheless treats these events as if they were typical to the New Spanish missions. Historian Maribel Lárraga notes of this quality:

> Villagutierre Sotomayor no hace ningún comentario crítico en torno a lo que significó Sor María de Agreda ni tampoco menciona en su manuscrito alguna razón que haya tenido para incluir este episodio en su obra. Concluyo que su fin principal para incluir la historia de María de Agreda fue de presentar una historia integra sobre el norte del Virreinato de la Nueva España y hacer hincapié en la meta evangelizadora que tenían los españoles.

> ———

> Villagutierre Soto-Mayor makes no critical commentary regarding what Sor María de Ágreda signified, nor does he mention in his manuscript any reason he might have had for including this episode in his work. I conclude that his principal aim for including the narrative of María de Ágreda was to present a complete history about the north of the viceroyalty of New Spain and to emphasize the Spanish evangelizing objective.[249]

In this way, Villagutierre Soto-Mayor's *Historia de la conquista, pérdida y restauración del reino de la Nueva México en la América Septentrional* affirms the Lady in Blue's place in the secular historical landscape of New Spain, while at the same time completely erasing the role of her writing.

Another historian, Andrés González de Barcia Caballido y Zúñiga, likewise included the Lady in Blue narrative as part of his regional history. His *Ensayo cronológico para la historia general de la Florida* (written under the pseudonym Don Gabriel de Cardenas Z'Cano) was printed in Madrid in 1723 as an appendix to El Inca Garcilaso de la Vega's *La florida del Inca*.[250] The text is a chronology of the exploration and settlement of the general region known as "La Florida" from 1512 to 1722. Barcia includes anecdotes recounting French, Danish, English, and Swedish explorations to the area to explain the risk their presence there presented to Spanish dominion.

Barcia opens the section "Década duodécima" (Twelfth Decade) with a list of the events described in the chapter, such as the expulsion of Franciscan friars from the English province of Acadia in 1628, and the political conflict between France and England for control over Canada in 1630.[251] He also deftly inserts the following anecdote in the list of historical events: "Predica à los Teguas [Tejas] la V.M. María de Jesús de Ágreda" (The Venerable Mother María de Jesús de Ágreda preaches to the Tejas).[252]

Barcia then presents a succinct, yet significant, version of the Lady in Blue narrative: "La V. Madre María de Jesús de Agreda, Predicó en la Provincia de los Tejas; si fue en Espíritu, o realmente, no pudo distinguirlo ella misma" (The Venerable Mother María de Jesús de Ágreda preached in the province of the Tejas; whether she went in her spirit or in her body, she herself did not know).[253] The dates of her time among the "Tejas" that Barcia provides are slightly later than those in other accounts of the narrative. Yet Barcia's commentary on the nature of Sor María's travel is revealing: he relays her expressed doubt as to the nature of her travel, a principal feature of her *vita*'s retelling of the episode. Although this allusion suggests that Barcia had read or was at least aware of her *vita* and/or *La mística ciudad de dios*, his *Historia general de la Florida* makes no mention of Sor María's writing at all.

Though the citation is brief, Barcia's casual inclusion of the Lady in Blue in the *Historia de la Florida* is indicative of how the narrative was perceived and considered in its time. In a text construed as an historical overview or "reflexión general"[254] in which historical briefs were assembled "para que se comprenda universalmente algún indicio, de lo mucho, que havia de decir" (so that one might gain a universal understanding through a hint of the much there is to say),²⁵⁵ the modest commentary on the Lady in Blue narrative is significant. Of the countless other anecdotes about Florida that Barcia could have included, "que especificarlas todas, era salir de los límites" (which, to detail all of them, would surpass the limits [of the text],²⁵⁶ Barcía includes Sor María as a protomissionary—but not as a writer—among those chosen. Through his regional history, Barcía legitimizes the Lady in Blue narrative, acknowledging Sor María's role in the evangelization of that region.

The 1764 manuscript of Franciscan friar and historian Francisco Antonio de la Rosa Figueroa, entitled *Becerro general menológico y chronológico*,²⁵⁷ documented the Franciscan leadership operating in the Province of Santo Evangelio from 1524 to 1764.²⁵⁸ The *Becerro*'s account of the Lady in Blue recorded the most important figures and events relating to the province and its operatives. In 1792, the New Spanish viceroy requested that Fray Figueroa compile and copy the chronicles and history of New Spain. But neither the thirty-two volumes the friar amassed nor the *Becerro* itself ever saw a printing press; their purpose was to create a standardized history, and Sor María was part of that project.²⁵⁹

In the *Becerro*'s entry on Fray Alonso de Benavides, Sor María and her conversions in New Mexico overtake the friar's biography. Fray Figueroa (erroneously) claims that Fray Vetancurt did not include this information in his discussion of the Province of Santo Evangelio in his *Teatro mexicano* because Fray Vetancurt "did not have information about these portents that recurred oftener in the custodiate of the said Venerable Father [Fray Benavides]."²⁶⁰ Fray Figueroa clarifies that Fray Benavides had sought a large number of missionaries for the region because the tribes there "had the amazing experience of seeing the prodigious and venerable Mother Madre de Jesús de Agreda appear to them really and visibly as an apostolic and catechizing preacher in those vast kingdoms."²⁶¹ In this historical record, the Lady in Blue's actions as a protomissionary in the New Mexico custodia were simple historical fact.

After offering considerable detail about Fray Benavides's travel to Spain in 1629, Fray Figueroa adds that information about the friar's 1631 visit to Ágreda can be found in *La mística ciudad de dios*. Rather than going into additional detail on that event, he "refer[s] the reader to the first part of the *Mística ciudad de Dios*, in the narrative of the life of the venerable virgin, paragraph no. 12, entitled 'Marvelous Conversions of the Heathens,' where are told all the marvelous details of what happened in her miraculous appearances and preachings here in the north in this boundless kingdom of the Indies."[262] He goes on to clarify the relationship between the 1730 Mexican printing of the *Tanto que se sacó de una carta* and the manuscript of the 1631 letter on which it was based. Figueroa adds that he himself submitted two copies of the printed document to the provincial archives for historical safekeeping.[263] The Franciscan historian was acquainted both with Sor María's own writing and with the documents describing her travels to New Mexico that had circulated within his order for decades. Although Fray Figueroa does not discuss Sor María's writing in any detail, it is clear he knew it well enough to cite it with precision and mention it in conjunction with her work in New Mexico.

The *Becerro* frames Fray Benavides's undertakings as *custos* of New Mexico in light of Sor María's conversions there. As Fray Figueroa presents it, it is almost as though the friar's activities played a supporting role to the nun's evangelization. In citing an earlier Franciscan biographical history to tell more about Fray Benavides, Fray Figueroa begins: "And to enhance the glory of the Venerable Mother, María de Jesús de Ágreda, miraculous apostle of New Mexico and its vast kingdoms of the north, as well as of this illustrious Venerable Apostle [Fray Benavides], and therefore of this holy province of the Holy Gospel, I shall translate literally what relates to this great apostle of New Mexico [Fray Benavides]."[264] The "miraculous apostle" Sor María is no small player in this episode of the province's history and its leadership; Sor María's conversions in the New Spanish northern provinces were integral to the region's historical narrative.

A final, poignant example of Sor María's importance in official New Spanish history is found in Fray José Antonio Pichardo's historical study of colonial-era Texas and Louisiana. Published in English translation in 1934 as *Pichardo's Treaty on the Limits of Texas and Louisiana*,[265] the original text was begun by Fray Pichardo's predecessor, Fray Melchor de Talamantes.[266] Fray Talamantes was charged with researching and composing the history, but he died as a result of illness contracted during the course of a court trial, during which he was accused of supporting the cause for Mexican independence from Spain.[267] The history Fray Talamantes began and abandoned was expanded and completed by Fray

Pichardo in 1812. In the course of finishing the report, Fray Pichardo revised, corrected, affirmed, and at times contradicted Fray Talamantes's research and conclusions.

Included among the papers Fray Talamantes worked with was an *opúsculo* (short treatise). It is a copy of the friar's notes on exploration in the Bahía de Espíritu Santo, which he drew from the work of a Padre L'Clerc.[268] Fray Pichardo incorporates parts of this document into his final *Treaty*, but he disagrees with the interpretations of various events relating to the Bahía that Fray Talamantes sets forth in the *opúsculo*.

In discussing Alonso de León's seventeenth-century exploration of the bay and neighboring areas, Fray Talamantes comments that it was commonly believed that Sor María was the first missionary to the tribes living there. As he explains it:

> Corrían entonces con la mejor aceptación las obras de la Venerable Madre María de Jesús de Agreda, de quien escribe el Padre Benavides, que fue arrebatada por el Señor para la conversión de los Indios del Nuevo-Mexico; y tanto por esta noticia, como la que dieron los Indios en una lengua que no entendían los nuestros, y que interpretaron entonces a su antojo o según sus preocupaciones, creyeron prontamente que el primer Apostol de los Texas fue la dicha venerable Madre.

——

> At the time, the writing of the Venerable Mother María de Jesús de Ágreda circulated with the greatest acceptance—she whom Father Benavides wrote about and who was spirited away by the Lord for the conversion of the Indians of New Mexico; and as much for this information as for that which the Indians gave in a language that our people did not understand, and which they then interpreted according to their whim or concerns, they soon believed that the first Apostle of Texas was the said Venerable Mother.[269]

After this explanation, Fray Talamantes censures several prominent authorities of that time (the *fiscal* and *asesor*) for having not taken a more critical view of these events and accepting the Lady in Blue narrative on its face: "no [se tomaron] el trabajo de reflexionar un poco adoptaron prontamente el prodigio" (without bothering to reflect a bit, they immediately accepted the miracle).[270] At the same time that Fray Talamantes reports that both secular and religious authorities believed Sor María to be "el primer Apóstol de los Texas" (the first apostle of Texas), he expresses his profound doubts on the matter. Equally important is the fact that, although Talamantes hesitates over her travels to New Mexico, he is perfectly clear regarding the popularity and acceptance of Sor María's writing in Mexico.

Fray Talamantes forges forward and walks a fine line as he circumspectly considers the nature of Sor María's mystical evangelization. A Mercedarian intellectual writing at the dawn of Mexican independence, he chooses his argument carefully:

> No es nuestro designio dar por falsas la apariciones de la Madre Agreda ni contradecir la opinion de los Religiosos Franciscanos. Sobran ejemplares de semejantes traslaciones o apariciones en que Dios ha querido ostentar su poder y no dudamos que dicho [*sic*] Venerable seria un instrumento a proposito escogido por el Señor para embiar su luz a los infieles.

> ⸻

> It is not our intent to take as false the apparitions of Mother Ágreda, nor to contradict the opinion of the Franciscans. There are plenty of examples of similar travels or apparitions in which God has wished to display his power, and we do not doubt that the said Venerable could be an instrument chosen for this purpose by the Lord to shine his light to the infidels.[271]

Fray Talamantes does not accuse his Franciscan brothers of believing in and promoting "falsas apariciones" (false apparitions). In fact, he affirms that spiritual occurrences such as Sor María's often occur, and that Sor María could have been one such agent. He qualifies this tacit reading, however, by debating the details attributed to Sor María's travels. The friar insists that all material goods that arrived to Tejas settlements were brought by Franciscan friars and not by Sor María. These items he cites include "caballos, pesos Fuertes, cucharas, ropas" (horses, money, spoons, clothing),[272] but the assertion also suggests that the rosaries and monstrance she was alleged to have transported arrived at the friars' hands instead of hers.

Fray Pichardo, reworking Fray Talamantes's opinions of Sor María, made certain that his predecessors' mild commentary regarding her bilocation would not be the narrative of record, rejecting Talamantes's doubts completely.[273] Fray Pichardo read Talamantes's *opúsculo* as a reproach of Franciscan support of the narrative, but not of the narrative itself: "[Fray Talamantes's critique was] due to a decided predilection [of the Franciscans] towards Mother Ágreda; they desire to prove valid her appearances in the province of Texas."[274] Fray Pichardo acknowledges the long history of the narrative in Texas, using Alonso de León's attempt to determine if Sor María had arrived prior to his exploration as a primary example.[275] He goes on to attack Fray Talamantes's interpretation: "If it were not the purpose of Father Talamantes to deny the appearances of Mother Ágreda, nor to contradict the statements of the Franciscan religious, it was his purpose to invent an enemy with whom to contend, that is, to make up, through caprice, a story [regarding the horses in Texas prior to Alonso de León's arrival], which he impugns."[276]

Later in the *Treaty*, Fray Pichardo continues his corrective presentation of Sor María as the Lady in Blue in Texas. He attacks Fray Talamantes's arguments against Sor María's presence there,[277] reads against the friar's interpretations of historical documents,[278] and presents counterpoints of a more personal nature: "Upon reading these words of Father Talamantes, the critic, I can only wonder that, in order to criticize the authors who believe in the appearances of Mother Ágreda to the Indians of New Mexico and Texas, he should have taken for granted any falsehoods so glaring as those he embodies in his context."[279] In reshaping Fray Talamantes's materials for his authoritative history of Texas and Louisiana, Fray Pichardo actively attempts to erase doubt regarding the validity of Sor María as the Lady in Blue or about the significance of the foundational narrative. Yet, for as persistently as Fray Pichardo promotes the Lady in Blue narrative, Sor María the writer is virtually invisible in his history of colonial Texas and Louisiana, whereas her writing *does* appear in Fray Talamantes's interpretation.

There are a few other important considerations in the *Treaty*. Although two Catholic friars wrote the *Treaty*, neither was a Franciscan: Fray Pichardo was a Congregant of the Oratorians of San Felipe de Neri, and Fray Talamantes a Mercedarian. It is unlikely either brought with him to the project the same zeal in promoting the Lady in Blue narrative that the Franciscans had. Both men wrote into the nineteenth century, reflecting an awareness of Enlightenment principles of history, if not necessarily the enaction of them. Finally, this documentary project was a secular history, ordered by the Mexican viceroy on behalf of

Carlos II, and Fray Talamantes was originally chosen for the task. Independent of their religious orders, Fray Pichardo and Fray Talamantes both considered the Lady in Blue absolutely essential to the project of documenting the secular history of the region. *Pichardo's Treaty on the Limits of Texas and Louisiana* is the final example of a significant historical work on the New Spanish borderlands that inscribed the Lady in Blue firmly into the history of the region and its people.

The narrative of Sor María de Jesús de Ágreda as the protomissionary Lady in Blue was fundamental to the story of colonization of the northern New Spanish frontier. As this chapter has shown, the inscription of this narrative correlated to the popularity of Sor María's writing even in the most remote areas of colonial Mexico, an extension of Sor María's large and diverse community of reading in Mexico and beyond.

The result of this unique intersection of writing and mystical narrative was the rooting of the Lady in Blue narrative into the historical landscape of northern New Spain and its subsequent evolution into folklore. The written historical record of the Lady in Blue narrative discussed here and in chapter 1 formed the basis for a body of folklore in which Sor María's writing and importance as an author all but evaporate.

CHAPTER FIVE

Blue Lady of Lore

The Lady in Blue Narrative and Sor María in the Folklore
of the American Southwest

> Who was she? Today, she can only be seen as a mysterious figure
> more than half obscured by the closed, gauzy curtains of more than
> three centuries.
>
> —James L. Cleveland[1]

The preceding chapters explored Sor María and the Lady in Blue in
the context of colonial-era Mexico and Spain. Chapter 1 focused on the
Lady in Blue narrative in text in the seventeenth and eighteenth centuries, paying special attention to which versions were most read and
shared. Chapter 2 described Sor María's rise to fame in Spain during
her lifetime and after, and concentrated on the popularity of her writing
and the promotion of her case for sainthood in relationship to that
writing. Chapter 3 defined the cultural impact of her writing and the
development of her devotional cult in colonial Mexican society. And
Chapter 4 examined how the Lady in Blue narrative was understood in
the context of Spanish colonization and conversion on the northern
New Spanish frontier, where familiarity with the narrative was complemented by awareness of Sor María's writing. This chapter studies the
next chronological step in the evolution of the Lady in Blue narrative—

and Sor María's history—in what was once New Spain: the transition from history to folklore.

Here I analyze what can be called "lore" treating the Lady in Blue, from the late nineteenth through twenty-first centuries. In many instances, the primary narrative of mystical travel and conversion is supplemented or even supplanted by stories in which the Lady in Blue engages in other sorts of activities, such as healing the sick, imparting wisdom to women, and inspiring commemorative practices involving the color blue. This lore often derives in part from written accounts of the Lady in Blue narrative (often the sources examined in previous chapters), and therefore walks a fine line between history and folk production.[2] For most folkloric artifacts discussed here, the connection between the Lady in Blue narrative and Sor María's writing is either absent or quickly glossed over in favor of the Lady in Blue narrative.

The first of this chapter's four sections examines the only example of lore that deals with Sor María's writing as its primary subject: an *alabado*, or prayer-song, of New Mexican origin. The second section considers how lore and history are invoked together, and to resistive ends, by three early twentieth-century Mexican American writers: Carlos Castañeda, Jovita González de Mireles, and Adina De Zavala. The third section examines stories about the Lady in Blue that depart from or add to the conversion narrative; the claimed provenance of that lore (Arizona, Texas, and New Mexico) is also considered. The chapter returns to New Mexico in the concluding section, relating a contemporary oral account based neither on the historical Sor María nor on the Lady in Blue narrative per se, but rather on a mural that includes the nun, located at the former St. Katharine's Indian School in Santa Fe, New Mexico. As chapter 6 will illustrate, contemporary renderings of the Lady in Blue often derive the narrative not from historical documents directly, but rather from lore of some type. Folklore therefore functions as both a temporal and ideational link between the narrative's colonial past and its creative present.

Coming from the field of literary studies, I cannot hope to fully represent the nuanced fields of ethnopoetics and folklore studies. The many critical perspectives involved in the analysis of lore likewise cannot be broached in this one chapter; however, some specific considerations are called for when thinking about manifestations of the Lady in Blue in folklore.

The first pertains to the lore's origins and its survival into the twenty-first century. The historical presence of writing by and about Sor María in the areas where lore has emerged, and the citation of written accounts about her by folklore informants, suggests that the lore refers back to and is reinforced by text. This foundation in writing has lent the folklore about the Lady in Blue uniformity across years and groups of production, and has undoubtedly contributed to its longevity.[3]

The connection to written sources might be seen by some to render lore about the Lady in Blue less "authentic." Yet as Mexican American studies scholars have shown, such interactions between textuality and orality are not uncommon in regional ethnopoetics. Enrique Lamadrid and Domino Perez, for example, consider both written and oral forms in their respective studies of the weeping woman, La Llorona, in Greater Mexico. In a similar vein, Mexican American folklorist Américo Paredes analyzed print and sung versions of the *corrido* of Gregorio Cortés in his analysis of the resistive borderlands lore, and considered the interplay between the two in his seminal work *With His Pistol in His Hand*.[4] These are by no means the only examples, nor are the borderlands the only place where intersectionality between written and spoken versions of a "folk" narrative reinforce and reinvent each other.[5]

As in the representative cases of La Llorona and the corrido of Gregorio Cortés, the Lady in Blue as lore has had cultural work done on it. The stories about the Lady in Blue that ascribe new abilities to her, that place her in contexts other than those of conversion, and that align her loyalties with groups other than Spanish colonizers are all examples of transformations of the narrative that occurred through collective evocation of the narrative. The cultural assimilation of the narrative's written legacy over time produced a profoundly modified Lady in Blue. But before examining the changed narrative in lore, we must consider how this lore is often imprecisely attributed.

Many of the examples discussed in this chapter disarticulate the folk stories from any specific origin, consolidating them as "regional lore." Historian Jean-Claude Schmitt warns of the risks inherent to interpreting such compilations of lore: "When scholars study these accounts in versions abstracted from their context and inserted into 'collections of folktales and legends,' they all too often tend to forget the people whose words these are, and the social and historical conditions in which they were spoken."[6] In the instances discussed here, it is the compilers of these accounts who turn them into Lady in Blue narratives by defining them as such, and (with very few exceptions) they do so without explaining who, when, where, and why the accounts were articulated originally.

Many casual folklorists and even some scholars seek out regional sources for the narrative other than the colonial-era New Spanish Franciscans, settlers, and colonizers whose roles in promulgating the narrative I have outlined in previous chapters. A popular folklore treatment of the Lady in Blue sums up this unsettling perspective: "Legend oftentimes has roots in reality. In many and varied parts of the Southwest there linger fragments of the story of the Blue Lady. This mysterious lady, although very real to the Indians, remains after centuries have passed still as unexplainable myth to the White Man."[7] The framing of the narrative as pertaining to some sort of generic, pan-indigenous community in this quote is not unique; it recurs throughout the documented lore about Sor María, even though it is, of course, in no way accurate and not in keeping with current ethnographic practice.

In the examples in this chapter, when a legend is attributed to indigenous sources, vital information about the informant is almost always missing: name(s) of informant(s), tribal affiliation, and other identifying details. The folklore collectors by and large do not self-identify as native; this means that they are reporting legends ascribed to cultures and groups that are not their own. The ascription of the lore to indigenous sources does not reflect documented provenance, and, in some sense, it says more about the individual recounting the narrative than it does about who produced it.

These two elements, combined with the dearth of documented extant native lore treating the Lady in Blue, demand that we as readers critically and deeply question the folklore collectors' designation of the Lady in Blue lore as one of exclusively indigenous origins. It also requires that we keep fully present postcolonial perspectives on cultural recasting in our understanding of what *is* presented by these sources.[8]

Contemporary Mexican American cultural critics also claim the Lady in Blue narrative as autochthonous lore. Ethnographer Lamadrid counts the Lady in Blue among the foundational *milagro* (miracle) narratives of New Mexico, one "situated at both the beginning and end times, continually emergent and current as times change."[9] The *Dictio-*

nary of Chicano Folklore's entry on "Agreda, María de Jesus Coronel de (The Blue Lady)" defines the Lady in Blue narrative as a Chicano *leyenda* (legend),[10] and compares it to those of La Llorona, Joaquín Murrieta (popularly known as Zorro), and the Chupacabras. By including this entry in the dictionary and presenting it in the context of other "Chicano" legends, the Lady in Blue lore is claimed by one of its communities of production.[11] The identification of Lady in Blue lore with the Mexican American community is reinforced in the writing of *Tejanos* Castañeda, González, and De Zavala.

Bearing in mind the complexity of the lore's interpretation, there is still great value in examining these stories of the Lady in Blue and Sor María. Classifying a narrative with historical and literary origins as lore is in and of itself a statement of possession and a gesture of meaning creation. In considering what follows, the reader is asked to take into account the content of the lore, the nature and context of its telling, the attribution of its source, and the individual(s) who conserves and selectively reproduces it.

"LA MÍSTICA SUIDÁ DE LUZ": A NEW MEXICAN *ALABADO* AND SOR MARÍA'S WRITING

All other examples of Lady in Blue folklore treated in this chapter deal with the narrative alone and, in the process, completely erase the memory of Sor María's writing and its historical impact. However, a New Mexican *alabado* (a devotional song sung at lay-directed Catholic religious events) is unique in that Sor María's writing takes center stage. The alabado alludes to and builds on the connection between Sor María, *La mística ciudad de dios*, and the Virgin Mary. There is no suggestion of the Lady in Blue narrative at all. This alabado is testament to a persistent cultural knowledge of Sor María's writing in New Mexico and to the legacy of her writing there in the nineteenth century and earlier, even if the meaning of the text is not clearly expressed in the song itself.

Alabados in New Mexico are associated with the *cofradía* (confraternity) of the Hermanos de Nuestro Padre Jesús Nazareno. Many alabados sung or read by the *hermanos* have their roots in the turn of the nineteenth century, when the cofradía was established in New Mexico, and have been preserved through oral transmission and in written form. Some *moradas* keep such materials private, as *hermano* practices have often been misunderstood and misrepresented,[12] yet at times they have permitted recording of the alabados and have shared written versions with researchers. The alabado to Sor María is one that has been documented.

As we discussed in chapters 3 and 4, the impetus for Sor María's canonization within the Franciscan Order was linked to Franciscan interest in promoting the Immaculate Conception theology and therefore to the promulgation of *La mística ciudad de dios*. We have already seen that copies of the text existed in New Mexico and elsewhere in the colonial Mexican north, where there was a strong Franciscan influence. The alabado's existence suggests that *La mística ciudad de dios* exerted popular influence in those regions, and within a population that may not have even read the text.

The alabado "Madre Agueda de Jesús" is included in a compilation of New Mexican folklore collected by Juan B. Rael, *The New Mexican Alabado* (1951). Rael derived the material for the book from notebooks loaned to him by Indo-Hispano residents of northern New Mexico and southern Colorado.[13] Rael organized the folk artifacts in his book thematically; he placed "Madre Agueda de Jesús" with petitions, prayers, and songs dedicated to the Virgin Mary. The alabado's lyrics make clear why Rael placed it there: throughout the oration, "Madre Agueda de Jesús" is conflated or interwoven with references to Mary.[14] The "Madre Agueda de Jesús" of the first stanza flows into "María, Madre de Jesús" ("Mary, Mother of Jesus") in the second, and "Eres Madre de Jesús" ("You are the Mother of Jesus") in the third. The fifth stanza takes this a step further, combining language from the prayer Hail Mary ("entre todas las mujeres," "among all women") with a refrain common to several other of Rael's Marian alabados ("bendita sea tu pureza," "blessed be your purity"): "entre todas las mujeres / bendita sea tu pureza." Other parts of the alabado deepen the interplay between Madre Agueda de Jesús and Mary.[15]

The element that ties Sor María to the alabado is the repetition of the phrase "mística suidá [ciudad] de *luz* [emphasis mine]" ("mystical city of *light*") in association with "Agueda." Though "luz" does not correlate perfectly to "dios" (as in "*Mística ciudad de dios*," "Mística ciudad de luz") nor "Agueda" to "Ágreda," the sound and stress patterns within each pair are the same. The reduction of the unstressed "r" of "Ágreda" to "Agueda" is consistent with observed tendencies in spoken Spanish, and the "dios" to "luz" evolution follows similar principles. Further, there is analogical pressure for the transition from Ágreda to Agueda, as the latter is the well-known name of a Catholic saint (Agatha), and the term "Ágreda" was considerably less well-known. Shifting to something recognizable from an unusual word is consistent with tendencies in oral Spanish. Finally, the movement from *Mística ciudad de dios* to "Mística ciudad de luz" is a likely instance of metaphorical extension, in which the correlated ideas of "dios" and "luz" are interchanged.

Alabado: María Agueda de Jesús

1.
Madre Agueda de Jesús,
María de más grandeza,
mística suidá de luz,
bendita sea tu pureza.
2.
María Madre de Jesús,
en la suidá eres princesa,
Agueda llena de luz,
bendita sea tu pureza.
3.
Eres Madre de Jesús,
pues es tanta su belleza,
los ángeles dan tu luz,
bendita sea tu pureza.
4.
Angeles y querubines,
coronan tu cabeza,
a tus pies postrados firmes,
bendita sea tu pureza.
5.
Agueda de Jesús eres,
el centro de su nobleza,
entre todas las mujeres,
bendita sea tu pureza.

6.
Suidá donde Dios alcanza,
y tienes tanta nobleza,
te entonen las alabanzas,
bendita sea tu pureza.
7.
Madre, Agueda de Jesús,
que fuistes en tu nobleza,
los misterios de la luz,
bendita sea tu pureza.
8.
Los treinta-y-siete consejos,
que distes a Santa Teresa,
de moralidad inmensa,
bendita sea tu pureza.
9.
De Dios fuistes elegida,
de coronar tu cabeza,
Madre Agueda de mi vida,
bendita sea tu pureza.
10.
Agueda de Jesús cuantos,
A tu singular belleza,
entonen en ti los santos,
bendita sea tu pureza.
11.
Angeles y Serafines,
entonen ya su grandeza,
te adoran los querubines,
bendita sea tu pureza.
12.
Agueda las profecías,
a ti a Dios las endereza,
Madre pues las cumplirías,
bendita sea tu pureza.
13.
Eres Madre de bondad,
todo el mundo de confiesa,

por Jesús, tenednos piedad,
bendita sea tu pureza.
14.
Dios a todas sus criatureas,
a ti las entrega y fija,
te pidemos, Virgen pura,
bendita sea tu pureza.
15.
El Padre eterno en María,
encarnó toda su belleza,
para darnos al Mesías,
bendita sea tu pureza.
16.
Madre Agueda te imploramos,
de corazón y franqueza,
el ir contigo a tu gloria,
bendita sea tu pureza.
17.
El Padre eterno y el Hijo,
a ti celestial princesa,
de virtudes y prodigios,
bendita sea tu pureza.

———

1.
Mother Agatha of Jesus,
Mary of the highest grandeur,
mystical city of light;
blessed be your purity.
2.
Mary, Mother of Jesus,
In the city you area a princess,
Agatha full of light;
Blessed be your purity.
3.
You are the mother of Jesus,
for your beauty is so great,
the angels give your light;
blessed be your purity.

4.
Angels and cherubim
crowned your head,
lie prostrate at your feet;
blessed be your purity.
5.
You are Agatha of Jesus,
the source of your nobility,
among all women;
blessed be your purity.
6.
City where God dwells,
and you have so much nobility
the mysteries of the light;
blessed be your purity.
7.
Mother, Agatha of Jesus,
you were in your nobility,
the mysteries of the light;
blessed be your purity.
8.
The thirty-seven counsels
that you gave to St. Theresa,
of immense moral worth;
blessed be your purity.
9.
By God you were chosen
to crown your head,
Mother Agatha dear as life,
blessed be your purity.
10.
Agatha of Jesus,
to your singular beauty
let the saints intone hymns;
blessed be your purity.
11.
Let angels and seraphim
now sing of your grandeur;

the cherubim worship you;
blessed be your purity.
12.
Agatha, God guides
the prophecies toward you,
mother, for you would fulfill them;
blessed be your purity.
13.
You are the mother of good,
all the world acknowledges you;
for Jesus' sake, have mercy upon us;
blessed be your purity.
14.
God delivers and entrusts
to you all His creatures;
we beg you, pure Virgin;
blessed be your purity.
15.
Eternal Father in Mary
embodied all his beauty
to give is the Messiah;
blessed be your purity.
16.
Mother Agatha, we implore you
with heartfelt sincerity
to go with you to your glory;
blessed be your purity.
17.
The Eternal Father and the Son
to you, heavenly princess
of virtues and wonders;
blessed be your purity.[16]

The collocation of "Madre Agueda" with "Mística suidá de luz" is the most compelling indication of a connection between the two concepts, linking back to Sor María and *La mística ciudad de dios*. And although the alabado does not specifically reference the theological content of *La mística ciudad de dios*,[17] its commingling of "Agueda," "mística ciudad de luz," and the Virgin Mary connotes a relationship among the three that does represent the broad themes of *La mística ciudad de dios*.

Two detailed stanzas refer either to *La mística ciudad de dios* itself or to other texts associated with Sor María and/or the Virgin Mary. Based on the apostrophe used in the seventh stanza ("Madre, Agueda de Jesús / que fuistes en tu nobleza / los misterios de la luz") ("Mother, Agueda of Jesus / you were in your nobility / the mysteries of the light"), the subject of the eighth stanza ("Los treinta-y-siete consejos / que diste a Santa Teresa, / de moralidad inmensa, / bendita sea tu pureza") ("the thirty-seven counsels / that you gave to St. Theresa / of immense moral worth/ blessed be your purity") appears to be Agueda/Ágreda. The unusual specificity of thirty-seven words of advice suggests a particular—likely textual—referent. The relationship indicated between Sor María and Santa Teresa of Avila is anachronistic, because the famed mystic died in 1582, well before Sor María's birth. However, the association between the two nuns is not surprising. Santa Teresa's mysticism was a precedent for Sor María's, and a short letter of Sor María's was at one point published by the nuns of Santa Teresa's convent along with some of Santa Teresa's own "Avisos," which could be understood as "consejos."[18] Both women were extremely influential in colonial-era mystical production, especially by women religious.[19] In chapter 3 we discussed several colonial Mexican publications that combined elements of Sor María's writing with Santa Teresa's, perhaps leading to a popular understanding of their writing as intermingled.

Another intertextual allusion occurs in the twelfth stanza, which addresses Agueda/Ágreda directly in reference to prophecies from God: "Agueda las profecías / a ti Dios las endereza, / Madre pues las cumplirías" ("Agueda, God guides / the prophecies toward you / Mother, you would fulfill them"). What the "profecías" consist of is not explained in the alabado, but they could refer to Mary's divine biography, imparted to Sor María and recounted in *La mística ciudad de dios*. The linkages explained here show a connection between that text and the long-term production and preservation of oral lore in New Mexico, reflecting the historical and literary precedent we explained in chapter 4.

The alabado itself is more widespread in New Mexico than Rael originally observed. As he recorded it, "Madre Agueda de Jesús" came from a single source in Arroyo Hondo, a small town in northern New Mexico. Many of the other alabados in his collection are attributed to three or more sources, dispersed geographically. Though Colahan and Rodriguez sought out other versions of the alabado, they were unsuccessful in locating additional sources or other versions of it.[20] However, in 1998, a fellow student from Torreón, New Mexico, shared with me an alabado dedicated to "Madre Agueda de Jesús," both in written and sung form. The lyrics of this alabado are identical to the Rael version; the Torreón alabado, therefore, does not offer any additional information that would help to clarify its origins or the relationship between Agueda/Ágreda and the Virgin Mary. Yet it tells us a great deal about the reach of her commemoration: through the alabado, Sor María and her writing were remembered far beyond Arroyo Hondo.[21] It also posits the possibility that the alabado was sung elsewhere in the region, but Rael did not record it.

Even though the alabado does not treat the Lady in Blue narrative directly, this fact does not make it any less relevant to the narrative's folk legacy. The reading and dissemination of *La mística ciudad de dios* led and/or followed the narrative's movement on the northern New Spanish frontier, and this manifested through the alabado. In the same way that the presence of Sor María's writing signals the Lady in Blue narrative on the northern New Spanish frontier (and vice versa), so too does this alabado portend the bilocation narrative in contemporaneous borderlands folkloric tradition. The three examples that follow bear this out explicitly and in a politicized manner within the Mexican American community of early twentieth-century Texas.

"THE GIFT OF SEEING TO THE HEART OF THINGS!": MEXICAN AMERICAN HISTORY IN TEXAS AND TEJANO LORE OF THE LADY IN BLUE

Three Mexican American Tejanos who worked in areas of academic or popular historical/cultural scholarship contributed to the lore about Sor María as the Lady in Blue in the early twentieth century. Carlos Castañeda (1896–1958), a Mexican-born historian who moved to Texas as a child, is best known as the author of *Our Catholic Heritage in Texas*, a comprehensive history of Catholicism in Texas, in which he includes both history and lore about the Lady in Blue. Jovita González de Mireles (1904–83) was a scholar, folklorist, and writer, and the protégée of controversial Anglo-Texan folklorist J. Frank Dobie. Her account of the Lady in Blue featured in an exhibition titled Catholic Heroines of Texas for the Texas Centennial celebration of 1936. A cultural activist integral to the preservation of San Antonio's Alamo Mission, Adina De Zavala (1861–1955) composed detailed folkloric and historical renderings of the Lady in Blue for her book *History and Legends of the Alamo and Other Missions in and around San Antonio* (1917).

Castañeda, González, and De Zavala are united based on how and to what ends they implemented the Lady in Blue narrative in the texts they wrote. They shared not only a moment in time but also other important characteristics. Castañeda, González, and De Zavala were Mexican Americans living in an Anglo-dominated social environment that limited and discriminated against Mexican Americans, and which also sought to erase Tejano agency from Texas history.[22] Each author responded to and resisted—to varying degrees—these conditions through their writing and social activism. In the process, they implemented the Lady in Blue in a contestatory manner to reinscribe the narrative—and by extension Mexican Americans—into the colonial-era history of Texas.

Carlos Castañeda: The Lady in Blue's Place in *Our Catholic Heritage in Texas*

Carlos Castañeda's historical text about Catholics and Catholicism in Texas is more encompassing than its title would suggest. As Castañeda wrote in the preface to the first book of his seven volume work: "The reader will find in the present volume for the first time the connected narrative of the history of Texas from 1519 to 1694. Incidents and events heretofore considered to have little or no relation with the subsequent history of the State are presented in a new light, as revealed by unused sources."[23]

Our Catholic Heritage in Texas was commissioned by the Texas Knights of Columbus Historical Commission in 1923 in response to the increasing prominence of the Ku Klux Klan in Texas. Reading between the lines of the appointment of Mexican American Castañeda as the project's director and the fact that most Tejanos identified as Catholic, the series was also indirectly a history of Mexican and/or Mexican American religious presence in Texas. The project documents Catholic history in Texas starting in 1519, and though the final volume, *The*

Church in Texas since Independence, 1836–1950, focuses on then-contemporary Catholic history, the preceding six volumes largely treat Mexican and Mexican American religious history in the state. The frontispiece to the first volume, "The Mission Era: The Finding of Texas, 1519–1693," places Sor María at the heart of this project: Castañeda used the 1730 printing of the *Tanto que se sacó de una carta* as his lead image for the Catholic history of Texas.

And Castañeda presents the narrative itself with comparable distinction. He recounts the Lady in Blue account in a chapter entitled "María de Agreda, the Jumano, and the Tejas, 1620–1654." Although the chapter treats several episodes in Texas's early Catholic history—mostly Spanish exploration and expeditions—Castañeda draws attention to Sor María's narrative alone, and it becomes the primary history of the chapter. In light of how Castañeda's historian contemporaries and predecessors treated Sor María in their writing, his prominent placement of the Lady in Blue narrative can be seen as fairly audacious.

In the 1916 notes to Fray Alonso de Benavides's *1630 Memorial*, Castañeda's historian colleagues Frederick Webb Hodge and Charles Fletcher Lummis flatly discredit the Lady in Blue narrative and Sor María, saying dismissively of Sor María's testimony regarding her bilocations that "some of the tribal names mentioned by Mother María de Jesús, as might be expected, were, like the journeys themselves, creations of the imagination; others it may be suggested, were derived from the *Memorial* published the year before."[24] According to Hodge and Lummis, the nun's writing was full of "preposterous things"[25] that "no doubt will prove sufficient to indicate the mental character of this nun."[26] They wrote her off as a woman who was not be believed on the basis of "other performances to which she laid claim."[27] This same critique was repeated in the notes to the *1634 Memorial*, published by Hodge, George Hammond, and Agapito Rey in 1945, in effect establishing an approach to the Lady in Blue narrative that later historians would parrot, when not ignoring Sor María completely.

Castañeda published his volume in 1936, in the midst of a decidedly antagonistic historical discourse concerning the Lady in Blue narrative.[28] Castañeda surely was aware of this, for as his contemporary, Texas historian Richard Sturmberg, noted of Sor María in his 1920 *History of San Antonio and the Early Days in Texas*, "volumes have been written about this venerable religious woman and quite a controversy is being carried on today about her visits to the Indian tribes."[29] Writing against the pre-vailing opinions of his contemporaries regarding Sor María's travel to Texas and New Mexico, Castañeda instead stressed its significance by framing it as a key moment in Texas's early Catholic history.

Castañeda's drew from several established historical sources in crafting the historical Lady in Blue narrative for this volume, cross-referencing Fray Benavides's *1630 Memorial*, Fray Agustín de Vetan-curt's *Chronica de la Provincia del Santo Evangelio* (1697), Juan Mateo Manje's account in *Luz de tierra incógnita* (1693–1721), and the *Tanto que se sacó de una carta* (1730), among others. External and internal mandates may have conditioned Castañeda's attention to historical detail. Castañeda's series was intended to reconstruct a detailed, histori-cally based chronology of Texas's Catholic past. The series editor, Rev. Paul J. Foik, C.S.C., notes in the forward: "In these series of volumes, *Our Catholic Heritage in Texas*, the historians have endeavored to present a critical and comprehensive treatment of the mission era fol-lowed by the modern period, stressing the narration of achievements and events in their relation to the Church through the various epochs to the present day."[30]

As we saw in chapter 4, most colonial-era accounts treating the Lady in Blue questioned neither the authenticity nor the importance of the narrative. Castañeda carries this sense over into his own entry, which is earnest in its presentation of the nun's historical role in Texas: "It was while they [the Jumanos] were living on a stream which the Spaniards called the Noeces or Nueces, that they were visited by María de Ágreda."[31] Although Castañeda cites the notes to the *Memorial* as im-portant sources for his own text ("Use of the excellent notes of Hodge to the *Ayer Memorial* [*1630 Memorial*] and of his and Bolton's mono-graphic studies of the Jumanos . . . has been made"[32]), not even a whisper of the editors' critical viewpoint emerges.[33] What Castañeda presents is not a metahistorical interpretation of the narrative; it is a sincere history that he anticipated his readers would understand as such.

Had Castañeda been aware of the ubiquity and impact of Sor Ma-ria's writing in colonial Mexico, including Texas, this presentation might have seemed more balanced. Yet in spite of his promotion of the Lady in Blue in early Texas Catholic history, he, like his historian predecessors and contemporaries, gives no weight to this vital element of Sor María's New Spanish history.

Perhaps to avoid raising any additional critical eyebrows of his historian colleagues, *Our Catholic Heritage in Texas* omits a folk narrative about the Lady in Blue that Castañeda cites in later writing. In his short story "The Woman in Blue," published in a special edition of the Marian magazine *Age of Mary* in 1958, his interest in Lady in Blue lore and history is evident.[34] That edition of the magazine was dedicated to Sor María and *La mística ciudad de dios*, and its distinctly hagiographic bent was expressed through articles defending *La mística ciudad de dios*; it affirmed the Lady in Blue narrative, outlined the institutional histories of book and nun, and contained creative pieces, such as Castañeda's. His short story presents a fictional account of the Lady in Blue narrative similar to his *Our Catholic Heritage in Texas* entry. Accompanied by an illustration of Sor María instructing what one assumes are Jumanos clustered about her, Castañeda's story changes the sound of his historical narrative by adding details and dialogue. This makes the same information appealing to the fiction reader, and establishes Fray Estevan de Perea, who both preceded and succeeded Fray Benavides, as the story's protagonist.

Most of the story proceeds along the lines of Sor María's biography in *Our Catholic History in Texas*. However, Castañeda disturbingly depicts native tribes as an infantilized blur. Their language is pidgin, constructed to seem ignorant and express simplistic thoughts ("Young, old, me no can tell . . . she came many times, many moons, again and again. We like her."[35]). The fictionalized Sor María herself delivers this opinion: "All Indian chiefs look much alike . . . they all wear headdresses and ornaments, all use paint to disfigure their features. . . . I know [native leader "Chief El Tuerto"] well, a good man who wants to be good."[36] The story, like many of the folk renderings of the Lady in Blue examined later in this chapter, is exceedingly troubling; its patronizing tone capitalizes on the colonizing view towards native populations that is part of many readings of the Lady in Blue narrative:

The story's conclusion makes a marked transition into borderlands lore: The last time the Woman in Blue appeared to them [the Texas Indians], she blessed them and was then slowly wafted away into the distant hills before she disappeared in the encircling gloom of eventide. Next morning the plains and fields were covered with a carpet of strange flowers, all of a deep blue shade that reminded them of the mantel she wore. It seemed to them that where her flowing cloak trailed as she was wafted away on the wings of air, the lovely flowers had sprung up over night.[37]

Castañeda's addition of folklore does not stand out for how it is written, or for its fit with the rest of the story. Nor is the bit of lore particularly unique; other lore sources attribute the story of Sor María's bluebonnets to the Mexican American community. Castañeda says it originates from an "Indian legend," exotifying the lore and at the same time suggesting its lack of consequence in the present day. But his choices about where to include the lore—namely, not in his historical text—is revealing. Castañeda seemingly acknowledges through this gesture that others could see lore as perhaps diminishing the rigor of his history, though he himself values and records it in his short historical story.

Castañeda's personal knowledge of Sor María was considerable, but, as mentioned earlier, he either did not know about or did not find important her writing's impact in colonial Mexico. His archive at the Dolph Briscoe Center for American History at the University of Texas at Austin provides insight into what he did know about her writing. The archive includes a copy of the *Tratado del grado de la luz*, a mystical travel treatise attributed to Sor María, and archival copies of her letters to Felipe IV. The historian seemed close to seeing at least some of Sor María's fuller picture, though he did not document it in his writing. Castañeda's historical representation of the Lady in Blue narrative points to a resistive position vis-à-vis Sor María in Texas's history, while his problematic story suggests an adherence to folklore as a marker of cultural preservation. Jovita González, Castañeda's contemporary and fellow scholar, takes a different approach in her own bold assertion of the Lady in Blue's place in the history of Texas's women.

Jovita González, Sor María, and the Catholic Heroines of Texas

In August 1936, Jovita González published a short historical article in the *Southern Messenger*, a Catholic newspaper published in San Antonio, Texas. Entitled "Our Catholic Heroines of Texas," it featured brief biographical accounts of twenty-two Catholic Texan women, most Spanish and Mexican, who "made every sacrifice within their power for the welfare of our people and advancement of our state."[38] Of the many "wonders and great events" in Texan history that González recounts, "none is more marvelous than our 'Woman in Blue,'" the first individual described in her article.

"Our Catholic Heroines of Texas" played a small part in the Texas Centennial of 1936, which commemorated Texas's 1836 independence from Mexico to form a sovereign nation. The *Southern Messenger* article was intended to complement González's exhibit at the Central Centennial Exhibition in Dallas. Her display of "photographs, short biographical narratives and material culture" was called "Catholic Heroines of Texas,"[39] a feature of the Catholic exhibit sponsored by the Diocese of Dallas.

Although the centennial was marketed as a shared civil commemoration, events and publications associated with the event directly and indirectly perpetuated the marginalization of the state's Mexican American population. In response, Tejano writers and scholars "formulate[d] literary responses that critiqued the link between racist representations and racial domination while envisioning a prominent and honored place for their community within the Lone Star State."[40] As literary scholar John Morán González notes, this Tejano effort resulted in the crystallization of a "new, politicized ethnic identity—Mexican American."[41] Through the publication of this article (and the composition of her novels *Caballero* and *The Dew on the Thorn*), Jovita González not only advanced the idea of Mexican American identity, but she also sought to establish an historical female agency within that group. The Lady in Blue narrative plays a part in this project.

"Catholic Heroines of Texas" opens with a description of long-standing Mexican American commemorative practices evoking the Lady in Blue: "To this day, beautiful legends, stories and beliefs are still told about her, and every Mexican cemetery in the state has its quota of blue crosses and blue fences around the grove, and blue coffins are still in popular use."[42] González then provides background for the popular practices she describes with a brief historical account of Sor María that includes specific dates and individuals from the nun's biography and references to Sor Luisa de Carrión and Fray Benavides, elements drawn from the friar's *Memorials*. González closes the account by citing Fray Damián Manzanet's report of the request for blue burial cloth for the mother of Tejas man. As González writes the Lady in Blue narrative, Mexican American traditions concerning narrative substantiate the historical narrative, not the reverse, as in Castañeda. Shared praxis within the community is prioritized above the purely "historical," and González's article defines the lore as Tejano, claimed by a Mexican American/Tejana.

González takes care to stress that Sor María's evangelization pre-dated that of all male mission friars who had traditionally been under-stood as founders of the Catholic Church in Texas: "Great then was the wonder of the first missionaries to find the Indians acquainted with the truths of Our Holy Religion and ready for the Salvation of the Lord."[43] González's heroine was comprehensive in her evangelization—more so than any of her male religious successors—as "no part of our state seems to have been neglected, for the Jumanos on the Concho River around present-day San Angelo knew her as well as the Tejas of East Texas."[44] Indeed, in Sor María, González challenges the idea of male primacy in Texas; the male friars and settlers who followed pale in comparison to Sor María and simply follow the path she laid straight.

John Morán González observes that the article as a whole "marked a milestone in the writing of tejanas into Texas history as perhaps the first published account in English by a tejana detailing their historical influ-ence and importance."[45] Through the "Woman in Blue" and the other female historical figures, Jovita González asserts female agency in Texas history that responded both to the "Anglo-Texan racial triumphalism"[46] and to a patriarchal view of women by other groups, including Mexican Americans themselves.

Because González's article progresses chronologically, the "Woman in Blue" is its first entry, lending it a prominence underscored by Gon-zález's introduction to the piece: "The historic past of our state is filled with wonders and great events, but none more marvelous than our 'Woman in Blue' and her supernatural bilocations to Texas from her convent in Spain."[47] In addition to its prominent placement and presen-tation, González develops the piece thoroughly; she dedicates more page space to the "Woman in Blue" than to most of the other Texan women she profiles further along in the article. In claiming both the lore and the history of the Lady in Blue for the Mexican American community, and for Tejanas particularly, González not only draws on the autochthonous folk traditions treating her to the forefront, but she also reinforces the connection between Sor María and the Mexican American community. Distressingly, but perhaps not unexpectedly, the authorial Sor María makes no appearance.

González's staging of the Lady in Blue narrative is affirming and subversive in this context, representative of the strategies she used that implemented folklore, history, and fiction discourses to question border modernity. In fact, by signaling the "Woman in Blue" as an important figure in lore and history, González may have provoked her mentor, J. Frank "Pancho" Dobie. As literary critics José Limón and María Cotera have noted, González's relationship with Dobie was at times fraught, particularly regarding issues relating to Mexican American identity, lore, and history in the context of a hegemonic Anglo Texas.[48] One cannot help but wonder if, years later, Dobie's categorization of the Lady in Blue narrative as "sacerdotal humbuggery" rather than "authentic" Mexican lore responded in some way to the perspective of his former student.[49] Their wildly divergent viewpoints on it are indicative of the deep rifts that existed between Tejanos and Anglo Texans; González's article is typical of her understated resistive stance within that dynamic.

Adina De Zavala and the Lady Who Lives under the Alamo

Adina De Zavala's rendering of the narrative and its legends is the most openly confrontational and overtly resistive of the three individuals presented here. De Zavala self-published her *History and Legends of the Alamo and Other Missions in and around San Antonio* in 1917.[50] It was a work consisting of "varied narrative forms,"[51] including folklore from a Mexican American perspective on the history and legends associated with the Alamo. For De Zavala, the mixed-race granddaughter of the first vice president the Republic of Texas, Lorenzo de Zavala, the Alamo was a site of acrimonious and ongoing debate. She had been locked in a long and bitter confrontation with a branch of the Daughters of the Republic of Texas and their leader, Clara Driscoll, for control over both the site of the Alamo (where the famous Battle of the Alamo between Mexican and Texan forces occurred in 1836) and the popular history of those events.

For more than ten years, De Zavala intensely lobbied from within the Daughters of the Republic of Texas (DRT) to preserve the original Alamo, then a commercial property owned by the Hugo and Schmeltzer Company; the DRT under Clara Driscoll had dismissed the building as irrelevant to the Alamo's history. De Zavala also sought to ensure that the Mexican protagonists and participants in the Battle of the Alamo were enshrined in the site's public history. Though De Zavala did successfully protect the original Alamo structure from demolition, her efforts to mitigate against what would become the Anglo-Texan–dominated master narrative of the Alamo were less successful. Nevertheless, after De Zavala formally resigned from the DRT (and her self-founded chapter was expelled from the organization),[52] De Zavala became "the organization's most vocal critic, constantly reminding the public of its failure to adhere to historical accuracy and its myopic vision of the Alamo's historical significance."[53] De Zavala's work to inscribe Mexicans back into the history of Texas and to preserve other structures important to Texas's history continued vigorously for many more decades. She founded the Texas Historical Landmarks Association and was active in both the Texas State Historical Society and the Texas Folklore Society. De Zavala's publication of *History and Legends of the Alamo* was another manifestation of her resistive career.

Judging from the book's dedication, the wounds from De Zavala's rounds with the DRT were still fresh. She dedicates the book to "The 'De Zavala Daughters,' Noble, Loyal, Unselfish, Patriotic Women in Whose Veins Course the Blood of the Heroes, Statesmen, Patriots, Pioneers, and Founders of Texas and to [sic] De Zavala Chapter [of the DRT]."[54] In dedicating the book to the organization that unsuccessfully sought to secure Mexican American's role in the state's public historical narrative, De Zavala sets up *History and Legends of the Alamo* to implicitly affirm those aims.[55] The book features several colonial-era and nineteenth-century historical narratives about the Alamo and surrounding missions, yet her treatment of the Lady in Blue narrative is unique in that it reaffirms De Zavala's own actions of preservation and resistance on the part of San Antonio's Tejanos. Among the three Mexican American accounts discussed in this section, De Zavala's example of Lady in Blue lore is the most elaborate, showcasing significant innovations on it that were of specific relevance to the Mexican American community.

De Zavala's "The Mysterious Woman in Blue and Her Gift to San Antonio by the Hand of One Woman Every Generation" is part of the chapter "Ghosts of the Alamo," and the Lady in Blue is one of the "Folk of the Underground Passages."[56] De Zavala does not attribute this legend to the Mexican American community directly, nor does she claim it as her own. She credits the story to local "folktellers," who are depicted in a troubling picture in the book that acutely contrasts with De Zavala's own elegant image.[57] She locates the folk narratives in pre-Republic, Mexican Texas; referencing the "old inhabitants of San Antonio de Béxar,"[58] she asserts that "it is a well-known fact that the papers of San Antonio, years ago, from time to time, chronicled marvelous tales of ghosts appearing at the Alamo."[59] Thus, although she does not claim the account directly for Tejanos, her framing of the lore—in particular the fact that it was written down—places it squarely in the domain of Mexican American Texas.

De Zavala's Lady in Blue of lore is very different from other versions; yet, as we will see, De Zavala unmistakably connects her with Sor María through the historical background on the nun near the book's end. De Zavala's Lady in Blue emerges from the Alamo's underground tunnels "once in a generation or when her gift has lapsed"[60] to give her gift to a worthy woman. This woman is always a native Texan (i.e., a Tejana) who is physically somewhat similar to De Zavala, with "eyes of grey . . . dark, fine hair—not black."[61] The recipient's personal character is "superior, pure and good, well-bred, intelligent, spiritual and patriotic."[62] Though the woman who receives the gift always uses it for the betterment of her people, she is not always aware that she has been given the gift.

What is the Lady in Blue's gift? It is, in De Zavala's words, "the gift of seeing to the heart of things! She sees with the clear-eyed vision of a Joan of Arc all that may vitally affect, for good or ill, the people of her city and State whom she ardently loves with a strange devotion. All the children are her children—all the people are her friends, and brothers and sisters! There is no can't, and no pretense—it is real."[63] The woman given this ability by the Lady in Blue frustrates her enemies' ill intents against the population she is poised to defend, "the whole people of San Antonio."[64] Though the most valiant of her actions on their behalf are kept secret, this champion of San Antonio is recognized by those who see with clear eyes what she has done to help "the rich, the poor, the artist, the artisan, the writer, the children."[65] De Zavala's account ends with an exhortation to those who would not believe in the Lady in Blue, her gift, and the woman who wields it: "If you do not profit by the Gift, the fault is yours, not that of the Mysterious Woman in Blue, nor of the Woman who holds the precious Gift as Almoner for San Antonio."[66]

De Zavala's account is intensely personal and resistive as she presents it. The woman endowed with the Lady in Blue's gift is always on the side of right, and she embodies the qualities of the De Zavala Daughters: "humanity, truth, justice and patriotism."[67] The characteristics De Zavala so clearly values in herself and others are portrayed as a type of a supernatural endowment, positing the possibility that De Zavala saw herself as the recipient of the Lady in Blue's gift, used to benefit the "native" inhabitants of San Antonio, at a moment when that help, according to De Zavala, was badly needed.

After her detailed and pointed explanation of the Lady in Blue lore, De Zavala parallels Castañeda's and González's approach; she provides historical background for the Lady in Blue/Sor María. As with González, De Zavala's lore is the featured element, and the narrative's history supports and justifies it. De Zavala ensures there can be no doubt about the veracity of Sor María's travels to Texas: "Numerous were her writings descriptive of these people, their country, customs and names of tribes, and it was afterwards found to be correct and true."[68]

De Zavala includes a historical description of Sor María, but she does not reveal her sources for that information.[69] Though she references Fray Alonso de Benavides earlier in the historical section of the book, in De Zavala's estimation, he is not the author of the narrative. Instead, De Zavala focuses on the chronicles of seventeenth-century explorer Alonso de León and Fray Damián Manzanet as historical evidence of the Lady in Blue's visits to Texas. De Zavala's historical treatment of Sor María, like González's, emphasizes the agency of women in Texas's early colonial history: "It being impossible for Mary de Agreda to remain long at a time with these Indians, she made them frequent visits, gaining the devoted love of the women and reverential respect of the men of the tribe."[70] In *History and Legends of the Alamo*, Adina De Zavala inscribes an entirely new Mexican American folkloric account of the Lady in Blue (one which, given the historical context, is clearly resistive); in incorporating the history of Sor María's travels, she further emphasizes the active nature of the lore's heroines, both the Lady in Blue and the present-day recipient of her gift.

A Resistive Lady in Blue in Early Twentieth-Century Tejano Scholarship

The works by Carlos Castañeda, Jovita González, and Adina De Zavala share a unique approach to the Lady in Blue narrative, making it function resistively on behalf of the early twentieth-century Mexican American community in Texas. Drawing on Mikhail Bakhtin, ethnographer Enrique Lamadrid notes that the way the three Tejanos deploy lore is not an uncommon strategy, especially among groups that have suffered repression. Through the recollection and evocation of legends and folkloric narratives, "tradition and identity are negotiated and endowed with value and prestige by tracing the group's origins back to a loftier, even supernatural, vision of initial events."[71] Castañeda, González, and De Zavala articulate and valorize Mexican Americans' roles in Texas's "initial events," resisting prevailing ideational bias and institutional opposition through their valorization of the Lady in Blue narrative.

All three implement both historical and folkloric versions of the Lady in Blue narrative as a means of establishing the primacy of Mexican Americans in Texas. The intentional deployment of the two genres together in these accounts is revealing. Although Castañeda was the only historian by profession, in each case, the evocation of an authoritative historical precedent provided a "rational" center for the folkloric narrative, even when, as in González and De Zavala, the lore was given precedence in the narrative's presentation. They wrote about the past in a manner considered at the time to be "lesser" or "unofficial"—through folklore—and therefore potentially threatened the hegemonic order that was in consolidation.[72] The tactic they employed anticipated and preemptively defended the folk tradition by providing it with what was perceived as a legitimizing context.

Of the three, Jovita González claims the Lady in Blue folklore as her own cultural praxis. Although retention and innovation on the narrative occurred in Mexican American/Indo-Hispano communities throughout Texas and New Mexico, Castañeda is vague on the folk account's origins. De Zavala leads the reader to understand that the lore has Tejano origins, but she does so indirectly. Yet regardless of how each author claims the lore, all take great pains to make sure that the folklore accounts are a significant element of what is recounted, an act of subtle defiance.

Why do these authors seek to establish historical precedence for Tejanos through what is essentially a colonizing figure? Because the Mexican American community strongly identified as Catholic, in a sense, their social significance was reinforced by the affirmation of a Catholic folkloric figure. Deploying the Catholic Lady in Blue in the context of Anglo Protestant cultural domination was itself an assertion of religious and cultural opposition. Perhaps it was less a case of historical colonization narrative versus real-time colonizing forces, and more one of the subversion of a prevailing social order through narrative. González and De Zavala use the narrative to an additional resistive end, namely, to articulate women's political and historical agency within the Mexican American community, affecting not only Mexican Americans but also Texas society as a whole.

Finally, how Castañeda, Jovita González, and De Zavala locate the Lady in Blue folklore in time is also important. The practices associated with the Lady in Blue in the lore—the legacy of the Texas bluebonnets, using blue casket linings and crosses, accepting and using her "gift"—are written about as contemporary events by these authors. They describe these beliefs and practices as active at the time they were writing. This imbues the lore, and thus the Lady in Blue narrative, with a relevance that continued into the early twentieth century (and beyond); the Lady in Blue was not a dim artifact of the past, but a figure relevant to early twentieth-century Texas. In contrast, many of the accounts described in the next section either relegate the practices and beliefs to bygone eras and/or localize them within marginalized communities. In effect, those renderings seek to preserve "lore" as a relic of a quaint, bygone, and largely irrelevant past. For Castañeda, Jovita González, and De Zavala, in contrast, the Lady in Blue functions actively on behalf of the contemporaneous Mexican American community, and in resistance to cultural pressures and behaviors prevalent in early twentieth-century Texas.

Extinguishing Canons, Healing the Sick, and Wailing along Roadsides: The Lady in Blue in Collections of Folklore

In the lore presented by Castañeda, Jovita González, and De Zavala, the Lady in Blue assumes dimensions aside from the conversion of native tribes in Texas and New Mexico. In many other folkloric accounts, the Lady in Blue's agency is similarly expanded. These other versions describe activities of the Lady in Blue that typically are presented as occurring after the colonial era, but before the time period in which the author of the story is writing. Unlike Castañeda, Jovita González, and

De Zavala, in these accounts, the Lady in Blue's actions are framed strictly as things of the past, either because of the narrative's historical constraints (it is associated with a specific earlier event) or because the author wishes to maintain the sense that such stories no longer pertained to the time when they were written. The folklore collectors who tell these stories are both engaged by and simultaneously distanced from the narrative because they locate the events in a supposed "prerational" period or among "superstitious" people.

Additive folk accounts of this nature frequently omit or obfuscate the sources for the folk elements of their texts, and they can be vague in their descriptions of the stories and practices they document; this occurs even though the stories are definitively correlated with the historical Sor María. *Arizona Twilight Tales*,[73] for example, includes a long historical narrative about Sor María that contextualizes her with La Llorona and the Virgin of Guadalupe as female folk icons of the Southwest. Author Jane Eppinga notes of Arizona lore that "[the Lady in Blue's] image has been seen in the gnarled roots of a mesquite tree, in the rust of leaking water pipes, and in many other unlikely places,"[74] but she does not provide any informant or source for the folk anecdote. *Ghost Stories from the American Southwest*[75] offers two versions of the Lady in Blue. The first is based on historical narrative, but the second is sourced from an indigenous-sounding but unidentified place "in the [unnamed] Pueblo."[76] This narrative claims that the Lady in Blue had been ill during her visits to the (anonymous) tribe, and when she left, she promised to send teachers (perhaps Franciscan friars?) who would "help the Indians who also suffered from illnesses."[77] This account offers the specific detail that although the Lady in Blue had never arrived as far as New Mexico, she continued to be commemorated in the present day by an unspecific native group in New Mexico—"and yet the Tanoan Indians remember her in legend and tell that where she walked, her footsteps had caused wild blue flowers to bloom."[78]

Most examples of Lady in Blue "lore" simply rewrite the history of the Lady in Blue in a folk mode. They add little new, but in framing it like lore, the narrative is abstracted from the realm of history and relocated in the (typically "bygone") world of folklore. Some examples of this include *The Lore of New Mexico*,[79] *Legends of Texas*,[80] *The Folklore of Texan Cultures*,[81] *Las Mujeres Hablan*,[82] *Ghost Stories from the American Southwest*,[83] *Texas Unexplained*,[84] *Folk Tales of New Mexico*,[85] and

Off the Beaten Trail.[86] The narrative as lore has also served as fodder for popular reading, including in the Texas Good Roads Association's October 1952 *Texas Parade Magazine*[87] and the American Catholic Church Extension Society publication *Extension Magazine.*[88] Numerous newspaper features, short magazine articles, and other types of publications also recount the narrative, usually in relationship to similar events in a given place.[89] The Lady in Blue is often invoked in these contexts to give "local flavor" or regional authenticity, a tendency we will see repeated in contemporary artifacts in chapter 6.

Other versions of the lore present a Lady in Blue who engages in activities other than converting indigenous tribes. In these cases, the relationship to the historical Sor María is almost nonexistent, and these stories are often distanced from the Lady in Blue as an evangelizer. Needless to say, Sor María the writer is not even a footnote—her authorial legacy is completely nullified in the "folk" tradition represented in these dramatically additive accounts. This type of lore is included in this book because, in naming the protagonist as the Lady in Blue, the collectors of the folk stories make such an interpretation possible, and not without reason—they write about regions in which there is a legacy of Lady in Blue history and lore.

In these additive versions, creative work has clearly been done on the narrative, modifying it significantly from the colonial-era version. Yet, *who* did this creative work? The anonymous informants? The authors of the texts who record the stories? Almost none of the other legends' compilers identify their sources with specificity. Most cite a "shared knowledge" arising from a generalized socio-racial group, but this, of course, is problematic for a variety of reasons. It is therefore difficult to determine in most cases when or where the work on the Lady in Blue narrative occurred. This complexity is compounded when one takes into account how the authors of the texts considered here portray their sources; the groups of production are often described in belittling terms that devalue them as the stories' sources, even as the folklore collectors themselves exploit the stories to their own ends.

What follows is a selection of these complicated but illustrative legends dealing with the Lady in Blue narrative, organized according to where the stories are alleged to have originated. The first site is Arizona, in Margaret Proctor Redondo's 1993 account of a nineteenth-century Lady in Blue who stops the advance of the U.S. Army to protect a Mexican church and the inhabitants of a nearby community. Next, Texas's multiple and entangled legends of the Lady in Blue are examined: Joe F. Combs's 1965 story of her intervention among ill nineteenth-century Texans near the Sabine River; Harry Pettey's account of a La Llorona–like Lady in Blue (1963); and Francis Abernethy's 1994 version of the Lady in Blue, which draws on elements of the Combs and Pettey stories, and also on an uncredited Adina De Zavala. Spanning Arizona, Texas, and New Mexico, Clive Hallenbeck and Juanita Williams's 1938 *Legends of the Spanish Southwest* offers three unique and elaborate stories the authors claim originated from the three states; their presentation of the legends and their sources is especially disconcerting. In New Mexico, legends of the Lady in Blue have both written and oral sources; Alice Bullock's *Living Legends of the Santa Fe Country* (1970) is of the former, as is May Raizizun's 1962 *New Mexico Magazine* piece, while four oral interviews from the Baughman Folklore Collection at the Center for Southwest Research at the University of New Mexico (1948–81), taken from interviews with G. L. Campbell, "Mrs. Ed Dwyer," Julia Keleher, and Mark Gens, record oral tellings of the Lady in Blue narrative. Taken together, these folk narratives illustrate the breadth and duration of the imaginative work done on the Lady in Blue since the nineteenth century.

A Foiled American Filibuster in Sonora: The Intrepid Lady in Blue of Caborca

Margaret Proctor Redondo's article "Valley of Iron: One Family's History of Madera Canyon," published in the *Journal of Arizona History*,[90] is a lore account corroborated by more than one source, allegedly including a published eyewitness account. Proctor Redondo's story, which includes an introduction by Arizona folklorist James Griffith, is very detailed, complete with historical data. In it, the Lady in Blue protects a Mexican Catholic church and the Sonorans who lived nearby in what is now southern Arizona from invading U.S. forces. Proctor Redondo's family had owned a ranch in the Madera Canyon area, in southeastern Arizona, and she claims Mexican descent, thus her connection to the lore. The version of the story Proctor Redondo retells was narrated by her mother, who in turn had heard it from other women in her family ("from her grandmother and her mother"[91]). Proctor Redondo maintains that her grandmother was four years old at the time the events of the story took place.

As the legend goes, a U.S. filibuster expedition (unauthorized military incursion to a foreign country) led by Henry Crabbe arrived on April 2, 1857, to a site near Caborca, Sonora, where his troops buried a small treasure before advancing on the town. The inhabitants of Caborca had barricaded themselves inside the town's church to defend against the filibusters (irregular U.S. soldiers), while Crabbe's troops holed up in a small, thatched-roof building in front of the church. They attacked the church from this base station over the course of two or three days. Eventually, Crabbe's troops tried to definitively end the assault: they rolled a barrel of gunpowder in front of the church's entrance, readying it for explosion. Curiously, the fuse to the gunpowder was repeatedly extinguished, and the Mexicans were able to withstand the assault for several more days inside the intact church. On April 6, the leader of the Mexican forces inside the church, José María Redondo, convinced a Tohono O'odham man named Francisco Xavier to shoot the roof of the Americans' hideout with a flaming arrow to chase the soldiers out. Crabbe's men fled from the burning building straight into advancing Mexican troops led by José María Girón. The U.S. troops surrendered, and all except a young sharpshooter named Charlie Evans were killed by the Mexican soldiers.

After these events concluded, Evans asked the Mexican survivors who the young woman dressed in blue was who had repeatedly extinguished the fuse on the barrel in front of the church. According to Evans, the Americans lit the fuse three different times, and each time the young woman snuck to the front of the church and extinguished the flame, much to the surprise of Crabbe's men. Evans tried to shoot at her and missed, and the other soldiers unleashed a "hail of bullets"[92] at her, which had no effect. Evans said this process was repeated "five or six times"[93] without causing any harm to the church or its occupants before the U.S. troops surrendered.

In this story, the Lady in Blue functions as the protector of a community under duress, shielding them from a dominating military force. In Caborca, she daringly protects Mexican citizens from unwanted U.S. Army incursions by repeatedly extinguishing a live cannon, actions that even Crabbe's soldiers considered terribly, terribly dangerous.

Within the folk narrative as Proctor Redondo writes it, the young woman dressed in blue at the Caborca church is not associated with the Lady in Blue; the story's narrators create that association. Griffith mulls over the young woman in his introduction: "Was she the Virgin of the Immaculate Conception protecting Her own church, or a post-humous appearance of Sor María de Agreda?"[94] He reflects on the "well-known narrative pattern in the Hispanic world"[95] that, from his perspective, the Lady in Blue narrative embodied. Proctor Redondo posits the connection between the Lady in Blue and the mysterious defender of Caborca, calling the former a legend "known throughout the Southwest and northern Mexico about a Spanish nun who appeared mostly to Indians."[96] Though Griffith's introduction to the story cites an account written by Charlie Evans and the testimony of eyewitnesses to the events as sources for the folk narrative, he offers no bibliography for either account.

A Mysterious Woman Who Heals and Frightens: Texas Lore of the Lady in Blue

As recorded by Joe F. Combs in his *Legends of the Pineys* (1965),[97] the Lady in Blue appeared in east Texas in the 1840s, also to help a local community under duress. Combs explains the events transpired in "historic old Sabinetown," a town near the Sabine River that was a "busy river port, and port of entry" in the early 1840s, but that had largely disappeared by the time Combs wrote his story. He notes that the account of the Lady in Blue and Sabinetown had no written record previous to his, but that it was "still told and retold with a feeling of deep respect for this mysterious lady with the soft white hands, black flowing hair, blue eyes and a body as graceful as a princess well covered with a blue silk dress."[98] Combs's account is quite detailed, citing local sources for the story, but Combs presents himself as an interloper in recounting the legend; he worries that in writing the story down he "might be invading the privacy of minds that hold the idea that because this legend has always been handed town from mouth to ear, and it should continue to be handed down in the same way."[99] Thus, the narrator avoids claiming the story for himself and is cognizant of the sensitivity of fixing oral stories in a written form.

As Combs tells it, when the Sabine River flooded in 1840 or 1841, locals suffered from a malady that they called "pernicious fever." It left them with high fevers, and made their tongues turn black and swell up, weakening its victims for several weeks or killing them. No doctors were nearby, and neighbors from other towns were too frightened to help the townspeople, who in their illness buried their own dead. Into this desperate situation appeared a "lady dressed in a blue silk dress. She was young, fresh and beautiful . . . a model of form and dignity . . . something about her tender approach brought a revival of their faith and kindled hope in their hearts."[100] She immediately comforted a family that had fallen ill, collecting herbs, roses, and other materials with which she made a tea for them, telling the mother, "Don't be afraid I have come here to help you."[101] Her remedy alleviated some of the symptoms, and she moved from home to home in the town without sleeping, compassionately sharing her cure with all the families without herself ever eating. She never shared her name. The afflicted improved, the healthy avoided contagion, and the townspeople were reinvigorated by her ministrations: "Her expression of profound interest, deep inner convictions and tenderness in dealing with ill persons caused them all to feel a thrill when she entered their rooms. There was something about the demeanor of the Lady in Blue that stirred their deepest emotions, and kindled their greatest faith."[102]

Combs notes a curious detail: while the woman was helping many of Sabinetown's ill, and somehow protecting those who were not sick from falling ill, she avoided patients who were severely ill: "On two or three occasions she was sent for when some ill person appeared to be approaching death, but she did not answer these calls. She treated them all, but seemed to be more interested in those who had a chance of recovery."[103]

Eventually, the recovering townspeople speculated as to her identity and wondered where she had come from. She discouraged too-pointed inquiries: "She stared at them long enough to give them the idea they were being too nosey [sic] and they would not press their point out of respect for her."[104] Others from outside the town, prevented from witnessing the events due to impassable, flooded roads, questioned the Lady in Blue's origins and if she really had been able to heal the black tongue illness. But the townspeople held firm that she had healed them, "for they had touched the soft hands, and looked upon the sympathetic eyes of the Lady in Blue too many times."[105]

As she made her last visit before leaving, the first little girl she had cured on arriving to Sabinetown insistently asked about her identity, and the Lady in Blue responded not with "Sor María" but with "Angelina," before walking away into the distance.[106] Combs proposes that perhaps the Lady in Blue was referring to the little girl herself, calling her "little angel," but he does not really answer the question of who the Lady in Blue was. In fact, although Combs calls her the Lady in Blue throughout his account, there is no obvious connection between the woman who saved the lives of the townspeople and either the Lady in Blue narrative or Sor María; the story's protagonist could have been associated with any female legend. As we will soon see, Texan folklore collector Frank Abernethy includes a summary of Combs's account in his 1994 *Legendary Ladies of Texas*, and it is he who connects Sor María/the Lady in Blue narrative with the legend of the Sabine River illness.

Harry Pettey published a legend linking the Lady in Blue to Texas geography in 1963, in the Nacogdoches, Texas, newspaper the *Daily Sentinel*.[107] Unlike most other variations on the Lady in Blue narrative, Pettey's story does not depict her in a mode of helping others. Instead, this account echoes a motif attributed to La Llorona, the crying woman of Borderlands lore. Pettey portrays the Lady in Blue as "an eerie ghost nun who walks the road . . . by night, crying."[108] As she wanders, "she cries for all the blood shed in violence along the ancient highway."[109] Pettey creates an explicit link between this figure and the Lady in Blue, stating that "this nun story may have partly grown out of the legend about Mother Agreda, or the Angel in Blue, who miraculously went among the Indians in spirit."[110] Pettey adds a detail connecting his story to the seventeenth-century account by Fray Damián Manzanet that mentioned a desire for blue cloth among the Tejas tribes; Pettey reports that "the Indians of Nacogdoches . . . treasured blue cloth"[111] and asked to be buried in it.

In *Legendary Ladies of Texas*, Abernethy links Combs's and Pettey's folk accounts with the historical narrative of the Lady in Blue.[112] The preface to his chapter is the image from the frontispiece to the 1730 *Tanto que se sacó de una carta*. Abernethy goes on to cite several historical sources for the Lady in Blue narrative, but he frames the narrative clearly as lore, not as history: "The first woman of Texas legend after the coming of Church and chains and armored horse and rider was a fair and loving figure somewhere between the world of legend and myth."[113] He justifies his linkage of what, to him, is obviously fictitious, to history by noting that "the legendary ones always have some touch with reality and real time and space and history."[114] Abernethy draws on the *1630 Memorial*, Carlos Castañeda's *Our Catholic Heritage in Texas* entry, José

Antonio Pichardo's report on Texas and Louisiana, and Fray Damián Manzanet's letter to Carlos Sigüenza y Góngora to reconstruct a rough historical account of Sor María. He even makes brief mention of her authorship of the "very controversial" *La mística ciudad de dios*, but describes how she came to write the text with a tone of barely tempered ridicule: "María claimed she was transported in 1627, this time to the Celestial City, where God commanded her to write the definitive biography of the Virgin. Not to be unreasonable, he gave her eight angels as assistants and then showed her all the stages of the Virgin's life."[115]

Abernethy centers the question of whether she did or did not actually travel to Texas at the heart of his historical discussion, but he comes to no conclusive answer, and his line of historical questioning locates the origin of the narrative with the native tribes of Texas, not with the colonial-era New Spanish sources he cites: "So what happened? Were the Lady in Blue's appearances examples of mass hysteria among the Indians? . . . Or was it the ultimate con game played by the Indians on the Spanish in order to get the gifts the priests handed out along with their more abstract blessings?"[116] This historical/mythical summary tangles back onto itself in attempting to explain the epistemology of the Lady in Blue, confusingly commenting that Texan folk legends about her and eighteenth-century Franciscan missionary Fray Antonio Margil de Jesús are "the last flickerings of the Medieval Age of Faith and were, in a sense, anachronisms,"[117] a muddling between reality and myth that was resolved by Erasmus and the "men of enlightment [*sic*] of the Renaissance."[118] He foregrounds his discussion of lore by stating that such stories "continued to circulate among the Indians and Spanish of East Texas,"[119] though he does not cite any specific sources.

In his treatment of lore about the Lady in Blue, Abernethy adds to the two accounts described above. The most interesting aspect of Abernethy's rendering is his decision to associate the legend of healing near the Sabine River with the Lady in Blue narrative. Abernethy cites Combs's account in his bibliography, so he must have known that Combs suggested the woman in that story was called Angelina, opening interpretation as to who the woman of legend actually was.[120] There was no a priori connection in Combs's version to the Sor María of Abernethy's chapter. Abernethy does not provide his reasoning for his association between the savior of Sabinetown and the Lady in Blue, but he certainly strives to associate them.

In summarizing Pettey's story of the Lady in Blue/Llorona, Abernethy does not need to forge a connection between the narrative and the wailing woman; Pettey already does that in his account. But Abernethy alters what that connection signifies in his summary of the lore. In Abernethy's conclusion, the Lady in Blue wanders along the "old Smugglers [*sic*] Road" outside of Nacogdoches, not for the death and violence that occurred there, but rather "in mourning for the vanished Tejas who she came to save."[121] Pettey's story has more to do with the historical conditions at the time of the legend's origination; Abernethy wills the Lady in Blue of the Nacogdoches roadway to conform explicitly to the ends of Catholic conversion he describes in his own historical narrative. Abernethy's two entries into the world of Lady in Blue lore, though well informed by historical texts, represent active exercises on the part of the author to locate Sor María in early Texan lore.

Lore across Arizona, Texas, and New Mexico: Hallenbeck and Williams's *Legends of the Spanish Southwest*

Cleve Hallenbeck and Juanita Williams's *Legends of the Spanish Southwest* (1938) presents three different folk narratives about the Lady in Blue, each attributed to a different region in the Southwest. As context, Hallenbeck and Williams provide some historical framing for her presence in Texas, Arizona, and New Mexico, drawing on many of the same colonial-era documents that the Tejano folklorists discussed above used in their texts. Their book demonstrates a preoccupation typical of historians and folklorists of their generation in that they define a position regarding the veracity of the Lady in Blue's alleged physical travel to the Southwest. Hallenbeck and Williams defend this aspect of the narrative by saying that "if it were impossible for Maria to leave Spain without being prominently recorded, why did Fray Benavides and Fray Manzanet accept her presence here as something not to be doubted?"[122] Yet the authors' concern for precision does not extend to their own ethnographic work: they do not name the sources for the folk narratives they recount in the text. Further, their treatment of indigenous tribes in the text in relationship to the narrative is extremely disturbing.

Hallenbeck and Williams make the peculiar claim that, while she was present in the Southwest, "[the Lady in Blue] avoided contact with others of her race in America. We find not a trace of evidence that she was ever seen by anyone, except Indians, on this side of the Atlantic."[123] They substantiate this by affirming that, whether in Arizona, Texas, or New Mexico, she spoke to the tribes she encountered in their native languages, and they "apparently had no difficulty in understanding her exposition of christian [sic] doctrines."[124] Hallenbeck and Williams locate the early narrative among indigenous Texans, and they later suggest that a corpus of "little stories of the Blue Lady, or the Lady in Blue, are to be found in the San Antonio valley of Texas,"[125] but only among the inhabitants "of part indian [sic] blood."[126] Since no actual sources are documented, it is impossible to know on what basis Hallenbeck and Williams make these claims for the lore's indigenous origins.

The book asserts that the (unattributed) Texas legends are legitimate, but casts doubt on the authenticity of Lady in Blue stories from New Mexico and Arizona, without any explanation for the differentiation. As the framing of the stories continues, Hallenbeck and Williams begin to confuse or meld the legends' groups of origin. Although they first declare indigenous roots for the narrative, they later cite Mexican "story-tellers" as their primary informants, who will not reveal their tales to just anyone: "A stranger will hear none of them from the lips of the Mexicans. Unless one has won the confidence and esteem of those people . . . they regard with suspicion, perhaps not unjustified, that Anglo-American who too obviously attempts to make their acquaintances."[127]

The first story shared by Hallenbeck and Williams is, they claim, a "typical one that has been told for one and one-half centuries"[128] in Texas. The story is very specific as far as the names of its characters, and the dates during which the story occurred (1780–1800), are concerned, but again it offers no information about who actually told the tale to them (which would provide validation for the narrative). The story takes place near San Antonio, Texas, and its protagonist is a Mexican American child named Ursula Valdez. Her father, José, gravely injured in a fight with the Comanche Indians, was unable to support his family, and therefore could not afford to travel to Mexico City where his injuries could be treated. While collecting flowers and playing with her playmates near the abandoned mission at San Antonio de Valero, Ursula disappeared. Her mother feared that she had been kidnapped by the Comanches, and the town searched for the little girl, eventually finding her asleep in a tower room in the former convent at San Antonio.

The girl explained that she had been playing with the other children nearby when a woman dressed in blue caught her garments on some shrubs and fell. Ursula disentangled the lady's dress and helped her to stand. In repayment, the lady gave Ursula a small, heavy package and left. Ursula hid in the convent as part of the game she was playing and fell asleep without opening the package. Once home, Ursula gave it to her mother, who found gold, diamonds, and pearls inside it. Ursula's family used this treasure to see the father treated, and he was able to resume work and support his family. Ursula's act of kindness towards a stranger was rewarded by the physical and economic restoration of her family that "so lately had been enveloped in despair."[129] Since the Lady in Blue's gift to Ursula resulted from her compassion, the narrators conclude that the interaction was a moral trial: "The Blue Lady had only pretended to be injured, in order to test Ursula's kindness of heart."

Some elements of the story are telling: the Lady in Blue appears in what is explained in the story as a formerly indigenous space (the mission site occupied what had been the natives' land), though the nature and purpose of the mission is neither elaborated nor questioned. The only line of dialogue is spoken by the man who finds Ursula, and it is indicative of the troubling patois Hallenbeck and Williams invent for the indigenous and Mexican characters in their stories: "*Sacramento! Diablita*! [Holy Sacrament! Little devil girl!] To cause us so much worry! Come you with me to your mother, quickly!" This same tendency is evident in the second story, which the authors reluctantly ascribe to New Mexico, as they cannot be sure whether stories of its ilk are "indigenous [to New Mexico] or have been imported from Texas."

In the second story, Hallenbeck and Williams claim to reproduce only a "general sense of the narrator's words,"[130] which is troublingly represented in a pidgin English that is supposed to represent the original narrator's voice. The narrator's identity is never stated and few clues point to it. Though the text is liberally sprinkled with Spanish phrases, many, like the reference to the "Jornada del muerte [*sic*],"[131] have linguistic errors no native speaker would make. The first-person narrator refers to "the war-chief of our pueblo," suggesting perhaps a native Puebloan identity, but there is no information that locates or defines his or her origins. The tale is foregrounded in an introduction consisting of generalities concerning the narrator's experience of the Lady in Blue: she brings blue flowers to the area, causes the natural environment to flourish, never appears at night, and vanishes if approached by people: in fact, the members of the narrator's community avoid getting too close to her: "*Que* [*sic*] *sacrilegio*! [What sacrilege!] Why molest her who brings only blessing with her?"[132] In the story that follows, the source of a natural spring of drinking water in southern New Mexico's arid south is explained via the Lady in Blue.

A "young Indian chief" out on a hunting expedition in the far southern mountains of New Mexico was called back to the tribe by a messenger informing him that his wife had become ill. The young man immediately turned for home, traveling through the desert, and became lost at night when clouds covered the stars he was using to guide his way. Desperately thirsty and close to death, he was saved when the "Blue Lady" guided him to a freshwater spring. He drank until he was well, at which point the clouds cleared and he found his way home, where his wife was cured upon seeing him. The storyteller concludes in his perplexing pidgin with a reference to the present day, speaking to a third party, who also remains anonymous: "And the spring is there today, Señor; the only water to drink that is to be found in the whole country of *la jornada del muerte* [*sic*]."[133]

The story seems to serve two purposes. It explains the existence of a spring of drinkable water in a remote location, found via the Lady in Blue's intervention, and it reinforces the value of loyalty to one's family in that the young man's attentiveness to his wife is rewarded with the valuable knowledge of where drinking water could be found in the desert.

Hallenbeck and Williams's final story is from Arizona, where they claim they unsuccessfully searched for native versions of "Kino's" story, referring no doubt to Fray Eusebio Kino's brief seventeenth-century mention of Sor María in his account of exploration in Pimería Alta. Their curious comment about that absent narrative—"if found it would have been the only existing legend of Maria Coronel that has come down from her own day exclusively through the Indians"[134]—shows that Hallenbeck and Williams perceived of their unnamed sources and of Lady in Blue lore in general as an artifact of indigenous groups, rather than of Spanish colonizing origin. Perhaps for this reason, the Arizona story is narrated in the first person by what seems to be a Tohono O'odham informant who speaks in stilted English peppered with Spanish-language references to "la Señorita Azul."[135] This story also occurred in the distant past — "before the grandfather of my grandmother's grandfather lived" — and is the only one of Hallenbeck and Williams's tales that mentions religion or evangelization specifically, as the Lady in Blue instructs the tribe in religious ideas,[136] and informs them that priests would follow in her wake: "The teachers came, as she foretold, and they told our people about the god of the white men."[137]

In the Arizona legend, a chief's grandson fell ill, and the tribe, gathered in worry for the child, was blinded by a flash of white light. A beautiful young woman dressed in blue appeared. She told the tribe that there was one God above all other gods, and her words were like "the music of a mountain stream to the ears of a thirsty man."[138] She asked if anyone in the tribe was ill. The chief led her to his grandson and daughter-in-law. The Lady in Blue "began saying prayers to the god whereof she had spoken," placing her hand on the child's head "for the time it would take to smoke a small pipe." The boy was miraculously healed and woke up hungry, at which point the visitor told the tribe to give him just water and wait until the next day to give him food.

The Lady in Blue did not stay, and she refused food for herself. Suddenly, the tribe was overcome by sleep, and the Lady in Blue disappeared. When they awoke, they doubted that the woman was real, but the boy was healthy and his mother confirmed that the Lady had visited and healed him. The narrator concludes the story by affirming that the priests the Lady in Blue foretold did arrive, and they taught the tribe to live "even as the white people lived."[139] The tribe and its chief are rewarded for accepting the Christianization and European colonization set out by the Lady in Blue.

In Hallenbeck and Williams's variations on the Lady in Blue, the authors posit that they relay folk narratives in good faith. They say that they distinguish between those legends from reliable sources and those whose sources they cannot verify.[140] Of course, if the informants' reliability was such an essential part of their selection of folk narratives, why is no informant named? Or identified? For his part, Cleve Hallenbeck was well aware of the historical precedent of the Lady in Blue. In his 1945 article in *New Mexico Magazine*, he takes the physical bilocation element of the Lady in Blue narrative to heart, presenting several arguments in support of her active role in the Southwest during the colonial era, such as naming the site of Gran Quivira.[141]

Blue Doorways and Bilocation Trances: Written and Oral Stories of the
Lady in Blue in New Mexico

The final grouping of folk narratives about the Lady in Blue is attributed to New Mexican sources by the people who collected the stories.
One such example is Alice Bullock's *Legends of the Santa Fe Country*,[142]
which locates the "Blue Lady" and stories about her near former Pueblo
settlement locations, specifically at Abó, Quarai, and Gran Quivira.[143]
Bullock describes commemorative practices she broadly ascribes to
"Indian and Spanish custom."[144] Though she avoids the derogatory
dialects used by Hallenbeck and Williams in their accounts, Bullock's
collection is nonetheless voyeuristic: she is clearly not a member of the
collective that produced the lore she recounts. After a brief historical
description of the Lady in Blue and a summary of other folk accounts,
Bullock introduces her (unattributed) story. It shares much in common
with one of Hallenbeck and Williams's tales. In Bullock's version, a girl
"lost on the Texas plain" is found by a woman dressed in a long blue
garment that the little girl describes as similar to a nun's habit.[145] The girl
is found three days later, and while she was lost she did not need food or
water because the Lady in Blue cared for her. In contrast to Hallenbeck
and Williams's Texas-origin story, there is no moral in this version to reinforce a particular behavior.

Bullock also describes a behavior she believes relates to the Lady
in Blue; it, too, originates in a community whose identity Bullock does
not clearly articulate. She notes that "occasionally one will hear that the
Indian and Spanish custom of painting window facings and doors 'Taos'
blue goes back to the Blue Lady." Bullock acknowledges that proving a
connection between the folk figure and the practices would be complicated ("this would be difficult to pin down"), but she nonetheless attempts to do so. In recounting her attempt to prove this connection, her
status as an outsider to the community she describes is made evident.
Bullock tells that she asked a "plump, kindly Indian matron" why she
painted her doorway blue. The answer to Bullock's question is brief:
"'It's pretty,' she said, and turned back to her task of painting her door
blue."[146] Though Bullock leaves the interpretation of this episode open
to her readers, her inclination to view the practice as associated with the
Lady in Blue is clear, as is the "Indian matron's" unwillingness to corroborate it for Bullock.

In a 1962 *New Mexico Magazine* article, the historical Lady in Blue narrative is correlated with a geological rock formation popularly known as the "Kneeling Nun," located near Silver City, New Mexico.[147] The article's author, May Raizizun, sister of prominent New Mexican folklorist Cleofas Jaramillo, couches the historical narrative in an oral folk-voice, saying that her family's indigenous household staff "told of a mysterious fair-skinned lady who had visited the Indian people 'long before the grandfather of the grandmother's grandfather was born.' This was the Blue Lady."[148] Raizizun goes on to recount several stories of what she claims are indigenous origins about the Lady in Blue, which she partially attributes to Irineo and Mateo, family "servants" whose tribes of origin she does not provide. Reducing even more the tribal or regional specificity of her accounts, she tells a tale about the grandson of the "chief of the Papago [Tohono O'odham]," who fell ill but was cured by a mysterious visit from the Lady in Blue: she "placed her soft white hand on the boy's head. At once his eyes opened and he smiled." She includes a more general story too, saying that Mateo's "people" believed the Lady in Blue lived under the earth, but when she came to the surface, "there was a gladness in nature felt even by the tiny creatures of the fields." Flowers sprung up where she stepped, and she brought with her "from out of the ground the precious turquoise, the blue *Sky Stone*."[149]

Several oral accounts from the Baughman Folklore Collection at the University New Mexico's Center for Southwest Research contribute brief, but intriguing, perspectives into the Lady in Blue in New Mexico, including one account in which she is an advocate for a (generalized) indigenous population. These stories were collected by students, who used an interview sheet to record informants' names, origins, and places of interview. This metadata about the interview—where it occurred, under what conditions the story was recounted, and so on—includes neither racial nor cultural information about the informants. In a 1977 interview, publisher G. L. Campbell of Palmer Lake, Colorado, related a story about the Lady in Blue he had first heard in the 1930s: "During the Pueblo Revolt [of 1680] she [the Blue Lady] reappeared, because she liked the Indians better, and led them to a place of hiding. It is said that one of the places that she led them was east of Bloomfield, N.M., in Governordor [*sic*] Canyon."[150] In Campbell's striking, if brief, account, the Lady in Blue favored Pueblo tribes over the Spanish in the colonial-era conflict between the two groups. Campbell states in the interview that the topic emerged in casual conversation, while he was "discussing the Pueblo Revolt with a friend."[151] As in the case of the Lady in Blue's obstruction of the nineteenth-century U.S. Army filibuster mission to Sonora, or Adina De Zavala's account, Campbell's story reveals a Lady in Blue who sides not with the dominant, colonizing group, but rather with vulnerable subalterns. J. M. Holman's oral contribution to *Hispanic Legends of New Mexico* (1955) partially corroborates Campbell's account in that it emphasizes the Lady in Blue's continued presence among the tribes she converted. Holman comments in his account: "This 'Lady in Blue' lived among [the tribes] at certain times of the year. . . . The people of the pueblo saw her many times."[152] Though Holman does not identify the Lady in Blue as Spanish per se, he does say that the story he recounted is told frequently in Spain. The lack of historical referents in his account suggests that he might have heard the story rather than read about it.

In 1960, retired University of New Mexico professor Julia M. Keleher shared another tale archived in the Baughman Folklore Collection.[153] What it recounts is complementary to Bullock's narrative. Keleher comments in her interview that not only the frames of windows and doors but also the "cement floors" of Native American homes were painted that "particular and peculiar shade" of blue in honor of the Lady in Blue.[154] Keleher provides a brief account similar to Adina De Zavala's gift-giving Lady in Blue, but her version lacks the geographical and sociological specificity of De Zavala's: "In another version of this tale it is told that this mystic endowed the power of prophecy upon the favorite daughters of certain families."[155]

The informants who shared the final two Baughman stories about the Lady in Blue display awareness of the historical narrative in their interviews, but many of the details they share are not historically accurate. Mark B. Gens's account[156] correlates the Lady in Blue's mystical reveries with "a Nun in France who had the phenomenal ability to put herself into a deep trance"[157] during which she could send "her personality and some semblance of her body"[158] to the Southwest. In the final oral narrative, a woman identified as "Mrs. Ed Dwyer" echoes the theme of a woman who would fall into a deep mystical state. In Mrs. Dwyer's account, the "nun back in Europe . . . always saw a land with many mountains, mud houses and dark-skinned people"[159] while in her reverie. The inhabitants of the "Indian village in New Mexico" she visited reported that she was "light-skinned and wore a blue dress." The informant then related an idea proposed by the "Indians": "After they [the tribal members] had learned about the Virgin Mary they decided it must have been her but the dress they described was exactly like the habit of the nun in Europe." The exact origins of Mrs. Ed Dwyer's story are not clear, but these concluding remarks echo the views of twentieth-century historians of Sor María, who have often noted the potential for conflation of the Virgin with Sor María, given the shared color blue.

EMERGENT LORE OF THE LADY IN BLUE

An emergent example of lore about the Lady in Blue/Sor María has different origins and ends altogether differently than the artifacts discussed so far. This final account is unique in that the oral narrative relates to the Lady in Blue indirectly, through a piece of contemporary artwork located at the former St. Katharine's Indian School in Santa Fe, New Mexico.

St. Katharine's was originally a Catholic boarding school operated by the Sisters of the Blessed Sacrament, a religious community founded by St. Katharine Drexel. Children from Pueblo tribes (in particular Laguna Pueblo) and other Native American communities in New Mexico, were sent to the school during its years of operation, from 1887 to 1998.[160] In 1966, Edward O'Brien, an artist who moved to Santa Fe in 1960, painted a mural on the school's dining room wall.[161]

O'Brien's mural is large, covering the full length of the room's longest wall, 19.25 feet by 10.5 feet. The entire painting will be discussed in greater detail in chapter 6 (see fig. 6.3), but for the purposes of the lore relating to it, the image's size and its striking depiction of the Lady in Blue are important. In the detail of the mural (see fig. 5.1), the Lady in Blue steps out from Sor María's temple, emerging towards a long line of what seem to be Pueblo people who are bowed towards her. The open blue-green eye in the close-up of Sor María's face looks out fixedly at the viewer. The eye's pupil is small, and the tone of the image projects intensity with a focus on the person looking at the mural. For the children who attended St. Katharine's, separated from their homes, families, and tribal communities, this blue-eyed figure assumed dimensions based on their readings of the mural, and experiences at the school and at home.

Figure 5.1. Detail of *Our Lady of Guadalupe's Love for the Indian Race* (1967), by Edward O'Brien. Author's image.

A former student at St. Katharine's, Shay Murray, explained in a conversation that the Lady in Blue in the painting held specific meaning for the children from Laguna Pueblo who lived at the school.[162] In Murray's 2007 oral account, recounted to me in a phone conversation, the Laguna children who left their families found the nuns of St. Katharine's distant and strict. Yet, they received some consolation in the form of a mysterious woman they called "Blue Eyes," whom they associated with the Lady in Blue of the mural. Blue Eyes would appear to the students at the school and comfort them in their new and unfamiliar surroundings. Murray suggested that Blue Eyes's name set her apart from the Laguna children, and from the nuns; Blue Eyes was not a "sister" like the religious women who operated the school. Murray stated that those who remained at Laguna Pueblo teased the children who attended St. Katharine's when they would return to Laguna, asking them if they had seen Blue Eyes while at St. Katharine's.

Murray's account of Blue Eyes at St. Katharine's is one whose creation is tied to a particular place and time, which is still relevant today. It is living lore that, paradoxically, bears witness to precisely the type of colonization that the Lady in Blue narrative itself problematically represents. Based not on the narrative itself, but rather on an artistic interpretation of it rendered in a specific context of enforced education, this account of the Lady in Blue, conceived of by school children, is one whose resonance continues.

This account, and the mural to which it relates, lead this study into chapter 6, which examines twentieth- and twenty-first-century cultural productions treating the Lady in Blue narrative. From artwork such as O'Brien's, to dance opera, theater, puppetry, poetry, and science fiction, the Lady in Blue—and Sor María—continues to engage audiences to the present day.

CHAPTER SIX

Sor María and the Lady in Blue in Contemporary Cultural Imagination

With enough love I can teleport like Mary of Agreda. That's got to be worth something here, right? Right? Transvective suburbanite (F, 38) unwittingly adding to the growing list of LRB Google-whacks at box no. 8556.

—David Rose[1]

In the preceding chapters I outlined Sor María de Jesús de Ágreda's historical role in Mexico and the American Southwest over the course of nearly four centuries, examining her as a writer, mystical missionary, and the subject of folklore. This chapter steps into the present day, incorporating contemporary treatments of Sor María and the Lady in Blue narrative into the long conversation. Taken together, these artifacts show cultural producers engaging with the narrative and the nun in creative and challenging ways. Sor María de Jesús de Ágreda remains utterly relevant in the twentieth and twenty-first centuries, and interest in her as a historical subject continues to grow.

But something is conspicuously absent in many of the texts that reimagine Sor María/the Lady in Blue narrative. Although tremendously varied in terms of genre (everything from dance operas to puppetry to cooking shows deal with Sor María), nearly all examples omit—and therefore erase—the reality of Sor María's writing in colonial Mexico, focusing instead solely on the bilocation narrative. Perhaps this should not be surprising, as many contemporary artifacts draw on folklore sources, and these, as we saw in chapter 5, are almost completely disarticulated from Sor María's writing. However, in contrast to the lore, there also is a hopeful reemergence of Sor María the writer in some contemporary literature, indicating interest in this powerful aspect of Sor María's history in the borderlands.

The contemporary examples treating Sor María are organized into seven categories.[2] The first grouping encompasses the works of Mexican American creators of Lady in Blue artifacts, which implement her narrative as an affirmation of cultural identity, or a means of claiming the lore for Chicanos. The second category presents works that frame the Lady in Blue as a feminine narrative, one of empowerment based on the protagonist's gender. Artifacts in the third group cast the narrative as one perpetuated by and exclusive to indigenous communities (although in no case are the stories defined as a firsthand Native American account). In 180-degree contrast, the fourth group casts the Lady in Blue as a colonizer, in which the focus is specifically on the conquest and Europeanization of indigenous tribes.

The fifth category comprises many genres that send the Lady in Blue narrative running in different directions, illustrating how it has been broadly and frequently interpreted in the present day, a quality that lends interpretive instability. Commemorative celebrations in the Southwest—two in San Angelo, Texas, in 2009 and 2010, and another in Abó, New Mexico, in 2014—make up the sixth grouping, which signals Sor María's regional relevance and the growing interest in her canonization in the U.S.-Mexico borderlands. The seventh and final group brings creative interpretation to rest on Sor María's writing; in the examples we examine (a puppet show, short story, and novel), the legacy of her written works is as prominent as the Lady in Blue narrative, an important indicator of the surviving memory of her as a principal author of the colonial period.

THE CHICANA LADY IN BLUE: SIGNIFYING CULTURAL CURRENCY AND PLACE

Several Mexican American writers and cultural producers frame the Lady in Blue narrative as a uniquely Chicano or Indo-Hispano legend.

Two novels by Chicano authors, Luis Alberto Urrea and Ana Castillo, and a painting by New Mexican artist Amy Córdova define the Lady in Blue narrative on the basis of its cultural affiliation with populations of the American Southwest. Deriving in part from lore originating in the region, and in part from historical sources, these texts relocate the narrative contemporaneously within the U.S.-Mexico border community.

As in other examples, the Lady in Blue is here decoupled from Sor María's written legacy. But why should this be so? If, as chapter 5 demonstrated, regional collective memory of Sor María's writing exists in the form of the New Mexican *alabado*, why are similar recollections absent from these Mexican American artifacts? One possible reason is the absence of scholarship on Sor María as a writer. In general histories, such as the contemporary editions of the Benavides *Memorials*,[3] her writing was not significantly discussed by the texts' editors; this was also the case in histories and commentaries about Mexican Americans in the Southwest; and in the lore, except for the reference in the New Mexican alabado and cursory remarks by Carlos Castañeda and Adina De Zavala, Sor María the writer is similarly absent. Though contemporary Mexican American scholarship has been eager to embrace the Lady in Blue narrative as part of its cultural legacy, her writing has not formed a meaningful part of that story.[4]

In *The Devil's Highway* (2004),[5] Mexican American writer and journalist Luis Alberto Urrea presents a fictionalized version of the tragic crossing of twenty-two undocumented Mexican immigrants on foot across the Arizona-Sonora desert. Subtitled *A True Story* and dedicated to "the dead and . . . those who rescue the living,"[6] the novel is an intense work that focuses on issues of social justice, specifically on the real, and often appalling, outcomes of human trafficking across the U.S.-Mexico border. Urrea begins the novel *in medias res*, portraying the state of the men who survived most of the terrible trip along the Devil's Highway, a bleak stretch of desert spanning southern Arizona and northern Sonora. Urrea writes, "They were burned nearly black, their lips huge and cracking, what paltry drool still available to them spuming from their mouths in a salty foam as they walked."[7] Urrea graphically describes their struggle to hold on to life in the harsh environment, with few or no life-saving measures in place for them along the way.

Before returning to narrate the beginning of the men's torturous journey, Urrea develops place as one of the story's protagonists, establishing the character and context of a site that "has set out to illuminate one notion: bad medicine."[8] For Urrea, the Devil's Highway is steeped in death, suffering, and darkness: "Those who worship desert gods know them to favor retribution over the tender dove of forgiveness. In Desolation, doves are at the bottom of the food chain."[9] The mythology Urrea creates for the Devil's Highway is brutal and hostile, from its landscape ("the plants are noxious and spiked," the wildlife "creeps through the nights, poisonous and alien"[10]), to its human history ("As [sixteenth-century Spanish explorer] Melchior [Díaz] died . . . on his stinking cot, he burned and howled. Flies settled in his entrails."[11]), to its legends ("the dreaded Chupacabras . . . has been seen attacking animals, lurking in outhouses, and even jumping in bedroom windows to munch on sleeping children"[12]). Though she is mentioned but briefly, the Lady in Blue contributes to the borderlands environment Urrea conjures by offering an example of untimely death, one particularly marked by the relationships between indigenous peoples and Spanish invaders: the predecessors of contemporary mestizo populations living and crossing there.

Urrea indirectly references what appears to be historical narration attributed to Fray Eusebio Kino and Juan Mateo Manje of the encounter between the Lady in Blue and the Pima (Akimel O'odham) tribe, saying that the account cited was "written down in 1699."[13] Though the tribes inhabiting the Devil's Highway thought they were free of the Spanish after the death of conquistador Melchior Díaz, they were continuously bothered by a "meddlesome white women who flew above their heads," "a white woman who came bearing a cross."[14] To eliminate these unwelcome visits, the "warriors did the only practical thing they could: they filled her with arrows." In Urrea's account, this little affected the airborne woman: "They said she said she refused to die. Kept on flying." The novel then references another, related account of similar visits, claiming that the 1699 account referred to a "Blessed Virgin UFO," adding that fifty years later "a female prophet came out of the desert. She was known as La Mujer Azul." The native tribes, wishing to eliminate these perturbances, again shot her with arrows, and "this time, she died." In the concluding references to the narrative, Urrea states that when Jesuit missionaries arrived to the region, the tribes killed the friars, because "they made the People as unhappy as the mysterious spirit-woman." Drawing on various historical and folkloric accounts,

Urrea's *Devil's Highway* presents the Lady in Blue as a border crosser before the border existed.

Urrea's inclusion of the Lady in Blue narrative is not lengthy, but it serves specific ends within the arc of the novel. Like everything else in contact with the Devil's Highway, the Lady in Blue is touched by death and represents a type of undesired transmigration.[15] Her death in the desert resonates with those of the Mexican and Central American men who, during the course of the novel, expire in the same badlands. Her narrative is at once representative of the Devil's Highway, subject to its cruelty, and in an encompassing manner part of the legacy shared by Mexican, Mexican American, Indo-Hispano, and indigenous peoples who live there. Urrea does not dwell on the details of bilocations, theological writing, conversions, and convents, nor does he name Sor María de Jesús de Ágreda as that figure, referring to her only as the "la mujer azul." Nevertheless, the Lady in Blue narrative resonates deeply with the place and peoples he portrays and offers a patina of cultural historical authenticity.

Chicana author Ana Castillo's novel *So Far from God* (1993),[16] a fictionalization of the Hispanic people and culture of New Mexico, incorporates a (not historically contextualized) Lady in Blue in a significant, identity- and region-marking cameo. Pulled from Indo-Hispano folk tradition, and relocated as an active agent in the novel's contemporary setting, the Lady in Blue assumes a dual function. The novel is set in the central New Mexico farming community of Tomé and revolves around four sisters—Esperanza, Caridad, Fe, and La Loca—and their mother, Sofia. In the course of the novel, three of the sisters die or disappear, leaving the idiosyncratic La Loca with her mother. As the novel draws to a close, the celibate and reclusive La Loca contracts an AIDS-like disease.

As she prepares to die, La Loca is visited by an unexpected guest, an individual who, according to La Loca, does not smell human, who is certainly a nun, and who "must be related to Francisco el Penitente,"[17] a cartoonish character who is also a member of the local *cofradía*, or chapter of the lay religious brotherhood. (This parallel evokes a comparison of the two as regional, culturally Catholic figures.) Putting on her sister Esperanza's blue bathrobe to go out on Good Friday, La Loca comments, "It's blue. Blue is good."[18] The narrator contextualizes La Loca's comment: "This was no naïve remark coming from a young woman who knew, among other things she was never given credit for knowing, that in her land, blue was a sacred color and, therefore, very appropriate for the occasion."[19] Soon after, the strange nun-like guest begins to visit La Loca regularly: "The Lady in Blue started coming to visit her, walked right into Loca's little room when no one was around one day."[20] During her stays, La Loca and the Lady in Blue play *lotería*, and "Loca beat the nun two out of three."[21] More importantly, the nun listened to and soothed La Loca: "[She] did not seem interested in talking about nobody besides La Loca and just making her feel better when she couldn't get out of bed no more."[22] There is no mention of bi-location directly, but the figure appears and disappears instantaneously and is defined as being from another place, likely the Iberian Peninsula. When the Lady in Blue sings La Loca a final song, comforting the young woman in her arms, the nun calls the tune a Portuguese "fade," likely meaning "fado," a classic Portuguese song form.

As the title to the chapter preceding La Loca's death indicates ("La Loca Santa Returns to the World via Albuquerque before Her Transcendental Departure"[23]), La Loca does not actually die. With a history of epileptic seizures, one such episode was mistaken for her death, but she instead experienced a "transcendental departure" that was aided by the Lady in Blue's intervention. Sofia, La Loca's mother, forms an organization for mothers of saints, the implication being that La Loca's transcendental departure and association with the Lady in Blue qualified her as a popular saint. By associating her most New Mexican of characters with the Lady in Blue, Castillo's resolution of the character's arc cashes in on specific cultural currency.

Castillo aims in the text to present a fictionalized New Mexico that evokes the place and people by incorporating regional and cultural elements (e.g., New Mexican religious culture, code-switching, agricultural practices, etc.) into the novel. As with other regionally specific Indo-Hispano markers Castillo deploys in the text, the Lady in Blue is a gesture towards regional and cultural authenticity. Her inclusion as a character in a significant role provides a culturally encoded valence to the work as a whole.

Taos, New Mexico, artist Amy Córdova's painting of Sor María is a vibrant contemporary reimagining of Sor María via a culturally inscribed art genre. Córdova is a painter, children's book author, and illustrator of children's books with New Mexican historical, cultural, and mythological themes. The painting depicting the Lady in Blue alludes to the image of Sor María that accompanied the *Tanto que se sacó de una*

Figure 6.1. Sor María de Jesús de Ágreda (2007), by Amy Córdova. Image courtesy of the artist.

carta, published in Mexico in 1730, which was discussed in chapters 3 and 4. In those printings Sor María is represented in a hagiographic manner as a missionary figure. She is upright, holding a cross in her hand, above the "Chichimecos" near her feet, whose faces register hesitancy and protectiveness (see fig. 3.3).

In Córdova's fanciful rendering (fig. 6.1), the Lady in Blue is still positioned above the tribe, but she is horizontal, extended above the people beneath her as if she were flying over them, her blue veil swooping upward to indicate descent from a celestial height. The faces of the leather- and turquoise-clad observers register a range of surprised and engaged emotions. The feather Sor María holds in her hand suggests flying rather than a quill for writing. The landscape beneath her is a stylized rendering of northern New Mexican landscapes: brown hills dotted with brush, mountains in the background, and a rainbow stretching behind Sor María, aesthetically reflective of the painting's color scheme and overall tone. As portrayed by Córdova, the Lady in Blue is a benevolent, whimsical figure, her ethnically inflected face similar to those of the people gazing up at her. The content of the piece does not reflect the colonizing legacy of the Lady in Blue; in fact, it seems to elide or even overwrite it.

Whether this particular painting was conceived of as a devotional piece or as a work of art directed at a youth audience, Córdova's choice of artistic genre inscribes the piece and the message it conveys, with an Indo-Hispano, New Mexican sensibility. As it is presented in this art form, the scene gains context and an implicit community of reading. Córdova's work locates the narrative and its commemoration in New Mexican popular memory. In this way, Córdova sets out the Lady in Blue as a marker for locality and Mexican American cultural affiliation.

Inscribing Female Colonial History through the Lady in Blue

Two works of fiction drawing from historical and folkloric sources situate the Lady in Blue as a historically contextualized and empowered female heroine. Both texts present the Lady in Blue as a Mexican figure arising out of the colonial or late-colonial period: in Jane Eppinga's collection of short stories, she is a cultural icon, and in a poem by Dee Strickland Johnson, she is a historical actor who defends a Mexican community from outside aggressors.

Southwestern folk collector Eppinga's ghost story collection *Arizona Twilight Tales* (2000)[24] does not so much reformulate the Lady in Blue narrative as it reimagines it in a historical cultural context centering on women. Grouping the narrative with those of two other well-known female folk figures that originate in the colonial period—La Llorona and the Virgin of Guadalupe—the text places the Lady in Blue narrative in dialogue with recognizable "powerful feminine spirits,"[25] as Eppinga calls them. While La Llorona weeps for her "heinous crime,"[26] the Lady in Blue and Guadalupe are classified as "pure goodness,"[27] marking the Lady in Blue in a positive light in this stereotypically dichotomous grouping.

Eppinga's short account, entitled "The Blue Nun," provides an exposition of Sor María's biography, including her mystical travels. Inexplicably, it simultaneously refers to Sor María as a "barely literate young girl"[28] and "a simple country girl,"[29] while also detailing the nun's composition of *La mística ciudad de dios* and her correspondence with Felipe IV. Eppinga's inclusion of Sor María's biography is less important to the reader than is the fact that the story creates a context for the narrative within borderlands lore about influential female figures. *Arizona Twilight Tales* presents Sor María's story as biography-laced fable, seeking to restore or locate her in a regional, colonial feminized space with other paradigmatic female figures.

Folklore enthusiast and performer Dee Strickland Johnson includes the poem "The Mysterious Lady in Blue" in her collection on Arizona's history and legends entitled *Arizona Herstory* (2003).[30] Though the title is not critically defined as a historiographical construct countering "history" in the book,[31] women are at the book's center and comprise its stated focus. In this compilation of lyric renderings of legends and stories relating to Arizona's early history that feature women prominently, Strickland Johnson offers historical sources for her material, commenting that "unlike most poetry books, [*Arizona Herstory*] includes copious footnotes."[32] The historical citations she provides lead the reader to conceive of the Lady in Blue narrative as one whose female protagonist displayed agency in defense of the Mexican inhabitants of the Arizona borderlands, protecting the people of Caborca from the attacks of U.S. soldiers.[33]

Attributing the legend ambiguously to "Mexican country,"[34] the poem changes little of the narrative. The emphasis is on transgression on the part of the Lady in Blue for traveling to the region ("Reincarnation? Out of body affair? / The church would have frowned in the face / Of such an idea! 'Twas evil! Occult!"[35]), and this creates a sense for her confrontation with male authority during the colonial period. This impression is expanded further along in the poem: "Had some strange nun really wandered among / The Indians? Could it be abuse / Of God's holy vows? No nuns in New Spain! / The church in Old Spain had confirmed!"[36] The poem fashions a Lady in Blue/nun who, within the historical milieu of "New Spanish" Arizona, acted freely, both against male authority and in defense of people and ideas she valued. The conclusion of the poem further evokes this sense as her legendary actions in Caborca are cited, reinforcing the contextualization of the narrative set out in the poem. Strickland Johnson impresses an audacious, intrepid Lady in Blue rooted onto Arizona's colonial past.

An "Indigenous" Narrative of Spanish Conversion

In keeping with several folkloric accounts about the Lady in Blue narrative, three recent texts consider the narrative part of the indigenous landscape of the Southwest. The works discussed here—Ted DeGrazia's short illustrated book, *The Blue Lady: A Desert Fantasy of Papago Land* (1957),[37] Julia Keleher's play *Lady in Blue* (1932),[38] and Lisa Sandlin's *You Who Make the Sky Bend* (2011)[39]—deviate from the homogenizing, nonspecific representation of native peoples prevalent in the folklore in that they specify the tribal groups with which they associate the narrative. In DeGrazia's book, the Lady in Blue is associated with the Papago (Tohono O'odham) tribe of Arizona, and Keleher's play takes place with the Laguna and Acoma nations of central New Mexico.[40] As in the folkloric accounts, however, the depiction of indigenous peoples, culture, and language in these works is uninformed by postcolonial perspectives on race, ethnicity, and the construction of the other; in this sense, how they present or frame the tribes is at times disturbing, and they do not problematize the relative positions of the literary subject and the creator.

The Blue Lady: A Desert Fantasy of Papago Land, the work of Arizona artist Ettore "Ted" DeGrazia, was published in a limited run in conjunction with the Arizona tourism magazine *Arizona Highway* (see fig. 6.2). The impressionistic, watercolor-like illustrations in the short book—one of its primary features—are representative of DeGrazia's Southwestern-themed paintings and drawings that were popularized in the 1960s and 1970s. The text opens with a romanticized and unspecific notion of the Arizona desert and its indigenous inhabitants, in keeping with the book's subtitle: "The desert is spiritual, mysterious and religious. It is a dream within a dream. . . . There is peace and quiet upon you in the desert."[41]

Figure 6.2. Cover art for *The Blue Lady: A Desert Fantasy of Papago Land* (1957), by Ettore "Ted" DeGrazia. Image courtesy DeGrazia Gallery in the Sun, DeGrazia Foundation, Tucson, Arizona. All rights reserved.

The text transitions into a story allegedly told by an old "Papago chief" to his tribe, gathered around a fire, "all the Indians lean[ing] forward to hear his words."[42] The elder's supposed account is seeded with elements of the *1630 Memorial*, and adds the important detail that the Lady in Blue left a legacy of happiness to the Papago tribe, who had welcomed her visits (unlike the Papago, the Yuma tribe shot her with arrows, an echo of historical accounts discussed in chapter 4). As the space where the "chief" tells his story becomes suffused with blue light, he concludes and "lift[s] his arm to speak to the Blue Lady. Voices, faint voices, could be heard. They were singing an ancient hymn to the cross."[43] With the closing imagery of Christian conversion, the old man disappears into the night.

The Blue Lady inscribes the Lady in Blue narrative among the tribes of Arizona, assigning it a fantastical indigenous, cultural designation. It uses the narrative to distinguish between Native American groups that accepted Christianity and those who rejected it, without any specificity at all or discussion of the historical facts regarding these representations. It is abstracted from any recognizable historical context, and is refashioned as an exclusively indigenous story, without questioning what the story might have signified in its time. DeGrazia's book locates the narrative in the distant, ahistorical past, and the anachronistic quality of the desert that it portrays (and the parallel presentation of indigenous groups) emphasizes its hermetic and self-referential nature.

University of New Mexico drama professor Julia Keleher's play *Lady in Blue*,[44] performed on May 17, 1932, at UNM's Rodey Theater, shares some of these attributes. The playbill and cast list for the play indicate that it was part of a series of "local interest" topic plays: short works based on New Mexico folk traditions or histories that were performed into 1934. The play merges a version of the Lady in Blue narrative with a story about the exchange of a Spanish painting between the north-central New Mexican Acoma and Laguna tribes.

According to the playbill's summary of the historical events that underpin the play, a painting was given to Acoma Pueblo by the king of Spain in 1629, stolen by members of the Laguna Pueblo around 1807, and returned to Acoma "by order of the District Court of New Mexico" in 1857.[45] By fusing the two histories (the story of the Acoma painting and the Lady in Blue narrative) and situating the resulting story among New Mexico's tribes, Keleher's play projects the narrative into a space shared by the two Pueblos. Keleher's rendition suggests specificity to the Laguna and Acoma tribes that does not appear in historical narratives of the Lady in Blue.

The script opens in a nonspecific past, in the home of Lorenzo, a tribal elder from prosperous Acoma Pueblo.[46] Lorenzo and his devoted daughter, Anita, discuss her upcoming marriage to Pablo, another man from Acoma. As she sits at her loom, weaving a cloth of black, grey, red, and blue thread, Anita asks her father to tell her a story she can weave into the fabric. Lorenzo, preoccupied about the tribe's future, tells her a story themed on the blue thread, that of the Lady in Blue. Lorenzo recounts her bilocation to the region, adding an important detail echoing the lore of the Alamo recorded by Adina De Zavala. He tells that the Lady chooses a woman "good of heart"[47] from each generation whom she gifts with the capacity to see into the future: "The gift that she gives is of the mind. Of being able to read what is happening in the hearts of men, of being able to tell of future happenings."[48] Lorenzo goes on to say that no Acoma woman had ever been chosen by the Lady in Blue to receive her gift, but adds that neighboring Laguna Pueblo had been chosen. They were the first tribe to receive the Lady in Blue's gift, and one of the Laguna grandmothers foresaw the Pueblo Revolt of 1680. Lorenzo dismisses the suggestion that the Lady in Blue lives in an enchanted underground castle (perhaps again echoing De Zavala's account) as "a story for the children to believe."[49]

While Anita mulls over her father's story, a knock at the door announces the arrival of four representatives from the demoralized Laguna Pueblo. The men describe their pueblo's misfortune to Lorenzo, comparing it to the prosperity and happiness at Acoma. The Laguna have come to ask for the object to which they attribute Acoma's well-being and their own miserable state: a painting of St. Joseph given to the pueblo by the king of Spain. Lorenzo attempts to determine fairly which of the two tribes will keep the painting by drawing straws. Although Acoma wins, one of the Laguna visitors stealthily absconds with the painting. As the play draws to its climax, tom-toms beat in the background as Acoma prepares to fight Laguna over the painting.

Anita, preparing to join the rest of Acoma, is suddenly confronted by the Lady in Blue, who "look[s] steadily at [Anita] with great concentration and power."[50] The Lady in Blue poses rhetorical questions to Anita about the future of her pueblo and its relationship with Laguna and the painting. Anita's clairvoyant answers demonstrate that she has received the Lady in Blue's gift of vision into the future. She predicts the painting will not return to Acoma for fifty years, and when it does return, it will not be by force of arms. Turning to the Lady in Blue as the percussive noise increases, Anita begs her to help convince the Acoma not to enter into battle with Laguna Pueblo. Through the Lady in Blue, Anita becomes the only character, male or female, capable of averting disaster for both tribes; whether she successfully does so is left open at the work's close.

Keleher's set, costumes, and dialogue are intentionally marked as regional indigenous dress. Anita's hair is "black . . . banged above her eyes, the side locks cut square, even with the mouth. Her back hair is wound around a red cord,"[51] reflective of a hairstyle common among some New Mexican tribes. Anita's and Lorenzo's clothes—concha belt, moccasins "with no stockings," strands of silver beads[52]—are suggestive of the same aesthetic, and Anita is seated at a loom weaving as the play opens. The indigenous characters' speech projects a stereotypical quality; Lorenzo, for example, says, "Is it not of wonderment that this woman wrote books telling of our customs, our beliefs and our language as if she had lived among us, or known us for a long time?"[53] Written by an author who was not a member of the communities represented in the play, the sources for Keleher's interpretation and development of the Lady in Blue narrative are not apparent, and the play, like De Grazia's book, ascribes/inscribes the Lady in Blue narrative onto Southwestern indigenous communities.[54]

University of Nebraska creative writing professor Lisa Sandlin's *You Who Make the Sky Bend* is a collection of vignettes on Catholic saints and holy figures, accompanied by retablo-style images created by Galisteo, New Mexico, artist Catherine Ferguson. The collection draws from historical and popular sources to produce an abbreviated "lives of the saints" collection.[55] The individuals featured are saints venerated in the American Southwest, along with figures of interest for the author and illustrator.

The retablo-style image for the chapter on Sor María, entitled "María de Ágreda (1602–1665),"[56] depicts Sor María wearing a blue mantle, similar in style to that of the Virgin of Guadalupe. The setting is evocative of northern New Mexican landscapes, with Sor María on the banks of a river curving through a high mountain desert. A variety of domesticated animals, roses, and honeysuckle blossoms border the central image, though their relationship to the story is not explained in the text.

The story itself is a recounting of Sor María's biography, with particular focus on the *1630 Memorial* and Fray Alonso de Benavides's role in corroborating the Lady in Blue narrative. The story adds that when the Inquisition sought Sor María out, she "defended herself agilely enough. She cited the faults of others 'I find the events in Father Benavides' report all mixed-up,' and qualified 'Whether or not I really and truly went in my body is something about which I cannot be certain.' The Inquisition retracted its claws, and María de Ágreda died in her convent bed."[57] The story specifically mentions her written legacy, in particular *La mística ciudad de dios*, comparing the battle between good and evil that it portrays to Milton's *Paradise Lost*.[58]

It is the story's conclusion that contributes to the indigenizing orientation of the piece. Recounting Fray Damián Manzanet's seventeenth-century report on the Tejas tribe and his conclusions regarding their previous contact with Sor María, the story connects Fray Manzanet's account with the present-day testimony of a Jumano tribal representative, noting that the west Texas tribe had "mostly assimilated into the peoples of the Apaches, but today . . . are on a mission to revive their tribe."[59] The story ends with a recollection from Jumano tribal historian Enrique Madrid: "When we saw the flower [a five-foot-tall bluebonnet] we knew the Lady in Blue had come back to help us again."[60] Given this conclusion, Sandlin's story as a whole locates the narrative within an indigenous tradition.

Converting Native Populations: Confronting the Lady in Blue as Colonizer

Inverting the theme of the previous section, we examine several texts that frame the Lady in Blue as representative of Spanish colonization projects carried out on indigenous populations in the American Southwest. Although most of these works imagine the narrative in a neutral or positive light—indigenous groups are depicted as indifferent to or benefiting from Spanish colonization—Marilyn Westfall's stories about the

California missions, discussed at the end of this section, offer essential critical perspective.

Our Lady of Guadalupe's Love for the Indian Race is one of three murals artist Edward O'Brien completed as part of his Our Lady of the Americas series, this one at the former St. Katharine's Indian School in Santa Fe, New Mexico (see fig. 6.3) (an inset of which we saw in fig. 5.1); the other two are located at Our Lady of Guadalupe Abbey (an Olivetan Benedictine monastery) in Pecos, New Mexico, and the Hacienda Guru Ram Das, a Sikh ashram in Abiquiú, New Mexico. All three murals feature the Virgin of Guadalupe as their focal point, with different auxiliary themes. The title of the St. Katherine's mural represents its motif: *Our Lady of Guadalupe's Love for the Indian Race*. O'Brien began work in 1965 and finished in 1967, and the mural's bright colors are the result of a mixture of acrylic paint mixed with egg tempera painted onto the school's plaster walls.[61] According to O'Brien's notes on the mural at St. Katharine's,[62] the artist conceptualized the mural as an attempt "to re-echo [the Virgin of Guadalupe's] words through ten significant events on the South and North American continents and to portray her role in drawing to God this race so close to her heart."[63] Five of these events or motifs pertain to the Catholic conversion of South America and appear on the left as one faces the mural; five pertaining to North American Catholic colonization are on the right. The left side includes Christopher Columbus's voyage, Cortez and Malinche, Juan Diego and the appearance of the Virgin of Guadalupe, among other images.[64] A horizontal band of Mesoamerican images extends from the left of the painting to the center, where it meets with the central, colorful image of the Virgin of Guadalupe.

The right-hand side features Sor María, the borderlands mission friars Junípero Serra and Eusebio Kino, Algonquin-Mohawk St. Kateri Tekakwitha, and St. Katharine Drexel, founder of the Sisters of the Sacred Heart, accompanied by her assistant, Mother Mercedes.[65] A horizontal band of ceremonial masks and profiles of indigenous people extends above the North American side of the mural, reflecting a collective "great spirit," according to O'Brien biographers Margaret Succop and Merle Armitage, each of which is converted into a church just below the image: "The Holy Spirit sent by Christ to abide with His church forever."[66] This band stretches from the central image of Guadalupe to the mural's right end.

Figure 6.3. Our Lady of Guadalupe's Love for the Indian Race (1967), by Edward O'Brien. Located in the former St. Katharine's Indian School in Santa Fe, New Mexico. Author's image.

In the image, which spans the wall of the former school's dining room, Sor María figures prominently. Her story forms a rectangle directly to the right of the Virgin of Guadalupe. Wearing a blue habit, Sor María is presented in profile, eyes opened, superimposed over an image of herself facing forward with her eyes shut. Her closed eye suggests a meditative, tranquil state, while her side-facing double gazes intently into the distance, an effect underscored by the detail of her wide-open eye. Behind the double nun, a stone wall indicates that she is located in a place very different from the adobe structures depicted to her right. Adjoining her is a picture of Baja California, lower Alta California, and Sonora, and the image of waves; the places presumably suggesting the mission fields where Fray Eusebio Kino and Fray Junípero Serra traveled and the friars are seen to the right of the map. Fray Kino (wearing a black hat) and Fray Serra (tonsured) gaze fixedly through Sor María's bilocating figure to the Virgin of Guadalupe. Completing the upper right leg of the rectangle, the Lady in Blue is shown stepping into the desert Southwest, mesas in the background, arms extended to a tribe that appears to welcome her.

In the mural, Sor María is contextualized among other figures of the religious colonization of the Americas. Its message is clearly one of conversion of indigenous groups in the Americas, carried out primarily by European agents. The Lady in Blue functions within her own motif to the right of the Virgin of Guadalupe, but her inclusion within the overall scheme of the painting contributes to a reading of her as a Catholic colonizing figure, a conduit (as represented by Kino's and Serra's gazes) to the principal figure of conversion, the Virgin of Guadalupe.

O'Brien imagined the mural as "a conversation piece, a background asserting and emphasizing in all ways its main theme—Our Lady's love for the Indian, making whoever dines in this room aware of her special love for this race to whom she gave her image,"[67] a message transmitted through the mural's images and its location at a Catholic school for Native American children. The intimacy of the mural in the dining room, where it was observed every day by students and staff, reinforced the narrative's association with the parochial education of the children who attended and lived at the school. But what she represents for the students (the nun who comforted them while at boarding school) and what she was intended to represent (a symbol of Catholic colonization of native populations) are different. The children changed the intended meaning of the image through their interpretation of it.

Victoria Edwards Tester's poem "The Blue Lady, 1635" expresses Sor María's first-person voice that asserts a claim to her bilocations, and to the Lady in Blue's authority over New Mexico's missions and northern frontier politics.[68] The poem, from Tester's 2002 collection *Miracles of Sainted Earth*, opens with a tone that is part confessional and part testimonial: "I, Sister María de Jesus de Agreda / made five hundred blessed journeys to New Spain."[69] In contrast to the oblique answers the historical Sor María often gave regarding her mystical voyages, Tester's Sor María says that she traveled, in no uncertain words. The voice speaks in the present, refusing to comment on "[Sor María's] three-hundred-year-old / body that refuses to corrupt in this glass coffin,"[70] asserting instead that her mystical travel occurred "at this very table [in her convent]."[71] The intimacy of the first-person poetic voice and the confirmation of her travels to New Mexico do not leave her colonizing agency in doubt.

Later in Tester's poem, Sor María's voice is directed towards the New Mexican friars in general, and to Fray Benavides in particular: "I saw you, Fray Alonso, baptizing the pueblos of Piro."[72] She continues, "I turned the Indians towards you desert fathers,"[73] emphasizing the Lady in Blue's explicit role in the evangelization and colonization of the indigenous tribes of New Mexico. In speaking to Fray Benavides, she references the colonial-era political divisions between secular and religious leadership: "I have prayed for harmony between the governors and you friars,"[74] saying that she found her travels to the "people as brown as Our Lord's sparrows"[75] a "duty sweet as the fold of a dove's wing."[76] In contrast to the physical conquest carried out by men in the New Spanish borderlands, she went "without a horse, / without the swords of Toledo,"[77] implying that her means of conversion were less violent and aggressive—but no less a process of indigenous colonization. This effect is mediated by her prayer/injunction that the friars, soldiers, and tribes emulate her actions of peaceful conquest: "I have prayed for swords and arrows to return to water,"[78] advising the mission friars that "Spanish and Indian must be one prayer, the two wings of the same Inca dove."[79] Tester's poem as a whole reinforces notions of Spanish colonization even as it attempts to mitigate the violence associated with it, and asserts Sor María's ultimate agency over such questions and actions.

Eric Kimmel's children's book *The Lady in the Blue Cloak: Legends from the Texas Missions* (2006),[80] illustrated by Susan Guevara, presents a modernized series of legends about Texas missions that tell of Native American tribes' cultural assimilation to Spanish mores and religion. The book's introduction cursorily acknowledges—but does not elaborate—the trauma endured by the tribes ("becoming farmers and Christians required a total break with their past")[81] and recognizes contemporary criticism of the missions, "the padres are often condemned as agents of imperialism," but again without much detail. Ultimately, the introduction casts friars' conversion of the tribes in a positive light: "They sincerely believed they were doing God's work, saving lives as well as souls," concluding with a rationalization of the conflict between European friars and indigenous tribes, because it "ultimately led to the growth of a new culture—one that combined elements of both European and American civilizations."

This same sense favoring colonization and creating the impression of a peaceful cultural integration is captured in the illustration prefacing the story. The Lady in Blue bows on one knee, holding a miniaturized version of a mission church in one arm, the other arm sweeping upward.

An angel wearing blue flies above her, indigenous people wearing European-style clothing greet her, and several domesticated animals are clustered at her knees in the foreground. The picture depicts a Lady in Blue bringing European religion (in the form of the mission building) and cultural practice (represented by the clothing) and portending the arrival of European agriculture and livestock, another aspect of Spanish colonization.

The story itself is based on Fray Manzanet's account of the Lady in Blue among the Tejas tribes. After requesting blue fabric to bury their dead, the Tejas are depicted as eager to convert to Catholicism on the basis of the Lady in Blue's assurances. A Tejas tribal leader says, "God is our friend. God and the Lady in Blue will protect us,"[82] and continues, enthusiastic about the Europeanization of his tribe's practices, "The Lady also promised you would bring us new plants, new animals. Everything she said has come true. We will never be hungry and cold." The story's conclusion lauds the Lady in Blue's colonization of the tribes by presenting the tribes welcoming her and the Spanish friars and soldiers. The introduction, illustration, and story downplay the destructive, violent aspects of the Spanish colonization of Texas by redirecting attention to—as the story reads—"beneficial" aspects of the interaction between Spanish colonizers and native populations, leaving the complicated historical meanings out of the narrative.

Taking the colonizing message of the previous examples a step further, the short story collection "Quartet in Blue" (1998) by Marilyn Westfall,[83] a four-part "dramatized spiritual history of California from 1776 to 1998,"[84] includes two entries openly critical of the Lady in Blue narrative as a story of indigenous colonization. Although Sor María's character is a sympathetic, if somewhat terrified, character in the first story, Westfall's depiction of the creation of the California missions by Franciscan friars presents violent and ambivalent facets of that process. The two stories recount the brutality suffered by California tribes, the inconsistency of the vocation of the friars who attended to conversions and directed the missions, and the tension embodied in the Lady in Blue/Sor María.

In the introduction to "Quartet in Blue," Westfall clarifies this last point. Her reading of the Lady in Blue sees the narrative as an exoneration of the aggressive actions of the Franciscan friars and Spanish military against indigenous Californians during and after the mission period: "In 'The Blue Lady,' this supernatural frame [of the narrative of the Lady in Blue] refocuses California history on the divine precepts employed by the Franciscans to justify their intrusion into Native domains."[85] To wit, Sor María/Lady in Blue is "a key to interpreting California,"[86] because she functions as "a source for sublimation on the part of the Franciscan friars."[87] Westfall modulates, to an extent, this interpretation through a sympathetic portrayal of the character of Sor María, who is powerless over the effect her experiences will have on future conditions or conflicts among the tribes and Franciscan missionaries.

The first story, "The Blue Lady," has the historical Sor María as its protagonist. Its primary themes include the mechanics of bilocation, Sor María's views regarding her mission to the Americas, the ultimate ends of such travel, and the nature of her legacy among native Californians. Sor María, weakened from bouts of "travel illness," is suddenly accompanied by angels who speak to her in tongues, as the nun had received the "Apostle's legacy"[88] of the gift of tongues. The reader sees her mystical travel from the points of view of the nuns in her convent, the California tribes, the Franciscan friars, and the angels. When Sor María speaks in tongues to various tribes, she projects compassion for them as they are evangelized by her message: "¡Qué triste! Her breast ached with pity. It was terrible to observe the torments they suffered when confronting God's will."[89] Sor María's mind wanders to her experiences writing *La mística ciudad de dios*, particularly her communication with the divine, while she continues speaking, attempting to convert as she is martyred. As Sor María continues in her draining journey, her ambivalence about her actions and misgivings about the perception of native populations by the Spanish soldiers begin to emerge: "In secret she worried equally for these pagans' lives. . . . She remembered Oviedo's comment that gunpowder used to kill pagans was the burning of incense to the Lord."[90] Exhausted by her travel, Sor María does not wish to continue preaching in California, but "a stern force" pulls her back there, under the threat of punishment by Michael the Archangel if she were to stop her mission.

Sor María opens her eyes from a reverie and is addressed by a character intended to offer her hope and a vision of the fruits of her efforts, namely, the Franciscan California missionary Fray Francisco Palóu, Fray Junípero Serra's companion. He informs her that her "divinely sanctioned journeys to the New World aroused conversos by the hundreds"[91] and that "the indios revere your story . . . in their legends, your mantle . . . filled you with supernatural powers."[92] Palóu relates how the California tribes wished to imitate the Lady in Blue, and how she inspired him personally to become a missionary. Sor María wants to take comfort in the successful future missions inspired by her travels, but cries when she notices an older native woman, beaten and with a gash on her head, inside the San Francisco mission. Though Palóu assures her that the friars follow guidelines for loving treatment of neophytes, Sor María feels that the mission endeavor in the California of the future is not what it seems, that something is amiss. Palóu, begging for forgiveness, confesses that the soldiers have been abusing the indigenous converts, and Sor María sees that her work has unfolded much differently than she had anticipated: "bitter harvest, and she was to blame! Her message had borne only a plague!"[93]

The scene fades to Sor María's encounter with an infirm, but jubilant, Fray Junípero Serra, calling out for the bells to be rung at Mission San Antonio. He reads to Sor María the part of the *Tanto que se sacó de una carta* that inspired him to join Propaganda Fide, and Sor María, incapable of believing the letter was penned by her, starts to turn away, praying for the sickly priest. Serra calls her back and reminds her to remain fixed on the Virgin and not lose hope. Sor María then receives a vision of the image of the Virgin of Guadalupe being venerated by indigenous women. This Marian vision is conflated with Sor María herself when an old woman addresses the image as "Ycaiut" or "La Dama Azul."[94] Sor María recalls the woman beaten by the Spanish as she hears the "strained enunciation, awkward pauses and flat trills"[95] of indigenous children singing hymns, while Serra exhorts her to take faith in how she has inspired such conversions, because "only from pain are children born."[96] She takes leave of the scene, floating away to be awakened in Spain by the arrival of Fray Alonso Benavides to her convent. But as she leaves California, her mantle falls, left behind for her followers and serving as a transition into the next story, "From the Diary of Cacnumaie," the second story treating the Lady in Blue.

In "The Lady in Blue," Sor María is an uncertain missionary, one who sees her role among the friars and neophytes in ambiguous terms. Although the appearance of Serra and Palóu is supposed to console her and offer her a sense of purpose for her mystical travels, the ultimate message of her colonizing moves, as Westfall portrays it, is not positive.

The primary critique lies in the means of conversion, rather than in the conversion itself, but the difficulty lies in the fact that Sor María's travels inspired the conversion endeavor. As the stimulus for others' compassionless and cruel actions, Sor María wonders if she is the reason indigenous people are taken advantage of and abused. The Lady in Blue herself is not subject to this critique: among the tribes she visits, she is depicted as a beloved, venerated, enduring symbol of hope. She is a positive figure who is compassionate, suffers through her travels, and remains consistent to the spirit of the work she is sent to do, independent of what devotion to her brings about. Here, the Lady in Blue has integrity in her actions and in her relationships with indigenous peoples, but critically questions how others *use* her travels to destructive, colonizing ends.

In "From the Diary of Cacnumaie," Westfall uses a fictional memoir to present a first-person account of what happened to native Californian tribes at the hands of the Spanish friars after Serra and Palóu. The story—the autobiography of a California mestiza raised among the missions during the late eighteenth and early nineteenth centuries—is prefaced by a lengthy foreword that presents the diary as if it were an anthropological artifact, leading the reader to treat it as if it were an actual historical source.[97] The subject of the autobiography, Cacnumaie, is the last recipient of the Lady in Blue's cloak—left behind at the end of the "Lady in Blue" story—which she received from her mother. Her mother found the cloak, bearing an image of María de Ágreda, as a girl when a trader to her village inadvertently proved that it possessed the power to heal and that it provided the recipient with the ability to understand and speak many languages. As a result of the unique abilities the cloak afforded her, Cacnumaie's mother was raised outside of her village to become a shaman healer, exercising her curing abilities until she was raped by a Spanish soldier, became pregnant with the narrator, and was relocated to a labor camp at the Mission Dolores (Mission San Francisco). The conditions at the camp were squalid, oppressive, and depressing, and Cacnumaie's mother, with the help of the blue mantle, tried to heal as many people as possible. However, as the shaman who trained her to heal had told her, the blue cloth can only work if the recipient of its aid believes in it, and thus not all cures were successful.

Cacnumaie receives a piece of the blue fabric from her mother, from whom she was separated when her mother fell ill. The girl was subsequently cared for by an indigenous novice nun, Teresa, who cleans, mends, and embroiders the blue mantle with gold thread. Being so near the priests, Cacnumaie is exposed to a variety of religious men, from the zealously faithful to the sadistic and syphilitic. She is paraded at Mass wearing her blue cloth so that the indigenous people in attendance can see her and can identify with Catholicism via the symbol of the Lady in Blue. When Cacnumaie and her mother are reunited by the same priests who separated them (a separation that was intended to force Cacnumaie's mother to recruit other tribes to convert and join the missions), it is so that both of them, acting as interpreters, can translate the theological lessons and liturgy into the many different languages of the California people to more effectively convert them.

At the end of the autobiography, which Cacnumaie writes under the patronage of a Californio ranch owner, Juana Briones, it is revealed that Cacnumaie received the mantle when the Spanish killed her mother for escaping from Mission Dolores. Cacnumaie uses what seems like the last of the mantle's powers to heal her aged and ill benefactress (Briones) before disappearing from the ranch.

In "From the Diary of Cacnumaie," Westfall more fully develops the idea of the Lady in Blue as the protector of native Californians, immediately invoking and then answering the question of why such protection is needed: to keep them safe from the Spanish soldiers and Franciscan friars, and at times act as a mediator between the conquerors and conquered. The friars in Cacnumaie's account invoke the narrative as their inspiration for their behaviors at the mission (presented as cruel bordering on sadistic), with the primary instigator of these perversions, Fray Landeata, calling out: "I once soared, inspired by a blessed lady's prophecy. Her beatific face is impressed on your mother's mantle, like the sacred figure of the Virgin on Juan Diego's cloak. Blessed María Agreda!"[98] Cacnumaie, however, sees the control over and manipulation of the Lady in Blue's life reflected in her and her mother's condition, having been forced to evangelize to others tribes: "The lady's life, I thought, somewhat resembled my own."[99] If the Lady in Blue's mantle bestowed great and important gifts to the bearer, those gifts were not permanent, perhaps because they required belief in the cloth's efficacy (and therefore in the Lady in Blue), and that hope did not last forever. The missions and conversion of the tribes are seen as almost wholly negative, yet the Native Californians' belief in the mantle leads them to develop faith in the Lady in Blue/Virgin Mary, if not in Catholicism in its entirety. The mantle is used both to undo abuse inflicted on the tribes by the Spanish (healing people who were hurt by them, including Cacnumaie's mother) and also to promote their ends (using the gift of tongues to recruit or convert neophytes). Though the cloak was used exclusively for the healing of tribal members before Cacnumaie's mother was captured, her tribe did not understand her mother's ability to heal. Cacnumaie's mother was ostracized by her tribe, indicating that they did not understand how she enacted the Lady in Blue's legacy. In short, the Lady in Blue's powers and even her healing gifts are presented in a complicated, ambiguous manner that emphasizes their positive elements while simultaneously showing how these abilities (and those who wielded them) were abused.

Westfall's stories offer a clear critique both of the colonizing Spanish missions and of the Lady in Blue narrative as a means of rationalizing and justifying the actions associated with the missions. However, Sor María's personal actions as the Lady in Blue are not presented in the same negative fashion; in fact, they are positive, but their ramifications lie beyond Sor María's control and have a greater impact than she could have anticipated—one that is decidedly negative. The only contemporary text to bring postcolonial critique fully to bear on the Lady in Blue narrative, these stories of Westfall's provide much food for thought in their unique approach to the far-reaching effects of the narrative in its historical mission context.[100]

From Chile Con Carne Chef to Dance Opera Protagonist: Multifaceted Manifestations of the Lady in Blue

The eight examples we examine in this section illustrate the breadth of creative interpretation of the Lady in Blue narrative across several genres. Joseph Webber and Michele Larson's treatment of the narrative in their dance opera *Sor María* is exceptional, combining movement and music with New Age notions of spirituality. In the works of Alton Brown, S. E. Schlosser, William Wallrich, and Bert Wall, the narrative shares the same characterization (it is Mexican or Southwestern Hispanic), but the end purpose of the narrative in each of these examples differs from piece to piece. Three texts—Frances Parkinson Keyes's novel *I, The King*, Lisa Sandlin's short story "Saint of Bilocation," and

Javier Sierra's novel *La dama azul*—are set in Spain, but with different meanings assigned to the Lady in Blue in each.

Written by Joseph Webber and choreographed by Michele Larson, the dance opera *Sor María* was performed in the 1980s in Albuquerque and surrounding communities in New Mexico.[101] The production's program[102] and publicity materials[103] project a Sor María whose mystical travel as the Lady in Blue acts as a metaphor for the nun's relationship with God and for her spiritual growth. Webber and Larson's piece is a "chamber opera/dance-theater work,"[104] featuring only two characters— Sor María and Fray Joseph Ximénez Samaniego (her seventeenth-century biographer)—and a chamber orchestra. The textual origins of the work are outlined in the program's discussion of Sor María's *vita*,[105] and the production as a whole is intended to portray "a blend of emotions of the heart and aspirations of the soul in the portrayal of Maria in her mystical states as human being undergoing transformational experience."[106] The photographs featured on the posters for the performance, and the tone observable in short clips of the production,[107] project a spare, emotional quality.

The program emphasizes the secular nature of the dance opera, stating that "the subject of the work is a religious person, [but] the work itself [the dance opera] is not a 'religious' piece."[108] Her bilocation is described circumspectly, "it is evident from her own and her biographer's writing that she experienced transcendental states and wrote about them,"[109] which are categorized in the publicity materials as "astral projections."[110] (Sor María's written work is called "trance-writing."[111]) The overall conceptualization of the piece is one of spiritual reconciliation with the divine. Sor María is portrayed "in her trances, ecstasies and mystical states, as a human being undergoing transformational experience"[112] who was "describing very real, personal experiences, however the external reality might appear to an 'objective' observer."[113] The work's third movement, "New Mexico," depicts the bilocation narrative specifically as a spiritual reconciliation: "The choreographer [Larson] uses this story of María's travels and preaching in the New World as a metaphor for María's struggles with her darker self and her attempts to convert her soul to the will of God."[114] In the opera's last two movements, the character of Sor María expresses her conformation with God's will and rejection of sins, her dance ecstatic rather than trance-like, as in the first scenes.[115] The genre of the work, and its markedly spiritual—but not religious—content, enact a unique version of the Lady in Blue narrative unexplored in other contemporary texts.

A recipe for a classic Tex-Mex dish, presented on a popular cooking show, takes the narrative about as far away from transcendental dance opera as possible. A 2007 episode on Texas-style chili on the Food Network television program *Good Eats* uses Sor María's travels to explain the origin of chile con carne in the Southwest.[116] The episode, "The Big Chili," hosted by Alton Brown, features a cowboy-hatted Brown (aka "Grumpy") and his sidekick "cowpoke" Rusty (wearing a brimmed hat with a leopard skin band) who ride horses as they talk about the pleasures of a well-cooked, traditional chili ("with an 'i'"). In the next scene, gathered around a campfire with harmonica music keening in the background, nutritionist Deb Duchon ("Mystery Stranger"), wearing a cowboy hat, false mustache, denim shirt and vest, joins the duo and begins a discourse on the origins of chile ("with an 'e'") con carne in the Southwest. She explains the recipe might have originated among Canary Island settlers who came to the San Antonio area in 1731, but also proposes Sor María as the source for the recipe: "Other people say that . . . the first recipe for chili con carne was written by a seventeenth-century nun named Mary of Agreda. She said that recipe came to her when she was in a trance." Mystery Stranger says that the most likely source for the recipe was nineteenth-century cooks in the region who combined basic ingredients together to make the dish. The episode purposefully, if whimsically, invokes the lore about Sor María as the stew's source, locating it through its staged retelling in an imagined frontier Southwest.

The source for Brown's episode may have been the recipe for "Chile con Carne Mary of Agreda" in *Bull Cook and Authentic Historical Recipes and Practices*.[117] According to the book's authors George and Berthe Herter, the recipe, appearing in the book's "Meats" section, was "created by the first missionary to Texas, New Mexico, Arizona and Southern California . . . she taught this recipe to the Indians in these areas and the recipe remains almost exactly the same in the southwest today."[118] Though Sor María's seventeenth-century biography fails to mention her aptitude in the kitchen, the authors categorize the recipe as Spanish as opposed to Mexican. Sor María's recipe includes specifications as to what meats it "originally" called for: venison or antelope (instead of beef or mutton) and javelina (instead of pork)—local game replacing European domesticated animals. In spite of the fact that one of the main ingredients in chile con carne is chile (*Capsicum annuum*), a New World food rarely used in present-day household Spanish cooking, the recipe is "not at all Mexican and [is] not popular in Mexico."[119] Through this commentary, the authors take great pains to mark the recipe as historically linked to the Southwest and to Sor María, but they are equally emphatic in differentiating it from other kinds of "Mexican" cuisine from the area. The rationale required to accomplish this reflects the authors' emphasis on the relationship between Spain and the Southwest via Sor María's cooking, using the strange exclusion of Mexican influence in her alleged cooking as proof of that connection.

As in the recipes for chile con carne, S. E. Schlosser's "The Lady in Blue" locates the Lady in Blue narrative in a nonspecific, Spanish-speaking Southwest context. The story, an entry in Schlosser's children's book on Southwestern folklore and ghost stories, *Spooky Southwest: Tales of Hauntings, Strange Happenings and Other Local Lore* (2004),[120] thematically echoes the didactic sentiment expressed in the folkloric artifacts in chapter 5 herein. Narrated in the first person from the point of view of a child named Sammy, the story primarily consists of a straightforward recounting of the Lady in Blue narrative by Sammy's mother. The premise for the narrative's recounting is that Sammy has brought his mother fresh blue flowers on her birthday. She praises her son's thoughtful gesture and asks if he ran into the Blue Lady while collecting them. Sammy replies that he had wanted to buy flowers at the florist shop but did not have enough money. A lady dressed in blue observed Sammy's disappointment and kindly directed him, in Spanish, to where he might pick some flowers for his mother. The mysterious woman then vanished. When Sammy relates this meeting to his mother, she exclaims that he must have met the Blue Lady, as only she would "stop and help a little boy trying to do something special for his mama."[121] Sammy's questioning of who the Lady in Blue was leads his mother to tell the narrative, which in this instance focuses on the doubts surrounding her mystical travel, and the folkloric tradition stating that she left blue flowers where she stepped. The mother concludes the story by commenting that although perhaps Sammy did not meet with the actual Lady in Blue, the woman who helped him "certainly acted in the same gracious manner as Maria Coronel de Agreda."[122] Echoing Hallenbeck and William's folktales that we discussed in chapter 5, Sammy is aided in and rewarded for his desire to do good for others by the "gracious" Lady in Blue. The story expresses the perceived transgressive nature of Sor María's travels through the mother's retelling of the narrative, even as it uses the Lady in Blue as a means of reinforcing the values of self-lessness and generosity in a contemporary Southwestern context.

Spanish is used in the story to suggest the identity of Sammy and his mother, situating the narrative among Hispanophone inhabitants of the "Spooky Southwest." In this English-language story, Sammy and his mother are coded as Spanish bilingual and/or Hispanic by how they communicate. Sammy is able to find the blue flowers for his mother because he understands what the Lady in Blue tells him in Spanish. His mother's exclamation is marked out by language and italics—"*Dios mío*"—an interjection into the English text that displays she knows and perhaps prefers Spanish.

William Jones Wallrich's children's book *The Strange Little Man in the Chili-Red Pants* (1949)[123] consists of stories Wallrich adapted from what he calls "northern Rio Grande" folktales, those with their origins in New Mexico. His tales modify traditional narratives attributed to individuals he calls "los cuentos" (in his translation, "the storytellers"). His interpretations of classic narratives are composed with "no attempt . . . made towards strict accuracy in the following of established patterns or to recount the most traditional versions."[124] As such, though Wallrich's "The Blue Lady" cleaves close to the folkloric Lady in Blue, the tale modifies the original with a strange portrayal of her. The story's setting, its Spanish-named, bilingual characters, and the evocation of the Lady in Blue as a folk legend inscribe the story as a northern New Mexican, didactic tale.

The story unfolds "high in the mountains of New Mexico,"[125] and its protagonist is Miguel San Jose Jesus de Alegreda Alfonzo Jones Martinez, "but he was called Mike."[126] Mike's original Spanish name is an exaggerated stereotype of Spanish nomenclature, and his Anglo nickname is suggestive of a cross-cultural setting in which English is the dominant language. Mike visits the local village for a feast day, where he sees an impressive store owned by Don Pablo, a man well respected in the village. When Mike asks his grandmother how Don Pablo became so beloved, she replies that when Don Pablo was a boy ("Pablito") he met the Lady in Blue while driving his father's goats to water. She was disguised as an old woman carrying a load of sticks, and while Pablito's brother Juan ran ahead, Pablito stopped to help the woman with her burden.

Suddenly, she changed from an old woman into the beautiful, young Lady in Blue, who offered him three wishes to reward him for his goodness. The boy's first wish benefited his community: he asked for shoes so that everyone in the village could go to school even when there was snow. His second wish was for his sister: a mechanism to help her walk with a bad leg. The Lady in Blue affirmed that both were good wishes. Pablito leaves his last wish up to the "gracious Blue Lady," who silently disappears as the boy's attention is distracted by a puppy barking in the distance. When Mike asks what wish the Blue Lady granted to Pablito, his grandmother replies that nobody knew, but that Don Pablo "has prospered, and is loved by all. A truly good and happy man."[127] Mike considers his grandmother's story, and decides he simply wants to be like Don Pablo. The next day, Mike offers to help his neighbor Mrs. Garcia, "even though he knew her and knew that she couldn't be the Lady in Blue,"[128] demonstrating that Mike, like Don Pablo, chooses to do good for others. The narrative suggests that the sense of kindness and responsibility shared in the village was the Lady in Blue's final gift and the reason why Don Pablo was happy, wise, and beloved in his old age.

Although Wallrich's story makes no mention of the bilocation narrative, it employs elements of the folk tales associated with the narrative and draws a connection between the northern New Mexico village and local familiarity with the narrative. Mike had heard of the Lady in Blue, "but, then again, who hadn't,"[129] and he was familiar with many elements of her history: "about her feet flowers of blue sprang up,"[130] and "everyone knew that she lived in a beautiful castle deep in the earth and that at times she came up to the surface to visit the earth people. And when she did so, she would grant wishes."[131] The story's didactic perspective reproduces the idea of the Lady in Blue as a dispenser of rewards for selfless behavior: Mike's decision to help an old woman even though he knows he will not benefit from it makes explicit the story's moral message.

Shifting the regional affiliation of the narrative from New Mexico to Texas, Bert Wall's *The Devil's Backbone II* (2001),[132] "stories of the supernatural told by old-timers,"[133] originates near Wall's ranch in the Devil's Backbone, a hill range in south-central Texas Hill Country between Blanco and Wimberly. In his story of the Lady in Blue, the protagonist is the ranch's cook, Ventura, a beautiful young woman with dark eyes and "flowing black hair."[134] As a youth she was an excellent student with leanings towards religious life.

Ventura and the ranch workmen and staff, exhausted from the August heat and ranch work, rest during the hottest hours of the day. Later in the evening, Ventura reluctantly approaches the narrator's office and tells her employer and his wife about something that occurred to her during the afternoon nap. Falling into a deep sleep, Ventura experienced a convergence of herself with the Lady in Blue: "I left my body and was floating high above myself. . . . I was dressed in a sky-blue habit; I was definitely a Catholic nun. . . . I saw Indians, tribes of Indians, all over Texas, east, west, all over, and then all seemed to know me, or at least the nun in the blue robes."[135] During Ventura's dream, she becomes one with the Lady in Blue as the nun travels spiritually through Texas. Shortly after describing her experience, Ventura leaves the ranch to "follow her religious calling"[136] and become a Catholic sister. Later, upon researching some of the stories originating in colonial-era Texas, the narrator speculates on Ventura's experience, wondering: "Did Ventura see the old spirit [of the Lady in Blue]? Did the old spirit call her to the sisterhood?"[137] The narrator concludes with the hope that the Catholic Church will dress Sister Ventura in the blue robes of the woman who influenced her decision to leave the ranch and enter religious life.

The story's focus on the Southwest regional, Catholic nature of the narrative is affirmed as Ventura's conflation with the Lady in Blue leads her closer to a more formal and permanent relationship with the Catholic Church. Yet the story's conclusion and its title leave the question of the blue nun's identity open to the reader: Was it Sor María or Ventura?

The earliest of three texts that treat the Lady in Blue in a Spanish context, Frances Parkinson Keyes's novel *I, The King* (1966),[138] centers on the life of the Spanish king Felipe IV. As such, Sor María's main role in this work of historical fiction is as the monarch's spiritual and personal advisor. She emerges in the novel, as in life, after the king dismissed his *válido* (political advisor) the Duke of Olivares. The last third of the book is punctuated by translated excerpts from Sor María's letters to the king, in which she advises him on personal issues and questions of governance. Her character provides a sense of immediacy to the events of Felipe IV's life through these letters. She, like the reader, is on the outside looking in on the monarch's life, and because Felipe IV often followed through on the advice Sor María provided in her letters—including on military and political issues—these passages provide insight into his reign and her influence over it. The explanation for how she became his counselor, entering into a relationship so close that "until death snapped the spiritual link that joined them, the heart of Philip was bared in all its sorrow, its weakness, to Sor María alone,"[139] is explained through her Lady in Blue persona.

The initial encounter between Felipe IV and Sor María is a fraught dialogue: Sor María is reluctant to advise the king because of her limited experience with worldly affairs outside of Ágreda. She explains that she traveled all over the world, including to the New World, but had done so spiritually rather than physically, and describes the people, languages, geography, and customs she observed. Her detailed recounting of visits to New Spanish kingdoms holds the king spellbound. As she concludes her recitation, Felipe IV gazes at her habit and murmurs, "the lady in blue, of course, was you, Sor María,"[140] looking at her "with a thoughtful smile."[141]

Dismissing the nun's misgivings about whether he would believe her experience of mystical travel, Felipe IV states that he believes her absolutely. He wonders aloud "why a woman who has been so favored of the Almighty that He has sent her on these mystical missions, and who has been so far successful in them . . . should doubt that she can give solace and support of one lonely man in his extremity?"[142] Though Sor María avers that she cannot be so favored by God since her travels to the New World have ceased, Felipe IV assures her that the abilities manifested via these experiences ("your intelligence, your judgment, your executive abilities and your integrity, not to mention your piety"[143]) have simply been channeled elsewhere, and that he seeks her counsel because of, not in spite of, her mystical travels.

In *I, The King* the Lady in Blue narrative is the reason Felipe IV chooses to confide in Sor María, taking her into his confidence as his political and personal advisor. The Lady in Blue narrative broadens, in his eyes, her sphere of knowledge and therefore her appropriateness to act in this capacity, echoing the historical interaction between Felipe IV and Sor María. Demonstrating attitudes of the period and place, the rationale of the character Felipe IV is based squarely on his esteem for Sor María as the Lady in Blue.

Also set in Spain, Lisa Sandlin's short story "Saint of Bilocation," from her collection *In the River Province* (2004),[144] frames the narrative from the point of view of a New Mexico mission friar, Fray Antonio. Fray Antonio is a fictional amalgamation of Fray Alonso de Benavides and the Inquisitorial officials sent to interview Sor María about her travels. The story plays with the limits and consequences of faith, that which is rational or can be rationalized, and the center versus the periphery, namely, seventeenth-century Spain versus New Mexico.

The story takes place over the course of Fray Antonio's visit to Sor María in her convent at Ágreda, loosely based on Fray Benavides's actual trip to Ágreda to meet the nun. Fray Antonio has traveled from New Mexico to Sor María's convent to interview her, the members of her convent, and Ágreda's citizens regarding her claims of bilocation to New Mexico and the conversion of the tribes there to Catholicism. Prior to his arrival in Spain, Fray Antonio meets with the Jesuit secretary to the Mexican archbishop, and the secretary emphasizes the importance of "mathematics" in establishing what is beautiful and truthful, suggesting the parameters by which objective reality should be determined in the case of Sor María's travels.[145] Fray Antonio's response, in which he is unable to couch his experience as a missionary as a mathematical, limited, or quantifiable truth, sets the stage for the story's primary question: Knowing that others will challenge one's personal faith—in which an individual could have his or her own doubts—should one stake his or her self and well-being on those beliefs and experiences?

The story is told primarily in a third-person perspective that focuses on Fray Antonio's point of view, but it is intercalated with the first-person narrative of Baptista, a mischievous novice nun at the Ágreda convent who is particularly close to Sor María. Baptista spies on a hesitant Fray Antonio in order to report on the validity of Sor María's claims ("The archbishop has charged me with this task, that the infant Church of the New World not be damaged by a fraud or by an insane woman."[146]), as he sits in the convent's courtyard. The face the startled friar observed was "plain as a painted angel's, yet dreadful as a demon's in its wicked mobility."[147]

The spritely Baptista has her own mystical experiences to contend with: she both witnesses Sor María's spiritual raptures and experiences a transcendental union similar to the abbess's. Believing unquestioningly in Sor María's mystical travels, she records them in a journal, and simultaneously plans to abandon the religious life to which her impoverished brothers have subjected her because she had no dowry for marriage. Baptista confides her future plans to Sor María: she will travel to Seville and live a life as an anonymous merchant. In the meantime, Fray Antonio's loyal and religious man-at-arms Juan carries on a secret, semi-anonymous nighttime liaison with Baptista, during which the novice seduces the soldier and tells him of her belief in Sor María.

Sympathetic and at times conflicted in his mission, Fray Antonio doggedly conducts interviews to determine if Sor María truly did travel to New Mexico. Wrestling with his duty to be objective, and following the advice of the Jesuit secretary, Fray Antonio literally weighs Sor María's testimony and that of the nuns and the citizens of Ágreda. He uses small pieces of paper and a scale to determine whether doubt or belief provides the more substantial body of evidence. Fray Antonio is acutely aware that if he disputes the validity of Sor María's travels, the Inquisition will certainly examine her: "If no one authenticated her claims, what happened to her then? The proofs of her innocence—or guilt—could be prolonged, terrible and bloody."[148] Although much of the testimony in her favor is inconclusive, Fray Alonso is impressed with Sor María's unemotional conviction in the events, echoed in the priest's own feelings of spiritual limitlessness and joy among the Jumanos in New Mexico. Because of this, he finds that he cannot dismiss the case.

Fray Antonio readies himself to leave the convent with a disguised Baptista, and an enamored Juan, in tow. He carries a document for Sor María to sign stating that he does not find sufficient evidence confirming her mystical travels. As they leave, Sor María gazes at Fray Antonio and speaks to him the words he whispered to himself at the Jumano conversion: "God, live in me as I live in You. . . . You have in this far world no humbler servant."[149] The only person who could have heard Fray Antonio say this was Juan, and Fray Antonio asks the perplexed soldier if he had revealed the words to Sor María. He had not. Fray Antonio is thus finally convinced of the truth of Sor María's claims, regardless of the Inquisitorial encounters it could entail for both of them.

Fray Antonio returns to New Mexico and, many years after the incident, continues to correspond with the nun, who by now has survived her questioning by the Inquisition. He asks her to describe what bilocation really is like, and she responds with an answer that reaffirms the boundlessness of the spiritual travel and of faith itself, and alludes to the syncretic faith experienced by Fray Antonio in New Mexico. She tells him, "One world lies without boundaries inside the other, Fray Antonio."[150] The story closes as the aged Fray Antonio reaches across the table at his mission towards the ghostly image of Sor María and extends his blessing to her, "[leaning] forward and [etching] the cross on the warm skin of the air."[151]

In Sandlin's "Saint of Bilocation," the Lady in Blue narrative is a crucible for ruminations on belief, faith, and on the "River Province," a part of "the New World . . . a place without bounds. Earth and heavens folding into one."[152] It is firmly seated in a Spanish context, and many of the characters' preoccupations have to do with Spanish paradigms and their relationship to conditions in the New World. The characters represent facets of this deliberation: Sor María is distant, intense, with hidden warmth and credibility; Fray Antonio is conflicted between mathematical, rational, limited European reason, and his own transcendent and indefinable experiences in the missionary field; Juan is marked by his firm belief; and Baptista by her ecstatic emulation of Sor María and desire to transform her own conditions and future. The story's fundamental affirmation of an encompassing, all-pervasive spirituality comes by means of understanding and accepting the essence of the Lady in Blue narrative.

Spanish popular fiction author Javier Sierra's *La dama azul* (2005)[153] is the most elaborate reimagining of the Lady in Blue narrative presented in this chapter. Subtitled *El vaticano nunca contó toda la verdad*, the novel is in conspiracy-theory style, interlacing four plotlines connected through the Lady in Blue bilocation narrative. At the heart of the book lie questions concerning the acquisition and application of new technologies (instantaneous physical travel) and their intentional concealment from the public through powerful hierarchical organizations (in this case, the Vatican and the CIA). The Lady in Blue narrative is the site for exploring the dynamics of control and secrecy, translating the seventeenth-century account seamlessly into twenty-first-century themes.

The intertwined stories involve (1) Sor María's seventeenth-century bilocation to the Jumano tribes of New Mexico and her confusion as to the nature of her travel; (2) the development of a cadre of "astral spies" by the U.S government; (3) the research conducted by four contemporary priests who secretly develop a technology called "Chronovision" that records sounds and pictures at points in the past; and (4) the experiences of a character loosely modeled on Sierra, a journalist who specializes in investigating supernatural and unexplained phenomena. Through the course of the novel, it is revealed that bilocation is an old technology, based on mastering certain types of energetic vibrations; that such travel functions on a mystical plane; that a certain class of half-angel/half-humans are imbued with the ability to travel on that plane; and that this technology had been controlled and manipulated over the centuries.

Bringing the idea of female bilocation into the present day, a working Spanish woman, María Coronel, discovers that she is capable of such travels. After exploring and questioning this ability, she encounters a group of priest-scientists near the novel's conclusion and is presented as a member of a rebel group called the *Ordo Sanctae Imaginis*, who frustrate the Church's exploitation of bilocation. Because the cadre of spirit-travelers failed in their original attempt to expose this conspiracy by calling on one of the priest-scientists to publish on it, the Spanish journalist is called to the task. The text closes with a metaliterary reference to the novel itself: "Why don't we simply invite this journalist to write the novel you propose? . . . He could even title it something like *The Lady in Blue*."[154] The novel leads the reader through a maze of schemes that entangle the spiritual, the political, and the implausible, but it maintains the Lady in Blue travel narrative, and its Spanish origins, as the work's unifying notion. *La dama azul* questions authority, and the motivations that underlie such powerful forces, and so the book's conclusion imagines a subversion of those hierarchies, with the Lady in Blue narrative the integral plot piece around which these issues revolve.

Drawing on techniques used by other contemporary authors of historical fiction and metafiction, the novel's appendix provides the sources Sierra used in composing the novel and adds suggestively that the materials are intended for "those readers who have already intuited that *The Lady in Blue* is more than a work of fiction."[155] The postscriptum assures the reader of the reality of the Chronovision technology, tantalizingly hinting at still-hidden secrets relating to bilocation, Sor María, and the Vatican, among other topics. At times fantastically eccentric, Sierra's entertaining novel brings Sor María and the Lady in Blue narrative—its principal focus—to bear on the present day.

Reviving the Lady in Blue: Community Commemorations in Texas and New Mexico

Contemporary reconsiderations of the Lady in Blue narrative are not limited to literary and artistic examples. A growing interest in Sor María as a saint-like patron figure in the American Southwest has recently culminated in three commemorative celebrations, two events, in 2009 and 2010 in San Angelo, Texas, and another in Abó, New Mexico, in 2014. The unifying theme for these celebrations was Sor María as a mystical missionary visitor to the region, a figure of informal local devotion, and a candidate for canonization (associated in the Abó event with the Franciscan Texas missionary Fray Antonio Margil de Jesús). These borderland commemorations echo efforts under way to advance Sor María's case for canonization.[156]

In 2009 and 2010,[157] San Angelenos and devotees of the Lady in Blue from other parts of the country celebrated the nun's seventeenth- and eighteenth-century visits to the central Texas region. Organized by local civic leaders, the Diocese of San Angelo, researchers interested in the topic, and present-day members of the Jumano tribe, the two-day festival sought to recognize and reestablish the Lady in Blue as a preeminent figure in the community's local history.[158] The two weekend-long events collectively included an opening Mass and ecumenical ceremony;[159] a procession emulating the rites described by Fray Benavides in the *1630 Memorial* (in which the Jumanos greeted the two friars sent to them with crosses decorated with flowers); a powwow;[160] special events featuring Jumano tribal members;[161] a visit to petroglyphs at a nearby farm;[162] and the presentation and singing of an album of music based on Sor María.[163]

This celebration is more complicated than it seems at first blush. A demonstration of popular religiosity,[164] it is also involved in the advancement of the Jumano tribe's ongoing petition for recognition as an official tribe by the U.S. government, in connection with the Lady in Blue narrative as part of the tribe's history.[165] A newspaper article discussing the 2010 event completely evades critical understanding of the Spanish colonization of indigenous tribes near San Angelo. Entitled "Sister Maria Saved Jumanos from Spanish Rule,"[166] the article does not explain how this occurred, and closes with a puzzling statement seemingly conflating La Llorona with Sor María: "She [Sor María] is looking for old San Clemente and its lost souls, but the old mission is no longer there. She walks until sunrise. Sometimes, she cries."[167] The San Angelo event focuses on what is perceived as Sor María's historical influence on the region, assuming her presence as a protomissionary figure there; any attention at the event to the impact of her writing appears to have been minimal.

In 2014, another commemoration was celebrated near Mountainair, New Mexico. On June 28, the "4th Annual Pilgrimage in Honor of Sor María de Ágreda" took place at the Abó Salinas Pueblo Missions National Monument, amid the ruins of the former San Gregorio de Abó mission church.[168] The event was described in the planning and summary material, provided by one of the organizers, Jerry Javier Luján, as part of an initiative to advance the canonization of Sor María and Fray Antonio Margil de Jesús, and it involved approximately two hundred participants. In contrast to the San Angelo celebration, the pilgrimage had a more clearly Catholic focus: it started at Isleta Pueblo's St. Augustine church, included a celebration of Mass at the ruins by parish priests from Mountainair and Isleta, and involved the participation of the local Knights of Columbus chapter.[169]

After Mass at the ruins, a sculpture of Sor María was unveiled and blessed. Created by local artist Reynaldo "Sonny" Rivera, the piece bears the description "Sor María of Ágreda, Mystical Lady in Blue," and shows the blue-cloaked nun seated, half embracing an indigenous child at her knee (see fig. 6.4); its composition echoes an image of Sor María popularized in the 1958 special edition of *Age of Mary* magazine.[170] After the sculpture's debut, a letter from the abbess of Sor María's convent in Ágreda was read, expressing the convent's enthusiasm for the pilgrimage and efforts on behalf of Sor María made by the organizers, and inviting those present at the pilgrimage to join in the May 2015 celebration honoring Sor María's birth.

Although the majority of the events focused on Sor María's relevance to the area based on her mystical travels and conversions of local tribes, an enthusiast of *La mística ciudad de dios*, Juanita Chávez, made a presentation on the book, encouraging the formation of study groups dedicated to the text. After a break for lunch, several presentations followed, primarily focused on Sor María in relationship to local Native communities. This segment of the pilgrimage began with a presentation by park ranger Marc LeFrançois, who discussed the history of the Sa-

Figure 6.4. Sor María of Ágreda, Mystical Lady in Blue (2014), bas-relief, by Reynaldo "Sonny" Rivera. Image courtesy Hope Rivera.

linas Valley missions. This was followed by a talk on Sor María's impact on the Jumano tribe by their representative Enrique Madrid.[171] The pilgrimage schedule indicated that these were to be the closing events; however, the transcript of the event includes additional information of particular relevance for Sor María's canonization case: the documentation of two miracles ascribed to the nun's intervention.

In the first, the late Henry Casso, who had been affiliated with the advancement of Fray Margil's and Sor María's canonization in New Mexico and Texas, attributed the retention of his leg, despite a grave

diabetes diagnosis, to Sor María's intercession. The second miracle described the case of Louise Baca (daughter of pilgrimage participants De-
siderio and Martha Baca), who suffered from leukemia but found a rare
bone marrow match for transplant in her sister Gloria. Louise Baca's
continuing improvement was attributed to Sor María by her parents,
who at the previous year's pilgrimage asked for the nun's intervention in
the case.

Both the San Angelo and New Mexico commemorations built upon
growing interest in Sor María as religious historical figure in the American Southwest. (In fact, in 2008, New Mexico's governor Bill Richardson
declared New Mexico a sister community with Ágreda, Spain.[172]) The
two events centered almost exclusively on Sor María as the Lady in Blue,
and her particular relevance was directly connected in both cases to the
conversion of indigenous groups originally located in these regions. Although the pilgrimage to Abó did make brief mention of *La mística
ciudad de dios* and Sor María as its author, the two events echo the focus
of other contemporary artifacts examined so far in this chapter: the mystical missionary eclipses the literary Sor María almost entirely.

A Return to Sor María's Writing

But Sor María the author is beginning to reappear: a handful of recent
reimaginings of Sor María treat her writing as a primary theme, sharing
equal space with the Lady in Blue. The fiction works of Costa Rican
author Rima de Valbona, of Guatemalan American writer and journalist
Francisco Goldman, and the puppetry of Ron and Laia Dans distinguish
themselves by incorporating Sor María's writing into their creative
pieces. These works draw our attention back to Sor María as an author,
and remind us that this, as much or more than her mystical bilocations,
is her most profound impact in what was New Spain. The imaginative
work these texts do on Sor María's written production and its reading
suggests the possibility of future creative works treating her long legacy
as a writer.

Rima de Valbona's short story "El Legado de la Venerable Sor María
de Agreda" (The Legacy of the Venerable Sor María de Ágreda) (1988)[173]
plays with the idea of bilocation as a narrational tool by presenting a
syncretism between the story's protagonist and her relationship to Sor

María's bilocation, using Sor María's writing as a framing device. The story begins with the first-person voice of the first narrator, an anonymous female university professor conducting research on a colonial-era topic at the Biblioteca Nacional in Mexico City in anticipation of a conference. While perusing the city's market one Sunday, she encounters a copy of the 1670 Madrid printing of *La mística ciudad de dios*, and thumbs through the book's introduction. In an instant, the narrative voice changes to that of a nun who lives in Sor María's convent, and the professor narrator observes Sor María as she writes and travels to convert the Moqui (Hopi) tribe: "La veo en uno de los momentos de arrobo, suspendida en el aire, transfigurada y tan ligera de peso, que la brisa de mañana mece su leve cuerpo con el mismo vaivén de las hojas de lirio que bordean el jardín del claustro" (I see her in one of her moments of rapture, suspended in the air, transfigured, and so light that the morning breeze caresses her slight body with the same soft sway as the leaves of the lilies that border the cloister's garden).[174]

The story continues, alternating between the voice of the professor, attempting in the present day to complete her research, yet driven to distraction by her involvement with Sor María's writings, and the voice of (the professor as) a seventeenth-century Agredan nun, who observes Sor María's correspondence with Felipe IV, and Sor María's pleas to send missionaries to the tribes she visited. The porosity between the two characters makes them feel as if they are one, as in the following: "Un semáforo. La luz se vuelve roja. Veo entonces a la Venerable María de Jesús de Ágreda, claramente, como si la tuviera frente a mí" (A stoplight. The light turns red again. I then see the Venerable María de Jesús de Ágreda, clearly, as if I had her in front of me).[175]

The story interpolates authentic historical materials into the fictional text, as if to underscore the temporality of the professor, who is "enredada en una confusa telaraña entre el ayer barroco y el hoy de la electrónica" (caught up in a perplexing web between the baroque past and the electronic present).[176] She decides she must set Sor María aside or risk losing her career. Yet, when immersed in her research at the Biblioteca Nacional, she finds a historical tract, dated 1746 and composed by Fray Carlos Delgado, a Franciscan friar who administered at the Hopi tribe in New Mexico.[177] The text claims that Sor María continued to be a presence among the Moqui during his time there: "nuestra apreciada misionera nos está ayudando a cultivar la Viña del Señor" (our prized missionary is helping us cultivate the vineyard of the Lord).[178] Disregarding weeks of research—echoing Sor María's burning of *La mística ciudad de dios*—the liberated professor requests a map of Mexico from the librarian, exclaiming: "¡Qué bueno liberarme así de la tiranía académica!" (How wonderful to free myself from academic tyranny!).[179] As the story closes, the narrative changes voice a final time to an omniscient third person that observes and describes the convergence of the past and the present, as it appears that the professor and conventual nun become one. The professor, "impecable . . . de gesto intelectual" (impeccable . . . of an intellectual appearance)[180] throws herself at the librarian, pleading in the language of seventeenth-century Spain: "Vuestra Ilustrísima, os ruego dejarme ir al Moqui. . . . Me lo manda la Venerable María de Jesús . . . en su lecho de muerte me legó esta misión y por lo mismo no puedo dejar de cumplirla. ¡Mandadme a Moqui, por el amor de Dios!" (Your Grace, I beg you to let me go to Moqui. . . . The Venerable María de Jesús thus orders me . . . on her deathbed she bequeathed me this mission and for this reason, and I cannot leave it undone. Send me to Moqui, for the love of God!).[181] The narrator informs us of the librarian's confusion at the professor/nun's continued pleas to be sent to the Moqui, "cueste lo que cueste" (whatever the cost),[182] as the two merge into one. Valbona leaves the reader without a clear idea of which of two "yo's" is the more "real" one, and questioning whether the past has merged into the present or the present into the past.

Literary critic Lee Daniels reads the story's title and its relationship to the narration through several definitions of the word "legado." In the first sense, that of a material inheritance transmitted to one's successors (and inheritance or bequest), Daniels sees *La mística ciudad de dios* as the object that is passed along,[183] the point of connection between the seventeenth and twentieth centuries.[184] In this reading, it is as if Sor María left the book for the professor to find as a bequest. Daniels simultaneously reads "legado" with another meaning: that of an ambassador sent by a Church official and charged with a particular mission. The professor, as a "legado," acts as Sor María's emissary, dispatched to complete the nun's objectives. In Daniels's reading, Sor María has reached back across centuries through her own text to compel the professor—"mientras está loca"[185]—to continue her incomplete missionary work.

As both the seventeenth-century, Agredan nun and the present-day professor are expressed in the first-person voice, and the liquid character

of the narrative seamlessly dovetails one "yo" into the other, borders between past and present, between the "real" and the "imagined" are dis-
solved. This literary convention reproduces the back-and-forth sense of
Sor María's bilocation, through its close cousin, bi-temporality:

> Mientras recorro la calle Bolívar de vuelta al hotel, experimento la
> más intensa enajenación, como si estas peregrinas calles del México
> dieciochesco fueran de tiempos muy lejanos, todo un mundo de-
> sconocido por mí racionalmente, pero que me es muy familiar en el
> ámbito de mi yo profundo. En aquel instante las otras monjas se
> cuchichearon a mi lado.

> _____

> As I traverse the Calle Bolívar, returning to the hotel, I experi-
> ence the most intense alienation, as if these wandering streets of
> eighteenth-century Mexico were from a time long ago, a whole
> world that I rationally do not know, but that is very familiar to me
> in the confines of my deepest self. At that very moment, the other
> nuns whispered at my side.[186]

Regardless of how this game functions, the story's focus remains as
much on the literary Sor María as it does on the bilocation; the notion
of Sor María as a writer is as prominent in the text as is the idea of her as
a mystical traveler. The protagonist's transformation occurs through repeated contact with Sor María's writing; the text becomes the means
through which times and places are merged. "El legado de la Venerable
María de Jesús de Ágreda" does major reimaginative work on her written
legacy, creating an innovative symbiosis between it and the bilocation
narrative.

In Francisco Goldman's 2004 novel *The Divine Husband*,[187] Sor
María is a secondary but nonetheless significant figure for the book's
protagonist, María de las Nieves Morán. A work of historical fiction, the
novel opens in nineteenth-century revolutionary Cuba. María de las
Nieves is the servant and companion to Francisca "Paquita" Aparicio,
who later marries Cuba's dictator and flees the country after his death.

At the beginning of the novel, María and Paquita are sent to a convent school. As Paquita is pursued ever more intensely by the dictator,
María becomes a novice nun in the convent. While observing a nun's

strict rules, María is introduced to Sor María's *vita*, to which she feels an immediate affinity: "Nothing she had ever read before had so impressed or stimulated her, or awoken such concentrated yearning."[188] María compares herself to Sor María, noting that the Agredan nun began her mystical travels when she was about the same age as María when María first reads the nun's *vita*. Through her reading of Sor María's life, the young girl perceives "several provocative parallels between her own life and that of the mystically bilocating Spanish nun."[189] As in Valbona's story, the theme of bilocation linked with reading is echoed throughout the novel, specifically in a plot twist relating to Cuban revolutionary José Martí.

Sor María's *vita* had been a favorite for generations among the nuns of the Cuban convent where María resides. The convent's novice mistress comments: "It is one of the few books in this library that was rescued from the rubble of our first convent in the old capital. Our predecessors must have loved it very much."[190] A miserable María gives herself over entirely to the book, immersing herself in "the methodically narrated adventures and inner dialogues inspired by the mystical travels of the Spanish nun."[191] She escapes through the text, imagining herself traveling, trying to "lose herself in meticulously guided day and night dreams of mystical bilocation"[192] in order to visit the family and friends she misses. Sor María's counsel comforts María de las Nieves during her novitiate, and she learns that the travel is a reward of sorts for spiritual forbearance: "María de las Nieves knew now that such flights and visions were won only through the most heroic discipline, suffering and selflessness, and by the twinned powers of reason and faith."[193] When she finally finishes the *vita*, María relinquishes the adored texts regretfully: "Goodbye beautiful, beloved book, goodbye, I love you."[194] She then makes a special request to read *La mística ciudad de dios*, but is denied that privilege:

> During novice class one afternoon, María de las Nieves finally dared to ask if Sor María de Agreda's "autobiography" of La Virgen María could be her next spiritual reading. The Novice Mistress replied that it had been one of her own favorite books when she was young, and promised to meditate on her request. But even before the end of that same class, Sister Gertrudis switched to English to announce: "It is certainly not up to me to decide whether the Most Holy Virgin did actually dictate *The Mystical City* to Sor María or

not. But it being true of this book that its author does openly identify herself with the heroism and even person of our Most Holy
Blessed Virgin, I wonder if it makes suitable reading for a mere
novice who *does* seem to identify just as strongly and openly with
its moral authority." [María de las Nieves] understood [Sister Ger-
trudis's] meaning: that she was not going to be allowed to read
the book.[195]

Although Sor María's work was deemed too nuanced or perhaps too
controversial for an impressionable novice nun, her superiors' understanding of and appreciation for the work speak volumes about how
Goldman's novel portrays the value of Sor María's writing in nineteenth-
century Cuba.

María de las Nieves carries Sor María's lessons throughout her life,
wishing at various times that she could mystically travel through the
convent's walls to talk to Paquita,[196] comparing her unexpected freedom
from urban poverty to "a mystical escape as wondrous as any she'd read
about in Sor María de Agreda,"[197] and recalling, upon seeing an image of
Cañon de Chelly, Arizona, the nun's alleged travel to the area.[198]

Eventually, the bilocation narrative becomes a major plot point, as
a possible explanation for the paternity of María de las Nieves's second
child. María de las Nieves's first child, Mathilde, suggests that her mother
trilocated to three different men, including José Martí, "herself [María
de las Nieves] corporally manifesting with all three! That—according
to Mathilde, as confided by her mother—was how the second child, her
son Charles/Carlos . . . was conceived. That anonymous young sailor so
resembled the mysterious muchacho that he was like his ghost was the
physical progenitor, and Martí the mystical one, thus her son's physical
resemblance to El Apóstol."[199] The narrator comments that such a lu-
dicrous story must have been concocted to disguise Martí's paternity,
but Mathilde's conviction and the lingering possibility of bilocation per-
sist. Goldman casts the Lady in Blue narrative, "María de las Nieves's
old favorite,"[200] as a metonym for escape, movement, and earned self-
determination, a concept she picked up through the literary Sor María.

In *The Divine Husband*, Goldman establishes the motif of Sor
María's travels early, and María de las Nieves's actions echo them
throughout the book. Without Sor María's writing, however, María de
las Nieves could not have accessed the narrative in the convent and
would not have fallen in love with her "beautiful, beloved book." By

focusing on Sor María's writing through the interpretation of María de las Nieves, Goldman highlights the nun's agency as an author and her reception in communities of reading.

The final example is found not between the pages of a book, but rather on the puppet stage. On February 15, 2009, Santa Fe puppeteers Ron Dans and Laia Obregón-Dans debuted a scene from their newest puppet show, *Lady Blue, Maria Jesus de Agreda*, in Eldorado, New Mexico.[201] (see fig. 6.5) The Dans's puppet troupe, called Puppet's Revenge,[202] creates and presents original puppet shows on a variety of topics, including one on the story of Alvar Núñez Cabeza de Vaca and Estebanico, and another on the Greek myth of Eros and Psyche. Though puppetry is a genre associated with children's entertainment, the meaning behind Puppets Revenge's pieces is often oriented towards adults, delivered with a sophisticated, tongue-in-cheek sense of humor. As the Puppets Revenge website states, "our work is irreverent, sometimes politically incorrect, always funny." The scene of the play presented in Eldorado bears this out.

Figure 6.5. Still image from *Lady Blue's Dreams* by Puppet's Revenge. Image courtesy Ron Dans.

It opens with a Dr. Phil Fraud (a masked Ron Dans), who is presenting a past life regression seminar. As he speaks to the audience about the topic (who chuckle in recognition of the local relevance of this New Age topic), he calls for a volunteer to participate in a regression. A masked participant wearing blue (Laia Obregón-Dans) is selected, and she begins to recount why she believes that she has a connection to a past life, saying that she feels like she is in two places at once, and that everyone around her is speaking Spanish. This linkage between the volunteer and the Lady in Blue sets the scene for the puppet interaction to follow.

While a voice-over narrates the past life regression process—describing experiences similar to what Sor María wrote about spiritual voyage—the puppet scene is assembled. When the lights come up, a Sor María puppet sits behind a confessional screen, while a priest/confessor puppet listens to her describe her pleasurable mysterious travels. The confessor, uncomprehending of the subtlety of what he is told, offers her a penance of three hundred and fifty rosaries and three hours of exercises of the cross, and disappears. The scene shifts to Sor María praying in her cell, where she is approached by various manifestations of the Virgin Mary, wearing dresses of flowers (including an outfit à la Carmen Miranda). One encourages her explicitly to explore her sexuality and the idea of what sex means and offers her a feather for tickling—a seeming playful and also innuendo-filled allusion to the nun's iconography, in which she holds a quill for writing. Another Virgin Mary puppet appears to Sor María and begins to recount her story to the nun, who writes it down as the early draft of *La mística ciudad de dios*. This Virgin encourages Sor María to consider Christ's life as one filled with joy, rather than only suffering.

The confessor priest puppet returns and offers Sor María two crowns, one of flowers and one of thorns. She chooses the latter and is blessed by the priest, who disappears as a voice-over tells of how she wrote the Virgin's biography for twelve years. The Virgin encourages Sor María to be creative "like the Father," and she continues to write. Eventually, the confessor puppet returns and with a high-handed tone tells her to burn the sacrilegious document immediately, which she does, obeying his command without question. She picks up some needlework, while the voice-over tells that seven years passed, and suddenly the confessor returns. With an air of capricious authority, he orders Sor María to rewrite *La mística ciudad de dios*. The scene closes.

This scene of the play treats Sor María's authorship of *La mística ciudad de dios* at great length; it is the central motif, along with Sor María's conflicted response to her raptures, and obedience to her male confessor. These themes are presented in a cheeky manner that underscores women's lack of agency, control, and permission to self-articulate during the early modern period. The framing for the story (and for later scenes, which were presented in subsequent performances of *Lady Blue, María Jesús de Ágreda*) center on Sor María's bilocation travel,[203] and the connection to place via the mystical travel notion is one of the most appealing elements of the play. According to the playwrights, "The general public loves this play because it illustrates the myths and history of the Southwest." Puppet's Revenge admirably illustrates the authorial side of the Lady in Blue, sharing with Valbona's and Goldman's texts Sor María's writing as a major thematic element.

Reflections on Contemporary Sor María

Recent creative production treating Sor María de Jesús de Ágreda imagines varied contexts and frameworks for the Lady in Blue narrative. The examples discussed above mold and modify the narrative in different ways, resituating and even at times overwriting the original story altogether. Yet what is remarkably consistent across this collection of artifacts—with a few exceptions—is the omission of Sor María as a writer. One could even say this is *the* unifying characteristic of contemporary understanding of Sor María, and not just as portrayed in the artifacts examined here.

And yet this exclusion is wildly ironic. As we know, were it not for the popularity of Sor María's writing in colonial-era (and even nineteenth-century) New Spain, the Lady in Blue narrative would have likely been forgotten, as so many stories of that time and ilk have been. At the very least, it would not be remembered with the persistence we see in lore and contemporary production. The ubiquity of *La mística ciudad de dios*, with the Lady in Blue in its prologue, provided the narrative with reach, consistency, and longevity.

In this book I have sought to establish this important facet of Sor María de Jesús de Ágreda's history in what was New Spain. Past scholarship's blind spot left an incomplete picture of Sor María, which in part contributed to popular productions that do not depict her as the influential writer she was. By making Sor María's writing in New Spain finally visible, I hope to have created a different narrative from which future creative work on Sor María may draw.

Quill and Cross in the Borderlands

¿Pero que raro misterio tiene la Venerable María de Jesús que
aún ahora, pasados los siglos, se instala en esta realidad moderna de
vehículos motorizados y aparatos electrónicos?

———

But what rare mystery does the Venerable María de Jesús possess
that even now, centuries later, she alights into this modern reality of
motorized vehicles and electronic devices?

—Rima de Valbona[1]

A narrative that has fascinated seventeenth-century audiences and
present-day ones, the story of Sor María de Jesús de Ágreda's bilocation
endures across centuries. As an archetypal episode in colonial Mexican
frontier history, as the protagonist of Southwestern folklore, and as the
subject of diverse contemporary reinterpretations, the cloistered, mystically traveling nun continues to command attention in the twenty-first
century.[2] Over and over, scholars, artists, and readers dive into the depths
of what her story could mean, and they will no doubt continue to
wrangle with it for years to come.

But perhaps the narrative's most significant feat is not necessarily
that it still compels us to consider it, but rather that it has sustained
Sor María as an historical figure of interest for almost four centuries.
The ongoing engagement with the Lady in Blue narrative has kept Sor

337

María in our contemporary sights, unlike other—especially female and marginalized—protagonists of her epoch. And although, as we have seen throughout the book, some past treatments of the Lady in Blue are peculiar or problematic, collectively they have kept us pondering Sor María, even though we haven't necessarily grasped the full range of what could be asked of her. Persistent revisiting has preserved her in our collective imagination, and that is the point of departure for new lines of inquiry.[3]

Asking other types of questions of the Lady in Blue has revealed Sor María's previously unarticulated role in colonial Mexican letters: it showed her writing's extraordinary influence over seventeenth-, eighteenth-, and nineteenth-century New Spanish culture.[4] In carefully analyzing the story of the Lady in Blue, and working away at the history surrounding her, Sor María the author has gradually emerged. Implementing what I have elsewhere called a "lateral approach to the archive,"[5] the exceptional reach and impact her writing achieved in New Spain is at last beginning to emerge. This methodology uncovered the remarkable publication of her written work in Mexico: more than twenty-five different texts, resulting in at least fifty-nine publications from 1693 to 1844. No doubt there are many more to be uncovered and studied. The texts' influence materialized in colonial Mexican art, architecture, and writing, and in sermons, public prayers, and other spoken forms, ensuring that one need not have been literate in Spanish to be exposed to what Sor María wrote. Her writing was an undeniable presence in colonial Mexican society, and the subtleties of what these works expressed and signified for that audience is the next frontier of research on Sor María.

We now know what was always apparent for New Spanish readers: that Sor María's legacy was defined by complex interactions between text and legend, and shaped by her writing. Perhaps the recovery of Sor María de Jesús de Ágreda in her complete historical and literary complexity will engage and provoke for years to come, as the Lady in Blue already has.

1. As quoted in Kate Risse, "Strategy of a Provincial Nun: Sor María de Jesús de Ágreda's Response," *Ciberletras* 17 (2007): 8.

2. Alonso de Benavides, *The Memorial of Fray Alonso de Benavides, 1630*, trans. Emma Augusta Burbank Ayer (Chicago: Priv. Print. [R. R. Donnelley and Sons Co.], 1916). Cited hereafter as *1630 Memorial*. Translations in the text are mine unless otherwise indicated.

3. The 1916 edition of Fray Benavides's *1630 Memorial* (notes by Frederick Webb Hodge and Charles Fletcher Lummis, translation by Emma Ayer) is the most frequently cited English language version of the narrative. In its notes, editors Hodge and Lummis dismiss Sor María's travel to New Mexico out of hand: "The miracles she claimed to have performed were marvelous in the extreme. . . . Some of the tribal names mentioned by Mother María de Jesús, as might be expected, were, like the journeys themselves, creations of the imagination" (Benavides, *1630 Memorial*, note 2 on 189–90). They cast aspersions on the nun's temperament using a strange and recursive logic that attributes to Sor María far more agency than historical documents indicate she exerted: "The so-called mystical manifestations of Maria de Jesú as set forth in her *La Mística Ciudad* are characteristic of those she professed to have had in connection with the Indians of New Mexico. We have an inkling of these in the *Memorial* of Benavides, and have already seen that he visited the nun at Ágreda in 1631 where he had every opportunity to hear from the lady's own lips of her marvelous 'flights' to New Mexico. . . . This no doubt will prove sufficient to indicate the mental character of his nun. For other performances to which she laid claim, see the letter of Benavides, together with her own communication" (ibid., note 55 on 276, 278). In Mexican historian Fernando de Ocaranza's 1934 transcription of the 1631 letter written by Fray Benavides and Sor María to the friars in New Mexico, in which Sor María's travels to New Mexico are described, Ocaranza derisively comments at the document's conclusion: "Así terminó el 'translado' de la carta, donde nos refiere Fr. Alonso de Benavides, su maravilloso cuento de hadas" (Thus concluded the "excerpt" of the letter, in which Fray Alonso de Benavides recounts for us his marvelous fairy tale); Fernando Ocaranza, *Establecimientos*

franciscanos en el misterioso reino de Nuevo México (México, 1934), 84. Even Sor María's earliest English-language biographer and advocate, T. D. Kendrick, viewed her travels with misgivings: "All this means that it is not unfair to suggest that the gullibility of Father Benavides [in believing Sor María had traveled to New Mexico] must almost have equaled that of Father Marcos of Nice [Fray Marcos de Niza], and that the tale of their nun told by the Jumanos, assuredly with the Virgin Mary in mind, was as fictitious as a tale told by the Turk"; T. D. Kendrick, *Mary of Ágreda: The Life and Legend of a Spanish Nun* (London: Routledge & K. Paul, 1967), 55.

4. As historian Ronald Rittgers has critically commented of historical scholarship on miracle narratives: "We can allow that people in the past believed in such things, and we can concede that some of our colleagues do as well, but we insist that such beliefs have no place in the modern historian's craft.... Our culture will not abide intrusions of the transcendent and the supernatural into the interpretation of history. Our purview and our methodology are both strictly mundane, that is, this-worldly; we operate in a closed universe"; Rittgers, "'He Flew': A Concluding Reflection on the Place of Eternity and the Supernatural in the Scholarhip of Carlos M. N. Eire," in *A Linking of Heaven and Earth: Studies in Religious and Cultural History in Honor of Carlos M. N. Eire*, ed. Emily Michelson, Scott K. Taylor, and Mary Noll Venables (Farnham, Surrey: Ashgate, 2012), 205–6.

5. Studies of this nature include Marilyn H. Fedewa, *María of Ágreda: Mystical Lady in Blue* (Albuquerque: University of New Mexico Press, 2009); Servite Fathers, *The Age of Mary: An Exclusively Marian Magazine*, "The Mystical City of God" Issue (January-February 1958); see http://www.bookemon .com/flipread/681374/the-age-of-mary-magazine-january-february-1958 #book; Zótico Royo Campos, *Agredistas y antiagredistas: Estudio histórico-apologético* (Totana: Tipografía de San Buenaventura, 1929).

6. Maria de Jesús de Ágreda and Joseph Ximénez Samaniego, *Mystica ciudad de Dios . . . : Historia divina, y vida de la Virgen Madre de Dios . . . : Manifestada en estos ultimos siglos por la misma Señora à su esclava Sor María de Iesus . . . "Prologo galeato" and "Relación de la vida de la venerable madre Sor María de Jesus"* (Madrid: B. de Villa-Diego, 1670).

7. A representative selection of such studies of early modern women's writing in Spanish America might include the following: Ellen Gunnarsdøttir, *Mexican Karismata: The Baroque Vocation of Francisca de los Ángeles, 1674–1744*, Engendering Latin America (Lincoln: University of Nebraska Press, 2004); Nora Jaffary, *False Mystics* (Lincoln: University of Nebraska Press, 2004); Electa Arenal, Schlau Stacey, and Amanda Powell, *Untold Sisters: Hispanic Nuns in Their Own Works*, rev. ed. (Albuquerque: University of New Mexico Press, 2010); Kathleen Ann Myers and Amanda Powell, *A Wild Country Out in the Garden: The Spiritual Journals of a Colonial Mexican Nun* (Bloomington: Indiana University Press, 1999); Jennifer Lee Eich, *The Other Mexican Muse: Sor María Anna Agueda de San Ignacio, 1695–1765* (New Orleans: University Press of the South, 2004); Josefina Muriel, *Cultura femenina novohispana*, 1st ed., Serie de historia novohispana (Mexico: Universidad Nacional Autónoma de

México, Instituto de Investigaciones Históricas, 1982); Muriel, *Las indias caciques de Corpus Christi*, 1st ed., Instituto de Historia: Serie histórica (México: Universidad Nacional Autónoma de México, 1963); Kathleen Ann Myers, *Neither Saints Nor Sinners: Writing the Lives of Women in Spanish America* (New York: Oxford University Press, 2003).

8. Some sources that frame the narrative this way are Tey Diana Rebolledo, *Nuestras Mujeres* (Albuquerque: El Norte/Academia, 1992); Rafaela Castro, *Dictionary of Chicano Literature* (Santa Barbara, CA: ABC-CLIO, 2000); Juliana Barr, *Peace Came in the Form of a Woman: Indians and Spaniards in the Texas Borderlands* (Chapel Hill: University of North Carolina Press, 2007); William Donahue, "Mary of Agreda and the Southwest United States," *Americas* 9 (1953), 291–314; Donald E. Chipman and Harriett Denise Joseph, *Notable Men and Women of Spanish Texas* (Austin: University of Texas Press, 1999); John Francis Bannon, *The Spanish Borderlands Frontier*, ed. Ray Allen Billington and Howard Lamar, Histories of the American Frontier (Albuquerque: University of New Mexico Press, 1974).

9. See, for example, Domino Perez, *There Was a Woman: La Llorona from Folklore to Popular Culture* (Austin: University of Texas Press, 2008); Enrique Lamadrid, "Las dos Lloronas de Santa Fe," in *Santa Fe Nativa: A Collection of Nuevomexicano Writing*, ed. Rosalie C. Otero et al. (Albuquerque: University of New Mexico Press, 2010); Lamadrid, "From Santiago at Ácoma to the Diablo in the Casinos: Four Centuries of Foundational Milagro Narratives in New Mexico," in *Expressing New Mexico: Nuevomexicano Creativity, Ritual, and Memory*, ed. Phillip B. Gonzales (Tucson: University of Arizona Press, 2007); José Limón, *Dancing with the Devil* (Madison: University of Wisconsin Press, 1994); Paul Vanderwood, *Juan Soldado* (Durham, NC: Duke University Press, 2004).

10. For more on Guadalupe, Santiago, and the Santo Niño de Atocha, see D. A. Brading, *Mexican Phoenix* (Cambridge: Cambridge University Press, 2003); Timothy Matovina, *Guadalupe and Her Faithful* (Baltimore: Johns Hopkins University Press, 2005); Linda Hall, *Mary, Mother and Warrior* (Austin: University of Texas Press, 2004); Stafford Poole, *Our Lady of Guadalupe: The Origins and Sources of a Mexican National Symbol, 1531–1797* (Tucson: University of Arizona Press, 1995). Lamadrid, "From Santiago at Ácoma to the Diablo in the Casinos"; Enrique Lamadrid, *Hermanitos Comanchitos*, Pasó por aquí (Albuquerque: University of New Mexico Press, 2003); Juan Javier Pescador, *Crossing Borders with the Santo Niño de Atocha* (Albuquerque: University of New Mexico Press, 2009).

11. Previous scholarship has considered the narrative's origins and early reproduction, but only cursorily. See Clark Colahan, *The Visions of Sor María de Agreda: Writing Knowledge and Power* (Tucson: University of Arizona Press, 1994); Daniel T. Reff, "Contextualizing Missionary Discourse: The Benavides Memorials of 1630 and 1634," *Journal of Anthropological Research* 50, no. 1 (1994); Katie MacLean, "María de Agreda, Spanish Mysticism and the Work of Spiritual Conquest," *Colonial Latin American Review* 17, no. 1 (2008); Nancy Hickerson, "The Visits of the 'Lady in Blue': An Episode in the History of

the South Plains, 1629," *Journal of Anthropological Research* 46, no. 1 (1990); Carroll Riley, "Las Casas and the Benavides Memorial of 1630," *New Mexico Historical Review* 48, no. 3 (1973); Cyprian Lynch, introduction to *Benavides' Memorial of 1630* (Washington, DC: American Academy of Franciscan History, 1954); Frederick Webb Hodge, "The Jumano Indians" (paper presented at the Proceedings of the American Antiquarian Society, 1910); Frances Scholes, "Problems in the Early Ecclesiastical History of New Mexico," *New Mexico Historical Review* (January 1932).

12. For the case of the New Mexico/Texas region, see José Rabasa, *Writing Violence on the Northern Frontier: The Historiography of Sixteenth-Century New Mexico and Florida and the Legacy of Conquest*, Latin America Otherwise (Durham, NC: Duke University Press, 2000); Ramón Gutiérrez, *When Jesus Came, the Corn Mothers Went Away: Marriage, Sexuality and Power in New Mexico* (Stanford, CA: Stanford University Press, 1991); James Brooks, *Captives and Cousins: Slavery, Kinship and Community in the Southwest Borderlands* (Chapel Hill: University of North Carolina Press, 2002).

13. The pioneering work of Miguel León-Portilla set the stage for this approach, revealing the lacunae and assumptions regarding the experiences, perceptions, and responses of indigenous peoples in previous readings of colonial-era documents. See Miguel León-Portilla, *Visión de los vencidos: Relaciones indígenas de la conquista* (México: Universidad Nacional Autónoma de México, 1959). Contemporary work in this postcolonial vein continues to shape the field of colonial studies, including studies by Carlos Montemayor, Louise Burkhart, Elizabeth Hill Boone, James Lockhart, Dennis Tedlock, Rolena Adorno, and, more recently, Kelly McDonough, Mónica Díaz, and Heather Allen, among many others.

14. Medieval historian Jean-Claude Schmitt's scholarship greatly clarified my approach to studying Sor María's bilocations: "If one considers the beliefs and practices described in the text, which are clearly quite startling, to be too startling 'to be true' . . . one might as well abandon one's research right then and there. If, on the other hand, one thinks that there may be a meaning to it all, and that the document ought to be taken seriously, then that clearly provides a tremendous opportunity for a new approach to medieval history"; Schmitt, *The Holy Greyhound: Guinefort, Healer of Children since the Thirteenth Century* (New York: Cambridge University Press, 1983), 7–8. Many thanks to Alison Frazier for introducing me to Schmitt's scholarship. Scholars since Schmitt have produced an extensive literature building on similar themes and examining miracles in historical contexts. A partial listing should include Rittgers, "'He Flew'"; Craig Harline, *Miracles at the Jesus Oak* (New York: Doubleday, 2003); Vanderwood, *Juan Soldado*; Kathryne Beebe, *Pilgrim & Preacher: The Audiences and Observant Spirituality of Friar Felix Fabri (1437/8–1502)* (Oxford: Oxford University Press, 2014).

15. This book's methodology is indebted to the scholarly work of many, including Serge Gruzinski, *Images at War: Mexico from Columbus to Blade Runner (1492–2019)*, trans. Heather MacLean (Durham, NC: Duke University Press, 2001); Limón, *Dancing with the Devil*; Américo Paredes, *With His*

Pistol in His Hand (Austin: University of Texas Press, 1958); Perez, *There Was a Woman*; Richard R. Flores, *Remembering the Alamo: Memory, Modernity, and the Master Symbol*, History, Culture, and Society Series (Austin: University of Texas Press, 2002); Lamadrid, *Hermanitos Comanchitos*.

16. Written by Fray Joseph Ximénez Samaniego, the *vita* was included with the *Prólogo galeato* in most editions of *La mística ciudad de dios* published in the seventeenth through nineteenth centuries. The *vita* was also published repeatedly as a separate document: see Joseph Ximénez Samaniego, *Relación de la vida de la venerable Madre Sor María de Jesús abadesa de el convento de la Inmaculada Concepción de la Villa de Agreda* (Barcelona: Impresa de Martin Gelabert, 1687). In this book I cite the version of the *vita* included in the following edition, held at the University of New Mexico Center for Southwest Research: *Prólogo galeato, relacion de la vida de la V. Madre Sor Maria de Jesus, abadesa, que fue, de el convento de la Inmaculada concepción, de la villa de Agreda, de la provincia de Burgos. Y notas a las tres partes de la Mystica Ciudad de Dios* (Madrid: En la Imprenta de la causa de la V. Madre, 1759).

17. Sor Juana names Sor María in her genealogy of learned women in her famed "Carta de Respuesta a Sor Filotea de la Cruz"; see Juana Inés de la Cruz, *Obras completas*, 12th ed., ed. Francisco Monterede (Mexico: Editorial Porrúa, 2001), 827–48.

18. The Lady in Blue narrative is not unique in this sense—ethnopoetic production is often marked by fluidity between text and nontext, and by interactions between the two forms. For examples of scholarship on movement through spoken and written manifestations of lore, see Lamadrid, "Las dos Lloronas de Santa Fe"; Paredes, *With His Pistol in His Hand*; Perez, *There Was a Woman*.

19. Muriel, *Cultura femenina novohispana*, 9.

20. Debra A. Castillo, "Exclusions in Latin American Literary History," in *Literary Cultures of Latin America: A Comparative History*, ed. Mario J. Valdés and Djelal Kadir (Oxford: Oxford University Press, 2004), 307.

21. Asunción Lavrín, *Brides of Christ: Conventual Life in Colonial Mexico* (Stanford, CA: Stanford University Press, 2008), 2. Lavrin names many historical scholars of women in religious enclosures, among them Rosalva Loreto, Manuel Ramos Medina, Nuria Salazar, Sister Pilar Foz y Foz, Jacqueline Holler, and Margaret Chowning, Alicia Bazarte Martínez, Enrique Tovar Esquivel, and Martha A. Tronco.

22. Ibid., 3.

23. To these scholars, one could add many others, including Stephanie Kirk, Mariselle Meléndez, Santa Arias, Mabel Moraña, and Sara Vicuña Guengerich.

24. Josefina Muriel, "Women Writers during the Viceroyalty," in *Literary Cultures of Latin America: A Comparative History*, ed. Mario J. Valdés and Djelal Kadir (Oxford: Oxford University Press, 2004), 279.

25. Ibid., 284.

26. J. Frank Dobie, *Tales of Old Time Texas* (Austin: University of Texas Press, 1984), xi.

27. Lamadrid, "From Santiago at Ácoma to the Diablo in the Casinos."

28. Although this book focuses on the dissemination of Sor María's writing and the legend of the Lady in Blue in what was New Spain, there is clear evidence that her legacy spread to other sites of Spanish conquest, including Peru, Bolivia, Argentina, Colombia, Chile, and the Philippines. See Anna M. Nogar, "Genealogías hagiográficas y viajes coloniales: Sor María de Ágreda en las Filipinas," *Revista de Soria* 89 (Summer 2015); Ricardo Fernández Gracia, *Iconografía de Sor María de Ágreda: Imágenes para la mística y la escritora en el contexto del maravillosismo del Barroco* (Soria, Spain: Caja Duero, 2003); Fernández Gracia, *Arte, devoción y política: La promoción de las artes en torno a sor María de Ágreda* (Soria, Spain: Diputación Provincial de Soria, 2002); Laurencio Atlas, "Árbol geneológico de la familia Coronel-Arana" (1759), Archivo Franciscano Ibero-Oriental, Madrid (printed in Manila).

ONE   Seventeenth-Century Spiritual Travel to New Mexico

1. Ricardo Fernández Gracia, *Iconografía de Sor María de Ágreda: Imágenes para la mística y la escritora en el contexto del maravillosismo del Barroco* (Soria, Spain: Caja Duero, 2003), 106.

2. Ágreda and Ximénez Samaniego, *Mystica ciudad de Dios.*

3. Other miraculous episodes in the *1630 Memorial* include these: "Provincia y nación de los Piros, Senecú, Socorro y Sevilleta," "Nación Mansa del Río del Norte," "Nación Picuries," and "Nación Taos."

4. Benavides, *1630 Memorial*, 83.

5. This intersection appears frequently in colonial texts, as Stephen Greenblatt and others have noted. Stephen Greenblatt, *Marvelous Possessions: The Wonder of the New World* (Chicago: University of Chicago Press, 1991).

6. Benavides, *1630 Memorial*, 125–29, 97–99.

7. Frederick Webb Hodge, "Bibliography of Fray Alonso de Benavides," *Indian Notes and Monographs* 3, no. 1 (1919): 36–39; Alonso de Benavides, *Fray Alonso de Benavides' Revised Memorial of 1634*, trans. Agapito Rey, Coronado Cuarto Centennial Publications, 1540–1940 (Albuquerque: University of New Mexico Press, 1945), 190–98. Hereafter cited as *1634 Memorial*.

8. The elevation of a *custodia* to a *provincia* was predicated on a demand for the services of religious, and involved the establishment of places of religious formation and education. A *provincia* functioned with a great deal more autonomy than a *custodia*, and was often headed by a bishop. Ximénez Samaniego comments on this in Sor María's *vita*; see Joseph Ximénez Samaniego, *Prólogo galeato*, 134.

9. "En solo distrito de cien leguas tiene [nuestra seráfica religión] bautizadas mas de ochenta mil almas y hechas mas de cinquenta Iglesias, y conventos muy curiosos y son mas de quinientos mil Indios los que tenemos pacificos y sujetos a V. Magestad en todas las naciones comarcanas y que poco se van catequizando para bautizarse" (In a district of just one hundred leagues, [our Seraphic Religion] has baptized more than eighty thousand souls, and con-

structed more than fifty churches, and tidy convents, and there are more than five hundred thousand Indians that we have pacified and who are subjects to Your Majesty in the neighboring nations, and bit by bit they are being catechized to be baptized); Benavides, *1630 Memorial*, 164.

10. "Bien se infiere de lo dicho de los bienes espirituales tan copiosos que nuestra Seráfica religion ha descubierto por todo el mundo i por esta parte ella sola es la que con tanto trabajo y riesgos haze estos descubrimientos tan grandiosos" (One may well infer from what has been said about the copious spiritual goods our Seraphic Religion has discovered throughout the world, and for just this part, just for this, through great work and risk, these discoveries are so magnificent) (ibid.). See also subsection titled "Ocupación santa, en que los Religiosos se entretienen"(ibid., 170–73).

11. Anthropologist Daniel Reff notes that competition among the Franciscans, Jesuits, and Dominicans for control of the mission field motivates some elements of the *1630 Memorial*: "The friar [Benavides] was a member of a religious order that saw itself as competing not only with Satan, but also with other religious orders, particularly the Jesuits. During the 1630s this competition intensified, as reflected in curious passages from the *Memorials* that deal with the Señora [Sonora] Valley, mining in New Mexico, and the purported martyrdom at Cíbola of Marcos de Niza. Benavides's discussion and treatment of these subjects, particularly his 'stretching the truth,' reflect rhetorical strategies that were designed to win support for the Franciscans at the expense of their Jesuit rivals"; Reff, "Contextualizing Missionary Discourse: The Benavides Memorials of 1630 and 1634," *Journal of Anthropological Research* 50, no. 1 (1994): 53.

12. Studies of the *1630 Memorial* suggest that the final twelve chapters are taken from works by other authors, because they contradict or repeat earlier sections of the text. The earlier chapters also guide the reader geographically from the Rio Grande basin, where the Pueblos were located, toward Texas, and the final chapters break with this eastward progression, further hinting at their foreignness to the original.

13. The Tompira and Salinero tribes of eastern New Mexico.

14. "Bolviendo el Padre fray Juan de Salas por los Salineros, dixeron los Xumanas, que gente que bolvia por los pobres, era buena, y assi quedaron aficionados al Padre, y le rogaban fuesse a vivir entre ellos, y cada año le venían a buscar, y como estaba también ocupado con los Christianos, por su lengua, y muy buen Ministro, y no tener Religiosos bastantes fui entreteniendo a los Xumanas, que le pedían, hasta que Dios enviase mas obreros como lo embió el año passado de [16]29" (As Father Juan de Salas returned via the Salineros, the Jumanos said that people who came for the poor were good, and they became fond of the friar, and they begged him to go and live among them, and every year they would come to look for him, and as he was also occupied with the Christians, on account of his ability to translate and because he was an excellent minister, and because there were not enough friars, I kept the Jumanos at bay, until the Lord would send more friars, as he sent the previous year of 1629) (Benavides, *1630 Memorial*, 157–58). In 1629, thirty missionaries were sent to New Mexico from Mexico City with the new *custos*, Fray Estevan de Perea.

15. Sor Luisa de la Ascención (1565–1636), popularly known as Luisa de Carrión, was a Spanish nun from the monastery of Santa Clara de Carrión (Carrión de los Condes, Spain). Devotion to this proponent of the Immaculate Conception theology was widespread in Spain and in Spanish colonial sites, including New Mexico, where devotional objects and paintings of her were common. See Patrocinio García Barriuso, "La monja de Carrión Sor Luisa de la Ascención y Sor María de Jesús, la monja de Agreda," *Verdad y Vida: Revista de las Ciencias del Espíritu* 49, no. 196 (1991); Patrocinio García Barriuso, *La Monja de Carrión, Sor Luisa de la Ascención Colmenares Cabezón* (Madrid, 1986).

16. Benavides, *1630 Memorial*, 159.

17. "Echó la voz que mudassen puesto, para buscar de comer, y ya que no vendrían los religiosos que embiaban a llamar, pues en seis años que los avian esperado, no ivan" (He announced that they should move sites, to look for something to eat, and that the friars that they had set out to request would not come, since in the six years they had been waiting for them, they hadn't come) (ibid.).

18. "Dixeron, que como aquella [Luisa de Carrión] estava vestida, pero que era mas hermosa y moça" (They said that she was dressed like her [Luisa de Carrión], but that she was more beautiful and younger) (ibid., 160).

19. Ibid.

20. Ibid.

21. "Pareciendoles a los Padres, que aquella mies era mucha, y los obreros pocos, y estar la gente bien dispuesta a poblar, y hazer su Iglesias, se bolvieron adonde estábamos, para llevar los aderentes para ello" (As it seemed to the friars that the harvest was great and the workers few, and the people well disposed to settle and build their churches, they returned to where we were, to bring more faithful for it) (ibid., 162).

22. "Padre, nosotros aun no podemos nada con Dios, que somos como venados, y animales del campo, y tu puedes mucho con Dios, y con esta santa Cruz, y tenemos muchos enfermos, curalos primero que te [Salas] vayas" (Father, we cannot accomplish anything through God, for we are like deer, and other animals of the field, and you can accomplish so much with God and with that Holy Cross, and we have many who are ill; cure them before you [Salas] depart) (Benavides, *1630 Memorial*, 162–63).

23. The invocation to common prayer, a prayer to the Virgin Mary, and a prayer to St. Francis, the founder of the friars' order.

24. Benavides, *1630 Memorial*, 163–64.

25. Ibid., 164.

26. Gerónimo Zárate Salmerón, *Relaciones de todas las cosas que en el Nuevo-Mexico se han visto y sabido, asi por mar como por tierra, desde el año de 1538 hasta el de 1626, por el padre Gerónimo de Zarate Salmerón*, in *Documentos para la historia de México* (Mexico: Imprenta de Vicente García Torres, 1856).

27. Hodge and Lummis conclude that it could not have been completed earlier than 1627, since the document is directed to Fray Francisco de Apodaca, who became commissary general in 1627; Benavides, *1630 Memorial*, 243.

28. Zárate Salmerón's *Relaciones* were published in 1856 in the *Documentos para la historia de México* series. They were translated by Alicia Ronstadt Milich in 1966: *Relaciones: An Account of Things Seen and Learned by Father Jeronimo de Zarate Salmerón from the Year 1538 to Year 1626*, trans. Alicia Ronstadt Milich (Albuquerque: Horn and Wallace, 1966).

29. Zarate Salmerón, *Relaciones*, 55.

30. Marilyn Fedewa, citing T. D. Kendrick, claims that Manso y Zúñiga was sent an account of Sor María's travels by her confessor, Sebastián Marcilla; see Marilyn H. Fedewa, *María of Ágreda: Mystical Lady in Blue* (Albuquerque: University of New Mexico Press, 2009), 54.

31. Zarate Salmerón, *Relaciones*, 55.

32. Ibid.

33. The date given in the transcription (1682) is an apparent transposition of the date of the report, 1628.

34. Zarate Salmerón, *Relaciones*, 55.

35. The historical accuracy of other parts of his work has been questioned: Milich, trans., *Relaciones*, 17–19.

36. "A poco tiempo corrió entre Religiosos, y Religiosas, que la Sierva de Dios era llevada corporalmente a las Indias" (Very quickly, it became known among male and female religious that the Servant of God had been taken in her body to the Indies) (Ximénez Samaniego, *Prólogo galeato*, 133).

37. Alonso de Benavides, "Alonso de Benavides Memorial (ZCH)" (1634), Propaganda Fide Archives, Vatican City, Italy; University of Notre Dame Archives; "Translado que se sacó de una carta que el P. Fr. Alonso de Benavides . . . embió a los Religiosos de la Santa Custodia de la Conversión de San Pablo desde Madrid el año de 1631," in *Biblioteca Nacional de México: Documentos Para la Historia del Nuevo Mexico* (Center for Southwest Research, University of New Mexico, Albuquerque); Fernando Ocaranza, *Establecimientos franciscanos en el misterioso reino de Nuevo México* (México, 1934), 73–84; Alonso de Benavides, "Translado que se sacó de una carta que el P. Fr. Alonso de Benavides . . . embió a los Relogiosos de la Santa Custodia de la Conversión de San Pablo desde Madrid el año de 1631," in *Facsimiles of Manuscripts in the Biblioteca Nacional de México* (Center for Southwest Research, University of New Mexico).

38. "Todos estos maravillosos sucessos comunicaba la Sierva de Dios con humildad profunda, y sincera verdad a su Confessor. . . . El General que conforme a la obligación, avia examinado el espíritu de Sor María de Jesús, por la fama de santidad que ya tenía . . . lo hizo firme de que esta Sierva de Dios era el instrumento, que tomaba el Señor, para obrar aquellas misericordias" (The Servant of God confessed all these miraculous events with deep humility and sincere truth to her confessor. . . . General [Bernardino Sena], who in conformation with his obligations, had examined Sor María's spirit on the basis of the fame of sanctity that she was reputed to have . . . made manifest that this Servant of God was the instrument that the Lord used to work those acts of mercy) (Ximénez Samaniego, *Prólogo galeato*, 133, 135).

39. Franciscan historian Cyprian Lynch summarizes this challenge: "Whether Mary of Agreda's sanctity was genuine, whether her revelations were

authentic, and whether she possessed the power of bilocation, are primarily theological problems whose definitive solution lies beyond the competence of the historian"; see Alonso de Benavides, *Benavides' Memorial of 1630*, trans. Peter P. Forrestal (Washington, DC: Academy of American Franciscan History, 1954), 59.

40. Hodge, "Bibliography of Fray Alonso de Benavides," 7.

.41. Not all of Benavides's contemporaries and mission colleagues corroborate the existence of the Lady in Blue narrative. Fray Estevan de Perea, Benavides's successor as *custos* of New Mexico, left Mexico City after Manso y Zuñiga's installation as archbishop, yet his extant reports do not mention Sor María, or the conversion of the Jumano tribe.

42. There are some variations in grammar ("errare" versus "errase" in the Benavides version) and in the spelling places of "Tidam" versus "Tidan," but Benavides's version closely parallels the Zárate Salmerón text.

43. Benavides, "Alonso de Benavides Memorial (ZCH)."

44. Ibid.

45. Ocaranza, *Establecimientos franciscanos*, 75.

46. According to historian Frances Scholes, the original manuscript of the letter remained in the Archive of the Province of San Pablo y San Pedro, and Scholes transcribed that manuscript; see photostat of transcription at the Center for Southwest Research, University of New Mexico. Benavides, "Translado que se sacó de una carta." Ocaranza, *Establecimientos franciscanos*, published a transcription of the same manuscript. Both the Scholes transcription and the Ocaranza version (which are nearly identical) differ notably from the *Tanto que se sacó de una carta*, the eighteenth-century version published in Mexico.

47. "Obedeciendo a lo que N. Rmo. mro. P. Gl. Y nro. Pe. Fr. Sebastian de Amarillas, Provincial desta Sta. provincia de burgos y nro. P. fr. Franco, ques quien gobierna mi alma y a N. P. Cussto del nuevo mexico, en nombre de V.P. me mandan diga lo que se contiene estos cuadernos, es lo que he dicho, tratado y conferido, que he ablado a V.P. de lo que por misericordia de Dios y de sus Santos juisios que son ynmutables a obrado en mi pobre alma" (Obeying what our Reverend Father General, and our Father Sebastian de Marcilla, provincial of this Holy Province of Burgos, and our Father Franco, who is he who governs my soul, and the father custodian of New Mexico, in the name of Your Holiness, you order me to say what is contained in those notebooks, which is what I have said, addressed, and provided, that which I have told Your Holiness regarding what God in his infinite mercy and his holy judgments (which are immutable) has wrought through my poor soul) (Ocaranza, *Establecimientos franciscanos*, 79). Ximénez Samaniego characterized her sharing of this information as a "sacrifice": "Haciendo sacrificio de su secreto, en obsequio a la obediencia" (Making a sacrifice of her secret, in conformation with her vows of obedience) (Ximénez Samaniego, *Prólogo galeato*, 135).

48. Sor María later explained and provided nuance to her role in authoring the letter. In her exchange with Fray Pedro Manero, she states that she was terrified when asked to write about her travels to New Mexico, and acted under the authority of male superiors, who asked her to sign a document that she had

scarcely read; see Clark Colahan, *The Visions of Sor María de Agreda: Writing Knowledge and Power* (Tucson: University of Arizona Press, 1994), 123.

49. Benavides was sent to Goa, India, in 1635, but seems to have died en route. Sor María alone was left to testify about what had been popularized regarding her travels.

50. Ocaranza, *Establecimientos franciscanos*, 73.

51. Ibid., 74.

52. Ibid., 75.

53. Ibid.

54. Ibid., 76.

55. Benavides, *1630 Memorial*, 159.

56. Ocaranza, *Establecimientos franciscanos*, 76.

57. Ibid., 77.

58. Ibid., 76.

59. Sor María skillfully explained what she meant by this in the letter to Manero: "[Father Benavides] says that Saint Michael and Our Father Saint Francis would accompany me, and that I said they were my wings and that Saint Michael used to go on the right side. That was a remark of mine in conversation. I said they were my wings, calling them that metaphorically and reflecting that just as wings help birds to fly, just so the intercession of Our Father Saint Francis and of Saint Michael help us fly to God. Among nuns, it is common to call the holy angel and Our Father Saint Francis wings, for we have them placed on either side of the church and they are our patrons and advocates. But Father Benavides understood it so literally that he thought they were wings that would always accompany me, turning my devout feelings into a mystery. And although I have received many favors from the glorious prince Saint Michael and Our Father Saint Francis and owe them much, and in many difficult moments have seen him and the holy angel, they have not accompanied me as Father Benavides claims" (Colahan, *Visions of Sor María de Agreda*, 123–24).

60. Ocaranza, *Establecimientos franciscanos*, 76.

61. Benavides does not go into detail about this incident, perhaps assuming that the friars already knew of the event to which he alludes.

62. Ocaranza, *Establecimientos franciscanos*, 77.

63. "Y preguntandola que por que no se dignava que la viesemos pues los yndios la via [*sic*]. Respondio que los indios tienen necesidad y nosotros no" (And I asked her why she did not deign to let us see her, for the Indians did see her. She responded that the Indians needed to and we did not) (ibid., 77–78).

64. Ibid., 78.

65. Ibid.

66. Ibid., 79.

67. Ibid., 80.

68. Ibid.

69. Ibid., 81.

70. "Si pudiera comprarla con la sangre vida y crueles martirios lo ysiera" (If I could purchase this experience with my lifeblood and cruel martyrdom, I would) (ibid., 81).

71. "Lo he oydo de sus santos angeles que me an dicho me tenian enbidia de que custodios de las almas que se ocupaban en conbertir y como son ministros que presentan al altissimo nuestras obras asegureme las que su Magestad resibe con mas agrado. Las que se obran con las conversiones del nuevo Mxco [*sic*]" (I have heard it from his holy angels, who have told me that they are envious of those custodians of souls who are occupied in conversion and as they are the ministers who present our works to the Highest One, they assure me that his Majesty receives them with great pleasure. Those who work in the conversions of New Mexico) (ibid., 82).

72. Ibid., 83.

73. "A todos los yndios doi tanbien mil parabienes pues merecen su principal amor" (I send to the Indians a thousand well-wishes, as they deserve his principal love) (ibid.).

74. Ibid.

75. This text is a transcription of Benavides's manuscript; photostat from the University of Notre Dame Hesburgh Library, Propaganda Fide Collection.

76. Hodge, "Bibliography of Fray Alonso de Benavides."

77. Benavides, "Alonso de Benavides Memorial (ZCH)," 183v.

78. "En este estado dejaron estos religiosos aquella milagrosa conversión y se vinieron entre nosotros a darnos parte de los que habían visto y a llevar más compañeros y adherentes para fabricar allí una iglesia" (These religious left the miraculous conversions in this state, and returned to us to tell us some of what they had seen, and to bring with them more companions and faithful to create a church there) (ibid.). The building of churches and convents were evidence that the *custodia* attended to demands that were the equivalent of those of a *provincia*.

79. Ibid., 182v.

80. The *1634 Memorial* cites May 18, 1628, as the date of the archbishop's order.

81. Benavides, "Alonso de Benavides Memorial (ZCH)," 182v.

82. Ibid., 182f.

83. "Sin alterar ni variar unos de estos" (Without any one of them altering or varying) (ibid.).

84. Ibid., 183v.

85. Benavides, *1630 Memorial*, 114.

86. Benavides, "Alonso de Benavides Memorial (ZCH)," 183r.

87. "Libro de revelaciones" (Book of revelations) (ibid.).

88. Ibid.

89. Ibid.

90. "Y aunque nos pudiéramos quietar solo con esto hay otras mayores razones que por vivir estas Benditas religiosa estarán en silencio hasta su muerte" (And although we could fall silent with just this, there are other, greater reasons that, since these two holy women still live, will remain silenced until their deaths) (ibid.).

91. The Inquisition sought to curtail the spread of the Luisa de Carrión's popular cult, which had spread quickly among Franciscans in Spain and abroad,

in response to suspicions that the nun was an "alumbrada" (false mystic); see Kimberly Lynn, *Between Court and Confessional: The Politics of Spanish Inquisitors* (Cambridge: Cambridge University Press, 2013), 207.

92. Benavides, *1634 Memorial*, 199.

93. P. Víctor Añíbarro, "El P. José Ximénez Samaniego, Ministro General O.F.M. y Obispo de Plasencia (Conclusión)," *Archivo Ibero-Americano* (1944).

94. Scholars have suggested that Ximénez Samaniego borrowed from Sor María's autobiographical writing in composing the *vita*; see Madres Concepcionistas de Ágreda, "Obras publicadas," http://www.mariadeagreda.org/rdr.php ?cat=40&n=1. For more information about Ximénez Samaniego's creation of the *vita*, prologue, and notes to *La mística ciudad de dios*, see Añíbarro, "El P. José Ximénez Samaniego."

95. Ximénez Samaniego, *Prólogo galeato*,132.

96. "Por especies abstractivas" (Through abstract means) (ibid.).

97. "Los Gentiles del Nuevo Mexico, y otros Reynos remotos de àzia aquella parte" (the Gentiles of New Mexico and other remote kingdoms toward that part); "más . . . se inclinaba" (towards which he was most inclined) (ibid., 132).

98. "Inopinadamente sin percibir el modo" (ibid.).

99. "Deshogasse sus ansiedades," "Predicando su Fe, y Ley Santa a aquellas gentes" (ibid.).

100. He draws this number from the five hundred or more visits to New Mexico that Fray Benavides cited in the 1631 letter. Sor María addresses this in her correspondence with Pedro Manero, saying of the number that if one were to interpret it as the number of times she was aware of or desired the conversion of the people of the region, then the total was greater than five hundred (Colahan, *Visions of Sor María de Agreda*, 126).

101. Ximénez Samaniego, *Prólogo galeato*, 132.

102. Clark Colahan notes of her Inquisition trials and testimony, "The Inquisition, set in motion on her case in 1635 and again in 1649 by the nun's supposed participation in a political plot tied to her friendship with the king, examined her about the bilocation. She first gave oral testimony to the inquisitors who interrogated her, and then sent a written account to Pedro Manero, minister general of the order in Spain" (Colahan, *Visions of Sor María de Agreda*, 94).

103. Ibid., 120.

104. Ximénez Samaniego, *Prólogo galeato*, 136.

105. Ibid., 133.

106. Ibid., 134.

107. Ibid., 133: "El Señor le hacia [a Sor María] tan patente lo recto de su voluntad, lo puro de su intencion, lo bueno de los efectos, que no quedaba lugar a la duda de que fuesse traza de la diabolica astucia" (The Lord made the correctness of her will, the purity of her intention, and the goodness of its effects so clear to Sor María that there was no reason to entertain doubt that it was the result of the devil's guile).

108. "La gran fama de santidad que entonces en España tenía" (The great fame of sanctity that she had in Spain at that time) (ibid., 134).

109. "principal fin de su jornada" (the primary end of his journey) (ibid., 135).

110. "esta Sierva de Dios era el instrumento . . . para obrar aquellas misericordias" (this Servant of God was the instrument [through which] to work those acts of mercy) (ibid., 135).

111. Ibid., 136.

112. "Una carta exortatoria a los Religiosos, que estaban en aquellas conversiones . . . alentándolos a la prosecución constante de su santa ocupación" (An exhortative letter to the religious who were in those missions . . . encouraging them in the constant pursuit of their holy occupation) (ibid., 137).

113. The preface of the 1730 Mexican printing of the letter from Benavides and Sor María (the *Tanto que se sacó de una carta*) claims that the original from which the printing was taken had been in the safekeeping of the Archives of the Custodia of New Mexico.

114. Ximénez Samaniego, *Prólogo galeato*, 137.

115. "inopinadamente llegó a [mis] manos" (it unexpectedly arrived to my hands) (ibid.).

116. Heather Allen, "The Languages and Literatures of Early Print Culture in the Colonia," in *A History of Mexican Literature*, ed. Ignacio Sánchez Prado, Anna M. Nogar, and José Ramón Ruisánchez Serra (Cambridge: Cambridge University Press, 2016), 19–22.

117. José Mariano Beristáin de Souza's *Biblioteca Hispanomaericana septentrional* documents Fray Zárate Salmerón's mission work in New Mexico and his writings, noting that Zárate Salmerón's *Relaciones* could be found in manuscript form in the Archivo de la Provincia del Santo Evangelio; see José Mariano Beristáin de Souza, *Biblioteca Hispanoamericana septentrional* (Mexico: Editorial Fuente Cultural, 1947), 5:189. José Toribio Medina's *La imprenta en México* does not document any publication of the *Relaciones*, indicating that its reading was likely limited to a closed group of Church officials and Franciscan prelates; see José Toribio Medina, *La imprenta en Mexico (1539–1821)*, Vol. 2, *(1601–1684)* (Mexico City: Universidad Nacional Autónoma de México, 1989).

118. Most contemporary historians of Sor María make no mention of the Lady in Blue narrative in Zárate Salmerón's *Relaciones*, in part perhaps because very few seventeenth-century historical documents cite or acknowledge it.

119. For some idea, see "Campeggi informs Barberini of Benavides' departure for Goa as Auxiliary Bishop, February 11, 1636," in Benavides, *1634 Memorial*, 199.

120. Henry Raupp Wagner, *The Spanish Southwest, 1542–1794: An Annotated Bibliography* (Berkeley, CA: J. J. Gillick, 1924), 232.

121. Ayer; Forrestal; Morrow; also see its serial publication in *Land of Sunshine* (vol. XIII no.4 to vol. IV no. 3); Benavides, *1630 Memorial*, note 2 on 193–94.

122. It was translated into French in 1631, Dutch in 1631, Latin in 1634, and German in 1634 (*1630 Memorial*, note 2 on 193–94). The *1630 Memorial* was also presented in summarized format in a 1633 edition of seventeenth-century Dutch historian Johannes de Laet's popular compendium of New World history, *Novus orbis, seu, Descriptionis Indiae Occidentalis*. Laet's work cites Benavides's

1630 Memorial as a source of New Mexican history and geography, but makes no mention of the Lady in Blue narrative and thus does not contribute to its dissemination; see Johannes de Laet, *Novus orbis, seu Descriptionis Indiae Occidentalis libri XVIII* (Leiden: Apud Elzevirios, 1633), http://openlibrary.org/books/OL17457394M/Novus_orbis_seu_Descriptionis_Indiae_Occidentalis_libri_XVIII.

123. Damián Manzanet, "Carta de Don Damian Manzanet á Don Carlos de Siguenza sobre el descubrimiento de la Bahia del Espiritu Santo," *The Quarterly of the Texas State Historical Association* 2 (1899): 255.

124. Ibid.

125. "Para que con otros papeles la presentase en el Real Consejo de indias en testimonio de lo que la religión de San Francisco continuamente obra en aquel Nuevo Mundo en la conversión de los infieles contra cierta emulación que le pretendía obscurecer esta gloria" (So that with other papers, it may be presented at the Real Consejo de Indias as a testimony to what the Order of Saint Francis continually labors in that New World in the conversion of souls, as a response to a certain emulation that seeks to obscure this glory); Carlos Contreras Servín, "Manifiesto que el decreto de este apostólico colegio hizo al rey en 26 de febrero de 1776: Sobre los nuevos descubrimientos en la alta California," *Revista de Historia de América* 130 (2002): 197.

126. Medina, *La imprenta en Mexico*, 2:142. Wagner, *The Spanish Southwest*, 343–45, 347.

127. José Toribio Medina, *La imprenta en Mexico*, 4:283; 5:49; Alonso de Benavides and María de Jesús de Agreda, *Tanto que se sacó de una carta que el R.P. Fr. Alonso de Benavides, custodio, que fue del Nuevo Mexico, embió a los religiosos de la Santa Custodia de la conversion de San Pablo de dicho reyno, desde Madrid, el ano de 1631* (México, 1760). Alonso de Benavides and María de Jesús de Ágreda, *Tanto que se sacó de una carta, que el R. Padre Fr. Alonso de Benavides, custodio que fue del Nuevo Mexico, embió a los religiosos de la Santa custodia de la conversión de San Pablo de dicho reyno, desde Madrid, el ano de 1631* (Mexico: Joseph Bernardo de Hogal, 1730).

128. Wagner, *The Spanish Southwest*, 232.

129. José Ximénez Samaniego, *Relación de la vida de la venerable madre sor Maria de Jesus: abadesa, que fue, del Convento de la purissima concepcion de la villa de Agreda* (En Madrid: En la Imprenta de la Causa de la Venerable Madre, 1727).

TWO   Sor María's Rise as Mystical Writer and Protomissionary in Early Modern Spain

1. Julio Campos, "Los Padres Juan de la Palma, Pedro Manero y Pedro de Arriola y la Mística Ciudad de Dios," *Archivo Ibero-Americano* 26 (1966): 247.

2. Ricardo Fernández Gracia, *Iconografía de Sor María de Ágreda: Imágenes para la mística y la escritora en el contexto del maravillosismo del Barroco*

(Soria, Spain: Caja Duero, 2003), 198–99. The painting is described elsewhere by Fernández Gracia as follows: "Las pequeñas viñetas que componen la orla de la escena principal nos narran diversos pasajes de la vida de sor María y de la fundación del convento. No están ordenados, pero resultan de un enorme didactismo. Todos emanan de las declaraciones de los Procesos Ordinario y Apostólico, así como de otros testimonios de las religiosas que convivieron con sor María" (The small vignettes that comprise the border of the principal scene narrate to us various episodes from Sor María's life and from the founding of the convent. They are not in order, but together they are enormously instructive. All the scenes come from declarations made through the Ordinary Process and Apostolic Process, and from other testimonies taken from the nuns who lived with Sor María); Ricardo Fernández Gracia, "Los primeros retratos de la Madre Ágreda: Consideraciones sobre su iconografía hasta fines del siglo XVII," in *El papel de sor María de Jesús de Ágreda en el Barroco español*, Monografías Universitarias (Soria, Spain: Universidad Internacional Alfonso VIII, Diputación Provincial de Soria, 2002), 169.

3. Fernández Gracia, *Iconografía de Sor María de Ágreda*, 197–204.

4. Colahan, *Visions of Sor María de Agreda*, 37–38.

5. Marilyn H. Fedewa, *María of Ágreda: Mystical Lady in Blue* (Albuquerque: University of New Mexico Press, 2009), 31.

6. Colahan, *Visions of Sor María de Agreda*, 117.

7. Ibid., 115–27.

8. Fedewa, *María of Ágreda*, 39.

9. Luis Villasante, "Sor María de Jesús de Agreda a través de su correspondencia epistolar con el rey," *Archivo Ibero-Americano* 25, no. 98-99 (1965): 148.

10. "El 24 de marzo de 1635 la Suprema oficia al Tribunal de Logroño para que, con premura, averigüe 'si la Monja de Agreda, que se llama María de Jesús, se arroba en público, y si reparte cruces y quentas qué grazias dice que tienen, con todo lo demás'" (The 24th of March of 1635, the Supreme Office of the Tribunal of Logroño so that, with haste, may determine "if the Nun from Ágreda, who is called María de Jesús, experiences raptures in public, and if she distributes crosses and rosaries, and what graces they might have, and all the rest"); Joaquin Pérez Villanueva, "Algo más sobre la Inquisición y Sor María de Agreda: La prodigiosa evangelización americana," *Hispania Sacra* 37, no. 76 (1985): 590, 92.

11. According to Pérez Villanueva, the questioning of mystical experiences by the Inquisition, including that of Fray de la Fuente and Sor María, responded to the increase in general of "maravillosismos" of the period (ibid., 585).

12. The provincial father had told de la Fuente that his travels were not all that unusual, as Sor María had done something similar, and he showed de la Fuente a notebook of her writing to that effect (ibid., 596).

13. Ibid., 593.

14. Ibid., 594.

15. Ibid.

16. Ibid., 595.

17. Ibid.

18. Campos, "Los Padres," 11; Colahan, *Visions of Sor María de Agreda*, 115–27. In this letter, her care in expressing the mystical and complicated nature of the travel are manifest, illustrating what Consolación Baranda Leterio aptly observed of Sor María in her public interactions: "[que] se hizo de la cautela una forma de vida" (she made caution a way of life); see Consolación Baranda Leturio, *Cartas de Sor María de Jesús de Ágreda a Fernando de Borja y Francisco de Borja (1628–1664)* (Valladolid: University of Valladolid, 2013), 65.

19. Carabantes decided to become a missionary to Venezuela after a meeting with Sor María; see "Carabantes, José de (1628–1694)," in *Pequeña Enciclopedia Franciscana*, http://www.franciscanos.org/enciclopedia/penciclopedia_c.htm.

20. "Es casi seguro que estas cosas [sus viajes a New Mexico] habían llegado a oídos del Rey, aunque en la correspondencia no se alude para nada a ellas" (It is nearly certain that these things [her travels to New Mexico] had arrived to the king's ears, although in the correspondence there is no allusion whatsoever to them) (Villasante, "Sor María de Jesús de Agreda," 148).

21. Ibid., 146. Villasante here references Carlos Seco Serrano, *Cartas de Sor María de Jesús de Ágreda y de Felipe IV*, vols. 108–9, Biblioteca de autores españoles (Madrid: Ediciones Atlas, 1958), 3.

22. Villasante, "Sor María de Jesús de Agreda," 149.

23. "Sor María revela, en efecto, tener sobre estos puntos ideas no precisamente originales, pero sí bien definidas, y marca al Rey directrices y consejos generalmente prudentes y acertados" (Sor María reveals, in effect, that she has ideas regarding these points that are not precisely original, but that are well defined, and that she offered directions and advice for the king that were generally prudent and appropriate) (ibid., 150).

24. Joseph Mary Madden, "A Brief Biography of Venerable Mary of Agreda," *The Age of Mary: An Exclusively Marian Magazine*, "The Mystical City of God" issue (January-February 1958); T. D. Kendrick, *Mary of Agreda: The Life and Legend of a Spanish Nun* (London: Routledge & K. Paul, 1967), 73–74.

25. Kendrick, *Mary of Agreda*, 77–78.

26. Kate Risse, "Strategy of a Provincial Nun: Sor María de Jesús de Agreda's Response," *Ciberletras* 17 (2007): 16.

27. As Spanish literary historian Leturio comments in her study on the letters exchanged between Sor María and the nobles Fernando and Francisco de Borja, these epistles offer the other side of the long conversation she maintained with Felipe IV: "muchos son el reverso de la correspondencia con Felipe IV, nos indican lo que pensaba íntimamente [de las intrigas políticas]" (many of these are the reverse side of the correspondence she kept with Felipe IV, and show us what she truly thought [of the political intrigue]) (Baranda Leturio, *Cartas de Sor María*, 65). As to be expected from a renowned abbess and mystic, Sor María corresponded with many individuals from secular and religious contexts in Spain during her lifetime; see Andrés Ivars, "Algunas cartas autógrafas de la Venerable Madre Sor María de Jesús de Ágreda," *Archivo Ibero-Americano* 3 (1915); Ivars, "Algunas cartas autógrafas de la Venerable madre sor María de Jesús de

Ágreda (Continuación)," *Archivo Ibero-Americano* 3 (1916); Seco Serrano, *Cartas de Sor María*.

28. Pérez Villanueva, "Algo más sobre la Inquisición," 603.

29. Ibid., 596.

30. Ibid., 604.

31. Ibid., 605.

32. Ibid., 606.

33. Ibid.

34. In addition to her two defenses before the Inquisition itself, Risse suggests that Sor María implicitly upheld her travels within *La mística ciudad de dios*: "In a scene in Book Three, Chapter Seven, an angel replaces the Virgin so that she can leave earth to receive more knowledge from God. Sor María later applies this explanation to her own situation in her 'Relación,' albeit in an inverted and therefore more acceptable form, when she claims that she remained in the convent, perceiving the New World through abstract images infused divinely while an angel acquired her physical appearance in New Mexico and preached to the Indians." Risse, "Strategy of a Provincial Nun," 12.

35. This brevity of this writing process, undertaken while Sor María was still prioress of her convent, may have been due to her using sections of the second copy of the text that she gave to Felipe IV for safekeeping (Madden, "A Brief Biography," 97).

36. Francisco Javier Fuente Fernández, "Obras ineditas de Sor María de Jesús de Ágreda: *El jardín espiritual*," in *I Congreso Internacional del Monacato Femenino en España, Portugal y América, 1492–1992* (León, Spain: Universidad de León, 1993), 230–34.

37. Clark Colahan and Celia Weller, "An Angelic Epilogue," *Studia Mystica* 13, no. 4 (1990).

38. José Antonio Pérez-Rioja, "Proyección de la Venerable María de Agreda," *Celtiberia* 15, no. 29 (1965): 23.

39. Fedewa, *María of Ágreda*, 281; Baranda Leturio, *Cartas de Sor María*.

40. Colahan, *Visions of Sor María de Agreda*, 18–28.

41. Fedewa, *María of Ágreda*, 280.

42. Colahan, *Visions of Sor María de Agreda*, 28–32.

43. A forthcoming study of the *Tratado* by Mónica Díaz and Grady Wray, entitled *Sor María Jesús de Agreda's Cosmographical Writing: Producing Knowledge across the Atlantic*, examines the controversy surrounding the authorship of the text, and the texts and ideas that informed its creation.

44. Antonio de León Pinelo, *Epitome de la bibliotheca oriental y occidental, náutica y geográfica de don Antonio de León Pinelo* (Madrid: La Oficina de Francisco Martínez Abad, 1737–38), 612.

45. Andrés González de Barcia Carballido y Zúñiga, *Ensayo cronologico, para la historia general de la Florida* (Madrid: N. Rodríguez Franco, 1723).

46. Agustín de Vetancurt, *Teatro mexicano* (Mexico: Editorial Porrúa, 1971).

47. León Pinelo, *Epitome de la bibliotheca*, 612.

48. "Para todas las operaciones de su vida Regular, desde que recibe el Hábito Santo, hasta la hora de su muerte" (For all the tasks of her Regular life,

from the time she received the Holy Habit, until the hour of her death): Antonio Arbiol y Diez, *La religiosa instruida: con doctrina de la sagrada escritura y santos padres de la Iglesia catholica: para todas las operaciones de su vida regular, desde que recibe el habito santo, hasta la hora de su muerte* (En Madrid: En la Imprenta de la causa de la V.M. Maria de Jesus de Agreda, 1753).

49. *La religiosa instruida: Con doctrina de la sagrada escritura, y santos padres de la Iglesia catholica, para todas las operaciones de su vida regular, desde que recibe el habito santo, hasta la hora de su muerte* (Madrid: En la Imprenta Real de la Gazeta, 1776), 70, 77, 553.

50. Ibid., 84, 353, 56, 75.

51. Ibid., 93, 559.

52. Ibid., 337.

53. Ibid., 401–10.

54. Grady Wray, "Seventeenth-Century Wise Women of Spain and the Americas: Madre Ágreda and Sor Juana," *Studia Mystica* 22 (2001).

55. Manuel Serrano y Sanz, *Apuntes para una biblioteca de escritoras espanolas desde el año 1401 al 1833* (Madrid: Atlas, 1903), 1:580.

56. Enrique Llamas, "Inmaculada concepción de María y corredención mariana en la 'Mística ciudad de Dios' de la Madre Ágreda," *Celtiberia* 55, no. 99 (2005): 527.

57. Benito Mendía, "En torno al problema de la autenticidad de la *Mistica Ciudad de Dios*," *Archivo Ibero-Americano* 42, no. 165-68 (1982).

58. Risse, "Strategy of a Provincial Nun"; Luis Miguel Fernández, "De la revelación a la escritura: El difícil viaje de sor María de Jesús de Agreda," in *Actas del IX Simposio de la Sociedad Española de Literatura General y Comparada*, ed. Túa Blesa et al. (Zaragoza: Universidad de Zaragoza, 1994).

59. Serrano y Sanz, *Apuntes para una biblioteca*, 1:575.

60. Risse, "Strategy of a Provincial Nun," 6.

61. Augustine M. Esposito and María de Jesús de Agreda, *La mística ciudad de Dios (1670): Sor María de Jesús de Agreda*, Scripta Humanistica (Potomac, MD: Scripta Humanistica, 1990), biography, appendix I.

62. Benavides, *1630 Memorial* (1954), 58.

63. Kendrick, *Mary of Agreda*, 80. Kendrick elaborates the implicit ramifications of the work for the Catholic reading audience of its time: "Through Sor María by God's will came a declaration that the Virgin Mary was everything that her most ardent devotees had already determined that she was. If this book were right, then the most profound devotion to Our Lady [the Immaculate Conception] was not wrong, but evident duty divinely imposed upon all Christians" (ibid., 81).

64. Ángel Uribe, "La inmaculada en la literatura franciscano-española," *Archivo Ibero-Americano* 15 (1955).

65. María de Jesús de Ágreda, *Mystica ciudad de Dios. Primera parte: milagro de su omnipotencia, y abysmo de la gracia: historia divina, y vida de la Virgen madre de Dios, reyna, y señora nuestra, Maria santissima, restauradora de la culpa de Eva, y medianera de la gracia* (En Madrid: Por Bernardo de Villa-Diego, 1670), bk. 1, chap. 17, 253, quoted in Risse, "Strategy of a Provincial Nun," 7.

66. Regarding her Marian writing, some theologians claim she wrote according to the tendency of the time: "la Madre Ágreda [era] un exponente manifiesto de la mariología de su tiempo" (Mother Ágreda was a manifest model of the Mariology of her time); Llamas, "Inmaculada concepción de María," 530.

67. Uribe, "La inmaculada en la literatura," 203.

68. Pérez Villanueva, "Algo más sobre la Inquisición," 607.

69. Thomas Campbell, "Maria de Agreda," in *The Catholic Encyclopedia* (New York: Robert Appleton Company, 1907).

70. Patricia Andrés González, "Iconografía de la Venerable María de Jesús de Ágreda," *Boletín del Seminario de Estudios de Arte y Arqueología* 62 (1996): 450.

71. José María Pou y Martí, "El arzobispo Eleta y el término de la causa de la Venerable María de Agreda (conclusión)," *Archivo Ibero-Americano* 12, no. 52 (1923/25): 365.

72. On December 8, 1854, Pope Pius IX emitted the ex cathedra apostolic constitution *Ineffabilis Deus*, in which the Immaculate Conception theology was defined. It acknowledged the history of informal veneration of the Immaculate Conception and confirmed the theology as Church dogma: "Accordingly, by the inspiration of the Holy Spirit, for the honor of the Holy and undivided Trinity, for the glory and adornment of the Virgin Mother of God, for the exaltation of the Catholic Faith, and for the furtherance of the Catholic religion, by the authority of Jesus Christ our Lord, of the Blessed Apostles Peter and Paul, and by our own: 'We declare, pronounce, and define that the doctrine which holds that the most Blessed Virgin Mary, in the first instance of her conception, by a singular grace and privilege granted by Almighty God, in view of the merits of Jesus Christ, the Savior of the human race, was preserved free from all stain of original sin, is a doctrine revealed by God and therefore to be believed firmly and constantly by all the faithful'"; Pope Pius IX, *Ineffabilis Deus* (1854), in *New Advent Catholic Encyclopedia*.

73. Pou y Martí, "El arzobispo Eleta," 426; Madres Concepcionistas de Ágreda, "María de Jesús de Ágreda," http://www.mariadeagreda.org/rdr.php.

74. Isaac Vázquez Janiero, "Un Franciscano al servicio de los Habsburgos en la Curia Romana: Francisco Díaz de San Buenaventura (1652–1728)," *Archivo Ibero-Americano* 23 (1962): 198.

75. Ibid.

76. Uribe, "La inmaculada en la literatura," 203.

77. Ibid.

78. Vázquez Janiero, "Un Franciscano al servicio de los Habsburgos," 23, 198; however, the edict was not published until August 4.

79. Fedewa, *María of Ágreda*, 253.

80. Campbell, "Maria de Agreda."

81. Fedewa, *María of Ágreda*, 253.

82. Ibid., 254. Later versions of the Index printed after 1681 still included *La mística ciudad de dios* among the prohibited books in its appendix. A printing of the Index made in 1704 appears to have initially included the erroneous entry in its appendix. The procurador's intervention on behalf of Felipe V re-

sulted in its removal in 1705: "determinó [la Congregación] que se quitaran de dicho Apéndice todos los pliegos donde estaban notados por prohibidos los dichos libros de la V.M. y que estos pliegos se volvieran a reimprimir, sin que en ellos se pusieran los dichos Libros" (The [Congregation] determined that all the pages in the Index in which the said books by the Venerable Mother were noted as prohibited were to be removed, and that those pages be reprinted, without the inclusion of the said books); Francisco de Santa María, "Copia de Carta Escrita en Roma, En el Mes de Julio desde presente año de 1705 a un devoto de la V.M. María de Jesús de Ágreda," (1705), Archivo Franciscano Ibero-Oriental, Madrid. This important announcement was printed so as to remove any doubt in the matter of the legitimacy of *La mística ciudad de dios* and the permissibility of its reading.

83. Andrés Ivars, "Expediente relativo a los escritos de la Venerable Madre Sor María de Jesús de Agreda," *Archivo Ibero-Americano* 8 (1917): 132.

84. Mendía, "En torno al problema de la autenticidad de la *Mistica Ciudad de Dios*," 42, 398.

85. Ibid., 399.

86. Ibid., 400.

87. Pérez-Rioja, "Proyección de la Venerable María de Agreda."

88. Diego Sarmiento de Valladares, "Edict Lifting the Embargo on the Mistica Ciudad de Dios" (1686) (Madrid), University of Notre Dame Rare Books and Special Collections.

89. "y no constando si convienen en todo con los impressiones en Madrid, o si en ellos se han añadido quitado o enmendado algunas cosas . . . hemos resuelto . . . que se recoja todos los Libros de estas Obras, que no fueren de la dicha impression de Madrid, que se permite hasta que se reconozcan" (and without knowing for a fact if they correspond perfectly with the imprints made in Madrid, or if in those [other] copies elements have been added, removed or amended . . . we have resolved . . . that all copies of that book be collected that are not from the Madrid imprint, which is permitted for as long as it is recognized) (ibid.).

90. Campbell, "Maria de Agreda."

91. Uribe, "La inmaculada en la literatura," 203.

92. Mendía, "En torno al problema de la autenticidad de la *Mistica Ciudad de Dios*," 42, 402.

93. The nature of this debate as it took shape in the eighteenth century is well documented in the publications supporting and challenging *La mística ciudad de dios* produced during that time. The apologia and critiques were numerous, several of the former having been printed on Sor María's propaganda press and circulated along with copies of *La mística ciudad de dios* to the Americas. Among Sor María's most consistent eighteenth-century detractors was Eusebius Amort, a Bavarian priest, whose numerous publications against the text were a source of vexation for the Spanish Franciscans, to the point that a decree was issued in November 1741 prohibiting Amort from publishing further on the topic.

This decree did not apparently deter Amort, as he continued to censure Sor María's writing by responding to the works of her supporters, among them the Franciscan theologian Dalmatius Kick. This resulted in yet more reprimands for Amort, as the apology and explanation for his behavior, written by the elector general of Bavaria, Maximiliano Joseph, in February of 1751, and published in Spain the same year, indicates: "contra nuestra voluntad hemos entendido, que contraviniendo nuestro decreto, y seria prohibición, el dicho P. Amort, con grande audacia, y sin rubor alguno, ha impreso nuevamente una Obra llena de indecentes oprobios, y afrentosos desprecios, bajo el escandaloso título: *Nueva demostración de la falsedad de las Revelaciones Agredanas, con un paralelo y comparación entre los Dogmas apuesto al Evangelio y dichas Revelaciones . . .* Por tanto, de ningún modo puede pertenecer al P. Amort prevenir con crítica precipitada el juicio de la Santa Sede, haciendo presente al Público su privado juicio y dando a la estampa por modo tan ilícito su desbocada particular opinión" (Against our will we understand that, in defiance of our decree—in actuality a prohibition—the said Father Amort, with great audacity, and without any shame whatsoever, has again printed a work full of indecent opprobium and insulting slights, under the scandalous title *Nueva demostración de la falsedad de las Revelaciones Agredanas, con un paralelo y comparación entre los Dogmas apuesto al Evangelio y dichas Revelaciones.* . . . Thus in no way should Father Amort anticipate with his hasty critique of the Holy See's judgment, making his private judgment public and his foulmouthed particular opinion seem as though it were official through illicit means); Maximiliano Joseph, "Copia de un decreto del Señor Elector de Bavaria al Padre Propósito Polingano" (1751), Archivo Franciscano Ibero-Oriental, Madrid.

94. Mendía, "En torno al problema de la autenticidad de la *Mistica Ciudad de Dios,*" 408.

95. This point is discussed at length in a series of exchanges archived at Santa Sede 150, Archivo de la Embajada de España Ante la Santa Sede, Ministerio de Asuntos Exteriores, Madrid.

96. Mendía, "En torno al problema de la autenticidad de la *Mistica Ciudad de Dios,*" 421.

97. Madres Concepcionistas de Ágreda.

98. Pou y Martí, "El arzobispo Eleta," 359–60.

99. Ibid., 363.

100. "de dicha separación era preciso proviniesen inconvenientes y escándalos muy graves en la Iglesia de Dios con evidente peligro de que naciese un cisma" (out of such a separation, undoubtedly problems and grave scandals will arise in God's Church, with the obvious risk that a schism could be born from it) (ibid.).

101. "Clarísima injusticia que se ha echo siempre a esta pobre e inocente Causa" (Crystal-clear injustice with which this poor, innocent *causa* has always been treated) (ibid., 351).

102. Luis Miguel Fernández, "De la revelación a la escritura," 350.

103. Mendía, "En torno al problema de la autenticidad de la *Mistica Ciudad de Dios,*" 405.

104. "La razón por qué muchos atribuían esta obra al confesor de la Venerable Madre, nimiamente afecto a la escuela de Escoto, era porque hallaban en ella doctrinas escotistas principalísimamante, la de la Inmaculada Concepción de María santísima" (The reason for which many attributed this work to the Venerable Mother's confessor, a trivial fan of the Scotus school, was because they found in the work Scotist doctrines, most principally that of the Immaculate Conception of Holy Mary) (ibid., 417).

105. Ibid., 421.

106. Sor María was not the only nun of her time to claim to have traveled mystically. As Jean Franco maintains, mystical separations of body and soul were temporary breaks in the general atmosphere of control to which cloistered women (and women in general) were subject during the early modern period and before. Ellen Gunnarsdøttir explains in *Mexican Karismata* that by the sixteenth and seventeenth centuries the Carmelite Order had adopted the tradition of Santa Teresa's mystical experiences; Gunnarsdøttir, *Mexican Karismata: The Baroque Vocation of Francisca de los Ángeles, 1674–1744*, Engendering Latin America (Lincoln: University of Nebraska Press, 2004), 7. Further, Elisa Sampson Vera Tudela comments on the not uncommon phenomenon of mystical travel by such nuns, noting that "in the didactic literature of [Sor María's day], there is a clear attempt to resolve and contain the contradiction between the nun's enclosure and her role as holy voyager"; Elisa Sampson Vera Tudela, *Colonial Angels* (Austin: University of Texas Press, 2000), 3.

107. Jean Franco, *Plotting Women: Gender and Representation in Mexico*, Gender and Culture (New York: Columbia University Press, 1989); Gunnarsdøttir, *Mexican Karismata*.

108. Gunnarsdøttir, *Mexican Karismata*, 7.

109. "The Franciscan friars, who go so far as to call their Mother Ágreda's writing their 'Second Bible'"; Servando Teresa de Mier, *Fray Servando Teresa de Mier*, Los imprescindibles (México: Cal y arena, 1953), 144–45.

110. Uribe, "La inmaculada en la literatura," 203.

111. Ibid., 204.

112. Manuel de Castro, "Legislación inmaculista de la Orden Franciscana en España," *Archivo Ibero-Americano* 57-58 (1955): 36, 53.

113. Uribe, "La inmaculada en la literatura franciscano-española," 203.

114. Manuel de Castro, "Legislación inmaculista de la Orden Franciscana en España," 79–85.

115. Ibid., 86–89.

116. Ibid., 89–94.

117. Ibid., 44.

118. Ibid., 61.

119. Ibid., 65.

120. Patrocinio García Barriuso, "La monja de Carrión Sor Luisa de la Ascención y Sor María de Jesús, la monja de Agreda," *Verdad y Vida: Revista de las Ciencias del Espíritu* 49, no. 196 (1991): 574.

121. Santa Sede 150.

122. Ibid.

123. Ibid.

124. Ibid.

125. This date is estimated because the original document suffered significant mold degradation.

126. Santa Sede 150.

127. Vázquez Janiero, "Un Franciscano al servicio de los Habsburgos," 198.

128. Écija, *Sagrado inexpugnable muro*, 2.

129. Ibid., 3.

130. Ibid. In doing so, Écija reiterates the outcome of the Spanish War of Succession and reaffirms the legitimacy of the regent.

131. Ibid., 4.

132. Ibid., 5.

133. Ibid.

134. Ibid.

135. Ibid., 7.

136. At the text's close, Écija includes an illustrative index in which he names the "varones ilustres" cited in the *Sagrado inexpugnable muro*, that is, individuals who had honored, venerated, and approved the celestial doctrine of Sor María ("honrado, venerado, y aprobado la doctrina Celestial de la Venerable Madre Sor Maria de Jesús de Ágreda"). The four-page-long list includes religious, royal, and secular individuals who had written or spoken in support of *La mística ciudad de dios*, including several of the people discussed in this chapter.

137. Santa Sede 150.

138. Ibid.

139. Vázquez Janiero, "Un Franciscano al servicio de los Habsburgos," 217–20.

140. Santa Sede 150.

141. Ibid.

142. Ibid. The cover materials for the letter, though nearly illegible, support the message regarding the Immaculate Conception: "El Rey ordena se repitan las . . . para que Su Señoría conzeda . . . Misterio de la Concepción . . . ba y de segunda clase . . . para toda la cristiandad" (The king orders that the [?] be repeated so that His Holiness concede . . . the Mystery of the [Immaculate] Conception . . . and of second class . . . for all of Christendom).

143. Pou y Martí, "El arzobispo Eleta."

144. Near the closing of Sor María's case for canonization in 1778, Manuel de Roda, then procurador for the *causa*, wrote to the Spanish ambassador to Rome, the Duque de Grimaldi, regarding the Crown's hope for a positive ruling on *La mística ciudad de dios* and on Sor María's case for beatification. In the letter, Roda mentions the Imprenta in the context of Sor María's beatification (Pou y Martí, "El arzobispo Eleta," 359).

145. Juan de Ascargota, *Manual de confessores ad mentem Scoti* (Madrid: Imprenta de la casa de la V.M. María de Jesús de Ágreda, 1757).

146. Juan Blázquez del Barco, *Trompeta evangelica, alfange apostolico y martillo de pecadores Alfange Apostolico y Martillo de Pecadores* (Madrid: Imprenta de la Causa de la Venerable M. María de Jesús de Agreda, 1742).

147. *Gaceta de Madrid*, February 7, 1758; May 26, 1761; November 20, 1759. Jáuregui's press was on the Calle de Toledo.

148. Blázquez del Barco, *Trompeta evangélica*.

149. *Gaceta de Madrid*, March 26, 1771.

150. Pérez-Rioja, "Proyección de la Venerable María de Agreda," 14; María de Jesús de Ágreda, *Mystica ciudad de Dios, milagro de su omnipotencia y abismo de la gracia* (Madrid: Imprenta de la Causa de la V. Madre, 1720).

151. Joseph Ximénez Samaniego, *Prólogo galeato, Relación de la vida de la V. Madre Sor María de Jesús: Abadesa que fue de el Convento de la Inmaculada Concepcion de la villa de Agreda, de la provincia de Burgos* (Madrid: Imprenta de la Causa de la V. Madre, 1720).

152. The estimated total publication production of the press tallies twelve editions of *La mística ciudad de dios*, four editions of the *Relación de la vida de la V. Madre Sor María de Jesús (Prólogo galeato)*, and at least forty-three texts by other authors.

153. María de Jesús de Ágreda, *Mystica ciudad de Dios, milagro de su omnipotencia y abismo de la gracia* (Madrid: Imprenta de la Causa de la V. Madre, 1765).

154. Joseph Ximénez Samaniego, *Prólogo galeato, Relación de la vida de la V. Madre Sor María de Jesús: abadesa que fue de el Convento de la Inmaculada Concepcion de la villa de Agreda, de la provincia de Burgos* (Madrid: Imprenta de la Causa de la V. Madre, 1765).

155. Francisco Jesús María de San Juan del Puerto, *Patrimonio seraphico de Tierra Santa: fundado por Christo Nuestro Redentor con su preciosa sangre, prometido por su magestad ‡ n.p. S. Francisco para sí, y para sus hijos, adquirido por el mismo Santo, heredado, posseído por sus hijos de la regular observancia, y conservado hasta el tiempo presente* (Madrid: Imprenta de la Causa de la v.m. Maria de Jesus de Agreda, 1724).

156. Juan de Soto and Juan de San Antonio, *Bibliotheca universa franciscana sive Alumnorum trium Ordinum S.P.N. Francisci, qui ab ordine seraphico condito, usque ad praesentem diem, latina, sivè alia quavis lingua scripto aliquid consignarunt Encyclopaedia . . . : in tres distributa tomos, adjectis necessarijs Indicibus* (Madrid: Ex Typographia Causae V. Matris de Agreda, 1732).

157. Basilio Iturri de Roncal, *Eco Harmonioso del Clarín Evangelico con duplicados Sermones, ó Pláticas de Assumptos Panegyricos, Mysticos, y Morales, para las fiestas solemnes de Christo Señor nuestro, de Maria Santisima, y Santos, cuyos dias son festivos*, 2 vols. (Madrid: Imprenta de la Causa de la Venerable Madre Maria de Jesus de Agreda, 1736); Pedro Rodríguez Guillén, *Sermones varios, panegyricos, politicos, historicos, y morales: Predicados en los principales templos . . . de la ciudad de . . . Lima* (Madrid: Imprenta de la Causa de la Venerable Madre Maria de Jesvs de Agreda, 1736); *Regla y constituciones para las religiosas clarisas recoletas, de el monasterio de nuestra señora de los angeles de . . . Arizcun, en el Bastau, obispado de Pamplona, año de MDCCXXXVI* (Madrid: Imp. de la Causa de la V. Madre de Agreda, 1737); Domingo Losada, *Compendio chronologico de los privilegios regulares de Indias* (Madrid: Impr. Casa de la V. Madre de Agreda, 1737); Petrus Polo, *Mensiones morales seu*

quadragesima continua per mensiones hebraeorum et mysticae ad fratres et mo-niales, 4 vols. (Madrid: Ex Typographia causae V. Matris de Agreda, 1737); Juan de San Antonio, *Primacia fundamental del V. Padre Fray Juan de Guadalupe, vindicada* (Madrid: Imprenta de la Causa de la V.M. de Agreda, 1737); Matías Velasco, *Demostración histórico-chronológica de un engaño o inconsideración, que padeció y trasladó a la prensa el R. Padre Fr. Marcos de Alcalá . . . sobre, y en assumpto de la fundación de el convento de la Señoras Descalzas Reales for-mala en defensa de la verdad . . . el R. P. Fr. Mathias de Velasco* (Madrid: Imp. causa de la V. Madre Sor María de Jesús de Agreda, 1737).

158. Nicolás Ángel, *Directorio predicable apostolico, que contiene una pru-dente Instruccion de los sentidos de la Escritura Sagrada; los Assumptos mas prin-cipales para hacer una Mission ; y la Explicacion de todo el Texto de la Doctrina Christiana, . . . Dedicalo N. Rmo. P. Fr. Juan Bermejo, . . . Con licencia* (Madrid: Imprenta de la Causa de la V.M. Maria de Jesus de Agreda, 1740); Lorenzo Bona, *Theatro evangelico de oraciones, panegyricas y sagradas* (Madrid: Imprenta de la Causa de la V. madre Maria de Jesus de Agreda, 1741); Francisco Echarri, *Direc-torio moral que comprehende en breve . . . todas las materias de la theologia moral y novissimos decretos de los sumos pontifices que han condenado diversas proposiciones . . . : contiene ocho partes*, 5th printing (Madrid: Imprenta de la Causa de la V. Madre de Agreda, 1741); Joseph Ximénez Samaniego, *Vida del venerable padre Juan Dunsio Escoto, doctor mariano y subtil* (Madrid: Imprenta de la Causa de la Venerable Madre Maria de Jesvs de Agreda, 1741); Juan Blázquez del Barco, *Trompeta evangelica, alfange apostolico y martillo de peca-dores sermones de mission, doctrina moral, y mystica, y relox de el alma, com-puesto* (Madrid: Imprenta de la Causa de la Venerable M. María de Jesús de Agreda 1742); Manuel Garay, *Sermones varios: Continuación de el parentesis de el ocio, quenta con el tiempo, enigma claro, dentro, y fuera de los nueves, nada de nuevo* (Madrid: Imprenta de la causa de la V. Madre de Agreda, 1743); *Regla de las monjas de la orden de la purissima y inmaculada concepcion de la Virgen Santissima Nuestra Señora: dada por el santissimo Papa Julio Segundo en el año de la encarnacion del Señor de M.D.XI. ‡ quince de las kalendas de octubre en el año octavo de su pontificado* (Madrid: Imprenta de la causa de la Venerable Madre de Agreda, 1744); Joseph Nava y Quijada and Bernardo Mendel, *Colo-phon crítico-canónico-legal, a el privilégio de fuero, y exempción, en las causas civiles, criminales, y mixtas de los ecónomos apostólicos, y syndicos de la religión serafica: y decreto que Don Sylvestre Verde . . . obtuvo en la Real Chancillería de Granada* (Madrid: Imprenta de la causa de la V. Madre de Agreda, 1744); Juan Ros, *Relacion historica de la portentosa anual maravilla, con que Dios . . . el dia 19 de agosto . . . festividad de San Luis . . . con las milagrosas flores, que aparecen todos los años en la Ermita . . . llamada San Luis del Monte, sita en la parroquial de Vega de Rengos, Concejo de Cangas de Tineo* (Madrid: Imprenta de la Causa de la V.M. de Agreda, 1744).

159. Diego González Matheo, *Mystica civitas Dei vindicata ab observatio-nibus R. D. Eusebii Amorti* (Madrid: Ex Typ. Causae Venerabilis Matris Mariae Jesu de Agreda, 1747); *Constituciones Generales para todas las Monjas, y Reli-giosas . . . de . . . San Francisco . . . : De nuevo recopiladas de las antiguas y aña-*

didas con acuerdo . . . del Capitulo General . . . de 1639 . . . (Madrid: Imp. de la Causa de la V. Madre María de Jesús de Agreda, 1748); Juan Vázquez del Valle, *Año christiano, en que compendiosamente se explican los Evangelios* (Madrid: Imp. de la Causa de la V. Madre María de Jesús de Agreda, 1748); Francisco Venegas, *Oracion panegyrica, que en accion de gracias por haverse celebrado con toda felicidad el capitulo provincial, que prestidiò el M. R. P. Fr. Eugenio Ibañez en el Perù en su Convento de Jesus de Lima . . . el dia 23. de noviembre, año de 1746* (Madrid: Impr. de la Causa de la V. Madre María de Jesús de Agreda, 1748).

160. Pérez-Rioja, "Proyección de la Venerable María de Agreda," 14.

161. Joseph Ximénez Samaniego, *Prologo galeato, Relacion de la vida de la v. Madre sor María de Jesús: Abadesa, que fue, del Convento de la Inmaculada Concepción, de la Villa de Agreda, de la provincia de Burgos ; y notas a las tres partes de la Mystica ciudad de Dios* (Madrid: Imprenta de la Causa de la V. Madre, 1721); Ximénez Samaniego, *Relación de la vida de la v. Madre sor María de Jesús, abadesa, que fue, del Convento de la Inmaculada Concepción, de la Villa de Agreda, de la provincia de Burgos. Y Notas a las tres partes de la Mystica ciudad de Dios* (Madrid: Imprenta de la Causa de la V. Madre, 1759); Ximénez Samaniego, *Prólogo galeato, Relación de la vida de la V. Madre Sor María de Jesús: abadesa que fue de el Convento de la Inmaculada Concepcion de la villa de Agreda, de la provincia de Burgos*; María de Jesús de Ágreda and Joseph Ximénez Samaniego, *Mystica ciudad de Dios, milagro de su omnipotencia, y abismo de la gracia : historia divina, y vida de la Virgen Madre de Dios, reyna, y señora nuestra* (Madrid: Impr. de la Causa de la V. Madre, 1720).

162. *Compilatio statutorum generalium pro Cismontana Familia regularis observantiae S. Francisci a Revisoribus ad hoc deputatis compaginata et jussu rev. P. Joannis de Soto S. Francisci ministri generalis prelo data* (Madrid: Ex typ. V. Matris de Agreda, 1734).

163. Écija, *Sagrado inexpugnable muro.*

164. González Matheo, *Mystica civitas Dei vindicata.*

165. *Apodixis agredana pro mystica, civitate Dei technas detegens eusebianas* (Madrid: Ex. Typ. Causae Venerabilis Matris Mariae Jesu de Agreda, 1751).

166. Dalmatius Kick, *Revelationum agredanarum justa defensio in tres tomos distributa*, 2nd ed., 3 vols. (Madrid: Ex typographia Causae V.M. Mariae à Jesu de Agreda, 1754).

167. Blázquez del Barco, *Trompeta evangelica*, frontispiece.

168. Arbiol y Diez, *La religiosa instruida.*

169. Under "Introduccion de esta obra y motivo de escrivirla" (Introduction to this work and reasons for writing it): "En pocas palabras nos dice el Profeta [Ezequiel] quanto se puede discurrir en este punto: mas para que lo veamos por extenso, oygamos lo que la reyna de los cielos dice a su Discipula la V. Madre Maria de Jesus de Agreda en la 3. parte de la Mystica Ciudad de Dios, lib. 8 cap.3 num. 426 . . . Todas son palabras de la reyna de los cielos en el lugar citado de la Mystica Ciudad, de las que con claridad podemos inferir la gran falta, que padecen los almas de quien las sense y doctrine, y las muchas omisiones que tienen los sacerdotes y Ministros de Dios en darles el alimento verdadero. No me atreviera yo a tanto, si no nos hiciera esto el decreto que nuestro

Santisimo Padre Benedicto XIII expidio en el ano de 1728 y quinto de sun pontificado, el que onde aqui traducido en Romance, para que conste a todos . . .
Tengamosle muy presente, para ponerlo en execucion y no olvidemos las doctrina que la reyna de los Cielos da a su sierva mi Venerable Maria de Jesus de
Agreda en los lugares citados: puse asi el decreto, como la doctrina con la con-
firmacion mas solida de la necesidad, que padecen las almas del alimento verdadero y la obligacion que los ministros del altisimo tienen" (In few words, the
prophet Ezekiel tells us the extent to which we may disagree on this point: but
so that we might have a better idea of the extent of this, let us hear what the
Queen of Heaven says to her disciple, the Venerable Mother María de Jesús de
Ágreda in the third part of *La mística ciudad de dios*, book 8, chapter 3, number
426 . . . All of these are the words of the Queen of Heaven in the cited portion
of *La mística ciudad de dios*, from which we can clearly infer the great lack, from
which the souls who are ministered to and taught, suffer, and the great omissions
of the priests and ministers of God in giving them true nourishment. I would
not go so far as to say such a thing myself, if our Holy Father Benedict XIII
hadn't made a decree in the year 1728 and a quarter of his pontificate, which I
here translate to Spanish so that all may have it . . . Let us keep it before us, to
carry it out, and not forget the doctrine that the Queen of Heaven gives to her
servant, my Venerable María de Jesús de Ágreda, in the cited passages: I have
here placed the decree, along with the doctrine with the solid and necessary confirmation, that souls are starved for true nourishment, and the responsibility that
the ministers of the Most High have [to them]) (Ángel, *Directorio predicable
apostolico*).

170. Pablo de Écija, *Novena a la Milagrosa Imagen que con el titulo de
Nuestra Señora de los Milagros y Misericordias se venera en el coro de el Con-
vento de Religiosas de la Purissima Concepcion de la Villa de Agreda* (Madrid:
Imprenta de la Causa de la V. Madre de Agreda, 1745).

171. Ximénez Samaniego, *Vida del venerable padre Juan Dunsio Escoto*.

172. Pedro Rodríguez Guillén and Luis Montt, *El Sol, y año feliz del Perú
San Francisco Solano, apostol, y patron universal de dicho reyno: hijo de la ilustre, y Santa Provincia de los Doce Apostoles. Glorificado, adorado, y festejado en
su Templo, y Convento Maximo de Jesus de la Ciudad de los Reyes Lima, en ocacion que regocijada la serafica familia celebró con demostraciones festivas la deseada canonizacion, y declaracion del culto universal, y publico, que le decretó
nuestro santissimo padre Benedicto XIII. de eterna memoria, y felice recordacion: de que hace relacion en esta regia corte de Madrid el reverendo padre Fr.
Pedro Rodriguez Guillen, lector jubilado del numero, ex-secretario de la sobredicha provincia, y actual custodio de ella, convocado al capitulo general* (Madrid:
Imprenta de la Causa de la V.M. de Agreda, 1735).

173. Ascargota, *Manual de confessores ad mentem Scoti*.

174. Antonio Arbiol, *La familia regulada con doctrina de la Sagrada Escritura y Santos Padres de la Iglesia Catholica*, 6th printing (Madrid: Imprenta de
la Causa de . . . Maria de Jesus de Agreda, 1760).

175. Antonio Arbiol y Diaz, *Mystica fundamental de Christo Señor Nuestro explicada por . . . San Juan de la Cruz . . . y el religioso perfecto conforme a*

los cien Avisos y Sentencias espirituales (Madrid: Imprenta de la Causa de la V. Madre Maria de Jesus de Agreda, 1761).

176. "Su autor el Padre fray Pablo de Écija, guardian del convento de Capuchinos de la Ciudad de Granada . . . se ha impresso, tassaron a seis maravedis cada pliego, y dicho libro parece tiene quarenta y dos, sin principios ni tablas, que a este respecto importa doscientos y cinquenta y dos maravedis, y al dicho precio, y no mas mandaron se venda" (Its author, Father Pablo de Écija, guardian of the Capuchin convent in the city of Granada . . . it has been printed, and assessed six maravedís per sheet, and the said book looks to have forty-two sheets, without prefatory materials, nor tables, which therefore means the book is worth two hundred and fifty-two maravedís, and at the said price—and no more—the book should be sold); see legal prefatory materials for the *Sagrado inexugnable muro.*

177. "Don Miguel Fernandez Munilla, secretario del rey nuestro senor su escrivano de camara mas antiguo y governador del consejo. Certifico que haviendo visto por los senores de el un libro intitulado . . . que con licencia de dichos senores concedida a este, has sido impresso, tassaron a seis maravedis cada pliego; y el referido libro parece tener cinquenta y siete, sin principios, ni tablas, que a este respecto importa trescientos y quarenta y dos maravedis y al citado precio" (Don Miguel Fernandez Munilla, the secretary of the king our lord, his oldest scribe and head of council. / I certify that, having seen via his functionaries a book entitled . . . that with the permission that the said functionaries cede to the work, it has been printed and assessed and six maravedís each sheet; and since the said work has fifty-seven pages, without prefatory materials or tables, it is worth three hundred and forty-two maravedís, and should be sold at the said price) (Ángel, *Directorio predicable apostolico*).

178. "Ha sido reimpresso, tassaron a seis maravedis cada pliego, y dicho libro parece tiene veinte y ocho, sin principios ni tablas, que a este respecto importa ciento y sesenta y ocho maravedis; y al dicho precio, y no mas, mandaron se venda" (it has been printed, and assessed six maravedís per sheet, and the said book looks to have twenty-eight sheets, without prefatory materials, nor tables, which therefore means the book is worth sixty-eight maravedís, and at the said price—and no more—the book should be sold) (Ascargota, *Manual de confessores ad mentem Scoti*).

179. "Tassaron los senores de el consejo este libro . . . a seis maravedis el pliego, el cual tiene noventa y cuatro pliegos, sin principios ni tablas que a dicho respecto importan quinientos y sesenta y cuatro maravedis, como parece de certificacion, dada por Don Miguel Fernandez Munilla" (The lords of the council assessed this book . . . at six maravedís per sheet, and the book has ninety-four sheets, without prefatory materials, or tables, which therefore means it is worth four hundred and sixty-four maravedís, as is certified by Don Miguel Fernández Munilla) (Blázquez del Barco, *Trompeta evangelica*).

180. The distribution of the press's publications extended to the American colonies and even to the Philippines. The Catalog of Rare Books at the University of Santo Tomas Library in Manila, Philippines, for example, documents a copy of Fray Domingo Losada's *Compendio Chronologico de los Privilegios*

Regulares de Indias, published by the Imprenta in 1737, among the library's archival holdings (Losada, *Compendio chronologico*).

181. *Gaceta de Madrid*, April 12, 1729.

182. *Gaceta de Madrid*, February 7, 1758; Antonio Arbiol, *Desengaños mysticos a las almas detenidas o engañadas en el camino de la perfección* (Madrid: Imp. de la Causa de la V.M. Maria de Jesús de Agreda, 1757).

183. *Gaceta de Madrid*, February 7, 1758; Ascargota, *Manual de confessores ad mentem Scoti*.

184. *Gaceta de Madrid*, November 20, 1759; Diego de Estella, *Tratado de la vanidad del mundo: Dividido en tres libros con sus indices muy copiosos y assumptos predicables, discurriendo por todas las dominicas y fiestas del año, y al fin un tratado de Meditaciones devotissimas del amor de Dios* (Madrid: Imprenta de la Causa de la V.M. Maria de Jesus de Agreda, 1759).

185. *Gaceta de Madrid*, May 26, 1761; Arbiol, *Mystica fundamental*.

186. *Gaceta de Madrid*, December 2, 1747.

187. *Gaceta de Madrid*, February 10, 1748.

188. "Que es un Compendio de la *Mystica Ciudad de Dios*," *Gaceta de Madrid*, April 13, 1762.

189. Ibid.

190. *Gaceta de Madrid*, March 6, 1771.

191. Pou y Martí, "El arzobispo Eleta," 359.

192. Pérez-Rioja, "Proyección de la Venerable María de Agreda," 4.

193. Mariano Alcocer Martínez, *Catalogo razonado de obras impresas en Valladolid, 1481–1800* (Valladolid: Impr. de la Casa social catolica, 1926), 898.

194. Valladolid also appears to have been a regional center of interest in the *causa* and in Sor María's writing.

195. Patricia Andrés González, *Iconografía de la Venerable Madre*.

196. Ricardo Fernández Gracia, *Arte, devoción y política: La promoción de las artes en torno a sor María de Ágreda* (Soria, Spain: Diputación Provincial de Soria, 2002); Fernández Gracia, *Iconografía de Sor María de Ágreda*.

197. Fernández Gracia, *Iconografía de Sor María de Ágreda*, 183–92.

198. There are numerous eighteenth-century Spanish publications that treated *La mística ciudad de dios* as a topic of theological discussion, a work of popular religiosity, and as a source for popular reimagination of Sor María's own life or of the individuals who feature in the Marian treatise. One such example is the *Obsequiosa reverente expresión* by Joseph de Figueroa, a poetic composition consisting of sonnet, décima, and quintilla published in 1757 in honor of Benedict XIV's declaration that Sor María was the authentic author of *La mística ciudad de dios*; see Joseph de Figueroa, *Obsequiosa reverente expression que en fuerza del decreto pontificio de Nuestro SS.mo Padre Benedicto XIV* (Madrid: Imprenta de Francisco Xavier Garcia, 1757). Another popular devotional work is Francisco del Casar, *Devocionario seraphico: Exercicios de la V.O.T. de Colmenar Viejo, deducidos de la Mystica Ciudad de Dios, y milagro de la Divina Omnipotencia. Indulgencias que se logran . . . y un Apéndice latino, forma de dar hábitos, Profesiones y otras curiosidades* (Madrid: L. F. Mojados, 1750).

199. Manuel Francisco de Armesto, *La coronista más grande de la más sagrada historia, Sor María de Jesús de Agreda* (Madrid: Mora, 1736).

200. "En el siglo XVIII, cuando las obras de Sor María eran más alabadas que nunca y su memoria más bendecida, se escribió acerca de ella una comedia de santos, en dos partes, rotuladas: Comedias nuevas, Primera, y Segunda parte" (In the eighteenth century, when Sor María's works were more praised than ever and her memory ever more blessed, a comedy of saints was written about her, in two parts, entitled *Comedias nuevas, Primera, y Segunda parte*); Serrano y Sanz, *Apuntes para una biblioteca*, 1:582.

201. *Gaceta de Madrid*, January 31, 1736.

202. *Gaceta de Madrid*, October 9, 1736.

203. Francisco Muñoz de Villalón, "La caída de Luzbel" (1789), Biblioteca Nacional de Madrid.

204. Giacomo Casanova, *Mèmoires de Jacques Casanova de Seingalt, Ècrits par lui-mème*, 6 vols. (Bruxelles: Rozez, 1881).

205. *La mística ciudad de dios* was published in Venice in 1740; see Pérez-Rioja, "Proyección de la Venerable María de Agreda," 14.

206. Giacomo Casanova, *History of My Life* (New York: A. A. Knopf, 2006), 484–85.

207. Ibid., 485.

208. Ibid.

209. Ibid., 486. The Piombi prison in Venice was called "The Leads" because of the lead shingles on the roof.

THREE   "Como si fuera natural de México"

1. Fernández Gracia, *Iconografía de Sor María de Ágreda*, 46.

2. Josefina Muriel, *Cultura femenina novohispana*, 1st ed., Serie de historia novohispana (México: Universidad Nacional Autónoma de México, Instituto de Investigaciones Históricas, 1982), 351.

3. Indiferente 3029, Archivo General de Indias, Seville.

4. Ibid.

5. "Pedir limosna, durante seis años, para la beatificación de la Madre María de Jesús de Agreda" (Solicit pious donations for six years, for the beatification of Mother María de Jesús de Ágreda); see Juan Ruíz and Francisco Saez, "Real Cédula dando licencia a Fr. Francisco Saez y Fr. Juan Ruiz, de la Orden de San Francisco para pasar al Perú a pedir limosna, durante 6 años, para la beatificación de la Madre María de Jesús de Agreda" (1692), Archivo General de Indias.

6. Indiferente 3029.

7. Ibid.

8. Apart from explaining who was authorized to collect limosna on Sor María's behalf, and what steps that procedure involved, this decree also implicitly defines where early communities of devotion to Sor María in Spain's colonies could have been established.

9. Indiferente 3029.

10. Ibid.

11. Lucas Álvarez de Toledo, "Patente de fray Lucas de Toledo autorizando pedir limosna para una beatificación/Comisario general de Indias" (1708), Convento de San Francisco de Madrid.

12. Indiferente 3029.

13. Juan de Soto, "Patente de fray Juan de Soto para atender las limosnas de una beatificación" (1724), Convento de San Francisco de Madrid.

14. Hortensia Calvo, "The Politics of Print: The Historiography of the Book in Early Spanish America," *Book History* 6 (2003), 279, 281.

15. Indiferente 3029.

16. Ibid.

17. Ibid.

18. Ibid.

19. Ibid.

20. "[para que] los mencionados Libros no se carezca[n] en la Nueva España y Perú donde más se necesitan" (So that the above mentioned books may not be found lacking in New Spain and Peru, where they are the most needed) (ibid.).

21. Ibid.

22. Ibid.

23. Ibid.

24. Ibid.

25. Pérez-Rioja, "Proyección de la Venerable María de Agreda," 14.

26. Magdalena Chocano Mena, "Colonial Printing and Metropolitan Books: Printed Texts and the Shaping of Scholarly Culture in New Spain, 1539–1700," *Colonial Latin American Historical Review* 6, no. 1 (1997): 80.

27. Indiferente 3029.

28. Ibid.

29. Ibid.

30. Ibid.

31. Ibid.

32. Ibid.

33. The petitions for taxation remission located at the Archivo General de Indias indicate that Fray García followed Fray Saenz de Cabezón as procurador, and was himself succeeded by Fray Tadeo de Lievenna.

34. Indiferente 3029.

35. Ibid.

36. Ibid.

37. Ibid.

38. Ibid.

39. Ibid.

40. Ibid.

41. This estimation is based on the weight standard that one *castellano* was the equivalent of 46 grams, one *tomín* weighed 5.75 grams, and a *libra* was worth 460 grams. See Junta de Castilla y León, "Artehistoria: Introducción," http://www.artehistoria.com/v2/contextos/10131.htm.

42. Indiferente 3029.

43. The commentator was probably the Marqués del Real Tesoro, Julián de Arriaga, or one of his functionaries (ibid.).

44. Pérez-Rioja, "Proyección de la Venerable María de Agreda," 48.

45. Ibid.

46. Ibid.

47. Ibid.

48. Ibid.

49. Peru and Venezuela—and the surrounding areas and sites served by their ports—participated in a transoceanic exchange of Sor María's writing. Communities of reading for her texts also emerged at those Spanish colonial sites. See Fernández Gracia, *Arte, devoción y política*.

50. Juana Inés de la Cruz, *Obras completas*, 12th ed., ed. Francisco Monterede (México: Editorial Porrúa, 2001), 827–48.

51. The works documented here are by no means an exhaustive list of New Spanish publications of Sor María's writing. There were many texts published in Mexico that treated the Immaculate Conception, the biography of the Virgin Mary, the Trinity, or St. Joseph that, although they do not cite Sor María directly, no doubt derived from or owed much to *La mística ciudad de dios* and other works of Sor María's writing.

52. The majority of these publications were brief, few measuring longer than sixty-four pages, and their compact length and small physical size translated into lower prices and greater portability for readers. This accessibility affected circulation not only of the excerpts printed in Mexico but of *La mística ciudad de dios*. Editions of the book that arrived in Mexico from Spain were of varying numbers of volumes, the smallest of which, printed on eighth- or sixteenth-sheet size, produced the books that made up an eight-volume set. These editions were intended for private use, as opposed to the large and heavy three-volume sets.

53. *Escuela Mystica de María en la Mystica Ciudad de Dios, en las Doctrinas que dictó la Reyna de los Angeles a la M. Ma. De Jesús de Agreda, al fin de los ocho libros impresos, al presente separados, los reimprime el Dr. J. Ignacio Ma. Castoreña y Ursúa* (Pérez-Rioja, "Proyección de la Venerable María de Agreda," 14). In February 1731, the *Gaceta de México* announced the publication of this book in a news piece accompanied by an exhortation by Juan Ignacio Castoreña y Ursúa that the book was intended for the members of his diocese in Yucatán; see *Gaceta de México*, Testimonios mexicanos: Historiadores (México: Secretaría de Educación Pública, 1722), 312.

54. Calvo, "The Politics of Print," 280.

55. Fernández Gracia, *Arte, devoción y política*, 227–28, 247–49.

56. Ibid., 248–49.

57. *Gaceta de México*, 217.

58. Medina, *La imprenta en México*, 3:106.

59. Reimpresso: Francisco de Rivera Calderón (ibid., 3:539).

60. Ibid., 3:106.

61. "El Ilustrissimo Señor Arçobispo de Mexico [*sic*], concede quarenta dias de Indulgencia à los que leyeren este Compendio" (The illustrious Lord

Bishop of Mexico concedes forty days of indulgence to whoever reads this Compendio) (ibid., 3:106).

62. Agustín de Vetancurt, *Chronografía sagrada de la vida de Christo Nuestro Redemptor: Predicación evangélica, con las circunstancias de lugar, y tiempo en que obró los misterios de nuestra redemption* [*sic*], *obras de su omnipotencia, y maravillas de su gracia en Maria Santíssima, y en el seraphico padre S. Francisco, y su apostólica religión* (México: Por Doña Maria de Benavides, Viuda de Juan de Ribera, 1696).

63. The citation of *La mística ciudad de dios* begins with book 1, part 1, chapter 15, number 209, according to the text's margin notes. The *Chronografía sagrada* is filled with other items of interest aside from the chronology, including a revised chronology of Church doctors and saints; twelfth-century prophesies about pontifical succession by St. Malachías of Calabria that were published in the mid-seventeenth century; and a biography of the life, ministry, and death of St. Francis of Assisi, the patron of Fray Vetancurt's order.

64. Vetancurt, *Chronografía sagrada*, "Dedicatoria," 3.

65. This description offers a curious detail about what was believed to be the difference in gestation time required to form a female body versus a male body, and the uniqueness of the Virgin Mary's creation: "Y aunque para que se organizen los cuerpos de los hombres son necesarios cuarenta dias, y en las mugeres sesenta, poco mas, o menos conforme el calor natural; en la formación corporal de María Santissima su virtud divina aceleró el tiempo natural, y se hizo perfectamente en siete dias en el vientre de Santa Ana" (And although forty days are necessary to organize the bodies of men, and sixty for women, more or less, given one's inborn nature; in the corporeal formation of Blessed Mary, her divine virtue accelerated natural time, and she was perfectly formed in seven days inside St. Anne's womb) (ibid., 2r).

66. Ibid., "Prólogo," 1.

67. The latter was published in Bologna in 1669 (ibid., "Prólogo," 2; 84v).

68. Cayetano Verdiguer, *Matemática demostración de las letras dominicales y exactas desde el principio del mundo hasta el año 1760 y siguientes. Hechas sus tablas . . . bajo del computo que refiere la V.M. María de Jesús de Agreda* (Biblioteca Nacional de España, 1760).

69. Vetancurt, *Teatro mexicano*.

70. "Después se lo refirió ella misma al padre fray Alonzo de Benavides" (Later, she herself [Sor María] would tell this to Fray Alonso de Benavides); Vetancurt, *Teatro mexicano*, Biblioteca histórica de la Iberia Crónica de la Provincia del Santo Evangelio de México (México: Imprenta de I Escalante, 1871), 3:303.

71. Medina, *La imprenta en México*, 3:445.

72. *La imprenta en México*, 4:37.

73. *Gaceta de México*, 22.

74. Medina, *La imprenta en México*, 4:174.

75. Medina, *La imprenta en México*, 6:14, 146; María de Jesús de Ágreda, *Septenario al gloriosissimo patriarca Sr. San Joseph: De los siete privilegios de su patrocinio que reifere la V.M. Maria de Jesús de Ágreda en su Mystica ciudad de*

Dios (México: Imprenta nueva de la calle de S. Bernardo [Joseph de Jáuregui], 1785); Medina, *La imprenta en México*, 7:424.

76. Florencio Gavito, José Toribio Medina, and Felipe Teixidor, *Adiciones a la Imprenta en la Puebla de los Angeles* (México, 1961), 226.

77. Ágreda, *Septenario al gloriosissimo patriarca Sr. San Joseph*.

78. Ibid.

79. "Estas dos prudentisimas Virgenes, elevadisimas plumas, encendidas antorchas, que en muchas luces, abren los ojos del conocimiento, y encienden los afectos del corazón para el amor de este admirable Santo, han estendido por gran parte del Mundo su devoción, siendo la experiencia testigo de sus milagros al ligero costo de los ruegos" (These two prudent virgins, noble quills, burning torches, which in many ways broaden our understanding and ignite the affects of our hearts out of love for this admirable saint; they have spread this devotion throughout a great part of this world, experience being the witness to their miracles, at small cost of prayerful pleas) (ibid.).

80. Francisco González de Cossío and Medina José Toribio, *La imprenta en México, 1594–1820; cien adiciones a la obra de José Toribio Medina* (México: Porrúa, 1947), 172.

81. José Toribio Medina, *La Imprenta en Puebla de los Ángeles (1640–1821)* (Santiago de Chile: Imprenta Cervantes, 1908), 636.

82. *Gaceta de México*, 214, 216.

83. Medina, *La imprenta en México*, 4:279.

84. The text's original Latin author also goes unnamed.

85. *Gaceta de México*, 165–66.

86. *Traducción verídica y authentica de tres sucessos prodigiosos . . . en que la bondad divina se ha dignado de acreditar los libros de la Mystica Ciudad de Dios* (México: Joseph Bernardo de Hogal, 1729), 1v.

87. Ibid., 3v. Printed in Mexico in 1729 by Joseph Bernardo de Hogal, the *Traducción verídica*'s translation from Latin to Spanish was attributed to an anonymous priest from Mexico City (ibid.). Écija's text was published in 1734 in Madrid.

88. Ibid., 4r.

89. Ibid., 4v.

90. Ibid. The French translations of *La mística ciudad de dios* were particularly fraught given the Sorbonne's critique of the text, which Spanish Franciscans attributed to a faulty rendering of the text into French from Spanish.

91. Écija, *Sagrado inexpugnable muro*, 145–52.

92. Medina, *La imprenta en México*, 4:301–2.

93. Francisco Antonio de Vereo, *Aurora alegre del dichoso día de la gracia María Santíssima digna Madre de Dios: Prosiguen los diez y seis últimos días de el mes de vida . . . epítome de los libros Mystica ciudad de Dios y Vida de la Virgen Madre de Dios* (México: Joseph Bernardo de Hogal, 1730), 5.

94. Ibid., 6.

95. Ibid., 7.

96. Ibid., 9.

97. Ibid., 146.

98. Ibid., 18.

99. Ibid.

100. Ibid., 21.

101. Alonso de Benavides and María de Jesús de Ágreda, *Tanto que se sacó de una carta, que el R. Padre Fr. Alonso de Benavides, custodio que fue del Nuevo Mexico, embió a los religiosos de la Santa custodia de la conversión de San Pablo de dicho reyno, desde Madrid, el ano de 1631* (México: Joseph Bernardo de Hogal, 1730).

102. In his study on the iconography of Sor María, Ricardo Fernández Gracia argues that the images of Sor María as a missionary published alongside the *Tanto que se sacó de una carta* originated in Spain and were reinterpreted by artists in New Spain. However, there are no documented Spanish versions of this image that predate the 1730 *Tanto que se sacó de una carta*. American and European artists alike would later rework the theme of Sor María as mystical missionary; see Fernández Gracia, *Iconografía de Sor María de Ágreda*, 184–85.

103. *Tanto que se sacó de una carta* was printed before the *vitae* of Margil de Jesús and Serra were published; missionary iconography predates the 1730 publication.

104. Benavides and Ágreda, *Tanto que se sacó de una carta*.

105. The term "Chichimecos" also appears in the 1760 image.

106. Wagner proposed the 1760 publication date in part to explain a different copper plate engraving similar to the 1730 one that he encountered among the José F. Ramírez papers: "This would appear to indicate that it had been published between 1730 and 1747; but on the whole, Mr. George Parker Winship and I are inclined to agree that it was printed after 1747, probably about 1760, for it was a copy of this edition that Fr. Rafael Verger sent to Spain in 1772"; Henry Raupp Wagner, *The Spanish Southwest, 1542–1794: An Annotated Bibliography* (Berkeley, CA: J. J. Gillick, 1924), 347. Wagner included a copy of this image in *Spanish Southwest* (348).

107. Pérez-Rioja, "Proyección de la Venerable María de Agreda," 15.

108. *Gaceta de México*, 330.

109. Medina, *La imprenta en México*, 5:333–34.

110. Medina, *La Imprenta en Puebla de los Ángeles (1640–1821)*, 304.

111. One of Sor María's manuscripts (archived at the Biblioteca Nacional de España) details the names and roles of the six angels who looked after and helped her: Graciel, Nunciel, Saciel, Barachiel, Agael, and Marachiel; see Clark Colahan and Celia Weller, "An Angelic Epilogue," *Studia Mystica* 13, no. 4 (1990).

112. María de Jesús de Ágreda, *Mystica ciudad de Dios: Milagro de su omnipotencia, y abismo de la gracia, historia divina, y vida de la Virgen madre de Dios, reyna, y señora nuestra Maria santissima, restauradora de la culpa de Eva, y medianera de la gracia*, Vol. 1 (Antwerp: Henrico y Cornelio Verdussen, 1696), "Índice."

113. Joachín Osuna, *Peregrinación christiana por el camino real de la celeste Jerusalén: dividida en nueve jornadas, con quatro hospicios, que son unas estaciones devotas al modo del Via-Crucis, guirnaldas a la sagrada Passión de*

Christo, y dolores de su santíssima Madre: añadida al fin una refección espiritual de oraciones para antes, y despues de recibir los santos sacramentos de la penitencia, y comunión (México: Biblioteca Mexicana, 1756); Joachín Osuna, *Peregrinación christiana por el camino real de la celeste Jerusalen: dividida en doce jornadas, con quatro hospicios, que son unas estaciones devotas al modo del via-crucis, y guirnaldas à la sagrada passion de Christo y dolores de su santissima madre ; añadida al fin una refeccion espiritual de oraciones para antes, y despues de recibir los santos sacramentos de la penitencia y comunion* (México: Biblioteca Mexicana, 1760).

114. Medina, *La imprenta en México*, 5:333–34.

115. The *Novena sagrada* was printed on sixteenth-sheet paper and was fifty-five pages long.

116. Joachín Osuna, *Perla de la gracia y concha del cielo: devoción mensal a la concepción y preñez virginea de la madre de Dios . . . / sacado todo de las obras de M. Agreda y dispuesto por Joachin de Ossuna* (México: Bibliotheca Mexicana, 1758).

117. Ibid.

118. Ibid., 3r.

119. Ibid., 4r.-4v.

120. Fernández Gracia, *Iconografía de Sor María de Ágreda*, 153.

121. Francisco Marin, *Triduo mariano mensual en honor, y reverencia del Felicissimo Transito, entierro y assumpcion de la Reyna del Cielo y tierra María Nuestra Señora, para alcanzar mediante su Protección una dichosa muerte . . .* (Mexico City: Herederos del LIc. D. Joseph de Jauregui, 1790).

122. Medina, *La Imprenta en Puebla de los Ángeles (1640–1821)*, 359.

123. Ibid., 557, 613, 712.

124. Gavito, Toribio, and Teixidor, *Adiciones a la Imprenta en la Puebla de los Angeles*, 241.

125. Medina, *La imprenta en México*, 6:381–82; Francisco Marin, *Triduo mariano mensual en honor, y reverencia del Felicissimo Transito, entierro y assumpcion de la Reyna del Cielo y tierra María Nuestra Señora, para alcanzar mediante su Protección una dichosa muerte . . .* (México: Herederos del Lic. D. Joseph de Jáuregui, 1790); Medina, *La imprenta en México*, 8:124.

126. María de Jesús de Ágreda, *Modo de andar la via-sacra, sacado de la Mystica ciudad de Dios* (México: Biblioteca Mexicana, 1763).

127. María de Jesús de Ágreda, *Modo de andar la Via Sacra: Sacado de la Mystica Ciudad de Dios* (México: Felipe de Zúñiga y Ontiveros, 1773); *Modo de andar la via-sacra, / sacado de la Mystica ciudad de Dios, 2. part. lib. 6. cap. 21. por uno de los fundadores del Colegio de la Santa Cruz de Queretaro. Y reimpresso à devocion de los missioneros del Colegio Apostolico de San Fernando de esta Ciudad de Mexico* (México: Biblioteca Mexicana, 1774); *Modo de andar la Via-Sacra: Sacado de la Mystica ciudad de dios* (México: Biblioteca Mexicana, 1777); *Modo de andar la Via-Sacra* (México: Felipe de Zúñiga y Ontiveros, 1779); *Modo de andar la Via-Sacra* (México: Imprenta de los Herederos de Joseph de Jauregui, 1789); *Modo de Andar la Via-Sacra* (México: Herederos de J. Jauregui, 1793); *Modo de Andar la Via-Sacra* (México: En la oficina de doña

María Fernández de Jáuregui, 1806); *Modo de Andar la Via Sacra: Sacado de la Mística Ciudad de Dios* (México: María Fernández de Jáuregui, 1808); Amaya Garritz Ruiz, *Impresos novohispanos, 1808–1821*, 2 vols., Serie bibliografica (Universidad Nacional Autonoma de Mexico. Instituto de Investigaciones Historicas) 9 (Mexico City: Universidad Nacional Autónoma de México, 1990), 106; 476; 591; 676; 1064; María de Jesús de Ágreda, *Modo de andar la Via Sacra* (México: Oficina del finado Ontiveros, 1826).

128. Medina, *La imprenta en México*, 6:239.

129. Pérez-Rioja, "Proyección de la Venerable María de Agreda," 16.

130. Medina, *La imprenta en México*, 6:16.

131. The Franciscan devotion to St. Joseph, manifested through the publication of Sor María's writing in New Spain, grew in part out of the order's focus on Christ's humanity.

132. *Viernes de María: En obsequio de su glorioso tránsito, provechosa devoción para conseguir una buena muerte, según lo que la misma Señora reveló á la venerable madre sor María de Jesús de Agreda, Lib. 8. Cap. 28. Num. 745 / escrita por un vecino de Celaya* (México: En la oficina de la calle de Santo Domingo, 1816).

133. Garritz Ruiz, *Impresos novohispanos, 1808–1821*, 373–74.

134. Ibid.

135. Diego Miguel Bringas y Encinas, *Índice apologético de las razones que recomiendan la obra intitulada Mistica Ciudad de Dios escrita por la Ven, Madre Sor María de Jesus Coronel y Arana . . . Con varias cartas apologeticas escritas en defensa de la misma obra, por algunos sábios franceses . . . Un apéndice que contiene la supuesta y despreciable censura falsamente atribuida al Ilmo. Señor Bosuet, su impugnacion y notas. Ultimamente un resumen de la admirable vida y ejemplarísimas virtudes de la misma venerable Madre Sor María de Jesus* (Valencia: D. F. Brusola, 1834).

136. Ibid., 273.

137. *Compendio histórico, y novena de Maria santisima nuestra Señora, que con la advocacion de la Cueva santa se venera en el Seminario de la Santa Cruz de la ciudad de Queretaro* (Puebla: Hospital de San Pedro, 1834).

138. Ibid., 92–93.

139. María de Jesús de Ágreda, *Mística ciudad de Dios: Historia divina y vida de la Santísima Vírgen María, Madre de Dios, Reina, Abogada y Señora Nuestra. Manifestada por la misma Señora su esclava sor María de Jesus, abadesa del Convento de la Purísima Concepcion de la villa de Ágreda* (México: Impr. de V. García Torres, 1844).

140. Basilio Arrillaga, *Defensa de la Mística Ciudad de Dios de . . . Sor María de Jesus Agreda contra la censura que en nombre propio y bajo el de el illmo. Bossuet ha publicado El Constitucional, etc* (México, 1844).

141. Other colonial sites where the Franciscan Order was involved in local religious administration developed their own communities of reading for Sor María's writing. In addition to the places mentioned earlier in this chapter, copies of *La mística ciudad de dios* emerged in collections in Nueva Granada (present-day Colombia); see María del Pilar López Pérez, "El objeto de uso en las salas de las casas de habitación de españoles y ciollos en Santafé de Bogotá:

Siglos XVII y XVIII en el Nuevo Reino de Granada," *Anales del Instituto de Investigaciones Estéticas* 74–75 (1999): 126. Interestingly, Jesuits stationed in Colombia also had copies of the text; see José del Ray Fajardo, "Marco conceptual para comprender el estudio de la arquitectura de las misiones jesuíticas en la América colonial," *Apuntes* 20, no. 1 (2007): 17.

142. Laurencio Atlas, "Árbol genealógico de la familia Coronel y Arana" (1759), Archivo Franciscano Ibero-Oriental.

143. Another version of Sor María's family tree exists in Lima, Peru (Fernández Gracia, *Iconografía de Sor María de Ágreda*, 174–75). I discuss this work and other manifestations of colonial-era Filipino interest in Sor María at greater length in Anna M. Nogar, "Genealogías hagiográficas y viajes coloniales: Sor María de Agreda en las Filipinas" *Revista de Soria* 89 (2015): 151–59.

144. Antonio de Robles, *Diario de sucesos notables (1665–1703)*, Vol. 2, ed. Colección de Escritores Mexicanos (México: Editorial Porrúa, 1972).

145. Ibid., 2:19.

146. Ibid., 2:211. Art historian Silvia Evangelisti notes that religious objects possessed by women mystics were particularly valuable to Spanish and New Spanish citizens for their miraculous powers, which they transferred to their possessor: "Rosaries, sometimes together with crosses, possessed miraculous powers precisely because they had been associated with mystic women. Sponsored by biographers as objects that attest to the holy and heroic virtues of the mystics, these beliefs concerning the rosaries were sometimes condemned by the authorities as symbols of superstition"; Silvia Evangelisti, "Spaces for Agency: The View from Early Modern Female Religious Communities," in *Attending to Early Modern Women: Conflict and Concord*, ed. Karen Nelson (Newark: University of Delaware Press, 2013), 120.

147. José de Arlegui, Antonio Gálvez, and Ignacio Cumplido, *Crónica de la provincia de n.s.p.s. Francisco de Zacatecas* (México: Reimpresa por Cumplido, 1851).

148. Ibid., 415.

149. Judging from one of the images used on the cover of the manuscript (the symbol for Christ's name—IHS—with a cross above the "H"), which is a symbol often used by the Jesuit Order, it is likely Verdiguer was a Jesuit himself and/or was educated by the Jesuits.

150. Verdiguer, *Matemática demostración*, "Frontispiece." Verdiguer draws further attention to his devotion to the Immaculate Conception by specifying in the chronology the year Duns Scotus defended the theology at Oxford University, 1302 (ibid., 31).

151. Ibid.

152. Verdiguer merges Rome with New Spain in his commemoration of the 1757 decision regarding *La mística ciudad de dios*. He refers to Pope Benedict XIV, who made the declaration, in distinctly Mexican terms, adding an additional title reflecting the importance of the Virgin of Guadalupe: "Esta declaración aprobò aquel tres vezes Maximo Guadalupano Pontifice el Señor Benedicto XIV" (This declaration was passed three times by his Highest Guadalupan Pontifice Benedict XIV) (ibid., "Prólogo").

153. Ibid.

154. Ibid., 29.

155. Ibid., 1–2.

156. Ibid., 1.

157. Ibid.

158. Ibid., 49.

159. Fernández Gracia, *Iconografía de Sor María de Ágreda*, 14. Fernández Gracia's research unearths a rich array of artistic production in Spain representing Sor María and her writing and also several pieces created in the Americas.

160. Ibid.

161. Antonio Rubial García, "Civitas dei et novus orbis: La Jerusalén celeste en la pintura de Nueva España," *Anales del Instituto de Investigaciones Estéticas* 20 (Spring 1998): 21.

162. De la Maza's reflections on Sor María's influence on paintings of Christ by New Spanish artists appeared in his discussion of the following book: Sonia de la Rozière and Xavier Moyssèn, *México, Angustia de sus Cristos* (México: Instituto Nacional de Antropología e Historia, 1967).

163. Francisco de la Maza, "Los Cristos de Mexico y la monja de Agreda," *Boletín del Instituto Nacional de Antropología e Historia* 30 (December 1967): 3.

164. Ibid.

165. Ibid., 2.

166. Ibid., 1, 2.

167. Elisa Vargas Lugo, *Juan Correa: Su vida y su obra* (México: UNAM, 1985), 15.

168. Ibid., 16.

169. "Enriquecer a sus ángeles y desvestirlos con cierto recato" (Enrich his angels, and undress them with a certain modesty); Francisco de la Maza, *El pintor Cristóbal de Villalpando* (Mexico City: Instituto Nacional de Antropología e Historia, 1964), 30.

170. Ibid., 28. Fernández Gracia agrees, citing Sor María's writing regarding the names of the six angels as another possible influence in novohispanic representation of angels. (Also discussed in Colahan and Weller, "An Angelic Epilogue."); Fernández Gracia, *Iconografía de Sor María de Ágreda*, 49.

171. The description of the Virgin Mary receiving communion can be found in part 2, book 6, chapter 11, number 1198 of *La mística ciudad de dios*. Art historian Elisa Vargas Lugo has noted that it is not apparent whether Correa chose the theme of *La comunión de María* "por su propia iniciativa" (of his own initiative) or because it was a patron request or suggestion. Fernández Gracia asserts that Correa painted under the influence of a Franciscan advisor, who would have encouraged familiarity with Sor María's writing; see Elisa Vargas Lugo, "La vida de María," in *Juan Correa: Su vida y su obra. Repertorio pictórico*, ed. Elisa Vargas Lugo and José Guadalupe Victoria (México: Universidad Nacional Autónoma de México, 1994), 85; Fernández Gracia, *Iconografía de Sor María de Ágreda*, 49.

172. Fernández Gracia, *Iconografía de Sor María de Ágreda*, 44–45.

173. Vargas Lugo, "La vida de María," 85.

174. Ibid.

175. Vargas Lugo cites one other example of this unique theme, a work signed "Arellano," located in a private Mexican collection in Tepepan. The topic was of great interest to ninth-century mystics, though it was not a popular topic in New Spanish art; Fernández Gracia, *Iconografía de Sor María de Ágreda*, 49.

176. Ibid., 49, 50. Correa's *San Pedro administrando la communion a Elías y Enoc* is held in a private Mexican collection. The description of Elías and Enoch receiving communion can be found in part 2, book 6, chapter 11, number 1198 of *La mística ciudad de dios*. Two renderings of the *Tránsito de la Virgen* by Correa can be found at the Templo de San José el Real and at the Secretaria de Hacienda.

177. Ibid., 49.

178. *La anunciación* is located at the monastery of Guadalupe de Zacatecas.

179. De la Maza, *El pintor Cristóbal de Villalpando*, 205.

180. María del Consuelo Maquívar, *De lo permitido a lo prohibido: Iconografía de la Santísima Trinidad en la Nueva España* (México: Instituto Nacional de Antropología e Historia, 2006), 122.

181. *La adoración de los pastores* is located at the San Antonio de Padua church in Puebla.

182. María de Jesús de Ágreda, *Mystica ciudad de Dios, milagro de su omnipotencia, y abysmo de la gracia : historia divina, y vida de la virgen, Madre de Dios, Reyna, y Señora Nuestra, Maria Santissima, restauradora de la culpa de Eva* (Madrid: En la Impr. de la Causa de la Venerable Madre, 1765), pt. 2, bk. 4, chap. 11, no. 489–97.

183. Fernández Gracia, *Iconografía de Sor María de Ágreda*, 50.

184. Cabrera's painting can be found at the Santa Prisca church in Taxco (ibid., 52).

185. Ibid., 52, 53.

186. Ibid.

187. Ibid., 52.

188. Ibid.

189. Ibid., 55. Fernández Gracia cites volume 2, part 2, numbers 1340 and 1342 of *La mística ciudad de dios* as the source for this image. Morlete may have also included Sor María in a tableau treating the "Heart of Mary"; a nun in the lower left-hand corner holds book and pen, echoing Sor María's well-known iconography; see Juan Patricio Morlete, *Heart of Mary*, Google Art Project, https://en.wikipedia.org/wiki/Juan_Patricio_Morlete_Ruiz#media viewer/File:Juan_Patricio_Morlete_Ruiz_-_The_Heart_of_Mary_-_Google _Art_Project.jpg.

190. *Gaceta de México*, December 1732.

191. Maquívar, *De lo permitido a lo prohibido*, 115. The painting is located in Puebla's cathedral, which is dedicated to the Immaculate Conception.

192. Ibid., 114.

193. Rubial García, "Civitas dei et novus orbis," 23. Images similar to this one accompanied editions of *La mística ciudad de dios* printed outside of Spain. María de Jesús de Ágreda, *Mystica ciudad de Dios: milagro de su omnipotencia y abismo de la gracia: historia divina y vida de la Virgen Madre de Dios, Reyna*

y Señora Nuestra Maria Santissima, Nueva impression adornada y enriquezida con muchas lindissimas estampas . . . y con un indice general de las cosas notables que se contienen en las tres partes desta divina historia, 3 vols. (Amberes: Por la viuda de Henrico Verdussen, 1736); Rubial García, "Civitas dei et novus orbis"; Marie Mauquoy-Hendrickx, "Les Wierix illustrateurs de la Bible dite de Natalis," *Quaerendo* 6, no. 1 (1976).

194. Fernández Gracia, *Iconografía de Sor María de Ágreda*, 148. Villalpando created another version of this image (entitled *La mística ciudad de dios*) that more closely followed the cover of the 1685 Lisbon edition of *La mística ciudad de dios* in that it included Duns Scotus along with St. John and Sor María. In addition, Villalpando was not the only artist who painted this theme: an anonymous painting at the museum of Santa Monica de Puebla shares much in common with Villalpando's second piece. Rubial García, "Civitas dei et novus orbis," 23.

195. Fernández Gracia, *Iconografía de Sor María de Ágreda*, 149.

196. Ibid.

197. Ibid., 150. The visual parity between St. John and Sor María in the painting prompted art scholar Francisco de la Maza to remark offhandedly of the weight given to Sor María's writing in colonial Mexico that "igual daba el águila que la grulla en [las] superficiales devociones" (the eagle [a traditional symbol of St. John] seems the same as the crane in superficial devotions) (de la Maza, *El pintor Cristóbal de Villalpando*, 20).

198. This central image was relatively popular in colonial Mexico, and was found in artwork throughout the region, from Querétaro (where the icon was called *Our Lady of el Pueblito*) to New Mexico; see Cristina Cruz González, "Our Lady of el Pueblito: A Marian Devotion on the Northern Frontier," *Catholic Southwest: A Journal of History and Culture* 23 (2012), 6–15.

199. Manuel Romero de Terreros, "El convento franciscano de Ozumba y las pinturas de su portería," *Anales del Instituto de Investigaciones Estéticas* 6, no. 24 (1956): 20.

200. Ibid.

201. Fernández Gracia, *Iconografía de Sor María de Ágreda*, 162.

202. For the image, see ibid., 166.

203. Ibid., 215–16.

204. A painting with a similar motif—a family tree of the Franciscan Order—is located in a Franciscan convent in Lima, Peru. In it, Sor María again appears, wearing a blue Conceptionist habit. As mentioned earlier in this chapter, copies of *La mística ciudad de dios* were sent to Peru from Spain, and there are indications of its popularization there (ibid., 216).

205. Fernández Gracia comments on this particular Ágredan portrait genre (ibid., 109–20).

206. Cristina Cruz González, *Sor María Writing La mística ciudad de dios* (painting), Museo Nacional del Virreinato, Tepozotlán.

207. Ibid.

208. Rogelio Ruíz Gomar, "La colección de pintura colonial del Ateneo Fuente, en la ciudad de Saltillo, Coahuila," *Anales del Instituto de Investigaciones Estéticas* 15, no. 60 (1989), 90–91.

209. Ibid., 91.

210. Fernández Gracia, *Iconografía de Sor María de Ágreda*, 115.

211. "Alguno de los Colegios Apostólicos de los franciscanos" (One or another of the Franciscan Apostolic Colleges [Colleges of Propaganda Fide]) (ibid.).

212. Vargas Lugo, *Juan Correa: Su vida y su obra*, 176.

213. Mina Ramírez Montes, "El testamento del pintor Antonio Torres," *Anales del Instituto de Investigaciones Estéticas* 15, no. 59 (1988): 268.

214. Eduardo Báez Macías, "El testamento de José Miguel Rivera Saravia, arquitecto del siglo XVIII," *Anales del Instituto de Investigaciones Estéticas* 13, no. 46 (1976): 191.

215. Records of many of these donations are held at Sor María's convent in Ágreda (Fernández Gracia, *Arte, devoción y política*, 199–246).

216. Ibid., 244–46.

217. Ibid., 218–23. Patricia Andrés González, "Un temprano cuadro de la Virgen de Guadalupe, con el ciclo aparicionista, en las Conceptionistas de Ágreda (Soria)," *Anales del Museo de América* 7 (1999).

218. Fernández Gracia, *Arte, devoción y política*, 246–52.

219. Ibid., 199–219.

220. Ibid., 209–16.

221. Ibid., 241–44, 322–24; Fernández Gracia, *Iconografía de Sor María de Ágreda*, 51–52.

222. Two of Lorenzo de Ávila's brothers were affiliated with the Franciscan Order: one was the provincial of the Custodia del Santo Evangelio, and another was a Franciscan preacher (Fernández Gracia, *Arte, devoción y política*, 240).

223. Ibid., 241–42. De Ávila wrote in one of his letters to the convent that his devotion to it and to Sor María was based on his reading of the nun's works: "Toda esta demostración que hago y haré más adelante es llevado al afecto grande que tengo a los escritos de la Venerable y religiosa Madre sor María de Jesús, los cuales humildemente venero y reverencio, con toda mi estimación y aprecio" (All that I do now and will do in the future is for the great affection I have for the Venerable and religious Madre Sor María de Jesús's writing, which I humbly venerate and reverence, with all my appreciation and esteem) (ibid., 241).

224. Ibid., 242.

225. Ibid., 243.

226. Ibid., 250–51.

227. Ibid., 247–49.

228. *Gaceta de México*, August 1733. Bishop Castoreña y Ursúa also assured the nuns in Ágreda that he was advancing Sor María's writing and her culture of devotion in New Spain, specifically among women: "he solicitado con todas mis fuerzas la extensión de sus doctrinas y culto [entre] los fieles de estos reinos, en las cátedras y púlpito y a su obsequio he dedicado un colegio de doncellas honestas que se erigió a mi devoción" (I have sought with greatest effort the extension of her doctrines and devotional cult among the faithful of these kingdoms, in the classroom and at the pulpit, and as a gift I have dedicated a

college of honest young women built upon my devotion) (Fernández Gracia, *Arte, devoción y política*, 249).

229. Fernández Gracia, *Iconografía de Sor María de Ágreda*, 53.

230. Fernández Gracia, *Arte, devoción y política*, 252.

231. Male religious were also influenced by Sor María's writing in their prayer lives and devotional practices, as we shall see in chapter 4. One example of this is Father Luis Felipe Neri de Alfaro (el Padre Alfaro), a member of the Congregation of San Felipe de Neri in Atotonilco, whose novena entitled "A la flor más Hermosa y salutífera de los campos" alludes to Sor María as a writer; the priest's penitential practices were also inspired by Sor María's; see Clementina Díaz y de Ovando, "La poesía del Padre Luis Felipe Neri de Alfaro," *Anales del Instituto de Investigaciones Estéticas* 15 (1947).

232. Muriel, *Cultura femenina novohispana*, 351.

233. Antonio Arbiol y Diez, *La religiosa instruída: Con doctrina de la sagrada escritura, y santos padres de la Iglegia catholica, para todas las operaciones de su vida regular, desde que recibe el habito santo, hasta la hora de su muerte* (Madrid: En la Imprenta Real de la Gazeta, 1776), 403–4.

234. Ibid., 404.

235. Ibid.

236. Ibid., 406.

237. Ibid., 407.

238. Ibid., 408.

239. Ibid., 356.

240. Ibid., 82.

241. Ibid., 70, 553.

242. Fernández Gracia, *Iconografía de Sor María de Ágreda*, 53; Fernández Gracia, *Arte, devoción y política*, 252.

243. Nina M. Scott, "'La gran turba de las que merecieron nombres': Sor Juana's Foremothers in 'La Respuesta a Sor Filotea,'" in *Coded Encounters: Writing, Gender, and Ethnicity in Colonial Latin America*, ed. Francisco Javier Cevallos-Candau, et al. (Amherst: University of Massachusetts Press, 1994), 206.

244. Ibid., 212.

245. De la Cruz, *Obras completas*, 843.

246. Ibid.

247. Ibid.

248. Santa Teresa was declared a doctor of the Church in 1970.

249. Juana Inés de la Cruz, *Ejercicios devotos*, in *Obras completas* (México: Editorial Porrúa, 2001), 848–66.

250. Scott, "'La gran turba de las que merecieron nombres,'" 222.

251. Sor Juana's "Docta explicación del misterio y voto que hizo de defender la purísima concepción de nuestra Señora, la madre Juana Inés de la Cruz," written shortly before she was prohibited from her studies, seemingly affirms the Immaculate Conception theology (de la Cruz, *Obras completas*, 872–73).

252. Grady Wray, "Seventeenth-Century Wise Women of Spain and the Americas: Madre Agreda and Sor Juana," *Studia Mystica* 22 (2001): 132.

253. De la Cruz, *Obras completas*, 848.

254. Wray, "Seventeenth-Century Wise Women," 126, 128. Wray indicates that some of the inaccuracies in elements borrowed from *La mística ciudad de dios* for the *Ejercicios devotos* might have resulted from Sor Juana's referencing "popular tradition" in colonial Mexico regarding Sor María's writing, rather than the text itself (ibid., 126).

255. Ibid., 128.

256. Ibid., 134.

257. Ibid., 135.

258. Wray's insights reflect certain contemporary considerations of the portrayal of the Virgin Mary in *La mística ciudad de dios*, and their socio-theological implications; see Enrique Llamas, *La Madre Ágreda y la Mariología del siglo XVII*, Estudios marianos (Salamanca: Sociedad Mariológica Española, 2003).

259. Jennifer Lee Eich, *The Other Mexican Muse: Sor María Anna Agueda de San Ignacio, 1695–1765* (New Orleans: University Press of the South, 2004), 15.

260. Ibid., 19.

261. Ibid., 136.

262. Ibid., 89–90.

263. Ibid., 255.

264. Ibid., 27–28.

265. Ibid. María de San José (1656–1719), a *criolla* originally from Tepeaca who later lived in Oaxaca, is another example of a female religious who lived in a non-Franciscan community and whose writing may have been influenced by Sor María. After many years unsuccessfully attempting to enter a convent due to limited family resources, Sor María de San José joined the Augustinian recollects at the Convent of Santa Mónica in Puebla. She later became a founder and novice master at Nuestra Señora de la Soledad in Oaxaca from 1697 through 1719. Although Sor María de San José does not appear to have cited Sor María directly in her copious writing, the Ágredan nun's writing was read by one of the cofounders of the convent in Oaxaca, and several copies of *La mística ciudad de dios* were found at the Santa Monica convent in Puebla. Indeed, Sor María de San José's representation of the Stations of the Cross is evocative of Sor María's focus on Mary's experience of Christ's passion.

266. Nora Jaffary, *False Mystics* (Lincoln: University of Nebraska Press, 2004), 208.

267. Ibid., 186.

268. José Antonio de Noriega y Escandón, "Inquisition Interrogation of Josefa Palacios" (1791), 60, Greenleaf Papers: Inquisition, Center for Southwest Research, University of New Mexico.

269. Ibid., 33.

270. Fray Villarejo was himself subsequently accused of being an *iluso* by the Inquisition, in part, Jaffary suggests, because his defense of Josefa Palacios presented a "gendered inversion of power" (Jaffary, *False Mystics*, 10, 186).

271. "Diciendo que si espantándola quasi" (asking if she were almost surprised by her) (Noriega y Escandón, "Inquisition Interrogation of Josefa Palacios," 77–78).

272. Ibid., 78.

273. Ibid.

274. Ibid.

275. Jaffary, *False Mystics*, 186.

276. Ibid., 137–39.

277. Edelmira Ramírez, *María Rita Vargas, María Lucía Celis, Beatas embaucadoras de la colonia: De un cuaderno que recogió la Inquisición a un iluso, Antonio Rodríguez Colodrero, solicitante de escrituras y vidas*, 1st ed. (México: Universidad Autónima de México, 1988), 226.

278. Ibid.

279. Ibid.

280. Ibid., 16.

281. Ibid., 108.

282. Josefina Muriel, *Las indias caciques de Corpus Christi*. Instituto de Historia: Serie histórica (México: Universidad Nacional Autónoma de México, 1963). Mónica Díaz, *Indigenous Writing from the Convent: Negotiating Ethnic Autonomy in Colonial Mexico*, First Peoples: New Directions in Indigenous Studies (Tucson: University of Arizona Press, 2010).

283. Díaz, *Indigenous Writing from the Convent*, 103.

284. Ibid., 94.

285. Ibid., 105.

286. Muriel, *Las indias caciques de Corpus Christi*, 381.

287. Ibid., 385–87.

FOUR   "Aquella voz de las conversiones"

1. Juan Mateo Manje, *Luz de tierra incógnita en la América Septentrional y Diario de las Exploraciones en Sonora*, Vol. 10, Publicaciones Archivo General de la Nación (México: Talleres Gráficos de la Nación, 1926), 183.

2. Eleanor Adams, "Two Colonial New Mexico Libraries: 1704, 1776," *New Mexico Historical Review* 29 (1944): 151.

3. He is so named by Donahue-Wallace for the detailed hemlines on the clothing depicted in his paintings. Kelly Donahue-Wallace, "The Print Sources of New Mexican Colonial Hide Paintings," *Anales del Instituto de Investigaciones Estéticas* 68 (1996): 48.

4. Marie Mauquoy-Hendrickx, "Les Wierix illustrateurs de la Bible dite de Natalis," *Quaerendo* 6, no. 1 (1976).

5. This painting, the largest remaining of its type, is located at the Millicent Rogers Museum in Taos, New Mexico. Donahue-Wallace claims that the 1722 printing was the source for the illustration, but Alena Robin disagrees with this date, citing the later study by Mauquoy-Hendrickx, "Les Wierix illustra-

teurs de la Bible dite Natalis," which asserts that the 1736 Antwerp printing, also by the Viuda de Verdussen, was the source text; see Alena Robin, "El retablo de Xaltocán: Las Imágenes de Jerónimo Nadal y la monja de Ágreda," *Anales del Instituto de Investigaciones Estéticas* 88 (2006): 53, 60. Editions by the Verdussen press were printed in Antwerp both years; see Pérez-Rioja, "Proyección de la Venerable María de Agreda."

6. Donahue-Wallace, "Print Sources of New Mexican Colonial Hide Paintings," 58.

7. Robin, "El retablo de Xaltocán," 59.

8. Donahue-Wallace, "Print Sources of New Mexican Colonial Hide Paintings," 68. Given that even among the California Jesuit missions there were fewer copies of Nadal's Bible than of Sor María's *La mística ciudad de dios*, Donohue-Wallace's hypothesis is reasonable. Michael Mathes, "Oasis culturales en la Antigua California: Las bibliotecas de las misiones de Baja California en 1773," *Estudios históricos novohispanos* 10 (1991). A similar relationship may have existed between the Wierix images in the 1736 edition of *La mística ciudad de dios* and an anonymous, late eighteenth-century retablo located at the Nuestra Señora de los Dolores de Xaltocán church near Xochimilco. The images that served as inspiration for the retablo, which treats Christ's passion, are found in the 1736 Verdussen edition, and art historian Alena Robin concurs with Donohue-Wallace that "la hipótesis de la asociación Nadal-Ágreda resulta muy sugerente" (the hypothesis of the Nadal-Ágreda association seems very suggestive). The painter of the Xaltocán retablo opted not to include the bloody details of the Passion as Sor María described them ("decidió no representar los cruentos detalles de la Pasión como los relata la monja franciscana en los momentos de la Flagelación y la Crucifixión"), but rather reproduced the Wierix images without adding further Agredan content; see Robin, "El retablo de Xaltocán," 61, 70.

9. This was part of an expedition involving Silvestre Vélez de Escalante and the cartographer Bernardo Miera y Pacheco.

10. Adams, "Two Colonial New Mexico Libraries," 145.

11. Ibid.

12. Francisco Atanasio Domínguez, *The Missions of New Mexico, 1776: A Description with Other Contemporary Documents*, trans. Eleanor Adams and Fray Angélico Chávez (Albuquerque: University of New Mexico Press, 1956), 221.

13. Full title: *Certamen marianum Parisiense ubi veritas examinatur in splendoribus Sanctorum, et opus mirabile mysticae civitatis Dei, a censura doctorum, à sacra facultate parisiensi deputatorum, exegitatur liberum*; Adams, "Two Colonial New Mexico Libraries," 157.

14. Antonio Arbiol, *Certamen Marianum Parisiense, vbi veritas examinatur in splendoribvs sanctorvm, et opvs mirabile Mysticae civitatis Dei, a censvra doctorum, sacra Facultate Parisiensi deputatorum, exagitatur liberum, & sententia, sub ementito ejusdem sacrae Facultatis nomine evulgata, propugnatur immune: conatvr ostendere caelicam Mysticae civitatis Dei consonantiam, Scripturae Sacrae, Sanctis Patribus, doctoribus approbatis, alijsque revelationibus*

particularibus, in Ecclesia Catholica huiusque legi permissis, Fr. Antonivs Arbiol (Saragossa: Apud Emmanvelem Roman, 1698).

15. Domínguez, *Missions of New Mexico*, 221: Joseph Nicolas Cavero, *Anti-agredistae parisienses expvgnati, sive, Apologeticae dissertationes adversvs qvosdam parisienses, censvris insectatos complures propositiones, venerabili matre Maria a Iesv, vvlgo de Agreda: sua prima parte Mysticae Civitatis Dei assertas* (Saragossa: In officina Dominici Gascon, 1698).

16. The Santo Domingo collection also included a number of volumes by or about Duns Scotus, and others by authors discussing the Immaculate Conception theology; Domínguez, *Missions of New Mexico*, 222.

17. Junípero Serra, *Writings of Junípero Serra*, 4 vols., trans. Antonine Tibesar (Washington, DC: Academy of American Franciscan History, 1955), 2:235; Maynard Geiger, "The Story of California's First Libraries," *Southern California Quarterly* 46 (1964).

18. Maynard Geiger, *The Life and Times of Fray Junípero Serra, O.F.M; or, The Man Who Never Turned Back* (Washington, DC: Academy of American Franciscan History, 1959), 2:291.

19. Online Archive of California, "Guide to the Mission Santa Clara Book Collection, 1548–1835" (2009), http://www.oac.cdlib.org/findaid/ark:/13030 /tf967nb3tr/dsc.

20. Mathes, "Oasis culturales en la Antigua California," 385–86. An earlier (1767) inventory of the same library showed a six-volume copy of *La mística ciudad de dios* (missing the second and fifth volumes), the notes to the book, and a copy of Sor María's *vita* (ibid., 402).

21. Ibid., 388–89.

22. Ibid., 393, 400.

23. Ibid., 394.

24. Nicolás López, "Report of Custodio of New Mexico and Procurador General Nicolás Lopez on New Mexico" (1687), Archivo General de Indias, Guadalajara Collection, Legajo 138, Spanish Colonial Research Center.

25. "Memorial de Fr. Nicolás Lopez acerca de la repoblación de Nuevo Méjico y ventajas que ofrece el reino de Quivira," in *Don Diego de Peñaloza y su descubrimiento del reino de Quivira* (Madrid: Imprenta y Fundación de Manuel Tello, Real Academia de la Historia, 1686), 44, http://es.wikisource.org /wiki/Don_Diego_de_Peñalosa_y_su_descubrimiento_del_reino_de_Quivira.

26. Ibid., 35.

27. Ibid., 36–38.

28. Ibid., 35.

29. Ibid., 44.

30. Ibid.

31. La Junta de los Ríos is located at the confluence of the Río Grande and Río Conchos; present-day Presidio, Texas, lies near the intersection.

32. López, "Report of Custodio of New Mexico," 3.

33. "Memorial de Fr. Nicolás Lopez," 45.

34. Benito Fernández, "Memorial of Father Benito Fernández Concerning the Canary Islanders, 1741; Translated by Benedict Luetenegger, OFM," *Southwestern Historical Quarterly* 82, no. 3 (1979).

35. Ibid., 295.

36. Ibid.

37. Ibid.

38. In the letter, Fray Vélez de Escalante primarily apologizes for the lack of documents predating the 1680 Pueblo Revolt, their absence justifying a major lacuna in his historical report and its late arrival: "para que V.R. vea que estas dilaciones no son escusas" (so that Your Reverence might see that these delays are not excuses); Silvestre José Vélez de Escalante, "Relaciones de Nuevo-Mexico," in *Documentos para la Historia de México*, Series 3 (México: Imprenta de Vicente García Torres, 1856), 115.

39. Ibid., 201.

40. Ibid., 202.

41. Ibid.

42. Ibid.

43. Ibid., 203.

44. Ibid.

45. Michael Brandon McCloskey, *The Formative Years of the Missionary Colleges of Santa Cruz de Querétaro, 1683–1733* (Washington, DC: Academy of American Franciscan History, 1955), 15.

46. Alberto María Carreno, "The Missionary Influence of the College of Zacatecas," *The Americas* 7 (1951): 298.

47. Isidro Félix Espinosa, *Crónica de los Colegios de Propaganda Fide de la Nueva España*, ed. Lino Gómez Canedo (Washington, DC: Academy of American Franciscan History, 1964).

48. Ibid., 284.

49. Ibid.

50. Ibid.

51. Damián Manzanet, "Carta de Don Damian Manzanet á Don Carlos de Siguenza sobre el descubrimiento de la Bahia del Espiritu Santo," *The Quarterly of the Texas State Historical Association* 2 (1899): 255.

52. Ibid., 279.

53. Ibid., 279–80.

54. Ibid., 280.

55. "Real Cédula Sobre el Descubrimiento de la bahía del Espiritu Santo" (1686), p. 53, Archivo General de Indias, Center for American History, the University of Texas at Austin.

56. Elizabeth Howard West, "De León's Expedition of 1689," *The Quarterly of the Texas State Historical Association* 8, no. 3 (1905).

57. Gaspar de la Cerda Sandoval, "Carta de [Gaspar de la Cerda Sandoval, VII] conde de Galve y virrey de España a su hermano [Gregorio de Silva Mendoza, IX]" (1689), Sección Nobleza, Archivo Histórico Nacional, Spain.

58. Several of these friars were stationed at the College of Guadalupe de Zacatecas at the time of the expedition.

59. Francisco Céliz, *Diary of the Alarcón Expedition into Texas, 1718–1719*, trans. Fritz Leo Hoffman (Los Angeles: Quivira Society, 1935), 13.

60. Ibid., 2.

61. Ibid., 76.

62. Isidro Félix de Espinosa and Antonio Margil de Jesús, "Representación hecha al Virrey por los PP Fr. Isidro Félix de Espinosa y Fr. Antonio Margil de Jesús sobre los motivos que hubo en la fundación de las misiones de Texas y que se impida el avance de los franceses" (1719), Archivo Histórico Provincial de los Franciscanos de Michoacán, Celaya, México.

63. Ibid.

64. Ibid.

65. Isidro Félix de Espinosa, "Carta del padre Espinosa dando las gracias al Virrey por las providencias dadas para las misiones de Texas y su restauración, Agosto 18 1721," Archivo Histórico Provincial de los Franciscanos de Michoacán, Celaya, Mexico. A 1721 document discussing the taking of possession of several Texas mission sites refers to the mission as "esta misión de más Señora Concepción": see "Posesión de las misiones de San Francisco de los Neycha, y de la Concepción y San José de Nasones: 5 julio-agosto 8, 1721," Archivo Histórico Provincial de los Franciscanos de Michoacán.

66. The notes to the translated diary suggest that Alarcón subsequently changed the name of the village and mission; Céliz, *Diary of the Alarcón Expedition into Texas*, 105. Aníbal A. González, "Nuestra Señora de la Purísima Concepción de Acuña Mission," in *Handbook of Texas Online* (Texas State Historical Association), http://www.tshaonline.org/handbook/online/articles /uqn09.

67. Francisco Hidalgo, "Relación del Padre Hidalgo de la Quivira, hecha al señor Virrey, pretendiendo su descubrimiento" (no year), Archivo Histórico Provincial de los Franciscanos de Michoacán, Celaya, México.

68. Ibid.

69. "Relación sobre Quivira por Francisco Hidalgo, a continuación," Archivo Histórico Provincial de los Franciscanos de Michoacán, Celaya, México.

70. Ibid.

71. "A los 40 grados de latitud y uno la asienta a los 50."

72. Hidalgo, "Relación sobre Quivira por Francisco Hidalgo, a continuación."

73. Santa Arias, "De Fray Servando Teresa de Mier a Juan Bautista Muñoz: La disputa guadalupana en vísperas de la independencia," *Revista Iberoamericana* 222 (2008): 6.

74. Servando Teresa de Mier, *Fray Servando Teresa de Mier*, Los imprescindibles (México: Cal y arena, 1953).

75. Ibid., 91.

76. Fray Servando's Dominican theological training would have prepared him to critique the principle of the Immaculate Conception promoted in *La mística ciudad de dios*, which may explain in part his humorous appraisal of the text, its author, and adherents.

77. Mier, *Fray Servando Teresa de Mier*, 124.

78. Ibid., 101.

79. Ibid., 144–45.

80. Fray Servando continued lambasting Mexican Franciscans later in his *Memorias*. In the midst of his critique of the image of the Virgin of Guadalupe,

Fray Servando comments of the Franciscans' vestments that they changed color in Mexico, "los franciscanos de Indias mudaron en azul su hábito pardo," perhaps as a result of the order's involvement with the Conceptionist theology (associated with the color blue) and with Sor María's writing about it. He posited that the Virgin of Guadalupe of Mexico herself was the result of "una visión de la monja de Agreda en el siglo XVI" (a vision of the nun of Ágreda in the sixteenth century) (ibid.).

81. "Libro Becerro de Provincia: Tablas Capitulares II and III," Archivo Histórico Provincial de los Franciscanos de Michoacán.

82. Ibid., 392.

83. *Gaceta de México*, December 1729 (México: Secretaría de Educación Pública, 1728–44), 220.

84. Ibid. The *Gaceta de México* reported that that establishment of the teaching position coincided with dedication of the "Insigne Colegio de la Purissima Concepción."

85. Ibid. The article also notes that the students were dressed in blue and white (Conceptionist colors), with the image of the Immaculate Conception on their cowls.

86. That position also disappears in 1799: "Libro Becerro de Provincia: Tablas Capitulares II and III" (1799), Archivo Histórico Provincial de los Franciscanos de Michoacán, Celaya, México.

87. *Gaceta de México*, 100.

88. Ibid., 231.

89. Ibid.

90. Another inventory of the librería común was made in 1815: "Inventory of Books in the Santa Cruz Library: Librería Común" (1815), Archivo Histórico Provincial de los Franciscanos de Michoacán, Celaya, México.

91. "Inventory of Books at Santa Cruz: Librería Común" (1766), pp. 129–30, Archivo Histórico Provincial de los Franciscanos de Michoacán, Celaya, México.

92. Ibid., 129.

93. Ibid., 130.

94. Ibid., 134.

95. Ibid., 73,146.

96. Ibid.

97. Ibid., 76.

98. Ibid., 129, 30, 34. Texts by or about Duns Scotus, including Fray Ximénez Samaniego's biography of him, are also well represented in the library.

99. Ibid., 80.

100. Ibid., 81.

101. Ibid., 82. Other texts in the library also argue one or another side of the Immaculist/Maculist theological debate.

102. Ibid.

103. Ibid., 143.

104. Ibid.

105. Ibid.

106. There were also several copies of Fray Vetancurt's and Fray Isidro Felix de Espinosa's works on the Franciscans in the mission field that discuss Sor María's role in that context.

107. "Inventory of Books at Santa Cruz: Biblioteca Chiquita" (1803), Archivo Histórico Provincial de los Franciscanos de Michoacán, Celaya, México.

108. Antonio Losilla, "Tesoro escondido hallado por quienes lo buscan en María Puríssima Señora Nuestra, y comunicado nuevamente . . . Tomo Segundo," Archivo Histórico Provincial de los Franciscanos de Michoacán, Celaya, México.

109. Juan José Sáenz de Gumiel, "Libro de pláticas y sermones del P. Fr. Juan José Sáenz de Gumiel," Archivo Histórico Provincial de los Franciscanos de Michoacán, Celaya, México.

110. Juan Murga, "Amenissimus Sacrae Theologiae Tractatus Dei param Virginem Mariam . . ." (1775), Archivo Histórico Provincial de los Franciscanos de Michoacán, Celaya, México.

111. Isidro Félix Espinosa, *Chrónica apostólica, y seráphica de todos los Colegios de Propaganda Fide de esta Nueva-España* (México: Viuda del D. J. J. Bernal, 1746), 529.

112. Ibid.

113. Ibid., 466.

114. Ibid., 506.

115. Ibid., 518.

116. "Repetía muchas veces esta diligencia" (ibid.).

117. Juan Domingo Arricivita, *Apostolic Chronicle of Juan Domingo Arricivita: The Franciscan Mission Frontier in the Eighteenth Century in Arizona, Texas, and the Californias*, trans. George Hammond and Agapito Rey (Berkeley, CA: Academy of American Franciscan History, 1996), 2:335.

118. Ibid., 2:381.

119. Ibid., 2:326.

120. Ibid., 2:353.

121. Ibid., 2:383.

122. Ibid., 2:364.

123. Ibid., 2:362.

124. Ibid., 2:171.

125. Ibid.

126. Ibid.

127. Lázaro Lamadrid, "The Letters of Margil in the Archivo de la Recolección in Guatemala," *The Americas* 10 (1953): 347.

128. Gunnarsdøttir, *Mexican Karismata*, 93–94.

129. Fray Francisco Casañas de Jesús María, returning to the college after the 1691 expedition into Texas, also was said to have experienced evangelizing bilocations to the areas near the mission sites (ibid., 93).

130. Ibid., 91.

131. Ibid., 97.

132. Ibid., 94.

133. Ibid., 95–96.

134. Ibid., 98.

135. Ibid., 99.

136. Ibid., 91–93.

137. "Denunciasion de Don Francisco Barba Coronado: El Señor fiscal del Santo Oficio, contra una mujer llamada Francisca de los Ángeles vecina de Querétaro, por alumbrada," p. 25. Richard E. Greenleaf Papers, Center for Southwest Research, University of New Mexico, Albuquerque.

138. Espinosa, *Chrónica apostólica*, 881.

139. Ibid.

140. The archives of the College of Guadalupe de Zacatecas were not available at the time this book was researched.

141. Clara Bargellini, "'Amoroso horror': Arte y culto en la series de la Pasión de Gabriel de Ovalle de Guadalupe, Zacatecas," in *Arte y violencia: XVIII Coloquio Internacional de Historia del Arte* (México: UNAM/IIE, 1995), 511.

142. Fernández Gracia, *Iconografía de Sor María de Ágreda*; Bargellini, "'Amoroso horror.'"

143. Bargellini, "'Amoroso horror,'" 512.

144. Fernández Gracia, *Iconografía de Sor María de Ágreda*, 148.

145. Historian Juliana Barr comments that Sor María's writing was also successfully used as a recruiting tool for the Texas missions: Juliana Barr, *Peace Came in the Form of a Woman: Indians and Spaniards in the Texas Borderlands* (Chapel Hill: University of North Carolina Press, 2007), 299.

146. Mercedes Gómez Mont and Rafael Camacho Guzmán, *Las misiones de Sierra Gorda* (Querétaro: Gobierno del Estado de Querétaro, 1985), 81–82.

147. Duns Scotus is also depicted on the church's ceiling.

148. Fernández Gracia notes that the estimated construction dates for the Landa church coincided with the declaration of the Virgin of the Immaculate Conception as patron of Spain and its colonies, perhaps influencing in the mission's name and theme. Fernández Gracia, *Iconografía de Sor María de Ágreda*, 153.

149. Monique Gustin, *El barroco en la Sierra Gorda: Misiones franciscanas en el Estado de Querétaro, Siglo XVIII* (Mexico City: Instituto Nacional de Antropologia e Historia, 1969), 146–47.

150. Francisco Palóu, *La vida de Junípero Serra* (Ann Arbor, MI: University Microfilms, 1966).

151. Ibid., 7.

152. Ibid., 8.

153. Ibid.

154. Ibid.

155. Ibid.

156. Ibid.

157. Ibid., 327.

158. Ibid., 290.

159. Ibid.

160. *Palóu's Life of Junípero Serra*, trans. Maynard Geiger (Washington, DC: Academy of American Franciscan History, 1955), 408.

161. Per an 1800 inventory of the San Fernando library, documented by Serra historian Maynard Geiger (ibid.).

162. Ibid.

163. Serra, *Writings of Junípero Serra*, 1:64.

164. Lino Gomez Canedo, *De México a la Alta California* (México: Editorial Jus, 1969), 79.

165. Serra, *Writings of Junípero Serra*, 1:184.

166. Ibid.

167. Ibid., 1:182.

168. Ibid., 1:184.

169. Palóu, *La vida de Junípero Serra*, 137.

170. Ibid., 127.

171. Ibid., 122.

172. Geiger, *Life and Times of Fray Junípero Serra*, 1:293.

173. Palóu, *La vida de Junípero Serra*, 124.

174. "Y por su intercesión [la de Sor María] llevó allí N.P. dos religiosos de nuestra orden y bautizaron al Rey y a mucha gente y allí los martirizaron" (And through her intervention [that of Sor María], our Father [Saint Francis] took two friars from our order there, and they baptized the king and many people, and they were there martyred); Benavides and Ágreda, *Tanto que se sacó de una carta* (1730).

175. Carlos Contreras Servín, "Manifiesto que el decreto de este apostólico colegio hizo al rey en 26 de febrero de 1776. Sobre los nuevos descubrimientos en la alta California," *Revista de Historia de América* 130 (2002): 210.

176. Geiger, *Life and Times of Fray Junípero Serra*, 1:295–96.

177. The text was in part written to address concerns regarding a threat to the region by Russian interests; see Carlos Contreras Servín, "La frontera norte de la Nueva España y las exploraciones en el Pacífico. Siglo XVIII," *Revista de Historia de América* 130 (2002): 179.

178. Friars Francisco Pangua, José García, Juan Antonio Pico, Rafael Verger, Juan Ignacio Gaston, Esteban Antonio Pérez de Arenaza, Juan Ramos de Lora, and Domingo Bengoechea are listed among the *Manifiesto*'s signers (ibid., 180).

179. "Manifiesto que el decreto de este apostólico colegio hizo al rey en 26 de febrero de 1776. Sobre los nuevos descubrimientos en la alta California" (ibid., 185).

180. Ibid.

181. Ibid., 193.

182. Ibid.

183. Ibid.

184. Ibid., 194.

185. Ibid., 197.

186. Ibid. As the *Manifiesto* cited the *Tanto que se sacó* to prove Sor María's knowledge about Quivira, a copy of it was attached to the letter, for the king's perusal (ibid.).

187. Ibid., 198.

188. Ibid.

189. Ibid., 199.

190. Ibid., 201.

191. "There is a common belief that she came from Spain in a miraculous manner."

192. Basilio Arrillaga, *Defensa de la Mística Ciudad de Dios de . . . Sor María de Jesus Agreda contra la censura que en nombre propio y bajo el de el illustrísimo Bossuet ha publicado El Constitucional, etc* (México, 1844).

193. Fray Kino's Río Azul has been hypothesized to be the present-day Río Hardy or Río Pescadero, or a branch of the Gila River.

194. Eusebio Francisco Kino and Francisco Fernández del Castillo, *Las misiones de Sonora y Arizona. Comprendiendo: celestiales y la Relación diaria de la entrada del padre Eusebio Francisco Kino (Kuhne)*, ed. Francisco Fernández del Castillo, Publicaciones del Archivo General de la Nacion (Mexico City: Editorial Cultura, 1913), 8:70.

195. Ibid., 8:70–71.

196. Manje, *Luz de tierra incógnita*, 10, 266.

197. Ibid., 267.

198. The introduction to *Luz de tierra incógnita* remarks of Manje's unknown biography that "no se tienen más noticias biográficas que las que él mismo intercala en su obra" (there are no other biographical details about him aside from those he himself includes in his work). Francisco Fernández Del Castillo, introduction to *Luz de Tierra Incógnita en la América Septentrional y Diario de las Exploraciones en Sonora*, ed. Francisco Fernández Del Castillo, Publicaciones Archivo General de la Nación (México: Talleres Gráficos de la Nación, 1926), vii.

199. Manje, *Luz de Tierra Incógnita*, 10, 7.

200. Ibid.

201. Ibid.

202. Ibid., 11.

203. Ibid.

204. Ibid.

205. Ibid., 14.

206. Ibid., 41–42.

207. Ibid., 42–43.

208. Ibid., 43.

209. Ibid., 44–46.

210. Ibid., 46–48.

211. Ibid., 59–64.

212. Ibid., 183.

213. Ibid.

214. Ibid., 187.

215. Ibid., 188, 92–93.

216. Ibid., 191.

217. Ibid., 192–93.

218. Ibid., 194–96.

219. Gerónimo Zarate Salmerón, "Relaciones de todas las cosas que en el Nuevo-Mexico se han visto y sabido, asi por mar como por tierra, desde el

año de 1538 hasta el de 1626, por el padre Gerónimo de Zarate Salmerón," in *Documentos para la historia de México* (México: Imprenta de Vicente García Torres, 1856).

220. Manje, *Luz de Tierra Incógnita*, 10, 197.

221. This may have been a reference to the painting of Sor Luisa de Carrión that the Jumanos reference in the *1630 Memorial* (ibid., 198).

222. Ibid.

223. Ibid., 199.

224. Ibid., 201.

225. Luis González Rodríguez, introduction to *Etnología y misión en la Pimería Alta: 1715–1740*, ed. Luis González Rodríguez (Mexico City: Universidad Nacional Autónoma de México, 1977), 9.

226. Manje borrowed some of his material from Fray Velarde also; historian Luis González Rodríguez suggests that the friar's writings "completaban perfectamente el plan de Manje y por eso los utilizó, dando pleno crédito al autor" (perfectly complemented Manje's plan, and for this reason he used them, crediting their author) (ibid., 20).

227. Manje, *Luz de Tierra Incógnita*, 10, 330–31.

228. In the early eighteenth century, the idea of "Florida" was expansive and mutable.

229. González Rodríguez, *Etnología y misión en la Pimería Alta*, 229.

230. Ibid., 232.

231. Ibid.

232. José Agustín de Campos, "José Agustín de Campos y la conquista del Moqui," in *Etnología y misión en la Pimería Alta, 1715–1740*, ed. Luis González Rodríguez (México: Universidad Autónoma de México, 1977), 256.

233. Ibid.

234. Rima de Valbona, *Cosecha de pescadores* (San José, Costa Rica: Editorial Costa Rica, 1988), 41–42.

235. Ibid.

236. *Chronografía sagrada de la vida de Christo Nuestro Redemptor: Predicación evangélica, con las circunstancias de lugar, y tiempo en que obró los misterios de nuestra redemption, obras de su omnipotencia, y maravillas de su gracia en Maria Santíssima, y en el seraphico padre S. Francisco, y su apostólica religión* (México: Por Doña Maria de Benavides, Viuda de Juan de Ribera, 1696).

237. He claims that the *1630 Memorial* was published in Mexico ("cuya [de Benavides] relación se imprimió en México, año 1630, en la imprenta de Bernardo Calderón," "whose [Benavides's] report was published in Mexico in 1630, on the press of Bernardo Calderón) at the order of Archbishop Francisco Manso y Zúñiga, corroborating José Toribio Medina's documentation of the text's seventeenth-century Mexican publication.

238. This is predicated on the assumption that the 1630 Mexican printing of the *Memorial* Fray Vetancurt cites does not name Sor María either.

239. Vetancurt, *Teatro mexicano*, 303.

240. Villagutierre Soto-Mayor held this position from 1695 to 1709; Maribel Lárraga, "La mística de la feminidad en la obra de Juan Villagutierre Sotomayor" (Albuquerque: University of New Mexico Press, 1999), 3.

241. Ibid., 8.

242. Juan de Villagutierre Soto-Mayor, *Historia de la conquista, pérdida y restauración del reino de la Nueva México en la América Septentrional. Historia de la Nueva México.*, ed. Alfred Charles Herrera (Madrid: Alfred Charles Herrera, 1953), 113.

243. Ibid., 115.

244. Ibid., 121.

245. Ibid., 145.

246. Ibid.

247. Ibid., 128.

248. Ibid., 127.

249. Lárraga, "La mística de la feminidad," 162–63.

250. Andrés González de Barcia Carballido y Zúñiga, *Ensayo cronologico, para la historia general de la Florida* (Madrid: N. Rodríguez Franco, 1723).

251. Ibid., 197.

252. The "Teguas"/"Tejas" were at times thought to be found in the region of "La Florida" that Barcia documents (ibid., 192).

253. Ibid., 193.

254. Ibid., 5.

255. Ibid.

256. Ibid.

257. Francisco Antonio de la Rosa Figueroa, "Becerro general menológico y chronológico," in *Alonso de Benavides' Revised Memorial of 1634*, ed. Frederick Webb Hodge, George P. Hammond, and Agapito Rey (Albuquerque: University of New Mexico Press, 1945), 200.

258. Hodge, Hammond, and Rey do not document where Fray Figueroa's manuscript was located, nor do they provide much information about the document beyond what they include in the appendix to their translation of the *1634 Memorial*. From the fact that others of Fray Figueroa's manuscripts (microfilms of which are available at the Bancroft Library) originated from the Convento de Nuestro Padre San Francisco in Mexico City, it is probable that the *Becerro* originated from that same collection; Francisco Antonio De la Rosa Figueroa and Hubert Howe Bancroft, "Vindicias de la Verdad. ms., 1774 Jan. 8" (Mexico City, Convento de Nuestro Padre San Francisco, 1774), Ayer Collection at the Newberry Library.

259. Francisco Antonio De la Rosa Figueroa, "Bezerro general menológico y chronológico," in Benavides, *1634 Memorial*.

260. Ibid., 201.

261. Ibid.

262. Ibid., 202.

263. Ibid. Fray Figueroa continues to reference *La mística ciudad de dios* as he reconstructs Fray Benavides's biography after his visit to Sor María's convent.

264. Ibid., 204.

265. José Antonio Pichardo, *Pichardo's Treatise on the Limits of Louisiana and Texas*, Vol. 2, trans. Charles Hackett (Austin: University of Texas Press, 1934).

266. Carlos Castañeda, "Pichardo, José Antonio," in *Handbook of Texas Online* (Texas State Historical Association), http://www.tshaonline.org/hand book/online/articles/fpi01.

267. Ibid.: "Talamantes, Melchor de."

268. Melchor de Talamantes, "Opúsculo VI: El Reverendo Padre Fray Doctor Melchor de Talamantes solicitando documentos para dar el lleno á su comision se entró en la Biblioteca de la Real y Pontifica Universidad de esta corte," Spanish Colonial Research Center, National Park Service, Albuquerque, NM, University of New Mexico.

269. Ibid., 31.

270. Ibid.

271. Ibid.

272. Ibid.

273. Pichardo, *Pichardo's Treatise*, 2:524, 525, 526.

274. Ibid., 2:523.

275. Ibid.

276. Ibid.

277. Ibid., 2:518–23.

278. Ibid., 2:519.

279. Ibid.

FIVE   Blue Lady of Lore

1. James L. Cleveland, "Did Lady in Blue Visit Arizona without Ever Leaving Spanish Convent?" *The Southwesterner*, February 1967, 13.

2. Some more contemporary interpretations of the narrative as lore invoke the history itself as folklore. See Jennifer Curtis, "Beyond Texas Folklore: The Woman in Blue," in *Cowboys, Cops, Killers, and Ghosts: Legends and Lore in Texas*, ed. Kenneth Untiedt (Denton: University of North Texas Press, 2013), 196–204.

3. As I suggest in this book, *La mística ciudad de dios* was the primary vehicle for the narrative's early transmission in colonial New Spain. Yet most of the folk stories that reference historical sources in this chapter cite Fray Benavides's *1630* and *1634 Memorials*, and the *Tanto que se sacó de una carta*. These three texts were republished in English in the early twentieth century, making them more easily accessible to readers at that time than *La mística ciudad de dios*. The ironic result of their repeated citation in folkloric and scholarly studies has contributed to an overestimation of their historical influence during the colonial era.

4. Enrique Lamadrid, "Las dos Lloronas de Santa Fe," in *Santa Fe Nativa: A Collection of Nuevomexicano Writing*, ed. Rosalie C. Otero et al. (Albuquerque: University of New Mexico Press, 2010); Domino Perez, *There Was a Woman: La Llorona from Folklore to Popular Culture* (Austin: University of Texas Press, 2008); Américo Paredes, *With His Pistol in His Hand* (Austin: University of Texas Press, 1958).

5. For studies that examine how certain historical, mythical, or religious figures are invoked and transformed through collective memory, see the following: Jean-Claude Schmitt, *The Holy Greyhound: Guinefort, Healer of Children since the Thirteenth Century* (New York: Cambridge University Press, 1983); Craig Harline, *Miracles at the Jesus Oak* (New York: Doubleday, 2003); Paul Vanderwood, *Juan Soldado* (Durham, NC: Duke University Press, 2004); Juan Javier Pescador, *Crossing Borders with the Santo Niño de Atocha* (Albuquerque: University of New Mexico Press, 2009); Perez, *There Was a Woman*.

6. Schmitt, *The Holy Greyhound*, 40.

7. May Raizizun, "A Lady Veiled in Mystery (Legend? or History?)," El Paso Public Library.

8. The fifth chapter of Perez's *There Was a Woman* is particularly useful in this sense and discusses occurrences of La Llorona produced by individuals not from the traditional group of production.

9. Enrique Lamadrid, "From Santiago at Ácoma to the Diablo in the Casinos: Four Centuries of Foundational Milagro Narratives in New Mexico," in *Expressing New Mexico: Nuevomexicano Creativity, Ritual, and Memory*, ed. Phillip B. Gonzales (Tucson: University of Arizona Press, 2007), 42.

10. Rafaela Castro, *Dictionary of Chicano Literature* (Santa Barbara, CA: ABC-CLIO, 2000), 150.

11. Even within the corpus of Mexican American folk legends, the Lady in Blue narrative is unique. Few colonial-era motifs or subjects have crossed into modern Mexican American imagination as readily as has the Lady in Blue. Only a handful of such legends have survived in the contemporary folk traditions of Mexican American and Mexican border communities.

12. For a brief but insightful discussion of the misconstrual of the Hermanos de Nuestro Padre Jesús Nazareno, see Enrique Lamadrid and Gabriel Meléndez, "Review Essay: The Penitente Brotherhood," *New Mexico Historical Review* 82, no. 1 (2007).

13. Juan Bautista Rael, *The New Mexican Alabado* (Stanford, CA: Stanford University Press, 1951).

14. The full text of the alabado can be found in Clark Colahan and Alfred Rodriguez, "A New Mexico Alabado about María de Jesús de Agreda: Reflections on Its Popular Retention and Transmission," *Liberal and Fine Arts Review* 5, no. 1 (1985).

15. Literary scholars Clark Colahan and Alfred Rodriguez surmise in their analysis of the alabado that Sor María de Ágreda was the song's original focus.

16. Original and translation in Clark Colahan and Alfred Rodriguez, "A New Mexico Alabado about María de Jesús de Agreda: Reflections on Its Popular Retention and Transmission." *Liberal and Fine Arts Review* 5, no. 1 (1985): 5–6.

17. The alabado's indirect reference to the Immaculate Conception involves the repetition of the common Marian phrase "bendita sea tu pureza," referencing the Virgin Mary's purity.

18. Among several possible sources for this conflation of Santa Teresa of Avila and Sor María de Jesús de Ágreda is St. Theresa of Ávila, María de Jesús de

Ágreda, Jerónimo Gracián, Francisco Herrero y Bayona, *Avisos originales de Santa Teresa de Jesús: dos de sus cartas, una preciosa oración y una promesa de escritura: además una carta de la v.m. María de Jesús, hija de la santa, y otra de v.p. fr. Gerónimo Gracián de la Madre de Dios, primer provincial de la descalcez* (Madrid: Imprenta y librería de Moya y Plaza, 1881).

19. Josefina Muriel, "Women Writers during the Viceroyalty," in *Literary Cultures of Latin America: A Comparative History*, ed. Mario J. Valdés and Djelal Kadir (Oxford: Oxford University Press, 2004), 284.

20. Colahan and Rodriguez, "A New Mexico Alabado," 9.

21. Arroyo Hondo and Torreón, New Mexico, are approximately 130 miles apart.

22. See, for example, Richard R. Flores, *Remembering the Alamo: Memory, Modernity, and the Master Symbol*, History, Culture, and Society Series (Austin: University of Texas Press, 2002); David Montejano, *Anglos and Mexicans in the Making of Texas, 1836–1986* (Austin: University of Texas Press, 1987).

23. Carlos Castañeda, *Our Catholic Heritage in Texas, 1519–1936*, 7 vols. (Austin, TX: Von Boeckmann-Jones Company, 1936–58), preface to Vol. 1.

24. Benavides, *1630 Memorial*, 190.

25. Ibid., 276.

26. Ibid., 278.

27. Ibid. It appears neither historian was aware of Sor María's writing and its influence in colonial Mexico.

28. As I mentioned in the introduction, even Sor María's twentieth-century biographer T. D. Kendrick expressed reservations about the nun's bilocations. See Kendrick, *Mary of Agreda*, 55.

29. Richard Sturmberg, *History of San Antonio and of the Early Days in Texas* (San Antonio, TX: Standard Printing Co., 1920), 28.

30. Castañeda, *Our Catholic Heritage in Texas*, foreword to Vol. 1.

31. Ibid., 1:200.

32. Ibid., 1:203.

33. Castañeda takes pains to describe Sor María and her mystical travel in positive terms. Here, he cites Fiscar Marison's (Fr. George Blatter) edition of *La mística ciudad de dios*: "The miracle of bilocation was in fact more remarkable and lasted a longer time than that recorded anywhere in the lives of the saints. Her good sense, her truthfulness, her sincerity, her humility, her unselfish love of God and man eminently adapted her for the communication of message from God to man" (Castañeda, *Our Catholic Heritage in Texas*, 199). Excerpt from María de Jesús de Ágreda, *City of God: The Divine History and Life of the Virgin Mother of God Manifested to Mary of Agreda for the Encouragement of Men*, 4 vols., trans. Fiscar Marison (George Blatter), (Mount Vernon, OH: Louis W. Bernicken, 1902).

34. Carlos E. Castañeda, "The Woman in Blue," *The Age of Mary: An Exclusively Marian Magazine*, January-February 1958, "The Mystical City of God" issue. This issue was dedicated to Sor María and *La mística ciudad de dios*.

35. Ibid., 24.

36. Ibid., 28.

37. Ibid., 28–29.

38. Jovita González, "Catholic Heroines of Texas," *The Southern Messenger*, August 20, 1936.

39. John Morán González, *Border Renaissance: The Texas Centennial and the Emergence of Mexican American Literature*, 1st ed. (Austin: University of Texas Press, 2009), introduction.

40. Ibid.

41. Ibid.

42. Jovita González, "Catholic Heroines of Texas," 2.

43. Ibid.

44. Ibid.

45. John Morán González, *Border Renaissance*, 178.

46. Ibid., 22.

47. Jovita González, "Catholic Heroines of Texas," 2.

48. For more on the fraught relationship between Jovita González and Dobie, and González's subtle resistance of dominant paradigms in Mexican American folklore studies, see Jovita González, *Dew on the Thorn*, Recovering the U.S. Hispanic Literary Heritage (Houston: Arte Público Press, 1997), xv–xxviii; José Limón, *Dancing with the Devil* (Madison: University of Wisconsin Press, 1994), 60–75; María Eugenia Cotera, "Engendering a 'Dialectics of Our America': Jovita González's Pluralist Dialogue as Feminist Testimonio," in *Las obreras: Chicana Politics of Work and Family*, ed. Vicki Ruiz (Los Angeles: UCLA Chicano Studies Research Center Publications, 2000); Anna M. Nogar, "La décima musa errante: Sor Juana en la ficción mexicana/americana," in *Asaltos a la historia: Reimaginando la ficción histórica en Hispanoamérica*, ed. Brian Price (México: Ediciones Eón, 2015).

49. J. Frank Dobie, *Tales of Old Time Texas* (Austin: University of Texas Press, 1984).

50. Flores, *Remembering the Alamo*, 75–76.

51. Ibid., 76.

52. Ibid., 66.

53. Ibid., 70.

54. Adina De Zavala, *History and Legends of the Alamo and Other Missions in and around San Antonio* (San Antonio, TX: privately published by author, 1917), dedication.

55. Regarding the organization's preservation of the Alamo structure, the book states: "It was the De Zavala Daughters versus commercialism!" (De Zavala, *History and Legends of the Alamo*, 50).

56. Ibid., 58.

57. Ibid., 59.

58. Ibid., 58.

59. Ibid., 55.

60. Ibid., 61.

61. Ibid.

62. Ibid.

63. Ibid.

64. Ibid., 62.

65. Ibid., 61.

66. Ibid., 62.

67. Ibid., 61.

68. Ibid., 106.

69. This lack of sourcing can be confusing, as De Zavala includes very specific anecdotes, the origins of which are not clear. For example, she claims: "These towns [of the Texas natives Sor María visited] consisted of a number of round straw houses roofed in conical shape. While they kept a perpetual fire burning, they were not exactly fire worshippers, though they believed that should the fire die out they would all perish. The fire was built of four logs, one log each pointing north, south, east and west. There was one Great house where they kept the principal fire and from whence the other fires were brought. Great piles of logs for the replenishing of the fire were kept outside the Great House near at hand" (ibid., 104).

70. Ibid., 104. In the historical section, De Zavala refers to Sor María by an Anglicized, secularized, and abbreviated version of her full Spanish name ("Mary Coronel").

71. Lamadrid, "From Santiago at Ácoma to the Diablo in the Casinos."

72. For more on the infantilizing and marginalizing representation of Mexican Americans and their lore, which had become a predominant paradigm when González and De Zavala wrote, see Limón, *Dancing with the Devil*, 43–59.

73. Jane Eppinga, *Arizona Twilight Tales: Good Ghosts, Evil Spirits and Blue Ladies* (Boulder, CO: Pruett, 2000).

74. Ibid., 144.

75. Richard Alan Young and Judy Dockrey Young, *Ghost Stories from the American Southwest* (Little Rock, AR: August House, 1991).

76. Ibid., 117.

77. Ibid.

78. Ibid.

79. Marta Weigle and Peter White, *The Lore of New Mexico*, 1st ed. (Albuquerque: University of New Mexico Press, 1988).

80. Charles H. Hemisath, "The Mysterious Woman in Blue," in *Legends of Texas*, ed. J. Frank Dobie (Dallas, TX: Southern Methodist University Press, 1976).

81. Frank Abernethy, ed. *The Folklore of Texan Cultures* (Denton: University of North Texas Press, 2000).

82. Elba C. de Baca, "The Lady in Blue," in *Las Mujeres Hablan*, ed. Tey Diana Rebolledo, Erlinda González-Berry, and Teresa Márquez (Albuquerque: El Norte Publications/Academia, 1988).

83. Young and Young, *Ghost Stories from the American Southwest*.

84. Jay Sharp, *Texas Unexplained: Strange Tales and Mysteries from the Lone Star State* (Austin: University of Texas Press, 1999).

85. Elba C. DeBaca, "Folk Tales of New Mexico," Center for Southwest Research University of New Mexico, Albuquerque.

86. William Edward Syers, *Off the Beaten Trail*, Vol. 3 (Ingram, TX: OBT, 1965).

87. Jimmy Banks, "The Lady in Blue," *Texas Parade Magazine*, October 1952.

88. "'The Lady in Blue' and 'A Mission under Our Lady's Care,'" *Extension Magazine*, June 1, 2007. The organization is dedicated to supporting Catholic missions.

89. Examples of these types of accounts abound in library collections, including those at the University of New Mexico Center for Southwest Research, and at the El Paso Public Library. The following sources were provided by the El Paso Public Library: Paul A. F. Walter, "Yesteryears in the Spanish Southwest," *Santa Fe New Mexican*, October 21, 1928; Raizizun, "A Lady Veiled in Mystery"; Edna Hoffman Evans, "The Mysterious Lady in Blye," *Arizona Highways*, 1959; Ed Syers, "Catholic Legend Brought Back from the Past," *El Paso Times*, May 30, 1965; Marjorie White, "Miraculous Visitations Form Gripping Southwest Mystery," *El Paso Times*, January 30, 1966; Ann Van Atta, "Pecos River Pageantry," *The Junior Historian*, May 1958; Cleveland, "Did Lady in Blue Visit Arizona"; Edmond J. P. Schmitt, "Ven. Maria de Jesus de Agreda: A Correction," *Texas State Historical Quarterly* 1, no. 2 (1897).

90. Margaret Proctor Redondo and James Griffith, "Valley of Iron," *The Journal of Arizona History* 34, no. 3 (1993), 234–36, 258–60.

91. Ibid., 258.

92. Ibid., 259.

93. Ibid., 260.

94. Ibid., 236.

95. Ibid., 236.

96. Ibid., 258. Proctor Redondo attributes her knowledge of the Lady in Blue narrative, and possibly the story of the thwarted filibuster mission, to a cowboy named Carlos Casasola: "Casasola was reluctant to tell the story of the Lady in Blue" (ibid., 259).

97. Joseph F. Combs, *Legends of the Pineys* (San Antonio, TX: Naylor Co., 1965).

98. Ibid., 76.

99. Ibid., 87.

100. Ibid., 79. Combs relates a physical description later in the story: "She always wore the same silk dress and walked in sandaled feet. She was described as about five feet nine inches tall, a model of form and dignity, and standing straight with a most penetrating and tender expression. She wore no jewels or beads, and there was nothing to detract from her beauty and manners. She had teeth as white as pearls and flowing black hair that was always hanging over her shoulders, but gracefully groomed. She walked with the air of a princess, and at all times appeared to be absolutely sure of herself. Her deep blue eyes could stare you into a feeling of inferiority, and everyone had a profound respect for her, it was said" (ibid., 84–85).

101. Ibid., 79–80.

102. Ibid., 80–81.

103. Ibid., 82.

104. Ibid., 81.

105. Ibid., 84.

106. Ibid., 88. Jovita González's article likewise mentions the lore of "Angelina," but she is clearly differentiated from the Lady in Blue.

107. Harry Pettey, "Names and Creeks along Historic Roads Are Stories in Themselves," *Daily Sentinel*, July 9, 1963.

108. Ibid.

109. Ibid.

110. Ibid.

111. Ibid.

112. Interestingly, the introduction to this text, written by the project director of the Texas Women's History Project, Mary Beth Rogers, states that the book's purpose is to demonstrate that "Texas women were influential in the development of this state." The book is careful to demarcate the differences between fact and fiction: "There should be no conflict between the legends that have grown up about some Texas women, and the actual facts about the lives of most Texas women—as long as we know what is factual and what is legendary. Facts inform us; legends enrich us"; Francis Edward Abernethy, ed., *Legendary Ladies of Texas* (Denton: University of North Texas Press, 1994), 6.

113. Ibid., 9.

114. Ibid.

115. Ibid., 13.

116. Ibid.

117. Ibid.

118. Ibid., 14.

119. Ibid., 12.

120. The entry following Sor María in *Legendary Ladies of Texas* is that of Angelina.

121. Abernethy, *Legendary Ladies of Texas*, 13.

122. Cleve Hallenbeck and Juanita H. Williams, *Legends of the Spanish Southwest* (Glendale: CA: Arthur H. Clark Co., 1938), 302.

123. Ibid., 301.

124. Ibid., 302.

125. Ibid., 305.

126. Ibid. Further racializing their informants, the authors add that the secret tunnels under San Antonio (the home to De Zavala's Lady in Blue) are familiar to "the Mexicans of San Antonio." They add to De Zavala's subterranean Lady in Blue the ability to leave her underground palace to bless those in need, particularly children.

127. Ibid., 306.

128. Ibid.

129. Ibid., 308.

130. Ibid., 309.

131. Ibid., 310.

132. Ibid., 309.

133. Ibid., 310.

134. Ibid., 314.

135. Ibid., 311.

136. Ibid., 312.

137. Ibid., 313.

138. Ibid., 312.

139. Ibid., 313.

140. They share with their contemporaries a reference to Will Robinson, who claimed the Navajo tribe anticipated the Lady in Blue's imminent return. No source is cited.

141. Cleve Hallenbeck, "The Blue Lady," *New Mexico Magazine*, February 1945. Hallenbeck writes, in support of the idea of Sor María's travels to the Southwest: "And what could have been that young woman's reason for secrecy? There is no evidence, not even a suggestion, that she ever was seen on this side of the ocean by any one [*sic*] of her own race. In New Mexico, she was but two or three day's travel from Spanish settlements along the Rio Grande, but she never visited any of them. I advance no supernatural theory: I merely recite the known facts. . . . I have suggested that Maria Coronel first applied the name Gran Quivira to Tabirá, or at least to the district wherein Tabirá is situated" (ibid., 31, 35).

142. Alice Bullock, *Living Legends of the Santa Fe Country* (Denver, CO: Green Mountain, 1970).

143. A caption under the picture of the Quarai ruins muses, "Did the Blue Lady visit here?" (ibid., 70).

144. Ibid., 72.

145. Ibid.

146. Ibid.

147. May Raizizun, "The Blue Lady," *New Mexico Magazine*, February 1962, 23.

148. Ibid., 22.

149. Ibid. Raizizun, like De Zavala, inserts herself indirectly into the Lady in Blue narrative, saying that her family's indigenous servants nicknamed her after the woman of legend: "'Why do you call me Little Blue Lady,' I asked [Irineo] once, and he replied, 'Because you are kind to us as the Blue Lady was kind to my people hundreds of years ago'" (ibid.).

150. G. L. Campbell, "The Blue Lady: Interview with Eileen Mattison," Baughman Folklore Collection, Center for Southwest Research, University of New Mexico, Albuquerque.

151. Ibid.

152. J. M. Holman, "The Lady in Blue," in *Hispanic Legends from New Mexico: Narratives from the R. D. Jameson Collection*, ed. Stanley Robe (Berkeley: University of California Press, 1980), 532.

153. Keleher's 1936 play *Lady in Blue* will be discussed in the next chapter.

154. Julia Keleher, "Lady in Blue: Interview with Stephanie Redd," Baughman Folklore Collection, Center for Southwest Research, University of New Mexico, Albuquerque.

155. Ibid.

156. Mark B. Gens, "The Blue Lady: Interview with M. Kathleen Nicoli" (ibid.).

157. Ibid.

158. Ibid.

159. Mrs. Ed Dwyer, "Interview with Margaret Castonguay" (ibid.).

160. Corinne P. Sze, "St. Catherine's Indian School," http://www.new mexicohistory.org/filedetails.php?fileID=21300.

161. Carol Vogel, Personal interview with Edward O'Brien, Santa Fe, NM, January 4, 2007.

162. Shannon Murray was the caretaker of the St. Katharine's grounds in 2007, when this interview took place. Shannon Murray, "Personal Interview," 2007.

SIX Sor María and the Lady in Blue in Contemporary Cultural Imagination

1. David Rose, ed. *They Call Me Naughty Lola: Personal Ads from the London Review of Books* (New York: Scribner, 2006), 139–40. Many thanks to my colleague Mary Quinn for this reference.

2. Domino Perez's cataloging of La Llorona artifacts in *There Was a Woman* was a model for this chapter's organization. See Perez, *There Was a Woman*.

3. Benavides, *1630 Memorial*; *Fray Alonso de Benavides' Revised Memorial of 1634*, trans. Agapito Rey, Coronado Cuarto Centennial Publications, 1540–1940 (Albuquerque: University of New Mexico Press, 1945).

4. Tey Diana Rebolledo, *Nuestras Mujeres* (Albuquerque: El Norte/ Academia, 1992); Castro, *Dictionary of Chicano Literature*; Enrique Lamadrid, "From Santiago at Ácoma to the Diablo in the Casinos."

5. Luis Alberto Urrea, *The Devil's Highway* (New York: Little, Brown and Company, 2004).

6. Ibid., dedication.

7. Ibid., 3.

8. Ibid., 5.

9. Ibid.

10. Ibid., 6.

11. Ibid., 10.

12. Ibid., 6.

13. Ibid., 11.

14. Ibid.

15. This is representative of a growing body of cultural and literary production denouncing the risk posed to immigrants during desert border crossings. Two other works allude to the Lady in Blue in this context: John Annerino, *Dead in Their Tracks: Crossing America's Desert Borderlands* (New York: Four Walls Eight Windows, 1999); Eric Holland, "Angel in the Desert," in *Without Borders*, created in 2004 by CD Baby, https://store.cdbaby.com/cd/ericholland.

16. Ana Castillo, *So Far from God: A Novel* (New York: W. W. Norton, 1993).

17. Ibid., 244.

18. Ibid., 241.

19. Ibid.

20. Ibid., 244.

21. Ibid., 245.

22. Ibid., 244.

23. Ibid., 238.

24. Jane Eppinga, *Arizona Twilight Tales: Good Ghosts, Evil Spirits and Blue Ladies* (Boulder, CO: Pruett, 2000).

25. Ibid., xi.

26. Ibid. As presented, this portrayal of La Llorona as guilty of "heinous crime" is unproblematized by contemporary critical readings of the folk figure, such as those of Chicana scholar Cherríe Moraga and others.

27. Ibid.

28. Ibid., 139.

29. Ibid., 149.

30. Dee Strickland Johnson, *Arizona Herstory: Tales from Her Storied Past* (Phoenix: Cowboy Miner Productions, 2003).

31. Ibid., 10.

32. Ibid. Strickland Johnson encourages the reader to hearken back to these sources after reading the poems (ibid., 11).

33. Strickland Johnson cites Jim Griffith's introduction to Margaret Proctor Redondo's account, which we discussed in chapter 5. See Proctor Redondo and Griffith, "Valley of Iron."

34. Strickland Johnson, *Arizona Herstory*, 170.

35. Ibid., 180–81.

36. Ibid., 181.

37. Ed DeGrazia, *The Blue Lady: A Desert Fantasy of Papago Land* (Tucson: DeGrazia Studios, 1957).

38. Julia Keleher, "Lady in Blue," Keleher Family Private Collection, 1936.

39. Lisa Sandlin and Catherine Ferguson, *You Who Make the Sky Bend: Saints and Archetypes of the Human Condition* (Montrose, CO: Pinyon, 2011).

40. Neither author was a member of the tribes they describe in their works.

41. DeGrazia, *The Blue Lady*, 1, 3.

42. Ibid.

43. Ibid.

44. Julia Keleher, "Lady in Blue Program and Playbill," College of Fine Arts Collection, Center for Southwest Research, University of New Mexico, Albuquerque.

45. Ibid. Historical sources for this claim not provided are currently unavailable.

46. Original script graciously provided by Keleher's nephew, William Keleher.

47. Keleher, "Lady in Blue," 5.

48. Ibid.

49. Ibid., 8.

50. Ibid., 17.

51. Ibid., 1.

52. Ibid.

53. Ibid., 4.

54. Many of the ethnographic details Keleher includes are much more specific to New Mexican tribes than De Grazia's generalizations, but neither work appears to have ethnographic accuracy as its goal.

55. The account draws on published English-language works on the topic: the *1630 Memorial*, and two more recent works, Clark A. Colahan, *The Visions of Sor María de Agreda: Writing Knowledge and Power* (Tucson: University of Arizona Press, 1994); and Marilyn H. Fedewa, *María of Ágreda: Mystical Lady in Blue* (Albuquerque: University of New Mexico Press, 2009).

56. Sandlin and Ferguson, *You Who Make the Sky Bend*, 27–30.

57. Ibid., 29.

58. Ibid.

59. Ibid., 30.

60. Ibid.

61. Peter E. Lopez, *Edward O'Brien, Mural Artist: 1910–1975* (Santa Fe, NM: Sunstone, 2013), 10–11.

62. O'Brien's niece, Carol Vogel, graciously provided these notes. Carol Vogel, "Personal Interview: Edward O'Brien," January 4, 2007.

63. Margaret Phillips Succop and Merle Armitage, *Painter into Artist: The Progress of Edward O'Brien* (Yucca Valley, CA: Manzanita, 1964), 1.

64. Edward O'Brien painted himself on the left-hand side of the image.

65. O'Brien used the students, priests, and nuns living and teaching at St. Katharine's as models for the images. Lopez, *Edward O'Brien, Mural Artist*, 26–27.

66. Succop and Armitage, *Painter into Artist*, 3.

67. Ibid., 1.

68. Victoria Edwards Tester, *Miracles of Sainted Earth* (Albuquerque: University of New Mexico Press, 2002).

69. Ibid., 108.

70. Ibid., 109.

71. Ibid., 108.

72. Ibid.

73. Ibid., 109.

74. Ibid.

75. Ibid., 108.

76. Ibid.

77. Ibid.

78. Ibid., 109.

79. Ibid.

80. Eric Kimmel, *The Lady in the Blue Cloak: Legends from the Texas Missions* (New York: Holiday House, 2006).

81. Ibid., vii.

82. Ibid., 3.

83. Marilyn Thomas Westfall, "Quartet in Blue" (PhD diss., Texas Tech University, 1998).

84. Ibid., 2.

85. Ibid., 10.

86. Ibid., 11.

87. Ibid.

88. Ibid., 16.

89. Ibid., 17.

90. Ibid., 20–21.

91. Ibid., 26.

92. Ibid.

93. Ibid., 31.

94. Ibid., 40.

95. Ibid.

96. Ibid., 43.

97. The introduction to "Diary" is a faux anthropological/archival report by a professor at UC Davis: the fictional M. Martinko. He or she gives an account on the finding of the diary on an old California ranch owned by a woman named Juana Briones in 1970, noting that "the document was donated to the University of California at Berkeley where it was initially examined then archived, though its authenticity was, and still remains, in doubt" (ibid., 47). The introduction goes on to imply that the Cacnumaie who authors the diary was perhaps related to Juana Briones, because she signed the document "María Dolores Briones." A description of the diary from historical and anthropological perspectives, which emphasize Cacnumaie's female agency and critique methods implemented at California missions, follows the initial introduction.

98. Ibid., 127.

99. Ibid., 128.

100. A 2002 talk Westfall presented at the First Unitarian Universalist Church in Lubbock, Texas, alludes to the themes manifested in the two stories, the focus being on the convergence between nationalism and religion in the Lady in Blue figure. Westfall speculated in the talk: "Would anyone in twenty-first century America use the rather innocent perspective of a religious woman to marry nationalism to religion?"; Marilyn Westfall, "Blue Lady of the Plains, Maria Agreda," talk delivered at the First Unitarian Universalist Church, Lubbock, TX, July 2002.

101. Webber and Larson's *Sor María* was performed at several venues in New Mexico over the course of several years. At least 2 three-day series of performances, one at the KiMo Theater in Albuquerque and another at Northern New Mexico Community College in Española, took place. The poster for the NNMCC performance indicates that is was preceded a year before by an earlier production of the work. The discussion of the dance opera is based on the following artifacts: Joseph Webber and Michele Larson, *Sor María* advertisement, Northern New Mexico Community College performance (author's collection); Joseph Webber and Michele Larson, *Sor María* program (author's collection); Joseph Webber and Michele Larson, *Sor María* advertisement, KiMo Theater performance (author's collection).

102. Webber and Larson, *Sor María*.

103. Ibid.

104. Ibid.

105. Ibid.

106. Ibid.

107. Madres Concepcionistas de Ágreda, "María de Jesús de Ágreda," http://www.mariadeagreda.org/rdr.php.

108. Webber and Larson, *Sor María*.

109. Ibid.

110. Ibid.

111. Ibid.

112. Ibid.

113. Ibid.

114. Ibid.

115. Ibid.

116. "The Big Chili," *Good Eats*, Food Network, 2007.

117. George Leonar Herter and Berthe Herter, *Bull Cook and Authentic Historical Recipes and Practices* (Waseca, MN: Herter's, 1970). The Herters' recipe is also cited in A. D. Livingston, *Strictly Chili: Cooking the Best Bowl of Red* (Short Hills, NJ: Burford Books, 2003). Another version of the recipe appears in Larry Torres, "Chile Con Carne María de Agreda/Mystic María Agreda Invents Chile Recipe," in "Blue Lady" Vertical File, Fray Angélico Chávez Library, Santa Fe.

118. Herter and Herter, *Bull Cook and Authentic Historical Recipes and Practices*, 52.

119. Ibid.

120. S. E. Schlosser, *Spooky Southwest: Tales of Hauntings, Strange Happenings and Other Local Lore* (Guilford, CT: Globe Pequot, 2004).

121. Ibid., 170.

122. Ibid., 173.

123. William Jones Wallrich, *The Strange Little Man in the Chili-Red Pants* (Fort Garland, CO: Cottonwood, 1949).

124. Ibid., introduction.

125. Ibid., 3.

126. Ibid., 4.

127. Ibid., 11.

128. Ibid., 12.

129. Ibid., 7.

130. Ibid., 8.

131. Ibid., 7.

132. Bert Wall, *Ghostly Chills: The Devil's Backbone 2* (Austin, TX: Eakin, 2001).

133. Ibid., vii.

134. Ibid., 88.

135. Ibid., 89.

136. Ibid.

137. Ibid., 90.

138. Frances Parkinson Keyes, *I, The King* (New York: McGraw-Hill, 1966).

139. Ibid., 212.

140. Ibid., 227.

141. Ibid., 228.

142. Ibid.

143. Ibid., 229.

144. Lisa Sandlin, *In the River Province* (Dallas, TX: Southern Methodist University Press, 2004).

145. Ibid., 130.

146. Ibid., 136.

147. Ibid., 132.

148. Ibid., 145.

149. Ibid., 159.

150. Ibid., 164.

151. Ibid., 165.

152. Ibid., 131.

153. Javier Sierra, *La dama azul* (Madrid: Ediciones Martín Roca, 2005). The book was translated and published in 2007 in English as *The Lady in Blue*, trans. James Graham (New York: Atria, 2007).

154. Graham, trans., *The Lady in Blue*.

155. Ibid., 329. The Spanish original has a much shorter appendix than the English edition.

156. The most recent of these commemorations, the "8th annual Sor María de Jesús de Ágreda 'The Lady in Blue' Celebration," was scheduled to take place May 22, 2016, in San Angelo, Texas, at the San Angelo Museum of Fine Arts. The materials announcing and promoting the event indicate that it was in keeping with previous celebrations in the series that sought to advance Sor María's case for canonization. A flier states that participants could "join in the effort to have the Church declare her a saint." A Mass concelebrated by the current bishop of San Angelo, Michal Sis, and Bishop Emeritus Michael Pfeifer is among the activities listed, and the bishops were scheduled to participate in a procession to members of the Jumano tribe (stationed by the Rio Conchas) to greet them in a manner "symbolic of the time the Jumanos greeted the Franciscan Friars at Isleta, New Mexico" (Jerry Javier Luján, announcement, April 19, 2016).

157. Brian Bethel, "Second Festival Likely to Atttract Diverse Interest," *San Angelo Standard-Times*, June 17, 2010.

158. Laurel L. Scott, "Event Honors Lady in Blue," *San Angelo Standard-Times*, June 11, 2010.

159. Brian Bethel, "Lady in Blue Calls across Time," *San Angelo Standard-Times*, June 17, 2010.

160. Ami Mizell-Flint, "Powwow Welcomes Culture to San Angelo," *San Angelo Standard-Times*, June 17, 2010.

161. "Mission Ongoing for Jumano Indians," *San Angelo Standard-Times*, June 20, 2009.

162. Laurel Scott, "Vision of the Past: Pain Rock Drawings Are Starts of Ceremony," *San Angelo Standard-Times*, June 21, 2009.

163. Becca Nelson Sankey, "Celebrating Lady in Blue," *San Angelo Standard-Times*, June 19, 2009; Cynthia Jordan, *The Lady in Blue* (San Angelo: Emerald Eagle Music, 2009).

164. The Diocese of San Angelo includes on its homepage a link to the "Lady in Blue," in which Bishop Emeritus Michael Pfeifer offers an explanation of her relevance to the diocese. See Diocese of San Angelo, "Lady in Blue," http://sanangelodiocese.org/lady-in-blue.

165. Rick Smith, "Rick Smith: Lady in Blue Stuck to Her Faith," *San Angelo Standard-Times*, June 20, 2009; Becca Nelson Sankey, "Lasting Effect of Lady in Blue's Story," *San Angelo Standard-Times*, June 19, 2009.

166. Ron Cosper, "Sister Maria Saved Jumanos from Spanish Rule," *San Angelo Standard-Times*, June 16, 2010.

167. Ibid.

168. Event organizer Jerry Javier Luján provided information about the 2014 event; I do not have information about the previous three pilgrimages. An article on the Lady in Blue, which documents what may have been a small pilgrimage in 2012, was published in the Archdiocese of Santa Fe newspaper *People of God* in May 2012. It mentions a roundtable talk at the National Hispanic Cultural Center. See Marilyn H. Fedewa and Henry Casso, "Sor Maria de Jesus de Agreda, The Blue Nun: Blue Threads in the Fabric of Time," *People of God*, May 2012.

169. Jerry Javier Luján, June 28, 2014. The communication included a timeline, and description and photos of the events of the pilgrimage.

170. Servite Fathers, *The Age of Mary: An Exclusively Marian Magazine*, January-February, "The Mystical City of God" Issue (1958).

171. The schedule of events indicates that talks by two more tribes were planned for the event: one on Isleta Pueblo (presented by its leadership), and one a discussion of the Piro-Tompiro nations by Juan Benavides. The relationship between Isleta Pueblo and Sor María is described in an article in the *People of God* concerning the pueblo mission's four-hundredth anniversary celebration. See Alan Cherino, "The 400 Year Celebration: St. Augustine, Isleta, NM," *People of God*, September 2013.

172. The official press release from the governor's office reads, in part: "'New Mexico and the historic town of Agreda have enjoyed a unique cultural connection for centuries,' said [Governor] Richardson. 'I am pleased to sign a sisterhood agreement so we can further our relationship while promoting tourism, educational opportunities, and to increase trade and investments.' . . . 'It is our intention to use this historical figure that binds New Mexico and Agreda, Sister Maria of Agreda, as a beginning for interaction for some innovative cultural and economic exchanges,' said Cultural Affairs Secretary [Stuart] Ashman." Bill Richardson, "Governor Bill Richardson Signs New Mexico Sisterhood Agreement with Agreda, Spain," press release, Office of the Governor of New Mexico, Santa Fe, December 2, 2008.

173. Rima de Valbona, *Cosecha de pescadores* (San José, Costa Rica: Editorial Costa Rica, 1988).

174. Ibid., 34.

175. Ibid., 37.

176. Ibid., 16.

177. We examined the reference to Sor María in his account in chapter 4.

178. Valbona, *Cosecha de pescadores*, 42.

179. Ibid., 43.

180. Ibid.

181. Ibid.

182. Ibid., 44.

183. Lee Daniels, "Bilocación en el ayer barroco pero, ¿el hoy de la electrónica?" in *Nuevos acercamientos a la obra de Rima de Valbona (Actas del Simposio-homenaje)*, ed. Jorge Chen Sham (San José, Costa Rica: Editorial de la U. de Costa Rica, 2000), 170.

184. Ibid., 166.

185. Ibid., 171.

186. Valbona, *Cosecha de pescadores*, 39.

187. Francisco Goldman, *The Divine Husband: A Novel* (New York: Atlantic Monthly Press, 2004).

188. Ibid., 41.

189. Ibid., 42.

190. Ibid., 44.

191. Ibid., 46.

192. Ibid.

193. Ibid., 49.

194. Ibid., 54.

195. Ibid., 56–57.

196. Ibid., 60.

197. Ibid., 91.

198. Ibid., 433–34.

199. Ibid., 432.

200. Ibid., 146.

201. The recording discussed here depicts only the first scene of the play. The complete production was presented April 24, 2009, at Lady in Blue: Sor María de Jesús de Ágreda, A University of New Mexico Homage Symposium, University of New Mexico. The play has since been retitled *Lady Blue's Dreams*; see http://puppetsrevenge.com/plays/lady-blue's-dreams.

202. The troupe's motto is "Small Actors, Big Meaning." See Puppet's Revenge Homepage, http://puppetsrevenge.com.

203. This was the case in the 2009 UNM presentation, as the troupe's webpage explains: "[The play is] structured in several parts. It begins in a Past Lives Therapy session with actors with masks which leads to subsequent scenes with hand puppets in the XVII century: a Convent in Spain, the deserts of New Mexico and in the middle of the Atlantic." See "The Blue Lady: A Brief History," http://www.imageevent.com/puppetsrevenge/theblueladyabriefhistory.

CONCLUSION

1. Valbona, *Cosecha de pescadores*, 38.

2. In some of these modern manifestations, she has become an icon for groups unaffiliated with canonization advocates or regional devotees. Two examples of this are the Library of Congress, whose American Memory series "'With Peace and Freedom Blest!' Woman as Symbol in America, 1590–1800" includes Sor María among their prominent American historical women, and the Hispano Roundtable of New Mexico's "Hispanas Distinguidas de Nuevo México," which features her as an important woman in the state's history. See Sara Day, "'With Peace and Freedom Blest!' Woman as Symbol in America, 1590–1800," in *American Women: A Library of Congress Guide for the Study of Women's History and Culture in the United States*, ed. Sheridan Harvey (Washington, DC: Library of Congress, 2001); Juan José Peña, "Hispano Roundtable of New Mexico Honors Hispanas Distinguidas de Nuevo Mexico," 2008.

3. I am indebted for this idea to a talk on Mary Magdalene by Sister Geneal Kramer, in which she contrasted what is known about the biblical figure with apocryphal constructs. The popularity of Mary Magdalene as a story continues to engage those interested in discovering more about the historical woman. See Geneal Kramer, O.P., "Mary of Magdala," Dominican Ecclesial Institute Talk Series, University of New Mexico Continuing Education Center, July 20, 2014.

4. Some contemporary scholarly studies briefly mention Sor María's writing in the context of colonial Latin American letters: Kathleen Ann Meyers, *Neither Saints Nor Sinners: Writing the Lives of Women in Spanish America* (New York: Oxford University Press, 2003); Gunnarsdøttir, *Mexican Karismata*; Kathryn Joy McKnight, *The Mystic of Tunja: The Writings of Madre Castillo, 1671–1742* (Amherst: University of Massachusetts Press, 1997); Josefina Muriel, *Cultura femenina novohispana*, 1st ed., Serie de historia novohispana (México: Universidad Nacional Autónoma de México, Instituto de Investigaciones Históricas, 1982). Sor María was also championed—controversially—as one of Spain's foundational Golden Age writers by nineteenth-century Spanish author Emilia Pardo Bazán. See the prologue for the late nineteenth-century publication of *Vida de la Virgen María*, an edition of *La mística ciudad de dios*: Emilia Pardo Bazán, introduction to *Vida de la Virgen María* (Barcelona: Montaner y Simón, 1899).

5. Anna M. Nogar, "New Spain's Archival Past and Present Materiality," in *The History of Mexican Literature*, ed. Ignacio M. Sánchez Prado, Anna M. Nogar, and José Ramón Ruisánchez Serra (Cambridge: Cambridge University Press, 2016).

Abernethy, Francis Edward, ed. *Legendary Ladies of Texas*. Denton: University of North Texas Press, 1994.

Abernethy, Frank, ed. *The Folklore of Texan Cultures*. Denton: University of North Texas Press, 2000.

Adams, Eleanor. "Two Colonial New Mexico Libraries: 1704, 1776." *New Mexico Historical Review* 29 (April 1944): 135–67.

Ágreda, María de Jesús de. *Mystica ciudad de Dios. Primera parte: milagro de su omnipotencia, y abysmo de la gracia: historia divina, y vida de la Virgen madre de Dios, reyna, y señora nuestra, Maria santissima, restauradora de la culpa de Eva, y medianera de la gracia*. En Madrid: Por Bernardo de Villa-Diego, 1670.

———. *Mystica ciudad de Dios: milagro de su omnipotencia, y abismo de la gracia, historia divina, y vida de la Virgen madre de Dios, reyna, y señora nuestra Maria santissima, restauradora de la culpa de Eva, y medianera de la gracia*. 3 vols. Antwerp: Henrico y Cornelio Verdussen, 1696.

———. *Mystica ciudad de Dios, milagro de su omnipotencia y abismo de la gracia*. Madrid Imprenta de la Causa de la V. Madre, 1720.

———. *Mystica ciudad de Dios: milagro de su omnipotencia y abismo de la gracia: historia divina y vida de la Virgen Madre de Dios, Reyna y Señora Nuestra Maria Santissima*. Nueva impression adornada y enriquezida con muchas lindissimas estampas . . . y con un indice general de las cosas notables que se contienen en las tres partes desta divina historia. 3 vols. Amberes: Por la viuda de Henrico Verdussen, 1736.

———. *Modo de andar la via-sacra, sacado de la Mystica ciudad de Dios*. México: Biblioteca Mexicana, 1763.

———. *Mystica ciudad de Dios, milagro de su omnipotencia, y abysmo de la gracia: historia divina, y vida de la virgen, Madre de Dios, Reyna, y Señora Nuestra, Maria Santissima, restauradora de la culpa de Eva*. Madrid: En la Impr. de la Causa de la Venerable Madre, 1765.

———. *Mystica ciudad de Dios, milagro de su omnipotencia y abismo de la gracia*. Madrid: Imprenta de la Causa de la V. Madre, 1765.

———. *Modo de andar la Via Sacra: Sacado de la Mystica Ciudad de Dios*. México: Felipe de Zúñiga y Ontiveros, 1773.

———. *Modo de andar la via-sacra, / sacado de la Mystica ciudad de Dios, 2. part. lib. 6. cap. 21. por uno de los fundadores del Colegio de la Santa Cruz de Queretaro. Y reimpresso â devocion de los missioneros del Colegio Apostolico de San Fernando de esta Ciudad de Mexico.* México: Biblioteca Mexicana, 1774.

———. *Modo de andar la Via-Sacra: Sacado de la Mystica ciudad de dios.* México: Biblioteca Mexicana, 1777.

———. *Modo de andar la Via-Sacra.* México: Felipe de Zuñiga y Ontiveros, 1779.

———. *Septenario al gloriosissimo patriarca Sr. San Joseph: de los siete privilegios de su patrocinio que reifere la V.M. Maria de Jesús de Ágreda en su Mystica ciudad de Dios.* México: Imprenta nueva de la calle de S. Bernanrdo [Joseph de Jáuregui], 1785.

———. *Modo de andar la Via-Sacra.* México: Imprenta de los Herederos de Joseph de Jauregui, 1789.

———. *Triduo mariano mensual en honor, y reverencia del Felicissimo Transito, entierro y assumpcion de la Reyna del Cielo y tierra María Nuestra Señora, para alcanzar mediante su Protección una dichosa muerte* . . . México: Herederos del Lic. D. Joseph de Jauregui, 1790.

———. *Modo de Andar la Via-Sacra.* México: Herederos de J. Jauregui, 1793.

———. *Modo de Andar la Via-Sacra.* México: En la oficina de doña María Fernández de Jauregui, 1806.

———. *Modo de Andar la Via Sacra: Sacado de la Mística Ciudad de Dios.* México: María Fernández de Jáuregui, 1808.

———. *Modo de andar la Via Sacra.* México: Oficina del finado Ontiveros, 1826.

———. *Mística ciudad de Dios: historia divina y vida de la Santísima Vírgen María, Madre de Dios, Reina, Abogada y Señora Nuestra. Manifestada por la misma Señora a su esclava sor María de Jesus, abadesa del Convento de la Purísima Concepcion de la villa de Ágreda.* 1 vol. México: Impr. de V. García Torres, 1844.

———. *City of God: The Divine History and Life of the Virgin Mother of God Manifested to Mary of Agreda for the Encouragement of Men.* 4 vols. Translated by Fiscar Marison (George Blatter). Mount Vernon, OH: Louis W. Bernicken, 1902.

Ágreda, María de Jesús de, and Joseph Ximénez Samaniego. *Mystica ciudad de Dios . . . Historia divina, y vida de la Virgen Madre de Dios . . . Manifestada en estos ultimos siglos por la misma Señora à su esclava Sor María de Iesus . . . 'Prologo galeato' y 'Relación de la vida de la venerable madre Sor María de Jesus.'* Madrid: B. de Villa-Diego, 1670.

———. *Mystica ciudad de Dios, milagro de su omnipotencia, y abismo de la gracia: historia divina, y vida de la Virgen Madre de Dios, reyna, y señora nuestra.* Madrid: Impr. de la Causa de la V. Madre, 1720.

Alcocer Martínez, Mariano. *Catálogo razonado de obras impresas en Valladolid, 1481–1800.* Valladolid: Impr. de la Casa social católica, 1926.

Allen, Heather. "The Languages and Literatures of Early Print Culture in the Colonia." In *A History of Mexican Literature*, edited by Ignacio Sánchez Prado, Anna M. Nogar, and José Ramón Ruisánchez Serra, 17–32. Cambridge: Cambridge University Press, 2016.

Álvarez de Toledo, Lucas. "Patente de fray Lucas de Toledo autorizando pedir limosna para una beatificación/Comisario general de Indias" (1708). Convento de San Francisco de Madrid.

Ángel, Nicolás. *Directorio predicable apostolico, que contiene una prudente Instruccion de los sentidos de la Escritura Sagrada: los Assumptos mas principales para hacer una Mission y la Explicacion de todo el Texto de la Doctrina Christiana.* Madrid: Imprenta de la Causa de la V.M. Maria de Jesus de Agreda, 1740.

Añíbarro, P. Víctor. "El P. José Ximénez Samaniego, Ministro General O.F.M. y Obispo de Plascencia (Conclusión)." *Archivo Ibero-Americano* (July-September 1944): 353–88.

Annerino, John. *Dead in Their Tracks: Crossing America's Desert Borderlands.* New York: Four Walls Eight Windows, 1999.

Arbiol, Antonio. *Certamen Marianum Parisiense, vbi veritas examinatur in splendoribvs sanctorvm, et opvs mirabile Mysticae civitatis Dei, a censvra doctorum, ‡ sacra Facultate Parisiensi deputatorum, exagitatur liberum, & ‡ sententia, sub ementito ejusdem sacrae Facultatis nomine evulgata, propugnatur immune: conatvr ostendere caelicam Mysticae civitatis Dei consonantiam, Scripturae Sacrae, Sanctis Patribus, doctoribus approbatis, alijsque revelationibus particularibus, in Ecclesia Catholica huiusque legi permissis, Fr. Antonivs Arbiol.* Saragossa: Apud Emmanvelem Roman, 1698.

——. "Desengaños mysticos a las almas detenidas o engañadas en el camino de la perfección." Madrid: Imprenta de la causa de la V.M. Maria de Jesús de Agreda, 1757.

——. *La familia regulada con doctrina de la Sagrada Escritura y Santos Padres de la Iglesia Catholica.* 6th ed. Madrid: Imprenta de la Causa de . . . Maria de Jesus de Agreda, 1760.

——. *Mystica fundamental de Christo Señor Nuestro explicada por . . . San Juan de la Cruz . . . y el religioso perfecto conforme a los cien Avisos y Sentencias espirituales.* Madrid: Imprenta de la Causa de la V. Madre Maria de Jesus de Agreda 1761.

Arbiol y Diez, Antonio. *La religiosa instruida: con doctrina de la sagrada escritura y santos padres de la Iglesia catholica: para todas las operaciones de su vida regular, desde que recibe el habito santo, hasta la hora de su muerte.* Madrid: En la Imprenta de la causa de la V.M. Maria de Jesus de Agreda, 1753.

——. *La religiosa instruida: Con doctrina de la sagrada escritura, y santos padres de la Iglegia catholica, para todas las operaciones de su vida regular, desde que recibe el habito santo, hasta la hora de su muerte.* Madrid: En la Imprenta Real de la Gazeta, 1776.

Arenal, Electa, Schlau Stacey, and Amanda Powell. *Untold Sisters: Hispanic Nuns in Their Own Works.* Rev. ed. Albuquerque: University of New Mexico Press, 2010.

Arias, Santa. "De Fray Servando Teresa de Mier a Juan Bautista Muñoz: La disputa guadalupana en vísperas de la independencia." *Revista Iberoamericana* 222 (2008): 6–13.

Arlegui, José de, Antonio Gálvez, and Ignacio Cumplido. *Crónica de la provincia de n.s.p.s. Francisco de Zacatecas*. México: Reimpresa por Cumplido, 1851.

Armesto, Manuel Francisco de. *La coronista más grande de la más sagrada historia, Sor María de Jesús de Ágreda*. Madrid: Mora, 1736.

Arricivita, Juan Domingo. *Apostolic Chronicle of Juan Domingo Arricivita: The Franciscan Mission Frontier in the Eighteenth Century in Arizona, Texas, and the Californias*. Translated by George Hammond and Agapito Rey. Vol. 2. Berkeley, CA: Academy of American Franciscan History, 1996.

Arrillaga, Basilio. *Defensa de la Mística Ciudad de Dios de . . . Sor María de Jesús Agreda contra la censura que en nombre propio y bajo el de el illmo. Bossuet ha publicado El Constitucional, etc*. México, 1844.

Ascargota, Juan de. *Manual de confessores ad mentem Scoti*. Madrid: Imprenta de la causa de la V. M. María de Jesús de Ágreda, 1757.

Atlas, Laurencio. "Árbol genealógico de la familia Coronel-Arana" (1759). Archivo Franciscano Ibero-Oriental, Madrid.

Avila, Santa Teresa de, and María de Jesús de Ágreda. *Avisos originales de Santa Teresa de Jesús: dos de sus cartas, una preciosa oración y una promesa de escritura: además una carta de la v.m. María de Jesús, hija de la santa, y otra de v.p. fr. Gerónimo Gracián de la Madre de Dios, primer provincial de la descalcez*. Madrid: Imprenta y librería de Moya y Plaza, 1881.

Banks, Jimmy. "The Lady in Blue." *Texas Parade Magazine*, October 1952, 24–25.

Bannon, John Francis. *The Spanish Borderlands Frontier*. Edited by Ray Allen Billington and Howard Lamar. Albuquerque: University of New Mexico Press, 1974.

Baranda Leturio, Consolación. *Cartas de Sor María de Jesús de Ágreda a Fernando de Borja y Francisco de Borja (1628–1664)*. Valladolid: University of Valladolid, 2013.

Barcia Carballido y Zúñiga, Andrés González de. *Ensayo cronológico, para la historia general de la Florida*. Madrid: N. Rodríguez Franco, 1723.

Bargellini, Clara. "'Amoroso horror': Arte y culto en la serie de la Pasión de Gabriel de Ovalle de Guadalupe, Zacatecas." In *Arte y violencia: XVIII Coloquio Internacional de Historia del Arte*, 499–524. México: Universidad Autónoma de México/Instituto de Investigaciones Estéticas, 1995.

Barr, Juliana. *Peace Came in the Form of a Woman: Indians and Spaniards in the Texas Borderlands*. Chapel Hill: University of North Carolina Press, 2007.

Barriuso, Patrocinio García. "La monja de Carrión Sor Luisa de la Ascención y Sor María de Jesús, la monja de Agreda." *Verdad y Vida: Revista de las Ciencias del Espíritu* 49, no. 196 (1991): 547–52.

Benavides, Alonso de. "Translado que se sacó de una carta que el P. Fr. Alonso de Benavides . . . embió a los Religiosos de la Santa Custodia de la Conversión de San Pablo desde Madrid el año de 1631" (1631). Biblioteca Nacional de México: Documentos para la Historia del Nuevo México, Center for Southwest Research, University of New Mexico.

———. "Translado que se sacó de una carta que el P. Fr. Alonso de Benavides . . . embió a los Religiosos de la Santa Custodia de la Conversión de San Pablo desde Madrid el año de 1631" (1631). In Facsimiles of Manuscripts in the Biblioteca Nacional de México, Center for Southwest Research, University of New Mexico, Albuquerque.

———. "Alonso de Benavides Memorial (ZCH)" (1634). Propaganda Fide Archives, Vatican City, Italy; University of Notre Dame Archives.

———. *The Memorial of Fray Alonso de Benavides, 1630*. Translated by Emma Augusta Burbank Ayer. Chicago: Privately Printed [R. R. Donnelley and Sons Co.], 1916.

———. *Fray Alonso de Benavides' Revised Memorial of 1634*. Translated by Agapito Rey. Coronado Cuarto Centennial Publications, 1540–1940. Albuquerque: University of New Mexico Press, 1945.

———. *Benavides' Memorial of 1630*. Translated by Peter P. Forrestal. Washington, DC: Academy of American Franciscan History, 1954.

Benavides, Alonso de, and María de Jesús de Ágreda. *Tanto que se sacó de una carta, que el R. Padre Fr. Alonso de Benavides, custodio que fue del Nuevo Mexico, embió a los religiosos de la Santa custodia de la conversión de San Pablo de dicho reyno, desde Madrid, el ano de 1631*. México: Joseph Bernardo de Hogal, 1730.

———. *Tanto que se sacó de una carta que el R.P. Fr. Alonso de Benavides, custodio, que fue del Nuevo Mexico, embió a los religiosos de la Santa Custodia de la conversion de San Pablo de dicho reyno, desde Madrid, el ano de 1631*. México, 1760.

Beristáin de Souza, José Mariano. *Biblioteca Hispanoamericana septentrional*. Vol. 5. México: Editorial Fuente Cultural, 1947.

Bethel, Brian. "Lady in Blue Calls across Time." *San Angelo Standard-Times*, June 17, 2010.

———. "Second Festival Likely to Atttract Diverse Interest." *San Angelo Standard-Times*, June 17, 2010.

"The Big Chili." *Good Eats*, Food Network, 2007.

Blázquez del Barco, Juan. *Trompeta evangelica, alfange apostolico y martillo de pecadores sermones de mission, doctrina moral, y mystica, y relox de el alma, compuesto*. Madrid: Imprenta de la Causa de la Venerable M. María de Jesús de Agreda, 1742.

Bona, Lorenzo. *Theatro evangelico de oraciones, panegyricas y sagradas*. Madrid: Imprenta de la Causa de la V. Madre Maria de Jesus de Agreda, 1741.

Bringas y Encinas, Diego Miguel. *Índice apologético de las razones que recomiendan la obra intitulada Mistica Ciudad de Dios escrita por la Ven. Madre Sor María de Jesus Coronel y Arana . . . Con varias cartas apologeticas escritas en defensa de la misma obra, por algunos sábios franceses . . . Un apéndice que contiene la supuesta y despreciable censura falsamente atribuida al Ilmo. Señor Bosuet, su impugnacion y notas. Ultimamente un resumen de la admirable vida y ejemplarísimas virtudes de la misma venerable Madre Sor María de Jesus*. Valencia: D. F. Brusola, 1834.

Bullock, Alice. *Living Legends of the Santa Fe Country*. Denver, CO: Green Mountain, 1970.

C. de Baca, Elba. "Folk Tales of New Mexico." Center for Southwest Research, University of New Mexico, Albuquerque.

———. "The Lady in Blue." In *Las Mujeres Hablan*, edited by Tey Diana Rebolledo, Erlinda González-Berry, and Teresa Márquez, 10–11. Albuquerque: El Norte Publications/Academia, 1988.

California, Online Archive of. "Guide to the Mission Santa Clara Book Collection, 1548–1835." 2009. http://www.oac.cdlib.org/findaid/ark:/13030/tf967 nb3tr/dsc.

Calvo, Hortensia. "The Politics of Print: The Historiography of the Book in Early Spanish America." *Book History* 6 (2003): 277–305.

Campbell, G. L. "The Blue Lady: Interview with Eileen Mattison" (Fall 1977). Baughman Folklore Collection, Center for Southwest Research, University of New Mexico, Albuquerque.

Campbell, Thomas. "Maria de Agreda." In *The Catholic Encyclopedia*. New York: Robert Appleton Company, 1907. http://www.newadvent.org/cathen /01229a.htm.

Campos, José Agustín de. "José Agustín de Campos y la conquista del Moqui." In *Etnología y misión en la Pimería Alta, 1715–1740*, edited by Luis González Rodríguez, 227–63. México: Universidad Autónoma de México, 1977.

Campos, Julio. "Los Padres Juan de la Palma, Pedro Manero y Pedro de Arriola y la Mística Ciudad de Dios." *Archivo Ibero-Americano* 26 (1966): 227–52.

"Carabantes, José de (1628–1694)." In *Pequeña Enciclopedia Franciscana*. http:// www.franciscanos.org/enciclopedia/penciclopedia_c.htm.

Carreno, Alberto María. "The Missionary Influence of the College of Zacatecas." *The Americas* 7 (1951): 297–320.

Casanova, Giacomo. *Mèmoires de Jacques Casanova de Seingalt, Ècrits par luimème*. 6 vols. Brussels: Rozez, 1881.

———. *History of My Life*. New York: A. A. Knopf, 2006.

Casar, Franciso del. *Devocionario seraphico: Exercicios de la V.O.T. de Colmenar Viejo, deducidos de la Mystica Ciudad de Dios, y milagro de la Divina Omnipotencia. Indulgencias que se logran . . . y un Apéndice latino, forma de dar hábitos, Profesiones y otras curiosidades*. Madrid: L. F. Mojados, 1750.

Castañeda, Carlos. "Pichardo, José Antonio." In *Handbook of Texas Online*. Texas State Historical Association. https://tshaonline.org/handbook/online /articles/fpi01.

———. "Talamantes, Melchor de." In *Handbook of Texas Online*. Texas State Historical Association. https://tshaonline.org/handbook/online/articles /fta04.

———. *Our Catholic Heritage in Texas, 1519–1936*. Vol. 1. Austin, TX: Von Boeckmann-Jones Company, 1936–58.

———. "The Woman in Blue." *The Age of Mary: An Exclusively Marian Magazine*, "The Mystical City of God" Issue (January-February, 1958): 22–30.

Castillo, Ana. *So Far from God: A Novel*. New York: W. W. Norton, 1993.

Castro, Manuel de. "Legislación inmaculista de la Orden Franciscana en España." *Archivo Ibero-Americano* 57-58 (1955): 35–105.

Castro, Rafaela. *Dictionary of Chicano Literature*. Santa Barbara, CA: ABC-CLIO, 2000.

Cavero, Joseph Nicolas. *Anti-agredistae parisienses expvgnati, sive, Apologeticae dissertationes adversvs qvosdam parisienses, censvris insectatos complures propositiones, ‡ venerabili matre Maria a Iesv, vvlgo de Agreda: sua prima parte Mysticae Civitatis Dei assertas.* Saragossa: In officina Dominici Gascon, 1698.

Céliz, Francisco. *Diary of the Alarcón Expedition into Texas, 1718–1719.* Translated by Fritz Leo Hoffman. Los Angeles: Quivira Society, 1935.

Cherino, Alan. "The 400 Year Celebration: St. Augustine, Isleta, NM." *People of God*, September 2013, 14–15.

Chocano Mena, Magdalena. "Colonial Printing and Metropolitan Books: Printed Texts and the Shaping of Scholarly Culture in New Spain, 1539–1700." *Colonial Latin American Historical Review* 6, no. 1 (1997): 69–90.

Cleveland, James L. "Did Lady in Blue Visit Arizona Indians without Ever Leaving Spanish Convent?" *The Southwesterner*, February 1967, 13, 15.

Colahan, Clark. *The Visions of Sor María de Agreda: Writing Knowledge and Power.* Tucson: University of Arizona Press, 1994.

Colahan, Clark, and Alfred Rodriguez. "A New Mexico Alabado about María de Jesús de Agreda: Reflections on Its Popular Retention and Transmission." *Liberal and Fine Arts Review* 5, no. 1 (1985): 4–14.

Colahan, Clark, and Celia Weller. "An Angelic Epilogue." *Studia Mystica* 13, no. 4 (1990): 50–59.

Combs, Joseph F. *Legends of the Pineys.* San Antonio: Naylor Co., 1965.

Compendio histórico, y novena de Maria santisima nuestra Señora, que con la advocacion de la Cueva santa se venera en el Seminario de la Santa Cruz de la ciudad de Queretaro. Puebla: Hospital de San Pedro, 1834.

Compilatio statutorum generalium pro Cismontana Familia regularis observantiae S. Francisci a Revisoribus ad hoc deputatis compaginata et jussu rev. P. Joannis de Soto S. Francisci ministri generalis prelo data. Madrid: Ex typ. V. Matris de Agreda, 1734.

Constituciones Generales para todas las Monjas, y Religiosas . . . de . . . San Francisco . . .: De nuevo recopiladas de las antiguas y añadidas con acuerdo . . . del Capitulo General . . . de 1639 . . . Madrid: Imp. de la Causa de la V. Madre María de Jesús de Agreda, 1748.

Contreras Servín, Carlos. "La frontera norte de la Nueva España y las exploraciones en el Pacífico. Siglo XVIII." *Revista de Historia de América* 130 (2002): 179–83.

———. "Manifiesto que el decreto de este apostólico colegio hizo al rey en 26 de febrero de 1776: Sobre los nuevos descubrimientos en la alta California." *Revista de Historia de América* 130 (2002): 184–211.

Cosper, Ron. "Sister Maria Saved Jumanos from Spanish Rule." *San Angelo Standard-Times*, June 16, 2010.

Cotera, María Eugenia. "Engendering a 'Dialectics of Our America': Jovita González's Pluralist Dialogue as Feminist Testimonio." In *Las obreras: Chicana Politics of Work and Family*, edited by Vicki Ruiz, 237–56. Los Angeles: UCLA Chicano Studies Research Center Publications, 2000.

Cruz González, Cristina. "Our Lady of el Pueblito: A Marian Devotion on the Northern Frontier." *Catholic Southwest: A Journal of History and Culture* 23 (2012): 3–21.

———. *Sor María Writing La mística ciudad de dios.* Painting. Museo Nacional del Virreinato, Tepozotlán.

Curtis, Jennifer. "Beyond Texas Folklore: The Woman in Blue." In *Cowboys, Cops, Killers, and Ghosts: Legends and Lore in Texas*, edited by Kenneth Untiedt, 195–204. Denton: University of North Texas Press, 2013.

Daniels, Lee. "Bilocación en el ayer barroco pero, ¿el hoy de la electrónica?" In *Nuevos acercamientos a la obra de Rima de Valbona (Actas del Simposio-homenaje)*, edited by Jorge Chen Sham, 165–72. San José, Costa Rica: Editorial de la University de Costa Rica, 2000.

Day, Sara. "'With Peace and Freedom Blest!' Woman as Symbol in America, 1590–1800." In *American Women: A Library of Congress Guide for the Study of Women's History and Culture in the United States*, edited by Sheridan Harvey. Washington, DC: Library of Congress, 2001.

DeGrazia, Ted (Ettore). *The Blue Lady: A Desert Fantasy of Papago Land.* Tucson, AZ: De Grazia Studios, 1957.

De la Cruz, Juana Inés. *Ejecicios devotos.* In *Obras completas*, 848–66. México: Editorial Porrúa, 2001

———. *Obras completas.* 12th ed. Edited by Francisco Monterede. México: Editorial Porrúa, 2001.

De la Maza, Francisco. *El pintor Cristóbal de Villalpando.* México: Instituto Nacional de Antropología e Historia, 1964.

———. "Los Cristos de Mexico y la monja de Agreda." *Boletín del Instituto Nacional de Antropología e Historia* 30 (December 1967): 1–3.

De la Rosa Figueroa, Francisco Antonio. "Becerro general menológico y chronológico." In *Alonso de Benavides' Revised Memorial of 1634*, edited by Frederick Webb Hodge, George P. Hammond, and Agapito Rey, 200–209. Albuquerque: University of New Mexico Press, 1945.

De la Rosa Figueroa, Francisco Antonio, and Hubert Howe Bancroft. "Vindicias de la Verdad: ms., 1774 Jan. 8" (1774) (originals). México: Convento de Nuestro Padre San Francisco.

"Denunciasion de Don Francisco Barba Coronado: El Señor fiscal del Santo Oficio, contra una mujer llamada Francisca de los Ángeles vecina de Querétaro, por alumbrada." Richard E. Greenleaf Papers, Center for Southwest Research, University of New Mexico.

De Zavala, Adina. *History and Legends of the Alamo and Other Missions in and around San Antonio.* San Antonio, TX: Privately published by the author, 1917.

Díaz, Mónica. *Indigenous Writing from the Convent: Negotiating Ethnic Autonomy in Colonial Mexico.* First Peoples: New Directions in Indigenous Studies. Tucson: University of Arizona Press, 2010.

Díaz y de Ovando, Clementina. "La poesía del Padre Luis Felipe Neri de Alfaro." *Anales del Instituto de Investigaciones Estéticas* 15 (1947): 51–101.

Diocese of San Angelo. "Lady in Blue." http://sanangelodiocese.org/lady-in-blue.

Dobie, J. Frank. *Tales of Old Time Texas*. Austin: University of Texas Press, 1984.

Domínguez, Francisco Atanasio. *The Missions of New Mexico, 1776: A Description with Other Contemporary Documents*. Translated by Eleanor Adams and Fray Angélico Chávez. Albuquerque: Univeristy of New Mexico Press, 1956.

Donahue, William. "Mary of Agreda and the Southwest United States." *The Americas* 9 (1953): 291–314.

Donahue-Wallace, Kelly. "The Print Sources of New Mexican Colonial Hide Paintings." *Anales del Instituto de Investigaciones Estéticas* 68 (1996): 43–69.

Dwyer, Mrs. Ed. "Interview with Margaret Castonguay" (October 27, 1967). Baughman Folklore Collection, Center for Southwest Research, University of New Mexico, Albuquerque.

Echarri, Francisco. *Directorio moral que comprehende en breve . . . todas las materias de la theologia moral y novissimos decretos de los sumos pontifices que han condenado diversas proposiciones . . . contiene ocho partes*. 5th ed. Madrid: Imprenta de la Causa de la V. Madre de Agreda, 1741.

Écija, Pablo de. *Sagrado inexpugnable muro de la Mystica Ciudad de Dios: Epitome historial theológio . . . Con un tratado-Apendice Alegórica Torre de David*. Madrid: Imp. de la Causa de la Venerable Madre Maria Jesus de Agreda, 1735.

———. *Novena a la Milagrosa Imagen que con el titulo de Nuestra Señora de los Milagros y Misericordias se venera en el coro de el Convento de Religiosas de la Purissima Concepcion de la Villa de Agreda*. Madrid: Imprenta de la Causa de la V. Madre de Agreda, 1745.

Eich, Jennifer Lee. *The Other Mexican Muse: Sor María Anna Águeda de San Ignacio, 1695–1765*. New Orleans: University Press of the South, 2004.

Eppinga, Jane. *Arizona Twilight Tales: Good Ghosts, Evil Spirits and Blue Ladies*. Boulder, CO: Pruett, 2000.

Espinosa, Isidro Félix. "Carta del padre Espinosa dando las gracias al Virrey por las providencias dadas para las misiones de Texas y su restauración, Agosto 18 1721" (1721). Archivo Histórico Provincial de los Franciscanos de Michoacán, Celaya, México.

———. *Chrónica apostólica, y seráphica de todos los Colegios de Propaganda Fide de esta Nueva-España*. México: Viuda del D. J. J. Bernal, 1746.

———. *Crónica de los Colegios de Propaganda Fide de la Nueva España*. Edited by Lino Gómez Canedo. Washington, DC: Academy of American Franciscan History, 1964.

Espinosa, Isidro Félix de, and Antonio Margil de Jesús. "Representación hecha al Virrey por los PP Fr. Isisdro Félix de Espinosa y Fr. Antonio Margil de Jesús sobre los motivos que hubo en la fundación de las misiones de Texas, y que se impida el avance de los franceses" (1719). Archivo Histórico Provincial de los Franciscanos de Michoacán, Celaya, México.

Esposito, Augustine M., and María de Jesús de Ágreda. *La mística ciudad de Dios (1670): Sor María de Jesús de Agreda*. Potomac, MD: Scripta Humanistica, 1990.

Estella, Diego de. *Tratado de la vanidad del mundo: dividido en tres libros con sus indices muy copiosos y assumptos predicables, discurriendo por todas las dominicas y fiestas del año, y al fin un tratado de Meditaciones devotissimas del amor de Dios.* Madrid: Imprenta de la Causa de la V.M. Maria de Jesus de Agreda, 1759.

Evangelisti, Silvia. "Spaces for Agency: The View from Early Modern Female Religious Communities." In *Attending to Early Modern Women: Conflict and Concord*, edited by Karen Nelson, 117–34. Newark: University of Delaware Press, 2013.

Evans, Edna Hoffman. "The Mysterious Lady in Blue." *Arizona Highways*, 1959, 32–35.

Fajardo, José del Ray. "Marco conceptual para comprender el estudio de la arquitectura de las misiones jesuíticas en la América colonial." *Apuntes* 20, no. 1 (2007): 8–33.

Fedewa, Marilyn H. *María of Ágreda: Mystical Lady in Blue.* Albuquerque: University of New Mexico Press, 2009.

Fedewa, Marilyn H., and Henry Casso. "Sor Maria de Jesus de Agreda: The Blue Nun Blue Threads in the Fabric of Time." *People of God*, May 2012, 18, 28.

Fernández, Benito. "Memorial of Father Benito Fernández Concerning the Canary Islanders, 1741; Translated by Benedict Luetenegger, OFM." *Southwestern Historical Quarterly* 82, no. 3 (1979): 265–96.

Fernández, Luis Miguel. "De la revelación a la escritura: El difícil viaje de sor María de Jesús de Agreda." In *Actas del IX Simposio de la Sociedad Española de Literatura General y Comparada*, edited by Túa Blesa, María Teresa Cacho, Carlos García Gual, Mercedes Rolland, Leonardo Romero Tobar, and Margarita Smerdou Altolaguirre. Zaragoza: Universidad de Zaragoza, 1994, 347–58.

Fernández Del Castillo, Francisco. *Luz de Tierra Incógnita en la América Septentrional y Diario de las Exploraciones en Sonora*, edited by Francisco Fernández Del Castillo. Publicaciones Archivo General de la Nación México, Talleres Gráficos de la Nación, 1926.

Fernández Gracia, Ricardo. *Arte, devoción y política: La promoción de las artes en torno a sor María de Ágreda.* Soria, Spain: Diputación Provincial de Soria, 2002.

———."Los primeros retratos de la Madre Ágreda: Consideraciones sobre su iconografía hasta fines del siglo XVII." In *El papel de Sor María de Jesús de Ágreda en el Barroco español*, 155–82. Monografías Universitarias. Soria, Spain: Universidad Internacional Alfonso VIII: Diputación Provincial de Soria, 2002.

———. *Iconografía de Sor María de Ágreda: Imágenes para la mística y la escritora en el contexto del maravillosismo del Barroco.* Soria, Spain: Caja Duero, 2003.

Figueroa, Joseph de. *Obsequiosa reverente expression que en fuerza del decreto pontificio de Nuestro SS.mo Padre Benedicto XIV: en el que declara ser de la mano y letra de la V. Madre Maria de Jesus de Agreda las obras intituladas, Mystica ciudad de Dios.* Madrid: Imprenta de Francisco Xavier Garcia, 1757.

Flores, Richard R. *Remembering the Alamo: Memory, Modernity, and the Master Symbol.* History, Culture, and Society Series. Austin: University of Texas Press, 2002.

Franco, Jean. *Plotting Women: Gender and Representation in Mexico.* Gender and Culture. New York: Columbia University Press, 1989.

Fuente Fernández, Francisco Javier. "Obras ineditas de Sor María de Jesús de Ágreda: *El jardín espiritual.*" In *I Congreso Internacional del Monacato Femenino en España, Portugal y América, 1492–1992,* 221–36. León, Spain: Universidad de León, 1993.

Gaceta de Madrid. April 12, 1729, January 31, 1736, February 7, 1758, November 20, 1759, May 26, 1761, December 2, 1747, February 10, 1748, April 13, 1762, March 26, 1771.

Gaceta de México. México: Secretaria de Educación Pública, 1722.

Gaceta de México. México: Secretaria de Educación Pública, 1728–44.

Garay, Manuel. *Sermones varios: Continuación de el parentesis de el ocio, quenta con el tiempo, enigma claro, dentro, y fuera de los nueves, nada de nuevo.* Madrid: Imprenta de la causa de la V. Madre de Agreda, 1743.

García Barriuso, Patrocinio. "La monja de Carrión Sor Luisa de la Ascención y Sor María de Jesús, la monja de Agreda," *Verdad y Vida: Revista de las Ciencias del Espíritu* 49, no. 196 (1991): 547–52.

Garritz Ruiz, Amaya. *Impresos novohispanos, 1808–1821.* Serie bibliografica (Universidad Nacional Autonoma de México. Instituto de Investigaciones Historicas 9). 2 vols. México: Universidad Nacional Autónoma de México, 1990.

Gavito, Florencio, José Toribio Medina, and Felipe Teixidor. *Adiciones a la Imprenta en la Puebla de los Ángeles.* México: Unión gráfica, 1961.

Geiger, Maynard. *The Life and Times of Fray Junípero Serra, O.F.M.; or, The Man Who Never Turned Back.* Washington, DC: Academy of American Franciscan History, 1959.

———. "The Story of California's First Libraries." *Southern California Quarterly* 46 (1964): 109–24.

Gens, Mark B. "The Blue Lady: Interview with M. Kathleen Nicoli." Baughman Folklore Collection, Center for Southwest Research, University of New Mexico, Albuquerque, November 15, 1971.

Goldman, Francisco. *The Divine Husband: A Novel.* 1st ed. New York: Atlantic Monthly Press, 2004.

Gomez Canedo, Lino. *De México a la Alta California.* México: Editorial Jus, 1969.

Gómez Mont, Mercedes, and Rafael Camacho Guzmán. *Las misiones de Sierra Gorda.* Querétaro: Gobierno del Estado de Querétaro, 1985.

González, Aníbal A. "Nuestra Señora de la Puríssima Concepción de Acuña Mission." In *Handbook of Texas Online.* Texas State Historical Association. https://tshaonline.org/handbook/online/articles/uqn09.

González, John Morán. *Border Renaissance: The Texas Centennial and the Emergence of Mexican American Literature.* Austin: University of Texas Press, 2009.

González, Patricia Andrés. "Iconografía de la Venerable María de Jesús de Ágreda." *Boletín del Seminario de Estudios de Arte y Arqueología* 62 (1996): 447–64.

———. "Un temprano cuadro de la Virgen de Guadalupe, con el ciclo aparicionista, en las Conceptionistas de Ágreda (Soria)." *Anales del Museo de América* 7 (1999): 237–47.

González de Cossío, Francisco, and José Toribio Medina. *La imprenta en México, 1594–1820: Cien adiciones a la obra de José Toribio Medina.* México: Porrúa, 1947.

González de Mireles, Jovita. "Catholic Heroines of Texas." *The Southern Messenger*, August 20, 1936.

———. *Dew on the Thorn.* Recovering the U.S. Hispanic Literary Heritage. Houston: Arte Público Press, 1997.

González Matheo, Diego. *Mystica civitas Dei vindicata ab observationibus R. D. Eusebii Amorti.* Madrid: Ex Typ. Causae Venerabilis Matris Mariae Jesu de Agreda, 1747.

———. *Apodixis agredana pro mystica, civitate Dei technas detegens eusebianas.* Madrid: Ex. Typ. Causae Venerabilis Matris Mariae Jesu de Agreda, 1751.

González Rodríguez, Luis. Prologue to *Etnología y misión en la Pimería Alta: 1715–1740*, edited by Luis González Rodríguez. México: Universidad Nacional Autónoma de México, 1977.

Greenblatt, Stephen. *Marvelous Possessions: The Wonder of the New World.* Chicago: University of Chicago Press, 1991.

Gruzinski, Serge. *Images at War: Mexico from Columbus to Blade Runner (1492–2019).* Translated by Heather MacLean. Durham, NC: Duke University Press, 2001.

Gunnarsdøttir, Ellen. *Mexican Karismata: The Baroque Vocation of Francisca de los Ángeles, 1674–1744.* Engendering Latin America. Lincoln: University of Nebraska Press, 2004.

Gustin, Monique. *El barroco en la Sierra Gorda: Misiones franciscanas en el Estado de Querétaro, Siglo XVIII.* México: Instituto Nacional de Antropologia e Historia, 1969.

Gutiérrez, Ramón. *When Jesus Came, the Corn Mothers Went Away: Marriage, Sexuality and Power in New Mexico.* Stanford, CA: Stanford University Press, 1991.

Hallenbeck, Cleve. "The Blue Lady." *New Mexico Magazine*, February 1945, 17, 29–35.

Hallenbeck, Cleve, and Juanita H. Williams. *Legends of the Spanish Southwest.* Glendale, CA: Arthur H. Clark Co., 1938.

Harline, Craig. *Miracles at the Jesus Oak.* New York: Doubleday, 2003.

Hemisath, Charles H. "The Mysterious Woman in Blue." In *Legends of Texas*, edited by J. Frank Dobie. Dallas, TX: Southern Methodist University Press, 1976.

Herter, George Leonar, and Berthe Herter. *Bull Cook and Authentic Historical Recipes and Practices.* Waseca, MN: Herter's, 1970.

Hickerson, Nancy. "The Visits of the 'Lady in Blue': An Episode in the History of the South Plains, 1629." *Journal of Anthropological Research* 46, no. 1 (1990): 67–90.

Hidalgo, Francisco. "Relación del Padre Hidalgo de la Quivira, hecha al señor Virrey, pretendiendo su descubrimiento." Archivo Histórico Provincial de los Franciscanos de Michoacán, Celaya, México.

———. "Relación sobre Quivira por Francisco Hidalgo, a continuación." Archivo Histórico Provincial de los Franciscanos de Michoacán, Celaya, México.

Hodge, Frederick Webb. "Bibliography of Fray Alonso de Benavides." *Indian Notes and Monographs* 3, no. 1 (1919).

Holland, Eric. "Angel in the Desert." In *Without Borders*. https://store.cdbaby .com/cd/ericholland.

Holman, J. M. "The Lady in Blue." In *Hispanic Legends from New Mexico: Narratives from the R. D. Jameson Collection*, edited by Stanley Robe, 531–32. Berkeley: University of California Press, 1980.

Indiferente 3029. Archivo General de Indias, Seville.

"Inventory of Books at Santa Cruz: Biblioteca Chiquita" (1803). Archivo Histórico Provincial de los Franciscanos de Michoacán, Celaya, México.

"Inventory of Books at Santa Cruz: Librería Común" (1766). Archivo Histórico Provincial de los Franciscanos de Michoacán, Celaya, México.

"Inventory of Books in the Santa Cruz Library: Librería Común" (1815). Archivo Histórico Provincial de los Franciscanos de Michoacán, Celaya, México.

Iturri de Roncal, Basilio. *Eco Harmonioso del Clarín Evangelico con duplicados Sermones, ó Pláticas de Assumptos Panegyricos, Mysticos, y Morales, para las fiestas solemnes de Christo Señor nuestro, de Maria Santisima, y Santos, cuyos dias son festivos*. 2 vols. Madrid: Imprenta de la Causa de la Venerable Madre Maria de Jesus de Agreda, 1736.

Ivars, Andrés. "Algunas cartas autógrafas de la Venerable madre sor María de Jesús de Ágreda." *Archivo Ibero-Americano* 3 (1915): 435–57.

———. "Algunas cartas autógrafas de la Venerable madre sor María de Jesús de Ágreda (Continuación)." *Archivo Ibero-Americano* 3 (1916): 413–38.

———. "Expediente relativo a los escritos de la Venerable Madre Sor María de Jesús de Agreda." *Archivo Ibero-Americano* 8 (1917): 131–42.

Jaffary, Nora. *False Mystics*. Lincoln: University of Nebraska Press, 2004.

Johnson, Dee Strickland. *Arizona Herstory: Tales from Her Storied Past*. Phoenix: Cowboy Miner Productions, 2003.

Jordan, Cynthia. *The Lady in Blue*. San Angelo, TX: Emerald Eagle Music, 2009.

Joseph, Maximiliano. "Copia de un decreto del Señor Elector de Bavaria al Padre Propósito Polingano" (1751). Archivo Franciscano Ibero-Oriental, Madrid.

Junta de Castilla y León. "Artehistoria: Introducción." http://www.artehistoria .com/v2/contextos/10131.htm.

Keleher, Julia. "Lady in Blue." Keleher Family Collection, 1936.

———. "Lady in Blue: Interview with Stephanie Redd." Baughman Folklore Collection, Center for Southwest Research, University of New Mexico, Albuquerque. Fall 1960.

———. "Lady in Blue Program and Playbill." College of Fine Arts Collection, Center for Southwest Research, University of New Mexico, Albuquerque.

Kendrick, T. D. *Mary of Agreda: The Life and Legend of a Spanish Nun.* London: Routledge & K. Paul, 1967.

Keyes, Frances Parkinson. *I, The King.* New York: McGraw-Hill, 1966.

Kick, Dalmatius. *Revelationum agredanarum justa defensio in tres tomos distributa.* 3 vols. 2nd ed. Madrid: Ex typographia Causae V.M. Mariae à Jesu de Agreda, 1754.

Kimmel, Eric. *The Lady in the Blue Cloak: Legends from the Texas Missions.* New York: Holiday House, 2006.

Kino, Eusebio Francisco, and Francisco Fernández del Castillo. *Las misiones de Sonora y Arizona. Comprendiendo: la crónica titulada: "Favores celestiales" y la "Relación diaria de la entrada al norueste" del padre Eusebio Francisco Kino (Kuhne).* Vol. 8. Pulicaciones del Archivo General de la Nacion. Edited by Francisco Fernández del Castillo. México: Editorial Cultura, 1913.

Kramer, Geneal, O.P. "Mary of Magdala." In Dominican Ecclesial Institute Talk Series. University of New Mexico Continuing Education Center, July 20, 2014.

"The Lady in Blue/A Mission under Our Lady's Care." *Extension Magazine,* June 1, 2007, 18–19.

Laet, Johannes de. *Novus orbis, seu Descriptionis Indiae Occidentalis libri XVIII.* Leiden: Apud Elzevirios, 1633. http://openlibrary.org/books/OL17457394M/Novus_orbis_seu_Descriptionis_Indiae_Occidentalis_libri_XVIII.

Lamadrid, Enrique. *Hermanitos Comanchitos.* Pasó por aquí. Albuquerque: University of New Mexico Press, 2003.

———. "From Santiago at Ácoma to the Diablo in the Casinos: Four Centuries of Foundational Milagro Narratives in New Mexico." In *Expressing New Mexico: Nuevomexicano Creativity, Ritual, and Memory,* edited by Phillip B. Gonzales, 42–60. Tucson: University of Arizona Press, 2007.

Lamadrid, Enrique, and Gabriel Melendez. "The Penitente Brotherhood." *New Mexico Historical Review* 82, no. 1 (2007): 121–27.

Lamadrid, Lázaro. "The Letters of Margil in the Archivo de la Recolección in Guatemala." *The Americas* 10 (1953): 323–55.

Lárraga, Maribel. "La mística de la feminidad en la obra de Juan Villagutierre Sotomayor." PhD diss., University of New Mexico, 1999.

Lavrín, Asunción. *Brides of Christ: Conventual Life in Colonial Mexico.* Stanford, CA: Stanford University Press, 2008.

León Pinelo, Antonio de. *Epitome de la bibliotheca oriental y occidental, náutica y geográfica de don Antonio de León Pinelo.* Madrid: La Oficina de Francisco Martínez Abad, 1737–38.

"Libro Becerro de Provincia: Tablas Capitulares II and III." Archivo Histórico Provincial de los Franciscanos de Michoacán, Celaya, México.

Limón, José. *Dancing with the Devil.* Madison: University of Wisconsin Press, 1994.

Livingston, A. D. *Strictly Chili: Cooking the Best Bowl of Red*. Short Hills, NJ: Burford Books, 2003.

Llamas, Enrique. *La Madre Ágreda y la Mariología del siglo XVII*. Estudios marianos. Salamanca: Sociedad Mariológica Española, 2003.

———. "Inmaculada concepción de María y corredención mariana en la 'Mística ciudad de Dios' de la Madre Agreda." *Celtiberia* 55, no. 99 (2005): 525–66.

López, Nicolás. "Memorial de Fr. Nicolás Lopez acerca de la repoblación de Nuevo Méjico y ventajas que ofrece el reino de Quivira." In *Don Diego de Peñaloza y su descubrimiento del reino de Quivira*. Imprenta y Fundación de Manuel Tello, Real Academia de la Historia, 1686. http://es.wikisource .org/wiki/Don_Diego_de_Peñalosa_y_su_descubrimiento_del_reino_de _Quivira.

———. "Report of Custodio of New Mexico and Procurador General Nicolás Lopez on New Mexico" (1687). Archivo General de Indias, Guadalajara Collection, Legajo 138, Spanish Colonial Research Center.

Lopez, Peter E. *Edward O'Brien, Mural Artist: 1910–1975*. Santa Fe, NM: Sunstone, 2013.

López Pérez, María del Pilar. "El objeto de uso en las salas de las casas de habitación de españoles y ciollos en Santafé de Bogotá: Siglos XVII y XVIII en el Nuevo Reino de Granada." *Anales del Instituto de Investigaciones Estéticas* 74–75 (1999): 99–134.

Losada, Domingo. *Compendio chronologico de los privilegios regulares de Indias*. Madrid: Impr. Causa de la V. Madre de Agreda, 1737.

Losilla, Antonio. "Tesoro escondido hallado por quienes lo buscan en María Puríssima Señora Nuestra, y comunicado nuevamente . . . Tomo segundo." Archivo Histórico Provincial de los Franciscanos de Michoacán, Celaya, México.

Luján, Jerry Javier. "Event Description." June 28, 2014.

Lynch, Cyprian. Introduction to *Benavides' Memorial of 1630*, translated by Peter P. Forrestal. Washington, DC: American Academy of Franciscan History, 1954.

Lynn, Kimberly. *Between Court and Confessional: The Politics of Spanish Inquisitors*. Cambridge: Cambridge University Press, 2013.

Macías, Eduardo Báez. "El testamento de José Miguel Rivera Saravia, arquitecto del siglo XVIII." *Anales del Instituto de Investigaciones Estéticas* 13, no. 46 (1976): 187–96.

MacLean, Katie. "María de Agreda, Spanish Mysticism and the Work of Spiritual Conquest." *Colonial Latin American Review* 17, no. 1 (2008): 29–48.

Madden, Joseph Mary. "A Brief Biography of Venerable Mary of Agreda." *The Age of Mary: An Exclusively Marian Magazine*, "The Mystical City of God" Issue (January-February 1958): 91–98.

Madres Concepcionistas de Ágreda. "Obras publicadas." http://www.mariade agreda.org/rdr.php?cat=40&n=1.

———. "María de Jesús de Ágreda." http://www.mariadeagreda.org/rdr.php.

Manje, Juan Mateo. *Luz de tierra incógnita en la América Septentrional y Diario de las Exploraciones en Sonora*. Publicaciones Archivo General de la Nación, Vol. 10. México: Talleres Gráficos de la Nación, 1926.

Manzanet, Damián. "Carta de Don Damian Manzanet á Don Carlos de Siguenza sobre el descubrimiento de la Bahia del Espiritu Santo." *The Quarterly of the Texas State Historical Association* 2 (1899): 253–80.

Maquívar, María del Consuelo. *De lo permitido a lo prohibido: Iconografía de la Santísima Trinidad en la Nueva España.* México: Instituto Nacional de Antropología e Historia, 2006.

Marin, Francisco. *Triduo mariano mensual en honor, y reverencia del Felicissimo Transito, entierro y assumpcion de la Reyna del Cielo y tierra María Nuestra Señora, para alcanzar mediante su Protección una dichosa muerte . . .* México: Herederos del Lic. D. Joseph de Jáuregui, 1790.

Mathes, Michael. "Oasis culturales en la Antigua California: Las bibliotecas de las misiones de Baja California en 1773." *Estudios históricos novohispanos* 10 (1991): 369–442.

Mauquoy-Hendrickx, Marie. "Les Wierix illustrateurs de la Bible dite de Natalis." *Quaerendo* 6, no. 1 (1976): 28–63.

McCloskey, Michael Brandon. *The Formative Years of the Missionary Colleges of Santa Cruz de Querétaro, 1683–1733.* Washington, DC: Academy of American Franciscan History, 1955.

McKnight, Kathryn Joy. *The Mystic of Tunja: The Writings of Madre Castillo, 1671–1742.* Amherst: University of Massachusetts Press, 1997.

Medina, José Toribio. *La Imprenta en Puebla de los Ángeles (1640–1821).* Santiago de Chile: Imprenta Cervantes, 1908.

——. *La imprenta en México (1539–1821)*: Vol. 2, *(1601–1684)*; Vol. 3, *(1685–1717)*; Vol. 4, *(1718–1744)*; Vol. 5, *(1745–1767)*; Vol. 6, *(1768–1794)*; Vol. 7, *(1795–1812)*; Vol. 8, *(1813–1821).* 8 vols. México: Universidad Nacional Autónoma de México, 1989.

Mendía, Benito. "En torno al problema de la autenticidad de la *Mistica Ciudad de Dios*." *Archivo Ibero-Americano* 42, no. 165-68 (1982): 391–430.

Mier, Servando Teresa de. *Fray Servando Teresa de Mier.* México: Cal y arena, 1953.

Mizell-Flint, Ami. "Mission Ongoing for Jumano Indians." *San Angelo Standard-Times*, June 20, 2009.

——. "Powwow Welcomes Culture to San Angelo." *San Angelo Standard-Times*, June 17, 2010.

Montejano, David. *Anglos and Mexicans in the Making of Texas, 1836–1986.* Austin: University of Texas Press, 1987.

Morlete, Juan Patricio. "Heart of Mary." Google Art Project. https://en.wiki pedia.org/wiki/Juan_Patricio_Morlete_Ruiz#mediaviewer/File:Juan _Patricio_Morlete_Ruiz_-_The_Heart_of_Mary_-_Google_Art_Project .jpg.

Muñoz de Villalón, Francisco. "La caída de Luzbel." Biblioteca Nacional de Madrid, 1789.

Murga, Juan. "Amenissimus Sacrae Theologiae Tractatus Dei param Virginem Mariaé . . ." Archivo Histórico Provincial de los Franciscanos de Michoacán, Celaya, México, 1775.

Muriel, Josefina. *Las indias caciques de Corpus Christi.* Instituto de Historia: Serie histórica. México: Universidad Nacional Autónoma de México, 1963.

———. *Cultura femenina novohispana.* Serie de historia novohispana. 1st ed. México: Universidad Nacional Autónoma de México/Instituto de Investigaciones Históricas, 1982.

Murray, Shannon. "Personal Interview." 2007.

Myers, Kathleen Ann. *Neither Saints Nor Sinners: Writing the Lives of Women in Spanish America.* New York: Oxford University Press, 2003.

Myers, Kathleen Ann, and Amanda Powell. *A Wild Country out in the Garden: The Spiritual Journals of a Colonial Mexican Nun.* Bloomington: Indiana University Press, 1999.

Nava y Quijada, Joseph, and Bernardo Mendel. *Colophon crítico-canónico-legal, a el privilégio de fuero, y exempción, en las causas civiles, criminales, y mixtas de los ecónomos apostólicos, y syndicos de la religión serafica: y decreto que Don Sylvestre Verde . . . obtuvo en la Real Chancillería de Granada.* Madrid: Imprenta de la causa de la V. Madre de Agreda, 1744.

Nogar, Anna M. "La décima musa errante: Sor Juana en la ficción mexicana /americana." In *Asaltos a la historia: Reimaginando la ficción histórica en Hispanoamérica*, edited by Brian Price, 77–99. México: Ediciones Eón, 2015.

———. "Genealogías hagiográficas y viajes coloniales: Sor María de Agreda en las Filipinas." *Revista de Soria* 89 (2015): 151–59.

———. "New Spain's Archival Past and Present Materiality." In *The History of Mexican Literature*, edited by Ignacio M. Sánchez Prado, Anna M. Nogar, and José Ramón Ruisánchez Serra, 128–40. Cambridge: Cambridge University Press, 2016.

Noriega y Escandón, José Antonio de. "Inquisition Interrogation of Josefa Palacios" (1791). Greenleaf Papers: Inquisition, Center for Southwest Research, University of New Mexico, Albuquerque.

Ocaranza, Fernando. *Establecimientos franciscanos en el misterioso reino de Nuevo México.* México, 1934.

Osuna, Joachín. *Peregrinación christiana por el camino real de la celeste Jerusalén: dividida en nueve jornadas, con quatro hospicios, que son unas estaciones devotas al modo del Via-Crucis, guirnaldas a la sagrada Passión de Christo, y dolores de su santíssima Madre : añadida al fin una refección espiritual de oraciones para antes, y despues de recibir los santos sacramentos de la penitencia, y comunión.* México: Biblioteca Mexicana, 1756.

———. *Perla de la gracia y concha del cielo: devoción mensal a la concepción y preñez virginea de la madre de Dios . . ./ sacado todo de las obras de M. Agreda y dispuesto por Joachin de Ossuna.* México: Bibliotheca Mexicana, 1758.

———. *Peregrinación christiana por el camino real de la celeste Jerusalen: dividida en doce jornadas, con quatro hospicios, que son unas estaciones devotas al modo del via-crucis, y guirnaldas â la sagrada passion de Christo y dolores de su santissima madre; añadida al fin una refeccion espiritual de oraciones para antes, y despues de recibir los santos sacramentos de la penitencia y comunion.* México: Biblioteca Mexicana, 1760.

Palóu, Francisco. *Palóu's Life of Junípero Serra.* Translated by Maynard Geiger. Washington, DC: Academy of American Franciscan History, 1955.

———. *La vida de Junípero Serra*. Ann Arbor, MI: University Microfilms, 1966.

Pardo Bazán, Emilia. Prologue to *Vida de la Virgen María*, by María de Jesús de Ágreda. Barcelona: Montaner y Simón, 1899.

Paredes, Américo. *With His Pistol in His Hand*. Austin: University of Texas Press, 1958.

Peña, Juan José. "Hispano Roundtable of New Mexico Honors Hispanas Distinguidas de Nuevo Mexico." Hispano Round Table, 2008.

Perez, Domino. *There Was a Woman: La Llorona from Folklore to Popular Culture*. Austin: University of Texas Press, 2008.

Pérez-Rioja, José Antonio "Proyección de la Venerable María de Agreda." *Celtiberia* 15, no. 29 (January-June 1965): 77–122.

Pérez Villanueva, Joaquin. "Algo más sobre la Inquisición y Sor María de Agreda: La prodigiosa evangelización americana." *Hispania Sacra* 37, no. 76 (1985): 28.

Pescador, Juan Javier. *Crossing Borders with the Santo Niño de Atocha*. Albuquerque: University of New Mexico Press, 2009.

Pettey, Harry. "Names and Creeks along Historic Roads Are Stories in Themselves." *Daily Sentinel* (Nacogdoches), July 9, 1963, 1.

Pichardo, José Antonio. *Pichardo's Treatise on the Limits of Louisiana and Texas*. Translated by Charles Hackett. Austin: University of Texas Press, 1934.

Polo, Petrus. *Mensiones morales seu quadragesima continua per mensiones hebraeorum et mysticae ad fratres et moniales*. 4 vols. Madrid: Ex Typographia causae V. Matris de Agreda, 1737.

Pope Pius IX. *Ineffabilis Deus* (1854). In *New Advent Catholic Encyclopedia*.

"Posesión de las misiones de San Francisco de los Neycha, y de la Concepción y San José de Nasones: 5 julio-agosto 8, 1721" (1721). Archivo Histórico Provincial de los Franciscanos de Michoacán.

Pou y Martí, José María. "El arzobispo Eleta y el término de la causa de la Venerable María de Agreda (conclusión)." *Archivo Ibero-Americano* 12, no. 52 (1923/5): 347–65.

———. "El arzobispo Eleta y el término de la causa de la Venerable María de Agreda." *Archivo Ibero-Americano* 10, no. 50 (1923/5): 425–60.

Puppet's Revenge. "Puppet's Revenge Homepage." http://www.imageevent.com/puppetsrevenge.

———. "The Blue Lady: A Brief History." http://www.imageevent.com/puppets revenge/theblueladyabriefhistory.

———. "Lady Blue's Dreams." http://puppetsrevenge.com/plays/lady-blue's -dreams.

Rabasa, José. *Writing Violence on the Northern Frontier: The Historiography of Sixteenth-Century New Mexico and Florida and the Legacy of Conquest*. Latin America Otherwise. Durham, NC: Duke University Press, 2000.

Rael, Juan Bautista. *The New Mexican Alabado*. Stanford, CA: Stanford University Press, 1951.

Raizizun, May. "A Lady Veiled in Mystery (Legend? or History?)." El Paso Public Library.

——. "The Blue Lady." *New Mexico Magazine*, February 1962, 22.

Ramírez, Edelmira. *María Rita Vargas, María Lucía Celis, Beatas embaucadoras de la colonia: De un cuaderno que recogió la Inquisición a un iluso, Antonio Rodríguez Colodrero, solicitante de escrituras y vidas.* México: Universidad Autónoma de México, 1988.

Ramírez Montes, Mina. "El testamento del pintor Antonio Torres." *Anales del Instituto de Investigaciones Estéticas* 15, no. 59 (1988): 265–73.

"Real Cédula Sobre el Descubrimiento de la bahía del Espiritu Santo" (1686). Archivo General de Indias, 52–59, Dolph Briscoe Center for American History, the University of Texas at Austin.

Rebolledo, Tey Diana. *Nuestras Mujeres.* Albuquerque: El Norte/Academia, 1992.

Redondo, Margaret Proctor, and James Griffith. "Valley of Iron." *The Journal of Arizona History* 34, no. 3 (1993): 233–74.

Reff, Daniel T. "Contextualizing Missionary Discourse: The Benavides Memorials of 1630 and 1634." *Journal of Anthropological Research* 50, no. 1 (1994): 51–67.

Regla de las monjas de la orden de la purissima y inmaculada concepcion de la Virgen Santissima Nuestra Señora: dada por el santissimo Papa Julio Segundo en el año de la encarnacion del Señor de M.D.XI. Quince de las kalendas de octubre en el año octavo de su pontificado. Madrid: Imprenta de la causa de la Venerable Madre de Agreda, 1744.

Regla y constituciones para las religiosas clarisas recoletas, de el monasterio de nuestra señora de los angeles de . . . Arizcun, en el Bastau, obispado de Pamplona, año de MDCCXXXVI. Madrid: Imp. de la Causa de la V. Madre de Agreda, 1737.

Richardson, Bill. "Governor Bill Richardson Signs New Mexico Sisterhood Agreement with Agreda, Spain." Press release, Office of the Governor of New Mexico, Santa Fe, 2008.

Riley, Carroll. "Las Casas and the Benavides Memorial of 1630." *New Mexico Historical Review* 48, no. 3 (1973): 209–22.

Risse, Kate. "Strategy of a Provincial Nun: Sor María de Jesús de Agreda's Response." *Ciberletras* 17 (2007).

Rittgers, Ronald. "'He Flew': A Concluding Reflection on the Place of Eternity and the Supernatual in the Scholarhip of Carlos M. N. Eire." In *A Linking of Heaven and Earth: Studies in Religious and Cultural History in Honor of Carlos M. N. Eire*, edited by Emily Michelson, Scott K. Taylor, and Mary Noll Venables, 205–16. Farnham, Surrey: Ashgate, 2012.

Robin, Alena. "El retablo de Xaltocán: Las Imágenes de Jerónimo Nadal y la monja de Ágreda." *Anales del Instituto de Investigaciones Estéticas* 88 (2006): 53–70.

Robles, Antonio de. *Diario de sucesos notables (1665–1703).* Vol. 2. Edited by Colección de Escritores Mexicanos. México: Editorial Porrúa, 1972.

Rodríguez Guillén, Pedro. *Sermones varios, panegyricos, politicos, historicos, y morales : predicados en los principales templos . . . de la ciudad de . . . Lima.* Madrid: Imprenta de la Causa de la Venerable Madre Maria de Jesvs de Agreda, 1736.

Rodríguez Guillén, Pedro, and Luis Montt. *El Sol, y año feliz del Perú San Francisco Solano, apostol, y patron universal de dicho reyno: hijo de la ilustre, y Santa Provincia de los Doce Apostoles. Glorificado, adorado, y festejado en su Templo, y Convento Maximo de Jesus de la Ciudad de los Reyes Lima, en ocacion que regocijada la serafica familia celebró con demostraciones festivas la deseada canonizacion, y declaracion del culto universal, y publico, que le decretó nuestro santissimo padre Benedicto XIII de eterna memoria, y felice recordacion: de que hace relacion en esta regia corte de Madrid el reverendo padre Fr. Pedro Rodriguez Guillen, lector jubilado del numero, ex-secretario de la sobredicha provincia, y actual custodio de ella, convocado al capitulo general.* Madrid: Imprenta de la Causa de la V.M. de Agreda, 1735.

Romero de Terreros, Manuel. "El convento franciscano de Ozumba y las pinturas de su portería." *Anales del Instituto de Investigaciones Estéticas* 6, no. 24 (1956): 9–12.

Ros, Juan. *Relacion historica de la portentosa anual maravilla, con que Dios . . . el dia 19 de agosto . . . festividad de San Luis . . . con las milagrosas flores, que aparecen todos los años en la Ermita . . . llamada San Luis del Monte, sita en la parroquial de Vega de Rengos, Concejo de Cangas de Tineo.* Madrid: Imprenta de la Causa de la V.M. de Agreda, 1744.

Rose, David, ed. *They Call Me Naughty Lola: Personal Ads from the London Review of Books.* New York: Scribner, 2006.

Royo Campos, Zótico. *Agredistas y antiagredistas: Estudio histórico-apologético.* Totana: Tipografía de San Buenaventura, 1929.

Rozière, Sonia de la, and Xavier Moyssèn. *México, Angustia de sus Cristos.* México: Instituto Nacional de Antropología e Historia, 1967.

Rubial García, Antonio. "Civitas dei et novus orbis: La Jerusalén celeste en la pintura de Nueva España." *Anales del Instituto de Investigaciones Estéticas* 20 (Spring 1998): 5–37.

Ruíz, Juan, and Francisco Saez. "Real Cédula dando licencia a Fr. Francisco Saez y Fr. Juan Ruiz, de la Orden de San Francisco para pasar al Perú a pedir limosna, durante 6 años, para la beatificación de la Madre María de Jesús de Agreda" (1692). Archivo General de Indias.

Ruíz Gomar, Rogelio. "La colección de pintura colonial del Ateneo Fuente, en la ciudad de Saltillo, Coahuila." *Anales del Instituto de Investigaciones Estéticas* 15, no. 60 (1989): 79–93.

Sáenz de Gumiel, Juan José. "Libro de pláticas y sermones del P. Fr. Juan José Sáenz de Gumiel." Archivo Histórico Provincial de los Franciscanos de Michoacán, Celaya, México.

San Antonio, Juan de. *Primacia fundamental del V. Padre Fray Juan de Guadalupe, vindicada.* Madrid: Imprenta de la Causa de la V.M. de Agreda, 1737.

San Juan del Puerto, Francisco Jesús María de. *Patrimonio seraphico de Tierra Santa : fundado por Christo Nuestro Redentor con su preciosa sangre, prometido por su magestad n.p. S. Francisco para sí, y para sus hijos, adquirido por el mismo Santo, heredado, posseїdo por sus hijos de la regular observancia, y conservado hasta el tiempo presente.* Madrid: Imprenta de la Causa de la V.M. Maria de Jesus de Agreda, 1724.

Sandlin, Lisa. *In the River Province*. Dallas, TX: Southern Methodist University Press, 2004.

Sandlin, Lisa, and Catherine Ferguson. *You Who Make the Sky Bend: Saints and Archetypes of the Human Condition*. Montrose, CO: Pinyon, 2011.

Sandoval, Gaspar de la Cerda. "Carta de [Gaspar de la Cerda Sandoval, VII] conde de Galve y virrey de España a su hermano [Gregorio de Silva Mendoza, IX]" (1689). Sección Nobleza, Archivo Histórico Nacional, Spain.

Sankey, Becca Nelson. "Lasting Effect of Lady in Blue's Story." *San Angelo Standard-Times*, June 19, 2009.

——. "Celebrating Lady in Blue." *San Angelo Standard-Times*, June 19, 2009.

Santa María, Francisco de. "Copia de Carta Escrita en Roma, En el Mes de Julio desde presente año de 1705 a un devoto de la V.M. María de Jesús de Ágreda" (1705). Archivo Franciscano Ibero-Oriental.

Santa Sede 150. Archivo de la Embajada de España Ante la Santa Sede, Ministerio de Asuntos Exteriores, Madrid.

Sarmiento de Valladares, Diego. "Edict Lifting the Embargo on the Mistica Ciudad de Dios" (1686). Madrid, University of Notre Dame Rare Books and Special Collections.

Schlosser, S. E. *Spooky Southwest: Tales of Hauntings, Strange Happenings and Other Local Lore*. Guilford, CT: Globe Pequot, 2004.

Schmitt, Edmond J. P. "Ven. Maria de Jesus de Agreda: A Correction." *Texas State Historical Quarterly* 1, no. 2 (1897): 121–24.

Schmitt, Jean-Claude. *The Holy Greyhound: Guinefort, Healer of Children since the Thirteenth Century*. New York: Cambridge University Press, 1983.

Scholes, Frances. "Problems in the Early Ecclesiastical History of New Mexico." *New Mexico Historical Review* (January 1932): 32–74.

Scott, Laurel. "Vision of the Past: Pain Rock Drawings Are Stars of Ceremony." *San Angelo Standard-Times*, June 21, 2009.

——. "Event Honors Lady in Blue." *San Angelo Standard-Times*, June 11, 2010.

Scott, Nina M. "'La gran turba de las que merecieron nombres': Sor Juana's Foremothers in 'La Respuesta a Sor Filotea.'" In *Coded Encounters: Writing, Gender, and Ethnicity in Colonial Latin America*, edited by Francisco Javier Cevallos-Candau, Jeffrey A. Cole, Nina M. Scott, and Nicomedes Suárez-Araúz, 206–23. Amherst: University of Massachusetts Press, 1994.

Seco Serrano, Carlos. *Cartas de Sor María de Jesús de Ágreda y de Felipe IV*. Biblioteca de autores españoles 108–9. Madrid: Ediciones Atlas, 1958.

Serra, Junípero. *Writings of Junípero Serra*. 4 vols. Translated by Antonine Tibesar. Washington, DC: Academy of American Franciscan History, 1955.

Serrano y Sanz, Manuel. *Apuntes para una biblioteca de escritoras espanolas desde el año 1401 al 1833*. Vol. 1. Madrid: Atlas, 1903.

Servite Fathers. *The Age of Mary: An Exclusively Marian Magazine*. "The Mystical City of God" Issue (January-February, 1958).

Sharp, Jay. *Texas Unexplained: Strange Tales and Mysteries from the Lone Star State*. Austin: University of Texas Press, 1999.

Sierra, Javier. *La dama azul*. Madrid: Ediciones Martín Roca, 2005.

———. *The Lady in Blue*. Translated by James Graham. New York: Atria, 2007.

Smith, Rick. "Rick Smith: Lady in Blue Stuck To Her Faith." *San Angelo Standard-Times*, June 20, 2009.

Soto, Juan de. "Patente de fray Juan de Soto para atender las limosnas de una beatificación" (1724). Convento de San Francisco de Madrid.

Soto, Juan de, and Juan de San Antonio. *Bibliotheca universa franciscana sive Alumnorum trium Ordinum S.P.N. Francisci, qui ab ordine seraphico condito, usque ad praesentem diem, latina, sivè alia quavis lingua scripto aliquid consignarunt Encyclopaedia . . .: in tres distributa tomos, adjectis necessarijs Indicibus*. Madrid: Ex Typographia Causae V. Matris de Agreda, 1732.

Sturmberg, Richard. *History of San Antonio and of the Early Days in Texas*. San Antonio, TX: Standard Printing Co., 1920.

Succop, Margaret Phillips, and Merle Armitage. *Painter into Artist: The Progress of Edward O'Brien*. Yucca Valley, CA: Manzanita Press, 1964.

Syers, Ed. "Catholic Legend Brought Back from the Past." *El Paso Times*, May 30, 1965.

Syers, William Edward. *Off the Beaten Trail*. Vol. 3. Ingram, TX: OBT, 1965.

Sze, Corinne P. "St. Catherine's Indian School." http://www.newmexicohistory.org/filedetails.php?fileID=21300.

Talamantes, Melchor de. "Opúsculo VI: El Reverendo Padre Fray Doctor Melchor de Talamantes solicitando documentos para dar el lleno á su comision se entró en la Biblioteca de la Real y Pontifica Universidad de esta corte." Spanish Colonial Research Center. University of New Mexico, Albuquerque, NM.

Tester, Victoria Edwards. *Miracles of Sainted Earth*. Albuquerque: University of New Mexico Press, 2002.

Torres, Larry. "Chile Con Carne María de Agreda/Mystic María Agreda Invents Chile Recipe." "Blue Lady" Vertical File, Fray Angélico Chávez Library, Santa Fe.

Traducción verídica y authentica de tres sucessos prodigiosos . . . en que la bondad divina se ha dignado de acreditar los libros de la Mystica Ciudad de Dios. México: Joseph Bernardo de Hogal, 1729.

Tudela, Elisa Sampson Vera. *Colonial Angels*. Austin: University of Texas Press, 2000.

Uribe, Ángel. "La inmaculada en la literatura franciscano-española." *Archivo Ibero-Americano* 15 (1955): 201–495.

Urrea, Luis Alberto. *The Devil's Highway*. New York: Little, Brown and Company, 2004.

Valbona, Rima de. *Cosecha de pescadores*. San José, Costa Rica: Editorial Costa Rica, 1988.

Van Atta, Ann. "Pecos River Pageantry." *The Junior Historian*, May 1958.

Vanderwood, Paul. *Juan Soldado*. Durham, NC: Duke University Press, 2004.

Vargas Lugo, Elisa. *Juan Correa: Su vida y su obra*. México: Universidad Autónoma de México, 1985.

———. "La vida de María." In *Juan Correa: Su vida y su obra*, edited by Elisa Vargas Lugo and José Guadalupe Victoria, 75–102. México: Universidad Nacional Autónoma de México, 1994.

Vázquez del Valle, Juan. *Año christiano, en que compendiosamente se explican los Evangelios.* Madrid: Imp. de la Causa de la V. Madre María de Jesús de Agreda, 1748.

Vázquez Janiero, Isaac. "Un Franciscano al servicio de los Habsburgos en la Curia Romana: Francisco Díaz de San Buenaventura (1652–1728)." *Archivo Ibero-Americano* 23 (1962): 197–266.

Velasco, Matías. *Demostración histórico-chronológica de un engaño o inconsideración, que padeció y trasladó a la prensa el R. Padre Fr. Marcos de Alcalá... sobre, y en assumpto de la fundación de el convento de la Señoras Descalzas Reales formala en defensa de la verdad... el R. P. Fr. Mathias de Velasco.* Madrid: Imp. causa de la V. Madre Sor María de Jesús de Agreda, 1737.

Vélez de Escalante, Silvestre José. "Relaciones de Nuevo-Mexico." In *Documentos para la Historia de México, Serie 3.* México: Imprenta de Vicente Garcia Torres, 1856.

Venegas, Francisco. *Oracion panegyrica, que en accion de gracias por haverse celebrado con toda felicidad el capitulo provincial, que prestidiò el M. R. P. Fr. Eugenio Ibañez en el Perù en su Convento de Jesus de Lima... el dia 23. de noviembre, año de 1746.* Madrid: Impr. de la causa de la V. Madre Maria de Jesus de Agreda, 1748.

Verdiguer, Cayetano. "Matemática demostración de las letras dominicales y exactas desde el principio del mundo hasta el año 1760 y siguientes. Hechas sus tablas... bajo del computo que refiere la V.M. María de Jesús de Agreda." Biblioteca Nacional de España, 1760.

Vereo, Francisco Antonio de. *Aurora alegre del dichoso día de la gracia María Santíssima digna Madre de Dios: prosiguen los diez y seis últimos días de el mes de vida... epítome de los libros Mystica ciudad de Dios y Vida de la Virgen Madre de Dios.* México: Joseph Bernardo de Hogal, 1730.

Vetancurt, Agustín de. *Chronografia sagrada de la vida de Christo Nuestro Redemptor: Predicación evangélica, con las circunstancias de lugar, y tiempo en que obró los misterios de nuestra redemption [sic], obras de su omnipotencia, y maravillas de su gracia en Maria Santíssima, y en el seraphico padre S. Francisco, y su apostólica religión.* México: Por Doña Maria de Benavides, viuda de Juan de Ribera, 1696.

———. *Crónica de la Provincia del Santo Evangelio de México.* Vol. 3. México: Imprenta de I Escalante, 1871.

———. *Teatro mexicano; descripción breve de los sucesos ejemplares de la Nueva-España en el Nuevo Mundo Occidental de las Indias.* Colección Chimalistac de libros y documentos acerca de la Nueva España, 8–11. Madrid: J. Porrúa Turanzas, 1960.

———. *Teatro Mexicano.* México: Editorial Porrúa, 1971.

Viernes de María: en obsequio de su glorioso tránsito, provechosa devoción para conseguir una buena muerte, según lo que la misma Señora reveló á la venerable madre sor María de Jesús de Agreda, Lib. 8. Cap. 28. Num. 745/escrita por un vecino de Celaya. México: En la oficina de la calle de Santo Domingo, 1816.

Villagutierre Soto-Mayor, Juan de. *Historia de la conquista, pérdida y restauración del reino de la Nueva México en la América Septentrional*. Edited by Alfred Charles Herrera. Madrid: Alfred Charles Herrera, 1953.

Villalpando, Cristóbal de. *La mística Jerusalén*. Zacatecas.

Villasante, Luis. "Sor María de Jesús de Agreda a través de su correspondencia epistolar con el rey." *Archivo Ibero-Americano* 25, no. 98-99 (1965): 145–72.

Vogel, Carol. Personal Interview. Santa Fe, NM, January 4, 2007.

Wagner, Henry Raupp. *The Spanish Southwest, 1542–1794: An Annotated Bibliography*. Berkeley, CA: J. J. Gillick, 1924.

Wall, Bert. *Ghostly Chills: The Devil's Backbone 2*. Austin, TX: Eakin, 2001.

Wallrich, William Jones. *The Strange Little Man in the Chili-Red Pants*. Fort Garland, CO: Cottonwood, 1949.

Walter, Paul A. F. "Yesteryears in the Spanish Southwest." *Santa Fe New Mexican*, October 21, 1928.

Webber, Joseph, and Michele Larson. *Sor María*, Advertisement: KiMo Theater performance. Author's collection.

———. *Sor María*, Advertisement: Northern New Mexico Community College performance. Author's collection.

———. *Sor María*, Program. Author's collection.

Weigle, Marta, and Peter White. *The Lore of New Mexico*. Albuquerque: University of New Mexico Press, 1988.

West, Elizabeth Howard. "De León's Expedition of 1689." *The Quarterly of the Texas State Historical Association* 8, no. 3 (1905): 199–224.

Westfall, Marilyn. "Quartet in Blue." PhD diss., Texas Tech University, 1998.

———. "Blue Lady of the Plains, Maria Agreda." Talk given at First Unitarian Universalist Church, Lubbock, TX, 2002.

White, Marjorie. "Miraculous Visitations Form Gripping Southwest Mystery." *El Paso Times*, January 30, 1966.

Wray, Grady. "Seventeenth-Century Wise Women of Spain and the Americas: Madre Agreda and Sor Juana." *Studia Mystica* 22 (2001): 123–49.

Ximénez Samaniego, Joseph. *Relación de la vida de la venerable Madre Sor María de Jesús abadesa de el convento de la Inmaculada Concepción de la Villa de Agreda*. Barcelona: Impresa de Martin Gelabert, 1687.

———. *Prólogo galeato, Relación de la vida de la V. Madre Sor María de Jesús: abadesa que fue de el Convento de la Inmaculada Concepcion de la villa de Agreda, de la provincia de Burgos*. Madrid: Imprenta de la Causa de la V. Madre, 1720.

———. *Prologo galeato, Relacion de la vida de la v. Madre sor María de Jesús: abadsa, que fue, del Convento de la Inmaculada Concepción, de la Villa de Agreda, de la provincia de Burgos; y notas a las tres partes de la Mystica ciudad de Dios*. Madrid: Imprenta de la Causa de la V. Madre, 1721.

———. *Relacion de la vida de la venerable madre sor Maria de Jesus: abadesa, que fue, del Convento de la purissima concepcion de la villa de Agreda*. En Madrid: En la Imprenta de la Causa de la Venerable Madre, 1727.

———. *Vida del venerable padre Juan Dunsio Escoto, doctor mariano y subtil.* Madrid: Imprenta de la Causa de la Venerable Madre Maria de Jesvs de Agreda, 1741.

———. *Relación de la vida de la v. Madre sor María de Jesús, abadsa, qu fue, del Convento de la Inmaculada Concepción, de la Villa de Agreda, de la provincia de Burgos. Y Notas a las tres partes de la Mystica ciudad de Dios.* Madrid: Imprenta de la Causa de la V. Madre, 1759.

———. *Prólogo galeato, relacion de la vida de la V. Madre Sor Maria de Jesus, abadesa, que fue, de el convento de la Inmaculada concepción, de la villa de Agreda, de la provincia de Burgos. Y notas a las tres partes de la Mystica Ciudad de Dios.* Madrid: En la Imprenta de la causa de la V. Madre, 1759.

———. *Prólogo Galeato, Relación de la vida de la V. Madre Sor María de Jesús: abadesa que fue de el Convento de la Inmaculada Concepcion de la villa de Agreda, de la provincia de Burgos.* Madrid: Imprenta de la Causa de la V. Madre, 1765.

Young, Richard Alan, and Judy Dockrey Young. *Ghost Stories from the American Southwest.* Little Rock, AR: August House, 1991.

Zárate Salmerón, Gerónimo. "Relaciones de todas las cosas que en el Nuevo-Mexico se han visto y sabido, asi por mar como por tierra, desde el año de 1538 hasta el de 1626, por el padre Gerónimo de Zarate Salmerón." In *Documentos para la historia de México*, 3–55. México: Imprenta de Vicente García Torres, 1856.

———. *Relaciones: An Account of Things Seen and Learned by Father Jeronimo de Zarate Salmerón from the Year 1538 to Year 1626.* Translated by Alicia Ronstadt Milich. Albuquerque: Horn and Wallace, 1966.

INDEX

Page numbers in italics indicate illustrations.

ANNA M. NOGAR is an associate professor of Hispanic Southwest studies in the Department of Spanish and Portuguese at the University of New Mexico.

CPSIA information can be obtained
at www.ICGtesting.com
Printed in the USA
LVHW010134291018
595164LV00007B/285/P